ALTERED STATES OF CONSCIOUSNESS

ALTERED STATES OF CONSCIOUSNESS

A BOOK OF READINGS

CHARLES T. TART

Editor
University of California, Davis

John Wiley & Sons, Inc.
New York · London · Sydney · Toronto

Library of Congress Catalog Card Number: 69-16040
SBN 471 84560 4
Printed in the United States of America

CONTENTS

INTRODUCTION 1

1. INTRODUCTION TO SECTION 1. SOME GENERAL
VIEWS ON ALTERED STATES OF CONSCIOUSNESS 7

   1 Altered States of Consciousness, Arnold M. Ludwig 9

   2 Deautomatization and the Mystic Experience, Arthur J.
Deikman 23

   3 A Special Inquiry with Aldous Huxley into the Nature
and Character of Various States of Consciousness, Milton
H. Erickson 45

2. INTRODUCTION TO SECTION 2. BETWEEN WAKING
AND SLEEPING: THE HYPNAGOGIC STATE 73

   4 Ego Functions and Dreaming during Sleep Onset, Gerald
Vogel, David Foulkes and Harry Trosman 75

   5 Some Preliminary Observations with an Experimental
Procedure for the Study of Hypnagogic and Related
Phenomena, M. Bertini, Helen B. Lewis and Herman A.
Witkin 93

3. INTRODUCTION TO SECTION 3. DREAM
CONSCIOUSNESS 113

   6 Theories of Dream Formation and Recent Studies of
Sleep Consciousness, David Foulkes 117

   7 Toward the Experimental Control of Dreaming: A
Review of the Literature, Charles T. Tart 133

   8 A Study of Dreams, Frederik van Eeden 145

   9 Dream Theory in Malaya, Kilton Stewart 159

10   The "High" Dream: A New State of Consciousness, Charles T. Tart   169

4.   INTRODUCTION TO SECTION 4.   MEDITATION   175

11   On Meditation, Edward W. Maupin   177

12   Individual Differences in Response to a Zen Meditation Exercise, Edward W. Maupin   187

13   Experimental Meditation, Arthur J. Deikman   199

14   Meditative Techniques in Psychotherapy, Wolfgang Kretschmer   219

5.   INTRODUCTION TO SECTION 5.   HYPNOSIS   229

15   Hypnosis and the Concept of the Generalized Reality-Orientation, Ronald E. Shor   233

16   Three Dimensions of Hypnotic Depth, Ronald E. Shor   251

17   Hypnosis, Depth Perception, and the Psychedelic Experience, Bernard S. Aaronson   263

18   The Psychedelic State, the Hypnotic Trance, and the Creative Act, Stanley Krippner   271

19   Psychedelic Experiences Associated with a Novel Hypnotic Procedure, Mutual Hypnosis, Charles T. Tart   291

20   Autogenic Training: Method, Research and Application in Medicine, Wolfgang Luthe   309

6.   INTRODUCTION TO SECTION 6.   MINOR PSYCHEDELIC DRUGS   321

21   Marijuana (Cannabis) Fact Sheet, Bruin Humanist Forum   325

22   The Effects of Marijuana on Consciousness, Anonymous   335

23   Psychedelic Properties of *Genista Canariensis*, James Fadiman   357

24   Subjective Effects of Nitrous Oxide, William James   359

25 Inhalation Psychosis and Related States, Frederick B. Glaser   363

7. INTRODUCTION TO SECTION 7. MAJOR PSYCHEDELIC DRUGS   377

26 Current Status and Future Trends in Psychedelic (LSD) Research, Robert E. Mogar   381

27 Implications of LSD and Experimental Mysticism, Walter N. Pahnke and William A. Richards   399

28 Attitude and Behavior Change through Psychedelic Drug Use, Joseph Downing   429

29 *Ipomoea Purpurea*: A Naturally Occurring Psychedelic, Charles Savage, Willis W. Harman and James Fadiman   441

30 Psychedelic Agents in Creative Problem Solving, Willis Harman, Robert McKim, Robert Mogar, James Fadiman and Myron J. Stolaroff   445

31 "Psychedelic" Experiences in Acute Psychoses, Malcolm B. Bowers Jr. and Daniel Freedman   463

32 Guide to the Literature on Psychedelic Drugs, Charles T. Tart   477

8. INTRODUCTION TO SECTION 8. THE PSYCHOPHYSIOLOGY OF SOME ALTERED STATES OF CONSCIOUSNESS   485

33 An Electroencephalographic Study on the Zen Meditation (Zazen), Akira Kasamatsu and Tomio Hirai   489

34 Some Aspects of Electroencephalographic Studies in Yogis, B. K. Anand, G. S. Chhina and Baldev Singh   503

35 Operant Control of the EEG Alpha Rhythm and some of Its Reported Effects on Consciousness, Joe Kamiya   507

REFERENCES   519

AUTHOR INDEX   557

SUBJECT INDEX   569

ALTERED STATES OF CONSCIOUSNESS

INTRODUCTION

CHARLES T. TART

Whenever I speak on the topic of dreams, I mention a very unusual sort of dream, the "lucid" dream (see Chapter 8) in which the dreamer knows he is dreaming and feels fully conscious in the dream itself. After discussing some of the philosophical and semantic difficulties in defining states of consciousness, I always ask whether anyone has the slightest doubt that he is awake, that is, in a "normal" state of consciousness at that moment; I have never found anyone who had difficulty in making this distinction.

In introducing a book of readings on altered states of consciousness, I find myself in a similar position: there is a multitude of philosophical and semantic problems in defining just what "normal" consciousness and "altered" states of consciousness are, yet at this instant I have not the slightest doubt that I am in my normal state of consciousness. Yet there have been a number of occasions in my life when I have not had the slightest difficulty in realizing that I was in an altered state of consciousness (ASC). Thus I shall give only the simplest sort of definition of what an ASC is here and let the articles in this book flesh it out: our knowledge of ASCs is too incomplete at this time for a tight conceptualization.

For any given individual, his normal state of consciousness is the one in which he spends the major part of his waking hours. That your normal state of consciousness and mine are quite similar and are similar to that of all other normal men is an almost universal assumption, albeit one of questionable validity. An altered state of consciousness for a given

1

individual is one in which he clearly feels a *qualitative* shift in his pattern of mental functioning,* that is, he feels not just a quantitative shift (more or less alert, more or less visual imagery, sharper or duller, etc.), but also that some quality or qualities of his mental processes are *different*. Mental functions operate that do not operate at all ordinarily, perceptual qualities appear that have no normal counterparts, and so forth. There are numerous borderline cases in which the individual cannot clearly distinguish just how his state of consciousness is different from normal, where quantitative changes in mental functioning are very marked, etc., but the existence of borderline states and difficult-to-describe effects does not negate the existence of feelings of clear, qualitative changes in mental functioning that are the criterion of ASCs.

This book is concerned with those states of consciousness in which the individual feels one or more qualitative (and possibly one or more quantitative) shifts in mental functioning, so that he believes himself to be in an ASC.

Within Western culture we have strong negative attitudes toward ASCs: there is the normal (good) state of consciousness and there are pathological changes in consciousness. Most people make no further distinctions. We have available a great deal of scientific and clinical material on ASCs associated with psychopathological states, such as schizophrenia: by comparison, our scientific knowledge about ASCs which could be considered "desirable" is extremely limited and generally unknown to scientists. One of the purposes of these articles is to begin to provide some balance; therefore almost all the ASCs treated here have *positive* qualities in that they are ASCs that many people will go to considerable trouble and effort to induce in themselves because they feel that experiencing a particular ASC is rewarding. Our understanding of mental processes has been greatly facilitated by focusing on psychopathology, but it cannot be complete without looking at the other side of the coin. Further, we need to drop the "good" or "bad" judgments about various ASCs and concentrate on the question: What are the characteristics of a given ASC and what consequences do these characteristics have on behavior in various settings?

A normal state of consciousness can be considered a resultant of living in a particular environment, both physical and psychosocial. Thus the normal state of consciousness for any individual is one that has adaptive value within his particular culture and environment; we would expect the normal state of consciousness to show qualitatively and/or quantitatively

---

*For those who prefer a behavioristic approach an ASC is a hypothetical construct invoked when an *S*'s behavior (including the behavior of verbal report) is radically different from his ordinary behavior.

different aspects from one culture to another. But one of the most common cognitive errors made is what Carl Jung has called the fallacy of the psychologist projecting his own psychology upon the patient, that is, we almost always make the implicit assumption that everybody else thinks and experiences about the same way as we do, with the exception of "crazy" people.

In a broader perspective it is clear that man has functioned in a multitude of states of consciousness and that different cultures have varied enormously in recognition and utilization of, and attitudes toward, ASCs. Many "primitive" peoples, for example, believe that almost every normal adult has the ability to go into a trance state and be possessed by a god; the adult who cannot do this is a psychological cripple. How deficient Americans would seem to a person from such a culture. In many Eastern civilizations, elaborate techniques have been developed for inducing and utilizing ASCs, such as the Yoga and Zen systems.* In some cases vocabularies have been developed for talking about these ASCs more adequately. I recall Fredrick Spiegelberg, the noted Indian scholar, pointing out that Sanskrit has about 20 nouns which we translate into "consciousness" or "mind" in English because we do not have the vocabulary to specify the different shades of meaning in these words. (Spiegelberg, Fadiman & Tart, 1964).

Within our Western culture we have several commonly used words for naming some ASCs, such as trance, hypnosis, dream, and ecstasy, but none of them are very clearly defined. It could be expected that within psychology and psychiatry there would be far more exact terms for describing various ASCs and their components, but except for a rich (but often not precise) vocabularly dealing with psychopathological states, this is not true. A few years ago, for example, I tried to find a clear definition of the word "trance," a very common psychological term, used in an explanatory as well as a descriptive sense. To my surprise, for every defining characteristic of a trance mentioned by one authority, another authority would use the opposite characteristic. Formal psychology in this century simply has not dealt with ASCs, especially positive ASCs, to any reasonable extent, considering their potential importance.

If one (perhaps naively) assumes that the distribution of expended energies in the psychological sciences should show some relation to what is important in affecting people's behavior rather than just being related to what is methodologically convenient to investigate, then this neglect of ASCs by the psychological sciences is strange and has become increasingly

---

*Many techniques for inducing ASCs were developed in Christian mysticism, but these were not as elaborate as the Eastern techniques and no longer represent an important element in contemporary Western culture.

incongruent with what has happened in American society in the past decade of the "psychedelic revolution." The discrepancies will almost certainly become even greater over the next decade as the present trends continue. I shall not attempt to describe the whole "hippie" movement since it is too diverse, but judging by the more conservative writers in the mass media, there are tens of thousands of people who are *obviously* hippies in their life style and hundreds of thousands (perhaps millions) of "respectable" middle-class people who are experimenting with drug trips, meditation, sensory awareness, encounter groups, intentional communities, dream interpretation, and so forth (see, e.g., Rosenfeld & Farrel, 1966). I see these trends primarily in terms of the interests and activities of psychologists, undergraduate psychology majors, and psychology graduate students in my everyday life; the change over the past few years has been remarkable. When I was a graduate student a few years ago, I found almost no one who shared my interest in ASCs: today it is commonplace for graduate students to discuss their meditation experiences, their drug experiences, and their plans to work in these areas as psychologists. Five years ago a person who mentioned at a party that he had taken LSD-25 became the center of attention: now descriptions of psychedelic experiences are too commonplace to attract special attention.

As further illustration, in the last month two graduate students in physics have come to talk to me about their experiences of their "souls leaving their bodies"; a sociology graduate student told me about a group of students he meets with regularly to discuss what to do with your state of consciousness and style of life after exhausting the LSD-25 experience; a mathematics graduate student asked for a guide to the scientific literature on marijuana so he may compare these findings to his own experiences. These are not hippie students and they are no longer unusual. They are representatives of a whole new generation entering the conventional social power structure who spend much effort in exploring their own consciousness.

This upsurge of serious interest in and personal exploration of ASCs is likely to cause an important change in psychology as a discipline. Students come to talk with me in my role as a psychologist because they believe that the science which treats the mind or behavior will help clarify their ASC experiences. I must tell them we have very little to offer. Undergraduates begin to major in psychology and find that we concentrate our research efforts of "methodologically sophisticated" approaches on what seem to them trivial problems. They can meditate for a month or take a psychedelic drug and have overwhelming psychological effects in their minds: if psychologists largely ignore this whole area, the students then dismiss psychology as an academic word game of no importance. And, in my experience, these are some of the very brightest students. Among graduate students I have talked to, particularly in West Coast universities, the same trend is evident: a great dissatisfaction with the conventional areas of psychology and a questioning of whether training in psychology is worth while in terms of their interests, I suspect that within a few years the psychology graduate school that does not offer course work and research opportunities in ASCs simply will not attract many bright students. Non-academic centers such as Esalen Institute, in Big Sur, California, are arising to fill some of this need.

This is not to denigrate the valuable research that has been done in psychology these many years: it is simply saying that the profession must pay adequate attention to these areas of such importance to students if we want to avoid losing some good, potential psychologists.

The need for a shift in emphasis in psychology is based on more important considerations than attracting bright students in the future, however. The actual behavior of an important segment of our population, the students and the middle-class intellectuals, is increasingly involved with producing and using ASCs. Yet our scientific knowledge of the nature and effects of these ASCs is so limited that we can offer little sound guidance on public policy with respect to such practices as psychedelic drug use. We cannot give much advice to individuals who wish to experience ASCs, nor can we adequately understand this significant portion of people's behavior.

This collection of articles is an attempt to begin to correct the situation by, hopefully, stimulating research on ASCs in the course of presenting material on them. To many people who are not involved in scientific research, valid knowledge about ASCs is to be obtained by experiencing them; they are somehow beyond the reach of scientific research. The most important obligation of any science is that its descriptive and theoretical language embrace *all* the phenomena of its subject matter; the data from ASCs cannot be ignored if we are to develop a comprehensive psychology. Psychology has often failed to meet this obligation because of premature conceptualizations, that is, investing in simplified and elegant theoretical systems that exclude the data of ASCs, but this has been more a matter of the cultural climate than any inherent shortcoming of scientific method. Man is a theorizing and conceptualizing animal and does not accept experience in and of itself: he always develops beliefs and theories about his experience. The difficulty with studying ASCs by simply experiencing them is that we run as much risk of systematizing our delusions as of discovering "truth." When we complement personal experience with scientific method the risk of simply systematizing our delusions is considerably reduced. Thus the hope of stimulating research on ASCs is the prime reason for assembling these articles.

The readings in this collection cover a wide range of ASCs; they are presented in groups, beginning with some ASCs available to almost everyone (the hypnagogic state and the dream state), continuing with more specialized and powerful ASCs (meditation, hypnosis, minor and major psychedelic drugs), and ending with the psychophysiology of some ASCs (including the most modern technique for producing an ASC—electroencephalographic feedback). More than 1,000 references to scientific literature relating to ASCs are contained in the articles and they should serve to guide the serious researcher to a vast amount of background literature. The papers range from relatively "hard-headed" experimental articles to very speculative ones. This variability occurs because our knowledge of ASCs is highly variable. My primary criterion for selecting papers is that they be provocative as well as sound: many of the phenomena reported will seem preposterous, impossible, and "unscientific." This simply reflects the limitations of our knowledge. I hope that those readers who are incensed by various articles will sublimate your anger into research.

ASCs are going to become increasingly important in modern life. With proper research our knowledge of them can be immensely enriched very quickly and it is my hope that this book will stimulate research in this area.

INTRODUCTION TO SECTION 1. SOME GENERAL VIEWS ON ALTERED STATES OF CONSCIOUSNESS

The number of discrete states of consciousness subsumed under the general heading ASCs is very large: exactly how large is unknown. This set of readings begins with Arnold Ludwig's "Altered States of Consciousness," one of the most comprehensive overviews available. Ludwig surveys the range of phenomena covered by ASCs and discusses their means of production and their various sociocultural functions. The latter are of particular interest: our Western culture makes virtually no use of ASCs and tends to regard all of them as pathological states. Ludwig's article provides a wide ranging perspective of the variety of *positive* functions that ASCs can serve, both for the individuals experiencing them and for the cultures the individuals live in.

Ludwig's article is primarily a survey of *what happens*, with little theorizing. His is followed by Arthur Deikman's "Deautomatization and the Mystic Experience," in which he looks at the types of ASC often reported by mystics and attempts an analysis of these states from a psychoanalytic point of view. Although our over-all knowledge of ASCs is so meager at this time that no theoretical explanation can be *completely* comprehensive and accurate, Deikman's article is an excellent illustration of the sort of first-class theorizing that can be done currently.

In order to add human relevance and richness to this survey of ASCs, the article by Milton Erickson that completes this section, a "Special Inquiry with Aldous Huxley into the Nature and Character of Various States of Consciousness," is a remarkable study of the ASCs experienced by one of the greatest minds of our generation. It was Huxley's lucid little book, "The Doors of Perception" (1954), that greatly stimulated my own interest in ASCs years ago: as a description of the psychedelic experience, this book has yet to be surpassed. Erickson's paper further illustrates the creative potentials of some ASCs, for he describes how Huxley did much of his writing in an ASC.

For further general readings on ASC the reader should see Belo (1960), Bucke (1961), Devereaux (1966), Gill & Brenman (1961), James (1958), King (1963), and Ludwig (1967).

1

ALTERED STATES OF CONSCIOUSNESS

ARNOLD M. LUDWIG

Beneath man's thin veneer of consciousness lies a relatively uncharted realm of mental activity, the nature and function of which have been neither systematically explored nor adequately conceptualized. Despite numerous clinical and research reports on daydreaming, sleep and dream states, hypnosis, sensory deprivation, hysterical states of dissociation and depersonalization, pharmacologically induced mental aberrations, and so on, there has been little attempt made to organize this scattered information into a consistent theoretical system. It is my present intention to integrate and discuss current knowledge regarding various altered states of consciousness in an effort to determine (a) the conditions necessary for their emergence, (b) the factors that influence their outward manifestations, (c) their relatedness and/or common denominators, and (d) the adaptive or maladaptive functions which these states may serve for man.

For the purpose of discussion I shall regard altered state(s) of consciousness [hereafter referred to as ASC(s)] as any mental state(s), induced by various physiological, psychological, or pharmacological maneuvers or agents, which can be recognized subjectively by the individual himself (or by an objective observer of the individual) as representing a sufficient deviation in subjective experience or psychological functioning from certain

Reprinted by permission from *Arch. Gen. Psychiat.*, Vol. 15, 1966, pp. 225–234.

general norms for that individual during alert, waking consciousness. This sufficient deviation may be represented by a greater preoccupation than usual with internal sensations or mental processes, changes in the formal characteristics of thought, and impairment of reality testing to various degrees. Although there will be some conceptual pitfalls in such a general definition, these pitfalls will be more than compensated for by the wide range of clinical phenomena which can now be considered and hence studied as presumably related phenomena.

PRODUCTION OF ASC

ASCs may be produced in any setting by a wide variety of agents or maneuvers which interfere with the normal inflow of sensory or proprioceptive stimuli, the normal outflow of motor impulses, the normal "emotional tone," or the normal flow and organization of cognitive processes. There seems to be an optimal range of exteroceptive stimulation necessary for the maintenance of normal, waking consciousness, and levels of stimulation either above or below this range appear conducive to the production of ASCs (Lindsey, 1961). Moreover, by adopting Hebb's views (1958), we also find that varied and diversified environmental stimulation appears necessary for the maintenance of normal cognitive, perceptual, and emotional experience, and that when such stimulation is lacking, mental aberrations are likely to occur. Although experimental evidence is sparse concerning the manipulation of motor, cognitive, and emotional processes, there seems to be ample clinical and anecdotal evidence to suggest that gross interference with these processes may likewise produce alterations in consciousness.*

In specifying the general methods employed to produce ASCs, I should like to emphasize that there may be much overlap among the various methods and that many factors may be operating other than those listed. Nevertheless, for the sake of classification (albeit artificial), I have categorized the various methods on the basis of certain variables or combinations of variables which appear to play a major role in the production of these ASCs.

A. *Reduction of exteroceptive stimulation and/or motor activity.* Under this category are included mental states resulting primarily from the absolute reduction of sensory input, the change in patterning of sensory data, or constant exposure to repetitive, monotonous stimulation. A drastic reduction of motor activity also may prove an important contributing factor.

---

*See R. Shor's excellent article (Chapters 15 & 16) concerning the conditions necessary for the emergence of trance, a term roughly similar to my usage of ASC.

Such ASCs may be associated with solitary confinement (Burney, 1952; Meltzer, 1956) or prolonged social and stimulus deprivation while at sea (Anderson, 1942; Gibson, 1953; Slocum, 1948), in the arctic (Byrd, 1938; Ritter, 1954), or on the desert; highway hypnosis (Moseley, 1953); "break-off" phenomena in high altitude jet pilots (Bennett, 1961); extreme boredom (Heron, 1957); hypnogogic and hypnopompic states; sleep and related phenomena, such as dreaming and somnambulism; or experimental sensory deprivation states (Heron, 1961; Lilly, 1956; Ziskind, 1958). In clinical settings, alterations in consciousness may occur following bilateral cataract operations (Boyd & Norris, 1941) or profound immobilization in a body cast or by traction (Leiderman et al., 1958). They may also occur in patients with poliomyelitis placed in a tank-type respirator (Mendelson et al., 1958), in patients with polyneuritis which is causing sensory anesthesias and motor paralyses (Leiderman et al., 1958), and in elderly patients with cataracts (Bartlett, 1951). Descriptions of more esoteric forms of ASCs can be found in references to the healing and revelatory states during "incubation" or "temple sleep" as practiced by the early Egyptians and Greeks (Ludwig, 1964) and "kayak disease," occurring in Greenlanders forced to spend several days in a kayak while hunting seals (Williams, 1958).

B. Increase of exteroceptive stimulation and/or motor activity and/or emotion. Under this category are included excitatory mental states resulting primarily from sensory overload or bombardment, which may or may not be accompanied by strenuous physical activity or exertion. Profound emotional arousal and mental fatigue may be major contributing factors.

Instances of ASCs induced through such maneuvers are as follows: suggestible mental states produced by grilling or "third degree" tactics (Sargant, 1957); brainwashing states (Sargant, 1957); hyperkinetic trance associated with emotional contagion encountered in a group or mob setting (LaBarre, 1962; Marks, 1947); religious conversion and healing trance experiences during revivalistic meetings (Sargant, 1957; LaBarre, 1962; Coe, 1916; Kirkpatrick, 1929); mental aberrations associated with certain *rites de passage* (Sargant, 1957); spirit possession states (Sargant, 1957; LaBarre, 1962; Belo, 1960; Ravenscroft, 1965); shamanistic and prophetic trance states during tribal ceremonies (Field, 1960; Murphy, 1964); fire walker's trance (Thomas, 1934); orgiastic trance, such as experienced by Bacchanalians or Satanists during certain religious rites (Dodds, 1963; Mischelet, 1939); ecstatic trance, such as experienced by the "howling" or "whirling" dervishes during their famous *devr* dance (Williams, 1958); trance states experienced during prolonged masturbation; and experimental hyperalert trance states (Ludwig & Lyle, 1964). Alterations in consciousness may also arise from inner emotional turbulence or conflict or secondary to external conditions conducive to heightened emotional arousal. Examples of these states would include fugues, amnesias, traumatic neuroses, depersonalization, panic states, rage reactions, hysterical conversion reactions (i.e., dreamy and dissociative possession states), berzerk, latah, and whitico psychoses (Arieti, & Meth, 1959), bewitchment and demoniacal possession states (Mischelet, 1939; Galvin & Ludwig, 1961; Jones, 1959; Ludwig, 1965), and acute psychotic states, such as schizophrenic reactions.

C. *Increased alertness or mental involvement.* Included under this category are mental states which appear to result primarily from focused or selective hyperalertness with resultant peripheral hypoalertness over a sustained period of time.

Such ASCs may arise from the following activities: prolonged vigilance during sentry duty or crow's watch; prolonged observation of a radar screen (Heron, 1957); fervent praying (Bowers, 1959; Rund, 1957); intense mental absorption in a task, such as reading, writing, or problem solving; total mental involvement in listening to a dynamic or charismatic speaker (Ludwig, 1965); and even from attending to one's amplified breath sounds (Margolin & Kubie, 1944), or the prolonged watching of a revolving drum, metronome, or stroboscope.

D. *Decreased alertness or relaxation of critical faculties.* Grouped under this category are mental states which appear to occur mainly as a result of what might best be described as a "passive state of mind," in which active goal-directed thinking is minimal.

Examples of such states are as follows: mystical, transcendental, or revelatory states (e.g., *satori, samadhi, nirvana, cosmic-consciousness*) attained through passive meditation or occurring spontaneously during the relaxation of one's critical faculties (Bucke, 1951; Ludwig, 1966); daydreaming, drowsiness, "Brown study" or reverie; mediumistic and autohypnotic trances (e.g., among Indian fakirs, mystics, Pythian priestesses, etc.); profound aesthetic experiences; creative, illuminatory, and insightful states (Ludwig, 1966, Koestler, 1964); free associative states during psychoanalytic therapy; reading-trance, especially with poetry (Snyder, 1930); nostalgia; music-trance resulting from absorption in soothing lullabies or musical scores; and mental states associated with profound cognitive and muscular relaxation, such as during floating on the water or sun-bathing.

E. *Presence of somatopsychological factors.* Included under this heading are mental states primarily resulting from alterations in body chemistry or neurophysiology (Hinkle, 1961). These alterations may be deliberately induced or may result from conditions over which the individual has little or no control.

Examples of physiological disturbances producing such ASCs are as follows: hypoglycemia, either spontaneous or subsequent to fasting; hyperglycemia (e.g., postprandial lethargy); dehydration (often partially responsible for the mental aberrations encountered on the desert or at sea); thyroid and adrenal gland dysfunctions; sleep deprivation (West et al., 1962; Tyler, 1956; Katz & Landis, 1935); hyperventilation; narcolepsy; temporal lobe seizures (e.g., dreamy states and *déja vu* phenomena); and auras preceding migraine or epileptic seizures. Toxic deleria may be produced by fever, the ingestion of toxic agents, or the abrupt withdrawal from addicting drugs, such as alcohol and barbiturates. In addition, ASCs may be induced through the administration of numerous pharmacological agents, such as anesthetics and psychedelic, narcotic, sedative, and stimulant drugs.

GENERAL CHARACTERISTICS OF ASCs

Although ASCs share many features in common, there are certain general molding influences which appear to account for much of their apparent differences in outward manifestation and subjective experience. Even though similar basic processes may operate in the production of certain ASCs (e.g., trance), such influences as cultural expectations (Wallace, 1959), role-playing (Sarbin, 1950; White, 1941), demand characteristics (Orne, 1959; 1962), communication factors, transference feelings (Kubie & Margolin, 1944), personal motivation and expectations (mental set), and the specific procedure employed to induce the ASC all work in concert to shape and mold a mental state with a unique flavor of its own.

Despite the apparent differences among ASCs, we shall find that there are a number of common denominators or features which allow us to conceptualize these ASCs as somewhat related phenomena. In previous research (Levine et al., 1963; Levine & Ludwig, 1965a, 1965b; Ludwig & Levine, 1966), Dr. Levine and I were able to demonstrate the presence of many of these features in alterations of consciousness induced by hypnosis, lysergic acid diethylamide (LSD-25), and combination of these variables. Similar features (described below), in greater or lesser degree, tend to be characteristic of most ASCs.

A. Alterations in thinking. Subjective disturbances in concentration, attention, memory, and judgment represent common findings. Archaic modes of thought (primary process thought) predominate, and reality testing seems impaired to varying degrees. The distinction between cause and effect becomes blurred, and ambivalence may be pronounced whereby incongruities or opposites may coexist without any (psycho)logical conflict. Moreover, as Rapaport (1951) and Brenman (1950) have commented, many of these states are associated with a decrease in reflective awareness.

B. Disturbed time sense. Sense of time and chronology become greatly altered. Subjective feelings of timelessness, time coming to a standstill, the acceleration or slowing of time, and so on, are common. Time may also seem of infinite or infinitesimal duration.

C. Loss of control. As a person enters or is in an ASC, he often experiences fears of losing his grip on reality and losing his self-control. During the induction phase, he may actively try to resist experiencing the ASCs (e.g., sleep, hypnosis, anesthesia), while in other instances he may actually welcome relinquishing his volition and giving in to the experience (e.g., narcotic drugs, alcohol, LSD, mystical states).

The experience of "loss of control" is a complicated phenomenon. Relinquishing conscious control may arouse feelings of impotency and helplessness, or, paradoxically, may represent the gaining of greater control and power through the loss of control. This latter experience may be found in hypnotized persons (Kubie & Margolin, 1944; Gill & Brenman, 1959) or in audiences who vicariously identify with the power and omnipotence which they attribute to the hypnotist or demagogue. This is also the case in mystical, revelatory, or spirit possession states whereby the person relinquishes conscious control in the hope of experiencing divine truths, clairvoyance, "cosmic consciousness," communion with the spirits or supernatural powers, or serving as a temporary abode or mouthpiece for the gods.

D. Change in emotional expression. With the diminution of conscious control or inhibitions, there is often a marked change in emotional expression. Sudden and unexpected displays of more primitive and intense emotion than shown during normal, waking consciousness may appear. Emotional extremes, from ecstasy and orgiastic equivalents to profound fear and depression, commonly occur.

There is another pattern of emotional expression which may characterize these states. The individual may become detached, uninvolved, or relate intense feelings without any emotional display. The capacity for humor may also diminish.

E. Body image change. A wide array of distortions in body image frequently occur in ASCs. There is also a common propensity for individuals to experience a profound sense of depersonalization, a schism between body and mind, feelings of derealization, or a dissolution of boundaries between self and others, the world, or universe.

When these subjective experiences arise from toxic or delerious states, auras preceding seizures, or the ingestion of certain drugs, etc., they are often regarded by the individual as strange and even frightening. However, when they appear in a mystical or religious setting, they may be interpreted as transcendental or mystical experiences of "oneness," "expansion of consciousness," "oceanic feelings," or "oblivion."

There are also some other common features which might be grouped under this heading. Not only may various parts of the body appear or feel shrunken, enlarged, distorted, heavy, weightless, disconnected, strange, or funny, but spontaneous experiences of dizziness, blurring of vision, weakness, numbness, tingling, and analgesia are likewise encountered.

F. Perceptual distortions. Common to most ASCs is the presence of perceptual aberrations, including hallucinations, pseudohallucinations, increased visual imagery, subjectively felt hyperacuteness of perception, and illusions of every variety. The content of these perceptual aberrations may be determined by cultural, group, individual, or neurophysiological factors and represent either wish-fulfillment fantasies, the expression of basic fears or conflicts, or simply phenomena of little dynamic import, such as hallucinations of light, color, geometrical patterns, or shapes. In some ASCs, such as those produced by psychedelic drugs, marihuana, or mystical contemplation, synesthesias may appear whereby one form of sensory experience is translated into other form. For example, persons may report seeing or feeling sounds or being able to taste what they see.

G. Change in meaning or significance. At this point I should like to dwell somewhat on one of the most intriguing features of almost all ASCs, the understanding of which will help us account for a number of seemingly unrelated phenomena. After observing and reading descriptions of a wide variety of ASCs induced by different agents or maneuvers, I have become very impressed with the predilection of persons in these states to attach an increased meaning or significance to their subjective experiences, ideas, or perceptions. At times, it appears as though the person is undergoing an attenuated "eureka" experience during which feelings of profound insight, illumination, and truth frequently occur. In toxic or psychotic states, this increased sense of significance may manifest itself in the attributing of false significance to external cues, ideas of reference, and the numerous instances of "psychotic insight."

I should like to emphasize that this sense of increased significance, which is primarily an emotional or affectual experience, bears little relationship to the objective "truth" of the content of this experience (Ludwig, 1966). To illustrate the ridiculousness of some of the "insights" attained during ASCs, I should like to cite a personal experience when I once took LSD for experimental purposes. Sometimes during the height of the reaction, I remember experiencing an intense desire to urinate. Standing by the urinal, I noticed a sign above it which read "Please Flush After Using!" As I weighted these words in my mind, I suddenly realized their profound meaning. Thrilled by this startling revelation, I rushed back to my colleague to share this universal truth with him. Unfortunately, being a mere mortal, he could not appreciate the world-shaking import of my communication and responded by laughing!

William James (1950, p. 284) describes subjective experiences associated with other alterations of consciousness. "One of the charms of drunkenness," he writes, "unquestionably lies in the deepening sense of reality and truth which is gained therein. In whatever light things may then appear to us, they seem more utterly what they are, more 'utterly utter' than when we are sober." In his *Varieties of Religious Experience*, he adds:

Nitrous oxide and ether, especially nitrous oxide, when sufficiently diluted with air, stimulate the mystical consciousness in an extraordinary degree. Depth upon depth of truth seems revealed to the inhaler. This truth fades out, however, or escapes, at a moment of coming to; and if the words remain over in which it seemed to clothe itself they prove to be the veriest nonsense. Nevertheless, the sense of a profound meaning having been there persists; and I know more than one person who is persuaded that in the nitrous oxide trance we have a genuine metaphysical revelation. (James, 1929, p. 378)

H. Sense of the ineffable. Most often, because of the uniqueness of the subjective experience associated with certain ASCs (e.g., transcendental, aesthetic, creative, psychotic, and mystical states), persons claim a certain ineptness or inability to communicate the nature or essence of the experience to someone who has not undergone a similar experience. Contributing to the sense of the ineffable is the tendency of persons to develop varying degrees of amnesias for their experiences during profound alterations of consciousness, such as the hypnotic trance, somnambulistic trance, possession fits, dreaming, mystical experiences, delirious states, drug intoxications, auras, orgiastic and ecstatic states, and the like. By no means is amnesia always the case, as witnessed by the lucid memory following the psychedelic experience, marihuana smoking, or certain revelatory or illuminatory states.

I. Feelings of rejuvenation. Although the characteristic of "rejuvenation" only has limited application to the vast panoply of ASCs, I have included this characteristic as a common denominator since it does appear in a sufficient number of these states to warrant attention. Thus, on emerging from certain profound alterations of consciousness (e.g., psychedelic experiences, abreactive states secondary to the administration of carbon dioxide, methamphetamine (Methedrine), ether or amytal, hypnosis, religious conversion, transcendental and mystical states, insulin coma therapy, spirit possession fits, primitive puberty rites, and even, on some occasions, deep sleep), many persons claim to experience a new sense of hope, rejuvenation, renaissance, or rebirth (LaBarre, 1962; Coe, 1916; Bucke, 1951; Ludwig & Levine, 1966; James, 1929; Blood, 1874; Ebin, 1961; Huxley, 1954; LaBarre, 1964; Pahnke, 1965).

J. Hypersuggestibility. Employing a broad view, I shall regard as manifestations of hypersuggestibility in ASCs not only the numerous instances of "primary" and "secondary" suggestibility but also the increased susceptibility and propensity of persons uncritically to accept and/or automatically to respond to specific statements (i.e., commands or instructions of a leader, shaman, demagogue, or hypnotist) or nonspecific cues (i.e., cultural or group expectations for certain types of behavior or subjective feelings). Hypersuggestibility will also refer to the increased tendency of a person to misperceive or misinterpret various stimuli or situations based either on his inner fears or wishes.

It is becoming increasingly apparent that the phenomenon of suggestibility associated with ASCs can be best understood by analysis of the subjective state itself. Recently, theoreticians seem to have become much more aware of the importance of the subjective state to account for many of the phenomena observed in hypnotized persons. Orne, for example, stated that "an important attribute of hypnosis is a potentiality for the subject to experience as subjectively real suggested alterations in his environment that do not conform with reality." (Meltzer, 1956, p. 237) Sutcliffe adds that "the distinguishing feature of this state is the hypnotized subject's emotional conviction that the world is as suggested by the hypnotist, rather than a pseudoperception of the suggested world." (1961, p. 200)

In attempting to account for the dramatic feature of hypersuggestibility, I believe that a better understanding of this phenomenon can be gained through an analysis of some of the subjective features associated with ASCs in general. With the recession of a person's critical faculties there is an attendant decrease in his capacity for reality testing or his ability to distinguish between subjective and objective reality. This, in turn, would tend to create the compensatory need to bolster up his failing faculties by seeking out certain props, support, or guidance in an effort to relieve some of the anxiety associated with the loss of control. In his attempt to compensate for his failing critical faculties, the person comes to rely more on the suggestions of the hypnotist, shaman, demagogue, interrogator, religious healer, preacher, or doctor, all representing omnipotent authoritative figures. With the "dissolution of self boundaries," which represents another important feature of ASCs, there would also be the tendency for the person to identify vicariously with the authoritarian figure whose wishes and commands are accepted as the person's own. Contradictions, doubts, inconsistencies, and inhibitions tend to diminish (all characteristics of "primary process" thinking), and the suggestions of the person endowed with authority tend to be accepted as concrete reality. These suggestions become imbued with even more importance and urgency owing to the increased significance and meaning attributed both to internal and external stimuli during alterations in consciousness.

With all these factors operating, a monomotivational or "supra-motivational" state is achieved in which the person strives to realize in behavior the thoughts or ideas which he experiences as subjective reality. The subjective reality may be determined by a number of influences working individually or in concert, such as the expectations of the authority figure, the group, culture, or even by the "silent inner voice" (e.g., during auto-hypnotic states, prayer, auditory hallucinations, guiding spirits) expressing the person's own wishes or fears.

When a person lapses into certain other ASCs, such as panic, acute psychosis, toxic delirium, etc., where external direction or structure is ambiguous and ill-defined, the person's internal mental productions tend to become his major guide for reality and play a large role in determining behavior. In these instances, he is much more susceptible to the dictates of his emotions and the fantasies and thoughts associated with them than to the direction of others.

FUNCTIONS OF ASCs

Now that we have considered certain characteristics associated with ASCs, we might raise the question whether they serve any useful biological, psychological, or social functions for man. It is my thesis that the very presence and prevalence of these states in man (Shor, 1960) attests to their importance in his everyday functioning. I find it difficult to accept, for example, that man's ability to lapse into trance has been evolved just so he can be hypnotized on stage or in a clinical or laboratory setting. Moreover, the widespread occurrence and use of mystical and possession states or aesthetic and creative experiences indicates that these ASCs satisfy many needs both for man and society. Although my thesis may prove teleological, I feel that this approach will shed some further light on the nature and function of these states.

My viewpoint, then, is that ASCs might be regarded (to use Sherrington's terminology) as "final common pathways" for many different forms of human expression and experience, both adaptive and maladaptive. In some instances the psychological regression found in ASCs will prove to be atavistic and harmful to the individual or society, while in other instances the regression will be "in the service of the ego" (Kris, 1952) and enable man to transcend the bounds of logic and formality or express repressed needs and desires in a socially sanctioned and constructive way.

A. Maladaptive expressions. The maladaptive expressions or uses of ASCs are numerous and manifold. The emergence of these ASCs may re-present (a) attempts at resolution of emotional conflict (e.g., fugues, amnesias, traumatic neuroses, depersonalization, and dissociation); (b) defensive functions in certain threatening situations conducive to the arousal of anxiety [e.g., lapsing into hypnoidal states during psychotherapy (Dickes, 1965)]; (c) a breakthrough of forbidden impulses (e.g., acute psychotic and panic reactions); (d) escape from responsibilities and inner tensions (e.g., narcotics, marihuana, alcohol); (e) the symbolic acting-out of unconscious conflicts [e.g., demoniacal possession, bewitchment (Galvin, 1961; Jones, 1959; Ludwig, 1965)]; (f) the manifestation of organic lesions or neurophysiological disturbances (e.g., auras, toxic conditions); and (g) an inadvertent and potentially dangerous response to certain stimuli (e.g., highway hypnosis, radar screen and sentry duty trance).

B. *Adaptive expressions.*   Man has employed a variety of ASCs in an effort to acquire new knowledge or experience, express psychic tensions or relieve conflict without danger to himself or others, and to function more adequately and constructively in society.

1. Healing: Throughout history, the production of ASCs has played a major role in the various healing arts and practices. The induction of these states has been employed for almost every conceivable aspect of psychological therapy. Thus, shamans may lapse into trance or possession states in order to diagnose the etiology of their patients' ailments or to learn of specific remedies or healing practices (Murphy, 1964). Moreover, during the actual treatment or healing ceremony, the shaman, hungan, medicine man, priest, preacher, physician, or psychiatrist may view the production of an ASC in the patient as a crucial prerequisite for healing. There are countless instances of healing practices designed to take advantage of the suggestibility, increased meaning, propensity for emotional catharsis, and the feelings of rejuvenation associated with ASCs. The early Egyptian and Greek practices of "incubation" in their sleep temples, the faith cures at Lourdes and other religious shrines, the healing through prayer and meditation, cures by the "healing touch," the laying on of hands, encounters with religious relics, spiritual healing, spirit possession cures, exorcism, mesmeric or magnetic treatment, and modern day hypnotherapy are all obvious instances of the role of ASCs in treatment (Ludwig, 1964).

Pharmacologically induced ASCs have also played a major role in the healing arts. Abreactive or cathartic techniques, employing peyote, ether, CO_2, amytal, methamphetamine, and LSD-25 have all had wide use in psychiatry (Sargant, 1957; Freeman, 1952). Kubie and Margolin (Kubie, 1945; Margolin & Kubie, 1945) have also commented on the therapeutic value of certain drugs to induce temporary dissociation and relieve repression.

Perhaps unrelated to the specific effects of ASCs in treatment are the nonspecific effects of certain other alterations in consciousness which aid in maintaining psychic equilibrium and health. For example, sleep, traditionally regarded as The Great Healer, and dreaming seem to serve important biological and psychological functions for man (Snyder, 1963). The ASC associated with sexual orgasm might be considered as another beneficial mental alteration which not only has biological survival value as a positive reinforcement for the sexual drive but also serves as an outlet for numerous human desires and frustrations.

2. Avenues of new knowledge or experience: Man often has sought to induce ASCs in an effort to gain new knowledge, inspiration, or experience. In the realm of religion, intense prayer, passive meditation, revelatory and prophetic states, mystical and transcendental experiences, religious conversion, and divination states have served man in opening new realms of experience, reaffirming moral values, resolving emotional conflicts, and often enabling him to cope better with his human predicament and the world about him. It is also interesting to note that among many primitive groups, spirit possession is believed to impart a superhuman knowledge which could not possibly be gained during waking consciousness. Such paranormal faculties as superlative wisdom, the "gift of tongues," and clairvoyance are supposedly demonstrated during the possession fit (Field, 1960).

ASCs appear to enrich man's experiences in many other areas of life. The intense esthetic experience gained while absorbed in some majestic scene, a work of art, or music may broaden man's subjective experiences and serve as a source of creative inspiration. There are also numerous instances of sudden illumination, creative insights, and problem solving occurring while man has lapsed into such ASCs as trance, drowsiness, sleep, passive meditation or drug intoxication (Koestler, 1964).

3. Social function: ASCs occurring in a group setting seem to serve many individual and social needs. Although a brief discussion cannot do justice to the wide variety of functions which ASCs serve for various cultures, we can at least mention a few.

If we may employ spirit possession as a paradigm for the potential value of ASCs, we find that its social import and ramifications are considerable. From the individual's vantage point, possession by one of the tribal or local deities or Holy Spirit during a religious ceremony would allow him to attain high status through fulfilling his cult role, gain a temporary freedom of responsibility from his actions and pronouncements, or enable him to act out in a socially sanctioned way his aggressive and sexual conflicts or desires (Mischel & Mischel, 1958). Tensions and fears are dissipated, and a new sense of spiritual security and confidence may supplant the despair and hopelessness of a marginal existence (Davidson, 1965).

From society's standpoint, the needs of the tribe or group are met through its vicarious identification with the entranced person who not only derives individual satisfaction from divine possession but also acts out certain ritualized group conflicts and aspirations, such as the theme of death and resurrection, cultural taboos, and so on (LaBarre, 1962; Belo, 1960; Field, 1960; Ravenscroft, 1965; Davidson, 1965; Deren, 1952). Moreover, the dramatic behavioral manifestations of spirit possession serve to convince the participants of the continued personal interest of their gods, reaffirm their local beliefs, allow them to exert some control over the unknown, enhance group cohesion and identification, and endow the utterances of the entranced person, shaman, or priest with an importance they might otherwise not have if spoken in an ordinary setting. In general, the existence of such practices represents an excellent example of how society creates modes of reducing frustration, stress and loneliness through group action.

In conclusion, then, it appears the ASCs play a very significant role in man's experience and behavior. It is also apparent that these states may serve as adaptive or maladaptive outlets for the expression of a multitude of man's passions, needs and desires. Moreover, there is little question that we have hardly scratched the surface in understanding fully the facets and functions of ASCs. As a final note, I should like to quote the very pertinent remarks of William James (1929, pp. 378–379).

. . . Our normal waking consciousness . . . is but one special type of consciousness, whilst all about it, parted from it by the filmiest of screens, there lie potential forms of conscious entirely different. We may go through life without suspecting their existence; but apply the requisite stimulus, and at a touch they are all there in all their completeness, definite types of mentality which probably somewhere have their field of application and adaptation. No account of the universe in its totality can be final which leaves these other forms of consciousness quite disregarded. How to regard them is the question—for they are so discontinuous with ordinary consciousness. Yet they may determine attitudes though they cannot furnish formulas, and open a region though they fail to give a map. At any rate, they forbid a premature closing of our accounts with reality.

SUMMARY

Despite numerous clinical and research reports on certain altered states of consciousness, there has been little attempt to conceptualize the relationship among these states and the conditions necessary for their emergence. To this end, the author has tried to integrate and discuss pertinent findings from many diverse areas in an effort to gain a better understanding of these states and the functions they serve for man and society.

As one views the many altered states of consciousness experienced by man, it soon becomes apparent that there are a number of essential conditions which contribute to their emergence. Moreover, although the outward manifestations and subjective experiences associated with various alterations in consciousness may differ, there are a number of basic features which most of these states share in common. From a functional viewpoint, it also becomes clear that many altered states of consciousness serve as "final common pathways" for many different forms of human expression, both maladaptive and adaptive.

2

DEAUTOMATIZATION AND THE MYSTIC EXPERIENCE

ARTHUR J. DEIKMAN

To study the mystic experience one must turn initially to material that appears unscientific, is couched in religious terms, and seems completely subjective. Yet these religious writings are data and not to be dismissed as something divorced from the reality with which psychological science is concerned. The following passage from *The Cloud of Unknowing*, a fourteenth-century religious treatise, describes a procedure to be followed in order to attain an intuitive knowledge of God. Such an intuitive experience is called mystical because it is considered beyond the scope of language to convey. However, a careful reading will show that these instructions contain within their religious idiom psychological ideas pertinent to the study and understanding of a wide range of phenomena not necessarily connected with theological issues:

... forget all the creatures that ever God made and the works of them, so that thy thought or thy desire be not directed or stretched to any of them, neither in general nor in special. ... At the first time when thou dost it, thou findst but a darkness and as it were a kind of unknowing, thou knowest not what, saving that thou feelest in thy will a naked intent unto God ... thou mayest neither see him clearly by light of understanding in thy reason, nor feel him in sweetness of love

Reprinted by permission from *Psychiatry*, Vol. 29 1966, pp. 324–338. This research was supported by Research Grant MH-07683, from the National Institute of Mental Health, USPHS; and by the Austen Riggs Center.

in thy affection . . . if ever thou shalt see him or feel him as it may be here, it must always be in this cloud and in this darkness. . . . Smite upon that thick cloud of unknowing with a sharp dart of longing love (Knowles, 1961, p. 77).

Specific questions are raised by this subjective account: What constitutes a state of consciousness whose content is not rational thought ("understanding in thy reason"), affective ("sweetness of love"), or sensate ("darkness", "cloud of unknowing")? By what means do both an active "forgetting" and an objectless "longing" bring about such a state? A comparison of this passage with others in the classical mystic literature indicates that the author is referring to the activities of renunciation and contemplative meditation. This paper will present a psychological model of the mystic experience based on the assumptions that meditation and renunciation are primary techniques for producing it, and that the process can be conceptualized as one of de-automatization.

PHENOMENA OF THE MYSTIC EXPERIENCE

Accounts of mystic experiences can be categorized as (a) untrained-sensate, (b) trained-sensate, and (c) trained-transcendent. "Untrained-sensate" refers to phenomena occurring in persons not regularly engaged in meditation, prayer, or other exercises aimed at achieving a religious experience. These persons come from all occupations and classes. The mystic state they report is one of intense affective, perceptual, and cognitive phenomena that appear to be extensions of familiar psychological processes. Nature and drugs are the most frequent precipitating factors. James cites the account of Trevor to illustrate a nature experience:

For nearly an hour I walked along the road to the "Cat and Fiddle," and then returned. On the way back, suddenly, without warning, I felt that I was in heaven— an inward state of peace and joy and assurance indescribably intense, accompanied with a sense of being bathed in a warm glow of light, as though the external condition had brought about the internal effect—a feeling of having passed, beyond the body, though the scene around me stood out more clearly and as if nearer to me than before, by reason of the illumination in the midst of which I seemed to be placed. This deep emotion lasted, though with decreasing strength, until I reached home, and for some time after, only gradually passing away. (James, 1929, p. 388).

For an example of a drug experience James cites Symonds' description of undergoing chloroform anesthesia:

. . . I thought that I was near death; when suddenly, my soul became aware of

God, who was manifestly dealing with me, handling me, so to speak, in an intense, personal present reality. I felt him streaming in like light upon me.... I cannot describe the ecstasy I felt. Then, as I gradually awoke from the influence of the anesthetics, the old sense of my relation to the world began to return, the new sense of my relation to God began to fade (James, 1929, p. 382).

More recent accounts of experiences with LSD-25 and related drugs fall into the same group (Watts, 1962).

The "trained-sensate" category refers to essentially the same phenomena occurring in religious persons in the West and in the East who have deliberately sought "grace," "enlightenment," or "union" by means of long practice in concentration and renunciation (contemplative meditation, Yoga, and so forth). One example of this group is Richard Rolle, who wrote:

... I was sitting in a certain chapel, and while I was taking pleasure in the delight of some prayer or meditation, I suddenly felt within me an unwanted and pleasant fire. When I had for long doubted from whence it came, I learned by experience that it came from the Creator and not from creature, since I found it ever more pleasing and full of heat.... (Knowles, 1961, p. 57).

A more elaborate experience is recorded by Julian of Norwich:

In this [moment] suddenly I saw the red blood trickle down from under the garland hot and freshly and right plenteously.... And in the same shewing suddenly the Trinity fulfilled my heart most of joy. And so I understood it shall be in heaven without end to all that shall come there (Warrack, 1952, p. 8).

Visions, feelings of "fire," "sweetness," "song," and joy are various accompaniments of this type of experience.

The untrained-sensate and the trained-sensate states are phenomeno-logically indistinguishable, with the qualification that the trained mystics report experiences conforming more closely to the specific religious cosmology to which they are accustomed. As one might expect, an experience occurring as the result of training, with the support of a formal social structure, and capable of being repeated, tends to have a more significant and persisting psychological effect. However, spontaneous conversion experiences are also noteworthy for their influence on a person's life. Typical of all mystic experience is a more or less gradual fading away of the state, leaving only a memory and a longing for that which was experienced.

Mystics such as St. John of the Cross and St. Teresa of Avila, commentators such as Poulain, and Eastern mystic literature in general, divide the effects and stages through which mystics progress into a lesser experience of strong emotion and ideation (sensate) and a higher, ultimate experience that goes beyond affect or ideation. It is the latter experience, occuring almost always in association with long training, that characterizes the "trained-transcendent" group. The trans-sensate aspect is stated specifically by a number of authors, such as Walter Hilton and St. John of the Cross:

> From what I have said you may understand that visions of revelations by spirits, whether seen in bodily form or in the imagination, and whether in sleeping or waking, do not constitute true contemplation. This applies equally to any other sensible experiences of seemingly spiritual origin, whether of sound, taste, smell or of warmth felt like a glowing fire in the breast or in other parts of the body, anything, indeed, that can be experienced by the physical senses (Hilton, 1953, pp. 14–15).

> ...that inward wisdom is so simple, so general and so spiritual that it has not entered into the understanding enwrapped or clad in any form or image subject to sense, it follows that sense and imagination (as it has not entered through them nor has taken their form and color) cannot account for it or imagine it, so as to say anything concerning it, although the soul be clearly aware that it is experiencing and partaking of that rare and delectable wisdom (St. John of the Cross, 1953, Vol. 1, p. 457).

A similar distinction between lower (sensate) and higher (transcendent) contemplative states may be found in Yoga texts. "Conscious concentration" is a preliminary step to "concentration which is not conscious (of objects)."

> For practice when directed towards any supporting-object is not capable of serving as an instrument to this [concentration not conscious of an object].... Mind-stuff, when engaged in the practice of this [imperceptible object], seems as if it were itself non-existent and without any supporting-object. Thus [arises] that concentration [called] seedless, [without sensational stimulus], which is not conscious of objects (Woods, 1914, p. 42).

In the transcendent state, multiplicity disappears and a sense of union with the One or with All occurs. "When all lesser things and ideas are transcended and forgotten, and there remains only a perfect state of imagelessness where Tathagata and Tathata are merged into perfect Oneness ...." (Goddard, 1938, p. 322).

> Then the spirit is transported high above all the faculties into a void of immense solitude whereof no mortal can adequately speak. It is the mysterious darkness wherein is concealed the limitless Good. To such an extent are we admitted and absorbed into something that is one, simple, divine, and illimitable, that we seem no longer distinguishable from it....In this unity, the feeling of multiplicity disappears. When, afterwards, these persons come to themselves again, they find

themselves possessed of a distinct knowledge of things, more luminous and more perfect than that of others. . . . This obscurity is a light to which no created intelligence can arrive by its own nature (Poulain, 1950, p. 272).

This state is described in all the literatures as one in which the mystic is passive in that he has abandoned striving. He sees "grace" to be the action of God on himself and feels himself to be receptive. In addition, some descriptions indicate that the senses and faculties of thought feel suspended, a state described in Catholic literature as the "ligature."

Human variety is reflected in the superficial differences between the various mystic records. However, perusal of these accounts leads one to agree with Marechal when he writes,

A very delicate *psychological problem* is thus raised: the consensus of the testimonies we have educed is too unanimous to be rejected. It compels us to recognize the existence in certain subjects of a special psychological state, which generally results from a very close interior concentration, sustained by an intense affective movement, but which, on the other hand, no longer presents any trace of "discursiveness," spatial imagination, or reflex consciousness. And the disconcerting question arises: after images and concepts and the conscious Ego have been abolished, what subsists of the intellectual life? Multiplicity will have disappeared, true, but to the advantage of what kind of unity? (Marechal, 1964, p. 185).

In summary, mystic literature suggests that various kinds of people have attained what they considered to be exalted states of mind and feeling, states that may be grouped in three divisions: untrained-sensate, trained-sensate, and trained-transcendent. The most important distinction would appear to be between an experience grounded in customary affect, sensations, and ideations, and an experience that is said to transcend such modalities.

BASIC MYSTIC TECHNIQUES

How is the mystic experience produced? To answer this question I will examine the two basic techniques involved in mystical exercises: contemplation and renunciation.

Contemplation is, ideally, a nonanalytic apprehension of an object or idea—nonanalytic because discursive thought is banished and the attempt is made to empty the mind of everything except the percept of the object in question. Thought is conceived of as an interference with the direct contact that yields essential knowledge through perception alone. The renunciation of worldly goals and pleasures, both physical and psychological, is an extension of the same principle of freeing oneself from distractions that interfere with the perception of higher realisms or more beautiful aspects of existence. The renunciation prescribed is most thorough and quite explicit in all texts. The passage that begins this paper instructs, "Forget all the creatures that ever God made . . . so that thy thought . . . be not directed . . . to any of them . . . " In the Lankavatra Scripture one reads, " . . . he must seek to annihilate all vagrant thoughts and notions belonging to the externality of things, and all ideas of individuality and generality, of suffering and impermanence, and cultivate the noblest ideas of egolessness and emptiness and imagelessness . . ." (Goddard, 1938, p. 323). Meister Eckhart promises: "If we keep ourselves free from the things that are outside us, God will give us in exchange everything that is in heaven, . . . itself with all its powers ..." (Clark & Skinner, 1958, p. 104). In Hilton one reads, "Therefore if you desire to discover your soul, withdraw your thoughts from outward and material things, forgetting if possible your own body and its five senses . . ." (Hilton, 1953, p.205). St. John calls for the explicit banishment of memory:

> Of all these forms and manners of knowledge the soul must strip and void itself, and it must strive to lose the imaginary apprehension of them, so that there may be left in it no kind of impression of knowledge, nor trace of aught soever, but rather the soul must remain barren and bare, as if these forms had never passed through it and in total oblivion and suspension. And this cannot happen unless the memory be annihilated as to all its forms, if it is to be united with God (St. John of the Cross, 1953, p. 227).

In most Western and Eastern mystic practice, renunciation also extends to the actual life situation of the mystic. Poverty, chastity, and the solitary way are regarded as essential to the attainment of mystic union. Zen Buddhism, however, sees the ordinary life as a proper vehicle for "satori" as long as the "worldly" passions and desires are given up, and with them the intellectual approach to experience. "When I am in my isness, thoroughly purged of all intellectual sediments, I have my freedom in its primary sense . . . free from intellectual complexities and moralistic attachments . . ." (Suzuki, 1959, p. 19).

Instructions for performing contemplative meditation indicate that a very active effort is made to exclude outer and inner stimuli, to devalue and banish them, and at the same time to focus attention on the meditative object. In this active phase of contemplation the concentration of attention upon particular objects, ideas, physical movements, or breathing exercises is advised as an aid to diverting attention from its usual channels and restricting it to a monotonous focus.* Patanjali comments,

---

*Breathing exercises can also affect the carbon dioxide content of the blood and thus alter the state of consciousness chemically.

Binding the mind-stuff to a place is fixed-attention. . . . Focusedness of the presented idea on that place is contemplation. . . . This same [contemplation] shining forth [in consciousness] as the intended object and nothing more, and, as it were, emptied of itself, is concentration. . . . The three in one are constraint. . . . Even these [three] are indirect aids to seedless [concentration] (Woods, 1914, pp. 203–208).

Elaborate instructions are found in Yoga for the selection of objects for contemplation and for the proper utilization of posture and breathing to create optimal conditions for concentration. Such techniques are not usually found in the Western religious literature except in the form of the injunction to keep the self oriented toward God and to fight the distractions which are seen as coming from the devil. (*The spiritual exercises of St. Ignatius* (Puhl, 1962) is a possible exception.)

The active phase of contemplative meditation is a preliminary to the stage of full contemplation, in which the subject is caught up and absorbed in a process he initiated but which now seems autonomous, requiring no effort. Instead, passivity—self-surrender—is called for, an open receptivity amidst the "darkness" resulting from the banishment of thoughts and sensations and the renunciation of goals and desires directed toward the world.

When this active effort of mental concentration is successful, it is followed by a more passive, receptive state of samadhi in which the earnest disciple will enter into the blissful abode of noble wisdom . . . (Goddard, 1938, p. 323).
For if such a soul should desire to make any effort of its own with its interior faculties, this means that it will hinder and lose the blessings which . . . God is instilling into it and impressing upon it (Hilton, 1953, p. 380).

It should not be forgotten that the techniques of contemplation and renunciation are exercised within the structure of some sort of theological schema. This schema is used to interpret and organize the experiences that occur. However, mere doctrine is usually not enough. The Eastern texts insist on the necessity for being guided by a guru (an experienced teacher), for safety's sake as well as in order to attain the spiritual goal. In Western religion, a "spiritual advisor" serves as guide and teacher. The presence of a motivating and organizing conceptual structure and the support and encouragement of a teacher are undoubtedly important in helping a person to persist in the meditation exercises and to achieve the marked personality changes that can occur through success in this endeavor. Enduring personality change is made more likely by the emphasis on adapting behavior to the values and insights associated both with the doctrinal structure and with the stages of mystical experience.

How can one explain the phenomena and their relation to these techniques? Most explanations in the psychological and psychoanalytic literature have been general statements emphasizing a regression to the early infant-mother symbiotic relationship. These statements range from an extreme position, such as Alexander's (1931), where Buddhist training is described as a withdrawal of libido from the world to be reinvested in the ego until an intra-uterine narcissism is achieved—"the pure narcissism of the sperm"—to the basic statement of Freud's (1961, Vol. 21, pp. 64–73) that "oceanic feeling" is a memory of a relatively undifferentiated infantile ego state. Lewin (1950, pp. 149–155) in particular has developed this concept. In recent years hypotheses have been advanced uniting the concepts of regression and of active adaptation. The works of Kris (1952, p. 302). Fingarette (1963), and Prince and Savage (1965) illustrate this approach to the mystic experience. This paper will attempt an explanation of mystic phenomena from a different point of view, that of attentional mechanisms in perception and cognition.

DEAUTOMATIZATION

In earlier studies of experimental meditation, I hypothesized that mystic phenomena were a consequence of a *deautomatization* of the psychological structures that organize, limit, select, and interpret perceptual stimuli. I suggested the hypotheses of sensory translation, reality transfer, and perceptual expansion to explain certain unusual perceptions of the meditation subjects (Deikman, 1966). At this point I will try to present an integrated formulation that relates these concepts to the classical mystic techniques of renunciation and contemplation.

Deautomatization is a concept stemming from Hartmann's (1958, pp. 88–91) discussion of the automatization of motor behavior:

> In well-established achievements they [motor apparatuses] function automatically: the integration of the somatic systems involved in the action is automatized, and so is the integration of the individual mental acts involved in it. With increasing exercise of the action its intermediate steps disappear from consciousness . . . not only motor behavior but perception and thinking, too, show automatization. . . .
>
> It is obvious that automatization may have economic advantages, in saving attention cathexis in particular and simple cathexis of consciousness in general. . . . Here, as in most adaptation processes, we have a purposive provision for the average expectable range of tasks.

Gill and Brenman (1959, p. 178) developed the concept of deautomatization:

> Deautomatization is an undoing of the automatizations of apparatuses—both

means and goal structures—directed toward the environment. Deautomatization is, as it were, a shake-up which can be followed by an advance or a retreat in the level of organization. . . . Some manipulation of the attention directed toward the functioning of an apparatus is necessary if it is to be deautomatized.

Thus, deautomatization may be conceptualized as the undoing of auto-matization, presumably by *reinvesting actions and percepts with attention.*

The concept of psychological *structures* follows the definition by Rapaport and Gill (1959, pp. 157–158):

> *Structures are configurations of a slow rate of change . . . within which, between which, and by means of which mental processes take place. . . . Structures are hierarchically ordered. . . .* This assumption . . . is significant because it is the foundation for the psycho-analytic propositions concerning differentiation (whether resulting in discrete structures which are then co-ordinated, or in the increased internal articulation of structures), and because it implies that the quality of a process depends upon the level of the structural hierarchy on which it takes place.

The deautomatization of a structure may result in a shift to a structure lower in the hierarchy, rather than a complete cessation of the particular function involved.

Contemplative Meditation

In reflecting on the technique of contemplative meditation, one can see that it seems to constitute just such a manipulation of attention as is required to produce deautomatization. The percept receives intense attention while the use of attention for abstract categorization and thought is explicitly prohibited. Since automatization normally accomplishes the transfer of attention *from* a percept or action to abstract thought activity, the meditation procedure exerts a force in the reverse direction. Cognition is inhibited in favor of perception; the active intellectual style is replaced by a receptive perceptual mode.

Automatization is a hierarchically organized developmental process, so one would expect deautomatization to result in a shift toward a perceptual and cognitive organization characterized as "primitive," that is, an organization preceding the analytic, abstract, intellectual mode typical of present-day adult thought. The perceptual and cognitive functioning of children and of people of primitive cultures have been studied by Werner, who described primitive imagery and thought as (a) relatively more vivid and sensuous, (b) syncretic, (c) physiognomic and animated, (d) de-differentiated with respect to the distinctions between self and object and between objects, and (e) characterized by a dedifferentiation and fusion of sense modalities. In a statement based on studies of eidetic imagery in children as well as on broader studies of perceptual development, Werner (1957, p. 152) states:

> ...The image...gradually changed in functional character. It becomes essentially subject to the exigencies of abstract thought. Once the image changes in function and becomes an instrument in reflective thought, its structure will also change. It is only through such structural change that the image can serve as an instrument of expression in abstract mental activity. This is why, of necessity, the sensuousness, fullness of detail, the color and vivacity of the image must fade.

Theoretically, deautomatization should reverse this development in the direction of primitive thought, and it is striking to note that classical accounts of mystic experience emphasize the phenomenon of Unity. Unity can be viewed as a dedifferentiation that merges all boundaries until the self is no longer experienced as a separate object and customary perceptual and cognitive distinctions are no longer applicable. In this respect, the mystic literature is consistent with the deautomatization hypothesis. If one searches for evidence of changes in the mystic's experience of the external world, the classical literature is of less help, because the mystic's orientation is inward rather than outward and he tends to write about God rather than nature. However, in certain accounts of untrained-sensate experience there is evidence of a gain in sensory richness and vividness. James (1929, pp. 243–244), in describing the conversion experience, states: "A third peculiarity of the assurance state is the objective change which the world often appears to undergo, 'An appearance of newness beautifies every object' ...." He quotes Billy Bray: "... I shouted for joy, I praised God with my whole heart ... I remember this, that everything looked new to me, the people, the fields, the cattle, the trees. I was like a new man in a new world." Another example, this one from a woman, "I pled for mercy and had a vivid realization of forgiveness and renewal of my nature. When rising from my knees I exclaimed, 'Old things have passed away, all things have become new'. It was like entering another world, a new state of existence. Natural objects were glorified. My spiritual vision was so clarified that I saw beauty in every material object in the universe. ..." Again, "The appearance of everything was altered, there seemed to be as it were a calm, a sweet cast or appearance of divine glory in almost everything."

Such a change in a person's perception of the world has been called by Underhill (1955, p. 235), "clarity of vision, a heightening of physical perception," and she quotes Blake's phrase, "cleanse the doors of perception." It is hard to document this perceptual alteration because the autobiographical accounts that Underhill, James, and others cite are a blend of the mystic's spiritual feeling and his actual perception, with the result that the spiritual content dominates the description the mystic gives of the physical world. However, these accounts do suggest that a "new vision" takes place, colored by an inner exaltation. Their authors report perceiving a new brilliance to the world, of seeing everything as if for the first time, of noticing beauty which for the most part they may have previously passed by without seeing. Although such descriptions do not prove a change in sensory perception, they strongly imply it. These particular phenomena appear quite variable and are not mentioned in many mystic accounts. However, direct evidence was obtained on this point in the meditation experiments already cited (Deikman, 1963, 1966). There, it was possible to ask questions and to analyze the subjects' reports to obtain information on their perceptual experiences. The phenomena the subjects reported fulfilled Werner's criteria completely, although the extent of change varied from one subject to the next. They described their reactions to the percept, a blue vase, as follows: (a) an increased vividness and richness of the percept—"more vivid," "luminous"; (b) animation in the vase, which seemed to move with a life of its own; (c) a marked decrease in self-object distinction, occurring in those subjects who continued longest in the experiments: " . . . I really began to feel, you know, almost as though the blue and I were perhaps merging, or that vase and I were. . . . It was as though everything was sort of merging . . . "; (d) syncretic thought and a fusing and alteration of normal perceptual modes: "I began to feel this light going back and forth," "When the vase changes shape I feel this in my body," "I'm still not sure, though, whether it's the motion in the rings or if it's the rings [concentric rings of light between the subject and the vase]. But in a certain way it is real . . . it's not real in the sense that you can see it, touch it, taste it, smell it or anything but it certainly is real in the sense that you can experience it happening." The perceptual and cognitive changes that did occur in the subjects were consistently in the direction of a more "primitive" organization.*

Thus, the available evidence supports the hypothesis that a deautomatization is produced by contemplative meditation. One might be tempted to call this deautomatization a regression to the perceptual and cognitive state of the child or infant. However, such a concept rests on assumptions as to the child's experience of the world that cannot yet be verified. In an oft-quoted passage, Wordsworth (1904, p. 353) writes:

> There was a time when meadow, grove, and stream,
> The earth, and every common sight,
> To me did seem

*See Chapter 33. As dedifferentiation of the vase progressed, however, a fusion of background and object tended to occur with a concomitant loss of color and vividness.

Apparelled in celestial light,
The glory and the freshness of a dream.

However, he may be confusing childhood with what is actually a reconstruction based on an interaction of adult associative capacities with the *memory* of the more direct sensory contact of the child. "Glory" is probably an adult product. Rather than speaking of a return to childhood, it is more accurate to say that the undoing of automatic perceptual and cognitive structures permits a gain in sensory intensity and richness at the expense of abstract categorization and differentiation. One might call the direction regressive in a developmental sense, but the actual experience is probably not within the psychological scope of any child. It is a deautomatization occurring in an adult mind, and the experience gains its richness from adult memories and functions now subject to a different mode of consciousness.

Renunciation

The deautomatization produced by contemplative meditation is enhanced and aided by the adoption of renunciation as a goal and a life style, a renunciation not confined to the brief meditative period alone. Poverty, chastity, isolation, and silence are traditional techniques prescribed for pursuing the mystic path: To experience God, keep your thoughts turned to God and away from the world and the body that binds one to the world. The meditative strategy is carried over into all segments of the subject's life. The mystic strives to banish from awareness the objects of the world and the desires directed toward them. To the extent that perceptual and cognitive structures require the "nutriment" of their accustomed stimuli for adequate functioning, renunciation would be expected to weaken and even disrupt these structures, thus tending to produce an unusual experience (Rapaport, 1951). Such an isolation from nutritive stimuli probably occurs internally as well. The subjects of the meditation experiment quoted earlier reported that a decrease in responsiveness to distracting stimuli took place as they became more practiced. They became more effective, with less effort, in barring unwanted stimuli from awareness. These reports suggest that psychological barrier structures were established as the subjects became more adept (Deikman, 1963, p. 338). EEG studies of Zen monks yielded similar results. The effect of a distracting stimulus, as measured by the disappearance of alpha rhythm, was most prominent in the novices, less prominent in those of intermediate training, and almost absent in the master (Kasamatsu & Hirai, 1963). It may be that the intensive, long-term practice of meditation creates temporary stimulus barriers producing a functional state of sensory isolation.* On the basis of sensory isolation experiments it would be expected that long-term deprivation (or decreased variability) of a particular class of stimulus "nutriment" would cause an alteration in those functions previously established to deal with that class of stimuli (Schultz, 1965, pp. 95–97; Solomon et al., 1961, pp. 226–237). These alterations seem to be a type of deautomatization, as defined earlier—for example, the reported increased brightness of colors and the impairment of perceptual skills such as color discrimination (Zubek et al., 1961). Thus, renunciation alone can be viewed as producing deautomatization. When combined with contemplative meditation, it produces a very powerful effect.

Finally, the more renunciation is achieved, the more the mystic is committed to his goal of Union or Enlightenment. His motivation necessarily increases, for having abandoned the world, he has no other hope of sustenance.

PRINCIPAL FEATURES OF THE MYSTIC EXPERIENCE

Granted that deautomatization takes place, it is necessary to explain five principal features of the mystic experience: (a) intense realness, (b) unusual sensations, (c) unity, (d) ineffability, and (e) trans-sensate phenomena.

Realness

It is assumed by those who have had a mystic experience, whether induced by years of meditation or by a single dose of LSD, that the truthfulness of the experience is attested to by its sense of realness. The criticism of skeptics is often met with the statement, "You have to experience it yourself and then you will understand." This means that if one has the actual experience he will be convinced by its intense *feeling of reality*. "I know it was real because it was more real than my talking to you now." But "realness" is not evidence. Indeed, there are many clinical examples of variability in the intensity of the feeling of realness that is not correlated with corresponding variability in the reality. A dream may be so "real" as to carry conviction into the waking state, although its content may be bizarre beyond correspondence to this world or to any other. Psychosis is often preceded or accompanied by a sense that the world is *less real* than normally, sometimes that it is more real, or has a different reality. The phenomenon

*It has been postulated by McReynolds (1960, p. 269) that a related stimulus barrier system may be operative in schizophrenia.

of depersonalization demonstrates the potential for an alteration in the sense of the realness of one's own person, although one's evidential self undergoes no change whatsoever. However, in the case of depersonalization, or of derealization, the distinction between what is external and what is internal is still clear. What changes is the quality of realness attached to those object representations. Thus it appears that (a) the *feeling* of realness represents a function distinct from that of reality *judgment*, although they usually operate in synchrony; (b) the feeling of realness is not inherent in sensations, per se; and (c) realness can be considered a quantity function capable of displacement and therefore, of intensification, reduction, and transfer affecting all varieties of ideational and sensorial contents.*

From a developmental point of view, it is clear that biological survival depends on a clear sense of what is palpable and what is not. The sense of reality necessarily becomes fused with the object world. When one considers that meditation combined with renunciation brings about a profound disruption of the subject's normal psychological relationship to the world, it becomes plausible that the practice of such mystic techniques would be associated with a significant alteration of the feeling of reality. The quality of reality formerly attached to objects becomes attached to the particular sensations and ideas that enter awareness during periods of perceptual and cognitive deautomatization. Stimuli of the inner world become invested with the feeling of reality ordinarily bestowed on objects. Through what might be termed "reality transfer," *thoughts and images become real* (Deikman, 1966, pp. 109–111).

Unusual percepts

The sensations and ideation occurring during mystic deautomatization are often very unusual; they do not seem part of the continuum of everyday consciousness. "All at once, without warning of any kind, he found himself wrapped around as it were by a flame colored cloud" (Bucke, 1961, p. 8). Perceptions of encompassing light, infinite energy, ineffable visions, and incommunicable knowledge are remarkable in their seeming distinction from perceptions of the phenomena of the "natural world." According to mystics, these experiences are different because they pertain to a higher transcendent reality. What is perceived is said to come from another world, or at least another dimension. Although such a possibility cannot be ruled

---

*Paul Federn's (1955, pp. 241–260) idea that the normal feeling of reality requires an adequate investment of energy (libido) in the ego boundary, points toward the notion of a quantity of "realness." Avery Weisman (1958) has developed and extended this idea, but prefers the more encompassing concept of "libidinal fields" to that of ego boundaries.

out, many of the phenomena can be understood as representing *an unusual mode of perception*, rather than an unusual external stimulus.

In the studies of experimental meditation already mentioned, two long-term subjects reported vivid experiences of light and force. For example:

> . . . shortly I began to sense motion and shifting of light and dark as this became stronger and stronger. Now when this happens it's happening not only in my vision but it's happening or it feels like a physical kind of thing. It's connected with feelings of attraction, expansion, absorption and suddenly my vision pinpointed on a particular place and. . . I was in the grip of a very powerful sensation and this became the center [Deikman, 1966, p. 109].

This report suggests that the perception of motion and shifting light and darkness may have been the perception of the *movement* of attention among various psychic contents (whatever such "movement" might actually be). "Attraction," "expansion," "absorption," would thus reflect the dynamics of the effort to focus attention—successful focusing is experienced as being "in the grip of" a powerful force. Another example: ". . . when the vase changes shape . . . I feel this in my body and particularly in my eyes . . . there is an actual kind of physical sensation as though something is moving there which recreates the shape of the vase" (Deikman, 1966, p. 109). In this instance, the subject might have experienced the perception of a resynthesis taking place following deautomatization of the normal percept; that is, the percept of the vase was being reconstructed outside of normal awareness and the *process* of reconstruction was perceived as a physical sensation. I have termed this hypothetical perceptual mode "*sensory translation*," defining it as the perception of psychic *action* (conflict, repression, problem solving, attentiveness, and so forth) via the relatively unstructured sensations of light, color, movement, force, sound, smell, or taste (Kris, 1952; Deikman, 1966, pp. 108–109). This concept is related to Silberer's (1951) concept of hypnagogic phenomena but differs in its referents and genesis. In the hypnagogic state and in dreaming, a *symbolic* translation of psychic activity and ideas occurs. Although light, force, and movement may play a part in hypnagogic and dream constructions, the predominant percepts are complex visual, verbal, conceptual, and activity images. "Sensory translation" refers to the experience of nonverbal, simple, concrete perceptual equivalents of psychic action.*

*Somewhat related concepts, although extreme in scope, are those advanced by Michaux (1963, pp. 7–9), who suggests that the frequent experience of waves or vibrations in hallucinogenic drug states is the result of direct perception of the "brain waves" measured by the EEG; and by Leary (1964, pp. 330–339), who suggests that hallucinogenic drugs permit a "direct awareness of the processes which physicists and biochemists and neurologists measure," for example, electrons in orbit or the interaction of cells.

The concept of sensory translation offers an intriguing explanation for the ubiquitous use of light as a metaphor for mystic experience. It may not be just a metaphor. "Illumination" may be derived from an actual sensory experience occurring when in the cognitive act of unification, a liberation of energy takes place, or when a resolution of unconscious conflict occurs, permitting the experience of "peace," "presence," and the like. Liberated energy experienced as light may be the core sensory experience of mysticism.

If the hypothesis of sensory translation is correct, it presents the problem of why sensory translation comes into operation in any particular instance.

In general, it appears that sensory translation may occur when (a) heightened attention is directed to the sensory pathways, (b) controlled analytic thought is absent, and (c) the subject's attitude is one of receptivity to stimuli (openness instead of defensiveness or suspiciousness). Training in contemplative meditation is specifically directed toward attaining a state with those characteristics. Laski (1961) reports that spontaneous mystic experiences may occur during such diverse activities as childbirth, viewing landscapes, listening to music, or having sexual intercourse. Although her subjects gave little description of their thought processes preceding the ecstasies, they were all involved at the time in intense sensory activities in which the three conditions listed above would tend to prevail. Those conditions seem also to apply to the mystical experiences associated with LSD. The state of mind induced by hallucinogenic drugs is reported to be one of increased sensory attention accompanied by an impairment or loss of different intellectual functions (Crocket et al., 1963; Watts, 1962; Michaux, 1963). With regard to the criterion of receptivity, if paranoid reactions occur during the drug state they are inimical to an ecstatic experience. On the other hand, when drug subjects lose their defensiveness and suspiciousness so that they "accept" rather than fight their situation, the "transcendent" experience often ensues (Sherwood et al., 1962). Thus, the general psychological context may be described as *perceptual concentration*. In this special state of consciousness the subject becomes aware of certain intra-psychic processes ordinarily excluded from or beyond the scope of awareness. The vehicle for this perception appears to be amorphous sensation, made real by a displacement of reality feeling ("reality transfer") and thus misinterpreted as being of external origin.

Unity

Experiencing one's self as one with the universe or with God is the hallmark of the mystic experience, regardless of its cultural context. As James (1929, p. 410) puts it,

This overcoming of all the usual barriers between the individual and the Absolute is the great mystic achievement. In mystic states we both become one with the Absolute and we become aware of our oneness. This is the everlasting and triumphant mystical tradition, hardly altered by differences of clime or creed. In Hinduism, in Neoplatonism, in Sufism, in Christian mysticism, in Whitmanism, we find the same recurring note, so that there is about mystical utterance an eternal unanimity which ought to make a critic stop and think, and which brings it about that the mystical classics have, as has been said, neither birthday nor native land. Perpetually telling of the unity of man with God, their speech antedates languages, and they do not grow old.

I have already referred to explanations of this phenomenon in terms of regression. Two additional hypotheses should be considered: On the one hand, the perception of unity may be the perception of one's own psychic structure; on the other hand, the experience may be a perception of the real structure of the world.

It is a commonplace that we do not experience the world directly. Instead, we have an experience of sensation and associated memories from which we infer the nature of the stimulating object. As far as anyone can tell, the actual *substance* of the perception is the electrochemical activity that constitutes perception and thinking. From this point of view, the contents of awareness are homogeneous. They are variations of the same substance. If awareness were turned back upon itself, as postulated for sensory translation, this fundamental homogeneity (unity) of perceived reality—the electrochemical activity—might itself be experienced as a truth about the outer world, rather than the inner one. Unity, the idea and the experience that we are one with the world and with God, would thus constitute a valid perception insofar as it pertained to the nature of the thought process, but need not in itself be a correct perception of the external world.

Logically, there is also the possibility that the perception of unity does correctly evaluate the external world. As described earlier, deautomatization is an undoing of a psychic structure permitting the experience of increased detail and sensation at the price of requiring more attention. With such attention, it is possible that deautomatization may permit the awareness of new dimensions of the total stimulus array—a process of *perceptual expansion.* The studies of Werner (1957), Von Senden (1960), and Shapiro (1960) suggest that development from infancy to adulthood is accompanied by an organization of the perceptual and cognitive world that has as its price the selection of some stimuli and stimulus qualities to the exclusion of others. If the automatization underlying that organization is reversed, or temporarily suspended, aspects of reality that were formerly unavailable might then enter awareness. Unity may in fact be a property of the real world that becomes perceptible via the techniques of meditation and renunciation, or under the special conditions, as yet unknown, that create the spontaneous, brief mystic experience of untrained persons.

Ineffability

Mystic experiences are ineffable, incapable of being expressed to another person. Although mystics sometimes write long accounts, they maintain that the experience cannot be communicated by words or by reference to similar experiences from ordinary life. They feel at a loss for appropriate words to communicate the intense realness, the unusual sensations, and the unity cognition already mentioned. However, a careful examination of mystic phenomena indicates that there are at least several types of experiences, all of which are "indescribable" but each of which differs substantially in content and formal characteristics. Error and confusion result when these several states of consciousness are lumped together as "the mystic experience" on the basis of their common characteristic of ineffability.

To begin with, one type of mystic experience cannot be communicated in words because it is probably based on primitive memories and related to fantasies of a preverbal (infantile) or nonverbal sensory experience.* Certain mystical reports that speak of being blissfully enfolded, comforted and bathed in the love of God are very suggestive of the prototypical "undifferentiated state," the union of infant and breast, emphasized by psychoanalytic explanations of mystical phenomena. Indeed, it seems highly plausible that such early memories and fantasies might be re-experienced as a consequence of (a) the regression in thought processes brought about by renunciation and contemplative meditation, and (b) the activation of infantile longings by the guiding religious promise—that is, "that a benign deity would reward childlike surrender with permanent euphoria" (Moller, 1965, p. 127). In addition, the conditions of functional sensory isolation associated with mystic training may contribute to an increase in recall and vividness of such memories (Suraci, 1964).

*Schachtel (1959, p. 284) regards early childhood, beyond infancy, as unrememberable for structural reasons: "It is not merely the repression of a specific content, such as early sexual experience, that accounts for the general childhood amnesia; the biologically, culturally, and socially influenced process of memory organization results in the formation of categories (schemata) of memory which are not suitable vehicles to receive and reproduce experiences of the quality and intensity typical of early childhood." It would follow that verbal structures would likewise be "unsuitable."

A second type of mystical experience is equally ineffable but strikingly different—namely, a revelation too complex to be verbalized. Such experiences are reported frequently by those who have drug-induced mystical experiences. In such states the subject has a revelation of the significance and interrelationships of many dimensions of life; he becomes aware of many levels of meaning simultaneously and "understands" the totality of existence. The question of whether such knowledge is actual or an illusion remains unanswered; however, if such a multileveled comprehension were to occur, it would be difficult—perhaps impossible—to express verbally. Ordinary language is structured to follow the logical development of one idea at a time and it might be quite inadequate to express an experience encompassing a large number of concepts simultaneously. William James suggested that "states of mystical intuition may be only very sudden and great extensions of the ordinary 'field of consciousness'." He used the image of the vast reaches of a tidal flat exposed by the lowering of the water level (James, 1920, pp. 500–513). However, mystic revelation may be ineffable, not only because of the sudden broadening of consciousness that James suggests, but also because of a new "vertical" organization of concepts.* For example, for a short while after reading *The Decline and Fall of the Roman Empire*, one may be aware of the immense vista of a civilization's history as Gibbon recreated it. That experience can hardly be conveyed except through the medium of the book itself, and to that extent it is ineffable, and a minor version of James's widened consciousness. Suppose one then read *War and Peace* and acquired Tolstoy's perspective of historical events and their determination by chance factors. Again, this is an experience hard to express without returning to the novel. Now suppose one could "see" not only each of these world views individually but also their parallel relationships to each other, and the cross connections between the individual conceptual structures. And then suppose one added to these conceptual strata the biochemical perspective expressed by *The Fitness of the Environment* (Henderson, 1958), a work which deals, among other things, with the unique and vital properties of the water molecule. Then the *vertical* interrelationships of all these extensive schemata might, indeed, be beyond verbal expression, beyond ordinary conceptual capacities—in other words, they would approach the ineffable.

Trans-sensate Phenomena

A third type of ineffable experience is that which I have described earlier as the "trained-transcendent" mystical experience. The author of *The Cloud*

*A similar distinction concerning "vertical" listening to music is made by Ehrenzweig (1964, pp. 385–387).

of Unknowing, St. John of the Cross, Walter Hilton, and others are very specific in describing a new perceptual experience that does not include feelings of warmth, sweetness, visions, or any other elements of familiar sensory or intellectual experience. They emphasize that the experience *goes beyond* the customary sensory pathways, ideas, and memories. As I have shown, they describe the state as definitely not blank or empty but as filled with intense, profound, vivid perception which they regard as the ultimate goal of the mystic path.* If one accepts their descriptions as phenomenologically accurate, one is presented with the problem of explaining the nature of such a state and the process by which it occurs. Following the hypotheses presented earlier in this paper, I would like to suggest that such experiences are the result of the operation of a new perceptual capacity responsive to dimensions of the stimulus array previously ignored or blocked from awareness. For such mystics, renunciation has weakened and temporarily removed the ordinary objects of consciousness as a focus of awareness. Contemplative meditation has undone the logical organization of consciousness. At the same time, the mystic is intensely *motivated* to perceive something. If undeveloped or unutilized perceptual capacities do exist, it seems likely that they would be mobilized and come into operation under such conditions. The perceptual experience that would then take place would be one outside of customary verbal or sensory reference. It would be *unidentifiable*, hence indescribable. The high value, the meaningfulness, and the intensity reported of such experiences suggest that the perception has a different scope from that of normal consciousness. The loss of "self" characteristic of the trans-sensate experience indicates that the new perceptual mode is not associated with reflective awareness—the "I" of normal consciousness is in abeyance.

CONCLUSION

A mystic experience is the production of an unusual state of consciousness. This state is brought about by a deautomatization of hierarchically ordered structures that ordinarily conserve attentional energy for maximum efficiency in achieving the basic goals of the individual: biological survival

*Ehrenzweig (1964, p. 382) proposes that mystic "blankness" is due to a structural limitation: " . . . the true mystic orison becomes empty yet filled with intense experience. . . . This full emptiness. . . . It is the direct result of our conscious failure to grasp imagery formed on more primitive levels of differentiation. . . . Owing to their incompatible shapes, [these images] cancelled each other out on the way up to consciousness and so produce in our surface experience a blank 'abstract' image still replete with unconscious fantasy."

as an organism and psychological survival as a personality. Perceptual selection and cognitive patterning are in the service of these goals. Under special conditions of dysfunction, such as in acute psychosis or in LSD states, or under special goal conditions such as exist in religious mystics, the pragmatic systems of automatic selection are set aside or break down, in favor of alternate modes of consciousness whose stimulus processing may be less efficient from a biological point of view but whose very inefficiency may permit the experience of aspects of the real world formerly excluded or ignored. The extent to which such a shift takes place is a function of the motivation of the individual, his particular neurophysiological state, and the environmental conditions encouraging or discouraging such a change.

A final comment should be made. The content of the mystic experience reflects not only its unusual mode of consciousness but also the particular stimuli being processed through that mode. The mystic experience can be beatific, satanic, revelatory, or psychotic, depending on the stimuli predominant in each case. Such an explanation says nothing conclusive about the source of "transcendent" stimuli. God or the Unconscious share equal possibilities here and one's interpretation will reflect one's presuppositions and beliefs. The mystic vision is one of unity, and modern physics lends some support to this perception when it asserts that the world and its living forms are variations of the same elements. However, there is no evidence that separateness and differences are illusions (as affirmed by Vedanta) or that God or a transcendent reality exists (as affirmed by Western religions). The available scientific evidence tends to support the view that the mystic experience is one of internal perception, an experience that can be ecstatic, profound, or therapeutic for purely internal reasons. Yet for psychological science, the problem of understanding such internal processes is hardly less complex than the theological problem of understanding God. Indeed, regardless of one's direction in the search to know what reality is, a feeling of awe, beauty, reverence, and humility seems to be the product of one's efforts. Since these emotions are characteristic of the mystic experience, itself, the question of the epistemological validity of that experience may have less importance than was initially supposed.

3

A SPECIAL INQUIRY WITH ALDOUS HUXLEY INTO THE NATURE AND CHARACTER OF VARIOUS STATES OF CONSCIOUSNESS

MILTON H. ERICKSON

INTRODUCTION

Over a period of nearly a year much time was spent by Aldous Huxley and by the author, each planning separately for joint inquiry into various states of psychological awareness. Special inquiries, possible methods of experimental approach and investigations and various questions to be propounded were listed by each of us in our respective loose-leaf notebooks. The purpose was to prepare a general background for the proposed joint study with this general background reflecting the thinking of both of us uninfluenced by the other. It was hoped in this way to secure the widest possible coverage of ideas by such separate outlines prepared from the markedly different backgrounds of understanding that the two of us possessed.

Early in 1950 we met in Huxley's home in Los Angeles, there to spend an intensive day appraising the ideas recorded in our separate notebooks and to engage in any experimental inquiries that seemed feasible. I was particularly interested in Huxley's approach to psychological problems, his

Reprinted by permission from *Amer. J. Clin. Hypnos.*, Vol. 8, 1965, pp. 17–33.

method of thinking and his own unique use of his unconscious mind which we had discussed only briefly sometime previously. Huxley was particularly interested in hypnosis and previous exceedingly brief work with him had demonstrated his excellent competence as a deep somnambulistic subject.

It was realized that this meeting would be a preliminary or pilot study, and this was discussed by both of us. Hence we planned to make it as comprehensive and inclusive as possible without undue emphasis upon completion of any one particular item. Once the day's work had been evaluated, plans could then be made for future meetings and specific studies. Additionally, we each had our individual purposes, Aldous having in mind future literary work, while my interest related to future psychological experimentation in the field of hypnosis.

The day's work began at 8:00 A.M. and remained uninterrupted until 6:00 P.M. with some considerable review of our notebooks the next day to establish their general agreement, to remove any lack of clarity of meaning caused by the abbreviated notations we had entered into them during the previous day's work and to correct any oversights. On the whole we found that our notebooks were reasonably in agreement but that naturally certain of our entries were reflective of our special interests and of the fact that each of us had, by the nature of the situation, made separate notations bearing upon each other.

Our plan was to leave these notebooks with Huxley since his phenomenal memory, often appearing to be total recall, and his superior literary ability would permit a more satisfactory writing of a joint article based upon our discussions and experimentations of that day's work. However, I did abstract from my notebook certain pages bearing notations upon Huxley's behavior at times when he, as an experimental subject, was unable to make comprehensive notations on himself, although post-experimentally he could and did do so, though less completely than I had. It was proposed that, from these certain special pages, I was to endeavor to develop an article which could be incorporated later in the longer study that Huxley was to write. Accordingly, I abstracted a certain number of pages intending to secure still more at a later date. These pages that I did remove Huxley rapidly copied into his own notebook to be sure of the completeness of his own data.

Unfortunately, a California brush fire sometime later destroyed Huxley's home, his extensive library containing many rare volumes and manuscripts, besides numerous other treasures to say nothing of the manuscripts upon which Huxley was currently working as well as the respective notebooks of our special joint study. As a result, the entire subject matter of our project was dropped as a topic too painful to discuss, but Huxley's recent death led to my perusal of these relatively few pages I had abstracted from my notebook. Examination of them suggested the possibility of presenting to the reader a small but informative part of that day's work. In this regard, the reader must bear in mind that the quotations attributed to Huxley are not necessarily verbatim, since his more extensive utterances were noted in abbreviated form. However, in the essence of their meaning, they are correct and they are expressive of Huxley as I knew him. It is also to be borne in mind that Huxley had read my notations on the occasion of our joint study and had approved them.

PROJECT INITIATION

The project began with Huxley reviewing concepts and definitions of conscious awareness, primarily his and in part those of others, followed by a discussion with me of his understandings of hypnotic states of awareness. The purpose was to insure that we were both in accord or clear in our divergences of understanding, thus to make possible a more reliable inquiry into the subject matter of our interest.

There followed then a review in extensive detail of various of his psyche-delic experiences with mescaline, later to be recorded in his book. (Huxley, 1954).

Huxley then proceeded with a detailed description of his very special prac-tice of what he, for want of a better and less awkward term which he had not yet settled upon, called "Deep Reflection." He described this state (the author's description is not complete since there seemed to be no good reason except interest for making full notations of his description) of Deep Reflec-tion as one marked by physical relaxation with bowed head and closed eyes, a profound progressive psychological withdrawal from externalities but without any actual loss of physical realities nor any amnesias or loss of orientation, a "setting aside" of everything not pertinent, and then a state of complete mental absorption in matters of interest to him. Yet, in that state of complete withdrawal and mental absorption, Huxley stated that he was free to pick up a fresh pencil to replace a dulled one to make "auto-matically" notations on his thoughts and to do all this without a recognizable realization on his part of what physical act he was performing. It was as if the physical act were "not an integral part of my thinking." In no way did such physical activity seem to impinge upon, to slow, or to impede "the train of thought so exclusively occupying my interest. It is associated but completely peripheral activity . . . I might say activity barely contiguous to the periphery." To illustrate further, Huxley cited an instance of another type of physical activity. He recalled having been in a state of Deep Reflec-tion one day when his wife was shopping. He did not recall what thoughts or ideas he was examining but he did recall that, when his wife returned that day, she had asked him if he had made a note of the special message she had given him over the telephone. He had been bewildered by her inquiry, could not recall anything about answering the telephone as his wife asserted, but together they found the special message recorded on a pad beside the telephone which was placed within comfortable reaching distance from the chair in which he liked to develop Deep Reflection. Both he and his wife reached the conclusion that he had been in a state of Deep Reflection at the time of the telephone call, had lifted the receiver and had said to her as usual, "I say there, hello," had listened to the message, had recorded it, all without any subsequent recollections of the experience. He recalled merely that he had been working on a manuscript that afternoon, one that had been absorbing all of his interest. He explained that it was quite common for him to initiate a day's work by entering a state of Deep Reflection as a preliminary process of marshalling his thoughts and putting into order the thinking that would enter into his writing later that day.

As still another illustrative incident, Huxley cited an occasion when his wife returned home from a brief absence, found the door locked as was customary, had entered the house and discovered in plain view a special delivery letter on a hallway table reserved for mail, special messages, etc. She had found Huxley sitting quietly in his special chair, obviously in a state of deep thought. Later that day she had inquired about the time of arrival of the special delivery letter only to learn that he had obviously no recollection of receiving any letter. Yet both knew that the mailman had undoubtedly rung the doorbell, that Huxley had heard the bell, had interrupted whatever he was doing, had gone to the door, opened it, received the letter, closed the door, placed the letter in its proper place and returned to the chair where she had found him.

Both of these two special events had occurred fairly recently. He recalled them only as incidents related to him by his wife but with no feeling that those accounts constituted a description of actual meaningful physical behavior on his part. So far as he knew, he could only deduce that he must have been in a state of Deep Reflection when they occurred.

His wife subsequently confirmed the assumption that his behavior had been completely "automatic, like a machine moving precisely and accurately. It is a delightful pleasure to see him get a book out of the bookcase, sit down again, open the book slowly, pick up his reading glass, read a little, and then lay the book and glass aside. Then some time later, maybe a few days, he will notice the book and ask about it. The man just never remembers what he does nor what he thinks about when he sits in that chair. All of a sudden, you just find him in his study working very hard."

In other words, while in a state of Deep Reflection and seemingly totally withdrawn from external realities, the integrity of the task being done in that mental state was touched by external stimuli, but some peripheral part of awareness made it possible for him to receive external stimuli, to respond meaningfully to them but with no apparent recording of any memory of either the stimulus or his meaningful and adequate response. Inquiry of his wife later had disclosed that when she was at home, Aldous in a state of Deep Reflection paid no attention to the telephone which might be beside him or the doorbell. "He simply depends completely on me, but I can call out to him that I'll be away and he never fails to hear the telephone or the doorbell."

Huxley explained that he believed he could develop a state of Deep Reflection in about five minutes but that in doing so he "simply cast aside all anchors" of any type of awareness. Just what he meant and sensed he could not describe. "It is a subjective experience quite" in which he apparently achieved a state of "orderly mental arrangement" permitting an orderly free flowing of his thoughts as he wrote. This was his final explanation. He had never considered any analysis of exactly what his "Deep Reflection" was nor did he feel that he could analyze it, but he offered to attempt it as an experimental investigation for the day. It was promptly learned that, as he began to absorb himself in his thoughts to achieve a state of Deep Reflection, he did indeed "cast off all anchors" and appeared to be completely out of touch with everything. On this attempt to experience subjectively and to remember the processes of entering into Deep Reflection, he developed the state within five minutes and emerged from it within two as closely as I could determine. His comment was, "I say, I'm deucedly sorry. I suddenly found myself all prepared to work with nothing to do and I realized I had better come out of it." That was all the information he could offer. For the next attempt, a signal to be given by me was agreed upon as a signal for him to "come out of it." A second attempt was made as easily as the first. Huxley sat quietly for some minutes and the agreed upon signal was given. Huxley's account was, "I found myself just waiting for something. I did not know what. It was just a 'something' that I seemed to feel would come in what seemed to be a timeless spaceless void. I say, that's the first time I noted that feeling. Always I've had some thinking to do. But this time I seemed to have no work in hand. I was just completely disinterested, indifferent, just waiting for something and then I felt a need to come out of it. I say, did you give me the signal?"

Inquiry disclosed that he had no apparent memory of the stimulus being given. He had had only the "feeling" that it was time to "come out of it."

Several more repetitions yielded similar results. A sense of a timeless spaceless void, a placid comfortable awaiting for an undefined "something" and a comfortable need to return to ordinary conscious awareness constituted the understandings achieved. Huxley summarized his findings briefly as "a total absence of everything on the way there and on the way back and an expected meaningless something for which one awaits in a state of Nirvana since there is nothing more to do." He asserted his intention to make a later intensive study of this practice he found so useful in his writing.

Further experiments were done after Huxley had explained that he could enter the state of deep reflection with the simple undefined understanding that he would respond to any "significant stimulus." Without informing him of my intentions, I asked him to "arouse" (this term is my own) when three taps of a pencil on a chair were given in close succession. He entered the state of reflection readily and, after a brief wait, I tapped the table with a pencil in varying fashions at distinct but irregular intervals. Thus, I tapped once, paused, then twice in rapid succession, paused, tapped once, paused, tapped four times in rapid succession, paused, then five times in rapid succession. Numerous variations were tried but with an avoidance of the agreed upon signal. A chair was knocked over with a crash while four taps were given. Not until the specified three taps were given did he make any response. His arousal occurred slowly with almost an immediate response to the signal. Huxley was questioned about his subjective experiences. He explained simply that they had been the same as previously with one exception, namely that several times he had a vague sensation that "something was coming," but he knew not what. He had no awareness of what had been done.

Further experimentation was done in which he was asked to enter Deep Reflection and to sense color, a prearranged signal for arousing being that of a handshake of his right hand. He complied readily and when I judged that he was fully absorbed in his state of reflection, I shook his left hand vigorously, then followed this with a hard pinching of the back of both hands that left deep fingernail markings. Huxley made no response to this physical stimulus, although his eyes were watched for possible eyeball movements under the lids and his respiratory and pulse rates were checked for any changes. However, after about a minute he slowly drew his arms back along the arms of the chair where he had placed them before beginning his reflection state. They moved slowly about an inch and then all movement ceased.

He was aroused easily and comfortably at the designated signal.

His subjective report was simply that he had "lost" himself in a "sea of color," of "sensing," "feeling," "being" color, of being "quite utterly involved in it with no identity of your own, you know." Then suddenly he had experienced a process of losing that color in a "meaningless void," only to open his eyes and to realize that he had "come out of it."

He remembered the agreed upon stimulus but did not recall if it had been given. "I can only deduce it was given from the fact that I'm out of it," and indirect questioning disclosed no memories of the other physical stimuli administered. Neither was there an absent-minded looking at nor rubbing of the backs of his hands.

This same procedure in relation to color was repeated but to it was added, as he seemed to be reaching the state of Deep Reflection, a repeated insistent urging that, upon arousal, he discuss a certain book which was carefully placed in full view. The results were comparable to the preceding findings. He became "lost", . . . "quite utterly involved in it", . . . "one can sense it but not describe it", . . . "I say, its an utterly amazing, fascinating state of finding yourself a pleasant part of an endless vista of color that is soft and gentle and yielding and all-absorbing. Utterly extraordinary, most extraordinary". He had no recollection of my verbal insistences nor of the other physical stimuli. He remembered the agreed upon signal but did not know if it had been given. He found himself only in a position of assuming that it had been given since he was again in a state of ordinary awareness. The presence of the book meant nothing to him. One added statement was that entering a state of Deep Reflection by absorbing himself in a sense of color was, in a fashion, comparable to but not identical with his psychedelic experiences.

As a final inquiry, Huxley was asked to enter the reflection state for the purpose of recalling the telephone call and the special delivery letter incidents. His comment was that such a project should be "quite fruitful." Despite repeated efforts, he would "come out of it" explaining, "There I found myself without anything to do so I came out of it." His memories were limited to the accounts given to him by his wife and all details were associated with her and not with any inner feelings of experience on his part.

A final effort was made to discover whether or not Huxley could include another person in his state of Deep Reflection. This idea interested him at once and it was suggested that he enter the reflection state to review some of his psychedelic experiences. This he did in a most intriguing fashion. As the reflection state developed, Huxley in an utterly detached dissociated fashion began making fragmentary remarks, chiefly in the form of self-addressed comments. Thus he would say, making fragmentary notes with a pencil and paper quickly supplied to him, "most extraordinary . . . I overlooked that . . . How? . . . Strange I should have forgotten that (making a notation) . . . fascinating how different it appears . . . I must look . . . ."

When he aroused, he had a vague recollection of having reviewed a previous psychedelic experience but what he had experienced then or on the immediate occasion he could not recall. Nor did he recall speaking aloud nor making notations. When shown these, he found that they were so poorly written that they could not be read. I read mine to him without eliciting any memory traces.

A repetition yielded similar results with one exception. This was an amazed expression of complete astonishment by Huxley suddenly declaring, "I say,

Milton, this is quite utterly amazing, most extraordinary. I use Deep Reflection to summon my memories, to put into order all of my thinking, to explore the range, the extent of my mental existence, but I do it solely to let those realizations, the thinking, the understandings, the memories seep into the work I'm planning to do without my conscious awareness of them. Fascinating . . . never stopped to realize that my deep reflection always preceded a period of intensive work wherein I was completely absorbed . . . I say, no wonder I have an amnesia."

Later when we were examining each other's notebook, Huxley manifested intense amazement and bewilderment at what I had recorded about the physical stimuli and for which he had no memory of any sort. He knew that he had gone into Deep Reflection repeatedly at my request, had been both pleased and amazed at his subjective feelings of being lost in an all-absorbing sea of color, had sensed a certain timelessness-spacelessness and had experienced a comfortable feeling of something meaningful about to happen. He reread my notations repeatedly in an endeavor to develop some kind of a feeling of at least a vague memory of subjective awareness of the various physical stimuli I had given him. He also looked at the backs of his hands to see the pinch marks but they had vanished. His final comment was, " . . . extraordinary, most extraordinary, I say, utterly fascinating."

When we agreed that, at least for the while, further inquiry into Deep Reflection might be postponed until later, Huxley declared again that his sudden realization of how much he had used it and how little he knew about it made him resolve to investigate much further into his "Deep Reflection." The manner and means by which he achieved it, how it constituted a form of preparation for absorbing himself in his writing and in what way it caused him to lose unnecessary contact with reality were all problems of much interest to him.

Huxley then suggested that an investigation be made of hypnotic states of awareness by employing him as a subject. He asked permission to be allowed to interrupt his trance states at will for purposes of discussion. This was in full accord with my own wishes.

He asked that first a light trance be induced, perhaps repeatedly, to permit an exploration of his subjective experiences. Since he had briefly been a somnambulistic subject previously, he was carefully assured that this fact could serve to make him feel confident in arresting his trance states at any level he wished. He did not recognize this as a simple direct hypnotic suggestion. In reading my notebook later he was much amused at how easily he had accepted an obvious suggestion without recognizing its character at the time.

He found several repetitions of the light trance interesting, but "too easily conceptualized." It is, he explained, "A simple withdrawal of interest from the outside to the inside." That is, one gives less and less attention to externalities and directs more and more attention to inner subjective sensations. Externalities become increasingly fainter and more obscure, inner subjective feelings more satisfying until a state of balance exists. In this state of balance, he had the feeling that, with motivation, he could "reach out and seize upon reality," that there is a definite retention of a grasp upon external reality but with no motivation to deal with it. Neither did he feel a desire to deepen the trance. No particular change in this state of balance seemed necessary and he noted that a feeling of contentment and relaxation accompanied it. He wondered if others experienced the same subjective reactions.

Huxley requested that the light trance be induced by a great variety of techniques, some of them non-verbal. The results in each instance, Huxley felt strongly, were dependent entirely upon his mental set. He found that he could accept "drifting along" (my phrase) in a light trance, receptive of suggestions involving primarily responses at a subjective level only. He found that an effort to behave in direct relationship to the physical environment taxed his efforts and made him desire either to arouse from the trance or to go still deeper. He also, on his own initiative, set up his own problems to test his trance states. Thus, before entering the light trance he would privately resolve to discuss a certain topic, relevant or irrelevant, with me at the earliest possible time or even at a fairly remote time. In such instances, Huxley found such unexpressed desires deleterious to the maintenance of the trance. Similarly any effort to include an item of reality not pertinent to his sense of subjective satisfaction lessened the trance.

At all times there persisted a "dim but ready" awareness that one could alter the state of awareness at will. Huxley, like others with whom I have done similar studies, felt an intense desire to explore his sense of subjective comfort and satisfaction but immediately realized that this would lead to a deeper trance state.

When Huxley was asked to formulate understandings of the means he could employ by which he could avoid going into more than a light trance, he stated that he did this by setting a given length of time during which he would remain in a light trance. This had the effect of making him more strongly aware that at any moment he could "reach out and seize external reality" and that his sense of subjective comfort and ease decreased. Discussion of this and repeated experimentation disclosed that carefully worded suggestions served to emphasize the availability of external reality and to enhance subjective comfort though Huxley was fully cognizant of what was being said and why. Similar results have been obtained with other highly intelligent subjects.

In experimenting with medium deep trances, Huxley, like other subjects with whom I have worked, experienced much more difficulty in reacting to

and maintaining a fairly constant trance level. He found that he had a subjective need to go deeper in the trance and an intellectual need to stay at
the medium level. The result was that he found himself repeatedly "reaching
out for awareness" of his environment and this would initiate a light trance.
He would then direct his attention to subjective comfort and find himself
developing a deep trance. Finally, after repeated experiments, he was given
both posthypnotic and direct hypnotic suggestion to remain in a medium
deep trance. This he found he could do with very little concern then. He
described the medium trance as primarily characterized by a most pleasing
subjective sense of comfort and a vague dim faulty awareness that there was
an external reality for which he felt a need for considerable motivation to
be able to examine it. However, if he attempted to examine even a single item
of reality for its intrinsic value, the trance would immediately become increasingly lighter. On the other hand, when he examined an item of external
reality for subjective values, for example, the soft comfort of the chair
cushions as contrasted to the intrinsic quiet of the room, the trance became
deeper. But both light and deep trances were characterized by a need to
sense external reality in some manner, not necessarily clearly but nevertheless to retain some recognizable awareness of it.

For both types of trance, experiments were carried out to discover what
hypnotic phenomena could be elicited in both light and medium deep trances.
This same experiment has been done with other good subjects and also with
subjects who consistently developed only a light trance and with those who
consistently did not seem to be able to go further than the medium trance.
In all such studies, the findings were the same, the most important seeming
to be the need of light and medium deep hypnotic subjects to retain at least
some grasp upon external reality and to orient their trance state as a state
apart from external reality but with the orientation to such reality, however
tenuous in character, sensed as available for immediate utilization by the
subject.

Another item which Huxley discovered by his own efforts unguided by me
and of which I was fully aware through work with other subjects, was that
the phenomena of deep hypnosis can be developed in both the light and the
medium deep trance. Huxley, having observed deep hypnosis, wondered
about the possibility of developing hallucinatory phenomena in the light
trance. He attempted this by the measure of enjoying his subjective state
of physical comfort and adding to it an additional subjective quality, namely,
a pleasant gustatory sensation. He found it quite easy to hallucinate vividly
various taste sensations while wondering vaguely what I would think if I
knew what he were doing. He was not aware of his increased swallowing
when he did this. From gustatory sensations he branched out to olfactory
hallucinations both pleasant and unpleasant. He did not realize that he

betrayed this by the flaring of his nostrils. His thinking at the time, so he subsequently explained, was that he had the "feeling" that hallucination of a completely "inner type of process," that is, occurring within the body itself, would be easier than those in which the hallucination appeared to be external to the body. From olfactory hallucinations he progressed to kinesthetic, proprioceptive and finally tactile sensations. In the kinesthetic hallucinatory sensation experience he hallucinated taking a long walk but remaining constantly aware that I was present in some vaguely sensed room. Momentarily he would forget about me and his hallucinated walking would become most vivid. He recognized this as an indication of the momentary development of a deeper trance state which he felt obligated to remember to report to me during the discussion after his arousal. He was not aware of respiratory and pulse changes during the hallucinatory walk.

When he first tried for visual and auditory hallucinations, he found them much more difficult and the effort tended to lighten and to abolish his trance state. He finally reasoned that if he could hallucinate rhythmical movements of his body, he could then "attach" an auditory hallucination to this hallucinated body sensation. The measure proved most successful and again he caught himself wondering if I could hear the music. His breathing rate changed and slight movements of his head were observed. From simple music he proceeded to an hallucination of opera singing and then finally a mumbling of words which eventually seemed to become my voice questioning him about Deep Reflection. I could not recognize what was occurring.

From this he proceeded to visual hallucinations. An attempt to open his eyes nearly aroused him from his trance state. Thereafter he kept his eyes closed for both light and medium deep trance activities. His first visual hallucination was a vivid flooding of his mind with an intense sense of pastel colors of changing hues and with a wavelike motion. He related this experience to his Deep Reflection experiences with me and also to his previous psychedelic experiences. He did not consider this experience sufficiently valid for his purposes of the moment because he felt that vivid memories were playing too large a part. Hence he deliberately decided to visualize a flower but the thought occurred to him that, even as a sense of movement played a part in auditory hallucinations, he might employ a similar measure to develop a visual hallucination. At the moment, so he recalled after arousing from the trance and while discussing his experience, he wondered if I had ever built up hallucinations in my subjects by combining various sensory fields of experience. I told him that that was a standard procedure for me.

He proceeded with this visual hallucination by "feeling" his head turn from side to side and up and down to follow a barely visible, questionably visible, rhythmically moving object. Very shortly the object became increasingly more visible until he saw a giant rose, possibly three feet in diameter.

This he did not expect and thus he was certain at once that it was not a vivified memory but a satisfactory hallucination. With this realization came the realization that he might very well add to the hallucination by adding olfactory hallucinations of an intense "unroselike" sickeningly sweet odor. This effort was also most successful. After experimenting with various hallucinations, Huxley aroused from his trance and discussed extensively what he had accomplished. He was pleased to learn that his experimental findings without any coaching or suggestions from me were in good accord with planned experimental findings with other subjects.

This discussion raised the question of anesthesia, amnesia, dissociation, depersonalization, regression, time distortion, hypermnesia (an item difficult to test with Huxley because of his phenomenal memory) and an exploration of past repressed events.

Of these, Huxley found that anesthesia, amnesia, time distortion, and hypermnesia were possible in the light trance. The other phenomena were conducive to the development of a deep trance with any earnest effort to achieve them.

The anesthesia he developed in the light trance was most effective for selected parts of the body. When generalized anesthesia from the neck down was attempted, Huxley found himself "slipping" into a deep trance.

The amnesia, like the anesthesia, was effective when selective in character. Any effort to have a total amnesia resulted in a progression toward a deep trance.

Time distortion was easily possible and Huxley offered the statement that he was not certain but that he felt strongly that he had long employed time distortion in Deep Reflection, although his first formal introduction to the concept had been through me.

Hypermnesia, so difficult to test because of his extreme capacity to recall past events, was tested upon my suggestion by asking him in the light trance state to state promptly upon request on what page of various of his books certain paragraphs could be found. At the first request, Huxley aroused from the light trance and explained, "Really now, Milton, I can't do that. I can with effort recite most of that book, but the page number for a paragraph is not exactly cricket." Nevertheless, he went back into a light trance, the name of the volume was given, a few lines of a paragraph were read aloud to him whereupon he was to give the page number on which it appeared. He succeeded in definitely better than 65 per cent in an amazingly prompt fashion. Upon awakening from the light trance, he was instructed to remain in the state of conscious awareness and to execute the same task. To his immense astonishment he found that, while the page number "flashed" into his mind in the light trance state, in the waking state he had to follow a methodical procedure of completing the paragraph mentally, beginning the next, then turning back mentally to the preceding paragraph and then "making a guess." When restricted to the same length of time he had employed in the light trance, he failed in each instance. When allowed to take whatever length of time he wished, he could reach an accuracy of about 40 per cent, but the books had to be ones more recently read than those used for the light trance state.

Huxley then proceeded to duplicate in the medium trance all that he had done in the light trance. He accomplished similar tasks much more easily but constantly experienced a feeling of "slipping" into a deeper trance.

Huxley and I discussed this hypnotic behavior of his at very considerable length with Huxley making most of the notations since only he could record his own subjective experience in relation to the topics discussed. For this reason the discussion here is limited.

We then turned to the question of deep hypnosis. Huxley developed easily a profound somnambulistic trance in which he was completely disoriented spontaneously for time and place. He was able to open his eyes but described his field of vision as being a "well of light" which included me, the chair in which I sat, himself and his chair. He remarked at once upon the remarkable spontaneous restriction of his vision, and disclosed an awareness that, for some reason unknown to him, he was obligated to "explain things" to me. Careful questioning disclosed him to have an amnesia about what had been done previously, nor did he have any awareness of our joint venture. His feeling that he must explain things became a casual willingness as soon as he verbalized it. One of his first statements was, "Really, you know, I can't understand my situation or why you are here wherever that may be but I must explain things to you." He was assured that I understood the situation and that I was interested in receiving any explanation he wished to give me and told that I might make requests of him. Most casually, indifferently he acceded, but it was obvious that he was enjoying a state of physical comfort in a contented passive manner.

He answered questions simply and briefly, giving literally and precisely no more and no less than the literal significance of the question implied. In other words, he showed the same precise literalness found in other subjects, perhaps more so because of his knowledge of semantics.

He was asked, "What is to my right?" His answer was simply, "I don't know." "Why?" "I haven't looked." "Will you do so?" "Yes." "Now!" "How far do you want me to look?" This was not an unexpected inquiry since I have encountered it innumerable times. Huxley was simply manifesting a characteristic phenomenon of the deep somnambulistic trance in which visual awareness is restricted in some inexplicable manner to those items pertinent to the trance situation. For each chair, couch, footstool I wished him to see specific instructions were required. As Huxley explained later,

"I had to look around until gradually it (the specified object) slowly came into view, not all at once, but slowly as if it were materializing. I really believe that I felt completely at ease without a trace of wonderment as I watched things materialize. I accepted everything as a matter of course." Similar explanations have been received from hundreds of subjects. Yet experience has taught me the importance of my assumption of the role of a purely passive inquirer, one who asks a question solely to receive an answer regardless of its content. An intonation of interest in the meaning of the answer is likely to induce the subject to respond as if he had been given instructions concerning what answer to give. In therapeutic work I use intonations to influence more adequate personal responses by the patient.

With Huxley I tested this by enthusiastically asking, "What, tell me now, is that which is just about 15 feet in front of you?" The correct answer should have been, "A table." Instead, the answer received was, "A table with a book and a vase on it." Both the book and the vase were on the table but on the far side of the table and hence more than 15 feet away. Later the same inquiry was made in a casual indifferent fashion, "Tell me now what is that just about 15 feet in front of you?" He replied, despite his previous answer, "A table." "Anything else?" "Yes." "What else?" "A book." (This was nearer to him than was the vase.) "Anything else?" "Yes." "Tell me now." "A vase." "Anything else?" "Yes." "Tell me now." "A spot." "Anything else?" "No."

This literalness and this peculiar restriction of awareness to those items of reality constituting the precise hypnotic situation is highly definitive of a satisfactory somnambulistic hypnotic trance. Along with the visual restriction, there is also an auditory restriction of such character that sounds, even those originating between the operator and the subject, seem to be totally outside the hypnotic situation. Since there was no assistant present, this auditory restriction could not be tested. However, by means of a black thread not visible to the eye, a book was toppled from the table behind him against his back. Slowly, as if he had experienced an itch, Huxley raised his hand and scratched his shoulder. There was no startle reaction. This, too, is characteristic of the response made to many unexpected physical stimuli. They are interpreted in terms of past body experience. Quite frequently as a part of developing a deep somnambulistic trance, subjects will concomitantly develop a selective general anesthesia for physical stimuli not constituting a part of the hypnotic situation, physical stimuli in particular that do not permit interpretation in terms of past experience. This could not be tested in the situation with Huxley since an assistant is necessary to make adequate tests without distorting the hypnotic situation. One illustrative measure I have used is to pass a threaded needle through the coat sleeve while positioning the arms and then having an assistant saw back and forth on the thread from a place of concealment. Often a spontaneous anesthesia would keep the subject unaware of the stimulus. Various simple measures are easily devised.

Huxley was then gently indirectly awakened from the trance by the simple suggestion that he adjust himself in his chair to resume the exact physical and mental state he had had at the decision to discontinue until later any further experimental study of Deep Reflection.

Huxley's response was an immediate arousal and he promptly stated that he was all set to enter deep hypnosis. While this statement in itself indicated profound posthypnotic amnesia, delaying tactics were employed in the guise of discussion of what might possibly be done. In this way it became possible to mention various items of his deep trance behavior. Such mention evoked no memories and Huxley's discussion of the points raised showed no sophistication resulting from his deep trance behavior. He was as uninformed about the details of his deep trance behavior as he had been before the deep trance had been induced.

There followed more deep trances by Huxley in which, avoiding all personal significances, he was asked to develop partial, selective, and total posthypnotic amnesias (by partial is meant a part of the total experience, by selective amnesia is meant an amnesia for selected, perhaps interrelated items of experience), a recovery of the amnestic material and a loss of the recovered material. He developed also catalepsy tested by "arranging" him comfortably in a chair and then creating a situation constituting a direct command to rise from the chair ("take the book on that table there and place it on the desk over there and do it now"). By this means Huxley found himself, unexplicably to him, unable to arise from the chair and unable to understand why this was so. [The "comfortable arrangement" of his body had resulted in a positioning that would have to be corrected before he could arise from the chair and no implied suggestions for such correction were to be found in the instructions given. Hence, he sat helplessly unable to stand, unable to recognize why. This same measure has been employed to demonstrate a saddle block anesthesia before medical groups. The subject in the deep trance is carefully positioned, a casual conversation is then conducted, the subject is then placed in rapport with another subject who is asked to exchange seats with the first subject. The second subject steps over only to stand helplessly while the first subject discovers that she is (a) unable to move, and (b) that shortly the loss of ability to stand results in a loss of orientation to the lower part of her body and a resulting total anesthesia without anesthesia having been mentioned even in the preliminary discussion of hypnosis. This unnoticed use of catalepsy not recognized by the subject is a most effective measure in deepening trance states.]

Huxley was amazed at his loss of mobility and became even more so when he discovered a loss of orientation to the lower part of his body and he was most astonished when I demonstrated for him the presence of a profound anesthesia. He was much at loss to understand the entire sequence of events. He did not relate the comfortable positioning of his body to the unobtrusively induced catalepsy with its consequent anesthesia.

He was aroused from the trance state with persistent catalepsy, anesthesia and a total amnesia for all deep trance experiences. He spontaneously enlarged the instruction to include all trance experiences, possibly because he did not hear my instructions sufficiently clearly. Immediately he reoriented himself to the time at which we had been working with Deep Reflection. He was much at a loss to explain his immobile state, and he expressed curious wonderment about what he had done in the Deep Reflection state, from which he assumed he had just emerged, and what had led to such inexplicable manifestations for the first time in all of his experience. He became greatly interested, kept murmuring such comments as "Most extraordinary" while he explored the lower part of his body with his hands and eyes. He noted that he could tell the position of his feet only with his eyes, that there was a profound immobility from the waist down, and he discovered, while attempting futilely because of the catalepsy to move his leg with his hands that a state of anesthesia existed. This he tested variously, asking me to furnish him with various things in order to make his test. For example, he asked that ice be applied to his bare ankle by me since he could not bend sufficiently to do so. Finally, after much study he turned to me, remarking, "I say, you look cool and most comfortable while I am in a most extraordinary predicament. I deduce that in some subtle way you have distracted and disturbed my sense of body awareness. I say, is this state anything like hypnosis?"

Restoration of his memory delighted him, but he remained entirely at loss concerning the genesis of his catalepsy and his anesthesia. He realized, however, that some technique of communication had been employed to effect the results achieved but he did not succeed in the association of the positioning of his body with the final results.

Further experimentation in the deep trance investigated visual, auditory and other types of ideosensory hallucinations. One of the measures employed was to pantomime hearing a door open and then to appear to see someone entering the room, to arise in courtesy and to indicate a chair, then to turn to Huxley to express the hope that he was comfortable. He replied that he was and he expressed surprise at his wife's unexpected return since he had expected her to be absent the entire day. (The chair I had indicated was one I knew his wife liked to occupy.) He conversed with her and apparently hallucinated replies. He was interrupted with the question of how he knew that it was his wife and not an hypnotic hallucination. He examined the question thoughtfully, then explained that I had not given him any suggestion to hallucinate his wife, that I had been as much surprised by her arrival as he had been, and that she was dressed as she had been just before her departure and not as I had seen her earlier. Hence, it was reasonable to assume that she was a reality. After a brief thoughtful pause, he returned to his "conversation" with her apparently continuing to hallucinate replies. Finally I attracted his attention and made a hand gesture suggestive of a disappearance toward the chair in which he "saw" his wife. To his complete astonishment he saw her slowly fade away. Then he turned to me and asked that I awaken him with a full memory of the experience. This I did and he discussed the experience at some length making many special notations in his notebook elaborating them with the answers to questions he put to me. He was amazed to discover that when I asked him to awaken with a retention of the immobility and anesthesia, he *thought* he had awakened but that the trance state had, to him, unrecognizably persisted.

He then urged further work on hypnotic hallucinatory experiences and a great variety (positive and negative visual, auditory, olfactory, gustatory, tactile, kinesthetic, temperature, hunger, satiety, fatigue, weakness, profound excited expectation, etc.) were explored. He proved to be most competent in all regards and it was noted that his pulse rate would change as much as twenty points when he was asked to hallucinate the experience of mountain climbing in a profound state of weariness. He volunteered in his discussion of these varied experiences the information that while a negative hallucination could be achieved readily in a deep trance, it would be most difficult in a light or medium trance because negative hallucinations were most destructive of reality values, even those of the hypnotic situation. That is, with induced negative hallucinations, he found that I was blurred in outline even though he could develop a deep trance with a negative hallucination inherent in that deep trance for all external reality except the realities of the hypnotic situation which would remain clear and well defined unless suggestions to the contrary were offered. Subsequent work with other subjects confirmed this finding by Huxley. I had not previously explored this matter of negative hallucinations in light and medium trances.

At this point, Huxley recalled his page number identification in the lighter trance states during the inquiry into hypermnesia and he asked that he be subjected to similar tests in deep hypnosis. Together we searched the library shelves, finally selecting several books that Huxley was certain he must have read many years previously but which he had not touched for twenty or more years. (One, apparently, he had never read, the other five he had.)

In a deep trance with his eyes closed, Huxley listened intently, as I opened the book at random and read a half dozen lines from a selected paragraph. For some, he identified the page number almost at once and then he would hallucinate the page, and "read" it from the point where I had stopped. Additionally, he identified the occasion on which he read the book. Two of the books he recalled consulting fifteen years previously. Another two he found it difficult to give the correct page number and then only approximating the page number. He could not hallucinate the printing and could only give little more than a summary of the thought content; but this, in essence, was correct. He could not identify when he had read them but he was certain it was more than twenty-five years previously.

Huxley in the post-trance discussion was most amazed by his performance as a memory feat but commented upon the experience as primarily intellectual with the recovered memories lacking in any emotional significances of belonging to him as a person. This led to a general discussion of hypnosis and Deep Reflection with a general feeling of inadequacy on Huxley's part concerning proper conceptualization of his experiences for comparison of values. While Huxley was most delighted with his hypnotic experiences for their interest and the new understandings they offered him, he was also somewhat at a loss. He felt that, as a purely personal experience he derived certain unidentifiable subjective values from Deep Reflection not actually obtainable from hypnosis which offered only a wealth of new points of view. Deep Reflection, he declared, gave him certain inner enduring feelings that seemed to play some significant part in his pattern of living. During this discussion he suddenly asked if hypnosis could be employed to permit him to explore his psychedelic experiences. His request was met but upon arousal from the trance he expressed the feeling that the hypnotic experience was quite different than was a comparable "feeling through" by means of Deep Reflection. He explained that the hypnotic exploration did not give him an inner feeling, that is, a continuing subjective feeling, of just being in the midst of his psychedelic experience, that there was an ordered intellectual content paralleling the "feeling content" while Deep Reflection established a profound emotional background of a stable character upon which he could "consciously lay effortlessly an intellectual display of ideas" to which the reader would make full response. This discussion Huxley brought to a close by the thoughtful comment that his brief intensive experience with hypnosis had not yet begun to digest and that he could not expect to offer an intelligent comment without much more thought.

He asked urgently that further deep hypnosis be done with him in which more complex phenomena would be induced to permit him to explore himself more adequately as a person. After a rapid mental review of what had been done and what might yet be done, I decided upon the desirability of a deep trance state with the possibility of a two-stage dissociative regression, that is, of the procedure of regressing him by dissociating him from a selected recent area of his life experience so that he could view it as an onlooker from the orientation of another relatively recent area of life experience. The best way to do this I felt would be by a confusion technique (Erickson, 1964). This decision to employ a confusion technique was influenced in large part by the author's awareness of Huxley's unlimited intellectual capacity and curiosity which would aid greatly by leading Huxley to add to the confusion technique verbalizations other possible elaborate meanings and significances and associations, thereby actually supplementing in effect my own efforts. Unfortunately, there was no tape recorder present to preserve the details of the actual suggestions which were to the effect that Huxley go ever deeper and deeper into a trance until "the depth was a part and apart" from him, that before him would appear in "utter clarity, in living reality, in impossible actuality, that which once was, but which now in the depths of the trance, will, in bewildering confrontation challenge all of your memories and understandings." This was a purposely vague yet permissively comprehensive suggestion and I simply relied upon Huxley's intelligence to elaborate it with an extensive meaningfulness for himself which I could not even attempt to guess. There were, of course, other suggestions but they centered in effect upon the suggestion enclosed in the quotation above. What I had in mind was not a defined situation but a setting of the stage so that Huxley himself would be led to define the task. I did not even attempt to speculate upon what my suggestions might mean to Huxley.

It became obvious that Huxley was making an intensive hypnotic response during the prolonged repetitious suggestion I was offering when suddenly he raised his hand and said rather loudly and most urgently, "I say, Milton, do you mind hushing up there. This is most extraordinarily interesting down here and your constant talking is frightfully distracting and annoying."

For more than two hours, Huxley sat with his eyes open, gazing intently before him. The play of expression on his face was most rapid and bewildering. His heart rate and respiratory rate were observed to change suddenly and inexplicably and repeatedly at irregular intervals. Each time that the author attempted to speak to him, Huxley would raise his hand, perhaps lift his head, and speak as if the author were at some height above him, and frequently he would annoyedly request silence.

After well over two hours he suddenly looked up toward the ceiling and remarked with puzzled emphasis, "I say, Milton, this is an extraordinary *contretemps*. We don't know you. You do not belong here. You are sitting on the edge of a ravine watching both of us and neither of us knows which one is talking to you; and we are in the vestibule looking at each other with most extraordinary interest. We know that you are someone who can determine our identity and most extraordinarily we are both sure we know it and that the other is not really so, but merely a mental image of the past or of the future. But you must resolve it despite time and distances and even though we do not know you, I say, this is an extraordinarily fascinating predicament, and am I he or is he me? Come, Milton, whoever you are." There were other similar remarks of comparable meaning which could not be recorded, and Huxley's tone of voice suddenly became most urgent. The whole situation was most confusing to me, but temporal and other types of dissociation seemed to be definitely involved in the situation.

Wonderingly, but with outward calm, I undertook to arouse Huxley from the trance state by accepting the partial clues given and by saying in essence, "Wherever you are, whatever you are doing, listen closely to what is being said, and slowly, gradually, comfortably begin to act upon it. Feel rested and comfortable, feel a need to establish an increasing contact with my voice, with me, with the situation I represent, a need of returning to matters in hand with me not so long ago, in the not so long ago belonging to me, *and leave behind but AVAILABLE UPON REQUEST practically everything of import- ance, KNOWING BUT NOT KNOWING that it is AVAILABLE UPON REQUEST.* And now, let us see, that's right, you are sitting there, wide awake, rested, comfortable, and *ready for discussion of what little there is.*"

Huxley aroused, rubbed his eyes, and remarked, "I have a most extraor- dinary feeling that I have been in a profound trance, but it has been a most sterile experience. I recall you suggesting that I go deeper in a trance, and I felt myself to be most compliant, and though I feel much time has elapsed, I truly believe a state of Deep Reflection would have been more fruitful."

Since he did not specifically ask the time, a desultory conversation was conducted in which Huxley compared the definite but vague appreciation of external realties of the light trance with the more definitely decreased aware- ness of externalities in the medium trance which is accompanied by a pecu- liar sense of minor comfort that those external realities can become secure actualities at any given moment.

He was then asked about realities in the deep trance from which he had just recently aroused. He replied thoughtfully that he could recall vaguely feeling that he was developing a deep trance but that no memories came to mind associated with it. After some discussion of hypnotic amnesia and the possibility that he might be manifesting such a phenomenon, he laughed with amusement and stated that such a topic would be most intriguing to discuss. After still further desultory conversation, he was asked à *propos* of nothing, "In what vestibule would you place that chair?" (indicating a nearby arm- chair.) His reply was remarkable. "Really, Milton, that is a most extraor- dinary question. Frightfully so! It is quite without meaning, but that word 'vestibule' has a strange feeling of immense anxious warmth about it. Most extraordinarily fascinating!" He lapsed into a puzzled thought for some minutes and finally stated that if there were any significance, it was undoubt- edly some fleeting esoteric association. After further casual conversation,

I remarked, "As for the edge where I was sitting, I wonder how deep the ravine was." To this Huxley replied. "Really Milton, you can be most frightfully cryptic. Those words 'vestibule,' 'edge,' 'ravine,' have an extraordinary effect upon me. It is most indescribable. Let me see if I can associate some meaning with them." For nearly 15 minutes Huxley struggled vainly to secure some meaningful associations with those words, now and then stating that my apparently purposive but unrevealing use of them constituted a full assurance that there was a meaningful significance which should be apparent to him. Finally he disclosed with elation, "I have it now. Most extraordinary how it escaped me. I'm fully aware that you had me in a trance and unquestionably those words had something to do with the deep trance which seemed to be so sterile to me. I wonder if I can recover my associations."

After about 20 minutes of silent, obviously intense thought on his part, Huxley remarked, "If those words do have a significance, I can truly say that I have a most profound hypnotic amnesia. I have attempted Deep Reflection, but I have found my thought centering around my mescaline experiences. It was indeed difficult to tear myself away from those thoughts. I had a feeling that I was employing them to preserve my amnesia. Shall we go on for another half hour on other matters to see if there is any spontaneous recall in association with 'vestibule,' 'edge' and 'ravine'?"

Various topics were discussed until finally Huxley said, "It is a most extraordinary feeling of meaningful warmth those words have for me, but I am utterly, I might say frightfully, helpless. I suppose I will have to depend upon you for something, whatever that may be. It's extraordinary, most extraordinary."

This comment I deliberately bypassed but during the ensuing conversation Huxley was observed to have a most thoughtful puzzled expression on his face, though he made no effort to press me for assistance. After some time, I commented with quiet emphasis, "Well, perhaps now matters will *become available*." From his lounging comfortable position in his chair, Huxley straightened up in a startled amazed fashion and then poured forth a torrent of words too rapid to record except for occasional notes.

In essence, his account was that the word "available" had the effect of drawing back an amnestic curtain, laying bare a most astonishing subjective experience that had miraculously been "wiped out" by the words "leave behind" and had been recovered *in toto* by virtue of the cue words of "become available."

He explained that he now realized that he had developed a "deep trance," a psychological state far different from his state of Deep Reflection, that in Deep Reflection there was an attenuated but unconcerned and unimportant awareness of external reality, a feeling of being in a known sensed state of subjective awareness, a feeling of control and a desire to utilize capabilities and in which past memories, learnings, and experiences flowed freely and easily. Along with this flow there would be a continuing sense in the self that these memories, learnings, experiences, and understandings, however vivid, were no more than just such an orderly meaningful alignment of psychological experiences out of which to form a foundation for a profound pleasing subjective emotional state from which would flow comprehensive understandings to be utilized immediately and with little conscious effort.

The deep trance state, he asserted, he now knew to be another and entirely different category of experience. External reality could enter but it acquired a new kind of subjective reality, a special reality of a new and different significance entirely. For example, while I had been included in part in his deep trance state, it was not as a specific person with a specific identity. Instead, I was known only as someone whom he (Huxley) knew in some vague and unimportant and completely unidentified relationship.

Aside from my "reality," there existed the type of reality that one encounters in vivid dreams, a reality that one does not question. Instead, one accepts such reality completely without intellectual questioning and there are no conflicting contrasts nor judgmental comparisons nor contradictions so that whatever is subjectively experienced is unquestioningly accepted as both subjectively and objectively genuine and in keeping with all else.

In his deep trance, Huxley found himself in a deep wide ravine, high up on the steep side of which, on the very edge, I sat, identifiable only by name and as annoyingly verbose.

Before him, in a wide expanse of soft dry sand was a nude infant lying on its stomach. Acceptingly, unquestioning of its actuality, Huxley gazed at the infant, vastly curious about its behavior, vastly intent on trying to understand its flailing movements with its hands and the creeping movements of its legs. To his amazement, he felt himself experiencing a vague curious sense of wonderment as if he himself were the infant and looking at the soft sand and trying to understand what it was.

As he watched, he became annoyed with me since I was apparently trying to talk to him, and he experienced a wave of impatience and requested that I be silent. He turned back and noted that the infant was growing before his eyes, was creeping, sitting, standing, toddling, walking, playing, talking. In utter fascination he watched this growing child, sensed its subjective experiences of learning, of wanting, of feeling. He followed it in distorted time through a multitude of experiences as it passed from infancy to childhood to school days to early youth to teenage. He watched the child's physical development, sensed its physical and subjective mental experiences, sympathized with it, empathized with it, rejoiced with it, thought and wondered and learned with it. He felt as one with it, as if it were he himself, and he continued to watch it until finally he realized that he had watched that infant grow to the maturity of 23 years. He stepped closer to see what the young man was looking at, and suddenly realized that the young man was Aldous Huxley himself, and that this Aldous Huxley was looking at another Aldous Huxley, obviously in his early fifties, just across the vestibule in which they both were standing; and that he, aged 52, was looking at himself, Aldous, aged 23. Then Aldous, aged 23 and Aldous aged 52, apparently realized simultaneously that they were looking at each other and the curious questions at once arose in the mind of each of them. For one the question was, "Is that my idea of what I'll be like when I am 52?" and, "Is that really the way I appeared when I was 23?" Each was aware of the question in the other's mind. Each found the question of "Extraordinarily fascinating interest" and each tried to determine which was the "actual reality" and which was the "mere subjective experience outwardly projected in hallucinatory form."

To each the past 23 years was an open book, all memories and events were clear, and they recognized that they shared those memories in common, and to each only wondering speculation offered a possible explanation of any of the years between 23 and 52.

They looked across the vestibule (this "vestibule" was not defined) and up at the edge of the ravine where I was sitting. Both knew that that person sitting there had some undefined significance, was named Milton, and could be spoken to by both. The thought came to both, could he hear both of them, but the test failed because they found that they spoke simultaneously, nor could they speak separately.

Slowly, thoughtfully, they studied each other. One had to be real. One had to be a memory image or a projection of a self-image. Should not Aldous, aged 52, have all the memories of the years from 23 to 42? But if he did, how could he then see Aldous, aged 23, without the shadings and colorations of the years that had passed since that youthful age? If he were to view Aldous, aged 23, clearly, he would have to blot out all subsequent memories in order to see that youthful Aldous clearly and as he then was. But if he were actually Aldous, aged 23, why could he not speculatively fabricate memories for the years between 23 and 52 instead of merely seeing Aldous as 52 and nothing more? What manner of psychological blocking could exist to effect this peculiar state of affairs? Each found himself fully cognizant of the thinking and the reasoning of the "other." Each doubted "the reality of the other" and each found reasonable explanations for such contrasting subjective experiences. The questions rose repeatedly, by what measure could the truth be established and of how did that unidentifiable person possessing only a name sitting on the edge of the ravine on the other side of the vestibule fit into the total situation? Could that vague person have an answer? Why not answer? Why not call to him and see?

With much pleasure and interest, Huxley detailed his total subjective experience, speculating upon the years of time distortion experienced and the memory blockages creating the insoluble problem of actual identity.

Experimentally, I remarked casually, "Of course, all that could be *left behind to become AVAILABLE at some later time.*"

Immediately there occurred a re-establishment of the original post hypnotic amnesia. Efforts were made to disrupt this reinduced hypnotic amnesia by veiled remarks, frank open statements, by a narration of what had occurred. Huxley found my narrative statements about an infant on the sand, a deep ravine, a vestibule "curiously interesting," simply cryptic remarks for which Huxley judged I had a purpose. But they were not evocative of anything more. Each statement I made was, in itself, actually uninformative and intended only to arouse associations. Yet no results were forthcoming until again the word "AVAILABLE" resulted in the same effect as previously. The whole account was related by Huxley a second time but without his realization that he was repeating his account. Appropriate suggestions when he had finished his second narration resulted in a full recollection of his first account. His reaction, after his immediate astonishment, was to compare the two accounts item by item. Their identity amazed him, and he noted only minor changes in the order of narration and the choice of words.

Again, as before, a posthypnotic amnesia was induced, and a third recollection was then elicited, followed by an induced realization by Huxley that this was his third recollection.

Extensive detailed notations were made of the whole sequence of events, and comparisons were made of the individual notations, with interspersed comments regarding significances. The many items were systematically discussed for their meanings and brief trances were induced to vivify various items. However, only a relatively few notations were made by me of the content of Huxley's experience since he would properly be the one to develop them fully. My notations concerned primarily the sequence of events and a fairly good summary of the total development.

This discussion was continued until preparations for scheduled activities for that evening intervened, but not before an agreement on a subsequent preparation of the material for publication. Huxley planned to use both Deep Reflection and additional self-induced trances to aid in writing the article but the unfortunate holocaust precluded this.

CONCLUDING REMARKS

It is unfortunate that the above account is only a fragment of an extensive inquiry into the nature of various states of consciousness. Huxley's state of

Deep Reflection did not appear to be hypnotic in character. Instead, it seemed to be a state of utterly intense concentration with much dissociation from external realities but with a full capacity to respond with varying degrees of readiness to externalities. It was entirely a personal experience serving apparently as an unrecognized foundation for conscious work activity enabling him to utilize freely all that had passed through his mind in Deep Reflection.

His hypnotic behavior was in full accord with hypnotic behavior elicited from other subjects. He was capable of all the phenomena of the deep trance and he could respond readily to posthypnotic suggestions and to exceedingly minimal cues. He was emphatic in declaring that the hypnotic state was quite different from the Deep Reflection state.

While some comparison may be made with dream activity, and certainly the ready inclusion of the "vestibule" and the "ravine" in the same subjective situation is suggestive of dream-like activity, such peculiar inclusions are somewhat frequently found as a spontaneous development of profound hypnotic activity in highly intellectual subjects. His somnambulistic behavior, his open eyes, his responsiveness to me, his extensive posthypnotic behavior all indicate that hypnosis was unquestionably definitive of the total situation in that specific situation.

Huxley's remarkable development of a dissociated state, even bearing in mind his original request for a permissive technique, to view hypnotically his own growth and development in distorted time relationships, while indicative of Huxley's all-encompassing intellectual curiosity, is suggestive of most interesting and informative research possibilities. Questioning postexperimentally disclosed that Huxley had no conscious thoughts or plans for review of his life experience nor did he at the time of the trance induction make any such interpretation of the suggestions given him. This was verified by a trance induction and making this special inquiry. His explanation was that when he felt himself "deep in the trance" he began to search for something to do and "suddenly then I found myself—most extraordinary."

While this experience with Huxley was most notable, it was not my first encounter with such developments in the regression of highly intelligent subjects. One such experimental subject asked that he be hypnotized and informed when in the trance that he was to develop a profoundly interesting type of regression. This was primarily to be done for his own interest while he was waiting for me to complete some work. His request was met and he was left to his own devices while sitting in a comfortable chair on the other side of the laboratory. About two hours later he requested that I awaken him. He gave an account of suddenly finding himself on an unfamiliar hillside and, in looking around, he saw a small boy whom he immediately "knew" was six years old. Curious about this conviction about a strange little boy, he walked over to the child only to discover that that child was himself. He immediately recognized the hillside and set about trying to discover how he could be himself at 26 years of age watching himself at the age of 6 years. He soon learned that he could not only see, hear, and feel his child-self, but that he knew the innermost thoughts and feelings. At the moment of realizing this, he felt the child's feeling of hunger and his wish for "brown cookies". This brought a flood of memories to his 26-year-old self, but he noticed that the boy's thoughts were still centering on cookies and that the boy remained totally unaware of him. He was an invisible man, in some way regressed in time so that he could see and sense completely his childhood self. My subject reported that he "lived" with that boy for years, watched his successes and his failures, knew all of his innermost life, wondered about the next day's events with the child, and, like the child, he found to his amazement that even though he was 26 years old, a total amnesia existed for all events subsequent to the child's immediate age at the moment, that he could not forsee the future any more than could the child. He went to school with the child, vacationed with him, always watching the continuing physical growth and development. As each new day arrived, he found that he had a wealth of associations about the actual happenings of the past up to the immediate moment of life for the child-self.

He went through grade school, high school, and then through a long process of deciding whether or not to go to college and what course of studies he should follow. He suffered the same agonies of indecision that his then-self did. He felt his other self's elation and relief when the decision was finally reached and his own feeling of elation and relief was identical with that of his other self.

My subject explained that the experience was literally a moment by moment reliving of his life with only the same awareness he had then and that the highly limited restricted awareness of himself at 26 was that of being an invisible man watching his own growth and development from childhood on, with no more knowledge of the child's future than the child possessed at any particular age.

He had enjoyed each completed event with a vast and vivid panorama of the past memories as each event reached completion. At the point of entrance to college the experience terminated. He then realized that he was in a deep trance and that he wanted to awaken and to take with him into conscious awareness the memory of what he had been subjectively experiencing.

This same type of experience has been encountered with other experimental subjects, both male and female, but each account varies in the manner in which the experience is achieved. For example, a girl who had identical twin sisters three years younger than herself, found herself to be "a pair of identical twins growing up together but always knowing everything about the other." In her account there was nothing about her actual twin sisters, all such memories and associations were excluded.

Another subject, highly inclined mechanically, constructed a robot which he endowed with life only to discover that it was his own life with which he endowed it. He then watched that robot throughout many years of experiential events and learnings, always himself achieving them also because he had an amnesia for his past.

Repeated efforts to set up as an orderly experiment have to date failed. Usually the subject objects or refuses for some not too comprehensible a reason. In all of my experiences with this kind of development in hypnotic trances, this type of "reliving" of one's life has always been a spontaneous occurrence and with highly intelligent well-adjusted experimental subjects.

Huxley's experience was the one most adequately recorded and it is most unfortunate that the greater number of details, having been left with him, were destroyed before he had the opportunity to write them up in full. Huxley's remarkable memory, his capacity to use Deep Reflection and his ability to develop a deep hypnotic state to achieve specific purposes and to arouse himself at will with full conscious awareness of what he had accomplished (Huxley required very little instruction the next day to become skilled in autohypnosis) augured exceedingly well for a most informative study. Unfortunately the destruction of both notebooks precluded him from any effort to reconstruct them from memory because my notebook contained so many notations of items of procedure and observation for which he had no memories and which were vital to any satisfactory elaboration. However, it is hoped that the report given here may serve, despite its deficiencies, as an initial pilot study for the development of a more adequate and comprehensive study of various states of consciousness.

INTRODUCTION TO SECTION 2. BETWEEN WAKING AND SLEEPING: THE HYPNAGOGIC STATE

When we lie down to sleep at night, there is a period of time in which it would be difficult to say with any certainty whether we are awake or asleep. This borderline period has been termed the hypnagogic period. The transitional state that occurs when we wake *from* sleep is called the hypnopompic period.

One of the few things we can say with certainty about the hypnagogic period is that it is highly variable, both physiologically and psychologically, among individuals. For some people this is an experientially nonexistent period, with no conscious recollection of any experience at all. For others this may be a period of enchantment, with beautiful visions, sweet music, and insights into themselves.

Despite the tremendous increase in reseach on nocturnal dreaming over the past 15 years, little has been done about studying the hypnagogic period: the prevailing scientific opinion has lightly dismissed this as an unimportant "transitional" period. Yet it seems clear that this period can be prolonged and yield material as rich as any noctural dream for at least some individuals. It can be studied easily, even at home.* What its potentials are is unknown

*The problem in studying the hypnagogic state in oneself or others is that the material experienced is generally forgotten rapidly, especially as subsequent sleep intervenes between experience and reporting. A simple method to overcome this in studying hypnagogic phenomena is to lie flat on your back in bed, as in going to sleep, but keep your arm in a vertical position, balanced on the elbow, so that it stays up with a minimum of effort. You can slip fairly far into the hypnagogic state this way, getting material, but as you go further muscle tonus suddenly decreases, your arm falls, and you awaken immediately. Some practice with holding the material in memory right after such awakenings will produce good recall for hypnagogic material.

at this point, but it should be noted that many of the comments in Chapter 7 on the experimental control of dreaming apply equally well to the hypnagogic period: indeed, control over this period may be much easier because it is so much closer in time to the waking state than nocturnal dreams are. Further, a number of occult magical procedures (see, e.g., Ophiel, 1961; Carrington, 1958) involved gaining conscious control over the events of the magician's hypnagogic state, using the state as a "doorway" to step through into another world of experience.

The hypnagogic state is by no means confined to the beginnings of nocturnal sleep: I would speculate that there are many times when we believe we are just "thinking deeply" or "concentrating" in which we momentarily slip into a hypnagogic state and perhaps utilize this ASC for enhanced creativity.

In the past few years there have been two major studies of the hypnagogic state using the new electrophysiological techniques for studying dreaming. The first of these (Chapter 4), "Ego Functions and Dreaming during Sleep Onset," by Gerald Vogel, David Foulkes, and Harry Trosman, studies the phenomenology of the hypnagogic state in laboratory Ss as they spontaneously fall asleep. The second article (Chapter 5), "Some Preliminary Observations with an Experimental Procedure for the Study of Hypnagogic and Related Phenomena," by M. Bertini, Helen Lewis, and Herman Witkin, uses similar methodology but employs an active approach, deliberately stimulating the Ss with emotionally significant material before they go into the hypnagogic state. Important data are gathered by this method on the effects of such presleep stimulation not only on the hypnagogic period itself but on subsequent nocturnal dreaming. Further information on this work may be found in the original paper (Bertini, Lewis, & Witkin, 1964) from which Chapter 5 has been condensed, and in Tart (1967), Witkin (1967), and Witkin & Lewis (1967). It is a straightforward step from the Bertini et al. research to attempt to control the hypnagogic state itself and explore the possible use of such control.

Chapters 6 and 8 also contain material pertaining to the hypnagogic state. Besides the references presented in this section, further studies of the hypnagogic state can be found in Buck & Geers (1967), Fiss (1966), Foulkes, Spear, & Symonds (1966), Goodenough, Lewis, Shapiro, Jaret, & Sleser (1965), Green (1967), Hollingworth (1911), Ladd (1892), Leaning (1925), Liberson & Liberson (1966), McKellar (1959), Rechschaffen & Dement (1966), Saul (1965), Wooley (1914), and Zuckerman & Hopkins (1966). Leaning's article in particularly is a very thorough study of the phenomenology of the hypnagogic state but is virtually unknown today.

4

EGO FUNCTIONS AND DREAMING DURING SLEEP ONSET

GERALD VOGEL, DAVID FOULKES, AND HARRY TROSMAN

In the past ten years the work of Aserinsky, Kleitman, and Dement (Aserinsky & Kleitman, 1955; Dement & Kleitman, 1957a, 1957b) has shown that by the EEG/EOG (electrooculogram) there are two different kinds of sleep, which, under ordinary circumstances, cyclically alternate throughout the night. One of these is emergent stage 1 EEG (a low-voltage, fast, random pattern) accompanied by intermittent bursts of rapid eye movements (REM). The second kind of sleep has no rapid eye movements (NREM) and is characterized electroencephalographically by 12–14 cps spindles without δ-waves (stage 2) or with 3–6 cps δ-waves (stage 3 and 4). In an ordinary night's sleep subjects begin with $1\frac{1}{2}$ hours of NREM sleep which then gives way to about 10–15 minutes of REM sleep. A total of 3–7 cycles of alternating NREM and REM sleep compose a night's sleep, with REM sleep taking up progressively more of each cycle. In terms of mental activity during sleep, REM periods are an indicator of dreaming because 80%–90% of REM awakenings produce dream reports (Dement & Kleitman, 1957b). Foulkes (1962) and Rechtschaffen et al. (Rechtschaffen, Verdone & Wheaton, 1963) have shown that NREM sleep also has a characteristic kind of mentation, which, compared with REM reports, is more plausible and less bizarre, more conceptual and less perceptual, more concerned with contemporary waking life, and in general more like

Reprinted by permission from *Arch. Gen. Psychiat.*, Vol. 14, 1966, pp. 238–248.

waking thought (Monroe, et al., 1965). Thus, these findings demonstrate that there is a regular variation of the EEG/EOG pattern during the night and that each of the two kinds of EEG/EOG patterns is associated with a different kind of mentation.

Recently Foulkes and Vogel (1965) extended these EEG/EOG mentation studies to the sleep onset (hypnagogic) period. Physiologically, they found a regular sequence of four successive EEG/EOG stages marking the period from relaxed wakefulness to unequivocal sleep. These were: α-EEG with waking REMs; α-EEG with slow eye movements (SEM); descending stage 1, usually with SEM*; and descending stage 2, occasionally with SEM*. Subjects were awakened at each of these four EEG/EOG stages and information was gathered about the subjects' preawakening mental activity.

In terms of sleep-onset mentation the following findings of the Foulkes and Vogel study are relevant to the present investigation.

1. A specific item of content was found in 95.3% of awakenings.

2. At the time of each awakening three questions about control over mentation and loss of contact with the external world were asked. (a) "Did you feel that you were controlling the course of your thoughts in the sense that you felt you were conjuring them up and could stop them if you wanted to?" (b) "Were you, while this experience was occurring, aware that you were here, in the lab, lying in your bed?" (c) "Were you during the experience aware that you were observing the contents of your own mind, or did you feel that you were observing or participating in events out in the real world?" Tabulation of the replies by EEG/EOG stage showed that loss of volitional control over mentation tended to occur first; then loss of awareness of surroundings; and finally, loss of reality testing (hallucination) occurred. In the present study these replies are taken to indicate increasing degrees of loss of contact with the external world (withdrawal). The first indicates

*The similarities and differences between descending stage 1 and ascending (emergent) stage 1 are as follows: Both have a low-voltage, fast, random EEG and so both are called EEG stage 1. However, the distinctions between them are important. Descending stage 1 occurs at sleep onset, usually lasts one-half to five minutes, is not accompanied by REMs, and has not been thought to be associated with dreaming. It is called descending stage 1 because the subject is "descending" from wakefulness to sleep. On the other hand, ascending stage 1 occurs after 60 to 90 minutes of NREM sleep, lasts 10 to 40 minutes, is accompanied by intermittent bursts of REMs, and is simultaneous with the experience of dreaming. It is called ascending stage 1 because at one time it was thought the sleeper "ascended" from deeper to lighter sleep as he passed from NREM to REM sleep.

*Stage 2 sleep at sleep onset is herein taken to be the electroencephalographic end point of the hypnagogic period and the electroencephalographic beginning of NREM sleep.

that the subject is so focused on internal events that he is carried along by them and is uninterested in the external world. The second indicates further withdrawal because the subject is not only uninterested in the external world but has lost awareness of his immediate surroundings. The third indicates a complete break with reality because the subject believes that his internal experience is actually happening in the external world, i.e., the subject is hallucinating.

3. As indicated above, the recent EEG literature contains many claims that dreaming does not occur at sleep onset and is limited to REM periods during emergent stage 1 (Aserinsky & Kleitman 1955; Dement & Kleitman, 1957; Dement & Kleitman, 1957). The only exception to the latter has been the finding of Vogel (Vogel, 1960) and of Rechschaffen et al. (Rechschaffen, 1963) that in narcolepsy there is a sleep onset REM period with dreaming. Foulkes and Vogel (Foulkes & Vogel, 1965), however, found that dreams, which they defined as hallucinated dramatic episodes, do occur with considerable frequency at sleep onset. The pooled frequencies of dream reports by stage were as follows: α-REM, 31%; α-SEM, 43%; stage 1, 76%; and stage 2, 71%. Though occasional hypnagogic dream reports appeared indistinguishable from typical REM reports, differences between typical hypnagogic and REM dreams were noticed. Compared with the latter, sleep-onset dreams were usually shorter, had less effect, and were more discontinuous; that is, more like a succession of slides than like a movie. Also, there appear to be no substantial individual differences in the incidence and EEG stage of hypnagogic dreams. With regard to the manifest content of hypnagogic dreams, some contained distorted, regressive content so typical of REM reports, while others had undistorted, nonregressive content similar to some NREM reports.

The finding of dreaming in all EEG/EOG stages of the hypnagogic period, and particularly in the absence of stage 1 and in the absence of REM, raises a question about the previous generalization in sleep research which related each kind of mentation to a different EEG/EOG pattern. It is possible however, that this generalization may still be preserved if an investigation of the differences among hypnagogic reports shows the differences to be related to specific EEG/EOG patterns. The present work is such an investigation. Our preliminary view of this problem suggested that a useful approach to the issue of stage specific mentation would be studying the relationship of EEG/EOG stages to sleep-onset changes in ego functions.

In order to do this we pursued further two findings of Foulkes and Vogel. The finding of regressive and nonregressive content in dreams centered out attention on the fact that the content of both dream (hallucinated) and nondream (nonhallucinated) reports varied from nonregressive thinking or remembering to more regressive images such as bizarre, implausible scenes. Thus, gauged by the kind of content reported, the ego function of maintaining nonregressive content was sometimes intact and sometimes impaired during sleep onset. The finding that withdrawal from the external world tended to occur in three degrees focused our attention on the fact that the ego function of maintaining contact with the external world changed in specific ways during sleep onset.

These considerations about the sleep-onset change in two ego functions, viz., maintenance of nonregressive content and the maintenance of contact with the external world, raised the following specific questions which this study was designed to investigate.

1. During the hypnagogic period is there a relationship between the EEG/EOG sequence and each kind of content as there is after sleep onset? For example, do dreams with regressive content occur in one and not in another?

2. During the hypnagogic period what is the temporal relationship between withdrawal and regressive content? For example, does regressive content occur before any withdrawal, or at the same time as withdrawal, or after complete withdrawal?

3. During the hypnagogic period, is it possible to dream, i.e., to hallucinate, while there is still some awareness of one's surroundings? This question was not answered by Foulkes and Vogel, who only showed that there is a statistical tendency for hallucination to occur after loss of awareness of surroundings but who did not indicate whether there were exceptional reversals of this sequence.

4. Psychologically, Freud's clinical data (Freud, 1958), and, physiologically, Dement's (Dement, 1960) laboratory finding of the dream deprivation effect have supported the notion that there is a need for night (REM) dreaming; that, in Freud's words, dreaming "discharges excitation and serves as a safety valve (Freud, 1958, p. 579)." Is there any evidence to suggest a need or function for the hypnagogic dream?

PROCEDURE

The data reported in the present paper were taken from the same hypnagogic reports which were the data for the Foulkes and Vogel (Foulkes and Vogel, 1965) paper. The method of collecting the reports is described in detail in that paper and summarized here.

Nine young-adult subjects (eight male and one female) who had "normal" MMPI profiles and who were students or worked at the University of Chicago were studied. Each subject reported to the laboratory at his bedtime, had the EEG/EOG electrodes attached to his scalp in the usual manner (Dement & Kleitman, 1957), went to bed in a dark, quiet room, and was encouraged to go to sleep. The scalp leads were connected from the sleeper to a separate EEG control room. Subjects were "awakened" according to an unsystematic schedule from one of the four EEG/EOG patterns of the sleep-onset period. When the EEG/EOG indicated a preselected one of the sleep-onset patterns, the subject was called over an intercom and asked to report his "preawakening" experience and then to answer verbally a standard set of questions about his preawakening mental activity. The entire interview was taperecorded. Upon completion of the interview, the subject was encouraged to return to sleep. When during this next sleep-onset period the EEG/EOG indicated an appropriate pattern, the subject was called and the same questioning process was repeated. This procedure was repeated six times each night and usually took about three hours. Each subject came to the laboratory on four nights which were usually spaced one week apart. With six "awakenings" per subject night, there were 24 hypnagogic awakenings per subject, or a planned schedule of 216 awakenings for all nine subjects.

In the present study each transcribed report, unlabeled for EEG/EOG stage, was assessed for the performance of each ego function. Criteria for the assessment were as follows:

1. In rating the function of maintaining nonregressive content we used the content of each report and classified it as either nonregressive or regressive. Content was rated as nonregressive if the mentation was plausible, realistic, coherent, and undistorted, whether it consisted of verbal thoughts or visual images. Content was rated as regressive only by the presence of one or more of six categories (which were suggested by pilot data): (a) Single, isolated images, such as the number 2,081 hanging in midair; or a meaningless pattern, such as oblique lines as seen on a poorly tuned TV screen. (b) An incomplete scene or bits and pieces of a scene, e.g., one subject reported that he was in the process of constructing a lab scene, but it was incomplete, i.e., people and objects not yet in their proper places. (c) Bizarre, inappropriate, or distorted images, e.g., the image of tiny, hairy, people sitting inside the chest cavity. (d) Bizarre sequence or superimposition of images, e.g., one subject reported seeing a train station on which was superimosed an image of strawberries. (e) Dissociation of thought and image, e.g., one subject reported he was driving a car and simultaneously thinking about a problem in linguistics. (f) Magical, omnipotent thinking, e.g., one subject reported that he was a giant waving his hand over an entire town, and with each wave of his hand the lights of the town became dimmer.

2. In tabulating the function of maintaining contact with external reality, we used subjects' replies to the three questions about the abilities to maintain volitional control, orientation to time and place, and discrimination between

an internal and an external event. Contact with reality was classified intact if all these abilities were unimpaired; partially lost if some but not all of these abilities were impaired; and completely lost if all of these abilities were impaired.*

Two judges independently rated each transcribed report, unlabeled as to EEG/EOG stage, for the performance of each ego function. One of these judges was an experimenter (G. V.) and the other, not formally educated in psychology, was trained to do ratings on pilot data and was, of course, unaware of any hypothesis under consideration. Interrater reliability was very high and is defined more precisely and quantitatively in the next section. Of the scheduled 216 reports which were available, 203 were usable for classification according to kind of content and degree of contact with the external world.

RESULTS

A. Ego Function and EEG Stages.   During α-EEG it was found that both ego functions were usually intact, or, at most, one function was impaired. (If the impaired ego function was contact with reality, this function was partially, not completely, lost.) Reports with this combination of ego functions (both unimpaired or only one unimpaired) accounted for 68.8% of α-awakenings. The frequencies of such reports in all EEG stages were: α-REM, 75%; α-SEM, 63%; stage 1, 20%; and stage 2, 15.4%. If the combined incidence of such reports during all EEG/EOG stages is taken as the expected frequency in any EEG/EOG stage, than, as evaluated by the binomial probability distribution function, the difference between the observed α-EEG frequency and the expected frequency is significant at the 0.001 level. Furthermore, on t-tests for correlated means, the α-EEG—stage 1 and α-EEG—stage 2 differences in frequency of such reports are significant at less than the 0.001 level.

During descending stage 1 both ego functions were usually impaired, i.e., there was regressive content and there was partial or complete loss of reality contact. This combination of ego functions accounted for 51.2% of descending stage 1 reports, whereas in other EEG stages, it was 19.2% of α-REM, 27.8% of α-SEM, and 26.9% of descending stage 2. If the combined incidence of such reports during all EEG/EOG stages is taken as the expect-

---

*At times subjects were unable to give an unequivocal answer to one or more of the three questions. This was usually because the ability under question changed during the reported experience or because the subject was simply unable to decide. In either case, because there was not unequivocal complete loss, we classified contact with external reality as partially lost.

ed frequency in any EEG/EOG stage, then, as evaluated by the binomial probability distribution function, the difference between the observed stage 1 frequency and the expected frequency is significant at less than the 0.002 level. Furthermore, on t-tests for correlated means, the stage 1 and a-REM difference in frequency of such reports is significant at the 0.09 level; the stage 1 and a-SEM difference was not significant; the stage 1 and descending stage 2 difference was significant at the 0.07 level.

During descending stage 2 there was usually a paradoxical return to non-regressive content, and a complete loss of contact with external reality. This combination of ego functions accounted for 57.7% of all descending stage 2 reports, whereas it represented 3% of α-REM reports, 5% of α-SEM reports, and 28.8% of descending stage 1 reports. If the combined incidence of such reports during all EEG/EOG stages is taken as the expected frequency in any EEG/EOG stage, then, as evaluated by the binomial probability distribution function, the difference between the observed stage 2 frequency and the expected frequency is significant at less than the 0.001 level. Furthermore, on t-tests for correlated means, the stage 2 α-REM and stage 2 α-SEM differences in frequency of such reports are significant at less then the 0.001 level; the stage 2 and stage 1 difference is significant at less than the 0.005 level.

There is, then, a statistically significant tendency for each EEG stage (alpha, stage 1, and stage 2) to be associated with a different combination of ego functioning, which we call a different ego state. Each of these states is reviewed here and given a name so that we can easily refer to it later. In the first state, usually during α-EEG, the ego maintains both functions, or, at most, shows an impairment of only one function. (If the impaired ego function is contact with reality, this function is partially, not completely lost.) We call this state a relatively intact ego (I). In the second state, usually during descending stage 1, both ego functions are impaired, and we call this a relatively destructuralized ego (D).* In the third, or terminal, state of the hypnagogic period, usually during descending stage 2, the mentation returns from regressive content to more plausible, realistic mentation, but the contact with reality is completely lost. Because of the return of content to the secondary process patterns, we call this a relatively restructuralized ego

---

*The term destructuralized is used in the sense that Rapaport and Gill give to the notion of psychic structure, viz., an abiding configuration of functions (Rapaport and Gill, 1959). Since the ego temporarily loses its abiding functions of contact with reality and of secondary process mentation, it has, in this definition, temporarily lost "its abiding configuration of functions." One of us (H. T.), however, believes the transient shifts in ego functioning do not represent structural changes within the ego, and he would prefer a nonspecific designation to label the hypnagogic changes, such as early, middle, or late.

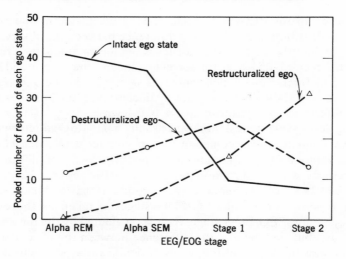

Figure 1.   Relationship of ego state to EEG/EOG stage.

(R). The frequency of these ego states at each EEG stage is plotted in Figure 1.

Reliability measures for the I-D-R ratings were made by an analysis of variance (Winer, 1962, pp. 124–128). The procedure was as follows: Each judge independently rated each transcribed report for regressive or non-regressive content and for degree of withdrawal. The ego function ratings of each judge were then used by the above criteria to assign an ego state I, D, and R judgments by assigning the numbers 1, 2, and 3 respectively to the three ego states. By this measure the reliability coefficient for the I-D-R judgments was 0.96.

Illustrative examples of the I-D-R sequence from two subjects follow. The impairment of contact with external reality in each report is not discernible from the content per se, but was determined from the subject's replies to the questions about this function.

Subject 8 α-SEM: Intact Ego (I)

I was thinking of sending clippings to a Russian pianist and I saw an envelope with 15¢ postage.

(The subject is a concert pianist. The content is not regressive. The subject had lost volitional control over content, was unaware of his surroundings, but knew that the image was in his mind and not in the external world.)

STAGE 1: DESTRUCTURALIZED EGO (D)

I was observing the inside of a pleural cavity. There were small people in it, like in a room. The people were hairy, like monkeys. The walls of the pleural cavity are made of ice and slippery. In the midpart there is an ivory bench with people sitting on it. Some people are throwing balls of cheese against the inner side of the chest wall.

(The report contains bizarre, implausibly associated elements, distortions, etc. There was a complete loss of contact with external reality during the reported experience.)

STAGE 2: RESTRUCTURALIZED EGO (R)

I was driving a car, telling other people you shoudn't go over a certain speed limit.

(In this report it will be noted that the content is again plausible and realistic. There was a complete loss of contact with external reality during the reported experience.)

Subject 7 α-REM: Intact Ego (I)

I was thinking about the lab secretary typing out my transcripts.

(This report is realistically oriented and an anticipation. There was loss of control and loss of awareness of surroundings during the experience, but the subject knew that the experience was mental.)

STAGE 1: DESTRUCTURALIZED EGO (D)

I was making Jello or pudding, following a recipe and putting powder in a pan, and then the "Communist" was in front of the pan.

(The report exemplifies a sequence of bizarrely associated images. There was a complete loss of contact with reality during the experience.)

STAGE 2: RESTRUCTURALIZED EGO (R)

I was writing an exam, probably in histology, and felt frustrated because I couldn't express myself clearly.

(The report indicates a plausible activity. There was a complete loss of contact with reality.)

B. Relationship of kinds of content to loss of contact with the external world. 1. An attempt was made to determine if some withdrawal from the external world was necessary for the appearance of regressive content.

Almost all regressive content reports (94%) occurred when there was some withdrawal from the external reality. The positive Pearson product moment correlation between regressive content and withdrawal was 0.944. This correlation is significantly greater than zero at less than the 0.001 level.

Further, in the category of regressive content reports, 6% have no impairment of reality contact, 12% have only loss of control, 31.3% have loss of control and disorientation, and 50.7% have loss of control, disorientation, and hallucination. Thus, it appears that greater withdrawal from the external world increases the probability for regressive content. A more precise test of this probability was made by using t-tests for correlated means. It was found that the difference in frequency between regressive content reports with no withdrawal and regressive content reports with disorientation is significant at less than the 0.05 level; the difference in frequency between such regressive content reports with no withdrawal and such reports with hallucination is significant at less than the 0.01 level.

These data indicate a correlation between withdrawal and regressive content. They also raise the question of whether early in the hypnagogic period one of these processes precedes the other, i.e., does withdrawal tend to begin before the appearance of regressive content, or does regressive content tend to appear before evidence of withdrawal? In order to provide data on this question, we tabulated for the early hypnagogic period, i.e., α-EEG, the number of reports with withdrawal and no regressive content (35) and the number of reports with regressive content and no withdrawal (2). Based on an equal probability for each, on the t-test for correlated means, this difference is significant at less than 0.001 level.

2. No reports of hallucination without loss of control and loss of awareness of surroundings were observed. A priori, there is no reason why one should expect that hypnagogic hallucinations cannot occur before "total" withdrawal from the external world. For example, it is theoretically conceivable that subjects could, during sleep onset, hallucinate some event or object and still be oriented to time and place. But in no instance was this observed. Hence, hypnagogic hallucinations are indistinguishable from REM reports (night dreams) on the basis of loss of contact with the external world. For this reason an hypnagogic hallucination is called a dream in this paper.

3. The statistically significant I-D-R sequence signifies that, following some withdrawal and regressive contents (D), there is return of the nonregressive contents and a further withdrawal indicated by a loss of reality testing or hallucination (R). This raises the question of whether at the end of the hypnagogic period hallucination tends to precede the return to nonregressive content or whether the reappearance of nonregressive content tends to precede hallucination. In other words, we are asking about the

comparative frequencies of two kinds of reports during the period immediately preceding R: (a) hallucinated reports without return to nonregressive content and (b) nonregressive content reports without hallucination.

An attempt was made to determine the incidence of each of these kinds of reports during the EEG stage immediately preceding the onset of R. For most subjects (eight out of nine) this is a relatively simple task, because R occurs almost exclusively during stage 2 and the incidence of each kind of report can be counted during stage 1. Hence, for subject 9 the frequency of each kind of report must be counted in α-SEM, and not in stage 1.

A tubulation of the incidence of each kind of report during the period preceding R was made. It shows that in this period hallucination with regressive content occurs 16 times, and in the same period nonregressive content without hallucination occurs six times. Based on an equal probability for each kind of report, and as evaluated by the binomial probability distribution function, this difference in frequency is significant at less than the 0.01 level.

Thus these results indicate that some withdrawal precedes or accompanies the appearance of regressive content; that, following the appearance of regressive content, loss of reality testing (hallucination) precedes or accompanies a return to non-regressive content; and, finally, that withdrawal from the external environment (disorientation to time and place) precedes the appearance of hallucination.

COMMENT

A. The relationship between EEG and ego state.   The data indicate that I is most likely to occur with α-EEG, D during descending stage 1, and R during descending stage 2. This psychophysiological parallel is consistent with the findings that after sleep onset different EEG/EOG patterns tend to be associated with different kinds of mentation (Aserinsky & Kleitman, 1955; Dement & Kleitman, 1957a, 1957b; Foulkes, 1962; Monroe et al., 1965; Rechtschaffen, Verdone & Wheaton, 1963). Thus the α-EEG had traditionally been associated with the relaxed waking state, so it is not unexpected that unimpaired ego functions are present during the α-rhythms of the hypnagogic period. Stage 1 after sleep onset (ascending stage 1 REM period) is associated with dreaming, so it is consistent that during the hypnagogic period the most bizarre and unrealistic dream reports come from stage 1, even though it is descending stage 1. Finally, stage 2 after sleep onset is a NREM stage and is associated with more plausible, less bizarre mentation than dreaming mentation. Again, it is not surprising that during the hypnagogic period stage 2 is associated with the return to more secondary process mentation than that reported from the previous descending stage 1. Hence, findings of the hypnagogic period are consistent with the notion gathered from NREM and REM periods that each variety of sleep mentation occurs with a unique EEG pattern.

However, at least two empirical findings make such a notion of sleep mentation seem an oversimplification. First, in Foulkes and Vogel's earlier paper (1965), it was pointed out that the finding of nonstage 1 and non-REM hypnagogic dreams contradicts the notion that "dreaming" is limited to one EEG/EOG pattern. And second, as shown in figure 1, there are many exceptions to an ideal psychophysiological parallel during sleep onset, viz., I occurs during non-alpha-EEG, D outside of descending stage 1, and R outside of descending stage 2. Because of these exceptions to the ideal psychophysiological parallel during the hypnagogic period, an alternative hypothesis about the relationship between ego states and EEG stages is proposed.

When viewed electroencephalographically, successful sleep onset is characterized by a sequence of patterns, α-REM, α-SEM, stage 1, and stage 2. When viewed psychologically, successful sleep onset is characterized by a sequence of ego states, I, D and R. In most instances of sleep onset, I occurs during α-EEG, D during stage 1, and R during stage 2. However, occasionally an ego state will occur in an EEG/EOG stage other than the expected or ideal one. We hypothesize that in these exceptional instances sleep onset is still marked by the same order of psychological events and the same order of EEG events, though the match between the stages of each has changed. For example, the I-D-R sequence may be finished in stage 1, so that reports from both stage 1 and stage 2 are characterized by R; or, at the opposite extreme, the I-D-R sequence may not progress until stage 2 is reached, so that both α-EEG and stage 1 reports are characterized by I. In short, from the psychological side, the hypothesis is that, with or without an ideal correlation between individual ego states and EEG stages, there is a sequence of ego states I, D, and R which marks the period from relaxed wakefulness to unequivocal sleep.

Evidence for this notion is as follows: (a) The usual correlations of I with alpha, D with stage 1, and R with stage 2 indicate the expected order of psychological events. (b) Subject 9 was an exceptional subject; all α-REM reports were D, almost all stage 1 and stage 2 reports were R. This illustrates a subject who regularly had an early onset of D and then maintained R throughout the remainder of the sleep-onset period. (c) Let us consider the exceptions to the ideal psychophysiological parallel during α-EEG, that is, D and R in α-EEG. The frequency of these ego states in α-EEG is such that D is greater than R (see Figure 1). This means that an R in α-EEG is more likely to be preceded by a D than an R. (d) Let us consider the exceptions to the ideal psychophysiological parallel during descending stage 2, that is, I and D during stage 2. The frequency of D in stage 2 is greater than the frequency of I. This means that an I in stage 2 is more likely to be followed by a D in stage 2 than by another I. Or, put in other terms, if an R in stage 2 is to be preceded by a different ego state during stage 2, it is more likely to be D than 1. Thus, from (c) and (d) the patterning of the exceptions to the ideal psychophysiological parallel is consistent with the hypothesis of a particular psychological order relatively independent of EEG stage. (e). Finally, there is evidence that for each subject, as well as for all subjects, each EEG stage had, on the average, a later ego state than the preceding EEG stage. Let us assign to ego states I, D, and R the numbers 1, 2, and 3 respectively. Then the rated means of ego states for each subject for each EEG stage can be calculated. The pooled results for all subjects show a monotonically increasing curve across all EEG stages. Of the 27 comparisons of consecutive stages for individual subjects (nine subjects, three comparisons among four consecutive stages for each subject), 23 are in the expected direction. The four exceptions were in three subjects and three of these exceptions concerned minimal differences between α-REM and α-SEM. Or, in other words, three of the four exceptions occured within α-EEG.

In summary, although there is substantial correlation between each EEG/EOG stage and a corresponding ego state, there are numerous exceptions to this ideal psychophysiological parallel. This raises two possibilities: (a) The ego states often do not occur in the expected order; or (b) during successful sleep onset the I-D-R sequence does occur and is an order of psychological events which exists independent of the linkage of ego states to an ordered EEG sequence. We have concluded that the data are more consistent with the latter possibility.

B. The relationship between kind of content and withdrawal from the external world. 1. The findings indicate that regressive content appears only with, or after, some loss of contact with the external world. This relationship seems so strong that we explain the rare empirical exceptions (5.9%) to this proposition by the notion that during these exceptional experiences there may have been some very early and minimal withdrawal which our questions were too gross or crude to detect.

The inference that some impairment of contact with the external world is a necessary precursor or accompaniment of regressive content is consistent with the results of sensory deprivation experiments and very reminiscent of them. In fact, several investigators of sensory deprivation, including Heron (1961), Ruff et al. (Ruff, Levy, & Thaler, 1961), and Freedman et al. (Freedman, Grunebaum, & Greenblatt, 1961), have explicitly mentioned its similarity to sleep onset. For example, Freedman et al. (1961) state that "visual illusions or hallucinations are very similar to those which have been described for . . . hypnagogic states . . . The significant aspect . . . is that the images . . . [are] not under the subjects control" (p. 68). And, "subjects slip into a dream-like transitional state between sleeping and waking, which makes coherent thinking difficult, thoughts cannot be anchored in reality, and the free flow of fantasy is promoted" (p. 69). Hence, regressive content follows loss of contact with the external world in both sensory deprivation and sleep onset. We are led to wonder if the regressive phenomena resulting from sensory deprivation might actually be caused by the subject's entering the hypnagogic state.

2. The findings indicate that the return to nonregressive content at the end of the hypnagogic period occurs only with or after the loss of reality testing. Again, the temporal relationship seems so strong that we offer an explanation of the six exceptions to this sequence of events. Let us begin by noting that the six exceptions are late hypnagogic reports in which nonregressive content appeared without loss of reality testing. Further, this kind of report is an I state. On the basis of previous arguments about the regularity of the I-D-R sequence and its independence from the EEG/EOG sequence, we suggest that these six I reports come from I-D-R sequences which have not yet progressed to D state. In other words, had sleep onset not been interrupted, we suggest that these I states would have been followed by regressive content (D), and still later by loss of reality testing and a return to nonregressive content (R).

The inference that loss of reality testing is a necessary precursor or accompaniment of a late hypnagogic return to nonregressive content is consistent with the effects of the sensory deprivation experiments. In these experiments subjects know that their perceptual "hallucinations" are not real, i.e., subjects do not lose reality testing (Heron, 1961). And under continuing sensory deprivation there is no return from regressive to nonregressive mentation. Hence, given regressive changes due to continuing reduction in sensory input, when reality testing remains intact (sensory deprivation experiments), the regressive changes persist, and when reality testing is lost (sleep onset), the regressive changes tend to disappear.

C. The psychodynamics of sleep onset.   We have concluded that the I-D-R sequence occurs during successful sleep onset whether or not each ego state is linked to its usually corresponding EEG/EOG stage. As a consequence, we reject the notion that each ego state is a psychic manifestation of a specific EEG/EOG stage. The question then arises, What determines this regular sequence of psychological events during sleep onset? In what follows we will use for this explanation a framework which has integrated the findings of sensory deprivation experiments into ego psychology. The major thesis of this integration is that "ego structures need [external] stimulus nutriment for their autonomous effectiveness and even for their maintenance" (Rapaport, 1958).

The evidence indicates that the desire for sleep produces a decathexis of the external world which occurs in three steps: first, a decathexis of perceptual information (indicated by a lack of interest in the external world); second, a decathexis of the perceptual apparatus (indicated by loss of awareness of the environment); and third, a decathexis of reality testing function (indicated by the belief that mental experience is really happening in the external world).

The evidence also indicates that at some point in this withdrawal from the external world the reduction of meaningful sensory input induces regressive changes in the ego which are manifested by the D state. Accordingly, the regressive changes are not in themselves necessary for sleep onset; rather, they appear to be unavoidable "side effects" of the reduced sensory input (withdrawal) which is essential for sleep onset.

Furthermore, because the D state is so quickly and regularly followed by a restitution (R), it appears that the tendency toward regression, which is represented by D, threatens the ego and produces the need for defense. Thus, at this point in the hypnagogic period, the ego, in order to sleep, needs a defense which will allow it to continue to withdraw and yet will overcome the threatened chaos (D) induced by the withdrawal. The finding that loss of reality testing is necessary for the return to non-regressive contents suggests that the inactivation of reality testing is a part of the needed defense which will resolve the conflict and allow the restitution represented by R. This is consistent with the notion that in other situations the decathexis of reality testing can be a defense which allows restitution of other ego functions, e.g., in the restitutional phase of schizophrenia (Fenichel, 1945, p. 442).

The fact that the subsequent R state contains only nonregressive content supports the notion that there is a successful defense against the regression represented by the D state. Further, the defense against regression—i.e., the loss of reality testing—persists for some time, because the entire subsequent NREM period contains mentation which is more thought-like than dream-like (Foulkes, 1962; Rechtschaffen, Verdone, & Wheaton, 1963; Monroe, et al., 1965), and which resembles a preconscious stream of thought (Rechtschaffen, Vogel & Shaikun, 1963).

This psychodynamic view of sleep onset provides an understanding of an important distinguishing characteristic of hypnagogic dreaming, viz., there are significant individual variations in the length, frequency, and EEG stage of sleep-onset dreams (Foulkes & Vogel, 1965). No such variations exist for REM dreams. We suggest that during sleep onset individuals differ in their tolerance of the potential threat of regression induced by the withdrawal and that these differences are responsible for the variations in the length, frequency, and EEG stage of hypnagogic dreams. This notion is consistent with our clinical impression that the subjects who are free to experience and enjoy their own fantasies had earlier and richer hypnagogic dreams than more anxious and rigid subjects. It appears likely that the more rigid subjects were more threatened by an impending regression and so held on to external reality longer or withdrew in some special way so as to minimize the regression. This is compatible with the clinical phenomena of hypnagogic dream-like experiences which abruptly awaken anxious patients who are particularly prone to insomnia.

D. Function of hypnagogic dreams. On the basis of association of manifest content of dreams (presumably REM reports), Freud (1958) found that night dreams are instigated by unconscious wishes. Since we did not elicit associations to hypnagogic dreams, we do not know if hypnagogic dreams *express* unconscious wishes. But even if they did, the inference is clear that the unconscious wishes do not instigate the hypnagogic dreams. In the case of D dreams the instigator is the reduced sensory input, or withdrawal, which produces a regressed state. Hence, unconscious wishes, if present, are only a secondary result of the regressed state which allows such everpresent wishes to emerge. Other investigators (Fenichel, 1945; Silberer, 1951) have also concluded, on the basis of different evidence, that hypnagogic dreams primarily represent a regressed ego state rather than unconscious wishes.

Freud (1958) also concluded that dream instigators (unconscious wishes) are sleep disturbers and that dreams function to protect sleep by an hallucinatory abolishment (wish fulfillment) of the dream instigator. The present work indicates a variety of dreams for which this formulation does not hold. Thus for hypnagogic D dreams the instigator (withdrawal) tends to promote sleep and the dream itself represents a process which tends to disturb sleep, viz., the regressive loss of effectiveness of ego structures. However, with regard to hypnagogic R dreams, it appears that they are instigated by a potential sleep disturbance (the regression) and that R dreams are the manifest representatives of a defense against this potential disturbance. Thus we conclude that different kinds of dreams have different kinds of instigators, and that some dream instigators tend to disturb sleep and others to protect it.

SUMMARY AND CONCLUSIONS

The psychology of the sleep-onset period was studied by gathering reports from four sequential EEG/EOG stages which mark the period from relaxed wakefulness to unequivocal sleep. These reports were rated for the performance of two ego functions, viz., the maintenance of secondary process mentation and the maintenance of contact with the external world. It was found that based on these two ego functions there is a sequence of three ego states during sleep onset. Thus, initially during sleep onset both functions are usually intact; somewhat later there is both regressive content and withdrawal from the external world; finally there is return to nonregressive content and a complete withdrawal indicated by a loss of reality testing.

Though the correlation between each ego state and a corresponding EEG stage is substantial, there are numerous exceptions to this ideal psychophysiological parallel. However, the sequence of three ego states occurs during successful sleep onset whether or not the ideal psychophysiological parallel holds. This indicates that generalizations from previous sleep research which relate one kind of EEG/EOG pattern to one kind of mentation are an oversimplification, and, more specifically, that during sleep onset the sequence of ego states is not simply a psychological reflection of the sequence of EEG/EOG stages.

The temporal relationship between loss of contact with the external world and presence of regressive or nonregressive mentation was studied. It was found that during the early hypnagogic period loss of contact with external reality precedes the appearance of regressive content. It was also found during the late hypnagogic period (after the appearance of regressive content) that loss of reality testing precedes the reappearance of nonregressive content.

These findings were united to construct a psychodynamic explanation of the sequence of ego states during sleep onset. Thus the initial loss of contact with the external world induces regressive changes in the ego. Accordingly, thought regression is not, in itself, necessary for sleep onset, but appears as an unavoidable side effect of the reduced sensory input. However, the regression threatens the ego and produces the need for a defense. Because loss of reality testing precedes the reappearance of nonregressive content, it is suggested that loss of reality testing is a part of the needed defense which allows sleep to continue.

Thus some hypnagogic dreams are instigated by withdrawal from the external world, and from a psychological point of view, they appear to reflect primarily a regressed ego state rather than the rise and disguised fulfillment of unconscious wishes which are expressed by night (REM) dreams.

5

SOME PRELIMINARY OBSERVATIONS WITH AN EXPERIMENTAL PROCEDURE FOR THE STUDY OF HYPNAGOGIC AND RELATED PHENOMENA

M. BERTINI, HELEN B. LEWIS AND HERMAN A. WITKIN

Although psychology and psychiatry have had a long-standing interest in altered states of consciousness (see Isakower, 1938; Kubie and Margolin, 1942; Kubie, 1953; Silberer, 1951; Federn, 1952), problems of technique have made systematic experimental study of such phenomena as dreams and hypnagogic reverie states difficult. In this paper we shall describe a special procedure for studying hypnagogic phenomena and present some preliminary observations obtained with the procedure which indicate that it may be useful for the study of a variety of problems.

The procedure has three salient features: (1) it facilitates drowsiness, (2) it simultaneously encourages imagery and (3) it permits observation of the "stream of consciousness". White noise is fed into the subject's ears at the same time that he sees a homogeneous visual field. While the subject is lying down in this special situation, he is asked to keep on talking

*Condensed from *Archivio di Psicologia Neurologia e Psichiatria*, 1964, Vol. 6, 493–534. From the Psychology Laboratory and the Psychiatric Treatment Research Center of the Department of Psychiatry. This work was supported in part by grant M-628 and grant MH-05518 from the United States Public Health Service National Institutes of Health.

continuously, describing any thoughts, feelings or images he may have. A tape recording is made of the subject's speech.

White noise, which creates a continuous monotonous sound, has been generally known to facilitate drowsiness. It also reduces auditory feedback from the subject's own voice while he is speaking and distorts the quality of the voice. A homogeneous visual field has been shown to facilitate imagery and to make the imagery more plausible to the subject. To create a homogenous visual field, the subject's eyes are covered with halves of pingpong balls over which is placed a source of diffuse red illumination. The resulting experience is of a relatively unvarying (except for eye-blinks) field of homogeneous stimulation or "ganzfeld" (Hochberg, Triebel & Seaman, 1951).

Our technique was originally developed for a study of the relation between experimentally induced pre-sleep experience and subsequent dreams by Witkin and Lewis (1965). Its purpose was to help follow the way in which thoughts, feelings and images stirred during the waking state might find expression "on the way down" through the hypnagogic reverie and in subsequent dreams.

For a variety of reasons it also seemed important to make a separate study of the experimental hypnagogic induction and monitoring procedure apart from the context of sleep. The transitional nature of the hypnagogic state makes it an especially fertile period for the production of primary process material. Loosened controls partly resulting from the drowsy state seem to make primary process thinking more accessible to observation. Reveries and fantasies, as well as dream-like images and experiences, are commonly reported. The reverie state is characteristically one in which fantasy life has freer expression in the stream of consciousness. A "free-association" period, which seeks to approximate the reverie state in its loosening of controls, is the foundation of many psychotherapeutic procedures, especially psychoanalytically based techniques. An experimental technique which could facilitate any of these states of drowsiness, reverie, or free association, while obtaining the content of consciousness, therefore seemed particularly valuable.

Preliminary observations have indicated that it is possible to induce a hypnagogic state by our procedure, not only when subjects are at their regular sleep time, but at other times of the day. Dreamlike transformations of elements from an exciting film may also occur during an experimental-hypnagogic interval in some subjects, again both at the regular sleep time and at other times.

This report is divided into two parts. In the first part, we present some observations which demonstrate the usefulness of our experimental-hypnagogic procedure in the study of the relationship between pre-sleep experience and subsequent dreams. In the second part we present some observations derived from a separate study of the experimental-hypnagogic procedure with subjects not at their regular sleep time.

CONTENT OF HYPNAGOGIC INTERVAL IN RELATION TO PRE-SLEEP EXPERIENCE AND SUBSEQUENT DREAMS

Procedure

The procedure used to study the content of the hypnagogic interval in relation to a pre-sleep event and subsequent dreams has been described by Witkin and Lewis (1965). In brief summary, in each of a series of five experimental sleep sessions subjects were exposed to a pre-sleep event which consisted, on some occasions, of the showing of an emotionally charged film, on other occasions of an encounter with another person through the medium of suggestion, and on still other occasions of a neutral film. In a sixth session, the subjects were shown an emotionally charged film of a mother monkey eating her dead baby and an attempt was made to retrieve the content of the ensuing hypnagogic interval and subsequent dreams. Study of the hypnagogic interval was made in this final session only.

To determine the occurrence of dreams in our subjects the recently developed method of monitoring the EEG and eye movements was used. It is now generally assumed from the work of Aserinsky and Kleitman (1953), Dement and Kleitman (1957) and the numerous other investigators that the coincidental occurrence of periods of rapid eye movements (REM) and Stage-1 EEG signifies the presence of dreaming. Subjects awakened at these Stage-1 EEG REM periods are very likely to report a dream experience.

At the end of each sleep session an inquiry was made into the subject's dreams, and into his associations to each dream. Each subject had been studied in advance by means of a psychiatric screening interview, projective tests and tests of perceptual field dependence. After the entire series of six experimental sleep sessions, he was interviewed at length for details of his biography. At the end of the interview he was asked to associate again to elements from all his dreams and to the elements from his hypnagogic reverie. The use of the same subjects throughout the series of experimental sleep sessions, together with extensive clinical inquiries into the subjects' dreams and biography, made it possible to amass a fund of clinical information about each subject.

We shall present observations based on study of transcripts of recordings of the experimental-hypnagogic interval of three subjects who participated in all six experimental sessions. These three subjects may be designated Mr. A, Mr. B and Mr. C. Mr. A is a clerical worker, 28 years old, married and the father of two children. Mr. B is an appliance repair man, 30 years old, married and the father of two children. Mr. C is 22 years old, single, a clerical worker and part-time college student. All three subjects were naive with respect to psychological or psychoanalytic theory.

The film which was used in the dream study as a prelude to the experimental-hypnagogic procedure was made in the Primate Laboratory of the Downstate Medical Center. It is a silent film, in black and white, and shows a mother monkey hauling her dead baby about by the arms and legs and nibbling at it. There are many scenes of the dangling legs of the dead baby.

Observations

A. During the experimental-hypnagogic period, which lasted for about an hour immediately following the showing of the film, a characteristic sequence could be observed in which relatively controlled ideation gave way to looser ideation and sluggish speech. As this latter period went on, visual and auditory imagery occurred which was quite dreamlike in quality. For example, the following is a transcript of the last portion of Mr. C's experimental-hypnagogic interval:

> white . . .* crunchy . . . can't keep them too long they go bad on you. (P—very long) (Inaud sentence) (Humming) (inaud) . . . someone's gonna eat the pumpernickel. (Inaud) . . . to the radio . . . to the phonograph . . . (sigh) 80. . . . (Long P) Well, another Florida license plate . . . not the only one . . . (P) Must have been funny . . . what a gorgeous day . . . look at the blue clouds . . . and the white . . . white and the blue intermixed in the distance. Pretty nice weekend. Except on Saturday. How come Monday's always nice? (P) What happened? Can you explain that? (P) Showed . . . one from them and one from us . . . one from them and one from us . . . supply. . . . (mumbling) I'd like to go soon. . . . They won't be doing this all the time. They can only be doing one thing at a time. The canary or the parakeet, or the monkey . . . (P) and add on two more and got six. I know him. What about him? 40 credits. . . . Taste soap? I just did. . . . Got cold in there again. Look at that tunnel . . . not tunnel . . . Long Island Expressway during the rush hour. . . . It's all lit up . . . one big travelling advertisement for something or other. . . . You could have been used as hatchet man . . . not necessarily hitters, but to (inaud) the ball . . . to (inaud) . . . (Inaud) like I said though . . . (snore).

It will be observed that Mr. C's ideation appears to be without any rational thread. The connections among his ideas cannot be followed by an outside observer. Mr. A fell asleep as he was talking, as have other subjects studied with this procedure.

Another subject, Mr. B, had a brief dream (so labelled by him) during the first part of his experimental-hypnagogic interval. Mr. B, who was extremely

---

*In transcripts, three dots indicate a very slight pause; "p" indicates a longer pause; and "P" a fairly long pause. Four dots indicate an omission.

sleepy, dozed and dreamed briefly that "this experiment was over and . . .I was leaving . . . through a basement step with Mr. F (the assistant) and he was saying, 'Don't be discouraged'." It is interesting that during this brief dream the EEG showed a fully waking record.

B. Elements from the film are apparent in transformation in the hypnagogic interval and in further transformation in subsequent dreams.

An example of traceable sequence of imagery from the film to the hypnagogic interval and thence into the dream can be found in Mr. B's texts. During his hypnagogic period, Mr. B said: ". . . It's getting very dark. I . . . I see the mother monkey sitting in the corner of a dark cage and cuddling her dead baby. A feeling of motion is again returning. I feel like I'm in a coal mine. . . . It's very dark, and there's very fine pieces of coal lying about. The feeling of motion has stopped, and just piles of coal around me. I see dirty black water and someone walking in it with bare feet. I see green plants with little blue flowers on them." The mother "cuddling" her dead baby is seen in a "dark cage." Darkness is emphasized and the image of a coal mine appears, with "dirty black water." This image is followed by an "opposite" image of pleasant living things: "green plants with blue flowers." In a subsequent dream Mr. B reported the following: ". . . There were some men and women . . . they had fairly large, well-developed feet. Uh, I think this is all going back to uh . . . Italian . . . Uh . . . you know, to Italy, probably to the grape regions or farm regions of Italy, and I believe these people were wine makers . . . these people were crushing grapes in the grape barrel." In this part of the dream Mr. B said he had a "feeling of well-being." It is possible to interpret this pleasant dream image of Italians making wine with their "feet" as a fusion of "opposites," i.e., a transformed and condensed representation of the darkness and dirt of the coal mine together with the green plants with blue flowers which appeared in the hypnagogic interval.

C. Images which appear in the hypnagogic interval can be shown to have uniquely personal meaning to the subject. Corresponding elements in the subsequent dreams can also be shown to refer to the film in a uniquely personal way.

For example, a "frog" which appeared to Mr. A in the hypnagogic interval had a special connection for him to the theme of mother and baby. Mr. A remembered, in the course of associating to elements presented from the text of his reverie, that he used to be "cruel" to frogs. He would throw them across a brick-wall incinerator and kill them. "After a while frog hunting became a little scarce. I suppose they *ran away* when they saw me." The "frog" in the hypnagogic interval was thus connected with memories of his own cruelty. The first image reported from his first subsequent REM awakening is of "someone *being chased*" (our emphasis).

D. Thoughts and images from the hypnagogic interval itself also find their way into subsequent dreams.

Following is an interesting example of imagery, in the hypnagogic interval, of being on a train, which was then followed by a dream about a train. During the hypnagogic interval, Mr. B said: "I have a feeling of motion, like I would be on a train. . . ." "I can identify the noise now with the motion of a train traveling at very fast speed. I dozed off for a moment, then, I'm awake now." At his fourth and last REM awakening from subsequent sleep, B's dream report contained the following: "This is strange . . . now I remember. The instant that uh . . . you woke me up . . . you see, we were walking off the lawn, and we were approaching the subway, but the approach was like a . . . you know, you walk down a slope and you went underground, and as we were approaching the subway, uh . . . there was a subway train coming out of the tunnel . . . of the subway portion of this . . . and it was ready to come up this high plane into the daylight. But . . . what I found very interesting is the way the subway . . . you see like the subway train would actually be uh . . . uh . . . there wasn't any station, but it would actually *come right onto the lawn, and then go underground again.* You know, right *from this big expanse of lawn* we could walk right over to the subway and there the train would be."

The dream image of a train coming right onto the lawn and going underground again seems very similar to the hypnagogic image right before he dozed off of being on a train. The imagery of the train coming right onto the lawn and going underground could represent, without too many steps of inference, the experience of going under in sleep and coming out again. It is interesting, also, that another subject, who had unusually great difficulty staying awake during the experimental-hypnagogic interval, had images of himself traveling on a train and descending "stone steps" (cf. subject S. K., p. 101).

E. The relation between the subject's method of handling feelings stirred by the film in full consciousness, in his reverie and in his dreams may also be explored by this experimental procedure.

An example of handling the cannibalistic theme of the monkey film in different ways in the reverie and in the dream came from Mr. C. The cannibalistic theme in the monkey film apparently had considerable emotional impact on Mr. C. The figure drawing he made at the end of the session was of "Count Dracula."

The following exchange took place between Mr. C and the experimenter on this point:

(*E*) Count Dracula? (*S*) Uh, a horror figure. (*E*) Uh hm, uh hm. (*S*) Huh, I don't know how it, how that eventually came out. I uh . . . (*E*) Count Dracula? (*S*) I just decided to draw a hat this time. (*E*) Oh, uh hm. (*S*) Then I just threw in a cape also.

(E) Uh hm. (S) And I said, "Well a hat and a cape." (E) Uh, hm. (S) "None other than Count Dracula." (E) Uh hm. What did Count Dracula do particularly? What is he noted for? (S) He was a vampire. (E) Uh hm. (S) In uh . . . in horror fiction. (E) Uh hm. (S) He, uh, thrived on the blood of others. (E) Uh hm. (S) And the implication is obvious. I didn't, I didn't, uh, I didn't think of . . . doing this originally, but then as it, as I started drawing I said, uh, "Oh boy. This movie had its effect."

Not only did the figure drawing carry a message about the fantasies evoked in Mr. C by the monkey film but the drawing provided a vehicle for Mr. C himself to see the connection, in the form of a sudden insight, between the drawing and the film.

Toward the middle of his hypnagogic interval, before he made the Dracula drawing, Mr. C saw a crane with "jaws" helping to "build up the rock jetties again . . . to protect the shoreline against erosion. It's low tide now and you can see the moss which has been growing on the rocks, and the wooden poles are completely uncovered. The seagulls are standing on the poles. . . . There's a seagull that caught a piece of something yesterday . . . looked like wet cardboard from the distance and it was flying around with it, and there was a few others trying to take it away. And he had to maneuver them for this piece of whatever it was. Eventually they left him alone and he was . . . I think he went out on the jetties to eat it."

In a very brief interval immediately following the end of the experimental-hypnagogic interval, right after the ping-pong balls were removed and the white noise shut off, Mr. C dozed and then reported the following very brief dream. He dreamed of his mother telling him about friends who had come to dinner when she was younger. He then said that it didn't make any sense, "My mother and I being the same age."

It is interesting to observe that in the hypnagogic interval, the cannibalistic theme is expressed in transformed images of a crane's jaws building up the shoreline against erosion, a seagull eating something and a tiger opening up his mouth. The figure drawing made after the session is of Count Dracula, a "vampire." In his brief hypnagogic dream, in contrast, there is a mundane eating scene: his mother is telling him about having some friends come for dinner. This is a very civilized, quiet image, in which all danger and all horror are gone. He and his mother are even the same age.

FURTHER OBSERVATIONS MADE WITH THE EXPERIMENTAL-HYPNAGOGIC PROCEDURES WITH SUBJECTS NOT AT THEIR REGULAR SLEEP TIME

As indicated earlier, it seemed important to make a separate study of the experimental-hypnagogic procedure apart from the context of sleep.

The technique seemed a promising one not only for the study of transformations and representations of an exciting film experience in the reverie state, but for the study of a variety of other phenomena as well.

Procedure

Transcripts of the experimental-hypnagogic interval* for 42 subjects, 38 men and 4 women, all normal young college or medical students, form the basis of this section of our report. These subjects, all paid volunteers, were seen during the day, i.e., not at their regular sleep time. Thirty-two subjects went through the experimental-hypnagogic procedure without any specific prior event. Twenty-two subjects were shown an exciting film before the experimental-hypnagogic procedure. Of these there were 12 subjects who went through both procedures. Included among the subjects studied were some selected as being extremely field dependent or field independent. Human figure drawings were obtained from each subject before and after the experimental-hypnagogic session. Because of the exploratory nature of this part of the study, no autonomic or EEG recordings were obtained.

Instructions of the following kind were given to the subjects: This is a study of imagination. You will be in the bed here. These cut ping-pong balls will be placed over your eyes. You will also wear these earphones, through which you will hear a uniform, continuous sound. Please try to be as still as you can on the bed. It is also important that you keep your eyes open during the entire procedure. What I would like you to do, when we are ready, is to start talking and to keep on talking. Talk about anything you please. Talk about anything that you see, anything you hear. In other words, any images you may have—and anything you feel in your body. The important thing is that you keep on talking continuously. Are there any questions you have?

Observations

The observations we shall report in this section are entirely preliminary and are intended to demonstrate the usefulness of the procedure. The data

*The "state" observed in subjects A, B and C described in the preceding section, who were studied at their regular sleep time, may appropriately be designated as a "hypnagogic state". We have not yet studied enough subjects at their ordinary sleep time to know how commonly this state occurs with the experimental-hypnagogic procedure at such times. Of the subjects observed in the studies to be reported now, all of whom were not at their regular sleep time, some showed a state similar to that observed in subjects A, B and C, whereas others did not. (The variety of reactions observed will be described in a later section." We shall continue to use the term "experimental-hypnagogic interval" to refer to the period of the subject's exposure to the experimental-hypnagogic procedure, without any implication, however, that in this interval the subject was necessarily in the kind of hypnagogic state described for subjects A, B, and C.

we have gathered touch on a variety of questions which point the direction for future research. We shall first consider some of the effects of the experimental-hypnagogic procedure itself, and of its several components. Next the variety of reactions to the procedure will be sampled. Then we will examine dreamlike transformations of elements from the films during the experimental-hypnagogic procedure. Sequences of imagery and ideation following increases of feeling will be described. Finally, some preliminary observations regarding more differentiated and less differentiated subjects will be presented.

   A. *Drowsiness and its effects on imagery.* A considerable number of subjects, though not at their regular sleep time, nevertheless reported that they felt very sleepy. Following are some typical examples of the subject's verbatim remarks: "I could fall asleep now if I wanted. Very easy." "Even with the noise, I conk right out now. Get to sleep very, very easily now." "Uh, I kept thinking. I would want to go to sleep."

   Although drowsiness was often reported by some subjects, others did not report it. Since we did not keep constant the point in the diurnal cycle at which we observed our subjects, we do not know how much this factor may have contributed to the observed differences in drowsiness.

   The drowsy state induced by the experimental-hypnagogic procedure seemed conducive to imagery and appeared to affect the kind of imagery produced. It is interesting to observe the imagery which appeared in one subject who was desperately trying to fight sleep during a good portion of his experimental-hypnagogic period. Following are excerpts from a middle portion and from an end portion of his transcript. Subject S.K., male, no film, middle portion of transcript.

"I'm falling asleep and talking, it's like I copied something that was (inaud mumbling)...Anyway...uh...uh...wonder if I'm supposed to feel like I'm drowsing? It sounds like water smashing against rocks. Why did I say that? That was part of a dream I slipped into as I just closed my eyes, impossible...Uhu... oh the image I have before my head where did it come from?... It's a broad green field...(P) It's a bluish building with a thin bottom...bluish building...thin bottom. Fell asleep. That's right...I actually had just fallen asleep. I found my lips moving...an image, a dream I was dreaming...then I woke up and then my eyes closed again...so easy (P). Jes, I'm almost going to sleep on you. Like I could fight it and fight it but it gets to be a pain." End portion of transcript: "Holy cow, I just fell asleep and then I woke up. Did somebody touch my elbow, or did I wake up by myself? (P) I don't even know.... I'll bet you I fell asleep...somebody sitting next to me...he realized I had stopped talking...he just very lightly tapped my elbow...And it was stimulus enough to wake up, to wake me up... 'Cause I don't care, I'll gladly go to sleep.... Gee, I'm having some nice little dreams.... I seem to be...in this...uh...a...stone staircase...no, stone handrail...with a vertical uh...pillar...and a...all of a sudden it's marble...

marble steps ... and a ... (P) But every time I'm about to fall asleep ... I realize it. You know, I can't fall asleep 'cause I know I'm not gonna sleep ... In other words, I ... uh'd like I'd like to fall asleep."

It is clear that brief, dreamlike images appeared to this subject as he was fighting his drowsiness. The auditory imagery involves "water smashing against the rocks"; the visual imagery is of a "broad green field ... it's a bluish building." These images can be understood as transformations of the monotonous sound and homogeneous light which the subject is experiencing. The transformations themselves may be understood as involving condensations of wishes for freedom of action—as opposed to the confined situation in which the subject actually is—with the sensory stimuli. "Water smashing against the rocks," "a broad green field" fuse wishes for freedom with the auditory and visual stimuli.

As the subject goes to sleep he also images "stone steps" which could be understood as visual imagery representing the experience of falling asleep. Again a condensation and fusion of many elements may be traced in the imagery. The "vertical pillar" is the opposite of the sinking sensation; the "stone steps" also represent hard surfaces. An image of a "hand-rail" occurs, perhaps to help the descent.

In the inquiry at the end of the session, this subject gave a very clear account of this last image. He said: "When I was falling asleep, as I was talking about one thing, I was falling asleep, and I suddenly had other images before me. Now I started to talk about one, I think. It was on the left of me ... descending. Um, stone and then it turned into a marble staircase ... of a Victorian type. And, uh, I was not walking down the stairs, it was as if I were traveling on a train, because I was moving at about a 30 miles an hour. Asleep I had little images of things which I don't recall clearly. But as I began to fall asleep like that ... every time ... I'd suddenly get images. If you want me to fall asleep again, I'll get another image for you."

This account of the formation of imagery at the point of falling asleep is particularly interesting. In the first place, it resembles the account given by Mr. B of feeling "motion" and "being on a train," just as he was falling asleep (p. 98). Also, it seems to be an example of the "labile balance" which Silberer thought was the condition for the formation of hypnagogic hallucinations. As this subject says, "If you want me to fall asleep again, I'll get another image for you." Finally, as the first excerpt also indicates, the imagery which appears can be understood as condensed transformation of the many experiences which the subject has in our procedure. In this last image of "stone steps" a fusion of many "opposite" elements can be discerned, hard and soft images, vertical pillar, marble steps, and moving at "30 miles an hour."

The imagery of descent to represent falling asleep is an example of a phenomenon described by Federn (1952). The experience of loss of self or loss of "body-ego" seems to evoke imagery which expresses the descent into nothingness. At the same time, opposite images of hardness and verticality represent the struggle to stay awake, i.e., to maintain "body-ego." The appearance of "marble" in the imagery might also perhaps be understood as an example of the appearance of breast imagery during the hypnagogic period, as described by Isakower.

B. *Variety of general reactions to the experimental-hypnagogic procedure.* A wide range of variation has been observed in the subjects' reactions to the conditions of the hypnagogic interval. Some subjects seem relatively unaffected by either the film or the experimental-hypnagogic situation. They talk quite doggedly about a series of personal themes, and make only brief, or tangential reference to the film or the experimental situation. Some subjects, in apparent reaction to the conditions of confinement in the situation, devote the entire period to thinking of recollections of travel and adventure. Other subjects seem to enjoy the experimental-hypnagogic procedure, finding it relaxing and pleasurable. In still other cases the subject's reaction shifted from feeling relaxed to feeling uneasy or even frightened by the experimental-hypnagogic procedure.

There was also considerable variation among subjects in their reactions to the showing of an exciting film before the hypnagogic interval. Some subjects, particularly field-independent perceivers, appeared relatively unaffected by the film. In contrast, the transcripts of other subjects (mainly field-dependent perceivers) were quite permeated with imagery which could be related to the film (cf. p. 106 for the transcripts of N. F., a field-dependent subject).

Other subjects appeared to use the experimental situation as a place for "free expression" of quite florid ideation after the film, at the same time observing themselves in this unusual procedure. The impression derived from these transcripts is that these subjects remained essentially in control of their ideational flow. We give below excerpts from a transcript which illustrates this pattern of reaction. This transcript came from Subject A. S., a male medical student who had seen the birth film which is divided between a description of the Malmstrom vacuum extractor and scenes of the delivery of a baby.

... and I thought how nice it would be starting perhaps at the under the baby's feet and taking the chopper and making nice thin sections going up the entire length of the baby, and I just thought of uh ... as I went ... (inaud) my slicing of the baby. I sort of winced or scrinched inside as my thoughts were directed towards chopping up the baby's genitals when I got to that area ... I like to think of the fact that there is nothing ... no thought which I would really be afraid of ... becoming aware of concerning myself. That is to say, uh . . . I'd like to think that I am not repressing anything in my consciousness. . . . what I'm thinking of presently I might as well . . . uh . . . having a sexual relationship with my cat. My cat happens to be castrated . . . he's a male. . . . I've always referred to the cat as she or her in knowing that it was a male. . . . I realized a while ago, my calling it a she might be uh . . . an attempt to alleviate any feelings of committing a homosexual act with the cat in my petting with it and playing with it . . . . I noticed that well, I hadn't been aware that the cat had a penis previously. I hadn't seen it, but there was some sort of (inaud) apparatus that was . . . protruded from . . . sort of wet, thin, short, pink thing, and I was surprised. I said, well maybe this cat is experiencing erotic sensations as I pet it, rather than just relaxing. . . . I was thinking about this but I can't remember what it was. Aha . . . my inability to recall, I imagine, is some sort of unconscious repression of the things I wanted to say . . . So maybe by a process of association I can reclaim the things I was gonna talk about.

Still other subjects, after a period of relatively controlled ideation, went over into what seemed like a trance-state. In this state, quite dreamlike imagery appeared which seemed traceable to the films. We give below excerpts from a transcript which illustrates the trancelike state and the dreamlike transformations of film elements. This transcript came from subject B. T., a medical student who had seen an anthropological documentary film made by Geza Roheim showing an initiation rite practiced by an Australian tribe. (Each initiate lies across the backs of the other initiates, all naked, and an incision is made across the dorsal surface of the penis with a sharp stone. The bleeding penis is then seen being held over a fire. The faces of the initiates clearly reflect their anguish. A hairdressing ritual is also shown. The film ends with a rhythmic ritual dance.) After about an hour of quite ordinary, controlled ideation, the quality of B. T.'s speech changed rather suddenly and he apparently went into a trancelike state. The tape at this point sounds as if B. T. were speaking from a dream, describing an ongoing dream experience. Since there was no EEG monitoring, it is impossible to know what the EEG record was like during the dreamlike ideation. Whatever the EEG record, however, B. T. was apparently in some special or unusual state, apparently different from what hypnosis is like and from his own ordinary dream experience, but closer to the latter. B. T.'s transcript follows:

Green bottle . . . interesting green bottle . . . (P) I just fell inside. (P) I keep falling inside the bottle. I can't tell whether I have any clothes on or not. (P) What am I gonna do in the green bottle? I can't get out. I only keep scratching at the walls. (P) I keep scratching at the walls. That's silly. (P) Why don't I do something? I'm gonna go out of the bottle. Ridiculous. (P) Looks kind of like W's wine bottle. Say, what happened to that? Did he give that away? (P) I think he said he wanted it. (P) Maybe I'm trapped in his wine bottle. (P) Now I'm up on a pink cloud. (P) Just laying on a pink cloud. (P) Am I having sex with the pink cloud? That's silly. (P)

Yes, I'm having sex with the pink cloud. Well. I'm going away from the pink cloud. That's ridiculous. Just that green wine bottle at the corner of the kitchen. (P) What's it doing hiding there for? I keep looking at the green bottle. Now that's silly too. (P) Here I am floating about the apartment. Kind of mysterious, but it's sort of pleasant. I just keep floating around from my room to the hall. . . . See, what painting was that? The Birthday Party? (P) Still remember when he showed that to me. That was pretty strange. Birthday party. . . . He floated around like that too. Peculiar head stuck out like that on his neck. And her neck stuck out. Gave him a little kiss. (P) He had flowers or something in his hand. She had something in her arms. . . . Seemed like it was gonna float right out the window. Kind of a funny painting actually. Seems to be floating, and yet it's so static. What an interesting technique. I wonder what B would have said, thought about it. He probably wouldn't like it; he doesn't like much. He's a kind of warped individual. (P) Looks all squeezed up in a little cave. He's just huddled there. Now I'm looking at him huddled there. He looks so pitiful. (P) He's just huddled there and I'm looking at him. Now he's moving a little. I think he's trying to dig himself in deeper. (P) There's snakes around. (P) A bird keeps passing over the sun. And the mountain has a mouth. (P) I don't like all these snakes around. (P) Perhaps I'll get in the cave with Bob. (P) Oh, there's snakes in here too. (P) Grass sure is high. Why don't they go away? I'm going away . . . walking across the field . . . cross a stream . . . into the woods . . . I'm looking around the woods. (P) Oh, there's a girl with blonde hair in the woods. She's got a big belly button. (P) Looks like she's tied up between two trees. (P) Seems strange, she's just, she's not moving. Very white skin . . . sure shows out in the woods. Kind of interesting to go over and touch her. (P) Looks rather inviting. (P) I guess I'm walking closer . . . I'm sticking my finger up her . . . and she isn't doing anything . . . Well now she's squirming a little. (P) Now the ropes came loose. Now she got down and we're walking out of the woods. (P) Now we're getting smaller there's sunshine . . . we're gone . . . (P) Well here comes a big dragon. (P) Now he's blotting out the sun . . . (P) The dragon keeps coming closer. I'm protecting the girl . . . throw her to the ground . . . Put my arm to shield off the dragon. (P) It's so big. Big as a four story house. It's ferocious. (P) Now I got a sword someplace and I knocked it down. It died. (P) Knocked off another head. And the girl got up and went off.

The subject's own account of what the state was like is most instructive. He said he felt "strange." Asked to compare his ideation to usual life, the subject said, "I would compare them to thoughts before going to sleep." Asked if he had this kind of thought often before going to sleep, the subject replied, "Well, not this last one. About going into the woods and so on, killing the dragon. I never had anything like that. Or a green bottle, being in a green bottle. I had that one a long time ago when I was a child. But I don't particularly have thoughts like that any more, or very rarely." The subject is thus describing a very vivid dreamlike experience which he said is not, however, exactly the same as what he experiences in dreaming.

The relation of the differences that have been described in general reaction to the experimental-hypnagogic procedure to differences in personality remains a subject for further investigation. The observations in the last section of this report on reactions of field-dependent and field-independent people provide one promising lead to such an investigation.

C. *Symbols and imagery related to the immediate experimental situation.* There are certain similarities among subjects in the visual and auditory imagery they reported under our experimental conditions. For example, images of "rushing water" or "waterfall," "trains" or "jet planes," "noisy crowd at a baseball game" were each observed in many records. These images are readily related to the monotonous white noise which does seem to vary in intensity. Along with these examples of a banal relationship between imagery and experience, there are many individual instances of original and poetic imagery which appeared in the transcripts. Both the uniformities and individual variations observed give promise that our procedure may be used to study the problems of imagery and symbol formation in relation to immediate sensory and social conditions. Images of motion, of spinning and floating, also occurred frequently in the records. These resemble the accounts of hypnagogic hallucinations given by Oswald (1963). Some subjects also commented on the unusual experience of difficulty in hearing their own voices.

D. *Dreamlike transformations of elements from the films during the experimental hypnagogic period.* The films previously seen provide another important source of imagery during the experimental-hypnagogic period, in addition to the immediate conditions of the experimental situation itself, considered in the preceding section.

For example, B. T.'s imagery during the trancelike state (described in *b* just above), can be connected back to the film, elements of which seem to be represented in transformed style. For example, imagery of having sex with a pink cloud and later with a girl with "white skin" can be understood as derived from the film in the same way that one would interpret dream transformations. This imagery is the "opposite" of the "filthy little people" B. T. saw in the film. In the reverie state, B. T. fights with a dragon to rescue the girl. The dragon is as big as a four story house; the number *four* can perhaps be derived from the groups of four shown in the film.

Other subjects who did not appear to be in the same special trancelike state into which B. T. entered also showed dreamlike imagery traceable to the film. Following are excerpts from the transcript of the hypnagogic interval of N. F., an extremely field-dependent subject, following the birth film. His transcript was permeated with imagery which can be traced to the film. The excerpts below are given in the order in which they occurred:

I just bit into an apple, and there was a worm inside of it, and . . . and half of the worm . . . the head and the first was inside the piece that I ate. And just the other half is sticking outside the apple and it's . . . I spit it out, and I got very nauseous and I throw up.

N. F. reported that he had actually had a nausea reaction at the moment he first saw the exposed vagina in the film. The imagery of biting into an apple and finding a worm clearly expresses the nausea reaction. It can perhaps also be understood as a transformed oral representation of the exposed vagina and protrusions seen in the film.

I see a caterpillar . . . a green . . . larvae or a caterpillar . . . like you see in the Walt Disney science films . . . shedding its skin, getting uh . . . and turning into a butterfly.

This is imagery representing growth and reproduction after seeing the film about the childbirth.

See a volcano . . . or a Polynesian island . . . erupting . . . and the black smoke is billowing up from the mouth of the volcano and the red lava in pouring down the sides on it, steaming and thick and jellylike. And it's just pouring down the sides.

Here is a classically transformed symbolic representation of the thighs of the woman with the blood gushing down them after the delivery.

See a lot of tourists leaving a country and the customs inspector wants to see this lady's suitcase. So he's suspicious and she's taking some jewelry or diamonds or liquor or perfume out of the country and she goes to open up the suitcase and the whole bag opens up. And all the contents fall out all on the floor.

Here we have a classic representation of the vagina as a "suitcase" and its precious contents, all opening out onto the floor, in other words, delivering the baby.

It is apparent from these protocols that the mechanisms of symbolism, displacement and condensation which characterize the dream work may be studied effectively in the content of the experimental-hypnagogic interval.

E. *The relation of feelings to imagery and ideation in the flow of free association.* A sequence can be observed in the flow of imagery in some records which might be interpreted as restitutive or wish-fulfilling. There is a suggestion in a number of other records, as well as in B. T.'s, that an increase of feeling at confinement immediately precedes either an increase in dreamlike imagery or a slight change in the direction of a more trancelike state. A flurry of feeling, not quite grasped cognitively, but reflected in autonomic activity, might be an immediate precursor of a special hypnagogic state. This is another kind of lead which may be checked in future work. Still another possible regularity of sequence has been observed in a number of transcripts. An indirectly expressed or muted expression of discomfort or irritation in the experiment may be followed by the appearance of anxious ideation or threatening imagery. One forms the impression that the throttled irritation might somehow be the anxious ideation and imagery. Anxiety has often been interpreted in psychoanalytic theory as the transformed product of repressed hostility. The complicated process of transformation has, however, remained obscure. It is possible that a careful scrutiny in the hypnagogic transcripts of the sequence which issues in anxious ideation and imagery may help to throw light on the process of transformation.

F. Usefulness of the experimental-hypnagogic procedure in study of free-association phenomena. It is apparent in the material already presented that having people in the experimental-hypnagogic procedure facilitates the flow of ideation and imagery and is evocative of feeling. Fantasies also frequently occur. Moreover, subjects often seem able to report a good deal of what they are experiencing. These characteristics of the experimental-hypnagogic productions make the procedure a useful one for the study of phenomena of free association. We summarize below several observations, some from material already presented, which reflect this.

1. Subjects in the course of their reverie recalled experiences, images and feelings from childhood, sometimes with the comment that these had not occurred to them in a very long time, in some cases even since childhood. These recollections from the past were woven in among thoughts about their current lives.

2. Some subjects specifically said that they had not talked like this in a long while, that they ordinarily keep their thoughts to themselves.

3. Subjects allowed themselves to have fantasies, sometimes quite lurid, and to report these fantasies to the experimenter.

4. Especially with subjects at their regular sleep time a sequence of thoughts, images and feelings typically occurred which, to an outsider, were disjointed and incoherent. We seem to be dealing here with an associational flow relatively removed from ordinary conscious control.

5. With regard to feelings evoked by the experimental situation, some subjects reported that they enjoyed the procedure, that it made them feel good. One subject commented that he could now see why psychiatrists are helpful, another said that he had gotten a lot off his chest. The basis of "feeling good" is not now clear, but the experimental-hypnagogic procedure may lend itself to further investigation of this kind of phenomenon.

6. Again with regard to feeling, some subjects showed open preoccupation with the experimenter—what he is doing, what he is like as a person, what his purposes may be, suggesting a "budding" transference as an important source of feelings in the experimental situation. Such feelings may be explored by means of the experimental-hypnagogic procedure.

7. Restitutive or wish-fulfilling sequences of ideation and imagery were frequently observed. On occasion anxious imagery and ideation were found

to follow immediately after "throttled feelings." Sequence analyses of the relation among feelings, thoughts and images thus seem possible in the productions obtained with the experimental-hypnagogic procedure.

8. Marked differences occurred among subjects in the associational flow. Whereas some generally showed a marked "loosening," others kept things very much in check. Identifying such differences may make possible explorations of their basis in differences in personality characteristics.

This listing suggests that the product of the experimental-hypnagogic procedure may be used in the study of a variety of phenomena of free association. To the extent that free association is at the heart of some forms of therapy, this line of work may in time prove to be of particular value for problems of therapy.

g. *Some observations of reactions of more differentiated and less differentiated subjects to the experimental-hypnagogic procedure.* As an approach to the study of individual differences in reaction to the experimental-hypnagogic procedure, we undertook to compare the reactions of relatively undifferentiated versus relatively differentiated personalities (Witkin, Lewis, Hertzman, Machover, Meissner, and Wapner, 1954; Witkin, Dyk, Faterson, Goodenough, and Karp, 1962).

Our earliest studies of the differentiation dimension focused on individual differences in styles of perceiving. Specifically, we established through three specially devised perceptual tests that people differ in the ability to keep an item separate from the embedding context around it. In one test the subject must tease out a simple hidden geometrical figure from a large organized figure designed to obscure it (embedded-figures test). In another test the subject, in a completely darkened room, must determine the position of a luminous rod contained within a tilted luminous frame (rod-and-frame test). In a third perceptual test the subject's task is to determine the position of his own body in space, when the chair in which he is seated is surrounded by a tilted room (body-adjustment test). We have called people whose perception is much influenced by the surrounding framework "field-dependent" perceivers. In research over the past twenty years we have shown that clusters of such personal characteristics as a relatively undifferentiated body concept (reflected, for example, in unarticulated human figure-drawings), a relatively undeveloped sense of separate identity and the tendency to use global defenses occur in field-dependent perceivers. We have come to regard these interrelated personal characteristics and the preceptual style associated with them as manifestations of a more general dimension which we have conceptualized as extent of psychological differentiation. The field-dependence-independence dimension of perceptual performance, as measured by the special battery of perceptual tests, is used as an indicator of extent of psychological differentiation.

The differentiation dimension provides a specific basis for making predictions, which can be checked in research, about how people may differ in their reaction to the experimental-hypnagogic procedure. The results of several studies suggest additional grounds for predicting how more differentiated and less differentiated persons may react to this procedure. For example, it has been found by Holt and Goldberger (1959) that field-dependent subjects are more uncomfortable than field-independent subjects in sensory deprivation situations. Cohen, Silverman and Shmavonian (1962) have reported that field-dependent subjects were more prone to hallucinatory experiences during sensory deprivation procedure. Taylor (1956) and Powell (1964) have also observed that hallucinating psychotic patients tend to be field dependent. These findings may be interpreted to mean that less differentiated subjects have more difficulty localizing stimulation as deriving from the self.

Our experimental-hypnagogic procedure resembles sensory deprivation procedures in its restriction of sensory input and in its isolation of the subject from the external world. It might therefore be expected that field-dependent subjects would be more uncomfortable in our experimental-hypnagogic procedure. It might also be expected that field-dependent subjects would be more influenced by the components of the experimental procedure: white noise, red light, continuous talking, the film.

In an analysis we made of data from a recent study by Lewis, Goodenough, Shapiro and Sleser (1966), field-dependent perceivers were found to show more overt references to the laboratory in their dreams. A study of the dreams of the eight most differentiated and eight least differentiated subjects in this group showed that the dreams of undifferentiated subjects were more concerned with the relationship to the experimenter and represented him more often in his own "proper person". It might also therefore be expected that the laboratory situation and relationship to the experimenter might figure more prominently in the experimental-hypnagogic interval of field-dependent subjects.

There are some examples of the ways in which the differentiation dimension may be used as a reference point in the study of individual differences in response to the hypnagogic-experimental procedure. Additional insight may be obtained with this reference point into differences in imagery formation, susceptibility to hypnagogic states and ways of reacting to "free association" procedures.

As we predicted, preliminary observation suggests that field-dependent and field-independent subjects are quite different in their reactions to the experimental-hypnagogic procedure. Field-dependent subjects appear to be made more uneasy or even frightened by the experimental situation. They appear to be more often caught up in an ongoing scene with imagery which, however bizarre, seems real to them. When they have been shown an exciting film, their imagery during the experimental-hypnagogic interval seems to be flooded with symbolic references to the film. In these specific ways they are more "influenced" by the experimental procedure, including the showing of an exciting film.

We present below excerpts from the transcript, the entire short protocol of a field-dependent subject in the experimental-hypnagogic procedure, administered without a film preceding it. (This is subject N. F., whose transcript for the hypnagogic interval following a film was given on p. 106 to illustrate symbolic transformations of elements from the film). He became so uncomfortable that he asked the experimenter to terminate the session.

I'm sitting in an airplane high up in the sky . . . and all of a sudden the door to the cabin is sucked out. And all we can see is clouds as the air rushes in. (Long P) A fishing vessel is caught in a stormy sea and there's lightning all around her. And the waves are hitting against her and tossing her about . . . helplessly in the storm. (Long P). An air-raid siren goes off in a big metropolitan city . . . mobbed with people in the streets, and there is chaos and everybody is running for shelter. And people are being trampled on. And there and everyone turns into animals, racing for life . . . for protection. And destroying themselves . . . as they fight for life. (Long P) I see a man on top a lighthouse in the middle of the ocean during a hurricane. Wearing his rain slicker and looking out over the seas with his binoculars. (Long P) Lumberjacks are cutting down trees in the forest by a river. . . . And they're tossing the logs into the river and sending them downstream to the sawmills.

In contrast, after subject T. E., a field-independent perceiver, saw the birth film, he first gave a very detailed and precise account of the film he had just seen and then proceeded on his own personal themes. Nothing like the dreamlike imagery which flooded N. F.'s record is apparent in T. E.'s transcript.

INTRODUCTION TO SECTION 3. DREAM CONSCIOUSNESS

If there is one ASC that is universal in all normal humans, it is the nocturnal dream. Indeed, the research of the last 15 years strongly indicates that we have no "choice" about dreaming; it is only in the degree to which people recall their dreams that men differ.

In spite of its being an ASC experienced by all men to various degrees, our knowledge of the nature of the dream is far from complete, and men's attitudes toward it have covered every extreme imaginable. The dream has been treated as the real experience of the soul wandering during sleep, as an indication of an upset stomach, as the Royal Road to the Unconscious, as a prophecy of things to come, as an epiphenomenon of the inefficient working of the brain, and even as something whose reality is disproven by the skillful subtleties of logical positivism* (Malcolm, 1959). The attitude of the scientific community toward the "respectability" of studying dreams has similarly varied. As a result of the discovery of distinct physiological cycling through the night, associated with dream recall, by Aserinsky and Kleitman some 15 years ago (Aserinsky & Kleitman, 1953, 1955), dreams are currently respectable. There are dozens of laboratories throughout the country engaged in the electrophysiological study of sleep and, to various degrees, the dreams that occur in sleep. The output of publications from these laboratories is currently reaching several hundreds per year.

In spite of this immense amount of scientific activity, most of the emphasis is on the *biology* of sleep rather than its psychology.

*The force of this argument affected me so strongly on first reading that I dreamed about it all night.

There is little doubt that our knowledge of the nature of dreaming has been and will continue to be vastly enriched by the use of the electrophysiological techniques for detecting dream activity. The first article in this section, "Theories of Dream Formation and Recent Studies of Sleep Consciousness," by David Foulkes, is an excellent illustration of how the psychological aspects of dreaming are linked with the biology of dreaming, as well as a good review of the current status of findings about sleep from the electrophysiological point of view.

The next article, one of my own, "Toward the Experimental Control of Dreaming: A Review of the Literature," indicates another way in which our methodology for studying dreaming may be expanded by moving toward an *active* approach to dreams. I have brought together a great deal of scattered evidence that indicates we may actively influence both the content and process of dreaming, rather than simply take dreams as they come along and, *post hoc*, try to correlate aspects of the dreams with other variables. Current research in my laboratory is designed to investigate the feasibility of some of these "active" approaches.

Nevertheless I feel that research on the nature of the dream *experience*, the qualities of that ASC which we call dreaming, is still too scarce, and rather than include more articles using the electrophysiological approach (the reader can easily find enough of that material to overwhelm himself), I have included some very provocative articles which deal more directly with the experiential nature of dreaming and some of its intriguing variations and potentials.

I believe that Chapter 8, the first article of this type is one of the most profound introspective studies ever made of dreaming, and because of its age (it was written in 1913) it is virtually unknown to modern dream researchers. This is a study of his own dreams by a Dutch physician, Frederik van Eeden. Through careful study of his recorded dreams, van Eeden was able to classify them into nine experientially distinct types (nine ASCs?). One of the distinctions he made sounds very much like that currently being made between the content of reports of mental activity reported from stage 1 EEG awakenings and nonstage 1 EEG awakenings. Of even more interest, however, is van Eeden's accounts of a particularly interesting type of dream he had—the lucid dream. This was an ASC in which he knew *while dreaming* that he was actually dreaming, despite the immediate experiential reality of the dream environment, *and* felt that he possessed all of his normal intellectual faculties, in contrast to the usual (retrospective) feeling that our consciousness is quite "dull" and otherwise modified in ordinary dreams. When I discovered this article several years ago I was very skeptical about it; as most people do, I naively accept all sorts of miraculous happenings in my everyday life (miraculous in the sense of exceptionally complex happenings about which we understand virtually nothing) but am overly skeptical about an unusual happening that is *unfamiliar*. Since then I have personally experienced the lucid dream for some brief moments and talked to others who have also experienced it. I am collecting detailed accounts now from several people who have had lucid dream experiences similar to van Eeden's. Further, there are other descriptions of lucid dreams scattered through the occult literature (Arnold-Foster, 1921; Fox, 1962).

The lucid dreams reported by van Eeden, and the various techniques I had reviewed suggesting that active control of dreaming for various positive ends was possible, made me decide to try to produce these phenomena in my laboratory some day. You can imagine my amazement when I read that a whole tribe of primitive people, the Senoi of Malaya, had been practicing dream control techniques for centuries. Chapter 9, by Kilton Stewart, "Dream Theory in Malaya," describes the dream practices of the Senoi. The Senoi apparently have dreams that are rather lucid as a matter of course, which, they believe, accounts for their splendid mental health. I have not been able to locate any other literature on the Senoi other than Stewart's, but even if much of what he has reported is too optimistic, the implications for understanding ASCs and various psychotherapeutic practices are extremely important, I hope that this article will provoke a great deal of research effort. The reader should also see Stewart's two other articles on this topic (Stewart, 1954, 1962).

Finally I have included a small article of my own, "The 'High' Dream: A New State of Consciousness," about the way in which some dreams undergo a distinct experiential shift toward a qualitatively different type of ASC, which I have tentatively called the "high dream" because of its experiential similarity to ASCs resulting from psychedelic drugs.

Chapters 8, 9, and 10 should clearly illustrate that there are a number of intriguing and potentially useful shifts in the nature of dream consciousness about which we know almost nothing. The articles on the hypnagogic state (Chapters 4 and 5) are also relevant to the study of dream consciousness.

For further reading I recommend the following books. All are relatively recent and, together with the many references in this section, should provide a comprehensive entry into the literature on sleep and dreams. They are Boss (1957), Foulkes (1966), Fromm (1957), Hall (1959), Hall & Van de Castle (1966), Kleitman (1963), Murray (1965), Oswald (1962), Witkin & Lewis (1967). Several other new books on the recent electrophysiological approach to the study of dreams are now in press.

6

THEORIES OF DREAM FORMATION AND RECENT STUDIES OF SLEEP CONSCIOUSNESS

DAVID FOULKES

Dement and Kleitman (1957b) reported data confirming earlier and more tentative findings by Aserinsky and Kleitman (1955) on the association of dreaming with the rapid eye movement (REM) periods of sleep. Studies of the undisturbed sleep of normal human subjects (Dement & Kleitman, 1957a) had revealed the cyclic recurrence during sleep of periods of low voltage, random EEG (Stage 1) accompanied by intermittent, conjugate REMs. Dement and Kleitman (1957b) made awakenings during periods of non-REM (NREM) sleep. Their criterion of dream recall was that

> Ss were considered to have been dreaming only if they could relate a coherent, fairly detailed description of dream content. Assertion that they had dreamed without recall of content, or vague, fragmentary impressions of content, were considered negative [p. 341].

Their results were that dream recall, thus defined, was obtained on 80% of REM-period awakenings but on only 7% of NREM-period awakenings. It was further noted that awakenings made within more than a few minutes of

---

Reprinted by permission from *Psychol. Bull.*, Vol 62, 1964, pp. 236–247.

the termination of undisturbed REM periods produced almost no dream recall, a finding taken to indicate that the content of a REM-period dream is swiftly forgotten unless an awakening occurs during the REM period.

The findings of this study have led to the widespread adoption of a new technique of dream retrieval—the interruption of REM periods by experimental awakenings. This technique seems to promise the dream researcher a more representative and complete sampling of the dreaming process than has been accessible previously and to provide an opportunity for the observation of dreams "in progress," that is, they may be interrupted at various points of their development and almost immediate recall obtained. Such a technique, therefore, also seems to present unique opportunities to test many of the formulations of psychoanalytic dream theory.

One might theorize about many aspects of dreaming. Psychoanalytic dream theorists have been much concerned with the meaning of dream content. They attempt to provide guidelines for the explanation and interpretation of "manifest" dream content, feeling that such content conceals, but may be made to reveal, information about the dreamer and his conception of his world. Dream theories are also concerned with the functional significance of the dreaming process, with statements as to why we dream at all, what psychological functions are served by dreaming, and at least inferentially, what might happen to us were we unable to dream. Comprehensive dream theories have also been concerned with describing dream formation and development, that is, they purport to describe the processes of construction through which the dream becomes an organized psychological event.

In this paper, we shall consider the implications of recent electrophysiological dream studies for the portions of two major dream theories, those of Freud (1956) and Adler (1958), which deal with dream formation and dream development. It is proposed, first, to present an outline of Freudian and Adlerian theories of dream formation and dream development, and then to examine these theories in the light of recent experimental data. In the presentation of Freudian theory, concentration will be focused upon those formulations which lend themselves to some kind of reasonably direct empirical verification.

TWO THEORIES OF DREAM FORMATION

The central proposition of Freud's (1956) theory of dream construction or dream formation are:

1. Dream formation and early phases of the organization of the dream

will not be represented in the conscious experience of the dreamer. The typical condition of sleep is a state of unconsciousness, a state in which no mental activity is available to personal awareness or to report to others. In discussing the "psychical conditions during the period of sleep which precedes dreams," that is, the period in which the dream is being "formed," Freud (1956) says "that we are dealing with an *unconscious* process of thought . . . [p. 281]." Much of the groundwork which has gone into the construction of the dream as an intelligible perceptual event takes place before the dream, in Freud's term, "attracts" consciousness to itself. Freud suggests that the dream "is like a firework, which takes hours to prepare but goes off in a moment." This preparation is achieved outside the boundaries of consciousness. It is only when the intensity of these unconscious processes becomes sufficient to arouse mechanisms of consciousness, or when, "just before waking, attention becomes more mobile and comes to meet it," that we experience the dream as a conscious event (p. 576).

2. The unconscious process which instigates dream formation is affective in character, and in particular, it is some derivative of the primary motives of sex or destructive hostility. In sleep, unexpressed and unexpressible sexual drives or hostility are freed from external monitoring, and also from the kinds of internal monitoring which require a high degree of cerebral vigilance. These impulses, long active, now press for some kind of expression. The dream provides the occasion for such expression.

In its final form, the dream is a distorted and symbolic rather than a manifest, direct expression of the impulses which instigate it. This reflects the fact that the forms of waking cortical inhibition exercised over primitive emotional processes are not entirely lacking during sleep. The dream is a fruit of compromise: on the one hand, it does provide an outlet for the expression of primitive emotional impulses; on the other hand, this expression is not (generally) so blatant that the dreamer's critical and inhibitory faculties will be extremely offended by its content. The manifest content of the dream, then, is not a direct reflection of the latent instigating "dream thoughts"; it is because of this disjunction that the manifest dream requires "interpretation."

3. If repressed affect provides the energy for dream construction, perceptual-memorial events provide the raw material. The impulses find their way to expression along sensory, rather than motor, pathways. The dreamer does not, with a patterned sequence of motor activities, inflict harm upon another person nor even go through all the appropriate motions (but, see Wolpert, 1960); he may, however, visually hallucinate that he is harming someone. The kind of thinking in which sensory hallucination of a goal serves as a substitute for its actual achievement Freud calls *primary process*

thinking. Dreams represent the most acute manifestation in the adult human of this developmentally primitive, perceptual-hallucinatory mode of thought.

The raw materials used in dream construction must, therefore, be traces of prior perceptual experiences of the dreamer. In particular, Freud (1956) feels, very recent experiences, experiences from the day immediately preceding the dream serve as basic elements in dream construction. These elements Freud calls *day residues*. The day residues will often consist of memories of what appear to be rather inconsequential happenings. But it is not what these memories are that is important; it is the fact that they can represent, or serve as screens for, the repressed impulses. The more inconsequential the day residues are, the better they may fulfill their function of disguising socially unacceptable impulses.

But Freud (1956) notes that dreams include much "infantile" perceptual material as well as the "recent and indifferent" material represented in day residues. Dreams, in fact,

> . . . can select their material from any part of the dreamer's life, provided only that there is a train of thought linking the experience of the dream-day (the "recent" impressions) with the earlier ones [p. 169].

It is through their association, then, with day-residue material that older sensory memories are contacted, and, in turn, it is the ability to contact such memories that plays a roll in the determination of which day residues shall figure most prominently in the formation of the dream.

4. The day residues, and their associated infantile memories, are the basic elements of the dream, but it would be misleading to conceive the dream as an orderly and logical sequence of such memories. Freud speaks, in particular, of day residues as being "worked over" so that the ultimate dream product is a complicated and bizarre patterning of the original elements. In fact, the elements may be so transformed in the dream that it will be difficult to establish precisely what they are. These transformations, which highly complicate the task of dream interpretation, appear for several reasons: so that the repressed impulses may be adequately expressed, that is, for purposes of dramatic representation; so that the repressed impulses may be successfully disguised, that is, for purposes of evading censorship; and so that the presentation will be as economical as possible, that is, for purposes of the conservation of psychic energy. These are the functions served by a series of processes to which Freud applies the term *dream work*. These processes include: condensation, displacement, and symbolization. The operations of these processes make the dream progressively less intelligible to waking consciousness and progressively detached from its moorings in unretouched sensory memory.

Let us now examine, briefly, one other theory of dream formation, that of Alfred Adler (1958). While Adler's theory of dreaming is by no means as comprehensive or detailed as is Freud's, it has gained much significance because it has formed a large part of the conceptual foundation of several recent and highly influential dream theories, those of Erich Fromm (1957) and Calvin Hall (1959). It is possible, moreover, to find some assertions about the processes of dream formation and dream development in Adler's (1958) own writings and in a recent restatement of the Adlerian position by Ullman (1962), assertions at considerable variance from those made by Freud.

1. Sleeping and waking thoughts are not totally incompatible with one another; we must recognize the essential continuity of all forms of thought. In particular, Adler objects to Freud's conception of dream thought as determined by a mechanism relatively inoperative in waking thought—the unconscious—and to the distinction of primary process and reality-centered thinking, with the former characterizing sleep and the latter wakefulness. There is, to be sure, some difference between dream thought and waking thought, but it is a relative, rather than an absolute, one. The dreamer maintains fewer relations with reality. Yet there is no complete break with reality; he is still in contact with it.

2. The instigation of dreams is not always, or even often, due to sexual or hostile motives, any more than waking thought is generally dominated by such motives. Again, Adler insists that the dream cannot be a contradiction of waking life; it is always consonant with one's waking style of life.

In common with Freud, Adler feels that we dream when we are troubled by something. We dream only when unresolved problems from waking life, which Ullman (1962, p. 20) characterizes as the "sore spots" of one's existence, press upon us during sleep. It is the task of the dream to meet and to try to solve such problems. The troublesome "something" which instigates the dream is, then, a problem from conscious experience, not a problem which has been repressed and of whose existence the waking organism is totally unaware. Freud (1956), on the other hand, relegates such problems to a "secondary position" (p. 554) with respect to dream formation.

3. The raw material of the manifest dream content comes from memories of prior perceptual experience, particularly from day residues. But, in Adlerian theory, the day residues are important in themselves, as representations of waking concerns; they are not important simply as "screens" for something else. Adler does not share Freud's (1956) feeling that day residues are "some cheap material" [p. 237] of little significance in determining the direction of the dream.

4. In the dream, these residues are transformed or worded over until the ultimate product becomes a deceitful working through of a waking problem. Adler (1958) speaks of the dream as being constructed "to fool us" (p. 107). As Ullman (1962, pp. 23–24) has pointed out, there is some contradiction here of Adler's basic theme of the continuity of waking and sleeping thought. The mechanisms of distortion which Adler seems to recognize include condensation, displacement of emphasis, and symbolization. There seems to be a greater stress in Adler than in Freud, however, upon the expressive nature of symbolic representation. In dreaming, we make use of those images and incidents which best agree with our style of life and which best express the present problem. This relatively strong emphasis on the symbol that expresses rather than the symbol which disguises is consistent with the notion of a continuity between waking and sleeping thought and becomes the keystone of Fromm's (1957) and Hall's (1959) theories of dreaming.

ELECTROPHYSIOLOGICAL STUDIES AND DREAM-FORMATION THEORY

It is apparent from the Dement and Kleitman data that both Freud and Adler misjudged the conditions under which dreaming occurs. Both seem to feel that we dream as it is needed, that is, in proportion to the number and intensity of our personal problems. But the facts seem to be that most adult human beings spend approximately 20% (e.g., Dement & Kleitman's figure, 1957a, is 18%) of their sleep in REM periods, periods which produce the kinds of mental content with which both theories are concerned. These periods recur in all individuals studied in a highly predictable cyclic fashion. Individual variations from the 20% figure have been minimal and there is little evidence that they are related to the nature of extent of personal problems. We seem to dream as physiological cycling indicates, not as relative degree of latent psychological trauma dictates. It is still possible, of course, that emotional complexes take advantage of the dreaming process, but apparently they do not, at will, precipitate that process.

The Dement and Kleitman (1957b) recall data were collected well after dream onset in the case of REM-period awakenings and other than immediately before REM onset in the case of NREM awakenings. For these reasons they provide an insufficient base for further evaluation of theories concerning events occurring at dream onset. Several more recent studies, however, have arrived at basically similar data which seem highly relevant to the characterization of the processes of dream formation and dream development.

Studies of Pre-REM Mentation

Foulkes (1962) conceived his study as an objective study of dream formation. Eight subjects were run for 7 nights each. Awakenings were made at various points in the sleep cycle clustered around the onset of REM periods, those portions of the sleep cycle in which, according to Dement and Kleitman (1957b), dreams would be occurring. It was reasoned that such awakenings might provide an empirical basis for theorization about dream onset and the characteristic sequence of dream development. Foulkes found, however, that subjects produce reports of mental phenomena from NREM sleep almost as often as they did from REM sleep. Apparently no point of absolute dream onset exists, in the sense that there is no point in the sleep cycle at which consciousness suddenly appears. It seems to be there all along.

There was, however, some indication of progressive changes in the quality of sleep consciousness around the point of REM onset. More generally, content from pre-REM and REM stages of sleep differed systematically along a number of dimensions. As assessed by direct questioning of the subject during the night and by responses to rating forms taken on the following morning, reports from the pre-REM periods were less likely than REM reports to be labeled as "dream," more likely to be called "thoughts"; less likely than REM reports to be vivid or highly elaborated; and more likely than REM reports to be intimately associated with recent and everydayish activities of the subject, sometimes to the point of consisting purely of memories of such events.

The nature of these differences may be appreciated more fully perhaps with several examples of REM and NREM reports. The following reports were obtained from an adult male subject who was employed by the Internal Revenue Service:

1. He asked an acquaintance at work for a hammer, so that he could fix something in his apartment. (NREM)
2. He was thinking of a point made in his tax class, that you have to provide over half of a person's support to claim him as a dependent. (NREM)
3. He received a phone call in the middle of the night from a girl identifying herself as from the University of Chicago. She said that it was time for his "35-day evaluation." He chided her for calling so late at night. She replied that was the only time they could get him in. (REM, 3 minutes after onset of eye movements)

The first two reports, which are typical of this subject's NREM reports, have an everydayish quality which the third one lacks. In commenting on the 35-day evaluation by the University of Chicago, with which his only connection was his service in the dream study, the subject noted that he was in a 90-day probationary period in his new job. He was to receive $35.00 for his services as a dream subject. It seems, then, that experimental and work experiences have been fused in the REM-period dream so that neither experience is portrayed with complete accuracy. In the second report, however, the subject is reexperiencing, in a completely undistorted manner, the recent experience of considering one of the details of his new job. The purely conceptual quality of this report was a fairly typical NREM characteristic for three of the eight subjects in this study.

The other subjects generally had somewhat more "dreamlike" NREM reports. The following examples come from such a subject, an undergraduate major in English literature.

1. He pictures Anna Karenina. She is sitting at a table, then gets up, turns to the left, and walks away (NREM)

2. He is in a sleep laboratory, filling out a pencil and paper form. Someone passes by, commenting that the task is a stupid one. (NREM)

3. In the first scene, he is standing on a street corner, holding his bicycle, and talking to someone about a girl who wanted to be a striptease dancer.

In the second scene, he is in a doctor's study with two women and the doctor. They are discussing two books. The heroine in the first book was a striptease dancer, but is no longer this, but a nurse. The women are discussing how much hardship she has as a nurse. A discussion then ensues of a second book, by John Steinbeck, in which the main character, also a nurse, did not, apparently, endure similar hardship. The women discuss this avidly, as if they were going to go into "this sort of thing." (REM, 3 minutes after onset of eye movements)

The first two reports of this series seem to be tied much more clearly, and with much less distortion, to recent manifest behaviors or concerns of the subject. In the first, he brings to life a character of a novel which he is reading; in the second, he takes notice of the questionnaire which he must fill out each evening at the laboratory, and makes, through a vaguely identified figure, a comment as to how he views this labor. Although these NREM reports are more detailed and dreamlike than those of the previous subject, there is still a striking difference with REM content in terms of distortion and elaboration.

Confirmation of the reliability of the differences found in the Foulkes (1962) study between REM and NREM material has been obtained by Rechtschaffen, Verdone, and Wheaton (1963). These authors studied the REM and NREM mentation of 17 normal subjects for a total of 30 nights and report that:

In every instance where the variable being measured was comparable, i.e., recall, thinking-dreaming, vividness, visual-conceptual, volitional control, plausibility, time referent, and emotionality, Foulkes' results were in the same direction as ours. The two studies were done entirely independently, and neither investigator knew the variables the other was studying [p. 410–411].

In the course of a study of the effects of presleep stimuli on dream content (24 subjects, 2 nights each), Foulkes and Rechtschaffen (1964) have reported still further confirmation of the reliability of the differences noted above between REM and NREM content.

But can the NREM reports of these three studies be accepted as valid indicators of mental processes occurring during NREM sleep? Can we be sure that these reports are not awakening artifacts, representing material experienced after the onset of the awakening stimulus? Can we be sure that these reports are not recollections of material experienced in previous REM periods? The available evidence, discussed elsewhere (Foulkes, 1962; Rechtschaffen, Verdone, & Wheaton, 1963) would seem to indicate that most NREM content is just what it appears to be: it represents experiences which occur during NREM sleep. The failure of Dement and Kleitman (1957b) to uncover this kind of material, which failure is responsible for raising the question of validity with respect to later findings on NREM recall, appears to be attributable to their very stringent criterion of recall, quoted above, and to several features of their awakening procedure which probably served to depress recall outside REM periods (Foulkes, 1962).

Pre-REM Mentation and Dream Formation Theory

What, then, do these apparently consistent and valid findings on mentation occurring outside REM periods suggest about the validity of the two theories of dream formation which we are examining?

1. Freud's characterization of the sleep in which full-fledged dreams are not occurring as periods of unconsciousness seems to be inaccurate. The typically bizarre and elaborate REM-period dream does not burst like sudden firework against a background of complete darkness; it develops in a context of already ongoing mental activity.

Parenthetically, we may inquire whether someone of Freud's stature could have been totally unaware of the existence of the everydayish thinking which seems to take place during much of the sleep cycle. As we might suspect, the answer is no. In Freud's (1959) paper "Dreams and Telepathy," he notes that there are mental events during sleep without condensation, distortion, dramatization, and wish fulfillment. These unaltered repetitions of actual daily experiences he calls *night phantasies* (p. 421). That the admission of night phantasies has not played any major role in Freud's theory of the dream process may be seen, however, in their treatment in *The Interpretation of Dreams* (Freud, 1956). There (p. 331) Freud indicates that he once considered the possibility of such a class of sleep mentation, but later dropped that category. The net impact of his total theoretical position, therefore, has been that we experience alternating periods of unconsciousness and consciousness during sleep, consciousness appearing when the dream is sufficiently well developed to "attract" it. This now seems to be a misleading characterization of sleep consciousness.

2. There is a strong resemblance between the NREM content which precedes dream periods and the Freudian concept of day residues from which dreams are presumed to develop. Insofar as the day-residue material reveals some of the "background thoughts" [Freud, 1956, p. 103] of the dream, collection of NREM material could facilitate dream interpretation in a more direct manner, perhaps, than even the waking free associations upon which psychoanalytic interpretations have heretofore depended so heavily. The whole body of NREM material occurring between REM-period dreams might be considered the conscious

exploring of one path and another, a swinging of the excitation now this way and now that, until at last it accumulates in the direction that is most opportune and one particular grouping becomes the permanent one [Freud, 1956, p. 576].

3. The rather dramatic shifts from plausible content to implausible content, from the everydayish to the bizarre, which attend REM onset suggest the engagement at this point of the sleep cycle of processes much like those which Freud calls the dream work. For example, 23% of 26 content-producing reports elicited by Foulkes (1962) from ascending EEG Stage 2 (Dement & Kleitman, 1957a), that portion of the sleep cycle immediately preceding REM periods, were undisguised memories or re-creations of recent events in the dreamer's life, while not a single one of 31 reports taken from awakenings made within 4–60 seconds of REM onset were of a comparable nature.

Moreover, Verdone (1963) has shown that longer REM periods produce reports judged by subjects as more vivid and emotional, and Foulkes' (1960) data reveal that reports from longer REM periods (9–24 minutes of REMs) produced greater mean values in subject ratings for activity, emotionality, anxiety, unpleasantness, frighteningness, dramatic quality, violence-hostility, and distortion than did reports elicited from within 4–60 seconds of REM onset. Whatever the processes are which become active at REM onset, they become increasingly predominant as the REM period progresses. And the highly organized (if often bizarre) drama they generally create supports Freud's attribution of dream distortion to active processes, to motivated condensation, displacement, and symbolization, rather than a conception that dream distortion is a sympton of general mental disorganization due to a sleepy, hence imperfectly functioning, cerebral cortex.

4. Strictly speaking, the fact that day-residue content is often experienced during pre-REM period EEG Stage 2 and that dreamlike experiences occur

in that stage of the sleep cycle which immediately follows, namely, EEG Stage 1 REM periods, does not establish that the first kind of material is dynamically transformed to produce the second kind of material. Is there any evidence that the day-residue content of Stage 2 forms the dynamic basis of the dream, that such material is "worked over" as the REM period commences? The following example seems to suggest that this may be the case:

> I was in the library and I was filing cards, and I came to some letter between "a" and "c." I was filing some, I think it was Burma, some country, and just as I put that in, there was this scene of some woman, who was sent to look for a little girl who was lost, and she was sent to Burma. They thought the little girl was going there, for some reason. This was sort of like a dramatization of what I was doing. I mean I was filing, and then this scene took place, right at the same time. In the setting it was sort of like you'd imagine it, but I had the feeling it was really happening.

In this dream, obtained 26 seconds after REM onset, a scene from the subject's daily work experience—she had a filing job in the university library—led to an elaboration which was far removed from her everyday experience. The daily-work element (filing), typical in Stage 2 content, preceded the unusual and somewhat unrealistic element (Burma), typical in REM-period content. The physiological recording shows a recent progression from Stage 2 to a REM period. This one case is not, of course, in itself conclusive, but it does suggest that REM-period dreams may begin with the working over of day residues of a sort most often experienced during NREM Stage 2.

Rechtschaffen, Vogel, and Shaikun (1963) have recently demonstrated, moreover, that discrete manifest elements and themes found in NREM reports are sometimes repeated in subsequent REM reports from the same night. Such finding led them to conclude that:

> On those nights when themes and images persist through both NREM and REM periods, the dreams do not arise *sui generis* as psychologically isolated mental productions, but emerge as the most vivid and memorable part of a large fabric of interwoven mental activity during sleep (p. 546).

5. Adler's assertion of a basic similarity of waking and sleeping thought finds support, at least when we consider NREM-period sleeping thought. Rechtschaffen, Verdone, and Wheaton (1963) have likened the content of NREM mentation to background mentation in waking experience. It is, in Stekel's (1951) image, a muted accompaniment rather than a melody. In NREM sleep the melody, or directive character of thought, seems less prominent and we become aware of this back-ground thought. Such an awareness is difficult to achieve in waking life; it is as if we might have direct

and immediate access to all those irrelevant things which passed along the borders of consciousness while we were more or less attentively engaged in some line of directed thought. Conditions of sensory deprivation or sensory monotony (Fiske, 1961) perhaps give us the best possible vantage point in waking life for viewing such phenomena. While the identification of NREM mentation with fringetype waking mentation may not be an apt characterization of all NREM mentation, it does underline the degree of continuity of NREM mentation and at least some forms of waking experience.

In the context of Freudian theory, what we do not find in pre-REM sleep mentation is worthy of note. We do not find a seething, libidinous turmoil, sharply at variance with waking thought. Rather we see a generally "relaxed" kind of thinking and imaging whose prominence becomes possible in the absence of a strong external focus or challenge for thought processes and whose nature is essentially similar to certain classes of incidental waking mentation.

6. But, if we find little evidence of libido or hostility in the pre-REM thought from which dreams may be presumed to develop, neither do we find much evidence for the Adlerian assertion that representations of pressing personal problems of a more general character are active at, and responsible for, dream formation. Awakenings made at various points leading into REM-period onset and during the early seconds and minutes of REM periods do not corroborate, at least in any obvious manner, the position that dreams begin with affective or ideational "sore spots." Transformations are noted in the quality of mental experience: from conceptualizing or vaguely perceiving to vivid visual imaging, from kaleidoscopic flux to continuity and integration, and from plausible content to distorted and bizarre content. However, these changes do not seem to be associated with any perception of particularly pressing personal problems which cry for some resolution or exploration. Rather than being sources of personal anxiety or insecurity, NREM contents of consciousness generally seem quite unconnected with basic psychodynamic concerns of the dreamer.

Because this last point is a particularly crucial one for both theories, we will do well to consider it in further detail. Will the dream theorist be impressed with evidence that the class of events-in-consciousness at or around REM-period dream onset fails to meet his specifications of dream-instigating events? Most likely not. He might comment that the analysis has, up to this point, relied too heavily upon appearances, upon manifest consciousness. It might be suggested that the everydayish, relaxed kinds of mentation which precede REM-period dreaming serve as screens for affective elements, based in infantile experience, which present a threat, or pose a challenge, to the dreamer. Such a contention raises a basic methodological question, however: since neither physiological nor experiential evidence seems to support the hypothesis that dream periods develop from or commence with such elements, with what kind of evidence does the dream theorist propose to confirm his theory of the affective instigation of dreams? At present, the assumption that pre-REM period contents are screens for something else seems entirely gratuitous. What we seem to have in NREM-period mentation is one level of cognitive functioning, a level which should at least tentatively be accepted for what it is, rather than be immediately interpreted as a disguised form of something else.

At this point we should, perhaps, consider the observation base upon which both Freudian and Adlerian theory rest, clinical dream collection. Ian Oswald's (1962) comments upon the adequacy of clinical dream collection as a basis for characterization of the dream process cut right to the heart of the matter. He notes that the patient probably describes only a very small fraction of his total dreams to his therapist, and that his "recall" of these dreams is more a construction than a reconstruction. This constructed, waking fantasy-material may tell the clinician a great deal about the patient, but "is not to be relied upon as evidence of what really happens during dream periods" [p. 143].

Yet both Freud and Adler, in the absence of systematic observations made at various phases of the (REM) dream process, have given us theories of that process. Quite clearly, what they have done is to read back into the dreaming process those events which it seems must have transpired in its early stages, given a certain dream outcome and/or a certain functional interpretation of that outcome. Now no one who has had experience in collecting, examining, or interpreting dreams can doubt that dreams often do express a person's basic feelings and indicate his problems. And yet, the pre-REM and early-REM recall data now available suggest that we err in assuming that since this may be the functional significance of the dream, the dream therefore must have started with the expression of such feelings or the posing of such problems. Rather it seems as if the dream allows the dreamer, eventually rather than immediately, to express himself in a rather profound way; it is not that the dream, by posing a basic challenge at its very onset, forces him to do this.

It is being suggested, then, that both Freudian and Adlerian theory are incorrect in their characterization of the dream process, that is, dream formation and dream development. But what, we may now ask, are the implications of this position for those portions of their dream theories which deal with dream meaning or the functional significance of dreaming? We have already noted that Freud's and Adler's theories of the dream process are generalizations from, rather than the inductive basis of, their theories of dream interpretation. This suggests that dream process data can confirm or disconfirm a particular theory of dream meaning only to the extent that

that theory is compatible with one, and only one, characterization of the dream process. Dream theorists have tended to assume such a necessary correspondence between interpretation theory and process theory; that is, they have generalized in a relatively direct fashion from what the dream is to how it must have started. But this overlooks the possibility that how a dream begins and what a dream becomes may be two entirely different matters. Both Freudian and Adlerian theories of dream meaning and function, therefore, may be compatible with the description of the dream process provided by recent electrophysiological research. To reject Freud's dream-process theory is not necessarily to reject his position that dreams serve the function of the fulfillment of repressed wishes. To reject Adler's dream-process theory is not necessarily to reject his position that dreams are attempts at problem solving which are consistent with the dreamer's life style.

Although the present data on the dream process are ambiguous with respect to theories of dream meaning, it is likely that further studies of the content of REM- and NREM-period dreams will provide some basis for choice among these theories. Dement's research on dream deprivation (1960) has already indicated the usefulness of electrophysiological studies in evaluating theories of the function significance of the dream.

In conclusion, it is hoped that this discussion has indicated some of the possibilities which the Aserinsky, Kleitman, and Dement dream-collection technique offers with respect to resolving or clarifying some of the major issues in classical, mainly psychoanalytic, dream theory. But the major contribution of this technique may well be the generation of altogether new theories of dreaming, theories solidly based upon experimentally derived dream-process data, and theories which articulate with modern neurophysiological evidence (e.g., Jouvet, 1962) upon the nature of the sleep phase in which dreaming occurs.

SUMMARY

Some of the implications of recent electrophysiological studies of sleep for dream theory, especially the theory of dream formation, are considered. Studies showing a variety of mentation in all stages of sleep fail to confirm Freud's belief that mental activity suddenly attracts consciousness at dream onset. The nature of pre-dream mentation, however, supports Freud's concept of day residues, and there is also evidence to support his position that dream-work processes distort these day residues into sometimes barely recognizable components of bizarre dream episodes. Adler's insistence on the continuity of waking and sleeping thought finds support in the nature and extent of nondreaming mentation in sleep. Both Freud and Adler are challenged on the alleged traumatic affective instigation of dreams; emotional complexes may take advantage of the dreaming state, but they seem neither to precipitate that state nor to determine its initial perceptual-ideational content.

7

TOWARD THE EXPERIMENTAL CONTROL OF DREAMING: A REVIEW OF THE LITERATURE

CHARLES T. TART

Scientific research is carried out with two basic kinds of procedures. One is the observational or correlational approach, where we observe "what happens naturally" and try to make sense of it by finding relations or correlations between various aspects of our observations. This approach leads to statements of the order, " . . . subjects classified as Sensitizers report recalling dreaming significantly more frequently than those classified as Repressors on the MMPI" (Tart, 1962). The other approach is the functional method, where we actively manipulate one factor or variable and observe the effect on some dependent variable. This approach leads to statements of the order, "A large dose of alcohol reduces the amount of EEG stage 1-REM time and inferred dreaming in normal Ss . . . " (Gresham, Webb, & Williams, 1963). Both approaches are used in most fields of science, as they are complementary.

Research into the nature of dreaming, on the other hand, has been, by and large, a matter of correlational research [ignoring for the moment the last decade's research using the electroencephalogram (EEG) and rapid eye movement (REM) techniques]. Researchers asked Ss how often they dreamed in color, whether their dreams are mainly pleasant or unpleasant,

Reprinted by permission from *Psychol. Bull.*, Vol. 64, 1965, pp. 81–91.

and the like, and then attempted to correlate these observed character-istics with personality characteristics, intelligence, sex, age, etc. Or the patient brought in a spontaneous dream and the therapist-researcher then attempted to "interpret" it in the light of what he knew about the patient.

We have, of course, learned a great deal about the nature of dreaming as a result of these correlational studies, and undoubtedly we will continue to learn from them. When we can complement correlational studies with functional studies, however, we shall advance our understanding of dream-ing much more rapidly.

The purpose of the present paper is to review and bring together for the first time those studies in which an experimental attempt to influence either the content or the process of nocturnal dreaming was made, in order to assess what possibilities they suggest for functional research on dreaming.

The past decade has seen an enormous increase in our knowledge of sleep and dreaming, resulting from application of EEG measures, and a brief summary of this body of results will be presented in order to provide an up-to-date background for assessing the studies to be reviewed herein. More detailed reviews and evaluations of the more than 75 studies contributing to the past decade's new knowledge of dreaming have been published elsewhere (Kamiya, 1961; Kleitman, 1960, 1963; Oswald, 1962, 1964; Snyder, 1963).

Sleep will be defined in this paper as a state of the organism indicated (in human Ss) by one of the four EEG stages (Dement & Kleitman, 1957a, 1957b). The stage I pattern consists of an irregular mixture of theta waves (4–8 cps), alphoid activity (waves of one to two cps slower than the S's waking alpha), and occasional alpha waves (8–13 cps). Stage 2 contains spindle activity (14 cps) in addition to the above, and stages 3 and 4 contain increasingly larger proportions (up to 100%) of delta waves (1–3 cps, high amplitude) in addition to spindle activity. The exact divisions between stages 2, 3, and 4 are arbitrary, based on the percentage of delta waves in given epochs. The stage 1 pattern is readily distinguishable from the other stages by its total lack of spindles and delta waves.

Stages 1 through 4 were initially conceived of as comprising continuum from "light" to "deep" sleep (Aserinsky & Kleitman, 1953, 1955; Dement, 1955), but as other measures of the "depth" of sleep contradict this con-ception (Berger, 1961; Hawkins, Puryear, Wallace, Deal, & Thomas, 1962; Kamiya, 1961; Snyder, 1963; Williams, Tepas, & Morlock, 1962), this paper will treat sleep as being of two qualitatively distinct types, viz., stage 1 as one type and stages 2, 3, and 4 as the other type. Distinctions between stages 2, 3, and 4 will not be made in this paper, and they will be collectively referred to as non-stage 1 sleep.

If Ss are awakened from the two types of sleep and asked to report what they have been experiencing, the reports may be classified into two rather distinct types. One type, awakenings from stage 1 sleep or shortly (within, roughly, 10–15 minutes) after stage 1 sleep has changed to non-stage 1 sleep, possesses, the characteristics traditionally associated with the experience of dreaming (Foulkes, 1962; Rechtschaffen, Verdone, & Wheaton, 1963). Reports from non-stage 1 sleep seem more like "thinking," and are generally called thinking by the Ss: these same Ss generally refer to their stage 1 experiences as dreams. The psychological differences reported so far are quantitative, rather than being completely dichotomous, but generally give the impression of distinct types of experiences.

Stage 1 sleep is almost always accompanied by binocularly synchronous, rapid eye movements (REMs), and the evidence is very convincing that these are closely associated with the content of the dream, if not actual scanning movements of the dream imagery (Berger & Oswald, 1962a; Dement & Wolpert, 1958a; Roffwarg, Dement, Muzio, & Fisher, 1962). Such REMs have not been reported in non-stage 1 sleep, although there are some slow, rolling movements (Kamiya, 1961).

In view of these findings, the following theoretical position will be taken in this paper as an aid in surveying the literature on functional studies of dreaming: that an experientially distinct type of phenomenon occurs concurrently with the presence of stage 1 sleep, which phenomenon will be called stage 1 dreaming, or just dreaming. The mental phenomena of non-stage 1 sleep will not be considered in this paper. Further, it is assumed that the experience of stage 1 dreaming is essentially continuous* during the presence of stage 1 EEG, whether the S can always recall this experience on waking or not. This position is, in the author's opinion, supported by all the studies using the EEG and REM technique, and directly refuted by none.

The term "process" of stage 1 dreaming is used to indicate the ongoing psychophysiological activity which is observed on a physiological level as the stage 1 EEG pattern and on an experimental level as the experience of dreaming (observed directly by the S and indirectly via the dream report). The terms "dream content," "reported dream," or simply "dream" refer to the particulars of the experience.

For normal Ss, stage 1 dreaming and non-stage 1 sleep alternate in a regular, cyclic fashion, referred to as the sleep-dream cycle. As an S falls asleep there is generally a brief (a few seconds to a minute or two) period of stage 1, without REMs, but Ss' reports indicate that this is apparently a

---

*Within a continuous period of stage 1 EEG, the content of the experienced dream may be divided into several distinct episodes so that, in a sense, there were several distinct "dreams" within a continuous period of dreaming. Dement and Wolpert (1958) present some evidence that such changes of topic may be accompanied by a gross body movement on the part of the S.

period of hypnagogic imagery, rather than typical dreaming (Dement & Kleitman, 1957a; Oswald, 1962). At approximately 90 minute intervals through the night there are periods of stage 1 dreaming, each dream period generally being longer than the preceding one. The first stage 1 period may last for 10 minutes; the fourth or fifth one may last as long as 50 minutes. Altogether, stage 1 dreaming occupies between 20 and 30% of the total sleep time of most young adults, spread over three to six stage 1 periods. While the exact percentage of dream time and the number of cycles varies from S to S, for a given S the sleep-dream cycle is generally quite stable from night to night (Dement, 1960; Dement & Kleitman, 1957b; Kleitman, 1960; Wood, 1962).

With this picture in mind of stage 1 dreaming occurring regularly through every night of sleep, let us now review those studies which have attempted to affect dreaming. Many of these studies were carried out before the discovery of the sleep-dream cycle and so lack precision, but do offer some data.

The studies will be reviewed under three convenient, but not mutually exclusive headings, viz.: (a) variables affecting the content of dreaming; (b) variables affecting the process of dreaming; and (c) discrimination during sleep.

VARIABLES AFFECTING THE CONTENT OF DREAMING

Variables affecting dreaming are of two types, viz., those applied before the onset of sleep, and those applied concurrently with sleep and dreaming. The latter type will be discussed first.

Naturally occurring stimuli, both external and internal (e.g., thunder, breezes, stomach cramps, falling out of bed), are sometimes incorporated into the content of dreams, and the older literature contains many anecdotal accounts of this (Ellis, 1911; Hennings, 1784; Hoffbauer, 1796; Jessen, 1855; Lhermittee, 1931; Meier, 1758; Schatzman, 1925; Spitta, 1882; Sully, 1905; Thompson, 1914; Walsh, 1920). Such accounts tell us little about the effectiveness of stimuli in modifying dream content, however, as they provide no baseline of how many naturally occurring stimuli were not incorporated, nor do they provide any systematic data on the manner in which the incorporated stimuli were represented in the dream.

A number of Es have experimentally presented stimuli to sleeping Ss (Claviere, 1897; De Sanctis & Neyroz, 1902; Hildebrandt, 1875; Maury, 1861; Max, 1935; Menuier, 1910; Stepanow, 1915; Straecke, 1913; Vaschide, 1902; Vold, 1910), and have further demonstrated that stimuli are sometimes incorporated into dreams. Despite great variation in method from study to study, there seems to be a general consensus in these studies that tactual stimuli are more effective in affecting dream content then stimuli in other sensory modalities.

Both the anecdotal and early experimental studies were, in the light of what is now known about the sleep-dream cycle, beset with an inherent lack of precision, as data concerning stage 1 sleep and non-stage 1 sleep were indiscriminately mixed together. A recent study (Dement & Wolpert, 1958), using the EEG and REM technique, has greatly increased our knowledge here. Briefly, a pure tone was incorporated in 9% of the trials, a bright light 23%, and drops of water 42%. As the water is a tactual stimulus, this is in agreement with the older studies. When these stimuli were presented during non-stage 1 sleep, stage 1 dreaming was *not* initiated, contrary to the old idea that dreaming was *caused* by stimulation, and when the Ss were awakened a few minutes later they had no recollection of the stimuli (or of dreaming).

An important and methodologically sophisticated study of stimulus incorporation into stage 1 dreams is that of Berger (1963). Spoken first names were presented at randomly chosen times during stage 1 dreaming. Some of the names were of persons with whom the Ss had important, emotional relationships, while others were neutral in this respect. Incorporation was objectively judged by having both the Ss and an independent judge later try to match reported dream content with stimulus names. The stimulus names were matched with the correct dream reports with considerably better-than-chance accuracy by both the Ss and the independent judge. The emotionally meaningful and the neutral names were incorporated with equal frequency. Incorporation was not associated with detectable EEG changes, or GSR responses. Berger reported the incorporations as falling into several descriptive categories, in order of decreasing frequency, as follows: (a) assonance, where a dream element or word sounded like the stimulus name, a sort of "clang association;" (b) direct incorporation, where the dreamer reported hearing the stimulus name in the dream; (c) associational incorporation, where a relatively direct personal association to the stimulus name appeared in the dream; and (d) representational association, where the stimulus name was represented or symbolized by an object or action in the dream.

There have been some studies of the incorporation of stimuli into hypnotic dreams (Benussi, 1927; Klein, 1930), but as there is strong evidence that hypnotic dreams may be quite different from stage 1 dreams (Barber, 1962; Tart, 1964b, in press), they will not be reviewed here.

Some Es applied various stimuli to their Ss before the latter went to sleep (Cubberly, 1923; Fisher, 1954, 1960; Malamud & Linder, 1931; Monfoe, 1899; Poetzl, 1917; Renshaw, Miller, & Marquis, 1933; Vold, 1912), and found that the stimuli sometimes appeared in the content of dreams reported the following day, often in "distorted" or "disguised" form. Such studies are difficult to evaluate, as there is a contaminating factor of waking suggestion to dream about the stimuli implicit in the design of stimulating Ss and then asking them to record their dreams. More serious difficulties in evaluating these studies arise from the heavy demand characteristics (Orne, 1959, 1962) undoubtedly operative as a result of the psychoanalytic orientation of many of the experimenters. About the most that can be concluded from these studies is that Ss will bring in "dreams" which seem to incorporate the stimulus material in disguised or distorted form, but this fact does not necessarily prove the validity of psychoanalytic theories of dream formation. These studies are also subject to other criticisms, discussed below.

A number of studies apparently demonstrated that posthypnotic suggestion could control the content of nocturnal dreaming to a high degree (Fisher, 1953; Nachmansohn, 1925; Newman, Katz, & Rubenstein, 1960; Schrotter, 1912), but as they did not use EEG monitoring of sleep, they were not controlled for the possibility that the dreams affected were hypnotic dreams interspersed with sleep, rather than ordinary nocturnal dreams. That such an event can happen, without the S being aware of it, has been shown in other studies (Barber, 1962; Schiff, Bunney, & Freedman, 1961; Tart, 1964b). These studies also are ambiguous in that effects on stage 1 dreaming and non-stage 1 mental activity would be indiscriminately mixed, and much of the early stage 1 dreaming of the night was undoubtedly forgotten by the time the Ss awoke in the morning.

Stoyva (1961), using the EEG and REM technique, was the first to demonstrate convincingly that the content of stage 1 dreaming could be influenced and manipulated to a very high degree in some Ss by means of posthypnotic suggestion. The content of non-stage 1 mental activity was also affected, although not as markedly. Tart (1964b) independently confirmed Stoyva's finding. As with Stoyva's Ss, the stage 1 dreams of some Ss were not affected at all, while those of other Ss were almost totally controlled by the posthypnotically suggested content. Stoyva also found that explicit waking suggestion affected dream content, as had been reported earlier by Fisher (1953) and Titchener (1895), but not as strongly as posthypnotic suggestion.

Wood (1962) found that social isolation for a period of one day affected the content of stage 1 dreaming occurring that night. The Ss seemed to be compensating for the isolation by increased "social intercourse" in their dreams.

The laboratory situation itself seems to have some effect on stage 1 dreaming, especially when psychiatric patients are used as Ss (Whitman, Pierce, Maas, & Baldridge, 1962). Feelings about the E and about being experimented on appeared in the reported dream content, often in "disguised" form. It has been reported, however (Dement, Kahn, & Roffwarg, in press), that this effect diminishes rapidly after a few nights in the laboratory, with normal Ss. About 24% of first night dreams were concerned with the experimental situation directly, but this fell to 9% for later nights.

Several studies have been carried out to investigate the effects of various drugs on dream content, e.g., chloropromazine and promazine (Lesse, 1959), meprobamate (Whitman, Pierce, & Maas, 1960); imipramine and prochlorperazine (Whitman, Pierce, Maas, & Baldridge, 1961). While these studies indicate some general changes in content, this area is still in a very exploratory stage, and no definite conclusions can be drawn yet.

At present, then, posthypnotic suggestion seems to be the most powerful and precise method for affecting dream content, although its use is restricted to a minority of Ss. The use of external stimuli presented to the dreaming S offers promise of strongly affecting dream content, but much research remains to be done in this area, using the EEG-REM technique, to discover the optimal types of stimuli and ways of presenting them.

VARIABLES AFFECTING THE PROCESS OF DREAMING

There are two powerful techniques which result in almost total disruption of the sleep-dream cycle. The first is total sleep deprivation, which has received considerable attention in recent years (Berger & Oswald, 1962b; Brauchi & West, 1959; Luby, Frohman, Grisell, Lenzo, & Gottlieb, 1960, 1962; Mirsky, & Cardon, 1962; Rodin, Luby, & Gottlieb, 1962; Simon, 1961; West, Janszen, Lester, Cornelisoon, 1962; Williams, Granda, Jones, Lubin, & Armington, 1962; Williams, Morris, & Lubin, 1962; Williams, Hammack, Daly, Dement, & Lubin, 1964). The second is selective deprivation of certain aspects of sleep, Dement's (1960) "dream deprivation" technique where Ss are awakened whenever a stage 1 pattern appears, and stage 4 deprivation (Agnew, Webb, & Williams, 1964), carried out in basically the same manner.

Dement found that if, on several consecutive nights, an S was awakened whenever stage 1 dreaming began, the S would have to be awakened more and more frequently to prevent stage 1 dreaming as the nights went on. Furthermore, if the S was allowed several undisturbed nights of sleep following this procedure, his stage 1 dream time was significantly increased for several nights. Control awakenings scattered randomly through non-stage 1 sleep produced no such effect. Dement concluded that there was a need for a given amount of stage 1 dreaming each night, although whether this is a need for the experience of dreaming or the physiological state represented by stage 1 EEG is unknown. Agnew et. al. followed the same procedure for stage 4 of sleep, although the stimuli given their Ss whenever stage 4 sleep started often served to have them shift to a different stage of sleep without awakening. They found results similar to Dement's, i.e., more and more need to stimulate the Ss to get them out of stage 4 as the deprivation nights went on, and an increase in stage 4 sleep time on undisturbed nights following this procedure.

As both the sleep deprivation and dream deprivation procedures represent a total disruption of the sleep-dream cycle, rather than a selective effect on dreaming *per se*, they will not be further discussed here.

The laboratory situation itself has an effect on dream process, just as it does on dream content. On an S's first night in the laboratory he is likely to miss his first stage 1 period of the night. This phenomenon has been called the "first night effect" (Dement, 1955; Dement, Kahn, & Roffwarg, in press; Rechtschaffen & Verdone, in press; Snyder, 1963) and it is now customary among dream researchers to have an S's first night count only as an adaptation night, rather than taking any precise measurements on it.

Social isolation also affects the process of stage 1 dreaming. Wood (1962) found that a day of social isolation resulted in a 60% increase of stage 1 dream time for the first two dream cycles of the experimental night, while the number of REMs/minute during this dreaming was decreased.

Gresham, Webb, & Williams (1963) studied the effect of alcohol and caffeine on stage 1 dream time, and found that alcohol produced a significant decrease in stage 1 dream time (a mean decrease of 22 minutes for the first 5 hours of sleep), while caffeine, in the dosage used, had no effect. Rechtschaffen and Maron (in press) found that a mixture of dextro amphetamine sulfate and pentobarbitol sodium may halve stage 1 dream time in many Ss. Dement (cited in Snyder, 1963) found that sodium amytal may also halve dream time. Heptabarbitone (Oswald, Berger, Jaramillo, Keddie, Olley, & Plunkett, 1963) also reduces stage 1 dream time.

Tactual stimuli, in the form of the hardness of the surface on which the S sleeps (a feather bed at one extreme and a board at the other) have been reported to affect sleep (Suckling, Koening, Hoffman, & Brooks, 1957), but the data are not presented in a form which allows careful assessment of the effect on stage 1 dreaming.

Stoyva (1961) found that posthypnotic suggestions intended to influence stage 1 dream *content* also affected the duration of stage 1 dreaming. In those of his Ss whose dream content was generally influenced by the suggestions in every dream of the night, Stoyva found a statistically significant decrease in stage 1 dream time for the early part of the night, what he termed the "shortening effect." For the first two stage 1 periods of the night, this effect was an average 7 minute decrease (21%), with a maximum decrease of 14 minutes.

Offering Ss money if they can dream more or less on different nights also has some effect (Rechtschaffen & Verdone, 1964), although the difference between the two conditions was only an average of 6.6 minutes per night ($\pm 3\%$ compared to baseline nights).

A particularly interesting problem is that of exerting control over waking from sleep. Ladd (1892), speaking of whatever "mechanism" caused sleep, reported that "I 'set' this mechanism so that it will dip down into sleep and dream-life, with a gradual curvature, as it were, and then come out of dream-life in an instant, i.e., by a steep curve." He provides no other information as to the nature of this sleep "mechanism" or how he went about "setting" it, although one might guess that he used some form of autosuggestion. Nor does he report how successful this technique was, although he mentions that it was more successful for arousing himself shortly after going to sleep than for late in sleep.

A very intriguing report on waking from sleep is that of Frobenius (1927), which shows that Ss can wake from sleep at a randomly preselected target time on most attempts. His Ss usually awoke within 10 minutes of the selected time, and felt rather disoriented. They had no idea as to how they had awoken, nor did the content of their dreams seem to reflect a waking process in any way on those occasions when they awoke from dreams. Elder (1941), in a brief abstract, reports that he had confirmed Frobenius' results, but provides no details. This material will soon be submitted for publication, however (Elder, personal communication, 1964). Ehrenwald (1923) also reports some anecdotal data on waking from sleep at a preset time.

Other investigators (Calkins, 1893; Dittborn, 1963; Nelson, 1888) have reported that they woke up frequently during the night and recalled dreaming, apparently as a result of their interest in studying dreams. In all these reports, however, there is no information on how often the Ss normally woke up during the night, although the effect seems to have been of considerable magnitude in at least one case (Nelson, 1888). The author (who was his own S) complained that his sleep was no longer refreshing as a result of waking too frequently, so that he dampened his interest in dreams in order to get more rest. Renneker (1952a, 1952b) reports on a patient who habitually awoke a few moments before the alarm was to go off, supposedly in order to prevent his dreams from becoming anxiety filled, and presents some psycho-analytic speculations about the nature of this behavior. Omwake and Loranz (1933) and Brush (1930) also report data which leave little doubt that some Ss can awaken at a preset time.

The most recent study in which the process of dreaming was affected was that of Tart (1963). Using posthypnotic suggestion and working intensively with two Ss, it was found that the Ss could be made to awaken at either the beginnings or ends of their stage 1 dreams, although the accuracy of this behavior was difficult to judge due to difficulties in defining criteria for "perfect" compliance with the suggestions. As in Frobenius' (1927) study, the Ss had no idea as to how they had awakened, and their dreams did not seem to reflect any processes of discrimination or waking. Tart also found that the stage 1 dream time of one of the Ss could be increased about 20% by means of posthypnotic suggestions to dream all night.

At present, then, posthypnotic suggestion would seem to be the most powerful technique for affecting the process of dreaming which is selective in its effect (although it is applicable only to a minority of Ss). Total sleep deprivation or dream deprivation is more powerful, but nonselective as it disrupts the phenomena we are trying to manipulate. In general the psychological variables (suggestion, hypnosis, laboratory setting, etc.) seem to have only a small effect on the actual amount of time spent in stage 1 dreaming.

DISCRIMINATION DURING SLEEP

Simon and Emmons (1956) played recorded questions and answers to their Ss once every 5 minutes while they slept. The Ss were asked to call out their own name if they heard the question and answer. The Ss showed essentially no responses to the questions and answers and no evidence of having learned them (judged by questioning them in the morning) whenever they showed non-stage 1 sleep patterns. The results of this study are difficult to interpret in terms of stage 1 patterns, however, as they were mixed with arousal patterns.

Granda and Hammack (1961) trained sleep-deprived Ss to press a microswitch on a certain schedule in order to avoid a noxious electrical shock. By avoiding the shock, the Ss could sleep. They found that their Ss could produce the required avoidance behavior in all stages of sleep, without showing signs of EEG arousal. Williams, Morlock, & Morlock (1963) extended this work and found that the Ss could discriminate between several tones, but that they tended not to respond during stage 1 dreaming unless the negative reinforcement was quite strong.

Li, Jasper, & Henderson (1952) report that a narcoleptic patient of theirs could sleep through the noise made by the E hitting a brass pail right beside her bed, but would awaken immediately if her name was softly spoken. Oswald (1962) carried out two studies of Ss' reactions to meaningful versus nonmeaningful stimuli during sleep. In one study, Ss showed more muscular responses to the sound of their own names and that of another designated name than to other, nonmeaningful names, although this response was usually accompanied by partial EEG arousal. In a second study, a series of first names was played repeatedly to Ss while they slept, but some of the names had been tape recorded backwards, making them meaningless sounds. The Ss showed more EEG responses without waking (K-complexes) to the meaningful sounds. A similar finding for tones, one of which had been associated with a noxious stimulus, was reported in cats (Rowland, 1957). Berger (1963), however, did not find any difference in frequency of incorporation into the reported dream content of names of persons with whom the Ss had emotional bonds versus emotionally neutral names.

Thus the literature indicates that the sleeping and dreaming S is not behaviorally inert, but may make, at least, some fairly simple discriminations and responses, sometimes accompanied by momentary awakening, but sometimes within the sleep or dream state itself.

DISCUSSION

There is little doubt that, in light of the past decade's discoveries, the conclusions of many of the earlier studies will be revised as the results of future research come in. And there are certain methodological problems to be solved even with the use of the EEG-REM technique.* In spite of these drawbacks, some conclusions may be drawn from the studies herein reviewed.

Sleep is *not* a state of behavioral inertness (a tradition long given implicit support by the extreme paucity of psychological studies of it). On the contrary, not only is a sleeping person having vivid experiences, dreams, periodically through the night, but: (a) he is capable of incorporating some external stimuli into the content of his dreams; and (b) at least some Ss are capable of sometimes altering their state of consciousness from sleeping (or dreaming) to waking, either by means of a discriminative response to external stimuli or by using the occurrence of dreaming itself or a given time of night as a stimulus. Furthermore, at least some sleeping Ss are able to carry out some relatively simple motor acts in response to external stimuli.

At present then, we know only that some Ss can make responses during sleep, make discriminations, incorporate stimuli, etc. But it should be emphasized that the exact percentages of Ss, the exact behaviors observed, or the methodological difficulties of these studies are not the most important things to be noted in this review. Rather, the fact that *any* Ss can carry out

---

*In Tart's (1963) study where Ss were supposed to wake from either the beginnings or ends of their dreams in accordance with posthypnotic suggestions to that effect, difficulties arose in evaluating the results because of a number of responses in which the Ss seemed to be complying on an experiential level with the suggestions, but could not meet strict criteria for the beginnings and ends of their dreams in terms of the amount of time stage 1 sleep had lasted.

these sorts of behaviors during sleep and dreaming, no matter how imperfectly at present, is the important thing, for it is highly probable that what has been done imperfectly by some Ss, using crude, exploratory methods, can be done far better by other Ss once these techniques are refined and developed. The immediate research need is not to show simply that some Ss can have their sleep and dreaming affected in these manners, but to investigate how well Ss can be trained to do these things, what the maximal level of performance and effect is. Then we shall possess a number of techniques for actively manipulating dreaming, leading to results which can only be speculated about now (Tart, 1964a), but which will almost certainly surprise us.

The most immediate need in this area is for extensive studies of stimulus incorporation, and of the potentialities for discriminative responses to stimuli, including experiential discriminations within the dream, waking from sleep at a preset time, and overt motor responses. How do various sensory modalities differ in the way in which stimuli are incorporated into the dream? Are stimuli in some modalities more distorted than in others? Can the degree of direct incorporation, with distortion, be affected by various experimental techniques? Can Ss learn to incorporate some stimuli effectively enough so that one could use these stimuli as "signals" to indicate to the S that he should carry out a specific action, e.g., dream about a particular topic, or carry out some motor act? What sorts of motor acts can be carried out? There are simple ones, such as raising a finger to indicate that he is dreaming, or that he is experiencing anger within the dream, but what about the possibility of more complex motor acts, say automatic writing, or sleep talking? Ultimately, to what extent could a "two-way communication system" be developed, whereby the E could instruct the S to do such and such while he is dreaming, and the S could report on the events of the dream while they are occurring? If such a development were possible, dreams would lose their status as a purely subjective event that can only be reported in retrospect, and become a much more immediate sort of behavior.

Besides these questions on what sorts of things can be made to happen, there are also many problems centering around the question of the best method or methods to bring these things about. Judging from the present status of the literature, posthypnotic suggestion seems to offer the most promise, but neither this method nor any of the others have really been adequately tested and explored. What potentialities are there in operant conditioning techniques, effects of increasing incentive, various combinations of drugs, etc.? What about combinations of these?

The studies reviewed herein, then, do not sum up our state of knowledge about this area so much as they serve a far more important function, viz., raising questions and pointing out some fascinating possibilities for future research and development.

8

A STUDY OF DREAMS

FREDERIK VAN EEDEN

Since 1896 I have studied my own dreams, writing down the most interesting in my diary. In 1898 I began to keep a separate account for a particular kind of dream which seemed to me the most important, and I have continued it up to this day. Altogether I collected about 500 dreams, of which 352 are of the particular kind just mentioned. This material may form the basis of what I hope may become a scientific structure of some value, if leisure and strength to build it up carefully do not fail me.

In the meantime, with a pardonable anxiety lest the ideas should not find expression in time, I condensed them into a work of art—a novel called *The Bride of Dreams* (van Eeden, 1918). The fictitious form enabled me to deal freely with delicate matters, and had also the advantage that it expressed rather unusual ideas in a less aggressive way—esoterically, so to speak. Yet I want to express these ideas also in a form that will appeal more directly to the scientific mind, and I know I cannot find a better audience for this purpose than the members of the Society for Psychical Research, who are accustomed to treat investigations and ideas of an unusual sort in a broad-minded and yet critical spirit.

This paper is only a preliminary sketch, a short announcement of a greater work, which I hope to be able to complete in later years.*

Reprinted from *Proc. Soc. Psych. Res.*, Vol. 26, 1913, pp. 431–461.

*Apparently van Eeden never completed this work—*Editor.*

I will as much as possible avoid speculation, and limit myself to facts; yet these facts, as I have observed them, bring me in a general way to the firm conviction that the theories on dream-life, as brought forward up to today, within my knowledge, are unable to account for all the phenomena.

Let me now give you an attempt at classification of the different forms of dreams, which I myself personally experienced and observed during a period of sixteen years. I have been able to distinguish nine different kinds of dreams, each of which presents a well-defined type. There are of course intermediate forms and combinations, but the separate types can still be recognized in their intermingling.

The first type of dreams I call *initial dreams*. This kind of dream is very rare; I know of only half-a-dozen instances occurring to myself, and have found no clear indication of them in other authors. Yet it is very characteristic and easily distinguishable. It occurs only in the very beginning of sleep, when the body is in a normal healthy condition, but very tired. Then the transition from waking to sleep takes place with hardly a moment of what is generally called unconsciousness, but what I would prefer to call discontinuity of memory. It is *not* what Maury (1878) calls a hypnagogic hallucination, which phenomenon I know well from my own experience, but which I do not consider to belong to the world of dreams. In hypnagogic hallucinations we have visions, but we have full bodily perception. In the initial dream type I see and feel as in any other dream. I have a nearly complete recollection of day-life, I know that I am asleep and where I am sleeping, but all perceptions of the physical body, inner and outer, visceral or peripheral, are entirely absent. Usually I have the sensation of floating or flying, and I observe with perfect clearness that the feeling of fatigue, the discomfort of bodily overstrain, has vanished. I feel fresh and vigorous; I can move and float in all directions; yet I know that my body is at the same time dead tired and fast asleep.

As the outcome of careful observations, I maintain my conviction that the bodily conditions of the sleeper have, as a rule, no influence on the character of dreams, with the exception of a few rare and abnormal cases, near the moment of waking up, or in those dreams of a second type which I have classified as *pathological*, in which fever, indigestion, or some poison, plays a rôle, and which form a small minority. For myself as the observer, I may state that I have been in good health all the time of observation. I had no important complaints of any nervous or visceral kind. My sleep and digestion both are usually good. Yet I have had the most terrible nightmares, while my body was as fresh and healthy as usual, and I have had delicious peaceful dreams on board ship in a heavy storm, or in a sleeping-car on the railway.

I wish, therefore, to define the true dream as *that state wherein bodily sensations, be they visceral, internal or peripheral, cannot penetrate to the mind*

directly, but only in the physical, nonspatial form of a symbol or an image.
I purposely avoid as much as possible the words "consciousness" and "unconsciousness." They may be convenient in colloquial language, but I am not able to attach any clear meaning to them. I have no idea what "unconsciousness," as a substantive, may stand for. And I found that I could do with the words memory and recollection and the word personality or person, in the primitive sense of *persona* (a mask, i.e., the mask worn by players). I do not think it accurate to call the body of a sleeper or a narcotized man unconscious. During my career as a psychotherapist, having by suggestion produced sleep in many people, I learned that the human body may act like a self-conscious person, without any participation of the recollecting mind. We know nowadays that a splitting-up of human personality is possible, not only into two, but into three or more. During my sittings with Mrs. Thompson (van Eeden, 1902) we observed that after a trance, in which Mrs. Thompson had been speaking as "Nelly," or as some other control, she herself remembered dreams, which had nothing whatever to do with the things of which she had been speaking to us. Her being could then be said to have been divided into three entities—the body in trance, apparently asleep; the "control," who spoke through her mouth; and Mrs. Thompson, who was dreaming in quite different spheres. All these persons or personalities were of course "conscious" in some way, as everything is probably conscious. The question is, where do the threads of recollection run that enable us to identify the persons?

I know that Mr. Havelock Ellis (Ellis, 1911) and many other authors will not accept my definition, because they deny the possibility of complete recollection and free volition in a dream. They would say that what I call a dream is no dream, but a sort of trance, or hallucination, or ecstasy. The observations of the Marquis d'Hervé, which were very much like mine, as related in his book, *Les Rêves et les moyens de les diriger* (1867), were discarded in the same way. These dreams could not be dreams, said Maury (1878).

Now this is simply a question of nomenclature. I can only say that I made my observations during normal deep and healthy sleep, and that in 352 cases I had a full recollection of my day-life, and could act voluntarily, though I was so fast asleep that no bodily sensations penetrated into my perception. If anybody refuses to call that state of mind a dream, he may suggest some other name. For my part, it was just this form of dream, which I call "lucid dreams," which aroused my keenest interest and which I noted down most carefully.

I quite agree with Mr. Havelock Ellis, that during sleep the psychical functions enter into a condition of *dissociation*. My contention, however, is that it is not dissociation, but, on the contrary, *reintegration*, after the dissociation of sleep, that is the essential feature of dreams. *The dream is a more or less complete reintegration of the psyche, a reintegration in a different sphere, in a psychical, nonspatial mode of existence. This reintegration may go so far as to effect full recollection of day-life, reflection, and voluntary action on reflection.*

The third type, *ordinary dreaming*, is the usual well-known type to which the large majority of dreams conform; probably it is the only kind that occurs to many people. It is not particularly pleasant or unpleasant, though it may vary according to its contents. It may occur in any moment of sleep, in day-time or in the night, and it does not need any bodily disturbance to produce it.

These dreams show dissociation, with very imperfect reintegration, and, as several authors have pointed out, they have in many respects a close likeness to insanity. The true conditions of day-life are not remembered; false remembrance—paramnesia—is very common in them; they are absurd and confused, and leave very faint traces after waking up.

The fourth type, *vivid dreaming*, differs from ordinary dreaming principally in its vividness and the strong impression it makes, which lasts sometimes for hours and days after waking up, with a painfully clear remembrance of every detail. These dreams are generally considered to be the effect of some abnormal bodily condition. Yet I think they must undoubtedly be distinguished from the pathological dreams. I have had them during perfectly normal bodily conditions. I do not mean to say, however, that some nervous disturbance, some psychical unrest, or some unknown influence from the waking world may not have been present. It may have been, but it escaped my observation in most cases. These vivid dreams are generally extremely absurd, or untrue, though explicit and well remembered. The mind is entirely dissociated and reintegration is very defective.

As a rule I find dreams of this kind unpleasant because of their absurdity, their insane character, and the strong lasting impression they make. Happily they are rare, at least with me. Sometimes they leave a strong conviction that they "mean something," that they have a premonitory, a prophetic character, and when we read of instances of prophetic dreams we find generally that they belong to this type. In my case I often found that they really could "mean" nothing; sometimes, however, I was not so certain. It depends in what direction we are looking for causes. One night, when I was on a lecturing tour, I was the guest of a family in a provincial town, and slept in what I supposed to be the guest-room. I had a night full of the most horrid dreams, one long confused nightmare, with a strong sentiment that it "meant something." Yet I felt in perfect health, cheerful and comfortable. I could not refrain from saying next morning at the breakfast table what an unpleasant night I had had. Then the family told me I had slept in the room of a daughter who was now in a sanatorium with a severe nervous disease, and who used to call that room her "den of torture."

It will be remarked that such vivid dreams are sometimes of a very pleasant character, filling whole days with an indescribable joy. This is true, but, according to my experience, my vividly pleasant dreams are now always of another and higher type. As a child I had these delicious vivid dreams. Now they have changed their character altogether and are of the lucid type.

In the fifth type, the *symbolic* or *mocking dreams*, the characteristic element is one which I call *demoniacal*. I am afraid this word will arouse some murmurs of disapproval, or at least some smiles or sneers. Yet I think I can successfully defend the use of the term. I will readily concede at once that the real existence of beings whom we may call "demons" is problematic. But the real existence of the interstellar ether is also problematic, and yet men of science find the conception very useful and convenient.

I hope to satisfy even the most skeptical of my audience by defining the expression "demoniacal" thus:

I call demoniacal those phenomena which produce on us the impression of being invented or arranged by intelligent beings of a very low moral order.

To me it seems that the great majority of dreams reported by Freud and his adherents, and used for the building up of his elaborate theory, belong to this type.

It may indeed be called a bold deed to introduce the *symbolism* of dreams into the scientific world. This is Freud's (1954) great achievement.

But now let us consider what the word "symbol" implies. A symbol is an image or an imaginary event, standing for a real object or event whereto it has some distant resemblance. Now the invention of a symbol can only be an act of *thought*—the work of some intelligence. Symbols cannot invent themselves; they must be thought out. And the question arises: who performs this intelligent act; who thinks out the symbol? The answer given by the Freudian school is: the subconscious. But here we have one of those words which come in "wo die Begriffe fehlen." To me the word "subconscious," indicating a thinking entity, is just as mysterious, just as unscientific, just as "occult" as the word "demon." In my view it is accurate to say only that in our dreams we see images and experience events, for which our own mind— our "person" as we remember it—cannot be held responsible, and which must therefore come from some unknown source. About the general character of these sources, however, we may form some judgment and I feel justified in calling them in the dreams of this type "demoniacal"—that is of low moral order.

It is in this class also, that the erotic element, or rather the obscene element, plays such an important part. And it is no wonder that some adherents of Freud's school, studying only this kind of dream, come to the conclusion that all dreams have a sexual origin.

The sixth type, which I call *general dream-sensations*, is very remarkable but not easy to describe. It is not an ordinary dream; there is no vision, no image, no event, not even a word or a name. But during a long time of deep sleep, the mind is continually occupied with one person, one place, one remarkable event, or even one abstract thought. At least that is the recollection on waking up. One night I was constantly occupied by the personality of an American gentleman, in whom I am not particularly interested. I did not see him, nor hear his name, but on waking up I felt as if he had been there the whole night. In another instance it was a rather deep thought, occupying me in the deepest sleep, with a clear recollection of it after waking up. The question was: Why can a period of our life be felt as very sad, and yet be sweet and beautiful in remembrance? And the answer was: because a human being knows only a very small part of what he is. Question and answer never left me; yet my sleep was very deep and unbroken.* These dream-sensations are not unpleasant and not absurd, so long as the body is in good health.

They often have an elevating or consoling effect. In pathological dreams, however, they may be extremely strange and harassing. The sleeper may have a feeling as if he were a square or a circle, or other sensations of an utterly indescribable character.

The seventh type of dreams, which I call *lucid dreams*, seems to me the most interesting and worthy of the most careful observation and study. Of this type I experienced and wrote down 352 cases in the period between January 20, 1898, and December 26, 1912.

In these lucid dreams the reintegration of the psychic functions is so complete that the sleeper remembers day-life and his own condition, reaches a state of perfect awareness, and is able to direct his attention, and to attempt different acts of free volition. Yet the sleep, as I am able confidently to state, is undisturbed, deep and refreshing. I obtained my first glimpse of this lucidity during sleep in June, 1897, in the following way. I dreamt that I was floating through a landscape with bare trees, knowing that it was April, and I remarked that the perspective of the branches and twigs changed quite naturally. Then I made the reflection, during sleep, that my fancy would never be able to invent or to make an image as intricate as the perspective movement of little twigs seen in floating by.

Many years later, in 1907, I found a passage in a work by Prof. Ernst Mach (1903) in which the same observation is made with a little difference. Like me, Mach came to the conclusion that he was dreaming, but it was because he saw the movement of the twigs to be *defective*, while I had wondered at the naturalness which my fancy could never invent. Professor Mach has not pursued his observations in this direction, probably because he did not

*van Eeden may be describing non-stage 1 mental processes—*Editor.*

believe in their importance. I made up my mind to look out carefully for another opportunity. I prepared myself for careful observation, hoping to prolong and to intensify the lucidity.

In January 1898 I was able to repeat the observation. In the night of January 19–20, I dreamt that I was lying in the garden before the windows of my study, and saw the eyes of my dog through the glass pane. I was lying on my chest and observing the dog very keenly. At the same time, however, I knew with perfect certainty that I was dreaming and lying on my back in my bed. And then I resolved to wake up slowly and carefully and observe how my sensation of lying on my chest would change into the sensation of lying on my back. And so I did, slowly and deliberately, and the transition— which I have since undergone many times—is most wonderful. It is like the feeling of slipping from one body into another, and there is distinctly a *double* recollection of the two bodies. I remembered what I felt in my dream, lying on my chest; but returning into the day-life, I remembered also that my physical body had been quietly lying on its back all the while. This obser- vation of a double memory I have had many times since. It is so indubitable that it leads almost unavoidably to the conception of *a dream-body.*

Mr. Havelock Ellis says with something of a sneer that some people "who dabble in the occult" speak of an astral body.* Yet if he had had only one of these experiences, he would feel that we can escape neither the dabbling nor the dream-body. In a lucid dream the sensation of having a body—having eyes, hands, a mouth that speaks, and so on—is perfectly distinct; yet I know at the same time that the physical body is sleeping and has quite a different position. In waking up the two sensations blend together, so to speak, and I remember as clearly the action of the dream-body as the restful- ness of the physical body.

In February 1899 I had a lucid dream, in which I made the following expe- riment. I drew with my finger, moistened by saliva, a wet cross on the palm of my left hand, with the intention of seeing whether it would still be there after waking up. Then I *dreamt* that I woke up and felt the wet cross on my left hand by applying the palm to my cheek. And then a long time afterwards I woke up *really* and knew at once that the hand of my physical body had been lying in a closed position undisturbed on my chest all the while.

The sensation of the *voice* during a lucid dream is most marvellous, and after many repetitions still a source of amazement. I use my voice as loudly as I can, and though I know quite well that my physical body is lying in pro- found sleep, I can hardly believe that this loud voice is inaudible in the

---

*For recent treatments of the phenomena of "astral projection," which seems phenomenologically similar to lucid dreams, see Broad, 1959; Eastman, 1962; Tart, 1967; 1968—*Editor.*

waking world. Yet, though I have sung, shouted, and spoken loudly in hundreds of dreams, my wife has never heard my voice, and in several cases was able to assure me that I had slept quite peacefully.

I cannot in this paper give even a short and superficial account of the many interesting details of these dreams. I must reserve that for my larger work. And I fear that only a repeated personal acquaintance with the facts can convince one of their significance. I will relate a few more instances in order to give some idea of their character.

On Sept. 9, 1904 I dreamt that I stood at a table before a window. On the table were different objects. I was perfectly well aware that I was dreaming and I considered what sorts of experiments I could make. I began by trying to break glass, by beating it with a stone. I put a small tablet of glass on two stones and struck it with another stone. Yet it would not break. Then I took a fine claret-glass from the table and struck it with my fist, with all my might, at the same time reflecting how dangerous it would be to do this in waking life; yet the glass remained whole. But lo! when I looked at it again after some time, it was broken.*

It broke all right, but a little too late, like an actor who misses his cue. This gave me a very curious impression of being in a *fake-world*, cleverly imitated, but with small failures. I took the broken glass and threw it out of the window, in order to observe whether I could hear the *tinkling*. I heard the noise all right and I even saw two dogs run away from it quite naturally. I thought what a good imitation this comedy-world was. Then I saw a decanter with claret and tasted it, and noted with perfect clearness of mind: "Well, we can also have voluntary impressions of taste in this dream-world; this has quite the taste of wine."

There is a saying by the German poet, Novalis, that when we dream that we dream, we are near waking up. This view, shared as it is by the majority of observers, I must decidedly reject. Lucid dreams occur in deep sleep and do not as a rule end in waking up, unless I wish it and do it by an act of volition. I prefer, however, in most cases to continue dreaming as long as possible, and then the lucidity vanishes and gives place to other forms of dream, and—what seems remarkable—the form that follows is often the "demon-dream," of which I will speak presently.

Then it often happens that I dream that I wake up and tell my lucid dream to some other person. This latter is then a dream of the ordinary form. From this dream I wake up in the real waking world, very much amazed at the curious wanderings of my mind. The impression is as if I had been rising through spheres of different depths, of which the lucid dream was the deepest.

*This corresponds with Mach's observation about the perspective of the twigs.

I may state that without exception all my lucid dreams occurred in the hours between five and eight in the morning. The particular significance of these hours for our dreams has often been brought forward—among others by Dante, *Purg. IX.*, where he speaks of the hour when the swallows begin to warble and our mind is least clogged by the material body.

Lucid dreams are also symbolic—yet in quite a different way, I never remarked anything sexual or erotic in them. Their symbolism takes the form of beautiful landscapes—different luminous phenomena, sunlight, clouds, and especially a deep blue sky. In a perfect instance of the lucid dream I float through immensely wide landscapes, with a clear blue, sunny sky, and a feeling of deep bliss and gratitude, which I feel impelled to express by eloquent words of thankfulness and piety. Sometimes these words seem to me a little rhetorical, but I cannot help it, as it is very difficult in dreams to control emotional impulses. Sometimes I conceive of what appears as a symbol, warning, consoling, approving. A cloud gathers or the light brightens. Only once could I see the disc of the sun.

Flying or floating may be observed in all forms of dreams, except perhaps the class of general dream sensations; yet it is generally an indication that lucid dreams are coming.

When I have been flying in my dreams for two or three nights, then I know that a lucid dream is at hand. And the lucid dream itself is often initiated and accompanied all the time by the sensation of flying. Sometimes I feel myself floating swiftly through wide spaces; once I flew backwards, and once, dreaming that I was inside a cathedral, I flew upwards, with the immense building and all in it, at great speed. I cannot believe that the rhythm of our breath has anything to do with this sensation, as Havelock Ellis supposes, because it is generally continuous and very swift.

Difficult, spasmodic floating belongs to dreaming of a lower class, and this may depend on morbid conditions of the body; but it may also be symbolic of some moral difficulty or distress.

On Christmas Day 1911 I had the following dream. It began with flying and floating. I felt wonderfully light and strong. I saw immense and beautiful prospects—first a town, then country-landscapes, fantastic and brightly colored. Then I saw my brother sitting—the same who died in 1906—and I went up to him saying: "Now we are dreaming, both of us." He answered: "No, I am not!" And then I remembered that he was dead. We had a long conversation about the conditions of existence after death, and I inquired especially after the awareness, the clear, bright insight. But that he could not answer; he seemed to lack it.

Then the lucid dream was interrupted by an ordinary dream in which I saw a lady standing on a bridge, who told me she had heard me talk in my sleep. And I supposed that my voice had been audible during the lucid dream.

Then a second period of lucidity followed in which I saw Prof. van't Hoff, the famous Dutch chemist, whom I had known as a student, standing in a sort of college-room, surrounded by a number of learned people. I went up to him, knowing very well that he was dead, and continued my inquiry about our condition after death. It was a long, quiet conversation, in which I was perfectly aware of the situation.

I asked first why we, lacking our organs of sense, could arrive at any certainty that the person to whom we were talking was really that person and not a subjective illusion. Then van't Hoff said: "Just as in common life; by a general impression."

"Yet," I said, "in common life there is stability of observation and there is consolidation by repeated observation."

"Here also," said van't Hoff, "And the sensation of *certainty* is the same." Then I had indeed a very strong feeling of certitude that it was really van't Hoff with whom I talked and no subjective illusion. Then I began to inquire again about the clearness, the lucidity, the stability of this life of shades, and then I got the same hesitating, dubious, unsatisfactory answer as from my brother. The whole atmosphere of the dream was happy, bright, elevated, and the persons around van't Hoff seemed sympathetic, though I did not know them.

"It will be some time probably before I join you," I said. But I took myself then for younger than I was.

After that I had several ordinary dreams and I awoke quite refreshed, knowing my voice had not been audible in the waking world.

In May 1903 I dreamed that I was in a little provincial Dutch town and at once encountered my brother-in-law, who had died some time before. I was absolutely sure that it was he, and I knew that he was dead. He told me that he had much intercourse with my "controller," as he expressed it—my guiding spirit. I was glad, and our conversation was very cordial, more intimate than ever in common life. He told me that a financial catastrophe was impending for me. Somebody was going to rob me of a sum of 10,000 guilders. I said that I understood him, though after waking up I was utterly puzzled by it and could make nothing of it. My brother-in-law said that my guiding spirit had told it to him. I told the story to somebody else in my dream. Then I asked my brother-in-law to tell me more of the after-life, and just as he was going to answer me I woke up—as if somebody cut off the communication. I was not then as much used to prolonging my dreams as I am now.

I wish to point out that this was the *only* prediction I ever received in a lucid dream in such an impressive way. And it came only too true, with this difference, that the sum I lost was twenty times greater. At the time of the dream there seemed not to be the slightest probability of such a catastrophe.

I was not even in possession of the money I lost afterwards. Yet it was just the time when the first events took place—the railway strikes of 1903—that led up to my financial ruin.

There may be deceit in the lucid dream. In March 1912 I had a very complicated dream, in which I dreamt that Theodore Roosevelt was dead, then that I woke up and told the dream, saying: "I was not sure in my dream whether he was really dead or still alive; now I know that he is really dead; but I was so struck by the news that I lost my memory." And then came a *false lucidity* in which I said: "Now I know that I dream and where I am." But this was all wrong; I had no idea of my real condition, and only slowly, after waking up, I realized that it was all nonsense.

This sort of mockery I call demoniacal. And there is a connection, which I observed so frequently that it must have some significance—namely, that a lucid dream is immediately followed by an eighth type of dream I call a *demon-dream*.

I hope you allow me, if only for convenience sake, to speak as if these intelligences of a low moral order exist. Let me call it also a working hypothesis. Then I wish to point out to you the difference between the symbolic or mocking dreams described earlier and the demon-dreams.

In the symbolic dreams the sleeper is teased or puzzled or harassed by various more or less weird, uncanny, obscene, lugubrious or diabolical inventions. He has to walk in slaughter-houses or among corpses; he finds everything besmeared with blood or excrement; he is drawn into obscene, erotic or horrible scenes, in which he even takes an active part. His moral condition is utterly depraved; he is a murderer, an adulterer, etc.; in a word, nothing is too low or too horrible for such dreams.

After waking up the effect is, of course, unpleasant; he is more or less ashamed and shocked; he tries to shake off the memory as soon as possible.

Now in the demon-dreams—which are always very near, before or after, the lucid dreams—I undergo similar attacks; but I *see* the forms, the figures, the personalities of strange non-human beings, who are doing it. One night, for instance, I saw such a being, going before me and soiling everything he touched, such as door-handles and chairs. These beings are always obscene and lascivious, and try to draw me into their acts and doings. They have no sex and appear alternately as a man, or a woman. Their aspect is very various and variable, changing every moment, taking all the fantastic forms that the old painters of the Middle Ages tried to reproduce, but with a certain weird plasticity and variability, that no painting can express.

I will describe one instance of these dreams (March 30, 1907, in Berlin), following immediately after a lucid dream. The lucidity had not been very intense, and I had some doubts about my real condition. Then all at once I was in the middle of demons. Never before had I seen them so distinct, so impertinent, so aggressive. One was slippery, shining, limp and cold, like a living corpse. Another changed its face repeatedly and made the most incredible grimaces. One flew underneath me shouting an obscenity with a curious slang-word. I defended myself energetically, but principally with invectives, which I felt to be a weakness. I saw the words written.

The circle of demons was close to me and grinning like a mob of brutal street-boys. I was not afraid, however, and said: "Even if you conquer me, if God wills it I do not fear." Then they all cried together like a rabble, and one said: "Let God then speak first!" And then I thundered with all my might: "*He* HAS spoken long since!" And then I pointed at one of them, saying: "You I know for a long time!" and then pointing to another: "And you!"

Then I awoke at once, and I believe I made some audible sound in waking up in the middle of my apostrophe.

And then—this will astonish you most—after this dispute I felt thoroughly refreshed, cheered up and entirely serene and calm.

This is the principal difference from the symbolic dreams that in the demon-dreams when I *see* the demons and fight them, the effect is thoroughly pleasing, refreshing and uplifting.

This is the principal point in these demon-dreams—that, whether these beings have a real existence or whether they are only creations of my fancy, to see them and to fight them takes away all their terror, all the uncanniness, the weirdness, of their tricks and pranks.*

I have not yet spoken about the ninth dream type, which I call *wrong waking up*, occurring always near awakening. Of this sort of dream I found an excellent instance described by Mach (1903). He calls it "Phantasma." We have the sensation of waking up in our ordinary sleeping-room and then we begin to realize that there is something uncanny around us; we see inexplicable movements or hear strange noises, and then we know that we are still asleep. In my first experience of this dream I was rather afraid and wanted nervously to wake up really. I think this is the case that most people who have it. They become frightened and nervous and at last wake up with palpitations, a sweating brow and so on.

To me now these wrong-waking-up-dreams have lost their terror. I consider them as demon-pranks, and they amuse me; they do not tell on my nerves any more.

In July 1906 sleeping at Langen Schwalbach a deep sleep after a laborious day, I had two or three dreams of this type. I seemed to wake up and heard a big luggage-box being *blown* along the landing, with a tremendous bumping. Then I realized that I had awakened in the demon-sphere. The second time I saw that my sleeping-room had three windows, though I knew there were

*Compare this with Stewart's article on the Senoi, chapter 9—*Editor*.

only two. Wishing to make sure, I woke up for a moment voluntarily and realized that my room had two windows and that stillness had reigned in the house all night.

After that I had a succession of lucid dreams, very beautiful. At the end of them, while I was still singing loudly, I was suddenly surrounded by many demons, who joined in my singing, like a mob of vicious semi-savage creatures. Then I felt that I was losing my self-control. I began to act more and more extravagantly, to throw my bedclothes and my pillows about, and so on. I drew myself up and saw one demon who had a less vicious look than the others and he looked as if he were saying "you are going wrong." "Yes," I said, "but what shall I do?" Then he said, "Give them the whip, on their naked backs." And I thought of Dante's shades, who also feared the whip. I at once made—created—a whip of leathern strings, with leaden balls at the end. And I threatened them with it and also struck at them a few times. Then suddenly all grew perfectly quiet around me, and I saw the creatures sneaking away with hypocritical faces, as if they knew nothing about it at all.

I had many more adventures that night, lucid and ordinary dreams, and I awoke fresh and cheerful, better in spirits than I had been for a long time.

This wrong-waking-up type is not to be confused with the dreams related on p. 152, in which I dreamt that I woke after a lucid dream and told that dream to some listener. Those dreams were of the ordinary sort. There was nothing uncanny about them. Dreams of the wrong-waking-up class are undoubtedly demoniacal, uncanny, and very vivid and bright, with a sort of ominous sharpness and clearness, a strong diabolical light. Moreover the mind of the sleeper is aware that it is a dream, and a bad one, and he struggles to wake up. As I said just now, however, the terror ends as soon as the demons are *seen*—as soon as the sleeper realizes that he must be the dupe of intelligences of a low moral order. I am prepared to hear myself accused of superstition, of reviving the dark errors of the Middle Ages. Well, I only try to tell the facts as clearly as possible and I cannot do it without using these terms and ideas. If anybody will replace them by others, I am open to any suggestion. Only I would maintain that it is not *my* mind that is responsible for all the horrors and errors of dream-life. To say that *nobody* is responsible for them will not do, for there is absolute evidence in them of some thought and intention, however depraved and low. A trick, a deceit, a symbol, cannot be without some sort of thought and intention. To put it all down to "unconsciousness" is very convenient; but then I say that it is just as scientific to use the names Beelzebub, or Belial. I, for one, do not believe in "unconsciousness" any more than in Santa Claus.

The remark may be made that in introducing intelligent beings of a low order to explain these phenomena, an element of arbitrariness is brought in, which excludes the possibility of finding a scientific order. It is, for instance, convenient to ascribe all the phenomena of insanity and of pathological dreams to demons, who make use of the weakness of the body to play their tricks. This is, in fact, the opinion of no less a man than Alfred Russel Wallace, as he freely confessed to me in a personal conversation.

I do not think, however, that even this idea, taken as a working hypothesis, will prevent us from trying to find a scientific order even in these apparently demoniacal tricks; the fact, for instance, that certain drugs bring about hallucinations of a well-defined kind; that cocaine produces delicious expectations and pleasant dreams, and alcohol causes visions of small white animals. This suggests that there must be some order behind it, which is not purely arbitrary.

We are here, however, on the borders of a realm of mystery where we have to advance very carefully. To deny may be just as dangerous and misleading as to accept.

9

DREAM THEORY IN MALAYA

KILTON STEWART

If you should hear that a flying saucer from another planet had landed on Gulangra, a lonely mountain peak in the Central Mountain Range of the Malay Peninsula a hundred years ago, you would want to know how the space ship was constructed and what kind of power propelled it, but most of all you would want to know about the people who navigated it and the society from which they came. If they lived in a world without crime and war and destructive conflict, and if they were comparatively free from chronic mental and physical ailments, you would want to know about their methods of healing and education, and whether these methods would work as well with the inhabitants of the earth. If you heard further that the navigators of the ship had found a group of 12,000 people living as an isolated community among the mountains, and had demonstrated that these pre-literate people could utilize their methods of healing and education, and reproduce the society from which the celestial navigators came, you would probably be more curious about these psychological and social methods that conquered space inside the individual, than you would about the mechanics of the ship which conquered outside space.

As a member of a scientific expedition travelling through the unexplored equatorial rain forest of the Central Range of the Malay Peninsula in 1935, I was introduced to an isolated tribe of jungle folk, who employed methods of psychology and inter-personal relations so astonishing that they might have come from another planet. These people, the Senoi, lived in long community houses, skillfully constructed of bamboo, rattan, and thatch, and held away from the ground on poles. They maintained themselves by

By permission of Mrs. Kilton Stewart.

practising dry-land, shifting agriculture, and by hunting and fishing. Their language, partly Indonesian and partly Non-Kamian, relates them to the peoples of Indonesia to the south and west, and to the Highlanders of Indo-China and Burma, as do their physical characteristics.

Study of their political and social organization indicates that the political authority in their communities was originally in the hands of the oldest members of patrilineal clans, somewhat as in the social structure of China and other parts of the world. But the major authority in all their communities is now held by their primitive psychologists whom they call *halaks*. The only honorary title in the society is that of *Tohat*, which is equivalent to a doctor who is both a healer and an educator, in our terms.

The Senoi claim there has not been a violent crime or an intercommunal conflict for a space of two or three hundred years because of the insight and inventiveness of the *Tohats* of their various communities. The foothill tribes which surround the Central Mountain Range have such a firm belief in the magical powers of this Highland group that they give the territory a wide berth. From all we could learn, their psychological knowledge of strangers in their territory, the Senoi said they could very easily devise means of scaring them off. They did not practise black magic, but allowed the nomadic hill-folk surrounding them to think that they did if strangers invaded their territory.

This fear of Senoi magic accounts for the fact that they have not, over a long period, had to fight with outsiders. But the absence of violent crime, armed conflict, and mental and physical diseases in their own society can only be explained on the basis of institutions which produce a high state of psychological integration and emotional maturity, along with social skills and attitudes which promote creative, rather than destructive, inter-personal relations. They are, perhaps, the most democratic group reported in anthropological literature. In the realms of family, economics, and politics, their society operates smoothly on the principle of contract, agreement, and democratic concensus, with no need of police force, jail, psychiatric hospital to reinforce the agreements or to confine those who are not willing or able to reach consensus.

Study of their society seems to indicate that they have arrived at this high state of social and physical cooperation and intergration through the system of psychology which they discovered, invented, and developed, and that the principles of this system of psychology are understandable in terms of Western scientific thinking.

It was the late H. D. Noone, the Government Ethnologist of the Federated Malay States, who introduced me to this astonishing group. He agreed with me that they have built a system of inter-personal relations which, in the field of psychology, is perhaps on a level with our attainments in such areas as television and nuclear physics. From a year's experience with these people working as a research psychologist, and another year with Noone in England integrating his seven years of anthropological research with my own findings, I am able to make the following formulations of the principles of Senoi psychology.

Being a pre-literate group, the principles of their psychology are simple and easy to learn, understand, and even employ. Fifteen years of experimentation with these Senoi principles have convinced me that all men, regardless of their actual cultural development, might profit by studying them.

Senoi psychology falls into two categories. The first deals with dream interpretation; the second with dream expression in the agreement trance or cooperative reverie. The cooperative reverie is not participated in until adolescence and serves to initiate the child into the states of adulthood. After adolescence, if he spends a great deal of time in the trance state, a Senoi is considered a specialist in healing or in the use of extra-sensory powers.

Dream interpretation, however, is a feature of child education and is the common knowledge of all Senoi adults. The average Senoi layman practises the psychotherapy of dream interpretation of his family and associates as a regular feature of education and daily social intercourse. Breakfast in the Senoi house is like a dream clinic, with the father and older brothers listening to and analyzing the dreams of all the children. At the end of the family clinic the male population gathers in the council, at which the dreams of the older children and all the men in the community are reported, discussed, and analyzed.

While the Senoi do not of course employ our system of terminology, their psychology of dream interpretation might be summed up as follows: man creates features or images of the outside world in his own mind as part of the adaptive process. Some of these features are in conflict with him and with each other. Once internalized, these hostile images turn man against himself and against his fellows. In dreams man has the power to see these facts of his psyche, which have been disguised in external forms, associated with his own fearful emotions, and turned against him and the internal images of other people. If the individual does not receive social aid through education and therapy, these hostile images, built up by man's normal receptiveness to the outside world, get tied together and associated with one another in a way which makes him physically, socially, and psychologically abnormal.

Unaided, these dream beings, which man creates to reproduce inside himself the external socio-physical environment, tend to remain against him the way the environment was against him, or to become disassociated from his major personality and tied up in wasteful psychic, organic, and muscular tensions. With the help of dream interpretations, these psychological replicas of the socio-physical environment can be redirected and reorganized and again become useful to the major personality.

The Senoi believes that any human being, with the aid of his fellows, can outface, master, and actually utilize all beings and forces in the dream universe. His experience leads him to believe that, if you cooperate with your fellows or oppose them with good will in the day time, their images will help you in your dreams, and that every person should be the supreme ruler and master of his own dream or spiritual universe, and can demand and receive the help and cooperation of all the forces there.

In order to evaluate these principles of dream interpretation and social action, I made a collection of the dreams of younger and older Senoi children, adolescents, and adults, and compared them with similar collections made in other societies where they had different social attitudes towards the dream and different methods of dream interpretation. I found through this larger study that the dream process evolved differently in the various societies, and that the evolution of the dream process seemed to be related to the adaptability and individual creative output of the various societies. It may be of interest to the reader to examine in detail the methods of Senoi dream interpretation:

The simplest anxiety or terror dream I found among the Senoi was the falling dream. When the Senoi child reports a falling dream, the adult answers with enthusiasm, "That is a wonderful dream, one of the best dreams a man can have. Where did you fall to, and what did you discover?" He makes the same comment when the child reports a climbing, travelling, flying, or soaring dream. The child at first answers, as he would in our society, that it did not seem so wonderful, and that he was so frightened that he awoke before he had fallen anywhere.

"That was a mistake," answers the adult-authority. "Everything you do in a dream has a purpose, beyond your understanding while you are asleep. You must relax and enjoy yourself when you fall in a dream. Falling is the quickest way to get in contact with the powers of the spirit world, the powers laid open to you through your dreams. Soon, when you have a falling dream, you will remember what I am saying, and as you do, you will feel that you are travelling to the source of the power which has caused you to fall.

"The falling spirits love you. They are attracting you to their land, and you have but to relax and remain asleep in order to come to grips with them. When you meet them, you may be frightened of their terrific power, but go on. When you think you are dying in a dream, you are only receiving the powers of the other world, your own spiritual power which has been turned against you, and which now wishes to become one with you if you will accept it".

The astonishing thing is that over a period of time, with this type of social interaction, praise, or criticism, imperatives, and advice, the dream which starts out with fear of falling changes into the joy of flying. This happens to everyone in the Senoi society. That which was an indwelling fear or anxiety, becomes an indwelling joy or act of will; that which was ill esteem toward the forces which caused the child to fall in his dream, becomes good will towards the denizens of the dream world, because he relaxes in his dream and finds pleasureable adventures, rather than waking up with a clammy skin and a crawling scalp.

The Senoi believe and teach that the dreamer—the "I" of the dream—should always advance and attack in the teeth of danger, calling on the dream images of his fellows if necessary, but fighting by himself until they arrive. In bad dreams the Senoi believe real friends will never attack the dreamer or refuse help. If any dream character who looks like a friend is hostile or uncooperative in a dream, he is only wearing the mask of a friend.

If the dreamer attacks and kills the hostile dream character, the spirit or essence of this dream character will always emerge as a servant or ally. Dream characters are bad only as long as one is afraid and retreating from them, and will continue to seem bad and fearful as long as one refuses to come to grips with them.

According to the Senoi, pleasurable dreams, such as of flying or sexual love, should be continued until they arrive at a resolution which, on awakening, leaves one with something of beauty or use to the group. For example, one should arrive somewhere when he flies, meet the beings there, hear their music, see their designs, their dances, and learn their useful knowledge.

Dreams of sexual love should always move through orgasm, and the dreamer should then demand from his dream lover the poem, the song, the dance, the useful knowledge which will express the beauty of his spiritual lover to a group. If this is done, no dream man or woman can take the love which belongs to human beings. If the dream character demanding love looks like a brother or sister, with whom love would be abnormal or incestuous in reality, one need have no fear of expressing love in the dream, since these dream beings are not, in fact, brother or sister, but have only chosen these taboo images as a disguise. Such dream beings are only facets of one's own spiritual or psychic makeup, disguised as brother or sister, and useless until they are reclaimed or possessed through the free expression of love in the dream universe.

If the dreamer demands and receives from his love partners a contribution which he can express to the group on awakening, he cannot express or receive too much love in dreams. A rich love life in dreams indicates the favor of the beings of the spiritual or emotional universe. If the dreamer injures the dream images of his fellows or refuses to cooperate with them in dreams, he should go out of his way to express friendship and cooperation on awakening, since hostile dream characters can only use the image of people for whom his good will is running low. If the image of a friend hurts him in a dream, the friend should be advised of the fact, so he can repair his damaged or negative dream image by friendly social intercourse.

Let us examine some of the elements of the social and psychological processes involved in this type of dream interpretation:

First, the child receives social recognition and esteem for discovering and relating what might be called an anxiety-motivated psychic reaction. This is the first step among the Senoi toward convincing the child that he is acceptable to authority even when he reveals how he is inside.

Second, it describes the working of his mind as rational, even when he is asleep. To the Senoi it is just as reasonable for the child to adjust his inner tension states for himself as it is for a Western child to do his homework for the teacher.

Third, the interpretation characterizes the force which the child feels in the dream as a power which he can control through a process of relaxation and mental set, a force which is his as soon as he can reclaim it and learn to direct it.

Fourth, the Senoi education indicates that anxiety is not only important in itself, but that it blocks the free play of imaginative thinking and creative activity to which dreams could otherwise give rise.

Fifth, it establishes the principle that the child should make decisions and arrive at resolutions in his night-time thinking as well as in that of the day, and should assume a responsible attitude toward all his psychic reactions and forces.

Sixth, it acquaints the child with the fact that he can better control his psychic reactions by expressing them and taking thought upon them, than by concealing and repressing them.

Seventh, it initiates the Senoi child into a way of thinking which will be strengthened and developed throughout the rest of his life, and which assumes that a human being who retains good will for his fellows and communicates his psychic reactions to them for approval and criticism, is the supreme ruler of all the individual forces of the spirit—subjective—world whatsoever.

Man discovers his deepest self and reveals his greatest creative power at times when his psychic processes are most free from immediate involvement with the environment and most under the control of his indwelling balancing or homeostatic power. The freest type of psychic play occurs in sleep, and the social acceptance of the dream would, therefore, constitute the deepest possible acceptance of the individual.

Among the Senoi one accumulates good will for people because they encourage on every hand the free exercise and expression of that which is most basically himself, either directly or indirectly, through the acceptance of the dream process. At the same time, the child is told that he must refuse to settle with the denizens of the dream world unless they make some contribution which is socially meaningful and constructive as determined by social consensus on awakening. Thus his dream reorganization is guided in a way which makes his adult aggressive action socially constructive.

Among the Senoi where the authority tells the child that every dream force and character is real and important, and in essence permanent, that it can and must be outfaced, subdued, and forced to make a socially meaningful contribution, the wisdom of the body operating in sleep, seems in fact to reorganize the accumulating experience of the child in such a way that the natural tendency of the higher nervous system to perpetuate unpleasant experiences is first neutralized and then reversed.

We could call this simple type of interpretation dream analysis. It says to the child that there is a manifest content of the dream, the root he stubbed his toe on, or the fire that burned him, or the composite individual that disciplined him. But there is also a latent content of the dream, a force which is potentially useful, but which will plague him until he outfaces the manifest content in a future dream, and either persuades or forces it to make a contribution which will be judged useful or beautiful by the group, after he awakes.

We could call this type of interpretation *suggestion*. The tendency to perpetuate in sleep the negative image of a personified evil, is neutralized in the dream by a similar tendency to perpetuate the positive image of a sympathetic social authority. Thus accumulating social experience supports the organizing wisdom of the body in the dream, making the dreamer first unafraid of the negative image and its accompanying painful tension states, and later enabling him to break up that tension state and transmute the accumulated energy from anxiety into a poem, a song, a dance, a new type of trap, or some other creative product, to which an individual or the whole group will react with approval (or criticize) the following day.

The following further example from the Senoi will show how this process operates:

A child dreams that he is attacked by a friend and, on awakening, is advised by his father to inform his friend of this fact. The friend's father tells his child that it is possible that he has offended the dreamer without wishing to do so, and allowed a malignant character to use his image as a disguise in the dream. Therefore, he should give a present to the dreamer and go out of his way to be friendly toward him, to prevent such an occurrence in the future.

The aggression building up around the image of the friend in the dreamer's mind thereby becomes the basis of a friendly exchange. The dreamer is also told to fight back in the future dreams, and to conquer any dream character using the friend's image as a disguise.

Another example of what is probably a less direct tension state in the dreamer toward another person is dealt with in an equally skillful manner. The dreamer reports seeing a tiger attack another boy of the long house. Again, he is advised to tell the boy about the dream, to describe the place where the attack occurred and, if possible, to show it to him so that he can be on his guard, and in future dreams kill the tiger before it has a chance to attack him. The parents of the boy in the dream again tell the child to give the dreamer a present, and to consider him a special friend.

Even a tendency toward unproductive fantasy is effectively dealt with in the Senoi dream education. If the child reports floating dreams, or a dream of finding food, he is told that he must float somewhere in his next dream and find something of value to his fellows, or that he must share the food he is eating; and if he has a dream of attacking someone he must apologize to them, share a delicacy with them, or make them some sort of toy. Thus, before aggression, selfishness, and jealousy can influence social behavior, the tensions expressed in the permissive dream state become the hub of social action in which they are discharged without being destructive.

My data on the dream life of the various Senoi age groups would indicate that dreaming can and does become the deepest type of creative thought. Observing the lives of the Senoi it occurred to me that modern civilization may be sick because people have sloughed off, or failed to develop, half their power to think. Perhaps the most important half. Certainly, the Senoi suffer little by intellectual comparison with ourselves. They have equal power for logical thinking while awake, considering their environmental data, whereas our capacity to solve problems in dreams is inferior compared to theirs.

In the adult Senoi a dream may start with a waking problem which has failed solution, with an accident, or a social debacle. A young man brings in some wild gourd seeds and shares them with his group. They have a purgative effect and give everyone diarrhea. The young man feels guilty and ashamed and suspects that they are poisonous. That night he has a dream, and the spirit of the gourd seeds appears, makes him vomit up the seeds, and explains that they have value only as a medicine, when a person is ill. Then the gourd spirit gives him a song and teaches him a dance which he can show his group on awakening, thereby gaining recognition and winning back his self-esteem.

Or, a falling tree which wounds a man appears in his dreams to take away the pain, and explains that it wishes to make friends with him. Then the tree spirit gives him a new and unknown rhythm which he can play on his drums. Or, the jilted lover is visited in his dreams by the woman who rejected him, who explains that she is sick when she is awake and not good enough for him. As a token of her true feeling, she gives him a poem.

The Senoi does not exhaust the power to think while asleep with these simple social and environmental situations. The bearers who carried out our equipment under very trying conditions became dissatisfied and were ready to desert. Their leader, a Senoi shaman, had a dream in which he was visited by the spirit of the empty boxes. The song and music this dream character gave him so inspired the bearers, and the dance he directed so relaxed and rested them, that they claimed the boxes had lost their weight and finished the expedition in the best of spirits.

Even this solution of a difficult social situation, involving people who were not all members of the dreamer's group, is trivial compared with the dream solutions which occur now that the Senoi territory has been opened up to alien culture contacts.

Datu Bintung at Jelong had a dream which succeeded in breaking down the major social barriers in clothing and food habits between his group and the surrounding Chinese and Mohammedan colonies. This was accomplished chiefly through a dance which his dream prescribed. Only those who did his dance were required to change their food habits and wear the new clothing, but the dance was so good that nearly all the Senoi along the border chose to do it. In this way, the dream created social change in a democratic manner.

Another feature of Datu Bintung's dream involved the ceremonial status of women, making them more nearly the equals of men, although equality is not a feature of either Chinese or Mohammedan societies. So far as could be determined this was a pure creative action which introduced greater equality in the culture, just as reflective thought has produced more equality in our society.

In the West the thinking we do while asleep usually remains on a muddled, childish, or psychotic level because we do not respond to dreams as socially important and include dreaming in the educative process. This social neglect of the side of man's reflective thinking, when the creative process is most free, seems poor education.

10

THE "HIGH" DREAM: A NEW STATE OF CONSCIOUSNESS

CHARLES T. TART

People have generally regarded a dream occurring at night as a unitary phenomenon: a dream is a dream is a dream.... Close questioning of people about the formal nature (as opposed to the particular content) of their dreams will reveal many differences between one person's dreams and another's. For example, we have always known some people dream in color while others never report color. This fact of individual differences suggests that there might be not only *quantitative* differences among various dreams of the same individual (such as in intensity of imagery, affect, feeling of control, etc.) but perhaps *qualitative* differences, i.e., that there may in fact be several psychologically and experientially distinct phenomena that have been indiscriminately lumped together under the term "dream."

Modern laboratory studies of sleep and dreaming have now indicated there are at least two distinct types of mental activity occurring during sleep, one associated with a stage 1 EEG pattern and the other associated with a stage 2, 3, or 4 EEG (Foulkes, 1962, 1964; Goodenough, Lewis, Shapiro, Jaret, & Sleser, 1965; Monroe, Rechtschaffen, Foulkes, & Jensen, 1965; Rechtschaffen, Verdone, & Wheaton, 1963). The stage 1 mental activity has the characteristics we usually associate with dreaming: vivid visual imagery, being located at some distant place, interacting with other

By permission of the author.

characters, intense emotions, lack of recognition that one is actually lying in bed asleep, etc. The mental activity in the other stages of sleep is thought-like, and has little or no visual imagery. Typical reports are on the order of "I was wondering what to buy at the store tomorrow." Further, non-stage 1 mental activity seems such less likely to be recalled by most subjects.

An even more interesting type of dream has been occasionally reported (Arnold-Forster, 1921; van Eeden, 1913, 1918) by introspective writers, which van Eeden called the "lucid" dream. This has the unusual characteristic that the dreamer "wakes" from an ordinary dream in that he feels he is suddenly in possession of his normal waking consciousness and knows that he is actually lying in bed asleep: *but*, the dream world he is in remains perfectly real. What stage of sleep this lucid dream might be associated with is unknown. There are occasional references to learning how to produce this sort of dream as a dream yoga, leading to liberation (Narayana, 1922; Chang, 1963), but other than that almost nothing is known about it. I have had a lucid dream about three times in my life, during the past ten years, and so can testify to its experiential reality. Each time it occurred from a normal dream: for a few seconds my state of consciousness would shift to a "full waking" state in which I seemed possessed of all my normal mental faculties, yet the dream world stayed perfectly real and I was experientially located "in" it. At the same time, I had to maintain a curious sort of mental "balance of activation" which I cannot describe adequately. If I pushed the activation too high I would actually wake up; if I didn't keep it high enough I would slip back into ordinary dream consciousness. I could not maintain the right balance for more than about half a minute on each occasion.

It appears then that there are at least three distinct types of mental activity that occur during sleep: "dreaming," associated with a stage 1 EEG pattern, "sleep thinking," associated with a stage 2, 3, or 4 pattern,* and the "lucid dream."

I would now like to describe what may be a fourth type of dreaming activity, which I shall term the "high dream."† I have had this type of

---

*I have noticed rational, thought-like activity in my dreams as a sort of background to the attention-attracting sensory and emotional action of ordinary dreaming on occasion, so it may be that "sleep thought" occurs continuously during sleep and is simply masked by the much more vivid activity of stage 1 dreaming.

†I use the popular term "high" rather than the more neutral term "psychedelic" to describe this type of dream for two reasons. First, the term "high" implies a positive, valued experience rather than a neutral one and this is true about the high dream. Second, the term "psychedelic" is currently being used in such loose and sloppy ways as to have lost much of its descriptive value.

dream about a dozen times in the past few years, subsequent to personal experience with psychedelic chemicals, although usually not in close temporal proximity to a psychedelic experience. This experience is a distinct shift to a new type of consciousness within the dream state, like being "high" on a psychedelic chemical, although not exactly the same. I have talked to many people who have had chemical psychedelic experiences but found only a few of them also noting high dreams. I will present a few dreams (mine and others) below to illustrate the phenomena before attempting a formal definition. All of these dreams are from people who have had many years interest in their dreams and so were good observers of dream processes, as well as having had chemically induced psychedelic experiences.

My first dream of this sort occurred several hours after the end of an LSD-25 session (dosage of 175 μg), so there was probably still some chemical activity occurring, although I had felt almost completely normal on going to bed. Several hours after falling asleep I found myself in a condition that was not sleep, dreaming, or waking. In it I was holding on to a gestalt concept of my waking personality, and with this nebulously articulated concept as a constant background I was examining statements about personality characteristics: slow to anger, high interest in outdoors, etc. Each concept would be examined and, if acceptable, "programmed" into the waking personality that would emerge on the morrow. If unacceptable the statement was thrown away rather than being programmed. Exactly what this programming operation was was clear in this high dream, but could not be recalled clearly on waking. Like many psychedelic experiences, the memory cannot be re-experienced in ordinary consciousness.

A high dream from a psychologist acquaintance goes as follows:

I was standing in the countryside talking with a friend of mine, Bill. In the dream he had recently returned from San Francisco, and he told me that he had obtained a new psychedelic drug there. He gave me a small white pill and we took the pills together. . . . Shortly after swallowing the pill I began to feel the effects. I was looking at the green grass and green hills of the countryside. Slowly the green changed into lavender, then violet, then purple. Soon I was enveloped in a purple cloud. My entire body was deep purple. It was an extremely pleasant sensation. It resembled sleeping between covers of purple velvet, an experience which I had at one time in my life and which was very sensuously enjoyable. There was no difference between inner and outer sensation: I felt the purple on the inside as well as on the outside. When I awakened I remembered this experience very clearly as it was very sensual, very unique, and very pleasant. The dream differed from my usual dreams in terms of the mental processes employed: most of my dreams include a great deal of conceptual activity, but by the end of this dream I was involved in a sheer sensing function. For example, I could see purple but I did not think "I am seeing purple." I put the experience in verbal terms only upon awakening.

The primary shift in this dream is the great intensification of sensory qualities and the dropping out of ordinary intellectual activity, to the point where the dreamer no longer experiences the usual split between the knower and the known. Another dream from a young woman illustrates the great shift in sensory qualities of the high dream:

I was sitting on a large square pillow, an intense blue (pillow), or lying across it at an angle, and it was large enough so that I could do this easily. The pillow was spinning slowly and all sorts of intense colors were happening at the corners and edges. Mostly it was the feeling rather than any visual cue, a feeling of being very much with it and whole. I woke up happy to have had a little glimpse of the peace I had gone to bed seeing.

Note that the dreamer emphasized that it is not simply the sensory quality alone which distinguishes the high dream from ordinary dreams. Asked to comment further on the differences between such dreams and her ordinary dreams she wrote:

Ordinary dreams usually center around action of some sort with other characters and usually take place in an everyday world. None of this is true of high dreams. The real distinction is the state of mind which in a high dream is one which would be found with marijuana or LSD, time and perceptual distortions which, however, are only pointers for the change, which is an altered and more exclusive point of view. . . .

At this point I shall attempt a formal definition of the high dream: it is an experience occurring during sleep in which you find yourself in another world, the dream world, *and* in which you recognize *during* the dream that you are in an altered state of consciousness which is similar to (but not necessarily identical with) the high induced by a chemical psychedelic. It is important to emphasize that it is not the *content* of the dream, but *what* is dreamed about that distinguishes the high dream from the ordinary dream: one could dream of taking LSD, e.g., without the change in the mental processes that constitute the high dream, just as one can dream of waking up without it being a lucid dream. This is a rough definition, but a more precise definition will not be possible until much more is known about the high dream.* It is quite possible that there may be several distinct types of high dreams also, just as there seem to be some differences in chemically

*I am collecting accounts of high dreams for research, and would appreciate hearing from readers who have had this experience. Such accounts of your high dream(s) are confidential and for research purposes. I would also appreciate information on your ordinary dreams and your experience with psychedelic chemicals.

produced highs which are a function of the particular chemical substance used (as well as set and setting).

Here is another high dream from a young woman, in which there is a clear progression from ordinary dreaming consciousness to the perceptual changes that occur with getting high and on to some characteristics specifically associated with being high.

(a) Someone had brought a tremendous amount of LSD into town and had been dispensing it freely. The cops were frustrated because they couldn't arrest everyone and they didn't know who to pin it on. In dispensing this there seemed to be a spirit of free giving and there were no strangers. Someone said to me that if you took the LSD with fish the way the Indians (American) do, it wouldn't make you sick, but if you took it medically, it might. I took some by itself, but I knew it wouldn't make me sick anyway. I continued walking, and noticed that I wasn't wearing any clothes. The other people in town were dressed, but my unclothed state didn't seem to bother them. I went into a room where there were a lot of young people, and also a man I know who is associated with young people as a teacher and counselor. (b) As I went in the whole room seemed to radiate life and color. The man was sitting on one end of a couch which was covered with a serape. The colors of the serape blended and moved in a free flowing maze. I went over and lay down on the couch with my head in the man's lap. He started stroking my hair as I looked up at the light. The light was shimmering with rainbow colors and seemed very close. (c) As I lay there looking up I felt the presence of all those in the room moving into my body as definite, discernible individual vibrations. I felt these vibrations in every cell of my body and I was raised to a state of ecstasy.

The dreamer then awoke and felt very ecstatic for several minutes before falling asleep again.

Part 1 of the dream seems to be ordinary dream consciousness: the dreamer confused her knowledge of LSD with that pertaining to peyote (more likely to cause nausea) and added a fantasy about taking it with fish to avoid nausea. She calmly accepts her nakedness in a town of normally clothed people. This is an acceptance of incongruities typical of ordinary dream consciousness. She dreams of taking LSD and then the ordinary dream continues for a while as she walks around. In the second part she knows the LSD has taken effect as sensory intensifications begins, and by the time the dream reaches part 3 she is experiencing a type of contact with the other dream characters that is often reported with real LSD experiences.

Note also that the dreamer reported feeling ecstatic for several minutes after awakening: this fascinating possibility, that some sort of high state of consciousness can be carried over from dream to waking, is illustrated by the following dream from a male:

I dreamed I got high on some sort of gaseous substance, like LSD in gas form. Space took on an expanded, high quality, my body (dream body) was filled with a delicious sensation of warmth, my mind "high" in an obvious but indescribable way. It only lasted a minute and then I was awakened by one of the kids calling out and my wife getting up to see what was the matter. Then the most amazing thing happened: I stayed high even though awake! It had a sleepy quality to it but the expanded and warm quality of time and space carried over into my perception of the (dimly lit) room. It stayed this way for a couple of minutes, amazing me at the time because I was clearly high, as well as recalling my high dream. Then I drifted back into sleep as my wife returned to bed. I think I slipped into a high dream state for a minute or two but can't recall clearly, as I fell asleep. . . . It was definitely a high condition, although not quite the same as an LSD high: I can't explain the difference. This high state was clearly different from ordinary dream consciousness, ordinary waking consciousness, and "ordinary" highs, and the high state itself was unchanged by the transition from dream to waking.

Thus we may not only have a pronounced shift in mental functioning during the dream state, but such a shift can carry over to a subsequent waking state.

Little more can be said about the high dream at this point: the examples presented above comprise almost my entire collection of them, and are from only a few individuals. How frequently does the high dream occur? Can all the characteristics of chemically induced highs be reproduced in it? Are there phenomena that do not occur in chemically induced highs? The high dream exists as a distinct entity from ordinary dreams in at least a few individualists,* but other questions about it cannot be answered until (a) many spontaneous high dreams are collected for analysis, or (b) we learn to produce high dreams at will for study.† The primary purpose of this paper has been to call others' attention to the existence of the high dream with the hope that this will spur investigation of this fascinating state of consciousness.

---

*With a large enough collection of dreams from single individuals, it might turn out that there were hitherto unobserved transitional dream forms between ordinary dreaming and the high dream.

†High dreams might be produced by administrations of psychedelic chemicals before or during sleep, or with the aid of psychological methods which affect dreaming, such as posthypnotic suggestion (Tart, 1965, 1966, and in press). The few published studies of the effect of LSD-25 on dreaming have been concerned with effects on sleep cycle variables in animals (Hobson, 1964) and time spent in stage 1 dreaming in man (Green, 1965; Kramer, Whitman, Baldridge, & Ornstein, 1966; Muzio, Roffwarg, & Kaufman, 1966), so dream content and psychological processes in dreams as affected by psychedelics is still an unknown area.

INTRODUCTION TO SECTION 4.
MEDITATION

Meditation is a practice that has been praised by a small, but highly vocal, portion of humanity all through recorded history, with its extolled virtues ranging from a way of achieving happiness and peace in everyday life to escaping the limitations of the human condition and attaining a mystical union with the Divine. One would expect that such a venerable practice would have been thoroughly studied by psychology, especially because of its mental health implications, but this is far from the case. The most popular and authoritative dictionary for psychological terms (English & English, 1958) defines meditation (quite inadequately) as simple serious thought, as does a standard English language dictionary (Webster, 1956). The latest dictionary of psychiatric terms (Hinsie & Campbell, 1960), although filled with definitions of rare and exotic mental processes, does not even list meditation. A glance through the indices of several current introductory psychology texts reveals no mention of meditation.

We have a great deal of nonscientific writing about meditation: how to do it, how it works, what effects it produces, etc. Most of these writings come from specific religious orientations, but certain universals can be gleaned from this literature, as the selections in this section illustrate. Our scientific knowledge of meditation, however, is virtually nil. This small section contains two-thirds of the published, English language experimental work, which sounds like a large amount of material until one realizes that there are only three published studies. Deikman's paper on "De-automatization and the Mystic Experience" (Chapter 2) is relevant, as well as his other experimental and theoretical article (Deikman, 1966). Thus this area is wide

open for experimental study. The dramatic nature of the effects obtaine
with ordinary subjects practicing meditation exercises,* as these paper
reveal, promises great yields for systematic investigation.

It seems likely that research in this area has been too long delayed throug
a combination of ignorance and prejudice. Scientists in general simply hav
not known anything about the rich tradition of meditation, and the intimat
connection of meditation practices with religion has further removed i
from the area of "acceptable" topics of study. The word is often use
with a negative value connotation in everyday speech, implying fuzzy day
dreaming or too much introversion. As the papers in this section point out
meditation can be viewed and studied with an areligious orientation; it i
not necessarily connected with mystical experiences. Although prediction i
premature, the potential contributions of the experimental study of medita
tion to such diverse areas as perceptual vigilance, psychotherapy, an
creativity, in both a theoretical and practical sense, warrant a greatl
expanded research effort.

Meditation has often been shallowly dismissed in the scientific literatur
by calling it "self-hypnosis" and then promptly forgetting about it. Ou
knowledge of the actual relationship between hypnotic states and meditativ
states is completely speculative rather than empirical at this time.

The section opens with an article by Edward Maupin, "On Meditation,"
which presents a number of practical techniques for meditating: in th
present state of our knowledge, any serious investigator of meditation mus
practice it himself to get an immediate "feeling" for it. Following this ar
two experimental studies. Chapter 12, by Edward Maupin, "Individua
Differences in Response to a Zen Meditation Exercise," is in the nature o
responses to a Zen meditation exercise and some of the personality variable
affecting this response. Chapter 13, by Authur Deikman, "Experimenta
Meditation," is on the phenomenology of responses to meditation and som
of its implications. Finally Chapter 14, by Wolfgang Kretschmer, "Meditative Techniques in Psychotherapy," illustrates some of the practical applications of meditation and related techniques to psychotherapy, applications
that can be based on much more solid ground when our basic knowledge o
meditation is expanded by research. Assagioli's (1965) system of psychosynthesis also makes use of meditative techniques in psychotherapy and
is must reading for the therapist interested in this area.

For further reading on meditation I recommend Noyes (1965), Reps
(1961), Suzuki (1959), and Underhill (1955), as well as the works cited in
these papers. Kamiya's paper (Chapter 35) is also quite relevant.

*John Heider (personal communication, 1967), in some as-yet-unpublished re-
search has confirmed Deikman's and Maupin's findings that strong effects can
result from short periods of meditation with ordinary Ss.

11

ON MEDITATION

EDWARD W. MAUPIN

Historically our Western culture appears to have been preoccupied with action. Our training has emphasized making and doing and controlling. With us the individualized and self-conscious self has been developed very carefully.

There has been a counter-tendency in the culture to turn to internal and spiritual concerns. Prayer, fasting, some varieties of psychotherapy, and now psychedelic drugs have been used to open up another aspect of the world. In contrast to the active, *doing* mode of the relation to the "external" world, this "internal" world ordinarily requires a passive, receptive attitude on the part of the experiencing person. Meditation is a classical way of developing the receptive attitude. It is practice in the skill of being quiet and paying attention.

Meditation has been used in the Western sects of Christianity. Roman Catholicism appears to have articulated a psychology, or map, of what happens with meditation. The conscious exercise of attention leads to a spontaneous flow of experience to which the person becomes a receptive onlooker. At its extreme, the feeling of a separate self is lost and union with the object of meditation is felt. This state is called contemplation. My impression is that, in practice, the meditative exercises in Catholicism have been oriented to specific content. In one manual, for example, the reader is led to imagine what Christ or Mary or various saints were experiencing at crucial points in their careers. I have no information about how effective this "discursive" meditation might be. The practices covered in this paper are not oriented toward specific content, but toward the more general problem of becoming open and aware of one's experience. Another meditation tradition within Christianity, that of silent prayer, is probably closer to this kind of content-less meditation. Especially in Quaker congregations the emphasis is on waiting and listening.

In general many of the traditions of prayer and meditation within Christianity have consisted of a kind of blabbing at God or some apart from-nature being about which one has all sorts of preconceived ideas. The present Western interest in meditation tends to be directed toward Eastern forms of practice, where there is a radical commitment to experiencing what one experiences—even God. Oriental rejection of verbal and conceptual substitutes for experience seems to appeal to our own growing investment in living experience.

The deepest objections to meditation have been raised against its tendency to produce withdrawn, serene people who are not accessible to what is actually going on in their lives. This is certainly a possible outcome. It has been very prominent in the history of Indian mysticism. (Although some observers feel that this was a reaction to the crushing defeats of the Moslem and British invasions of India. The earlier Hindu mysticism was not so other-worldly. In Japan, of course, the Zen-trained *samurai* were very much engaged in practical affairs.)

Krishnamurti is very critical of meditation. He attacks "special" cross-legged meditation practices on grounds that the meditative attitude must be directed toward the whole of one's living, not invested in precious, encapsulated practices (1966). Fritz Perls is, of course, even more savage in his antagonism to meditation,* even though his Gestalt Therapy (Perls, Hefferline, & Goodman, 1951) is very similar to meditations which attempt to observe the flow of experience in the here-and-now. He criticizes catatonic-like withdrawal and coercive interference with the spontaneous flow of one's life.

These are serious objections. The primary problem seems to be that people who engage in practices designed to produce personal growth tend to split these practices off from the rest of their lives. True growth must take place in ordinary living. It happens in psychotherapy, where what happens in the analyst's office is somehow of a different order, split off and more important than the more mundane remainder of life. Christianity has a strong historical tendency to split God from the apparent world. The Christian has tended to feel that his real growth has less to do with how he deals with his moment-to-moment living than with special and apart procedures. Within this model, the secluded monk who can devote full time to prayer is the person who is felt to be grappling with what is most real.

---

*Personal communication, 1966.

Bonhoeffer (1953) and Teilhard de Chardin (1960) are both explicitly concerned with this split. Both emphasize that the apparent life *is* the arena of growth, or, in their terms, of realizing God. The same split seems to occur in the LSD culture, where the insights afforded by the drug often profoundly alter the taker's beliefs about ultimate reality. But the experience of the drug is behind a curtain, so identified with the drug that the task of realizing the same reality in ordinary life tends to be ignored. There are very important exceptions to this.

Allied to this split is another, even more subtly potent one between "internal" and "external" experience. As a culture we are so inclined to overdraw this distinction that it is difficult to discuss alternatives. We have tended to place great importance on what is "objective," observable by other people, in contrast to what is "subjective," subject to our own "distortions." This overlooks how totally our experience of the world is molded by the observer, his present states and the arbitrary filters of his upbringing. With meditation it is easy to overvalue the internal at the expense of the external so that they remain split apart. It is possible, though, to use it to awaken the subjective life in contact with the external world. Then, rather than a secret closet, the internal becomes a huge space of many dimensions joined with the external world and adding meaning and richness to it. In this paper several meditations on external objects or other people are described. They seem to be particularly direct ways of bringing the meditative attitude into contact.

Admitting the dangers, I still feel it is worthwhile to engage in special activities directed at expanding awareness. In this paper I will outline several techniques of meditation in enough detail for the reader to try them for himself. From what is presented in the literature and from my own observations, I think meditation can bring important benefits. It is a powerful way to learn to be quiet and pay attention. The special combination of suspended action and waking attention make it possible to become aware of small cues. Calm, greater ability to cope with tense situations, and improved sleep are frequently reported. Better body functioning seems to result (Sato, 1958), and the pattern of psychosomatic benefits closely follows the well-researched effects of relaxation procedures such as Autogenic Training (Schultz & Luthe, 1959). A more solid feeling of oneself often seems to result, ("oneself" including both "body" and "mind") and, with that, more direct awareness of what one is experiencing. One Japanese psychiatrist reports that when his patients meditate in addition to their sessions with him, they seem to have more energy for constructive work on their problems (Kondo, 1958).

GENERAL PRINCIPLES

Meditation is first of all a deep passivity, combined with awareness. It is not necessary to have a mystical rationale to practice meditation, but there are marked similarities in the psychological assumptions which underlie most approaches. The ego, or conscious self, is usually felt to be only a portion of the real self. The conscious, striving, busy attempts to maintain and defend myself are based on a partial and misleading concept of my vulnerability, my needs, and the deeper nature of reality. In meditation I suspend this busy activity and assume a passive attitude. What I am passive *to* is conceived in many different ways, but I need only assume that deeper resources are available when I suspend my activity. Instead of diffusing myself in a welter of thoughts and actions, I can turn back on myself and direct my attention upstream to the out-pouring, spontaneous, unpredictable flow of my experience, to the states of mind which produce all the busyness and thinking. It is well at this point to distinguish the practice of meditation from special experiences of mystical union or *satori*. These dramatic states have probably been overemphasized in the meditation literature. Meditation may be worthwhile in itself without such states, which are unlikely to come about without prolonged practice under skilled supervision.

The position used in meditation is important. It should be such that you can let go and relax in it, yet not fall asleep. The relaxation is not the totally heavy kind you get when you lie down, but balanced and consistent with alertness. In Asia the cross-legged lotus positions are ordinarily used. If you want to try, sit on the floor and cross your legs so that your right foot rests on your left thigh and your left foot rests on the right thigh. This is very difficult to do. You might try the slightly easier procedure of getting only one foot on one thigh and crossing the other leg so that it is underneath the opposite thigh close to the buttock (the half-lotus position), or simply sit tailor fashion. In all three positions your rump should be raised by means of cushions so that knees and buttocks form a stable three-cornered base. Now see if you can let your back rest down into this base in such a way that it is a straight column which requires no strain to keep straight. The hands rest in the lap; the head is erect; the eyes should be open and directed without focussing at a point a few feet ahead of the knees. (All this is following Zen procedure most closely. Yoga practice usually omits the cushion and permits closing the eyes—which leads more easily into trances than to wakeful awareness.)

The cross-legged positions are not essential. You can meditate effectively in a straight-backed chair with your feet planted wide apart and flat on the floor, your back straight, head erect, and eyes open as before. The most comfortable height should be adjusted with cushions. A less erect posture in an ordinary easy chair can also be used.

After you get into position, sway back and forth for a while to settle in, take a few deep breaths, and begin to let go. You may find it useful to contact various parts of your body with your attention, especially your base, the legs and pelvis on which you are resting. Now you are ready to begin directing your attention according to the technique you have decided to use.

The techniques presented are fairly simple ones, classically used in the early stages of training. You may wish to experiment with more than one to find which is the most effective for you. They are all suitable for daily use for between a half hour and an hour. Although they are apparently different, they all seem to aim at increasing awareness of what is happening inside and making possible a detached look. It is extremely misleading to strive toward any particular state of mind, but all of these exercises will sometimes make possible a state of clear, relaxed awareness in which the flow of thought is reduced and an attitude of detached observation is maintained. In contrast with the usual thinking activity, which carries one off into abstractions or fantasies, this observing attitude keeps close contact with the here-and-now of experience. Thoughts are not prevented, but are allowed to pass without elaboration. It is not a blank state or trance, and it is different from sleep. It involves deep physical relaxation as well as letting go of the usual psychological busy-ness. Actually, one discovers very early how closely psychological and physical relaxation are related.

How you handle distractions is extremely important. Do not try to prevent them. Just patiently bring your attention back again and again to the object of your meditation. This detaching from fantasies and thoughts and outside stimuli is some of the most important work of meditation. If you attempt to prevent distractions in some other way, you may get into unproductive blank states, or get distracted by the task of preventing distractions, or become tense. If you patiently return to the meditation, gradually your attention to the object will replace the distractions, and your physical relaxation will make it possible for the flow of thoughts to decrease.

It is also very important that you not have some preconceived notion of what *should* happen in a "good" session. You may become relaxed and clear, but you may also remain tense and distracted, or you may uncover extremely painful kinds of experience. Allowing yourself to be honestly aware of whatever you experience is more constructive than the most pleasant relaxation. Accepting the session wherever it leads is essential. You may feel sleepy. Try observing the process of falling asleep itself— perhaps it is a response to some feeling you want to avoid. If sleep continues to be a problem, get up and walk around and breathe deeply for a while. You may feel bored and restless with the task. Observe and experience these feelings. In this culture you may well find yourself taking a negative attitude, beating yourself over the head, as it were, to do a good job of meditating. Try to observe this self-critical, hostile attitude in yourself. There is a kind of friendly neutrality you can bring to bear on any experience which emerges.

As the ego activity is reduced, inner material, some of it formerly outside awareness, begins to emerge. Herrigel writes:

> This exquisite state of unconcerned immersion in oneself is not, unfortunately, of long duration. It is likely to be disturbed from inside. As though sprung from nowhere, moods, feelings, desires, worries and even thoughts incontinently rise up, in a meaningless jumble.... The only successful way of rendering this disturbance inoperative is to ... enter into friendly relations with whatever appears on the scene, to accustom oneself to it, to look at it equably and at last grow weary of looking [1953, pp. 57–58].

This is one reason why you should probably be supervised if you want to practice meditating more than an hour at a time. With more time the emerging material may become more dense and impelling, more difficult to treat as an illusory distraction. Supposedly it was a Zen student in Japan who burned down the golden pavilion on grounds it was so beautiful that all it lacked was transience. The emerging material may change form, become predominantly visual imagery in contrast to the verbal form of the earlier distractions, and so on. However, it is not necessary to be *too* cautious about this material. My psychotherapy patients, when they have meditated at home, have had no special difficulty in treating their distractions as distractions. All that is required is to observe them and return to the meditation.

SPECIFIC EXCERCISES

The first group of meditation techniques focuses on the body or on breathing.

A Taoist meditation described by Rousselle (1960), directs that attention be placed in the center of the torso at about the level of the navel. Thoughts, when they arise, should be "placed" in this center of the body, as if they arose there. "Consciousness, by an act of the imagination, is shifted to the solar plexus." This procedure especially helps to promote a feeling of vitality and strength from the belly.

Breathing is a function which may be either voluntarily or involuntarily controlled. To meditate on breathing, then, is to deal with how you allow your spontaneity to flow. It is important not to force the issue, though. If you cannot allow your breathing to become fully involuntary, just observe how you *do* handle it, or move on to another exercise. The simplest breath meditation is as follows:

Sit with a straight back and relax. Let your breathing become relaxed and natural, so that the movement is mainly in the abdomen. Then keep your attention on this movement.

Wienpahl (1964) gives excellent instructions for breath concentration as used in his Japanese Zen training:

Breathe through the nose. Inhale as much as you require, letting the air come in by distending the diaphragm. Do not draw it in, rather let it come to you. Then exhale slowly. Exhale completely, getting all of the air out of your lungs. As you exhale slowly count "one". Now inhale again. Then exhale slowly to the count of "two". And so on up to "ten". Then repeat....

You will find this counting difficult as your mind will wander from it. However, keep at it, striving to bring your mind back to the process of counting. As you become able to do this with reasonable success, start playing the following game with the counting. As you count "one" and are slowly exhaling, pretend that this "one" is going down, down, down into your stomach. Then think of its being down there as you inhale and begin to count "two". Bring the "two" down and place it (in your imagination, one might say) in your stomach beside the "one"....
Eventually you will find that your mind itself, so to speak, will descend into your stomach.

The shift of attention down to the lower part of the body, the pelvis or the abdomen, is accompanied by a relaxation in which thoughts seem slow and distant. Preliminary evidence from several sources suggests that brain-wave recordings show an increase of slow, high amplitude (alpha) activity in subjects using these types of techniques (Chapter 33).

Another group of meditative exercises focuses the attention directly on the contents of consciousness. For example, Chaudhuri, drawing on yoga practice, writes:

The radical approach begins with the resolve to do nothing, to think nothing, to make no effort of one's own, to relax completely and let go one's mind and body ... stepping out of the stream of everchanging ideas and feelings which your mind is, watch the onrush of the stream. Refuse to be submerged in the current. Changing the metaphor, it may be said, watch your ideas, feelings and wishes fly across the mental firmament like a flock of birds. Let them fly freely. Just keep a watch. Don't allow the birds to carry you off into the clouds. (1965, pp. 30–31)

Another method is to focus attention, not on the thought activity, but on the state of mind which lies behind the thoughts. This was the exercise which first excited me about meditation:

Benoit (1959) suggests that attention be kept on the feeling of physical and personal existence from moment to moment—to what I scan when someone asks me "how are you?" At first this contact is only momentary. As soon as words try to describe it, the feeling of what it is like to be me at this instant is lost. Gradually it becomes possible to prolong the contact. "This inward glance . . . is that which I make towards the center of my whole being when I reply to the question: 'How are you feeling at this moment from every point at the same time?'" It is relaxing to make this move, and it promotes detachment, because you move upstream from the thoughts, fantasies and excited involvement to the states of mind which produce them.

A variant of this is to ask who is doing this thinking, feeling, acting. Brunton writes:

First watch your own intellect in its working. Note how thoughts follow one another in endless sequence. Then try to realize that there is someone who thinks. Now ask: "Who is this thinker?" (1935, p. 56)

Writing about a similar exercise used in Chinese Ch'an (Zen) Buddhism, Luk (1960) adds, "As mind is intangible, one is not clear about it. Consequently some slight feeling of doubt should be cultivated and maintained."

The same kind of attention with which one meditates on breathing can be directed to outside objects. Arthur Deikman, in a psychoanalytic study of meditation (Chapter 2), had his experimental subjects meditate on a small blue vase: The instructions were as follows:

Your aim is to concentrate on the blue vase. By concentration I do not mean *analyzing* the different parts of the vase, or thinking a series of thoughts about the vase, or associating ideas to the vase, but rather, *trying to see the vase as it exists in itself*, without any connections to other things. Exclude all other thoughts or feelings or body sensations. Do not let them distract you but keep them out so that you can concentrate all your attention, all your awareness on the vase itself. Let the perception of the vase fill your entire mind.

Another person may be encountered and received in the same way:

Place yourself face to face with another person. Look at him and be aware when your mind wanders. Be aware when you treat his face like an object, a design, or play perceptual games with it. Distortions may appear which tell you what you project into the relationship: angels, devils, animals and all the human possibilities may appear in his face. Eventually you may move past these visual fantasies into the genuine presence of another human being.

The meditative attitude can also be brought into sexual encounter. Use an intercourse position in which you can look at your partner and in which you can comfortably lie motionless for a long time. This exercise could probably be practiced for more than an hour at a time without supervision.

There are many other kinds of meditative exercises which have not been covered here. Once the student has learned generally how to settle into meditation many schools bring in more complex techniques. Tantric yoga introduces visual imagery, contemplation of symbols and concentration on parts of the body. Comprehensive surveys are given by Govinda (1959) and Zimmer (1960). The aim seems to be a systematic exploration of deeply unconscious, prelogical, archetypal experience. Kundalini yoga combines certain breathing patterns with concentration on nerve plexi in the pelvis, the abdomen, chest, throat, neck and head (Aurobindo, 1955; Behanan, 1937; Garrison, 1964; Woodroffe, 1931; Yeats-Brown, 1958). Each of these sites yields different universes of feeling and fear which can systematically be worked through. In some sects of Zen Buddhism paradoxical statements are introduced for meditation. For example:

The sixth Patriarch said to the monk, Emyo, "Think neither of the good nor the evil, but tell me what are your original features before your parents gave birth to you?" (Ogata, 1959)

These *koans* are not to be understood with ordinary logic. One must penetrate to the state of mind which they express. Usually a graded series of *koans* is used which focuses the student's mind toward *satori* and gives the Zen master a means of judging the progress of his student. All of these more advanced meditations require supervision.

*   *   *

This paper is intended as an introduction for someone who wants to begin to meditate. Gary Snyder, who has spent several years in Zen training in Japan, has written a poem which may be reassuring to those who wish to try:

What I Think When I Meditate

Well, I could tell you that I could tell
    you but wouldn't understand but I won't
You'd understand but I can't, I mean dig,
        this here guitar is gone bust
        I hate to sit crosslegged
my knees hurt my nose runs and I have to go
            to the crapper
tootsweet and damn that timeclock keeper won't ding.
WHAT I think about when I meditate is emptiness.
            I remember it well
the empty heads   the firecracker phhht
But what I *really* think about is sex
            sort of patterns of sex
like dancing hairs and goosebumps
            No, honestly

what I think about is what am I thinking about?
                    and
who am I? and 'MU?' and 'the clouds
                              on
          the
                southern mt'
Well: what I really honestly think about, no fooling . . . (etc.)

(from *Ark III*)

12

INDIVIDUAL DIFFERENCES IN RESPONSE TO A ZEN MEDITATION EXERCISE

EDWARD W. MAUPIN

In a previous paper (Maupin, 1962) the literature in English was surveyed in an attempt to extract a coherent picture of Zen Buddhism, its training procedures, and the psychological experiences which result. It was noted that the training seems analogous in some respects to Western insight-oriented psychotherapy. Moreover, the responses to training described in the literature seemed partly interpretable in terms of concepts of ego function which are subject to quantitative measurement. The present study was designed to obtain basic information about the meditation process by correlating differences in the meditation experience with psychological tests of relevant ego functions. Although the nature of the meditation process rather than its therapeutic merits was the subject of investigation, the information developed may be basic to later therapeutic studies.

ZEN BUDDHISM

Zen, a sect of Mahayana Buddhism, originated in China and has played an important role in Japanese culture since its introduction there in the

Reprinted by permission from *J. Consult. Psychol.*, Vol. 29, 1965, pp. 139–145.

thirteenth century. A variety of training techniques are employed by the Zen master to guide the student to a turning point, *satori*, which appears to be a major shift in the mode of experiencing oneself and the world.

The specific training procedures used are extremely variable, but certain generalizations are possible. The beginning student spends a portion of the day sitting motionless and engaging in concentration. The object of concentration varies and may be changed as the student progresses. The aim of the practice is to suspend the ordinary flow of thoughts without falling into a stupor. Usually there is an initial phase in which concentration is extremely difficult. With greater success, relaxation and a kind of pleasant "self-immersion" follow. At this point internal distractions, often of an anxiety-arousing kind, come to the fore. Herrigel (1953) indicates that the only way to render this disturbance inoperative is to "look at it equally and at last grow weary of looking." Eventually another phase begins, in which concentration is accompanied by a sense of calm stillness, a sense of energy and vitality, and a feeling of invulnerability. This state of mind is traditionally described with the analogy of a mirror, which reflects many things yet is itself unchanged by them. Much of this is reminiscent of the stance taken by the psychoanalytic patient, who experiences his associations as derivatives of his own mental processes regardless of the reality of the objects represented. An observing attitude can be maintained until anxiety or other affect become too intense. One difference has been pointed out by Sato (1958) who notes that the Zen student, unlike the analysand, does not dissect what he is experiencing with ideational operations. The ideas, if they appear, need not be grasped or verbalized. This writer has suggested that Zen meditation procedures, just because they are nonlogical and nonverbal, may enable one to deal with certain problems which are inaccessible to verbal communication—for example, problems hinging on pre-Oedipal experience antedating the development of language and logical structure.

To our knowledge, long-term alterations in personality factors as a result of Zen training have not been systematically observed, although meditation in conjunction with psychoanalysis has facilitated therapeutic progress in some instances (Fromm, 1959; Kondo, 1958). Conversely, individual variations in response to meditation training have not been studied with respect to their dependence on personality factors or ego functions. It is the latter problem with which the present study is concerned. Personality factors are considered the independent variables of the study; response to meditation is the dependent variable.

METHODS AND PROCEDURES

The strategy of the present study is this: if a specific function, such as attention, is important in the meditation process, then individuals who are relatively efficient in this function will tend to meditate more successfully and hence respond more extensively during the first few weeks of practice. The importance of various functions in determining response to meditation can then be judged by correlating response to meditation with appropriate measures of these functions. This section describes the subjects who participated in the experiment, the meditation exercise and the procedure for scaling response, and finally the procedures for assessing relevant personality functions.

Sample

Male subjects were recruited by means of an advertisement in the campus newspaper offering instruction in a Zen meditation exercise to persons interested enough to spend additional time taking tests. Thirty-nine men responded and were seen for an initial interview. A series of psychological tests was given in later appointments, after which the meditation sessions were begun. Eleven of the 39 subjects dropped out either before the meditation sessions began or before completing enough sessions to permit a good estimate of response. The remaining 28 subjects, all of whom completed at least nine meditation sessions, were included in the sample.

As might be expected, many of the subjects appeared to have a therapy-seeking motivation. They evidently felt enough subjective discomfort to look, sometimes explicitly, for new ways of dealing with personal problems. (Overt psychosis was not encountered, and no subject presented any other symptoms which seemed grounds for exclusion.) In other ways, too, the sample seemed atypical of the general college male population. The rater, who had scored Rorschach protocols for several other studies, commented on the unusually high incidence of primary-process responses to the test in this sample. It is not clear that any of the biases operating in the sample would have a consistent effect on the relationships between experimental measures. The generally high level of motivation to carry out the meditation instructions, while unusual, should facilitate better understanding of the meditation process. With regard to prior knowledge of Zen, some subjects had read the popular works on the subject, but the extent of their reading had no relationship with their response to the exercises.

Meditation Exercise

The meditation exercise used in this study required concentration on the breathing as described by Kondo (1958). The 45-minute practice sessions, followed by short interviews, were conducted each weekday for a two-week period. Before the first sessions, the subject was shown the correct sitting position—back straight, not resting on the chair back, feet flat on the floor—and given the following instructions:

While you are sitting let your breathing become relaxed and natural. Let it set its own pace and depth if you can. Then focus your attention on your breathing: the movements of your belly, not your nose or throat. Do not allow extraneous thoughts or stimuli to pull your attention away from the breathing. This may be hard to do at first, but keep directing your attention back to it. Turn everything else aside if it comes up.

You may also find yourself becoming anxious or uncomfortable. This is because sitting still and concentrating like this restricts the ordinary ways of avoiding discomfort. If you have to feel uncomfortable, feel uncomfortable. If you feel pleasant, accept that with the same indifference. Gradually, perhaps not today or even after several days, it will grow easier for you to concentrate. I will come and tell you when the time is up. Do you have any questions?

These instructions were repeated before the second session. At subsequent sessions the subject entered the experimental room, adjusted the chair height with firm cushions, and began concentrating without comment. The practice room was dimly lit and sparsely furnished. Two chairs were arranged so that subjects could not see one another but faced an unadorned wall. The experimenter remained in an adjacent room while one or a pair of subjects practiced the breathing exercise. If someone asked what was supposed to happen as a result of the practice, he was told:

I cannot tell you that, mainly because I don't know that much about you. Whatever happens will come from within you. It is better not to be distracted by preconceived ideas about it. The important thing is to accept whatever happens. Don't move, and keep your attention on your breathing.

After each session the interview was initiated with the question, "How did it go?" Further questions by the experimenter were limited to asking for clarification and for an estimate of the degree of concentration. These interviews were recorded verbatim and serve as the basis for scaling response.

PROCEDURE FOR SCALING RESPONSE TO MEDITATION

Frequently, especially after the early meditation sessions, subjects simply reported difficulty in concentrating, and their remarks indicated that little else had happened. Most subjects, however, proceeded beyond this point, reporting a variety of experiences in later sessions more or less comparable to those described in Zen literature. For purposes of scaling, five responses patterns were distinguished which appeared to recur in the protocols. The description of these patterns, as submitted to the raters, is as follows:

Type A. The identifying characteristic of these sessions is dizziness, some type of "befogged" consciousness, which occurs when a subject begins to concentrate. Typically, subjects report feeling dizzy or having sensations "like going under anesthetic" or "like being hypnotized." The experience is somewhat unpleasant, and it is common to find the subject retreating from the task of concentrating into increased thinking.

Type B. These are sessions in which the subject reports feeling quite calm and relaxed. His concentration need not have been very sustained.

Type C. In this pattern pleasant body sensations occur. They are often reminiscent of hypnotic phenomena and sometimes involve feelings which would be strange in the ordinary states of waking consciousness. They may be rather erotic-sounding as they are described. Sensations like "vibrations" or "waves" are often reported, or the subject feels his body is "suspended" or "light." Typically, concentration is somewhat more sustained that in Type A or B sessions.

Type D. The distinguishing feature of this pattern is the vivid way in which the breathing is experienced. Often the belly movements seem larger, or the subject feels "filled with air." Concentration seems almost effortless in such sessions.

Type E. This is the experience described by Herrigel (1953, pp. 56ff.) It appears to be a very lucid state of consciousness which is deeply satisfying. There is a "nonstriving" attitude, and the subject is able to take a calmly detached view of any thoughts and feelings which happen to emerge. Concentration seems to be easy and fairly complete. A frequent accompaniment of this pattern is extensive loss of body feelings.

The procedure for scaling subjects began with identifying the patterns they reported after each session. Rating was done independently by two advanced graduate students in clinical psychology who were unaware of the hypotheses of the study. The two raters agreed that 214 of the 330 session reports failed to show any of the five patterns. The remaining 116 sessions, then, were critical for identifying response. Here the judges agreed in only 54 cases, or 48%. Compared with the expectancy of chance agreement, however, this obtained agreement is significant ($X^2 = 137.4$, $df = 3$, $p < .001$).

The next step in scoring response to meditation consisted of grouping subjects according to their "highest" response in any of the first 10 sessions. Three groups were defined: a "high-response" group, consisting of subjects who reported a Type E response (detachment) at least once; a "moderate-response" group, including subjects who failed to report a Type E response, but reported a Type C or a Type D response (pleasant body sensations or vivid breathing) at least once; and a "low-response" group composed of subjects who reported nothing more than relaxation or dizziness (Types A or B). With this grosser grouping of subjects, the raters agreed on the placement of all but 3 (89%) of the 28. Table 1 presents the number of subjects assigned to each group as well as the number of subjects in each group who indicated a given pattern of response at least once. The subjects within each group are to be considered as having tied scores on a 3-point ordinal scale ranging from high to low response to meditation. Some support for the ordinal relationship is adduced from the fact that high-response subjects experienced not only the detached pattern but also reported the body alterations of the moderate-response group fairly frequently. This high group also had fewer uneventful (unscorable) sessions than the others.

PERSONALITY FACTOR APPRAISAL

Five aspects of personality functioning were considered in the study: receptive attention, concentration, breadth of attention deployment, tolerance for unrealistic experience, and capacity for adaptive regression.*

Tolerance for Unrealistic Experience

Three measures were used to assess the reaction of subjects in the face of unrealistic experience. The first is the Rorschach measure used by Klein, Gardner, and Schlesinger (1962). Tolerance on this dimension refers to acceptance of experiences which do not agree with what is known to be "true," while intolerance implies resistance to such precepts or cognitive experiences. In the Rorschach ratings, major weight was placed on the subject's attitude toward his responses rather than on formal scores. The tolerant person was characterized as one who naturally and comfortably accepted the blots as an opportunity for projection. The intolerant person, in contrast, was one who maintained a critical and cautious attitude of reality testing toward his responses.

These criteria were applied to the Rorschach records by two judges trained in the use of the system for a previous study (Lichtenstein, 1961). Records which could not be assigned by the raters to either the tolerant or the intolerant categories were placed in a "mixed" category which was interpreted as a midpoint on the scale. The judges agreed in their ratings of 19 of the 28 records. In only two instances was a record rated tolerant by

---

*Details of the attention measures used have been omitted.—*Editor.*

TABLE 1
Frequency of Response Patterns for High, Moderate, and Low Responders

Group	Number of Subjects	Pattern (Greater Response →)				
		Dizziness and Fogginess	Relaxation and Calmness	Pleasant Body Sensations	Vivid Breathing Sensations	Concentration and Detachment
High	6	0	2	3	4	6
Moderate	10	2	3	8	5	0
Low	12	6	8	0	0	0
Total	28	8	13	11	9	6

one and intolerant by the other. Computing reliability by means of the rank correlation coefficient, tau, gives .63 ($p < .001$).

The results of Klein et al. (1962) and Lichtenstein (1961) suggested a link between the tolerance dimension and the rate of alteration of reversible figures. The four figures used appeared to vary markedly in the extent to which tolerance influenced response. In the present study the Necker cube, Rubin figure-vase, and windmill and staircase figures were presented, the subject looking into an illuminated box at the figures 28 inches away. Number of reversals for each figure during the 30-second presentation plus the total number of reversals for all four figures were the scores used.

The third estimate of the subject's tolerance for unrealistic experience was the amount of autokinetic movement he reported. The median estimated movement for 20 trials was the experimental score. It was expected that subjects who are less comfortable in such an unstructured situation would give small estimates of movement.

Capacity for Adaptive Regression

During the course of meditation, the student must pass through a phase of internal distractions in order to reach the stillness of mediation. We infer that these distractions will occasionally express the drive-dominated content or organization of primary-process cognition. Furthermore, feelings such as omnipotence erupt, and the thinking function must be abandoned. Clearly, then, lowering of the level of psychic functioning is involved, and the concept of "regression in the service of the ego" may be applicable. Two measures of the ability to regress were therefore included in the present study: Holt's (Holt & Havel, 1961) scoring for primary-process thinking on the Rorschach, and visual imagery during free association.

The Rorschach scoring system is designed to identify not only the emergence of primary-process form and content but also the adequacy with which these manifestations are controlled. Goldberger (1958) related the system to capacity for regression in the service of the ego in a study of reactions to perceptual isolation. He distinguished three general modes of handling primary-process material: (a) a mode which admits such derivatives into awareness in a modulated, controlled fashion without disruption; (b) a mode which wards off the emergence of such material into awareness through defensive operations; and (c) a mode in which the person, although finding primary-process derivatives threatening, is unable to prevent their appearance in consciousness due to inadequate defenses. The Rorschach scores, rated by a clinical psychologist trained for another study, were used to identify these modes, considered to lie along a single dimension. Subjects were identified as showing a "large amount of controlled primary process" if they ranked high on amount of primary-process responses and also high on effectiveness of defense. They were considered to show a "small amount of controlled primary process" if they ranked low on "amount" and low on "effectiveness," and they showed a "large amount of poorly controlled primary process" if they ranked high on "amount" and low on "effectiveness."

Whether or not the subject tended to report spontaneous visual imagery during a short free-association task served as a second measure of capacity for adaptive regression. It was felt that the emergence of imagery represents a clear shift away from the primarily verbal thought of adults to a genetically more primitive mode of recognition. The free-association task was that used by Gardner et al. (1959). The subject is asked to report, for 3 minutes, everything that came to mind after hearing each of two stimulus words: *Dry* and *House*. Imagery (for example, "I see a picture of mud") was identified in 23 of the 56 work protocols, and each subject received 1 point for each of his 2 protocols in which imagery was identified, thus giving a 3-point scale. Average percentage of agreement between the three raters was 92.8.

Correlations between Measures

Since tolerance for unrealistic experience and capacity for adaptive regression seem to be overlapping concepts, correlations between measures of the two were calculated. The tau correlation between the Rorschach rating of tolerance and the Rorschach measure of capacity for regression was .18, but the actual relationship seemed to be curvilinear. The "amount of primary process" and "effectiveness of control" components of the latter dimension were each correlated with tolerance .28 ($p < .05$) when taken individually. Subjects responding with a small amount of poorly controlled primary process were thus likely to be identified as "tolerant." The visual imagery scores were correlated with tolerance ratings (tau = .34, p < .01) better than with the Rorschach dimension (tau = .04). There appears to be overlap between the three measures, yet not so much that they can be considered to be measuring identical phenomena.

RESULTS

Inasmuch as linear relationships were predicted between the ordinal scale for response to meditation and the measures of the independent variables, Kendall's rank-correlation coefficient, tau (Siegel, 1956), was used to express these relationships. A two-tailed probability of .05 was the level of significance required to reject the null hypothesis in all comparisons.

Meditation and Attention Functions

It was expected that response to meditation would be correlated positively with digit span scores (measuring receptive attention) and average sums in continuous additions (measuring active concentration) and negatively with variability scores in continuous additions (measuring fluctuations in active concentration). None of these hypotheses was borne out. No relationship was found, either, between response to meditation and size estimation error (measuring scanning control or breadth of attentional scanning). A relationship may exist between receptive attention and response to meditation but of a more complex type than originally thought. Both high- and low-response subjects received higher Digit Span scores than the moderate-response group. Tested *post hoc* with Kruskal-Wallace one-way analysis of variance, this curvilinear relationship gives $H = 6.38$ (p < .05).

Meditation and Tolerance for Unrealistic Experience

A subject's comfort in the face of unrealistic experience was expected to influence his ability to meditate in the early phases of practice. This led to the prediction that response to meditation would be positively correlated with the Rorschach measure of the tolerance control principle, with the frequency of perceived reversals of reversible figures and with the amount of autokinetic movement reported. The Rorschach measure of tolerance was positively correlated with response to meditation (tau = .37, p < .01). Autokinetic movement and figure reversals were not significantly related to response.

Meditation and Capacity for Adaptive Regression

The two measures used to assess capacity for adaptive regression were the Rorschach measure based on amount and degree of primary-process thinking and visual imagery during free association. Both of these measures were positively correlated with response to meditation (tau $= .49, p < .001$, and tau $= .35, p < .01$, respectively). Because of the complex nature of the Rorschach dimension, the relative contributions of its various components was explored in a multivariate chi-square analysis (Lancaster, 1949). It appears that the main contribution to the relationship with response to meditation comes from the "effectiveness of control" component ($X^2 = 7.82$, $df = 2, p < .02$), but the contributions from the "amount" component and the interaction between "amount" and "control," while not significant, are still noteworthy ($X^2 = 4.26$ and 3.84, respectively, with $df = 2$ in each case).

DISCUSSION

Certain inferences about the nature of the meditation process may be drawn from the correlations between response to meditation and measures related to regression in the service of the ego. As suggested elsewhere (Maupin, 1962) *satori* seems to fit into the class of psychologically adaptive regressions described in the psychoanalytic literature. The meditation process may then be conceptualized as a sequence of states of regression, each of which develops functions on which succeeding states must depend. For example, the early response pattern includes a kind of relaxed drowsiness in which primary-process derivatives appear. The ability to deal with them in an accepting, undisruptive fashion enables the student to get through to the next stage, past alterations in body feelings, to "mirrorlike" detachment, in which more "regressed" elements may emerge. The "nonstriving" quality of this state, presumably a lesson of the previous phase, constitutes a safeguard against maladaptive reactions, even though further impulse derivatives are emerging. *Satori* is said to grow out of this stage, and we may guess that it is based on certain internal safeguards developed there.

While the correlations between response to meditation and the Rorschach measures of tolerance for unrealistic experience and capacity for controlled primary process underline the relevance of such experience in the meditation process, it seems unlikely that attention functions are as irrelevant to meditation as the obtained correlations would indicate. More probably, when issues related to capacity for adaptive regression are resolved, a subject can easily learn to use attention properly. One way to study this problem further would be to observe the response to meditation of two groups, both having high capacity for regression but differing in their attention skills.

The response scale used in the study by no means taps all aspects of the response observed. Subjectively felt benefits similar to those resulting from relaxation therapies were reported by several subjects. The amount of such benefit did not appear to be correlated with level of response. Subjects in the high- and moderate-response groups occasionally mentioned the emergence of very specific and vivid effects other than anxiety while they were practicing. These included hallucinoid feelings, muscle tension, sexual excitement, and intense sadness. Although subjects differed in the extent to which they tried to puzzle out the meanings of such experiences, none appeared to reach any deeper understanding of the material which emerged. On the other hand, several reported an increased awareness of previously elusive subjective events when they occurred. Perhaps the period of observation was too short to permit the development of deep insight, or perhaps meditation leads naturally to a different type of outcome—an acceptance of feelings without further inquiry into their significance.

SUMMARY

In order to explore the psychological functions involved in meditation, 28 male college student volunteers were instructed in a concentration exercise related to Zen Buddhist procedures. Their response to the exercise was rated as high, moderate, and low from verbal reports taken after daily 45-minute sessions over a 2–3 week period. Response was then compared with pre-meditation test results related to attention, tolerance for unrealistic experience, and capacity for regression in the service of the ego (derived from Rorschach expressions of "primary process" and from spontaneous visual imagery). Capacity for regression and tolerance for unrealistic experience significantly predicted response to meditation, while attention measures did not. Once issues related to comfort in the face of strange inner experience are resolved, attention functions necessary to the exercise probably became available.

13

EXPERIMENTAL MEDITATION

ARTHUR J. DEIKMAN

If credence is given to accounts of the mystic experience, we are forced to recognize that certain mystics have succeeded in achieving a special state that goes beyond the usual feelings and perceptions of ordinary life. These men and women describe an experience of union, of Unity with life or God or the Ultimate. Visions, feelings of love, and similar sensate phenomena are regarded as transitional stages on the way to a higher, transcendent state—the "cloud of darkness"—in which thoughts and images no longer exist but, instead, a new dimension is perceived. Although the lower sensate pheno-mena can occur regardless of religious orientation, prior training or life context, the transcendent state seems always to require long practice in contemplative meditation and is achieved only by a few. Both the sensate and the transcendent experience raise questions pertinent to the study and understanding of a wide range of psychological problems not usually associ-ated with theological issues.

A selective review of the mystic literature led the writer to the following general hypotheses: (a) that the procedure of contemplative meditation is a principal agent in producing the mystic experience; (b) that training in contemplative meditation leads to the building of intrapsychic barriers against distracting stimuli; and (c) that many of the phenomena described in

Reprinted by permission from *T. of Nervous & Mental Dis.*, *Vol. 136*, pp. 329–373. Copyright © 1963 by The Williams & Wilkins Co., Baltimore, Md.

mystic accounts can be regarded as the consequence of a partial deautomatization of the psychic structures that organize and interpret perceptual stimuli.

The first hypothesis, that mystic experience is achieved through the use of the technique of contemplative meditation, was derived from noting the close resemblance between descriptions of mystic exercises from widely varying cultures and times. For example, the instructions of Walter Hilton (1957), a fourteenth-century Roman Catholic canon, are similar to those of Pantanjali (Woods, 1914), a Yogi from about the sixth century. Both described a procedure of concentration without thinking (contemplative meditation), for achieving a mystic state. Similar instructions are given by other authors of widely disparate backgrounds.

The second hypothesis, that with long practice intrapsychic barriers are built against distracting stimuli, is derived from the consistent reports that a stage in meditation is reached in which it is no longer necessary to struggle against unwanted thoughts, feelings and perceptions: concentration becomes effortless.

The third hypothesis, that mystic phenomena are a consequence of a partial deautomatization of psychic structures, was suggested initially by the emphasis on focused attention and not thinking found in meditation instructions and by the phenomenon of "fresh vision," described in some accounts of mystic experiences. These accounts describe seeing a new brilliance in the world, seeing everything as if for the first time and noticing beauty and details which for the most part have previously been passed by without being seen.* The concepts of automatization and deautomatization have been developed by Hartmann (1958) and by Gill and Brenman (1959). Briefly, automatization is assumed to be a basic process in which the repeated exercise of an action or of a perception results in the disappearance from consciousness of its intermediate steps. Deautomatization is the undoing of automatization, presumably by reinvestment of actions and percepts with attention.

In order to gather data on the process and phenomena of meditation, as well as to evaluate the hypotheses outlined above, an experimental study of contemplative meditation was undertaken.

PROCEDURE

The experiment was designed according to the general descriptions of meditation, incorporating the specific instructions found in the mystic

---

*A more detailed account of the mystic experience and the deautomatization hypothesis has been prepared (Deikman, Chapter 2, this book).—*Editor.*

literature. The setting for meditation should be one in which there are minimal distractions, simple surroundings and a rather neutral meditative object, although the meditative object may have rich associations (such as a Christian cross). The experiment was performed in a quiet room, approximately 12 by 12 feet, with pale green walls and a beige carpet. Lighting was from two windows on one wall and one overhead incandescent fixture. In general, the colors and the lighting were subdued. The subject (S) sat in a comfortable armchair with his eyes approximately eight feet from the meditative object, which was a blue vase ten inches high, which stood on a simple brown end table against the opposite wall. To S's right and slightly behind him was a desk at which the experimenter (E) sat and on which a tape recorder was placed.

Although in classical accounts meditation is performed in quiet surroundings, in this study, distracting sounds were deliberately introduced. The purpose was to test the hypothesis that with practice Ss would develop psychological barriers to the registration of distracting stimuli. In addition, it was assumed that a struggle against a single source of distracting stimuli would provide intensive training in the process of meditation.

Contemplative meditation requires that the S relinquish his customary mode of thinking and perceiving. Thoughts must be stopped, sounds and peripheral sensations put out of one's mind, and the contemplation of the meditative object be conducted in a nonanalytic, nonintellectual manner. This aim determined the instructions which E read to each S as S sat in the armchair directly facing the vase. The instructions were as follows. "The purpose of these sessions is to learn about concentration. Your aim is to concentrate on the blue vase. By concentration I do not mean analyzing the different parts of the vase, or thinking a series of thoughts about the vase, or associating ideas to the vase, but rather, trying to see the vase as it exists in itself, without any connections to other things. Exclude all other thoughts or feelings or sounds or body sensations. Do not let them distract you but keep them out so that you can concentrate all your attention, all your awareness on the vase itself. Let the perception of the vase fill your entire mind.

"While you concentrate I am going to play a variety of sounds on the tape machine. Try not to let the sounds occupy your attention. Keep the sounds out so that they do not disturb your concentration. Likewise, if you find you have drifted into a stream of thought, stop and bring your attention back to the vase. At the end of about five minutes [ten minutes and 15 minutes for the second and subsequent sessions respectively] I will tell you that the session is over. Take as much time as you like to stop." In general, the initial instructions had to be supplemented in subsequent sessions by additional explanations and emphases owing to the inherent difficulty of the procedure. For example, one S revealed by his retrospective account of the meditation that he had been systematically scanning the vase. It was explained to him that his intent should be to suspend thinking about the vase, or analyzing it, so that he could perceive it as directly, as completely, as intensely as possible. The amount of supplementary instruction required varied considerably from one S to another.

After the instructions were read, the tape recorder was turned on and the meditation session began. Length of the session was five minutes on the first day, ten minutes on the second, and 15 on the third and following days. Certain Ss wished to prolong the later sessions of meditation beyond 15 minutes and were allowed to do so. In those cases the sessions lasted from 22 to 33 minutes before S terminated them spontaneously. The 12 meditation sessions for each S were conducted over a period of three weeks.

During the first five sessions the taped auditory stimuli consisted of 15 one-minute selections, played without interruption according to the following program: music, word list, music, prose, music, poetry, music, prose, music, word list, music, prose, music, poetry, music. A different tape was prepared for each session. The volume was low but the material was clearly audible. The sixth, seventh, and eighth sessions were carried out in silence. The ninth and tenth sessions were carried out either in silence or with continuous music in the background. The eleventh and twelfth sessions were again accompanied by a tape of mixed selections of verbal material and music. In the twelfth session Ss were tested for recognition of background stimuli. The test and its results will be described below. In the thirteenth session, Ss listened to a tape without meditating and were again tested for recognition as a control procedure for the recognition test of Session # 12.

The classical literature on meditation emphasizes that instructions themselves are not sufficient to orient a subject adequately in meditation nor to guide him as he progresses in his meditation. The "guru," or teacher, is regarded as absolutely essential for success in attaining enlightenment. In Western religions the need for such a teacher receives less emphasis, but it often appears that the mystic has had a strong apprentice relationship to his spiritual "instructor" or "advisor." Accordingly, this experiment was designed in the belief that E should not be removed from the situation. It was anticipated that unconscious aspects of S's relationship to E would play an important part in the meditation training and, possibly, in the effects observed. No attempt was made to analyze such factors, however.

In the course of the meditation sessions E found it necessary to assume an active role, encouraging Ss to adopt the unfamiliar mode of thinking required and allaying anxiety arising from the experience of strange phenomena. This was done primarily by emphasizing the interesting nature of the phenomena, and by pointing out to Ss that they were capable of limiting the intensity and duration of the effects that occurred.

Immediately after each meditation session, E conducted an informal inquiry, designed to elicit information about S's affect, perception of the vase, awareness of background stimuli and perception of the landscape outside. It contained the following questions: (a) "How do you feel?" (b) (S is asked to go to the window.) "Look out the window and describe what you see and the way it looks." (c) (S returns to the armchair.) "Describe the course of the session." (d) "How much of the time were you able to concentrate so that you were aware only of the vase and nothing else?" (e) "What means did you use to maintain concentration?" (f) "Was the sound difficult to keep out?" (g) "Can you recall any of the sounds that were played?" (h) "What thoughts did you have during the session?" (i) "What feelings did you have?" (j) "What was your experience of the vase?" (k) (Optional, introduced as sessions progressed.) "What is your intent as you look at the vase?" (l) "Is there anything you would like to add about the session?"

Usually, Ss began commenting on their experiences without any prompting from E. After about five minutes, they were interrupted, if necessary, and asked to go to the window. Most Ss spontaneously covered the topics of the questions. The entire inquiry was recorded on tape and later transcribed.

Although meditation is usually practiced for months and years by those seeking enlightenment, practical considerations of time and the exploratory nature of the study required a much briefer period. A limit of twelve sessions was arbitrarily decided upon, in the hope that this would be a sufficient trial of meditation to provide material for further study.

Eight unpaid Ss were employed in the experiment. Four performed meditation for twelve sessions and four performed brief meditation control procedures. Ss were normal adults in their thirties or forties, well educated and intelligent. Most had a professional involvement in some phase of psychiatry. They were personally known to E and were selected primarily on the basis of having time available to give to the experiments. None had made a study of the mystic experience, although each recognized that meditation was connected with mystic practice.

RESULTS

Certain phenomena were experienced to some degree by all Ss, but highly individual phenomena also occurred.

Phenomena Common to All Subjects

Perception of the vase: Common to all Ss was the reported alteration of their perception of the vase. Sooner or later they experienced a shift to a deeper and more intense blue. "More vivid" was a phrase they used frequently. Ss experienced the vase as becoming brighter while everything in their visual field became quite dark and indistinct. The adjective "luminous" was often applied to the vase, as if it were a source of light. For example, subject B., Session 6, "The vase was a hell of a lot bluer this time than it has been before . . . it was darker and more luminous at the same time." A second effect experienced by Ss was an instability of the shape of the vase. This was most commonly reported as a felt change in the size or the shape of the vase, a loss of the third dimension and a diffusion or loss of its perceptual boundaries either partly or entirely. In addition, movement of the vase was sometimes reported. For example, subject C, Session 8, "Then it seemed to change its shape rather drastically. I mean it was always in a vase—pot shape, but there was a change symmetrically and undulating up and down more than a sideways movement." Subject A, Session 4, "The outlines of the vase shift. At that point they seem almost literally to dissolve entirely . . . and for it to be a kind of fluid blue . . . a very fluid kind of thing . . . kind of moving."

Time-shortening: For the most part, Ss felt that less time had elapsed than was recorded on the clock. This sense of time having passed very quickly occurred despite the Ss' occasional feelings during the meditation that the session had been going on for a very long time. For example, subject A stated, "I thought, I'm sure it must be longer and I don't know if I can keep myself concentrated on it, then when you did stop and I went back to it, it seemed as though it couldn't possibly have been ten minutes or twice as long as yesterday." If the struggle to concentrate was continuous, without periods of success, then Ss reported wearily, "It seemed like a long time."

Conflicting perceptions: Ss' reports indicated that they experienced conflicting perception. For example, in the third session, subject B stated, about the vase, "It certainly filled my visual field," but a few minutes later, stated, "It didn't fill the field by any means." In the seventh session, referring to the landscape, he commented, " . . .a great deal of agitation . . . but it isn't agitating . . . it's . . . pleasurable." In general, Ss found it very difficult to describe their feelings and perceptions during the meditation periods— "It's very hard to put into words," was a frequent comment. This difficulty seemed due in part to the difficulty of describing their experience without contradictions. Part of the problem was probably due also to the inadequacy of their descriptive vocabulary for reporting the meditation experiences.

Development of stimulus barriers: A major premise to be tested by the experiment was that with practice an S could develop organized, stable, intra-psychic barriers to incidental stimuli, external or internal. These Ss' statements seemed to support this hypothesis: a gradual increase in ability to keep out distracting stimuli was reported. This phenomenon appeared to have two components: (a) a decrease in the distracting effect of the stimuli, and (b) a decrease in conscious registration of the stimuli. Subject A stated that what was initially an effortful activity finally, toward the end of the series, did not seem to require effort. As she put it, "shutting out" began to "come naturally." More specifically, after the sixth session, subject A reported, "I am sure that at that point all sounds were obliterated. At that point somehow everything was out of my consciousness . . . when I came back my awareness that suddenly I could hear the tape again and for whatever infinitesimal space of time it was . . . it seemed that I heard absolutely no sound . . . it was as though the world was absolutely silent during that time". None of the other subjects seemed to reach this point of absolute silence, but subject B, in his ninth session, stated, "I think I heard maybe one-fourth of the clock ticks. I am sure I didn't hear them all. Other sounds were almost non-existent. The music changed or disappeared . . . decided changes of level." (In this session the taped sounds were continuous music.) In the twelfth session subject B stated, ". . . the distractions are not intrusive in a jarring way. There is a certain amount of control . . . a general . . . familiarity . . . a kind of learning which is that I keep them out at some level." An increased ability to bar distractions from awareness was also demonstrated with respect to new, unexpected stimuli. Subject A came to the fifth session complaining of a bad cold and expressed concern that her running nose and watery eyes would interfere with the meditation. Following the session she reported further progress in concentration and stated, " . . . at one point when I did start to cough I was aware of having a tear in my eye but then I forgot about it until suddenly it was just dripping down my face."

The least intrusive stimulus was continuous music of homogeneous texture and low volume. Very intrusive were clear prose passages whose content was of personal interest to the subjects (e.g., a discussion of diet fads). The most intrusive was the change from one type of sound material on the tape to another (e.g., music to prose). Ss said they found that this brought them "out" each time it happened. Although this effect was still manifest toward the end of the experiment, it, too, appeared then to be less disturbing and to have a less disrupting effect. In general, Ss found that as the experiment progressed, all distracting stimuli were less intrusive.

Personal attachment to the vase: Very striking was the personal involvement of Ss with the vase, as judged by their reactions to the thirteenth session (listening to a tape without meditation). In order to minimize the possibility that Ss would meditate, the vase was removed from the room before the session. As Ss entered and their eyes went to the place where the vase usually sat, it was apparent that its absence shocked them. Subject B remonstrated with E in a half-joking way by saying, "hey, cut it out. Put it back. Where have you got it?" He repeatedly looked back to the former location of the vase and seemed uncomfortable. "I am disappointed not to see that damn thing there, it's strange, if I look down it isn't there." He later stated that the vase had always seemed the most important thing in the room and its absence was disturbing. Subject *A* made no verbal comments but displeasure and some distress was evident. In a later interview, A stated, "You remember how excited I became when it first happened, as if I had found a toy? Well, this was as if I had lost it, lost something important . . . much more important than some inanimate object you're used to . . . losing some kind of emotional experience . . . I was nostalgic . . . it was like saying good-bye to a teacher in a course you had learned something in, had become involved in and was sorry to leave it . . . the most vivid thing in the room." While listening to the tape in Session 13, subject A was less able to concentrate than she would have expected and kept seeing the vase in her mind. After the thirteenth session she became mildly depressed. Subject C felt that the vase was very striking in its absence, and kept seeing it in his mind. In general, all *S*s reacted as if they had lost something they were very attached to.

Pleasurable quality: All *S*s agreed that the sessions were usually pleasurable, valuable and rewarding. Although one *S* "forgot" a testing appointment following a significant experience in the previous session, he returned and completed the series. All *S*s achieved the 15 minutes or longer meditation period, even those who experienced some anxiety. When displeasure with the procedure occurred, it seemed to be due to (a) anxiety over the loss of controls required, (b) a feeling of failure to perform as expected.

Individual phenomena

Merging: "Merging" was reported by subject A, who from the very beginning reported striking alterations in her perception of the vase and her relation to it. She reported, "one of the points that I remember most vividly is when I really began to feel, you know, almost as though the blue and I were perhaps merging, or that vase and I were. I almost got scared to the point where I found myself bringing myself back in some way from it . . . It was as though everything was sort of merging and I was somehow losing my sense of consciousness almost." This "merging" experience was characteristic of all of this *S*'s meditation sessions, but she soon became familiar with it and ceased to describe it as anything remarkable. Following the sixth session she reported, "At one point it felt . . . as though the vase were in my head rather than out there: I knew it was out there but it seemed as though it were almost a part of me." "I think that I almost felt at that moment as though, you know, the image is really in me, it's not out there."

This phenomenon of "perceptual internalization" did not recur although she stated that she hoped it would.*

In subsequent sessions subject A described a "film of blue" that developed as the boundaries of the vase dissolved. It covered the table on which the vase sat and the wall behind it, giving them all a blue color. In the tenth session the "film" became a "mist," and in the eleventh it became a "sea of blue." She reported after the eleventh session, "I am convinced now that what I initially . . . called merging was this kind of thing that happened (now) for practically 30 solid minutes." (By this time subject A was allowed to terminate the meditation "when it feels completed.") She experienced some anxiety during the session in that "it lost its boundaries and I might lose mine too" and described the general experience as "I was swimming in a sea of blue and I felt for a moment I was going to drown . . ." However, despite the anxiety it occasioned, she felt that the experience was very desirable.

A related phenomenon was reported by subject C in the tenth session, ". . . I felt this whole complete other plane where I was nothing, I mean where my body was nothing. I wasn't aware of my body, it could not have been there and I wouldn't be surprised."

Radiation: In the ninth session, subject C reported: "It started radiating. I was aware of what seemed like particles . . . seemed to be coming from the highlights there and right to me. I seemed fascinated with that. I felt that it was radiating heat. I felt warm from it and then realized that it was all shut out, that everything was dark all around, a kind of brown, lavender, eerie color and it was during this incandescent kind of radiating inner glow thing I could feel my pulse beating in my head and then there was . . . a twinge in my penis, I could feel my pulse beating in my penis and in my temples . . . I felt that there was a light coming down from above, too, that something was happening up there and I started getting an erection and this thing danced and it was very active. It moved, it pulsated and it also jumped around like this. It seemed like many colors around the edges of the table." (During this experience the vase appeared to him in a variety of different colors.)

Dedifferentiation: When subject B looked out the window in the sixth session (the first session without taped sounds), he gave the following description: "I don't know how to describe it, it's scattered. Things look scattered all over the lot, not hung together in any way. When I look at the background there is much in the foreground that is kind of drawing my attention. A very strong word would be clamoring for my attention. It isn't

---

*It is interesting that the session was the first in which no sounds were played on the tape machine and the meditation was conducted in relative silence.

really clamoring but looks like a call for attention from all over the lot and no way of looking at the whole or any individual part of it." (Somewhat later.) "This session strikes me as quite different . . . The view didn't organize itself in any way. For a long time it resisted my attempt to organize it so I could talk about it. There were no planes, one behind the other. There was no response to certain patterns. Everything was working at the same intensity . . . like a bad painting which I didn't know about until I got used to it so I could begin to pick out what was going on in the painting. I didn't see the order to it or the patterning to it or anything and I couldn't impose it, it resisted my imposition of pattern." The characteristics of this experience might be summarized as: (a) resistance of the stimuli to visual organization; (b) all stimuli appearing at equal intensity; (c) all stimuli actively calling for attention at once. Subject B's description suggests that the experience resulted from a deautomatization of the structures ordinarily providing visual organization of a landscape (30–500 feet). The ability to focus attention selectively and the normal figure-ground relationships were apparently deautomatized. It should be noted that subject B did not experience the room itself in this way.

Transfiguration: In Session 7 (the day after the dedifferentiation episode), subject B's perception of the landscape might be termed "transfigured." He described very few objects or details but instead talked mostly in terms of pleasure, luminescence and beautiful movements. For example, "the building is a kind of very white . . . a kind of luminescence that the fields have and the trees are really swaying, it's very nice . . . lean way over and bounce back with a nice spring-like movement. The sky behind them now is also very filled with light, there's a very blue patch in the sky . . . there are a couple of blue patches in the white, it's quite remarkable—quality to it." Again, "The movements are nice, the brightness is. I would have thought it was a terribly overcast day but it isn't. (The sky was a white overcast with some patches of blue.) It's perception filled with light and movement both of which are very pleasurable. Nobody knows what a nice day it is except me." Subject B later stated, "It was coming in to me in a sense, I wasn't watching myself watching . . . the antithesis of being self-aware." In succeeding sessions there seemed to be a gradual decline from the enhanced perception of Session 7 and a gradual diminution in the amount of light and pleasure perceived in the scene.

After the experiment had been concluded, subject B said, about looking out of the window, "What stands out in my mind are the organized occasions and the disorganized ones. The organized ones which then tended to organize themselves in various ways about the centers which seemed dominant or on planes which seemed a way of kind of organizing it. The disorganized ones are kind of scattered."

In summary, the group of four Ss, taken together, present a continuum ranging from subject A, who had the most intense personal experience and the least difficulties with the method, through subject D, who reported the fewest phenomena and had the greatest difficulty complying with the instructions. Subject D reported phenomena of lower intensity than the other Ss, required more sessions of practice and instruction before she noticed any effects, and did not report any striking individual phenomena. Common to all or most Ss were: (a) perceptual changes relating to the vase (darkening of hue, increased color saturation, loss of the third dimension, changes in size and shape, blurring or dissolving of outlines and movement of the vase itself); (b) development of a personal attachment to the vase; (c) modification of the state of consciousness; (d) increased ability to "keep out" distracting stimuli; and (e) a general feeling that the sessions were pleasurable and valuable. Phenomena which were apparently individual responses to the procedure were: (a) merging and perceptual internalization; (b) radiation with heat effect and sexual stimulation; (c) dedifferentiation of the landscape; and (d) transfiguration.

Recognition test

Incorporated in the design of the experiment was a test of recognition utilizing the word lists included in the background tape material. The test was based on the work of Schwartz and Rouse (1961, p. 22), who found that on a multiple-choice recognition test, Ss tended to choose close associates of "forgotten" test words. On the basis of their findings, it was expected that in the meditation experiment, registration of the word list without awareness would be revealed by a significant choice of close associates.

During the twelfth sessions, Ss were interrupted in the midst of meditation immediately after the playing of the second word list. They were given a multiple-choice recognition test containing the words that had just been played and instructed to "see how much your mind remembers" by checking any words that sounded as if they had been on the list.

The next day, the thirteenth session, Ss were tested sitting at the desk with the vase removed from the room and the instruction given: "This time I want you to listen to the tape and try to remember what you hear." After the second word list of that tape was played, Ss were again given a recognition test.

As a control for the effect of practice in meditation, a second group of four Ss was given the procedures of Sessions 12 and 13 only.

In all eight cases S was able to recognize more words when he was not meditating. There was no significant difference, however, in the ability of practice and control Ss to recognize words played while they were meditating, and no significant choice of close associates. An S's report that he had no memory of the word list was not necessarily related to his score on the test.

DISCUSSION

Meditation and the Mystic Experience

Ss' reports support the hypothesis that the procedure of contemplative meditation is a principal agent in producing the mystic experience. On the basis of the mystic literature, two classifications of mystic experience were distinguished: "sensate" experiences of strong emotion, vivid perception or heightened cognition, and "transcendent" experiences beyond the usual modes of affect, perception or cognition (Deikman, Chapter 2, this book). The reports of these Ss are analogs of the sensate mystic experience and, in the case of subject A, who continued further meditation sessions beyond the conclusion of the experiment itself, a possible preliminary phase to the transcendent state.

Subject B's experience of the landscape in the seventh session (see above) is similar to descriptions of untrained sensate mystic experience. William James, for instance, cites the following: ". . . everything looked new to me, the people, the fields, the trees, the cattle, I was like a new man in a new world" (1929, p. 244). "It was like entering another world, a new state of existence. Natural objects were glorified. My spiritual vision was so clarified that I saw beauty in every material object in the universe" (p. 244). "The appearance of everything was altered, there seemed to be, as it were, a calm, sweet cast for appearance of divine glory in almost everything" (p. 243). The difference between subject B's report and those of the untrained persons cited by James might depend on the presence of a religious viewpoint in the latter. The "luminescence" and "beauty" reported by subject B may be equivalent to "divine glory" as descriptive terms, and if subject B had been a mystic yearning to be touched by God, his vision of the landscape on that day probably would have seemed to him like a divine communion.

Another analog is subject C's experience of the "radiation" of heat from the vase, as well as pulsations in shape, lighting and color, felt as sexually exciting and pleasurable (see above). Richard Rolle, a fourteenth-century English mystic, wrote, ". . . I was sitting in a certain chapel, and while I was taking pleasure in the delight of some prayer or meditation, I suddenly felt within me an unwanted and pleasant fire. When I had for long doubted from whence it came, I learned by experience it came from the Creator and not from creature and I found it ever more pleasing and full of heat . . ."

(Knowles, p. 57). Other Western mystics have described a "sweet fire," a vivid physical experience that often has strong sexual implications. If subject C were a Christian mystic contemplating a statue of Christ or the Virgin Mary, he might well have reported his experience in religious terms.

In the Vedantic literature, particularly in the Yoga of Pantanjali (Woods, 1914), there is great emphasis on the independence of the mind and the location of the percept in the mind of the beholder. It is emphasized that objects exist but that our ideas about them are functions of our mental operations. The perception of the world as distinct from the self is regarded as false, but through the practice of meditation a true perception of reality may be achieved. Subject A's experience of the vase being in her head rather than in the external world (see above) could readily produce or support the Yoga philosophy.

Even more striking was the report of subject A from a session (21) conducted after the end of the experimental series. It is possible that she entered a preliminary phase of the "transcendent" state, and that what she describes is an analog of the trained-transcendent mystic experience. She reported that a diffuse blue occupied the entire visual field and that she felt merged completely with that diffuseness. She had a sense of falling, of emptiness, of loneliness and isolation as if she were in a vacuum. Her sudden realization that there were absolutely no thoughts in her mind made her anxious and she searched for thoughts to bring herself back. "It was as if I leaped out of the chair to put the boundaries back on the vase . . . because there was nothing there . . . the vase was going and I was going with it . . ." This description is strikingly similar to that found in *The Cloud of Unknowing*, where the author states, "And [to] do that in thee is to forget all the creatures that ever God made and the works of them, so that thy desire be not directed or stretched to any of them, neither in general nor in special . . . At the first time when thou dost it, thou findst but a darkness and as it were a cloud of unknowing, thous knowest not what . . ." (Knowles, 1961, p. 77).

What I have described are analogs of mystic experiences, not true mystic experiences. These *S*s did not have a sense of ineffable communication with the absolute, of profound illumination into the nature of Reality, nor of being in a state of Unity. However, their accounts do suggest that important basic elements of the mystic experience were achieved, and this in turn suggests that contemplative meditation as a psychological technique is a central element in the production of the trained mystic experience.

Stimulus barriers: The hypothesis that training in contemplative meditation leads to the building of intrapsychic barriers against distracting stimuli was supported by the subjective reports but not by the recognition test. All *S*s in the practice group reported an improvement in their ability to keep out of awareness internal and external stimuli that were potentially very distracting. These stimuli were internal as well as external, were often rich in meaning, and were sometimes accidental intrusions into the experimental situation (e.g., subject A's head cold). The combination of increased effectiveness and decreased effort suggests that psychic structures were established to keep out stimuli more efficiently—more work accomplished with less effort. (The automatization of such structures could conceivably account for the transition to effortless contemplation reported by mystics.) The recognition test data, however, did not show a difference between the practice and control groups. In view of the improvement in keeping out stimuli reported by Ss, it seems probable that this test was not a measure of the existence of stimulus-barrier structures. The question must then be asked: "By what process is an incoming stimulus barred from attention while still registering sufficiently to permit recognition?" The data do not supply an answer, so far.

Deautomatization: The concept of deautomatization would appear to be specifically demonstrated in the experience of de-differentiation reported by the subject B as he looked out the window. His description of the unorganized stimuli "clamoring" for his attention and "no way of looking at the whole or any individual part" is very similar to the quality of visual experience reported in Von Senden's (1960) survey of cataract patients seeing for the first time. It is precisely such a perceptual condition that would be expected in the absence of automatic processes responsible for organizing visual stimuli. Of course, in the case of subject B, considerable organization of vision was still present as compared to the Von Senden accounts; yet it seems clear that a partial disorganization, a deautomatization, took place briefly as he gazed out the window. The ability to focus attention selectively and the perception of normal figure-ground relationships would appear to have been affected.

The alteration of ego boundaries experienced by subject A, and the release of sexual feeling in the case of subject C, might be viewed as a deautomatization of self-object differentiation and of affect controls, respectively. Similarly, the loss of the third dimension of the vase, the diffusion of its boundaries, and its increased intensity of color is consistent with a deautomatization of formal organization of visual stimuli resulting in a shift to a more direct, less organized sensory experience.

Related phenomena

Color perception: The changes in perception of the vase which most Ss reported would seem to be composed of elements of color adaption, color contrast and color summation. For example, color summation is suggested by the diffuse film of blue that subject A reported, which in later sessions completely occupied and filled the field of vision. Color adaptation would similarly seem involved in S's perception of the vase. Cohen, however, in an experiment using binocular trichromatic colorimeters, reported that "the course of adaptation to color consists of a gradual but never complete loss of saturation, of no change in hue, and of an increase in intensity" (Cohen, 1946, p. 110). In contrast to his results, saturation of the vase in the meditation experiment was often reported to be increased, with a shift in the hue toward purple. Although the conditions of the Hochberg (1951) experiments (color adaptation using a Ganzfield) are not duplicated here, the darkening of the visual field and the shift in hue of the vase seem in accord with his finding that red or green adapted to black or dark grey. Yet the overall darkening of the meditation room "as if the lights had been turned down," was accompanied by an increased "luminous" and "vivid" quality of the vase. "It was as if light were coming from it." This finding does not parallel Hochberg's results. Thus additional central processes must probably be considered to account for the meditation color phenomenon. Experimental evidence for central factors over and above the mechanisms of neuronal adaption is provided by Pritchard (1958) in his studies of the stabilized retinal image. "When a subject views a pattern in a stabilized condition, he can still alter the amount which he perceives in a certain region of the pattern by deciding to transfer his attention to that region." This finding is relevant to an understanding of meditative concentration, for the allocation of attention appears to be the principal process involved in meditation, above and beyond the more peripheral processes of adaptation and summation.*

Hypnosis: The experimental procedure and setting suggest a similarity to hypnosis and raise the question of whether the phenomena are due to the same process. As discussed by Gill and Brenman (1959), three of the main features of hypnotic induction are: (a) extensive limitation is placed on S's sensory intake; (b) S's bodily activity is strictly limited; and (c) stimulation is provided of a particular and narrow kind. The first two features are found in the meditation procedure. With regard to the latter point, the music selections played on the background tapes, the simple meditative object, and the repeated instructions might all be viewed as such narrow stimulation. However, the prose and poetry selections were different for each session, were varied in type, and were often rich in meaning. A fourth point mentioned by Gill and Brenman, the attempt to alter the quality of the bodily

---

*One may infer from the Hochberg experiment, from the work with after-images (Osgood, 1956, p. 222) and from recent work on the stabilized retinal image (Eagle & Klein), that the more meaningful the percept, the more it resists breakdown.

awareness of Ss, was not part of the meditation procedure. The absence of this feature is in accord with the absence in the meditative Ss of vivid spontaneous changes in body experience which Gill and Brenman believe are the most prominent phenomena of hypnotic induction. A striking similarity between hypnosis and the meditation experiment concerns the expectations of S. Gill and Brenman wrote, "During the course of the steps of any successful hypnotic induction process, the hypnotist progressively persuades the subject that he is gradually losing control of himself and that this control is being responsibly taken over by the hypnotist. Usually implied, though sometimes explicitly stated, is the promise to the subject that if he permits the hypnotist to bring about the deprivations and losses of power we have discussed, he will be rewarded by an unprecedented kind of experience; the precise nature of this experience is usually left ambiguous. Sometimes the implication is that new worlds will be opened to him, providing an emotional adventure of a sort he has never known" (Gill & Brenman, 1959, p. 10). All Ss in the present meditation experiment revealed by their comments a more or less vague expectation of this sort. Two of the meditation Ss used the term "hypnotic" to characterize some aspects of their concentration process. Clearly there are certain similarities in the physical setting, the expectations of S and the relationship to E in the two procedures.

In spite of these similarities, the phenomena of meditation seem to represent a state of ego organization different from that associated with hypnosis. The intense affective phenomena often found in the phypnotic induction period did not occur in the meditative sessions. Except for feelings of surprise or fear at the occurrence of a new phenomenon, Ss' emotional intensity could be described as mild. Subject C did experience a combination of physical and mental excitement during the most vivid of the perceptual phenomena but even this does not seem comparable in quality to the more intense hypnotic phenomena "ranging from the relatively minor explosions of uncontrolled weeping to the enactment of waking nightmares on a level of symbolism and with a quantity of feeling very similar to that known to us only in dream-life; poetry, or fairy tales" (Gill & Brenman, 1959, p. 19), found sometimes in the induction period of hypnosis. The surrender of will power, which is the cardinal feature of the hypnotic state, is encountered in meditation only insofar as S renounces his normal intellectual activities— he does not consciously feel that he is turning control over to E. As in hypnosis, this renunciation itself is undertaken voluntarily, but the meditation Ss seem always to have been aware that they were able to bring themselves back at any time that they wished, whereas in the hypnotic state fluctuations in the depth of hypnosis appear to take place involuntarily (Brenman, Gill & Knight, 1952).

The basic difference between hypnosis and the classical mystic experience is the difference in the experience itself. Hypnotic experiences do not appear to have the ineffable, profound, uplifting, highly valued quality of the mystic state and are not remembered as such. It may be argued that the difference is a function of suggestion. Orne has studied the nature of the hypnotic process and proposes that "the behavioral characteristics of hypnosis can be understood in terms of the subject's previous knowledge and the cues transmitted during the process of induction" (Orne, 1962, p. 1098). The hypothesis might be advanced that the phenomena of experimental meditation and of the mystic experience in general represent, as Orne suggests of hypnosis, "an historically developed artifact occurring along with a process, the essential behavioral manifestations of which are little known" (1962, p. 1098). Thus the difference between hypnosis and contemplative meditation might lie in the differing expectations of Ss and the "demand characteristics" of the two situations. Coe (1917, p. 253) has pointed out that the form and content of the mystic experience is usually congruent with the mystics' cultural and religious background; to put it simply, a Yogin will have a Nirvana experience, while a Roman Catholic will report communion with Christ. Such an hypothesis of demand characteristics, however, is not consistent with the fact that the highest mystic experiences are similar in their basic content despite wide differences in cultural backgrounds and expectations. These similarities are: (a) the feeling of incommunicability; (b) transcendence of sense modalities; (c) absence of specific content such as images or ideas; and (d) feeling of unity with the Ultimate. Lower forms of mystic experience do embody specific content related to each S's beliefs, and the absence of religious motifs from the accounts of Ss performing meditation as a psychological experiment indicates a definite role of S-expectation in determining the presence of or absence of the secondary features of mystic experiences. However, the phenomena common to all Ss do not permit such an explanation. Also, there are reasons for believing that the idiosyncratic phenomena, such as "merging," were neither a function of Ss' knowledge of the role of meditator, nor of the total demand characteristics imposed by the experimenter and the experimental design. To begin with, the occurrence of the phenomena of "merging," "radiation" and the like surprised both S and E. One S was sufficiently alarmed to end the phenomena by shifting her attention. On the other hand, the "deautomatization" effect was not noticed by subject B as being a special event, whereas it seemed of great significance to E. In addition, the two Ss (A and C) who took to the procedure with greatest facility and interest, developed markedly different effects. Finally the later experience of subject A, clearly a further development of "merging," appears to be a preliminary phase of the Unity phenomenon of the transcendent mystic experience. This S had no conscious knowledge of the mystic literature and her retrospective account emphasized the strangeness, the unexpectedness and the startling quality of her experience.

The considerations discussed above do not rule out the presence of unconscious expectations on the part of Ss, nor unconscious as well as explicit expectations of the part of E. For the reasons given, however, it seems that the phenomena cannot be adequately explained as due to suggestion, and a careful examination of the transcripts gives one the strong impression that a unique process is involved.

Sensory deprivation: The meditation procedure also invites comparison with experimental sensory deprivation. In meditation, a narrowing and decrease in variation of the stimulus field are created, rather than sensory deprivation as such. However, the meditation instructions aim towards a situation in which very little meaningful information is taken in by Ss. Homogeneity of external stimulation is established by environmental conditions, but the narrowing of the perceptual field is accomplished primarily by S's own psychological actions. It is interesting that many studies point to the absence of meaningful stimuli as the primary determinant of deprivation phenomena (Solomon et al., 1961). A very important difference between the two procedures is that meditation involves an active striving for a definite goal (see the meditation instructions), while sensory deprivation fosters and creates complete psychological passivity.

The phenomena reported by the meditation Ss are similar in a number of respects to those encountered during and immediately after sensory deprivation: alterations in ego boundaries with accompanying feelings of estrangement; increased brightness of color; movement of stationary objects; and apparently idiosyncratic "hallucinations." It should be noted, however, that these effects occurred during the meditation and not when Ss turned their attention once more to the room and E. In the case of subject B, who experienced an apparent perceptual change in the nature of the landscape after meditation, this change was not the sort described as occurring after periods of deprivation. The sharp transition from the meditation state to the "normal" condition may be an indication of how completely the meditative state is under the control of S himself, in contrast to the deprivation procedure which is imposed upon S. It was clear that during the meditation Ss could control the rate of progression of phenomena as well as the extent of stimulus limitation which they experienced.

The meditation procedure and that of sensory deprivation both reveal a continuum between Ss who can abandon themselves to the required state and Ss who seem unable to adapt (Freedman et al., 1961; Holt & Goldberger, 1959). In contrast to Ss' usual experience in sensory deprivation, the meditation experience was generally felt to be pleasurable, rewarding and positively valued, even by those who did not seem able to adapt to it. No restlessness was observed and distress was momentary or absent.

It should be emphasized that sensory deprivation, even when enjoyed by S, is not the same experience as that recorded by mystics, and in the aspects mentioned above is different from the phenomena of experimental meditation.

Implications

The meditation procedure described in this report produces alterations in the visual perception of sensory and formal properties of the object, and alterations in ego boundaries—all in the direction of fluidity and breakdown of the usual subject-object differentiation. The phenomena are consistent with the hypothesis that through contemplative meditation deautomatization occurs and permits a different perceptual and cognitive experience. The change in perception of the vase (increase in color intensity, loss of the third dimension and diffusion of boundaries) are in the direction of the undifferentiated visual experience of Von Senden's patients. The meditation Ss, however, showed an appreciation for the "richness" and esthetically pleasing elements in the experience. Subject B's "deautomatization" episode was followed by his experiencing the landscape as transfigured with light and movement, as being pleasurable and beautiful. Deautomatization is here conceived as permitting the adult to attain a new, fresh perception of the world by freeing him from a stereotyped organization built up over the years and by allowing adult synthetic and associative functions access to fresh materials, to create with them in a new way that represents an advance in mental functioning. The search of the artist to find a new expressive style may be viewed as the struggle to deautomatize his perception and the evolution of styles is accordingly necessary to regain vivid, emotionally significant experience. The struggle for creative insight in all fields may be regarded as the effort to deautomatize the psychic structures that organize cognition and perception.

In this sense, deautomatization is not a regression but rather an undoing of a pattern in order to permit a new and perhaps more advanced experience. The crayfish sloughs its rigid shell when more space is needed for growth. The mystic, through meditation, may also cast off, temporarily, the shell of automatic perception, of automatic affective and cognitive controls in order to perceive more deeply into reality. The temporary nature of mystic deautomatization is seen in the episodic course of the mystic's progress toward Union. Mystics report achieving ecstatic peaks of experience succeeded by a fading away (reautomatization) until another high moment restores the state. The general process of deautomatization would seem of great potential usefulness whenever it is desired to break free from an old pattern in order to achieve a new experience of the same stimulus or to open a perceptual avenue to stimuli never experienced before. The effects of LSD and mescaline, the "break-off phenomenon" of high altitude flights and other related phenomena, may be due to a partial deautomatization of a mode or modes of perception and cognition. Such deautomatization achieved through external environmental changes appears to be more transient and less transcendent than those produced by individual efforts over long periods of time, however.

A most striking finding of the meditation experiment is the ease and rapidity with which the phenomena were produced. Comparable phenomena have required more or less elaborate procedures of sensory deprivation or the use of potent drugs. In this study a natural environment was employed and the process was performed by *S*s themselves. In less than half an hour, phenomena occurred that in other contexts have been described as "depersonalization," "hallucination," "delusion" or "visual distortion," "intensification" and the like. Such rapid, intense effects point to a capacity under minimal stress conditions, for alteration in the perception of the world and of the self far greater than what is customarily assumed to be the case for normal people.

The procedure of experimental meditation appears to be a valuable research tool and research problem in its own right. Further investigation is planned.

14

MEDITATIVE TECHNIQUES IN PSYCHOTHERAPY

WOLFGANG KRETSCHMER

The psychotherapist who wants to employ techniques of meditation must first be able to meditate himself. The book by the German psychiatrist, J. H. Schultz (Schultz, 1953, 1956; see Schultz and Luthe, 1959, for English translation) offers a step-by-step introduction to one technique of meditation. However, with meditation, as with psychotherapy, a study of the literature is seldom enough. A personal dedication is necessary. Without it, individual practice of meditation can be dangerous; especially the advance stages of genuine meditation described by Schultz. In these advanced stages, after a general bodily relaxation has been achieved, symbolic fantasies are skillfully induced. Then colors and objects are visualized. One endeavors to experience a symbolic representation of ideas which are understood only abstractly, of one's feelings, of friends, and finally of higher moral questions, in a way which allows the psyche to make unconscious tendencies symbolically visible. Dreams are similar to meditation, except meditation gains the reaction of the unconscious by a systematic technique which is faster than depending on dreams.

But the Schultz technique only serves to raise, with a special emphasis, the question, "What is the goal of meditation?" Schultz sees this question clearly, but that this question is basically a religious one, or at least

Reprinted by permission of *Psychologia*, Vol. 5, (1962) 76–83.

connected with religion, Schultz does not conclude. Therefore, he limits himself to the formulation of "basic existential values." This means the meditator is encouraged to strive toward a reasonable view of life oriented toward self-realization, psychic freedom and harmony, and a lively creativity. At best, one achieves a Nirvana-like phenomena of joy and release. Maybe Schultz conceals decisive experiences which go further; because of the basically unlimited possibilities of meditation, we can always await such an extension of his ideas.

The technique developed by Carl Happich, the former Darmstadt internist, is meditation of the most systematic kind, and also of the widest human scope. It begins with physiology and ends in religion. Happich developed it out of his literary and practical knowledge of Oriental techniques. He combined their wisdom with the experience of modern depth psychology. He set forth his fundamental principles in two small works (Happich, 1932, 1939), and beyond these left only a small *Introduction to meditation* (Happich, 1948), which is concerned with religious symbolism. Unfortunately, he did not live to set forth his life experiences in a grand scientific frame. His importance lies, above all, in the practical techniques which he began to spread among theologians when physicians demonstrated no interest in them.

Happich took the level of consciousness he called "symbolic consciousness," which seems to lie between consciousness and unconsciousness, as the point of departure for all creative production and, therefore, also for the healing process. On this level the "collective unconscious" can express itself through symbolism. It is in the activation of the possibilities of symbolic expression that Happich, as Schultz, sees the point of departure for meditation and its therapeutic possibilities.

How can we proceed practically? Assumed, as always, is the bodily solution which is attained systematically with the Schultz method or by more direct means. Happich placed great value in breathing as a graduated measure of the affective states which alters itself in the permissiveness of meditation. He encouraged, both before and during the therapeutic session, an increasing passivity of respiration. Most men can only achieve this through progressive breathing exercises.

After some experience with physiological reactions to breathing exercises has been gained, the first psychological exercise, the so-called "Meadow Meditation," can be attempted. The meditator must repeat to himself the words of his meditation-master and imagine that he (the meditator) leaves the room, goes through the city, over the fields, to a meadow covered with fresh grass and flowers and looks upon the meadow with pleasure. Then, he psychically returns the same way to the room, opens his eyes, and relates what he has experienced. When this exercise can be done freely (which usually requires a number of sittings) it is followed by the "Mountain Meditation."

The meditator, as in the first meditation, goes into the country and then slowly climbs a mountain. He passes through a forest, and finally reaches a peak from which he can view a wide expanse. In the third step, the "Chapel Meditation" is explored. In it, the meditator passes through a grove and reaches a chapel which he enters and where he remains for a long time. Lastly, Happich has the meditator imagine himself sitting on a bench by an old fountain listening to the murmur of the water.

What does all this mean? One who is familiar with dream symbolism knows immediately that the three central symbols (meadow, mountain, and chapel) to which the meditator is led have an "archetypal" significance even though, in everyday life, they are quite ordinary and in no way help to bring about an especially deep knowledge.

However, when a certain depth of meditation is attained, such symbols lose their ordinary meaning and their symbolical value is slowly revealed. As the meditator returns to the meadow, he does not experience things as he would in the ordinary world. Rather the meadow provides a symbol of the hypnotic level of consciousness and stimulates the emotions on this level. The individual takes an ordinary situation as the means of experiencing the primordial content of the symbol of the meadow. The meadow presents youthful Mother Nature in her serene and beneficent aspect. In contrast a forest is also inhabited by demons. The meadow represents the blossoming of life which the meditator seeks. It also represents the world of the child. When one meditates on the symbol of the meadow, he regresses to his psychic origin in childhood. Once there, he does not uncover sexual dreams of his childhood as might be expected. Nor does he find a "stump," which can also be a meaningful symbol. Rather he returns to the positive, creative basis of his life.

Every healthy man has in his psychic depths something corresponding to this meadow. He retains with him an active and creative "child." As the realm of this "child" is revealed through meditation on the symbol of the meadow, the meadow becomes a point of departure and crystallization for other symbols related to this psychic realm. These self-crystallized symbols are unmeditated expressions of the individual's adaptation to the realm of the "child" within his psyche. A healthy man will have a satisfying experience of a meadow in the flush of spring. He will populate the meadow with children or with the form of an agreeable woman. He will, perhaps, pick flowers and so on. In this way, the meditator discovers a symbolic representation of his psychic condition.

The psychically ill find it impossible to visualize a fresh meadow and during meditation cannot find one. Or the meadow may be seen as wilted or composed of a single stump. Or all sorts of disturbing, negative symbols may be scattered around. From such manifestations of illness, one gains a diagnosis which must then be translated into a therapy. Often, the meditation must be repeated many times until the crippling effects of the fundamental psychic problem are undone and the meditation can proceed normally. Analytic conversation with the psychotherapist normally aids the whole process.

In climbing the mountain, the meditator will generally symbolize some obstacle in his way so that he must prove himself. Climbing in this psychic sphere always implies "sublimation," in the Jungian rather than the Freudian use of the term. The words transformation, spiritualization, or humanization might convey the idea better than the word "sublimation." In any case, the climbing is a symbol of a movement during which man demonstrates his capacity to develop toward the goal of psychic freedom, the peak of human being. The passage through the forest on the way up the mountain gives the meditator the opportunity to reconcile himself with the dark, fearful side of nature.

With the symbol of the chapel, the meditator is led into the innermost rooms of his psyche where he faces the simple question of how he relates to the possibilities of psychic transformation within man. When the meditator is able to comprehend the symbolic significance of the chapel, he can learn to use it to uncover and face in himself the central problems of human life. The chapel also provides a stage on which the resolution of these central human problems can be symbolically revealed. It is Happich's idea that the "religious function" is the most intimate and not an invisible factor in human life. Further, he believed that man, if he will be really healthy and psychically free, sometime and somehow must face these questions. One cannot avoid the fact that the special efficacy of Happich's therapy was the result of his religious attitude. He developed a Christian meditation.

That his system of meditation is based on sound psychological principles is confirmed by the work of the Jungian school. Dreams have been recorded where a mountain is seen in a landscape and on the mountain stands a church. Such symbolic pictures have been valued psychically as an indication of the end of the process of "individuation," as a symbol of the attainment of "spirituality." But in meditation one does not wait until the needed symbols are produced spontaneously, as during dream analysis. Rather, the meditator is forced to occupy himself with certain symbols selected by the therapist until he has explored the fullness of their meaning.

Happich directed his meditators to a higher step which he called "Design (or Mandala, a Sanskrit word literally meaning circle, but more specifically an abstract design used especially in Tibetan Buddhism as a stimulus during meditation) Meditation." The design which is meditated upon is a kind of condensation, an abstraction of many symbols which are united into a generalized form. In the course of meditation on these designs, the meaning of the inherent symbolism can become obvious. With Mandala Meditation, the goal is not production of extensive fantasy, but rather a lively meditation revolving around the central meaning of the design. Eventually, the meditator is directed to psychically identify himself with the symbol and to integrate the meaning of the symbol with his psychic life. Properly speaking, these designs are not used as a technique of therapy, but rather in furthering the highest development of personality. An example of what can be experienced through meditation on a design can be read in the opening of Geothe's *Faust*, where Faust beholds the design of the macrocosmos.

A still more abstract form of meditation is "Word Meditation," directed toward unfolding the central human importance of a word or a saying. Meditation on designs and words are of the greatest importance in furthering religious development.

Happich holds the healthy principle of the equality of rational and irrational activity during the course of meditation.

On the other hand, one should not meditate on symbols or designs which stimulate dangerous negative emotions, as for example, a snake or a scorpion. The subject of meditation should be purified through thousands of years' experience of the wisest men, and be of proven value as is the case with many Egyptian, Hindu, and German symbols and also the holy symbols of the Greek church. The first requirement of such symbols is the impression of their positive transforming power, which can be regulated by man's psyche.

R. Desoille, a Frenchman, described one of the newest and most original techniques (Desoille, 1945, 1947, 1950). His procedure is not meditation in the classical sense. The emphasis is shifted toward more conventional depth psychology. But it deserves discussion as a technique of actively relating to the unconscious.

Desoille treats his patients in a state of limited consciousness, in which he suggests that symbols be plastically visualized and actively experienced. He directs his patients to psychically wander wherever they choose, availing themselves of any means, a kind of wandering into which most patients soon fall. They experience, for example, the climbing of a mountain or a tower, ascent into the clouds, etc. Especially important is the climbing, for reasons already discussed. In this wandering, all possible hindrances are eliminated. As in dreams, various symbolic forms are manifested from the "personal and collective unconscious"—in both auspicious and horrible aspects. Meeting "archetypal" symbols is considered especially effective. The patient relates his psychic experiences as he has them, and the turning point of the method is the therapist's reaction to them. As he is informed in each moment of the psychological scene, the therapist suggests to the patient a symbolic means of changing his (the patient's) situation by climbing or descending. The therapist does not suggest the whole fantasy; rather, he gives only a direction and maintains control of the fantasy by offering helpful symbols which can serve as points of crystallization for the fantasy. The technique is a good one. In the climb, Desoille realizes and makes use of the human ability for creative sublimation. In the descent, the patient comes to know psychic productions from the sphere of man's instinctual nature. The patient is led to the psychological execution of what Goethe poetically described as the way "from heaven through the world to hell." In other words, he penetrates through the patient's whole psychic report and provides symbolic expressions of inherent libidinal tendencies which motivate men on various psychic levels. Decisive for Desoille is the experience of meeting the "archetypes" which lead man to the absolutes of existence and the last decision, a decision of absolute and vast importance.

Desoille's valuation of the "collective unconscious" is more radical and consequential than Jung's; in this he (Desoille) holds that the meeting with the "collective unconscious" is a decisive and unavoidable presupposition of the therapeutic process.

Desoille holds that when the patient can relate himself to the "archetypes of the collective unconscious," he can find in them the appropriate adjustment to the problems of life. The patient must learn to control the "archetypes" within himself, to be free from them, and thereby lose his fear of them. He can then comprehend and resolve his personal conflicts within the larger context of man's inherent problems. Thus, the patient experiences his personal conflicts as having an impersonal and collective background. The motivational (libidinal) conflict is not resolved by being transferred upon the therapist, as in psychoanalysis; rather, the patient uncovers, in himself, the basic roots of the conflict. The goal of the technique is to direct the patient toward the fulfillment of his human potentialities through the creative development of man's basic biological impulses into a higher and harmonic order. With this idea, Desoille enters the realm of ethics and religion. Religious sensitivity is, for Desoille, the highest psychic state and the source of great activity.

Desoille's techniques require the therapist to possess a rare knowledge and understanding of symbolism and great psychological intuition in order to evaluate the waking dreams of his patients and to retain control of the process of psychological development which the waking dreams initiate.

The technique is, in a unique way, both diagnostic and therapeutic and the seemingly irrational procedure is worthy of note. Penetration of the psychic situation using reasonable conversation is given up. The therapeutic principle lies in the acceleration and furthering of effective development. It is a healing process which seeks the maximum transcendence of psychic limitations through symbolic ascensions and descensions. In this simple but most important principle, an earnest reminder can also be seen. Any therapist who would lead others to psychic heights and depths must, himself, be able to attain these heights and depths of the psyche. Contemporary psychotherapists will have to begin by training themselves to ascend and descend through their own psyche and thereby experience the manifold components within man and the driving forces behind human life. Who will accept Desoille's hypothesis and begin to look up and climb?

Walter Frederking calls his psychotherapeutic technique "Deep relaxation and symbolism" (Frederking, 1948). Frederking's technique is unsystematic, which implies nothing about its value.

Frederking also seeks freedom from dependence upon dreams by stimulating the unconscious to spontaneous productions of other kinds. To do this, he directs his patients in a progressive bodily relaxation during which they continue to describe their discoveries. One could also say he simply allows fantasy. The patient soon progresses from unclear visions to increasingly clearer productions of a kind of "symbolic strip thought." This symbolic thought, which has a significance similar to dream life, is allowed to flow by, scene by scene. The patient is both the playwright and the actors. He meets the contents of his "personal unconscious" and, to a degree, the "collective unconscious" and is able to relate their contents directly and dramatically to his psychic problems. One could also say that the patient is directed to enter "hell" to conquer the fiendish demons. This meeting with generally unrecognized aspects of himself brings about a spontaneous healing through various transforming symbols. Frederking holds that "in dreams and symbols man is led through every sphere of the psyche, during which the forms of psychic force are able to resolve themselves without the use of other means and deep-going transformations are effected."

Frederking also allows the therapy to be regulated by the autonomous healing force of the psyche. The technique is also irrational. Frederking knows, as all who work in these spheres know, that the therapist is in no way indifferent during the course of the therapy. It is true that he only occasionally interjects himself to clarify and point out the course of the healing. But the therapist knows that the patient can only experience the most favorably significant symbols at his own opportunity. Although the therapist remains essentially passive and does not interfere, the patient is still in the therapist's psychic field and may receive direction or formulation of impulses.

Friedrich Mauz has described another technique (Mauz, 1948). This technique is not meditation in the strictest sense, but it is related to it in many ways. With psychotics, the previously described methods are very dangerous and, therefore, rejected. Accordingly, the Mauz method is a severely restricted form of meditation in which the unconscious is most carefully tackled and channelled into productive performance.

Mauz does not mention preference for any technical preparation. The technique develops directly out of conversation considering the role of conditioned reflexes occurring daily at the same time. This conversation is almost a monologue in which the therapist depicts the patient in plastic and sympathy-evoking representative pictures from childhood; the experience of a procession, Christmas celebration in the family, a children's song, etc. The depiction must have, for the patient, an appropriate and intuitive power as a "solvent picture." It should unlock and enliven the suppressed emotions of the psychotic so that later a real conversation can develop.

Mauz aims, as does meditation in other respects, at the emotional level of the patient. Basically, he also leads the patient to the Happich childhood meadow, the creative ground of the psyche. But rather than wait for the patient to produce, Maus impregnates the meadow with symbols he knows will awaken positive feelings and meanings within the patient, such as the "security" of childhood with its guiltless pleasures. Through such feelings and symbols, the psychotic can again connect with the world around him. The creative power which flows from these feelings and symbols aids in closing the breach in the patient's personality.

It is noteworthy how Mauz describes important fundamental principles of meditation which he apparently discovered completely intuitively in genuine human behavior. The symbolic scene is the effector of the therapy, but only if it is experienced as real and actual; that is, as in meditation. "The picture must be personal and impersonal at the same time." It leads into the "sphere" of impersonal knowledge and reality." "All that is loud, obtrusive, and harsh must be avoided." The decisive experiences of the past present themselves in the stillness. We must "identify ourselves with the psychotic opposites." "The therapist mixes himself into a common solution with the patient and allows his own comfort to wait." One could say that the therapist must meditate on the patient. He must allow himself to be caught by the patient as the patient is caught by formulations of their psychic power. This is the mystical unity between the therapist and the sick. One must "not only analyze the illness," but also "know the possible health." The therapist must have before him a conception of the completely harmonic man and seek where he can find it again to develop it.

WOLFGANG KRETSCHMER 227

What happens here is biologically and ethically one. "The emotion of security," says Mauz, "is both vegetative and psychic." With this idea Mauz grasps the whole anthropological aspect of therapy.

Decisive for Mauz before all else, is "the simple human relationship." It appears most significant to the writer that a professional scientist like Mauz comes through his experience with meditation with the conclusion that "humanness" is the highest principle of therapy, an idea which is still far from scientific medicine today.

Now to gather together the viewpoints which characterize and are combined in the various techniques. All involve the active provocation of the unconscious, as the writer wishes to call it, in which the therapist chiefly has the function of a "birth helper." The patient is directed to place himself in relation to his unconscious, and thus make its creative possibilities available in the healing process. In contrast with the conscious, passive attitude employed in analytical methods of treatment, one takes an active, conscious, and oriented part in the healing process when using meditative techniques. Also in contrast with analytical methods, the meditative technique strives for a goal-directed, but individually adapted, formulation of man's nature in which a picture of the transformed man stands in the background. In this respect, Frederking is a relative exception. In contrast with the analytical-psychological techniques, the basic exercises of meditation are not only applicable to healthy men, but are very useful.

There is a value in the analysis of abnormality. Emphasis on the analytical is usually emphasis on our psychic past. During meditation, there is more dependence on the tendency toward health in the psyche. The orientation is synthetic rather than analytic.

Meditation helps the patient to an expanded consciousness and impersonal experience and knowledge. Meditation has an advantage in that it allows the transition to religious problems to consummate itself in a completely natural way. The course of therapy is shorter with meditation because one is not dependent upon the mood of dreams and comes more quickly, both diagnostically and therapeutically, to the psychic conflict. Finally, with meditation, the patient does not ordinarily transfer his problem onto the therapist and, therefore, the resolution of transference is usually unnecessary.

Opposed to the great range and efficiency of meditation is only one severe limitation. Meditation is limited by the subjectivity of both the therapist and the patient. Not without purpose are all the described experiences ascribed to a creator which none of the important schools has equalled. Unfortunately, each successful therapist forms his own school. Desoille and Mauz certainly demonstrate most unusual intuitions and artistic ability. Not every patient is equally able to fruitfully experience the deeper levels of the psyche. Decisive is the problem of the psychic field of force described by Heyer, which is valid for all techniques which explore the deeper levels of the psyche. If the patient would resolve his intimate psychic problems, he must bring the symbols which expose them, either in dreams or in meditation, into higher levels of consciousness. Stimulation of the deeper levels of the unconscious is the art of psychotherapy, which really can be described only by the unscientific term "exorcism." Exorcism is not only the result of a learnable technique, but is rather the result of the whole personal influence of the therapist on the patient. Therefore, with all these techniques, competent therapists are required. With one therapist, the patient may experience only the most banal contents of his unconscious; and with another, the patient may have a decisive experience of psychic depths. Thus, the psychotherapist must have a sense of vocation as well as a technique. A sense of vocation is the consequence of natural gifts and skill. Such skill is not learned as a craft nor as a medical training, but rather through personal skill as it develops in the relationship between master and disciple. Great psychotherapy is unique and cannot be copied any more than a work of art. It is because the work of a master cannot be copied that one can learn from him.

Meditation has a good chance of eventually becoming one of the leading therapeutic techniques. All the newer systems with which the writer is familiar look for a development in this direction. But whether or not this development takes place depends completely on a deep-going reformulation of psychotherapeutic training and the practice of psychotherapy. It is of the greatest importance whether psychotherapy continues to be sought in the direction of meditation. We can only hope that psychotherapy will continue to develop into a genuine technique which can aid men in their goal of developing their highest psychic potentialities.

INTRODUCTION TO SECTION 5. HYPNOSIS

"Hypnosis" is a rather vague term and refers to a *range* of ASCs, rather than to one clearly defined ASC. That is, investigators have used the term hypnosis as if there is general agreement on exactly what is meant, but an examination of the variability from S to S and from laboratory to laboratory suggests that there are probably several ASCs produced as a result of procedures all confusingly termed "hypnosis." The first two chapters in this section elaborate this point at great length.

In selecting articles to include in this section, the main problem was to select only a few out of many dozens of good studies carried out in the last two decades. The final choice is in no sense a representative survey of the past two decades' work on hypnosis, nor even the "best" work, using "best" in the sense of tightness of experimental design. Rather, I have selected five articles which I feel are very provocative in that they illustrate the complexity, wide-ranging applicability, and challenge of hypnosis research. Further, they all focus on the *experience* of hypnosis, rather than on its external behavioral manifestations. The past decade has seen a great increase in sophistication and tightness of experimental procedure in studying hypnotic *behavior*, but, in the process of this worthwhile and needed improvement, we have often lost sight of the *experience* of the hypnotized S.

There should be no need to justify the study of experience *per se* today, but there is another very important reason why the experience of the hypnotized S needs much greater emphasis, viz., quite different experiences can lead to the same externally observable behavior. If one then attempts to correlate this observable behavior with other factors, for instance, personality variables, one may not be able to find any strong relationships. The presence of posthypnotic amnesia, for example, is assessed in the objective suggestibility scales (Barber, 1965; Weitzenhoffer & Hilgard, 1959, 1962) by counting the number of hypnotic tasks the S can recall afterwards: if it is below a certain number, the S is considered amnesic. In work I have just completed, which involved interviewing Ss about their hypnotic experiences, the unitary concept of hypnotic amnesia was found to be quite misleading, since the Ss described *qualitatively* different ways (across Ss) of being amnesic. One way involves a lack of access to memory: they really cannot retrieve the information. A second involves an interference with memory retrieval, the appearance of "noise," distracting thoughts that mask the desired memory information. A third involves no interference with memory access at all, but a motor block develops so that they cannot *tell* the E what happened. All three different types of experience could lead to the same external behavior, viz., reporting less than the criterion number of items. Indiscriminately lumping them together under the term "amnesia," however, produces a measure with so much error variance that it would be difficult to find meaningful correlations with other factors.

Hypnosis is one of the most important ASCs that can be studied in the laboratory. It is easy to produce in many ordinary Ss and, in general, seems to be a very flexible state of consciousness which could be structured with appropriate procedures to simulate other ASCs or to produce ASCs that are well suited to a particular task, such as psychotherapy or creative endeavor. This point is discussed in greater detail elsewhere (Tart, 1967).

This section begins with two articles by Ronald Shor, "Hypnosis and the Concept of the Generalized Reality-Orientation," and "Three Dimensions of Hypnotic Depth," which provide a comprehensive theoretical orientation to hypnosis, as well as noting variables that may account for some of the variability in hypnosis. Shor's concept of the generalized reality-orientation and his emphasis on *several* dimensions of hypnotic depth may be applied to other ASCs with great profit.

Bernard Aaronson's article (Chapter 17), "Hypnosis, Depth Perception, and the Psychedelic Experience," on the far-reaching changes produced by posthypnotic suggestions designed to alter perceptual experience, is a highly challenging example of frontier research in hypnosis. He describes psychedelic experiences produced by one type of perceptual change and schizophreniclike experiences produced by another. The idea that our ordinary state of consciousness is heavily supported by and dependent on a relatively unvarying input from "reality" is not new but receives dramatic support in Aaronson's work. Aaronson has carried out a number of other studies to replicate and expand the work reported here (Aaronson, 1964, 1965a, 1965b, 1966a, 1966b, 1967a, 1967b).

Stanley Krippner's article (Chapter 18), "The Psychedelic State, the Hypnotic Trance, and the Creative Act," draws a number of intriguing parallels between hypnosis, the creative process, and the psychedelic state; it is full of ideas for future research.

My own article, "Psychedelic Experiences Associated with a Novel Hypnotic Procedure, Mutual Hypnosis," draws attention to a new procedure, in hypnosis which may be useful for studying psychedelic experiences as well as hypnosis *per se*.

Another paper in this book relevant to hypnosis is Milton Erickson's article (Chapter 3), on Aldous Huxley's experiences while hypnotized.

The final article in this section, "Autogenic Training: Method, Research and Application in Medicine," by Wolfgang Luthe, is a brief introduction to a large body of literature on this form of autohypnosis which is widely used in Europe but virtually unknown in the United States. Of particular interest are some of the observations of physiological parallels to those reported for Yoga and Zen meditation in Chapters 33 and 34. This paper is merely an overview of a very extensive literature; the reader who would like to do further reading should consult Schultz and Luthe's classic book, "Autogenic Training" (1959).

The references in this section will provide a very adequate guide to the modern literature on hypnosis. Some other recent books on hypnosis are Estabrooks (1962), Gill & Brenman (1959), Gordon (1967), Hilgard (1965), Kline (1962), Moss (1967), and Shor & Orne (1965).

15

HYPNOSIS AND THE CONCEPT
OF THE GENERALIZED REALITY-ORIENTATION

RONALD E. SHOR

Hypnotic theory has long been encumbered by concepts such as dissociation, suggestion, ideomotor activity, and automatism. Although useful distinctions are embedded in these concepts, they are incomplete and at times misleading. This paper will attempt to re-synthesize the implications of these concepts in a somewhat different fashion.

A significant advance in thinking about hypnosis became available with White's publication of *A Preface to a Theory of Hypnotism* (1941) in which he viewed hypnosis as the result of two intertwined processes: (a) goal-directed striving which (b) takes place in an altered psychologic state. White recognized that hypnosis cannot be understood without bearing in mind its motivational field and insisted that hypnosis must become a sophisticated chapter in social psychology before its proper contribution to the understanding of behavior can be made. White recognized that his views were not utterly unique, but his clarity and insistence on their broad meaning made his formulation a significant advance in theory construction even though admittedly heuristic.

In the first part of his theory White defined hypnosis as "meaningful goal-directed striving, its most general goal being to behave like a hypnotized person as this is continuously defined by the operator and understood by the

Reprinted by permission from *Amer. J. Psychotherapy*, Vol. 13, 1959, pp. 582–602.

subject ... Goal-directed striving [does not] necessarily imply either [conscious] awareness or intention."

White's view of goal-directed striving is sufficiently well known that there is little need to review it further.

The second part of White's theory, that of the altered psychologic state, has never received more than peripheral attention. Although White considered the notion of altered state vital to any adequate theory of hypnosis, he did not develop what he meant by it beyond asserting its importance. Happily, there are a number of indirect references to the specifications of the altered state spread throughout White's paper so that it is possible to reconstruct his underlying conception of it to some extent from his descriptive statements.

In speaking about trance induction White comments, "When a person is drowsy, his images and experiences tend to become more vivid, more concrete, and more absolute. Abstract processes and complex frames of reference seem to be highly vulnerable to fatigue. The operator avails himself of this vulnerability, reduces as far as possible the perceptual supports which might serve to sustain a wider frame of reference ... and thus encourages drowsiness to take a small toll from the higher integrative processes." Implicit in this quotation is the recognition that drowsiness *per se* is not the altered state, but rather that drowsiness helps reduce the abstract, integrative frames of reference that usually support and give context for all daily experiences. When the perceptual supports that sustain this wide frame of reference are withdrawn, the frame of reference itself fades."*
From the quotation it would appear then that White equates the altered state with the loss of a wide, complex, supportive frame of reference which is a kind of mental superstructure used in waking life to give substance and meaning to all experiences. Of special interest is White's observation of the high vulnerability of such supportive frames of reference to fatigue. He implies that the usual state of waking alertness is so fragile that simple drowsiness or fatigue can debilitate it, and implies furthermore that the altered state seen in hypnosis is akin to many related states, that is, wherever the significant aspect of the usual state of waking alertness is temporarily decomposed.

White further states, "It is significant that one of the commonest complaints of unsusceptible [hypnotic] subjects is that they could not forget the situation as a whole ... insofar as [these] are not signs of unfavorable

---

*The present writer would insist that the altered state can exist without any drowsiness whatsoever. Drowsiness has a certain indirect instrumental value in teaching an individual how to achieve the altered state, but it is not intrinsic to it nor is it essential to go through drowsiness to achieve it.

motivation, they imply that the frame of reference has refused to contract, that in spite of external circumstances there remains an internal alertness to 'other considerations' which is the opposite of drowsiness and the enemy of successful hypnosis." In this passage White emphasizes further that the altered state is a contraction of the usual frame of reference. When this occurs there is a consequent forgetting of the situation as a whole, and a loss of the internal alertness to the whole universe of other considerations which usually fills our waking minds.

In a later statement White (personal communication, in Sarbin, 1950) recognizes the desirability of expanding his views about the altered state.

"It would have been better, I think, to develop at more length the idea of a contracted frame of reference, or, as I would now prefer to put it, a contracted frame of activation. What has to be explained is how the hypnotic suggestions achieve their peculiar success, and I think the explanation should include two things: first the presence of a single ruling motivation, and second the exclusion by quieting of all promptings and even the sensory avenues of such prompting that might set up competing processes." White thus reasserts that hypnosis is to be understood as a complex of two processes; first, the single ruling motivation which is a clear reference to his view of goal-directed striving, and second, the quieting of all avenues of promptings, which refers to the altered state. White goes on to describe how these two processes interact in hypnosis and in some related states.

"...A fruitful comparison [is possible] between hypnosis and other states, such as great fear or excitement, in which volition is transcended. All such [latter] states are monomotivational ... in the sense that one extremely powerful motive or one strong preoccupation momentarily towers over all other processes. Hypnosis achieves the same relative effect at low dynamic intensities [by] quieting the competitors rather than heightening the chief process." The relative isolation of the hypnotic strivings is thus viewed as occurring partially by default, i.e., because the usual competitors for attention have been artificially quieted rather than because of an overpowering single motivation, as in states of great fear.

In recent years Sarbin (1950) has extended White's theory, rephrasing it into the language of social psychology. White's concept of striving becomes with Sarbin a special case of role-taking, and the altered state a simple derivation of profound organismic involvement in the role. Sarbin views even the deepest hypnotic phenomena as a kind of as-if behavior, which is not sham, but involves such a submergence of the self in the role that the subject can perceive the situation in no other way. He does not try to theorize, however, about the kinds of processes which might underlie such an inability to perceive the situation in another way. That Sarbin's view of this condition is not opposed to White's conception of the altered state can be seen in the following quotation. "When the subject takes the hypnotic role... a shift occurs from a sharp, alert, objective and critical attitude to a relatively relaxed, diffuse, and uncritical one... The alert orientation is highly valued and supported in our society... [subjects] must shift their focus to a relaxed, diffuse orientation which... allows for more active [role-taking]" (Sarbin, 1950).

The present paper attempts to develop the system of ideas implicit in White's descriptions of the altered state. A series of twelve propositions has been formulated in regard to the processes that produce the altered state, along with their implications and ramifications for hypnosis, related states, and cognitive theory in general.

1. The usual state of consciousness is characterized by the mobilization of a structured frame of reference in the background of attention which supports, interprets, and gives meaning to all experiences. This frame of reference will be called the usual generalized reality-orientation.

Perhaps the best way to explain what is meant by this proposition is to describe a state of consciousness in which the usual generalized reality-orientation is not mobilized, in order to see more clearly the psychic functions that are imputed to it. Many experiences could be cited as illustrations—from literature, "mystic" experiences, or pathologic states. The best of these have the quality of *merging* of self and world (as in the typical Nirvana experience), whereas the clearest illustration of our proposition would be an instance of the *loss* of self and world entirely. A personal subjective experience of the writer's meets the requirement. The experience is cited purely as illustrative material. It is understood that such material cannot constitute proof but it does supply a useful basis with which to discuss our conception.

Although the experience may appear unusual and idiosyncratic, the writer has been able to secure reports of similar experiences from a variety of people whenever it is clearly understood what kind of experiences are being referred to. Characteristically, people have such experiences but pay no attention to them and are not aware that anything significant has happened. Perhaps the reader may recall similar experiences of his own.

I had been asleep for a number of hours. My level of body tonus was fairly high and my mind clear to dream-images so that I believe I was not asleep but rather in some kind of trance-like state. At that time I was neither conscious of my personal identity, nor of prior experiences, nor of the external world. It was just that out of nowhere I was aware of my own thought processes. I did not know, however, that they were thought processes or who I was, or even that I was an *I*. There was sheer awareness in isolation from any kind of experiential context. It was neither pleasant nor unpleasant, it was not goal-directed, just sheer existing. After a time a "wondering" started to fill my awareness; that there was something more than this, a gap, an emptiness. As soon as this "wondering" was set into motion there was immediately a change in my awareness. In an instant, as if in a flash, full awareness of myself and reality expanded around me. To say that "I woke up" or that "I remembered," while perhaps correct, would miss the point of the experience entirely. The significant thing was that my mind changed fundamentally in that brief instant. In rediscovering myself and the world, something vital had happened; suddenly all of the specifications of reality had became apparent to me. At one moment my awareness was devoid of all structure and in the next moment I was *myself* in a multivaried universe of time, space, motion, and desire.

It will be noted that in this experience the sudden recollection was not of specific things about the world as such; rather what enveloped me was the whole abstract superstructure of relationships which serves as the foundation for my viewing the world. Into the immediate background of my awareness a framework, or orientation to the world, was reintroduced in which the world existed and in which I as a separate entity existed also. A mental representation of the world suddenly took a position in my mind where it could serve to interpret everything else. I, therefore, "rediscovered" the world, and, as a by-product, found myself in it. It was not simply that the distinction between self and world was remade. Both self and world and the distinction between them were all dependent upon reforming something more profound in which they all existed as by-products.

For whatever complex of reasons, the orientation or framework of experiences which I usually have in my normal waking life—to interpret automatically and give context to all my thought and experiences—was at this time not operating. And although I could reorganize it almost instantly, *until* I had reorganized it, nothing could exist for me except the vaguest awareness without even awareness of self. Before its return, self, world, past, or logic were totally incomprehensible, indeed, they could not even begin to exist. This experience illustrates our proposition that everything which is consciously known is predicated upon there existing in the immediate background of one's awareness a structured complex of recollections that support, give substance to, and critically integrate every further item of experience. Moreover, this usual orientation to reality cannot be taken for granted as a constant *given*, but rather can temporarily disintegrate in special states of mind, such as the one described. This brings us to the second proposition.

2a. The generalized reality-orientation does not maintain its regnancy as the cognitive superstructure in the background of awareness without active mental effort constantly devoted to its maintenance. However, this active effort is not usually consciously directed

2b. Whenever its supportive energy diminishes, the generalized reality-

orientation fades into the more distant background of attention and becomes relatively non-functional.

In this regard it is proper to reiterate White's reference to the fragility of wide frames of reference; their vulnerability to fatigue and drowsiness on the one hand and to hyperpreoccupation on the other. It has not gone unrecognized that under certain circumstances such as panic, sleep, toxic state of deprivation, toxic delirium, and, perhaps, sensory-deprivation and brainwashing, the generalized reality-orientation has less functional strength, and that consequently, inhibitions, awareness of surroundings, critical capacities, intellectual skills, and the ability to reality-test deteriorate.

Although it is sensible to hypothesize that the generalized reality-orientation is upheld by active efforts on the part of the organism, it should not, however, be conceived as necessarily consciously directed effort. It is consciously directed when we study, i.e., when we deliberately try to structure our mind with various ideas. Most of the time, however, the direction is essentially nonconscious and even seemingly "automatic" (as when we drive our car or play tennis or comprehend a social situation). The organism must maintain an adequate reality-orientation both in the special sense of driving a car or in the more general sense of generalized awareness. He must do this because it is the only "tool" he has to deal effectively with the masses of complex reality stimuli which bombard him throughout waking life. To let it lapse in average day-to-day living is to invite an automobile accident, or more generally, chaos and catastrophe in his commerce with reality.

The special aspect of the generalized reality-orientation necessary for driving—which can be called the special driving orientation—once learned becomes automatic and "reflexive" and is usually maintained without apparent effort by the driver. But actually it is fragile and probationary, dependent upon its active maintenance by nonconscious forces. The special driving orientation may lapse to a serious extent in fatigue and monotony states (so-called "highway hypnosis"). Every driver has moments of "temporary inattention." Such "inattention" is only secondarily a lack of attention to external reality; even more important is a lack of full and ready mobilization of the special driving orientation by the driver. The central fact is the lapsing of the special orientation from its regnancy in the immediate background of attention. Note that the special driving orientation may be fully mobilized in spite of conversations or concurrent thoughts while driving, and that it may temporarily fade at other times for no other reason than that the roadway does not call for its exercise. These factors can also be observed in regard to the more generalized reality-orientation.

In many circumstances, however, it is all right for the individual to allow his reality-orientation to slip away. Sleep is the prime example, but there are other situations, equally nonpathologic, where the individual feels safe and protected enough to do so. Hypnosis is one example. The complete absorption in music, especially of the abstract type, is another; it also occurs in focal attention (Schachtel, 1947), peak experiences (Maslow, 1964), mystic experiences (Huxley, 1945, 1956; James, 1936), B-cognition (Maslow, 1962), and the inspirational phase of creativity (Ghiselin, 1952; Hutchinson, 1949). In these latter examples the generalized reality-orientation may not just inadvertently slip away but may be voluntarily and deliberately renounced. Kris gives many examples under the concept of "voluntary regression in the service of the ego" (1952).

The freudian concept of regression thus refers in some fashion to the giving up of the usual orientation to reality but it implies that in its stead a new reality-orientation more appropriate to a prior state of psychosexual development is integrated. The concept that the reality-orientation *per se* may fade is alien to the freudian view. This is understandable given Freud's interest in psychopathology rather than cognitive organization, but makes the concept of regression too tangential for our use.*

3. The generalized reality-orientation is developed slowly throughout the life-cycle.

The work of Piaget (1951), Werner (1940), and others has demonstrated that an individual's orientation to reality is built up slowly through many stages of development. There is thus little need to expound this proposition further here. Graphic discussions have been long available of the child's first distinction of himself from his environment, the development of a body image, and the emergence of the concept of an external reality, as separated from the self (Allport, 1937; Baldwin, 1895; Cooley, 1902; Mead, 1934).

4. The concept of generalized reality-orientation is not equivalent to the many processes that derive from it, nor is it a mere sum total of them.

The generalized reality-orientation is a structured complex of recollections, an abstractive superstructure of ideas or superordinate gestalt of interrelationships. From its totality are derived various concepts and functions, some of which are reality-testing, body-image, critical self-awareness, cognition of self, world, other people, time, space, logic, purpose,

---

*Those who wish to view our discussion in general freudian terminology may consider the generalized reality-orientation roughly equivalent to the cognitive components of the ego or the secondary-process orientation (Freud, 1925). The gestaltist and lewinian concepts of structured psychologic field or life-space are also applicable if one were to modify the concepts to include nonconscious components.

various inhibitions, conscious fears and defenses. Just as the number seven has mathematical meaning only when it is embedded within the whole number system, so, for example, the idea of *self* has no sensible meaning unless embedded within an adequate orientation to reality. This goes beyond the simpler distinction between self and external world. Before the time when a child makes the distinction between self and world, he nevertheless has some kind of reality-orientation, albeit an immature one.

Moreover, the reality-orientation does not exist just to "test" reality. While reality-testing is certainly an important derivation, the conception goes beyond it. The reality-orientation *is* reality, at least in the sense that it is the inner surrogate for reality which the person must have in order to interpret anything (to "test" anything for that matter). All entities and events (self, time, space, purpose) exist for an individual only because they are predicated upon the mobilization of an adequate reality-orientation in which such secondary functions (such as reality-testing and differentiation of self from environment) can exist.

5. *The generalized reality-orientation is not an inflexible entity but is of shifting character with many facets. What emerges into the central background of attention depends on the special cognitive requirements of the immediate situation.*

It is almost trivial to observe that the mind is devoted to different things at different times, and that the cognitive orientation to the task at hand varies considerably with the differing requirements of the task.* The generalized reality-orientation cannot be conceived of as inflexible, but rather must be viewed as allowing different aspects of itself to emerge into more central focus while other aspects are relegated to more distant positions.

The reality-orientation is, therefore, always in some flux in normal waking life, so that certain aspects of it are temporarily given more central focus and other aspects are made so distant as to be nonfunctional, except as a mass of vague apperceptions which lies far behind the immediate background of attention. When watching a baseball game, for example, the rules of baseball are given a central position in the background of our attention and many other aspects of the generalized reality-orientation—such as the system of skills used in swimming—are so formless as to be temporarily inoperative. But the important thing about our waking life is that although there can be a relative emphasis on this or that, the remainder of the reality-orientation is still vaguely within the bounds of conscious awareness. If

---

*There is a considerable body of experimental work on these relationships in academic psychology under the concepts of attention, mental set, and selective perception. See also Bartlett's work on schemas (1932).

someone asks us about the Australian Crawl, for example, we can pull the relevant information into central focus quickly with no profound shift in mental state, even while watching a baseball game.

This brings us to the next proposition.

6a. *In normal waking life, even where special aspects of the generalized reality-orientation are in central focus, the rest of it is in close communication at all times. When close communication is lost, the resultant state of mind may be designated as trance.*

6b. *Any state in which the generalized reality-orientation has faded to relatively nonfunctional unawareness may be termed a trance state.*

It is only when we become so absorbed in one segment of reality (and so oblivious to the rest of it that we lose easy contact with it) that we begin to approach the special state of disintegration of the reality-orientation which is trance. Indeed the induction of hypnotic trance takes place in just this way: focusing one's attention on a small range of preoccupations and concurrently allowing the usual orientation to reality to slip away into temporary oblivion so that certain behaviors can function in *isolation* from the totality of generalized experiences.

The concept of isolation stems from Goldstein's work with brain-injured individuals (1939). The concept refers to the fact that an altered organism no longer has functionally available the usual background for his reactions, and thus the behavior functions in isolation. Some of the formal character-istics of the brain-injured individual—concretization, stimulus bounded-ness, rigidity—are paralleled by certain analogous characteristics in hypnosis, for example, suggestibility.

In this view then suggestibility and hypersuggestibility are not con-ceptualized as the primary processes of hypnosis as in the theories of Bernheim (1889) and Hull (1933), but as secondary or derivative con-sequences of isolation.

The notion of relatively nonfunctional unawareness can be best under-stood with an illustration of a common experience.

I was reading a rather difficult scientific book which required complete absorption of thought to follow the argument. I had lost myself in it, and was unaware of the passage of time or my surroundings. Then, without warning, something was in-truding upon me; a vague, nebulous feeling of change. It all took place in a split-second, and when it was over I discovered that my wife had entered the room and had addressed a remark to me, I was then able to call forth the remark itself which had somehow etched itself into my memory, even though at the time it was spoken I was not aware of it.

It will be noted that the experience took place while I was reading a passage in a scientific work which required great absorption of thought for its comprehension. By *absorption* is meant that in order to understand the written statements, it was necessary for me to keep my mind actively structured in regard to the specifications and details of the intricate, technical niche of reality that was being referred to. This meant that I had to keep in mind, actively and continuously, a whole complex of details and interrelationships which were essential at each step of the argument in order to follow it. This does not mean that all details and interrelationships were full-blown and vividly conscious at each instant, but in some fashion there was created in my mind a mental superstructure within which each *new* statement derived its comprehension, and thereby was added, in turn, to the intricate mental superstructure.

This intricate mental superstructure thus referred to a specific, technical segment of reality. But the larger superstructure of notions about reality in general (of which this is but an infinitesimal part) which I usually use most of my waking life to interpret events was temporarily minimized in importance in my mind, and, by default, was pushed far back into the background of my attention and awareness. Note, however, that the book's special superstructure was also in the background of my awareness. But it was in the *immediate* background; it was the "thing" I was using to constantly interpret each new written item. The generalized reality superstructure was in the *more distant* background, and was of little consequence to the immediate task.

It was while I was thus absorbed in the book that my wife entered the room and spoke to me. As noted above, I did not know that she had entered the room, nor did I know that she had spoken to me. In some dim way I was aware of *something*—something intruding. In my phenomenal awareness this something was nothing so formal and structured as my wife speaking to me. Somewhere out of the vaguest depths of awareness an uncomfortable something created a problem in me—a feeling of nebulous discomfort: that there was something to do, something I had to do. An instant later and without apparent discontinuity, I reinstituted into my mind's immediate background of attention an orientation to generalized reality in which things such as other people, spoken language, wives, sitting and reading, and people entering rooms had sensible meaning and existence to me. Once the usual reality-orientation was reinstituted into the immediate background of conscious attention everything was clear to me. The jumble-of-something which had occurred a moment before I now knew to be words; indeed, words spoken by my wife, to *me*. Moreover, the jumble-of-something of a moment before had somehow remained reverberating in my mind, and now that I had reconstituted within my mind an orientation which was *adequate* to it, I thereby and immediately knew what the words were. That is, I remembered something which I had not really known before except as a senseless jumble-of-something (it was not at that time identified even as sounds). The process of recollection was in terms of a new frame of reference to generalized reality so that the same "things" of an instant before were thereby different from what they had been before. In the previous frame of reference such things could only be a jumble-of-something; in the new referential schema they were my wife's remark.

What had happened to the generalized reality-orientation when I was absorbed in the book? Nothing, except that it had receded far away into the background of my mind, far from the field of conscious awareness. The generalized reality-orientation had reference to the features of the everyday world. Comprehension of the book required a specific referential schema adequate to the particular character of the book's contents, and this was constructed in the immediate background of my attention. The generalized everyday frame of reference still existed far out on the periphery of awareness-unawareness as a vague, unobtrusive, formless thing, serving as some kind of distant support for my special structuring. Moreover, I was not aware that it had faded except afterwards when it was reinstated.

In some fashion the comment by my wife communicated with the generalized, everyday frame of reference, and the processes were initiated which brought it into the central arena of my attention. In the process of re-instituting this orientation, however, I concurrently relinquished in part my book's orientation and it took me a number of moments to again "get back into the book." Note that I did not really have to "get back into the book" but rather had to get the orientation of the book back into me.

It will be observed that in this illustration reference is made not only to an extensive fading of the usual generalized reality-orientation, but also to the production of a special little task-orientation. Such a special task-orientation is usually embedded upon the generalized reality-orientation, but can, as in this instance, function with relative isolation. It is these two cognitive processes which the writer views as composing the hypnotic trance, to wit:

7. *Hypnosis is a complex of two fundamental processes. The first is the construction of a special, temporary orientation to a small range of preoccupations and the second is the relative fading of the generalized reality-orientation into nonfunctional unawareness.*

Although these two processes are cited as the fundamental core of hypnosis, they are not exhaustive of the variables relevant to understanding it. They refer only to the underlying skeleton, i.e., the fundamental cognitive basis of hypnosis which may be assumed universal to all human beings. The flesh and blood of hypnosis—its multidimensional clinical richness and variation—only appears when hypnosis is viewed in terms of the dynamic interrelationships between real people. There is certainly no inherent

antagonism between the present conceptualization and more psychodynamically oriented formulations; indeed, they must supplement each other
for a complete theory.*

Hypnosis, as noted in the example in the above section, is not unique
in manifesting these two processes. Unlike related conditions, however,
hypnosis has the character of occurring within a special kind of interpersonal
situation where the task at hand (the special orientation) is to produce
certain expected phenomena and act like a hypnotic subject. When the
task at hand is instead a personal preoccupation in a small range of interests,
the resultant complex is not labeled hypnosis but rather absent-mindedness,
or daydreaming, or intense meditation.

Absent-mindedness is the proverbial occupational hazard of the academic
profession. It is not difficult to show its formal similarities with hypnotic
trance. A composite picture of absent-mindedness has been drawn by the
writer derived from many informal interviews with absent-minded people.
It is presented in the following paragraph.

When they become absorbed in something, every nook and cranny of their
minds is filled with affect-charged information that vibrates in vivid availability. "Reality" itself becomes almost exclusively the features and interrelationships of the task at hand, and the rest of the world which does not
"fit" into the task (the day-to-day world of petty business) slips far away
from their immediate concerns. They become so involved in the specific task-
orientation that the more generalized reality-orientation in which it resides
has faded like a weak Ground behind an attention-compelling Figure. They
still operate within the faded reality-orientation to some extent; they will eat
lunch unless they forget, keep an appointment if something reminds them,
or drive their cars without mishap. Their commerce with reality via the
generalized reality-orientation is minimal but just enough to be adequate.
Most of their energies are placed within the special task-orientation, and not
much remains to support the frame of reference in which day-to-day meanings exist. External events must be especially forceful, with their own
inherent organizations, to force their way through their preoccupations so
that the meaning will be grasped. Otherwise, they see everything in the
terms of the special task-orientation and since, for example, "picking up the
laundry" has no place or meaning in the task-orientation, it may flit away
until the generalized reality-orientation is reintroduced into a more central
focus. After they have refocused on everyday reality they may suddenly
rediscover that the laundry has been there all the time.

*For a careful exposition of some of the ways that these two fundamental processes
are implemented and affected by personality dynamics and the structure of the
cognitive and interpersonal situation in hypnosis see our forthcoming publications
from the *Studies in Hypnosis Project*.

In absent-mindedness, then, we find to a lesser degree the same two cognitive processes viewed as fundamental to deep hypnotic trance.

8. The generalized reality-orientation does not fade away completely either in deepest trance or deepest sleep.

Even in the deepest trance the generalized reality-orientation never disappears entirely. Whatever of it does remain, however, is so distant from consciousness that it has little effect upon the content of consciousness. That some modicum of the reality-orientation remains in the psychic distance can be seen in the fact that people do not usually fall out of bed at night and that dreams are censored. Even when the generalized reality-orientation seems utterly disintegrated something of it remains, continuing to function at a deeper level. Any situation arising which calls forth vigilance by the organism rapidly reinstates it. This can be observed in hypnosis where for one reason or another the subject experiences a minor trauma, and as a result the trance begins to lighten or he awakens entirely, In such circumstances subjects will report that suddenly they became aware of noises, of their surroundings, and that thoughts began again to fill their minds, i.e., that they again began to experience the world and themselves in waking terms. Typically, however, they scarcely recall the trauma itself.

Even in psychosis where the generalized reality-orientation is profoundly disturbed (conceptualized in part as breakdown of ego-organization) some aspects of the reality-orientation always remain.

One is usually not aware, moreover, that the wide orientation has faded. Awareness that it has faded itself requires its partial mobilization. One can sometimes feel it slipping away, however. This is an experience which may frighten an insecure hypnotic subject.

9. When the generalized reality-orientation fades (a) experiences cannot have their usual meanings; (b) experiences may have special meanings which result from their isolation from the totality of general experiences; and (c) special orientations or special tasks can function temporarily as the only possible reality for the subject in his phenomenal awareness as a result of their isolation from the totality of general experience.

The meaning of this postulate has been sufficiently clarified in previous sections so that there is little need to expand on it. The postulate is not exhaustive, however, of all the things that may happen when the generalized reality-orientation fades. The next two postulates consider additional occurrences.

10. When the generalized reality-orientation fades, special orientations or special tasks can be made to persist beyond the bounds of awareness and/or remain nonconsciously directive of further activities, even when the generalized reality-orientation is again mobilized.

Reference is made here to the nonconscious maintenance of special orientations in relative isolation from the generalized reality-orientation even after the latter has been returned to functional awareness. This is the familiar basic sequence in repression where impulses are initially repressed, and although kept out of awareness, nevertheless exist, are relatively impervious to conscious direction, and exert indirect expression. That the fundamental cognitive processes underlying these very well-known occurrences can be evoked in an artificial manner in hypnosis (once the generalized reality-orientation has sufficiently faded) can be observed clinically and is the basis for such hypnotic phenomena as artificial "neurotic" complexes, posthypnotic acts with amnesia, automatic writing, and various other dissociated activities.

When the generalized reality-orientation returns, the dissociated complex of strivings is somehow sealed off and kept relatively isolated. It is necessary to assume that this very sealing-off process—whatever one wishes to call it—implies that some communication with the generalized reality-orientation must remain, although this communication may be far beyond the bounds of conscious awareness. As far as phenomenal awareness is concerned, however, there may be an utter and complete dissociation between one's intentions and awareness and the form and contents of the dissociated activities.

Implicit in this formulation is a recognition that when the generalized reality-orientation fades, one can come closer to the sources of his nonconscious functioning. This leads us to the next postulate.

11. When the generalized reality-orientation fades (a) various mental contents excluded before can now flow more freely into phenomenal awareness, and (b) primary-process modes of thought may flow into the background of awareness to orient experiences.

Schachtel (1947) has observed that there are basically two ways in which capacities and memories are kept out of phenomenal awareness by the usual structuring of the waking mind. The first mode of exclusion is active repression. The second is a passive accomplishment, i.e., certain contents cannot fit into the conventionalized schemata which are the symbolic fabric of the waking mind. In other words, many things simply cannot fit into the logic and specifications of the usual reality-orientation. But as the usual reality-orientation fades, its derivative distinctions between wishes, self, other, imagination and reality fade with it, as do many inhibitions, conscious fears and defenses, and primary-process material and primary-process modes of thought can flow more easily into awareness, and *if* they do, a new kind of orientation is created which shares some of the qualities of the dream. Thus, trance states can be in much greater communication with an individual's nonconscious functioning than in the usual waking tate, and it is not surprising that nonconscious strivings may be more easily implemented. All of this becomes the more true the deeper one sinks into hypnotic trance. At first, the subject can hardly distinguish whether he is doing things intentionally or whether they are happening all by themselves, i.e., whether his behavior is consciously directed or directed by nonconscious motivations. As the subject sinks deeper it becomes more apparent to him that things occur without his conscious direction, sometimes even contrary to his conscious attempts at resistance, and these things may then be made to persist even after the usual reality-orientation is remobilized.*

A number of themes in the last three postulates may be summarized to serve as background for the next postulate.

To the extent that the usual reality-orientation fades from the background of awareness, the greater the possibility that other experiences will occur which could not have fit into the usual reality-orientation, the greater the possibility that new, special orientations may be constructed at profound levels without recourse to the logic, knowledge, and critical functions of the usual reality-orientation, and the greater the possibility that primitive, syncretic contents and modes of thought will come into awareness. With this as background we may define our conception of a good hypnotic subject.

12. A good hypnotic subject may be defined as a person who has the ability to give up voluntarily his usual reality-orientation to a considerable extent, and who can concurrently build up a new special orientation to reality which temporarily becomes the only possible reality for him in his phenomenal awareness.

While the concept of new, special orientation is defined from the standpoint of cognition, it is identical with what White has called goal-directed striving from the standpoint of motivation or what Sarbin has called role-taking from the standpoint of social psychology.

One important exception must be made clear. In a minority of hypnotic subjects, after the special orientation has outfitted the mind, many skills of the usual generalized reality-orientation may be brought back into communication with the special orientation, but in a position so subordinated to it that they do not critically undermine it (do not lighten trance). This exceptional ability is not to be confused with what is described above as the construction of a dissociated complex of strivings. A dissociated complex remains relatively isolated when the generalized reality-orientation is

---

*Erickson (1941) maintains that when posthypnotic suggestions are carried out, a spontaneous, self-limited trance occurs for the duration of the posthypnotic act. While this may be true, some complex of strivings or ideas must remain in the interim nonconsciously vigilant for the cues of the posthypnotic act.

reintegrated. In this new instance communication is made between the special orientation and the generalized orientation but in such a way that the latter is kept in a subordinate position rather than becoming superordinate. Only the very best subjects can do this, and they form what might even be considered a qualitatively different group from everyone else. For most subjects, however, when such general features are evoked, the whole inner superstructure of reality tends to be remobilized into superordinate position and trance lightens, even though role-taking may remain intense.

Many variations in special, temporary reality-orientations are possible and these account for many of the apparent variations in types of hypnotic trance (Orne, 1957). But unless there is a fairly extensive breakdown of the usual reality-orientation it is fallacious to speak of hypnosis at all, no matter how committed the subject is to the special orientation to reality he builds up in regard to the operator's tasks. To the extent that the usual reality-orientation remains in awareness all "hypnotic" behavior must be *as-if* a sheer playing of a role.† To the extent that the usual reality-orientation fades into unawareness, the special reality-orientation constructed in regard to the role of the subject becomes temporarily, by the very fact of isolation, the only possible reality to the subject.

We can thus speak of hypnosis as having two dimensions of depth: (a) the depth of *trance*, which may be defined as the extent to which the generalized everyday, reality-orientation has sunk into nonfunctional unawareness, and (b) the depth of *role-taking*, which may be defined as the extent to which the subject builds up a new, special orientation from the instructions of the hypnotist. Although closely interrelated, considerable confusion results if one confounds these two dimensions of hypnotic depth, based as they are on two logically distinct processes.

It is useful, therefore, to reiterate our distinction between trance and hypnosis. Trance is the superordinate concept used to refer to states of mind characterized by the relative unawareness and nonfunctioning of the generalized reality-orientation. Hypnosis is *a special form of trance* developed in Western civilization, achieved via motivated role-taking, and characterized

---

*Although the best subjects can do this without lightening trance, the most profound somnambulistic phenomena, such as convincing age-regression or time distortion, demand that the usual orientation remain faded.

†Orne capitalizes methodologically on this distinction by using a special control group of unsusceptible subjects who are treated experimentally like real hypnotic subjects but who "fake" hypnosis by intensively role-playing without otherwise going into trance (Orne, 1957).

by the production of a special, new orientation to a range of preoccupations.*

Hypnosis is thus an impure concoction of trance and role-playing. Not
only is the usual orientation still somewhere in the psychic distance, but
the role-playing aspects of hypnosis are in some ways antagonistic to the
process of trance. Many of the technical problems faced by a hypnotist are
to be found here. All other things being equal, certain special limited
orientations tend to reintegrate the generalized orientation, others tend
to help it slip away. Certain difficult hypnotic phenomena usually can be
produced only in deep trance. If they are attempted in lighter trance, they
tend to reintegrate the generalized orientation (lighten trance). Thus the
two processes can work together or be opposed. A great deal of the
hypnotist's skill consists in balancing these two processes, i.e., attuning the
tasks given to subjects to their depth of trance so as to help deepen trance
rather than lighten it.

Only in the fetus can one conceive of an ideally pure trance state, i.e., a
state in which there is a total absence of a functioning reality-orientation.
In the developing organism iń utero the first momentary experiences exist
concretely, independent of any structured background of experience. The
only organization that can take place at first is that which is genetically
given. But except for this natural, ontogenetically undeveloped state there
is always some degree of structuring. It must take tremendous organismic
effort, however, for an infant to learn to construct a generalized reality-
orientation and hold it in the background of awareness throughout waking
life. The spontaneous, intense absorption which occurs so easily in children,
or for that matter the easy deterioration of a child's reality-oriented behavior
with fatigue, suggests that children have a less rigid grip on their generalized
orientation and its temporary loss is more frequent at first than its maintenance. As the child grows older—at least in our culture—the usual
orientation takes on a more rigid and demanding character. Trances
occur with less frequency and intensity. Man's *second nature* (widely

*Once deep trance is achieved, however, hypnosis need not involve the playing
of any role other than pursuing one's own inner dynamics. In other words, the
hypnotist may act as a collaborator to help achieve a state of mind which transcends
the playing of an externally defined role, freeing the individual for hypnotic experiences more closely akin to states of profound fascination and absorption of peak
experiences or mystic states of inner contemplation. Maslow believes that an over-
emphasis on "striving-hypnosis" (role-playing) rather than "being-hypnosis"
(expressive inner experiencing) has led to a narrow and one-sided conceptual view
of hypnosis in the theories of White and Sarbin (Maslow, personal communication).
Compare in this regard Orne's belief that what is seen in hypnosis today in our
culture is essentially an historical accident (Orne, 1957).

oriented experiencing) becomes so firmly entrenched that it intuitively feels more primary than trance experiencing. If this analysis is correct then the mystery is in the usual state of waking alertness and not in trance. The mystery is not why some people can achieve deep trance states. Rather it is why most people are *not* able to do so. If it is true that active mental effort must be constantly devoted to the maintenance of the usual orientation then what accounts for our inability to let go of it? What kind of learning processes interfere with one's natural capacity to relinquish voluntarily his functional orientations? What enculturation processes interfere with the facile development of trance states so easy for us in childhood? It is with this problem that the paper ends.

SUMMARY

White's theory that hypnosis is a combination of (a) goal-directed striving in (b) an altered psychologic state of the organism was a significant advance in hypnotic theory construction. While the first part of White's theory has received considerable attention, the second part has been relatively ignored. Twelve propositions are formulated in regard to the altered state, which is defined as the relative breakdown of the usual orientation to generalized reality into nonfunctional awareness. Hypnosis, as conventionally understood, is viewed as the production of a special task-orientation with the concomitant breakdown or voluntary relinquishing of the usual reality-orientation so that the former functions in relative isolation from the totality of general waking experiences. Ramifications of this view are presented, along with a distinction between trance and hypnosis. The relationship between hypnosis and certain states such as absent-mindedness is discussed. The propositions are phrased so as to refer to human cognition in general.

16

THREE DIMENSIONS OF HYPNOTIC DEPTH

RONALD E. SHOR

A RECOGNITION OF THREE SEPARATE DIMENSIONS

White's (1941) two dimensions—eager obedience and oblivion—do not cover what Schilder and Kauders (1956) meant by psychic depth. White's two dimensions, however, do roughly cover the recognition of three separate dimensions of hypnotic depth, each of which appears capable of varying independently of the other two.

White's two dimensions of depth have already been fully embraced by the writer in his original twelve propositions. We spoke there of (a) depth of role-taking* and (b) depth of trance. In the present paper Schilder and Kauders' dimension of psychic depth will be incorporated into our propositional system as a third factor, which we will call the dimension of archiac involvement.

Reprinted by permission from *Interno. J. of Clinical & Experimental Hypnosis*, Vol. 10, 1962, pp. 23–38. To conserve space the first section of this paper has been deleted in the present volume since the main tenets of Shor's additional postulates are readily understood in relation to his preceding paper. The specialist who wishes to know the derivation of the theory more fully is advised to consult the original publication—*Editor*.

*See proposition 14 for a revision of this concept.

NINE ADDITIONAL PROPOSITIONS

13. Hypnotic depth may be defined as some complex of depth along three conceptually separate dimensions. These three dimensions are: (a) the dimension of hypnotic role-taking involvement; (b) the dimension of trance; and (c) the dimension of archaic involvement.

This proposition states in formal terms the three-factor theory of hypnotic depth discussed previously. The next three propositions define each of the three factors individually.

14. Hypnotic role-taking involvement depth is the extent to which the complex of motivational strivings and cognitive structurings regarding the role of hypnotized subject has sunk below the level of purely conscious compliance and volition, and has become nonconsciously directive.

In our initial series of propositions reference was made to *hypnotic role-taking* as one dimension of hypnotic depth. Since the publication of that earlier report, however, it became apparent that two quite different concepts were subsumed under that single rubric which we now feel bound to separate. A sharp distinction must now be drawn between the concepts: (a) hypnotic role-taking (as such) and (b) hypnotic role-taking involvement. Only the second of these two concepts do we consider a dimension of hypnotic depth.*

Hypnotic role-taking (as such) is the complex of motivational strivings and cognitive structurings to take as one's own the role of being a hypnotized subject. In order to be or become a hypnotized subject it is necessary that at some level an individual try to fulfill the requirements of what he perceives as the role of hypnotized subject. He must endeavor in a goal-directed, cognitively organized manner to conduct himself in consonance with his continuously evolving perception of the required hypnotic role. Responses to the directions of a hypnotist do not emerge in the subject's behavior without an adequate cognitive and motivational basis *within the subject*. The hypnotist's directions are effective because at some level these directions become translated into the subject's own cognitively structured strivings.

It is not the taking of the hypnotic role as such, however, which is a dimension of hypnotic depth. Rather, it is the extent to which whatever hypnotic role-taking there may be has become nonconsciously involved; i.e., the extent to which the hypnotic role-taking has sunk below the level of purely conscious compliance and volition and has become nonconsciously directive.

Hypnotic role-taking as such, regardless of its intensity, does not necessarily in itself imply any nonconscious involvement. Even intense hypnotic

*The earlier part of our propositional system will be revised eventually to account for this new distinction.

role-taking may often be an entirely conscious, deliberate, voluntary endeavor, with no nonconscious component.

When role-taking involvement deepens, a compulsive and involuntary quality derives from it. As a consequence of the progressive nonconscious involvement, the ongoing hypnotic experiences and behaviors become executed by the subject without the experience of conscious intention and often in defiance of it. The task of being a hypnotized subject has become not a consciously controlled choice.

15. Trance depth is the extent to which the usual generalized reality-orientation has faded into nonfunctional unawareness.

The concept of the generalized reality-orientation has already been expounded in our initial series of twelve propositions. It remains here only to identify trance depth as the progressive fading of the generalized reality-orientation, which leaves the ongoing contents of awareness increasingly more functionally isolated.

Trance, so defined, is not a strange mystic occurrence happening only in hypnosis, religious ecstasies, and such esoterica. Trance becomes seen as a daily, commonplace occurrence, a somewhat larger way of conceptualizing "selective attention," and as familiar as the chaotic oblivion of the mind during sleep.*

It is useful here to draw an example to show how trance depth makes the distinction between reality and imagination progressively less relevant. The example selected is from the writer's own experience but it is hardly unique. The writer has failed to find anyone among his acquaintances who could not identify minor variants of this experience as also his own. The particular scene happens to pertain to sleep and dreaming, but these are mere stage-settings. Our chief character is the meaning of trance depth.

I had been dreaming when the alarm-clock rang. Opening my eyes, I awakened suddenly. For the barest moment before the dream disappeared, I was aware both of waking reality and the dream "reality" together. I was forcefully struck by the realization of how unreal the dream "reality" was when observed by my mostly awake mind.

In this experience the waking reality and the dream "reality" existed together for a fleeting instant. Then, like a superimposed fade-out in a motion-picture sequence, the dream "reality" quickly dissolved into unawareness and only the waking reality was left in view. Yet for that prior

---

*Trance may be facilitated by, but may occur independently of, the physiological processes attendant to sleep. Our remarks should not be viewed as any identification of trance (or hypnosis) with sleep.

instant both the dream and the waking worlds existed entirely clear and intact together, superimposed yet unjoined. In that fleeting instant I could compare the two worlds, and a startling comparison it was: two universes, fundamentally disparate, with different logic, different boundaries. Chiefly startling was the recognition that my dream was but an unkempt, faded world when compared against the vivid, detailed, unbounded waking world. Imagery was meager, background was hardly painted in.

Nonetheless, during the dream itself the dream world had been an emotionally compelling world to dwell in. It was as vivid and as detailed as it needed to be in order to be totally "real" to me. Only when compared against waking standards did it seem constricted. But, only beginning with the fleeting instant of superimposition could waking standards be applied. Throughout the dream the only "reality" was the dream, and the usual reality was utterly irrelevant and unavailable to it.

All this description illustrates that my ongoing phenomenal experience while asleep (the dream) was functionally isolated from the usual abstract schemata of waking life—which is our definition of profound trance depth. It is clear that during this profound trance the ongoing contents of awareness had no need to mimic in every regard the actual occurrences. It was sufficient only that they possessed a "reality" value at the moment of the experience.

For an individual with excellent visual imagery, a dream (or a hypnotically hallucinated scene) might very well visually mimic the actual scene. For an individual like myself with no visual imagery whatsoever in the waking state and rather meager visual imagery even in dreams, his best dream (or hypnotic hallucination) might only be a faint copy of the original when judged by waking standards. But for both types of individuals the dream (or hallucination) may be unequivocally "real" at the moment of the experience—provided that trance is sufficiently deep.

16. Depth of archaic involvement is (a) the extent to which during the hypnosis archaic object relationships are formed onto the person of the hypnotist; (b) the extent to which a special hypnotic "transference" relationship is formed onto the person of the hypnotist; (c) the extent to which the core of the subject's personality is involved in the hypnotic processes.

It may strike the reader as noteworthy that on the one hand we embrace fully a psychoanalytic concept, and yet, on the other hand, we do not *formally* mention the usual phrasing of this conception; i.e., unconscious fixation of the libido on the person of the hypnotizer by means of the masochistic component of the sexual instinct; nostalgic reversion to that phase of life when passive-receptive mastery represented the primary means of coping with the outside world; an appeal to that universal core which longs for wholesale abdication, unconditional obedience; security through participation in the limitless powers of the all-powerful parent; the evocation of archaic, infantile wish-fantasies regarding the parent-like "magic" omnipotence of the hypnotist.

Our reluctance to embrace these phrasings is not because we are in disagreement with them. They entirely fit within the above definition of archaic involvement. We suspect, however, that profound archaic involvement may occur with somewhat different dynamic constellations than the above notion of masochistic surrender implies. Empirical clarification is needed, and until it is available we feel it best to leave our formal statement somewhat uncommitted.

17. When depth is profound along all three dimensions, a situation exists with the following characteristics: (a) the role-enactments have permeated down to nonconscious levels; (b) the hypnotic happenings become phenomenologically the only possible "reality" for the moment; (c) intense, archaic object relations are formed into the person of the hypnotist; (d) in general, all classic hypnotic phenomena can be produced.

When depth is profound along all three dimensions, the cognitively structured strivings to take the required hypnotic role have sunk below the conscious level and become nonconsciously directive and persistent. From the standpoint of phenomenal awareness the resulting strivings are totally compelling and involuntary. In the extreme the usual background of awareness has slipped so far away that even the little disembodied self off in the psychologic distance—which somewhat less entranced subjects often report as watching from afar their own hypnotic behavior—has itself faded out of the bounds of conscious awareness. The hypnotic experiences are isolated unto themselves and thus by default become phenomenally the total "reality" for the time. The larger personality is profoundly involved with the hypnotic performances, satisfying archaic longings and bestowing an importance, vitality, and energetic meaning upon the hypnotic processes.

When depth is profound along all three dimensions, it is not possible to disentangle clearly the dimensions as conceptually separable entities. Whenever depth is less than profound, but of roughly equivalent depth along all three dimensions, it is equally impossible to disentangle clearly the dimensions. If such parallel variation were always the case, moreover, there would be no merit in conceiving of more than one dimension. The three would most profitably merge in our thinking as but three ways of conceptualizing the same psychologic totality; as different aspects of—or frames of reference for viewing—this single dimension. It is only as we observe instances of gross imbalance among them that the need to conceptualize separate dimensions becomes apparent. The next proposition formally recognizes the conditions and effects of imbalance.

18. When depth along the three dimensions is not in relative balance the resultant hypnosis will have characteristics corresponding to the existing imbalance configuration.

The appearance of hypnosis when the configuration of depth is imbalanced is a question which is most meaningful when considered against the problem of how to measure the three hypnotic dimensions separately. The diagnosis or measurement of the three hypnotic depths is, however, too complex a problem to be dealt with here, and will be the topic of a later report. In this paper we wish merely to report a few examples in order to clarify the preceding proposition. It should be understood of course that estimations of depth from any one hypnotic item, from subjects' reports, and without taking account of the entire context of events can hardly be entirely reliable, but it illustrates the general meaning of variable configurations. Three examples are cited, each referring to the hallucination item in a widely used objective depth rating scale.*

Example I. "I knew very well there wasn't a mosquito in the room but when I was told it would bother me I felt an overpowering need to act as if it were. But I didn't feel it and I didn't hear it."

From this subjective report three tentative estimates regarding depth and imagery can be drawn: (a) the subject's feeling of strong compulsion to act as if the mosquito were bothering him suggests that hypnotic role-taking involvement was quite deep; (b) the subject's clear awareness that there really was no mosquito present would suggest that trance was far less deep; (c) his neither feeling nor hearing the mosquito would suggest at best meager touch and auditory imagery representation. The report yields no clue, however, about the depth of archaic involvement.

The second report suggests a somewhat different configuration of depth.

Example II. "I knew you wanted me to feel the mosquito. I tried hard to do it for you but I felt guilty because I couldn't imagine it too well. I acted as if I felt it though, and I felt rather upset that I really wasn't able to feel it."

Four tentative estimates of depth and imagery can be made: (a) the twin statements, "I tried hard but I just couldn't imagine" and "I acted as if" have the ring of voluntary deliberation and thus suggest that hypnotic role-taking involvement was not very deep; (b) the subject's awareness of the "true" state of affairs suggests a rather slight trance depth if any; (c) imagery representation also appears to be rather slight, through possibly somewhat greater than in the first example; (d) the subject's disquietude, guilt, and feelings of wanting to please the hypnotist suggest at least moderate archaic involvement.

The third report implies still another configuration.

*Item 9, Form B, *Stanford Hypnotic Susceptibility Scale*, Weitzenhoffer and Hilgard, 1959.

Example III. "When you told me there was a mosquito I heard him right away and felt him buzzing around my face. Looking back at it now the buzzing wasn't really very clear, but at the time it didn't occur to me that there wasn't a real mosquito".

Three tentative estimates of depth and imagery can be made: (a) the subject's immediate sensory perception of the mosquito without any feeling of voluntarily trying to do so suggests that hypnotic role-taking involvement was deep; (b) since the buzz was not really very clear when later judged by waking standards it appears that auditory imagery was only moderate; (c) the subject's statement that it did not occur to him to doubt the reality of the mosquito at the moment of the experience would suggest that trance was quite deep. The report itself yields no basis, however, for an estimate of archaic involvement depth.

It should be obvious from even these three examples that all combinations of imbalance are possible: depth may be light along two of the dimensions but deep along the third; depth along one dimension may be light, another medium, and the third deep; two may be light and one medium; and so forth.

It is unnecessary to describe the consequences of all configurations of depth in propositional form since a few configurations of greatest theoretical interest carry the underlying meaning of them all. The following three propositions depict the configurations where depth is profound along two of the three dimensions but superficial (or light) along the third.

19. *When both hypnotic role-taking and archaic involvement are deep but trance is superficial, a situation exists with the following characteristics: (a) the hypnotic role-enactments have permeated down to nonconscious levels; (b) intense, archaic object relations are formed onto the person of the hypnotist; (c) in general all classic hypnotic phenomena can be produced; but (d) the hypnotic happenings occur along with a relatively intact awareness within the phenomenal field of the more usual state of affairs.*

A small percentage of well-trained hypnotic subjects can learn to reintegrate a generalized alertness to outer reality during deep hypnosis so that they have immediate and full availability of critical, waking standards of judgment and yet remain deeply hypnotized along the dimensions of hypnotic role-taking involvement and archaic involvement. These individuals, who are often called active somnambulists, can open their eyes, walk about, talk and appear fully alert and attuned to the real world, yet at the same time remain keenly responsive to the hypnotist and produce all classic hypnotic phenomena except those which require profound trance as an intrinsic component.*

---

*Such as age-regression or time distortion.

These individuals are not to be confused with those less active somnambulists who still remain in at least medium trance. The latter may open their eyes and talk, but there is a glassy-eyed perplexed quality to their stare; alertness is decreased as is concern and contact with the usual generalized reality.

The fully active somnambulist, although still profoundly responsive to the hypnotist, is not entranced at all nor out of tune with any feature of abstractive appraisal. He may, for example, be vividly hallucinating an object while at the same time describing it as an hallucination and introspecting upon his own mental processes in abstractive terms.

20. *When both trance and archaic involvement are deep but hypnotic role-taking is superficial, a situation exists with the following characteristics: (a) the hypnotic happenings become phenomenologically the only possible "reality" for the moment; (b) intense, archaic object relations are formed onto the person of the hypnotist; (c) all classic hypnotic phenomena may emerge spontaneously; but (d) the subject is generally disinclined to follow hetero-suggestions.*

The importance of this configuration of factors can be best illustrated by a close evaluation of the processes which Gill and Brenman (1959) have called the induction phase of hypnosis. These authors have drawn a sharp distinction between (a) the induction phase of hypnosis and (b) the established state itself. Our dimensional analysis would suggest that this distinction derives from particular methods of hypnotic induction and is not an invariant accompaniment of hypnotizing.

In Gill and Brenman's (1959) theory the induction phase of hypnosis is the bringing about of a regression, a regressive *movement*. The hypnotic state itself is an established regression in Kris' sense of a regression in the service of the ego. In the established state, a regressed sub-system of the ego is set up within the overall ego. This sub-system is an organized structure; during the induction phase this structure has not yet been built. The induction phase is characterized by the mutual operation of two factors: (a) a sensori-motor and ideational deprivation leading to alteration in ego-functioning, and (b) the stimulation of an archaic object relationship onto the hypnotist. The regressive movement can be set into motion by either of these two factors, and once initiated the other factor inexorably develops. The induction phase is further characterized by a freer expression of repressed affect and ideas, the availability of motility to repressed impulses, the appearance and disappearance of hysterical phenomena, spontaneous age-regression, changes in body experience, feelings of depersonalization, and so forth. The authors report that such spontaneous occurrences almost never happen, however, once the established hypnotic state itself is produced.

Gill and Brenman's (1959) two intertwined induction phase factors correspond to two of our three dimensions of hypnotic depth. The first factor (sensori-motor and ideational deprivation leading to alterations in ego functioning) is our trance dimension. The second factor (stimulation of an archaic object relationship onto the hypnotist) is our archaic involvement dimension. Also, when the authors view the established hypnotic state as a regressed sub-system within the overall ego, they are referring in psychoanalytic terminology to what we have called profound hypnotic role-taking involvement; i.e., the complex of motivational strivings and cognitive structurings to be a hypnotized subject has become nonconsciously directive.

Gill and Brenman's (1959) descriptions of their modal induction techniques show their tendency to use induction strategies which emphasize both trance and archaic involvement but which place little weight at first upon active hypnotic role-enactments. Only later, when trance and archaic involvement are both quite extensive, is emphasis placed upon deepening hypnotic role-taking involvement. The spontaneous emergence of primary-process materials which Gill and Brenman (1959) observe during their induction phase is entirely consistent with a configuration of (a) extensive trance, (b) extensive archaic involvement, but (c) little hypnotic role-taking as such and little of its involvement depth. In the induction strategies which we tend to favor, much more emphasis is placed upon hypnotic role-taking and hypnotic role-taking involvement from the very beginning. Consequently, there is little occasion to observe a dichotomy between induction phase and established state. In other words, our dimensional analysis suggests that, given induction strategies with considerable emphasis upon hypnotic role-taking and hypnotic role-taking involvement from the very beginning the kind of distinction between induction phase and established state as described by Gill and Brenman (1959) will not occur.

21. *When both hypnotic role-taking and trance are deep but archaic involvement superficial, a situation exists with the following characteristics: a) the strivings to take the hypnotic role have permeated down to nonconscious levels; (b) the hypnotic happenings become phenomenologically the only possible "reality" for the moment; (c) in general all classic hypnotic phenomena can be produced; but (d) the hypnosis is relatively superficial to the core of the subject's personality.*

Most clinicians have such little opportunity to observe profound hypnosis where there is minimal archaic involvement that it is doubtful they would easily believe that such a state of affairs might exist. The therapeutic process itself obliges a reaching down into the core issues of the patient's personality. Even when engaged in experimentation instead of therapy, the clinician's habitual manner usually tends to initiate considerable archaic involvement.*

It is only the psychological researcher (especially when working in an academic setting) who might regularly see profound hypnoses with minimal archaic involvement. The experimentalist often maintains a greater psychologic distance from his subject than does the clinician (or the stage hypnotist). There is usually the implicit understanding that some larger scientific question is under test; often there is little requirement that the subject enter into the hypnotic experiences in a deeply personal fashion. Usually it is understood that issues dealing with the core of the subject's personality are to be avoided scrupulously. The researcher's manner, however, often belies mysticism and power fantasies. Sometimes the subject has never before seen or heard about the particular hypnotist who may work with him during a particular session. The routine of experimental method may introduce an added note of impersonality; the experimenter may even be slightly bored or otherwise mentally occupied. With sufficiently capable subjects such happenings need not interfere with the successful attainment of the most profound depths of trance and role-taking involvement. But under these circumstances there is far less impetus for archaic involvement to become profound.

How do otherwise profound hypnoses look when archaic involvement is minimal? All classic hypnotic phenomena are readily produced, but the fireworks (evoked primitive meanings) are lacking. The subject puts his whole role-taking "heart" into it but his archaic involvement "soul" is much less entangled. Fewer personal interpretations occur; less emotive, dynamic materials emerge. The subject is fully cooperative but the hypnotic happenings do not strike him to the core. His relationship to the hypnotist has not become infused with an unusual importance and wish to please. Whether classic hypnotic phenomena—though outwardly looking much the same—are really subtly different when archaic involvement is minimal is a vitally important theoretical and practical question demanding empirical clarification. Resolution of much of the dispute in the hypnotic literature between the clinicians and the experimentalists may hinge on answers to this question.

22. Interactions and interrelationships may occur among the dimensions.

Our recognition of separate dimensions does not at all deny that usually potent interactions and interrelationships occur among the dimensions. For example, the deeper the trance, the easier it is for archaic contents and

---

*The stage-hypnotist's manner has similar results but for different reasons. His stress on mysticism and omnipotence tends to evoke infantile fantasies of magical power and dependency.

modes of functioning to flow into the background of awareness to orient experiences. Thus the deeper the trance the more easily available will be modes of functioning for forming archaic object relationships. The experienced hypnotist will often try to fuse and intertwine all three dimensions into one tangled skein—using trance as a wedge to help establish his authority and parent-like image; archaic involvement as a wedge to help increase motivations and further relax generalized alertness; role-taking involvement as a wedge to achieve greater unity with more primitive modes of interpersonal relationship and to further selectively focus attention.

Not all interactions and interrelationships among the dimensions are so productive of greater mutual depth, however. Schilder and Kauders (1956), for example, observe that too much "sleep-consciousness" (trance) prevents "suggestibility" (in this context, role-taking and role-taking involvement), and vice versa. Too profound an infusion of archaic interpersonal meanings into the hypnotic relationship, moreover, may very well interfere with accuracy in comprehending the hypnotist's directions. Experimental investigation is needed to help clarify the exact conditions of mutual aid or disharmony among the dimensions.

SUMMARY

Nine additional formal propositions are presented which extend the writer's earlier presentation of a dual-factor theory of hypnosis to include a third factor, archaic involvement, a feature of hypnosis often stressed by psychoanalytically oriented theorists. Although interactions and interrelationships usually occur among these three factors, the three are viewed as conceptually separate; i.e., the depth of each may vary independently. Many ramifications of these views are presented. The theory is most properly seen as a synthesis of the enduring insights embedded in many prior theories of hypnosis. In a later paper the problem of measuring depth along the three dimensions will be dealt with directly.

17

HYPNOSIS, DEPTH PERCEPTION, AND PSYCHEDELIC EXPERIENCE

BERNARD S. AARONSON

Although mystic states have been experienced and sought by men in all cultures throughout history, the experiential variables which determine them are poorly understood. The technology for producing these altered states of consciousness is well developed and ranges from the rites of witchcraft to the practices of Yoga. The relatively easy success of all of these methods in producing these states has resulted in accounts of them in which the changing sequences of experience are slighted in favor of the putative goals of the induction of the experience.

The recent emphasis on pharmacological means for producing psychedelic conditions has brought along with it a spate of explanations couched in biochemical and neurophysiological terms. While the changes induced by these psychedelic substances may correlate with the patterns of biochemical and neurophysiological events observed, from the standpoint of the experiencing organism they involve events of a totally different kind. Consciousness may depend upon the functioning of the reticular formation, but it is not just the sets of events in the reticular formation. In fact, in order to produce more accurate mapping of the neural substrate, it is important to delineate what changes of experience occur in response

Reprinted by permission from Society for the Scientific Study of Religion, Paper, New York, 1965.

to particular kinds of stimulation and how the succession of these changes interacts with the changes themselves.

Data on the action of many hallucinogens (Ban, Lohrenz and Lehmann, 1961; Cohen, Silverman and Shmavonian, 1962; de Ropp, 1957; De Vito and Frank, 1964; Lawes, 1963; Malitz, Esecover, Wilkens and Hoch, 1960; Ostfeld, 1961; Savage, 1955) have shown characteristic spectra of behavioral effects for each drug which may be modified by the range of behaviors exhibited by each individual subject and by the situation in which the drugs are administered. These characteristically involve alterations in both the form and content of thought, emotional changes, changes in time perception, changes in the perception of space, and distortion of body image. Hallucinations in a number of sensory modalities are reported which may derive from physical anomalies or other characteristics of the perceptual apparatus (Horowitz, 1964; Oster, 1964). Distortions of space perception are noted in most of these accounts, although it is often not clear just how space seems distorted.

As part of a program in which the effects of hypnotic suggestions of perceptual and conceptual change on behavior are being studied (Aaronson, 1964), the effects of suggested alterations in depth perception were considered. A 22-year-old well-trained male hypnotic subject was told that the dimension of depth was gone. He at once showed marked schizophreniform behavior with catatonic features. Left alone for a second in a room as he lay down, he perceived the ceiling and walls closing in on him. Much of his behavior seemed reminiscent of that reported by Beers (1950) about the onset of his own psychosis in *The Mind That Found Itself*, a book that the subject had never read.

When the dimension of depth was expanded, a psychedelic state resulted similar to that described by Huxley (1954) in *The Doors of Perception*. Lines seemed sharper, colors intensified, everything seemed to have a place and to be in its place, and to be esthetically satisfying. The hand of God was manifest in an ordered world. It should be stressed that this subject knew nothing about the reported effects of psychedelic substances nor of Huxley's experiences.

None of these changes occurred when blurred vision or clear and distinct vision were suggested. The former yielded a hysteroid condition, the latter an anxiety reaction. Hypnosis without any suggestions of behavioral change produced no behavioral effects at all.

The present study deals with two attempts to replicate these phenomena. The first set of studies was carried out with a conventionally hypnotized subject, the second with a simulator, unhypnotized, but instructed to act out the suggestions. If similar results were obtained with these subjects, then it could be asserted that the phenomenon has some generality and that the experience of expanded depth is related to the development of psy-chedelic experiences.

METHOD

Two subjects were employed in this study. The hypnotized subject was a 22-year-old English major. He had little background in psychology and had spent one summer previously as a recreational aide at a ward for disturbed children. His favorite activity was painting and he hoped to make this a vocation. In personality, he was a hypomanic, extroverted person, who was always ready to turn any situation into a party. At the time the experiments reported here were begun, he had been a subject in this series for about $3\frac{1}{2}$ months.

The role-playing subject was a 22-year-old English major who had just graduated from college. He had no background in psychology. He had some previous experience in acting, but was not a method actor. In personality he was a brooding, irritable, introspective individual with good capacity for self-observation and good verbal facility. He was chosen as a simulator after extensive attempts at hypnotizing him failed to produce anything deeper than a light trance.

In carrying out these studies, the subjects first completed a Q-sort based upon Plutchik's (1962) theory of emotions. They then were administered a battery of visual perceptual tasks, including a test of depth perception. The subjects were then hypnotized, amnesia for all previous hypnotic experiences was suggested, and a posthypnotic suggestion of perceptual change imposed.

A two-hour free interval then followed. In the case of the hypnotized subject, the painting of a standard scene, the view from the windows of the room in which the experiments were conducted, was requested at the end of $1\frac{1}{2}$ hours. The subjects then went for a ride in a car over a standard course and then wrote an account of how their day had been. They were then interviewed by an outside observer,* a trained clinician who conducted an independent clinical evaluation of each subject. He knew that the subject had been hypnotized, but did not know what, if any, suggestion had been imposed.

After the interview was completed, the Minnesota Multiphasic Personality Inventory (MMPI) was administered. The Q-sort and perceptual battery were readministered. The subject was reinterviewed by the experimenter,

*Drs. A. Moneim El Meligi, Humphrey Osmond, Stanley R. Platman, Hubert Stolberg and A. Arthur Sugerman kindly assisted in these evaluations.

rehypnotized, and the earlier posthypnotic suggestions removed. The subject was then reinterviewed about his experiences and any residual feelings were dealt with. The simulator then wrote a secret account of what his day had really been like. The elapsed time for all these procedures ranged between $5\frac{1}{2}$ to 7 hours.

The conditions involved in this series included *no depth*, *expanded depth*, *blurred vision*, *clear and distinct vision*, and two *control* sessions. The instructions for *no depth* were, "When you open your eyes, the dimension of depth will be gone. The world will seem two-dimensional." The instructions for *expanded depth* were, "When you open your eyes, the dimension of depth will be expanded. Have you ever looked through a stereoscope? Do you know what depth looks like there? That's how the world will seem to you." The instructions for blurred vision were, "When you open your eyes, everything you look at will seem blurred." The instructions for *clear and distinct vision* were, "When you open your eyes, everything will seem clear and distinct." In the *control* conditions, the subjects were hypnotized, but no suggestions of perceptual change were imposed.

RESULTS

Because of the extensive amount of data collected and the limited amount of space available in which to present these data, I shall attempt to summarize the responses to each of the conditions without specific reference to the tests employed. They form a part of the evaluation, but will be referred to only when appropriate. The order in which the conditions are presented does not reflect the order in which they were imposed for each subject, but has been adopted for didactic reasons.

When the *expanded depth* condition was imposed on the hypnotized subject, he became very happy. He seemed uncertain of himself in his adjustment to space at first, but quickly adapted. Space seemed to extend through and beyond any physical limitations imposed on it. He tended to become confused in large open areas, but was able to contain his confusion in more limited spaces which the suggestion rendered more beautiful. Colors seemed intensified, lines more distinct, and sounds crisper.

The consciousness expanding effects and the personality change noted with the previous subject were not observed. He did report, however, that when his eyes were closed, he felt larger and seemed to himself to be growing. He also reported that he was able to contain the experience by painting it, and that this was a function his painting served for him.

Because this condition was induced much earlier in the hypnotic series than was the case with the previous subject, and because the painting had helped him to contain the suggestion, the condition was reinduced four months later. This time he was not allowed to paint. All of the phenomena noted previously were reported. In addition, he began to talk about how everything around him seemed to have been shaped into a world of super-reality and unspeakable beauty. In his account he remarked,

Riding in a car was like taking a wonderfully exhilarating roller coaster ride to everywhere. The landscape was at once a gargantuan formal garden and a wilderness of irrepressible joyous space. Even now, I feel dumb struck and pre-posterous in trying to describe this perceptual miracle which has somehow been given me. My feelings and perceptions are unspeakable. . . .

This time he seemed to become euphoric and many of the phenomena noted by Huxley and others under psychedelic drugs were noted by him. The outside observer and the MMPI both concurred in suggesting a euphoric, creative state.

The simulating subject became rather happy under this condition. He became involved with the shapes of objects and the relation of objects to space. As he did this, he found himself becoming less self-concerned and more concerned with people and their relationships to one another. He became more alert, active and involved. He found that by concentrating on perspective and the relation of lines and sizes to one another, he was able to actually change the usual way he perceived depth. He felt that the ex-perience had made him aware that the world we live in is three- and not two-dimensional. He felt, too, that the perception of depth is itself an illusion. The outside observer felt that he seemed somewhat happier and more spontaneous. The MMPI suggested a decline in obsessiveness.

Induction of the *no depth* condition with the hypnotized subject produced a sense that everything was flattened out which he attributed to excessive fatigue from the final exams which he had just completed. Colors, shapes, and sounds all seemed less intense. He reported a loss of sensitivity to touch. He became bored, withdrawn, and hostile. He painted the standard scene under protest. He was again able to use the painting to enable him to contain the experience. He also used his experience as a painter to permit him to orient himself in this altered world. The outside observer reported a bored withdrawal. The MMPI showed little change.

The *no depth* condition was reintroduced about four months later for the same reasons noted before in this paper. This time he was not allowed to paint. The responses observed before were repeated in much stronger form. He became apathetic and withdrawn. He showed little affect. He did not seem hostile, but felt that his environment had become alien and the people around him dehumanized. The outside observer felt that something similar to a schizophrenic reaction had occurred and the MMPI profile supported this interpretation.

When the simulator was given the *no depth* instruction, he became extremely hostile, apathetic and withdrawn. He felt bored, uninterested in anything, and unwilling to become so. He reported in his private diary that he had capitalized on an initial feeling of depression and exacerbated it. The outside observer and the MMPI raised the question of an ambulatory schizophrenia.

Under the first *control* condition, the hypnotic subject seemed happy and quite normal. This condition was run over a period of two sessions. During the interval between the first and second session, spring had burgeoned. As the second session was run with a time regression back to the time of the first session, the subject seemed confused by the way the trees had put forth leaves since the morning. The outside observer wondered if he had been given some kind of strange instruction to see green. The MMPI showed no change.

Under the *control* condition, the simulator, too, showed no change from his normal state. The outside observer and the MMPI both concurred in the no change observation.

Clear and distinct vision produced an elevated mood in the hypnotic subject. His painting of the standard scene shows his increased sensitivity to colors and textures. An elevated mood was noted by all, including the MMPI.

The simulator responded to this condition with an increased interest in his environment and in working. In his private diary he reported that by investing himself in his environment, he had succeeded in overcoming an earlier feeling of depression. The outside observer and the MMPI suggested more energy and more involvement.

When the *blurred vision* condition was imposed on the hypnotic subject, he attributed the blurring to his hay fever. Apart from a mild condition of belle indifference, he showed little change in mood, affect or behavior. The standard scene painting suggests the blurred quality of the environment rather well.

The simulator withdrew from the environment under the *blurred vision* instructions. He became uninterested in anything around him and unmotivated to do anything in particular. He was hostile to others and resistant to even minor demands that they might place on him. The MMPI and the outside observer record a movement in a schiziod direction.

The hypnotic subject was euphoric before the second *control* condition was introduced because of the kind of day it was.

No change was observed from his original high mood by any person or test all day.

The simulator was in a good mood when the second *control* condition was induced, and his mood became better as the day progressed. No change in behavior or personality was noted.

DISCUSSION

The data suggest that expanding depth yields a psychedelic experience, while ablating depth yields a schizophreniform response. These responses are not produced by suggestions of clear and distinct or of blurred vision, or by hypnotizing someone without accompanying suggestions of perceptual change. All three subjects responded in much the same fashion to the suggestions of *no depth* and *expanded depth*. The hypnotic subjects responded in similar fashion to *blurred vision*, while the simulator did not. The second hypnotic subject and the simulator responded in a similar fashion to *clear and distinct vision*, while the first hypnotic subject did not.

Heightened depth perception seems accompanied by a general increase in the overall clarity of perception in all modalities. This heightened clarity is in itself not sufficient to account for the observed effects, as the response to the *clear and distinct vision* condition shows. The important variable seems to be the relationship of the objects in the environment to space and the manner in which they seem to interact with it. The usual perception of objects in the environment as things in themselves, independent of their surroundings, seems replaced by a perception of objects as being in interaction with their surroundings and with the active properties of the space around them. The account of the simulator suggests that necessary to the development of these conditions is an interest in and an investment of the self in the objects of the environment, so that "the Universe grows I."

The *no depth* condition seems accompanied by a general dulling of perceptual experience. The crucial variable here in determining the schizophreniform response seems to be an increased insubstantiality of all objects in the environment, including the self. *Blurred vision* in and of itself does not produce a schizoid pattern of behavior unless there is a failure to interact with an environment that has become without relevance. The decreased relevance of events in the environment is associated with a tendency to respond to all attributes of stimuli in much the same way. This kind of general response is attainable if the intensities of stimuli can be reduced to a point at which the same no response can be given to all of them. The hallucinogenic drug, Sernyl, was originally developed for its anaesthetic properties (Greifenstein, De Vault, Yoshitake, & Gajewski, 1958), but it was soon observed that the reduction of stimulus input produced schizophreniform responses.

The contrast between the response to the expanded depth and the ablated depth conditions involves a contrast between mystic experience and psychosis. The psychedelic substances, such as LSD, were originally called psychotomimetics (Osmond, 1957) and regarded as providing a chemical model for psychosis. These data suggest that a valid distinction may be drawn between psychotomimetic agents, such as Sernyl, and psychedelic agents, such as LSD. Far from being the same, mystic experience seems the opposite of psychosis. Mystic experience seems characterized by profound involvement and expansion of the boundaries of self, psychotic experience by profound alienation and shrinking of the self boundaries.

The fact that the effects from a later induction of a hypnotic state are more profound than those from an earlier induction suggests the importance of the training procedures involved in many of the formal systems for inducing mystic experience. Kroger (1963) has pointed out the similarity of the systems of inducing religious experience in many of the world's religions to systems of autohypnosis. The fact that one subject was able to contain the experience by painting also suggests the importance of self-expressive devices to enable the organism to contain events that might otherwise overwhelm it. It also suggests the reason that many systems for inducing mystic experience require their aspirants to forego such expression while the experience is being sought.

The fact that expanded depth is associated with mystic experience recalls the observation of William James (1902) that most mystic experience tends to occur outdoors. The traditional predeliction of religious devotees for mountain tops and desert places may not be merely a desire to get away from the distractions of the social world, but a movement to a place where experiences of enhanced depth are possible. The traditional association of mountain tops with the abode of Deity may be less because they are higher than the areas around them than because they make possible those experiences of expanded depth in which the self can invest itself in the world around it and expand across the valleys.

18

THE PSYCHEDELIC STATE,
THE HYPNOTIC TRANCE,
AND THE CREATIVE ACT

STANLEY KRIPPNER

Sergei Rachmaninoff, the gifted Russian conductor, pianist, and composer, plunged into morbid brooding at the age of 21 because of the unfavorable reception accorded his first piano concerto. No amount of success as a conductor or pianist could revive his morale. Extremes of emotion were characteristic of Russian composers and depression was especially fashionable at the turn of the century, but Rachmaninoff's misery was so relentless that his friends became alarmed. They eventually persuaded him to visit Dr. Nikolai Dahl who specialized in hypnotic treatments.

During their first session together, the spare, gothic Rachmaninoff recoiled in distaste as he eased his slender frame into the doctor's chair. Following some preliminary instructions, Dahl repeated—over and over—such statements as, "You will begin to write another concerto; you will work with great facility." Rachmaninoff continued in treatment for three months, visiting Dr. Dahl daily for half hour sessions.

In this instance, hypnotic suggestion was remarkably effective. Rachmaninoff's gloom evaporated and he began composing again, working with speed and inspiration. Musical ideas flowed from his pen, were expanded, and became unforgettable melodies. The finished work, Rachmaninoff's Concerto Number Two in C Minor for Piano and Orchestra, was first performed in 1901 by the Moscow Philharmonic. Rachmaninoff openly acknowledged his debt to Dr. Dahl and dedicated the concerto to him; the

271

composition was a critical success and is still a favorite with concert audiences (Foley, 1963).

Psychedelic ("mind-manifesting") drugs have also been used for creative purposes. In 1966, Navy Captain John Busby reported using LSD to solve an elusive problem in pattern recognition while developing equipment for a Navy research project. He stated, "With LSD, the normal limiting mechanisms of the brain are released and entirely new patterns of perception emerge" (Rosenfeld, 1966).

In 1965 psychiatrist Humphrey Osmond and architect Kyo Izumi announced that they had utilized psychedelic drugs in the designing of a mental hospital. Izumi took LSD during visits to traditionally designed mental hospitals to determine their effect upon persons in altered conscious states. He found the long corridors and pale colors frightening and bizarre. The result of the Osmond-Izumi collaboration was a decentralized series of unimposing buildings with pleasant colors and no corridors; Izumi recalled that under LSD the corridor had "seemed infinite, and it seemed as if I would never get to the end of it" (Trent, 1966).

Altered states of consciousness, such as those induced by hypnosis and psychedelic chemicals, may assist in fostering the creative act because creativity is basically preverbal and unconscious in origin. Torrance (1962) has recognized the preverbal origins of creativity, defining it as the process of sensing gaps or missing elements, forming ideas or hypotheses about them, testing the hypotheses, and communicating the results. Freud (1938) has associated curiosity with unconscious drives, noting that "in the case of a creative mind . . ., the intellect has withdrawn its watchers from the gate, and the ideas rush pell-mell. . . ." Vinacke (1952) has stressed the necessity of intellectual freedom for creation to occur; to him, "there must be . . . an ability to reorganize experience with relative independence of external restraints."

Hypnosis appears to focus consciousness so intensely that subthreshold stimuli are perceived; in fact, hypnosis is frequently defined in terms of a heightened responsiveness to suggestion. Psychedelic substances (e.g., LSD, psilocybin, mescaline, marijuana, peyote) seem to affect consciousness in such a way that the nervous system is flooded with external and internal stimuli.

It may be that both hypnosis and the psychedelics can assist breakthroughs into the preverbal realm where creative inspiration has its origins. Many artists and scientists claim that their efforts at innovation exist as moods and feelings before they are expressed in words and other symbols. For Robert Frost, a poem began as "a lump in the throat, a sense of wrong, a homesickness, a lovesickness;" it was "never a thought to begin with." Richard Wagner is reported to have heard music spontaneously; Johannes

Brahms once disclosed that he heard fragments of his themes as "inner harmony." Aaron Copeland has stated that a musical theme comes to him almost like automatic writing. The German chemist August Kekule produced a conceptualization of the benzene ring which was inspired by a dream of a snake holding its tail in its mouth.

Some individuals, especially religious mystics, attempt to foster this type of phenomenon. Ben-Avi (1959), while discussing Zen Buddhism, has counseled that "change, illumination, or growth must be rooted in the immediate, the concrete experience of the individual" rather than being based on conscious abstractions and intellectual formulations. Zen Buddhism, with its emphasis on concentration, is often regarded as a modification of autohypnosis. In autohypnosis, as in Zen, meditation can lead to increased concentration, a focusing of attention, and an increased receptivity to creative ideas.

When an individual is most relaxed, his conditioned reactions to stimuli are characteristically "off guard" and flashes of creative insight may occur. It is as though a series of closed doors barred off a passageway of dark antechambers which ranged from the deep unconscious through several preconscious rooms, into the light of conscious awareness. We forget our unsolved problem, sleep on it, let go, and relax. A. E. Housman found that lines of poetry would flow into his mind during afternoon walks. Mozart stated that he composed most easily while riding or walking. Charles Darwin gathered specific biological data during many years of conscious struggle; however, his theory of evolution came to him while taking a carriage ride.

Henri Poincaré, the French mathematician, spent months at a work table but got nowhere in his attempts to investigate Fuchsian functions (a type of differential equation). Further insights developed over the next few weeks while Poincaré was vacationing and walking on the bluffs near the seaside—but not during his periods of conscious effort (1955).

HYPNOTHERAPY AND CREATIVE PRODUCTIONS

A number of psychoanalysts have combined hypnosis with attempts to stimulate creative activity with their patients. Raginsky (1963) encouraged his hypnotized patients to construct images from clay. Not only was Raginsky able to utilize in therapy his patients' descriptions and associations of the clay models, he also found that the patients' reactions to the clay's texture, color, and odor could play a part in the therapeutic process.

Stating that the creative act may be an attempt to organize and integrate past emotional experiences with one's entire life pattern, Margaret Bowers (1966) presented a provocative psychiatric case history of a patient,

"Walter," a musician who was 24 years of age when hospitalized. Suffering from tension and anxiety, Walter was unable to work. He was diagnosed as schizophrenic, emotionally withdrawn, and as having little interest in his environment.

Because Walter was a poor hypnotic subject, it took 50 hours to secure a valid age regression. When this point was reached, the patient could be sent back into his past to relive traumatic experiences. It soon became apparent that one aspect of Walter's personality was childlike, while another resembled an angry parent. The patient referred to these two aspects of himself as "Walter Positive" and "Walter Negative." Day after day, the psychiatrist and her assistants gave their complete support to Walter Positive while attempting to "exorcise" Walter Negative.

The paintings which Walter did in occupational therapy seemed to have no psychological significance at first glance. One, for example, was essentially nondescript; it depicted the left hand with fingers extended upward. The back of the hand was showing, there was a ring on the little finger, and the pink finger nails contrasted with the flesh-colored hand and the green sleeve.

One day the patient was hypnotized by Bowers and taken back to the day and hour when he painted the picture of the hand. Walter was asked to open his eyes and look at the picture, then told that he could see it in a mirror. Staring in the mirror, Walter drew the picture again. At this point, Bowers asked him several questions about his production:

WALTER.   The wrist and hand is Walter Positive. The fingers look stronger, the nails are longer. Hand is strong. He's got to be strong.

BOWERS.   What else do you see?

WALTER.   The pinkie is Walter Positive. The pinkie feels stronger because of the ring. Ring means positive, sureness, success. . . .

BOWERS.   When did the ring get on the pinkie?

WALTER.   Just now.

BOWERS.   What does it mean?

WALTER.   It means it's strong. It's a success. . . . I see myself in front of an audience. I'm singing and everybody is enjoying it. . . . I can see myself in a tuxedo, wearing the ring. I'm in a group of people sitting at a table in a night club. I'm friendly with them and having a good time. They're laughing and I'm laughing. . . . I've found myself. . . .

BOWERS.   Is that what the painting means?

WALTER.   Yes.

The session lasted for nearly four hours; within this period of time the patient gave a more complete picture of himself than he had during the previous four months. Besides discussing his magic ring, he told about his father's masturbation of him as a child, of his seductive and possessive mother, and of his frequent witnessing of his parents in the act of sexual intercourse. He was so preoccupied with these sexual concerns that he did poorly in school and in musical auditions.

As Walter's therapy proceeded, his anxiety lessened, he went back to work, he made several successful appearances as a singer, and began to take an interest in other people. Bowers concluded that the method used successfully with Walter could be utilized with other patients who could not be reached by traditional therapeutic techniques.

HYPNOSIS AND ACADEMIC PROFICIENCY

McCord (1961) reported a provocative experiment with a mathematics professor, a university colleague of his. After assisting the mathematician in entering a hypnotic trance McCord suggested that when awakened he would be given some calculus problems and would be able to do them with high accuracy and at a faster rate than he had ever done such work before. The subject was then roused from his trance, provided with the calculus problems, and asked to solve as many of them as possible in 20 minutes.

The subject completed in 20 minutes a task that normally would have taken him two hours. This gain was accomplished by the skipping of steps in the mathematical process, performing "in his head" some of the calculations that he would normally have written out, and by writing down necessary calculations at a rapid rate of speed. There was no loss of accuracy despite the increased speed.

The mathematician reported that he enjoyed doing the calculus and that he felt his unconscious mind had participated in the calculations to a greater extent than usual.

Despite these frequently reported clinical instances of improved performance under hypnosis, Barber (1965) and Uhr (1958) in two thorough reviews of the psychological literature found the results "inconclusive" because so few well-designed studies had been done to measure the effect of hypnosis on problem-solving.

HYPNOTIC SUSCEPTIBILITY AND CREATIVITY IN CHILDREN

Several experimental studies assume significance in tracing the association between the hypnotic trance and the creative act. For example, children appear to become less susceptible to hypnosis as they grow older as well as less creative.

London (1962) has reported, after studying 57 boys and girls aged five and older, that children are significantly more susceptible to hypnosis than are adults. In standardizing the Children's Hypnotic Susceptibility Scale, he also found that the older children could "simulate" hypnosis with a great deal of effectiveness. Furthermore, susceptibility and age had a curvilinear relationship.

London's study bears a striking resemblance to the findings of Torrance (1962:97–98). His subjects showed drops in originality—as measured by objective tests—upon entering kindergarten, fourth grade, and junior high school. Torrance's data suggest that each time the child leaves one cultural setting (the home, the primary grades, elementary school) for another (kindergarten, the intermediate grades, junior high school), more attention is paid to newly encountered problems in adaptation and less attention is devoted to creative activity.

It may follow that stereotyped thinking is an inevitable result of cultural indoctrination. As the growing child learns to see the world through the eyes of his culture, he surrenders his individualistic outlook, becoming less original, less open to new experiences, and less imaginative. Not only is it the more imaginative individual who is less likely to give up his interest in creative activity, it is also the imaginative person rather than the unimaginative one who reacts more quickly to hypnotic suggestion.

COGNITIVE ACTIVITY WITHOUT AWARENESS

Another piece of research which bears on the association between creativity and hypnosis was reported by Tinnin (1963) who has recalled how common it is for an individual to put a difficult problem out of his mind and then, suddenly, to experience a spontaneous flash of insight or even a sudden solution. Tinnin attempted to bring about this phenomenon through hypnosis. He used three male college students who were able to attain post-hypnotic suggestibility and who reported complete amnesia for the hypnotic experience.

Tinnin's subjects entered a hypnotic trance and were told that upon awakening they would be asked a specific algebraic question such as, "How much is Y^2 plus Z^2?" The subjects were told that the correct values of Y and Z would be indirectly supplied in the waking state before the question would be asked.

The value of Y, for one subject, was the second digit in the left hand column of a card shown immediately after awakening. The value of Z was the fifth digit in the right hand column. This particular subject was told, while in a hypnotic trance, that he would be able to select the correct numbers unconsciously when he saw the card. He would then compute the correct answer unconsciously, whereupon that answer would enter his conscious mind.

None of the subjects claimed to be able to remember their instructions. Nevertheless, they almost invariably gave the right answers to the questions posed. None of the subjects gave indications of remembering the clues but all three of them did well in stating the correct answers.

One of the subjects saw the answer as a momentary visual hallucination. The other two experienced it as a sudden flash of certain knowledge; "It just popped into my mind," was a typical report. Tinnin concluded that cognitive activity could utilize clues without full awareness and that this activity could run parallel to, without intruding upon, concurrent conscious activity.

Murphy (1958:129–130) has incorporated the "flash of insight" into his delineation of stages in the creative process. First there is the long immersion of the sensitive mind in a fulfilling medium with the world of color, of images, of social relationships, of contemplation, etc. Secondly, experiences are acquired in "great storehouses" by this immersion and consolidate themselves into structured patterns. From these great storehouses of experience comes an inspiration or illumination such as Archimedes leaping from the bathtub shouting, "I have it!" upon conceptualizing the law of specific gravity. Finally, the creative act sifted, tested, "hammered out," and integrated into the individual's other experiences with which it combines to produce the new poem, painting, invention, or other creative product.

CREATIVITY AND DEFENSIVENESS

An experiment with 80 female college students, susceptible to hypnotic induction, has been reported by Patricia Bowers (1965). Previous research had suggested to Bowers that creative persons have greater access to fluid, undeveloped realms of ideas than non-creative persons and that creative individuals are less defensive than others. However, Bowers noted that data were lacking on whether or not the lack of defensiveness plays a *causative* role in creative expression.

Surmising that hypnotic trance induction would lower defenses temporarily, Bowers told a hypnotized group of students that they had the ability to be creative if they would allow themselves to make use of all their relevant experiences.

The group also was told to perceive in unconventional ways, to notice aspects of problems overlooked previously, to ignore the possibility of criticism, to recall past moments of insight and the emotional feelings associated with these moments, and to feel confident about their ability to do well on creativity tests. The same set of instructions was given to the non-hypnotized group; these subjects had participated in a program of relaxation which had lasted as long as the hypnotic induction period for the other group.

Each of the two groups was administered a number of creativity tests devised by Guilford before the instructional period. A comparable series of tests was administered following the instructions. There were no significant differences between the two groups' test scores attained in the preinstructional period. Following the instructional period, the difference between the hypnotized group's scores and those of the non-hypnotized group were highly significant, with the hypnosis group doing significantly better. The hypnotized subjects also raised their scores above those obtained during the first test administration while the nonhypnotized subjects did not. Bowers concluded that the greater originality displayed by the hypnotized subjects indicated that instructions administered under hypnotic conditions can increase creative thinking, at least insofar as it can be objectively measured.

Bowers attempted to control many more factors than had most previous research workers. She equated the instructions for each group as well as the time spent by the experimenter with each group and the experimenter's attempts to motivate the subjects. Both groups had been given clerical ability tests which were non-creative in nature. The fact that hypnotized subjects did not raise their scores on the clerical ability tests to a significant degree indicated to Bowers that a general heightening of motivation under hypnosis was not the main factor accounting for the superiority of her hypnotized subjects.

P. Bowers (1965) also selected two additional groups and administered a different set of instructions encouraging the subjects to be clever, original, flexible, and fluent, but not mentioning attitudes which would reduce defensiveness. Although the resulting data were not as dramatic as the results obtained when defense reduction suggestions were given, there was still a statistically significant difference favoring the hypnotized subjects. This finding indicates that reduced defensiveness is not the only factor involved in creativity.

Bowers* later conducted an experiment with a group of subjects who pretended to be hypnotized. This group did about as well on the creativity tests as did the hypnosis subjects, suggesting that the lack of personal defense is more important than formal hypnotic trance induction in fostering creativity. Bowers stated that the subjects who pretended to be hypnotized may have abandoned responsibility for their typical personal behavior patterns

---

*Personal communication, Sept. 22, 1966.

while responding to the creativity test items, thereby increasing their powers of originality.

ATTENTION AND DISTRACTIBILITY

The work of As (1962) involved the hypnotized subject's ability to pay more attention to the hypnotist's suggestions than to other stimuli. There are, As suggested, two ways of explaining this process of selective in-attentiveness to signals which do not emanate from the hypnotist. Perhaps the subject withstands distractions and irrelevant stimuli by making a conscious effort to do so, thus leaving his field of attention open for the hypnotist to manipulate. On the other hand, the subject may occupy himself with the cues and suggestions presented by the hypnotist; as a result, other stimuli become the objects of less attention. The first proposition emphasized the ability to actively block out distracting stimuli while the second proposition emphasized the ability to become absorbed in relevant material.

As prepared a list of 60 questions designed to investigate these two propositions. This list was administered to 152 subjects whose hypnot-izability was subsequently measured by two standardized scales. The items in the list which tested the first proposition included such questions as, "When there are sounds that you do not want to listen to, can you block them from your mind so that they are no longer important to you?" and "Are you able to change easily from one task to another, excluding ideas, associations, and actions of the former task?" The subjects' responses to these questions were not positively related to the subjects' degree of hypnotic susceptibility as measured by the standardized scales.

The second proposition was tested by questions which inquired as to the subjects' experiences of involvement in nature, art, literature, music, or dance to such an extent that they forgot about their surroundings: "Have you ever been completely immersed in nature or in art (e.g., in the mountains at the ocean, viewing sculpture, painting, etc.) and had a feeling of awe, inspiration, and grandeur sweep over you so that you felt as if your whole state of consciousness was somehow temporarily changed?" "Have you ever acted in a play and found that you really felt the emotions of the character and 'become' him (or her) for the time being, forgetting both your-self and the audience?" "Have you ever focused on something so hard that you went into a kind of benumbed state of consciousness or a state of extraordinary calm and serenity?" These items and the subjects' hypno-tizability were related to a highly significant degree.

As concluded that it is the positive focusing of attention that is important in hypnosis rather than the negative warding off of distractions. It is the absorption of the individual in the cues provided by the hypnotist that enables the subject to become oblivious or inattentive to irrelevant stimuli. This phenomena resembles the fusion of subject and artist reported by many creative artists. This fading of boundaries between the self on the one hand and the outer environment on the other hand facilitates hypnotic experience as well as creative activity.

CREATIVITY AND TIME DISTORTION

The pioneer work on time distortion by Cooper and Erickson (1954) is pertinent to the cultivation of creativity. Hypnotic techniques were used to slow the subjective perception of time by 14 subjects. Time distortion was defined as occurring when there was a marked difference between the expected duration of a given interval and the clock reading of the interval. Suggestions were given to imagine oneself performing a certain activity. It was mentioned that a termination signal would be given when the time had expired, but that sufficient time would be available for the completion of the activity.

Work with the individual began by scheduling training sessions several times per week. The ability to lengthen time required from three to twenty hours of training, depending on the subject. Cooper and Erickson found that time distortion ability was associated with a high degree of immersion, by the subject, in the world which was suggested by the hypnotist—and by an accompanying inattentiveness to his actual surroundings. This state of detachment, in which the individual became completely involved in the imaginary experience, constituted the basic goal for the training sessions.

One of Cooper and Erickson's subjects was a college student who exhibited talent in dress designing. She reported that she would customarily work for several hours at a time on from four to ten occasions to design a dress. Under hypnosis, a dress designing task was assigned six times. The subject was awakened immediately after the completion of each trance and asked to draw a picture of the dress and to describe it briefly. For example, one report went as follows:

EXPERIMENTER.   Where were you?
SUBJECT.   I was at home.
EXPERIMENTER.   How long did you seem to be working at it?
SUBJECT.   Oh, about an hour. I was sitting at a table, looking out of the window and thinking.

EXPERIMENTER.   Did you do some drawing?
SUBJECT.   Yes, after I had thought it all through.

Although the subject experienced the session as an hour in length, the actual time of the trance was 10 seconds. Cooper and Erickson suggested that distorted time could be utilized for creative mental activity in the field in which a subject is adept. The experimenters also called for additional research, noting that their investigation was a pilot study and quite exploratory in nature.

Barber and Calverley (1964) repeated these experiments and did not feel that their results supported the assertions made by Cooper and Erickson. However, the actual technique utilized by Barber and Calverley for inducing the effect was somewhat different than that used in the original study.

Wollman (1965), in an attempt to follow the Cooper and Erickson approach, made use of time distortion with an actor who was offered the lead in a Broadway play one week before opening night. The actor was seen twice a day; time distortion reportedly enabled him to compress a great deal of learning into a short period of time. Practice sessions continued at home after the actor's wife had been trained to serve as a substitute for the hypnotist. The actor was successful in mastering his part and received favorable reviews from the critics on opening night.

R.E.L. Masters*, has reported a number of successful attempts to repeat the time distortion phenomenon for creative purposes. In one instance, 125 micrograms of LSD rather than hypnosis was used and the subject, a male psychologist, was informed, without warning, that he would be given a minute of clock time to create a story. He was also told that this minute would be all the time he would need for the task as his subjective experience of time would be slowed down and lengthened. Almost at once, the subject laughed. At the end of a minute, the subject produced a well-constructed short story complete with character delineation and descriptive material:

By God, it was strange. I have never had an experience like that. Well, it seemed to be the beginning of a novel. It was an English country estate and there was a car. It had a woman sitting in it, a rather middle-aged, attractive but not beautiful woman, and a little dog, and the chauffeur came up to her and—but this is why I laughed. Talk about a writer "getting inside" his characters! First I was inside of this woman, then I was inside the chauffeur, and then I was inside of the dog, and I really could feel my body and my personality change in each case as I became first one and then the other. I tell you, I was really getting into those characters in a very literal sense but it would take forever, in that way, to do a novel. I recognized this and so I kind of pulled back and the rest of the time I just observed what was happening, as if I were watching a film. But it wasn't a novel,

*Personal communication, Aug. 3, 1966.

it was kind of a little, strange vignette, very poignant, and very curious. This woman, you see, was going down to the pier where the body of her husband was being returned to her from some place where he had died. He had been in the diplomatic service. All of the time she is driving down to pick up the body, this little dog is sitting there with her in the back seat of the big old touring car and is looking from side to side. Both the woman and the dog have perfectly inscrutable faces, so one has no idea at all what she is thinking or feeling. And she meets the ship where her husband's body is being brought off and a lot of dignitaries are on hand to posthumously give him medals and there are salutes being fired and evidently he has performed some great act that this country is honoring him for. She attends the ceremony. Through it all she just stands there, and it isn't possible at all to guess what she is thinking or feeling, and when it is over she gets back into her car. The chauffeur is driving her back to the estate, the little dog is sitting there as before, looking from side to side impassively, not very interested in anything. But then suddenly a rabbit jumps alongside the road. The dog gets very, very excited and causes this woman to notice the rabbit. And then, in an instant, this same woman seems to display a kind of murderous fury and she reaches down and picks up a gun and shoots the rabbit right through the head—and everything freezes for a minute right there—the excited expression on the face of the dog, the curious look of fury on the face of the woman, the rabbit just as its brains are blasted out, only the chauffeur as he was before. This scene just hangs together for a strange, terrible few moments, and then time and movement go back to their normal pace, the face of the woman is entirely inscrutable again, the dog looks from side to side impassively. They turn up into her driveway and the car stops at her house. But you have this strange, frightening sense of that one instance when she and the dog came to life and she blew the rabbit's brains out—that just for a moment something awful had been revealed about this woman and possibly about her relationship to her husband. Although what was revealed is left undefined, you know that there is something latent in her and the inscrutable face and the utterly conventional manner cover something that has the possibility of breaking through.

Island, the last novel written by Aldous Huxley (1962), describes a Utopian realm in which the educational system develops intuitive and problem-solving ability among children by utilizing time distortion. The educators assess each child's ability at an early age and ask:

> . . . how suggestible is he going to be when he grows up? All children are good hypnotic subjects—so good that four out of five of them can be talked into somnambulism. In adults the proportion is reversed. Four of five of them can never be talked into somnambulism. Out of any hundred children, which are the twenty who will grow up to be suggestible to the pitch of somnambulism . . .? The potential somnambulists are the twenty per cent who can go into very deep trance. And it's in very deep trance—and only in very deep trance—that a person can be taught how to distort time . . . . One starts by learning how to experience twenty seconds as ten minutes, a minute as half an hour. In deep trance it's really very easy. You

listen to the teacher's suggestions and you sit there quietly for a long, long time. Two full hours—you'd be ready to take your oath on it. When you've been brought back, you look at your watch. Your experience of two hours was telescoped into exactly four minutes of clock time.... For example..., here's a mathematical problem. In your normal state it might take you the best part of half an hour to solve. But now you distort time to the point where one minute is subjectively the equivalent of thirty minutes. Then you set to work on the problem. Thirty subjective minutes later it's solved. But thirty subjective minutes are one clock minute.... You can imagine what happens when somebody with a genius IQ is also capable of time distortion. The results are fantastic.

Most investigators regard Aldous Huxley's enthusiasm as premature. However, his biologist brother, Julian Huxley (1963), has stated that the use of hypnosis to maximize creativity "is in harmony with the future evolution of man."

MESCALINE, PSILOCYBIN, AND CREATIVE ARTISTS

A number of creative people claim to have benefitted from psychotherapy

attributed "a new assess-

she came into

(Gaines, 1963).

Only five major research projects in the area of psychedelic drugs and creative performance have been reported and most of these have been described by the experimenters as "pilot studies" rather than full-scale experiments with conclusive results. L. M. Berlin (1955) investigated the effects of mescaline and LSD upon four graphic artists of national prominence. There was an impairment of finger-tapping efficiency and muscular steadiness among the four artists, but all were able to complete paintings. A panel of art critics judged the paintings as having "greater aesthetic value" than the artists' usual work, noting that the lines were bolder and that the use of color was more vivid. However, the technical execution was somewhat impaired.

The artists themselves spoke of an increased richness of imagery and of pleasurable sensory experiences. One said, "I looked out of the window into the infinitely splendid universe of a tiny mauve leaf performing a cosmic ballet." Another spoke of "light falling on light."

Frank Barron (1963) administered psilocybin to a number of highly creative individuals and recorded their impressions. One of Barron's subjects stated, "I felt a communion with all things." A composer wrote, "Every corner is alive in a silent intimacy." Barron concluded, "What psilocybin does is to . . . dissolve many definitions and . . . melt many boundaries, permit greater intensities or more extreme values of experience to occur in many dimensions."

Some of Barron's artists, however, were wildly enthusiastic about their apparently increased sensitivity during the drug experience only to discover, once the effects wore off, that the production was without artistic merit. One painter recalled, "I have seldom known such absolute identification with what I was doing—nor such a lack of concern with it afterwards." This statement indicates that an artist is not necessarily able to judge the value of his psychedelically inspired work while he is under drug influence.

McGlothlin, Cohen, and McGlothlin (1967) made an intensive study of 72 volunteer graduate students following a preliminary study (1964) which involved 15 subjects. (In the preliminary study, no significant changes in creativity were noted following a 200 microgram LSD session; a number of creativity tests were given before the session and one week after the session. However, some significant changes were reported on anxiety and attitude tests.)

A large battery of psychological tests was administered prior to a series of three 200 microgram LSD sessions, and again at intervals of two weeks and six months following the third session. Among the tests in the battery were three art scales, a measure of artistic performance, a test of imaginativeness, a test of originality, four tests of divergent thinking, and a test of remote associations.

Three groups were created: an experimental group receiving 200 micrograms of LSD per session, a control group receiving 25 micrograms of LSD per session, and another control group receiving 20 milligrams of an amphetamine per session. As there were no systematic differences between the two control groups at the end of the study, they were combined for purposes of comparison with the experimental group.

The most frequently reported change in the experimental group on a questionnaire filled out after six months was "a greater appreciation of music"; 62 per cent of the subjects made this assertion. The increase in number of records bought, time spent in museums, and number of musical events attended in the post-drug period was significantly greater for the experimental group. However, the subjects' scores on the art tests did not show a significant increase; the authors concluded that the data "do not indicate that the increase in aesthetic appreciation and activities is accompanied by an increase in sensitivity and performance."

On the questionnaire filled out after six months, 25 per cent of experimental subjects felt that LSD experience had resulted in enhanced creativity in their work. However, the creativity tests showed no evidence to substantiate this subjective report for the experimental group as a whole or for those claiming greater creative ability.

The other tests in the battery produced provocative results in regard to personality variables and the taking of LSD. The authors reported that "persons who place strong emphasis on structure and control generally have no taste for the experience and tend to respond minimally if exposed. Those who respond intensely tend to prefer a more unstructured, spontaneous, inward-turning (though not socially introverted) life, and score somewhat higher on tests of aesthetic sensitivity and imaginativeness. They also tend to be less aggressive, competitive, and conforming."

On the one measure of artistic performance used (the Draw-A-Person Test), the LSD subjects showed a significant decrease after six months.

Zegans, Pollard, and Brown (1967) investigated the effects of LSD upon creativity test scores of 30 male subjects chosen from a group of volunteer graduate students. Upon arrival, the first battery of tests was given and certain physiological measures (blood pressure and pulse rate) were taken. A dose of LSD equal to 0.5 micrograms per kilogram body weight was added to the water of 19 subjects randomly selected to receive the drug; the other 11 subjects did not receive LSD. After ingestion (of the drug), the subject was escorted to a lounge where he relaxed for two hours. Immediately prior to the second half of the test battery (which consisted of alternate forms of the same tests previously given), the physiological measures were repeated. The battery of tests included a measure of remote association, a test of originality for word associations, a test for ability to create an original design from tiles, a free association test, and a measure involving the ability to perceive hidden figures in a complicated line drawing. A tachistoscopic stimulation task was also included; this determined speed of visual perception.

When the creativity test data were investigated, it was discovered that the LSD group did significantly better than the control group on the re-test for originality of word associations (a modified form of the Rapaport Word Association Test). Although most other comparisons favored the LSD group, no other results were statistically significant. The authors concluded that "the administration of LSD-25 to a relatively unselected group of people for the purpose of enhancing their creative ability is *not* likely to be successful."

A further analysis of the data demonstrated that the authors were able to predict physiological reactions to a significant degree of accuracy on the basis of previously administered personality tests. It was also noted that the LSD subjects (although doing significantly better than control subjects on the word association test) made their poorest showing on those tests requiring visual attention (e.g., the tachistoscopic task, the tile design test, the hidden figures test). It was suggested that LSD "may increase the accessibility of remote or unique ideas and associations" while making it difficult for a subject to narrow his attention upon a delimited perceptual field. As a result "greater openness to remote or unique ideas and associations would only be likely to enhance creative thought in those individuals who were meaningfully engaged in some specific interest or problem."

The Institute of Psychedelic Research of San Francisco State College employed mescaline in an attempt to facilitate the creative process (Fadiman et al., 1965; Harman et al., 1966). The subjects were professional workers in various fields, who were instructed to bring a professional problem requiring a creative solution to their sessions. A number of them had worked for weeks or months on their chosen problems without success. After some psychological preparation, subjects worked individually on their problem throughout their single mescaline session. Virtually all subjects produced solutions judged highly creative and satisfactory by practical standards. Details will not be given here as the study is reported in detail in Chapter 30 of this book.

Two of the five cited studies suggest that unselected graduate students cannot expect an increase in creative ability as a result of their participation in an LSD experiment. On the other hand, creative workers in three studies utilizing psychedelic drugs showed an enhancement of creative functioning. The results must be regarded as tentative until additional work has been done in this field and until a greater control is exerted over the many variables present.*

---

*An additional study (Janinger, personal communication, 1967) is being evaluated at the present time. Fifty prominent artists painted a picture of a standard object (an American Indian doll) before ingesting LSD. During their psychedelic sessions, they again painted the doll. The 100 paintings are being evaluated on the basis of several artistic criteria in an attempt to determine what type of change took place as well as the artistic merit (or lack of merit) reflected by the change.

NINETY-ONE ARTISTS

During 1967, in an attempt to discover the types of psychedelic drugs being used illegally by artists, as well as the subjective opinions of the users, Krippner (1967) surveyed 91 artists who were reputed to have had one or more "psychedelic experiences." Among the 91 were an award-winning film-maker, A Guggenheim Fellow in poetry, and a recipient of Ford, Fulbright, and Rockefeller study grants in painting.

A remarkably large number of the artists surveyed (93 per cent) agreed with a broad definition of the "psychedelic artist" and 81 per cent felt that the term could be applied to them personally. It was concluded that the "psychedelic artist" is one whose work shows the effects of psychedelic experience—usually, but not necessarily, chemically induced. The work may have been produced as a *result* of psychedelic experience, *during* psychedelic experience, or in attempt to *induce* a psychedelic experience. In addition, the work may *remind* someone of a previous psychedelic experience or it may be used to *facilitate* psychedelic experience brought about by something other than the work of art.

Of the 91 artists in the survey, 100 per cent reported having had at least one psychedelic experience. When asked if they had ever taken a psychedelic substance, 96 per cent answered "yes" while 4 per cent answered "no."

Of the chemical substances, LSD was mentioned by more artists than any other drug, followed by marijuana, DMT, peyote, mescaline, morning glory seeds, psilocybin, hashish, DET, and yage. A few artists had tried Kava-Kava, ibogaine, bufotenin, Ditran, the amanita muscaria mushroom, and the Hawaiian wood rose. One artist reported experimenting with STP, a powerful and long-lasting drug manufactured by an "underground chemist" in California while several others had toasted and smoked the inside of banana skins, usually with extremely mild and inconsequential results. A few artists claimed to have obtained psychedelic effects from substances generally not considered psychedelic—benzedrine (an amphetamine or psychic energizer), opium (a narcotic), ritalin, kinotrine, amyl nitrate, and nitrous oxide.

The artists surveyed were asked if their psychedelic experiences (chemically as well as non-chemically induced) were generally pleasant. An unqualified "yes" response was given by 91 per cent of the group while 5 per cent gave a qualified "yes" response. In the latter cases, it was stated that some of their initial "trips" were unpleasant but that their later experiences were pleasurable. One artist answered this question negatively and three others did not respond.

When the artists were asked, "How have your psychedelic experiences influenced your art?" none of them felt that their work had suffered as a result of psychedelic experience, although some admitted that their friends might disagree with this judgment. Three per cent of the artists stated that their psychedelic experiences had not influenced their work one way or the other. The others cited a number of effects which fell into three broad categories: content, technique, and approach. In most cases, the artists reported effects that fell into more than one category.

Seventy per cent of the group stated that psychedelic experience had affected the content of their work, the most frequently cited example being their use of eidetic imagery as subject matter.

Fifty-four per cent of the artists surveyed said there had been a noticeable improvement in their artistic technique resulting from their psychedelic sessions; a greater ability to use color was the example mentioned most frequently.

Fifty-two per cent of the artists attributed a change in their creative approach to the psychedelics. Frequently made was the claim that psychedelic experience had eliminated superficiality from the artists' work and had given them greater depth as people and as creators. Some referred to their first psychedelic experience as a "peak experience," as a turning point in their lives. "My dormant interest in music became an active one," said a musician, "after a few sessions with peyote and DMT." Another said that a psilocybin experience "caused me to enjoy the art of drawing for the first time in my life."

The impact of psychedelic experience upon an individual was illustrated in the case of Isaac Abrams, one of Krippner's subjects. In an interview, the artist stated that "psychedelic experience has deeply influenced all aspects of my life. It was an experience of self-recognition, under LSD, which opened my eyes to drawing and painting as the means of self-expression for which I had always been seeking. During subsequent experiences, many difficulties, personal and artistic, were resolved. When the personal difficulties were solved, energy was released for the benefit of my art."

Upon graduation from college, Abrams got married, toured Europe, and went to work selling furniture. "I had been taught," he said, "that the most important things in life were to look neat, act nice, and make money. Yet, I knew that something was missing. There was something to do that I wasn't doing. I had a sense of mission but no idea what the mission might be."

Abrams was offered mescaline by a friend but turned it down. Several years later, in 1962, he was offered psilocybin and decided to give it a try. On Washington's birthday, Abrams and his wife took psilocybin. Abrams watched the ceiling whirl, turned off the lights, and realized for the first time that during all the years of his life he had been behaving "like a person who had no mind."

Abrams enjoyed his psilocybin experience and a few months later had another opportunity to try mescaline. "We took it in the country and it was beautiful." His next psychedelic experiences were with marijuana; once again, these were pleasant and positive in nature.

The inner life having been opened up by these episodes, Abrams thought that he might discover his "life's mission." The search was in vain. He sold more furniture. He wrote a play. He entered graduate school, but this was not for him and he dropped out.

Early in 1965, Abrams took LSD. During his session, he began to draw. "As I worked," he recalled, "I experienced a process of self-realization concerning the drawing. When the drug wore off, I kept on drawing. I did at least one ink drawing every few weeks."

Abrams attended art classes to learn about technique and materials. His wife went to different classes, took notes, and passed on the information to her husband. The skills developed quickly and he began to paint.

Abrams entered psychoanalysis with a well-known psychoanalyst who specialized in the creative process. The artist mused, "Analysis helps me to mobilize the psychedelic experience and externalize it. I think any individual can go just so far on his own. At some point he needs a spiritual teacher or guru. A good psychoanalyst can be a guru.

"For me," Abrams continued, "the psychedelic experience basically has been one of turning on to the life process, to the dance of life with all of its motion and change. Before 1962, my behavior was based on logical, rational, and linear experience. Due to the psychedelics, I also became influenced by experiences that were illogical, irrational, and non-linear. But this, too, is a part of life. This aspect is needed if life is to become interrelated and harmonious.

"Psychedelic drugs give me a sense of harmony and beauty. For the first time in my life, I can take pleasure in the beauty of a leaf; I can find meaning in the processes of nature. For me to paint an ugly picture would be a lie. It would be a violation of what I have learned through psychedelic experience."

Abrams continued, "I have found that I can flow through my pen and brush; everything I do becomes a part of myself—an exchange of energy. The canvas becomes a part of my brain. With the psychedelics, you learn to think outside of your head. My art attempts to express or reproduce my inner state." Abrams concluded, "Psychedelic experience emphasizes the unity of things, the infinite dance. You are the wave, but you are also the ocean."

Krippner noted that he rarely had found artists among the casualties of illegal drug usage, suggesting that an artist must stand somewhat apart from his culture in order to create. "To invent something new," Krippner concluded, "one cannot be completely conditioned or imprinted. Perhaps it is this type of an individual—the person who will not be alarmed at what he perceives or conceptualizes during a psychedelic session—who can most benefit from these altered states of consciousness."

Cohen (1964) summarized the research data on creativity and the psychedelics by stating, "Whether LSD does or does not increase creativity remains an open question. No systematic research is available to help in finding an answer. All that can be said at this time about the effect of LSD on the creative process is that a strong subjective feeling of creativeness accompanies many of the experiences."

CONCLUSION

A great deal of evidence exists at the anecdotal and clinical level which suggests that the psychedelic state and the hypnotic trance can facilitate the creative act. Much less evidence exists at the experimental level. Three tentative conclusions can be drawn but each demands further data before its validity can be established.

In the first place, alterations in consciousness resulting from hypnosis and the psychedelics share certain characteristics with those mental states associated with creativity. Hypnosis and the psychedelics, for example, often permit access to preverbal impressions, to unconscious material, and to intuitive processes.

Secondly, the therapeutic use of hypnosis and the psychedelics seems to have been especially successful with artists. Perhaps the therapist, in producing an altered state of awareness on the part of his artist patients, not only appeals to their sense of the dramatic but brings about a mental state similar to that in which they have previously functioned at a mature, creative level.*

Finally, it should be noted that the transcendence of culturally imposed imprints and of societal conditioning always has been a goal for creative persons. Hypnosis and the psychedelics, when used properly, enable artists to stand apart from their culture, at least for a brief period of time. In so doing, they sometimes make an artistic statement that encompasses all cultures, a statement which in time may become a classic painting or poem. For all these reasons, the hypnotic trance, the psychedelic state, and other forms of altered consciousness are worthy of serious study if the act of human creation is to be better understood, guided, and encouraged.

*Levine & Ludwig (1965) have combined psychotherapy, hypnosis, and LSD producing a "hypnodelic state" which they have found to be more beneficial to patients than any of the approaches tried alone.

19

PSYCHEDELIC EXPERIENCES ASSOCIATED WITH A NOVEL HYPNOTIC PROCEDURE, MUTUAL HYPNOSIS

CHARLES T. TART

One of the most intriguing aspects of hypnosis has been its ability to produce, in the best Ss, very unusual subjective experiences. In the past decade these phenomena have been largely overlooked, as the emphasis in hypnosis research has been on the development of objective measures of suggestibility (Shor & Orne, 1962, Weitzenhoffer & Hilgard, 1959, 1962, 1963), the nature of hypnotic suggestibility (Hilgard & Tart, 1966), and psychological factors affecting responses to hypnotic suggestion (Hilgard, 1965). In comparing the reports of some of the older hypnotic phenomena, usually termed deep trance phenomena, I was struck by their resemblance to many of the experiences now being reported in conjunction with the use of psychedelic drugs. This resemblance suggested that the combination of hypnotic techniques and psychedelic drugs might be very fruitful.

In the past few years several articles have reported on psychedelic-like experiences occurring with hypnosis (Aaroneon, 1964, 1965a, 1965b, 1965c, 1965d; Erickson, 1966, Forgel & Hoffer, 1962b, 1963) and on the use of hypnosis to control or guide drug-induced psychedelic experiences (Fogel & Hoffer, 1962a; Levine & Ludwig, 1965, 1966; Levine, Ludwig, & Lyle, 1963; Ludwig & Levine, 1965). Some indirect evidence further indicating that hypnosis may offer a powerful technique for guiding psychedelic experiences also is suggested by the work of Sjoberg and Hollistar (1965), who found that suggestibility was markedly enhanced by LSD-25 and mescaline.

The purpose of the present paper is to present examples of psychedelic phenomena arising with the use of a novel hypnotic technique, "mutual hypnosis," as a further indication of possible relationships between deep hypnotic phenomena and drug-induced psychedelic experiences, with the hope that these relationships will be further explored and lead to greater understanding of both the deep hypnotic and psychedelic experiences.

In 1962 I was interested in the problem of whether the depth of hypnosis an S could reach was a relatively constant factor for a given S or whether it could be substantially increased by more effective hypnotic techniques. Data published since that time generally indicate that Ss have a fixed level of response to hypnotic suggestions that is not greatly altered by further training (As, Hilgard, & Weitzenhoffer, 1963; Cooper, Banford, Schubot, & Tart, 1967; Shor, Orne, & O'Connell, 1966), but at the time I carried out this study most hypnotists believed any S's hypnotic abilities could be increased by training. The particular technique I decided to try was based on the idea of *rapport*, the special relationship supposed to exist between hypnotist and S: I reasoned that if *rapport* was greatest in deep hypnotic states, a technique which markedly increased *rapport* would likely increase the depth of hypnosis. The method I decided to try for markedly increasing *rapport* was to have two Ss simultaneously fill the roles of both hypnotist and hypnotized S, what I will call mutual hypnosis. That is, I would have A hypnotize B, and when B was hypnotized he would (while still hypnotized and *en rapport* with A) then hypnotize A: then when A was also hypnotized by B (and *en rapport* with B), A would deepen B's hypnotic state, then B would deepen A's hypnotic state, and so on. Ordinary *rapport* is a one-way relation: the S is highly attentive to the hypnotist. This procedure would make it a two-way relation, with each S highly attentive to the other. I had never heard of such a hypnotic procedure at the time the experiment was carried out.*

Three experimental sessions were carried out over a period of several months with three fellow graduate students as Ss. Some background on the Ss will be provided below, as well as a description of a self-report scale of hypnotic depth which was used throughout the sessions. Highlights from the three sessions will then be presented and commented on, followed by a discussion of the mutual hypnosis technique and its effects.

---

*Two years later I discovered that Milton Erickson (1964, also Chapter 3 in this book) had tried a mutual hypnosis procedure in 1933, but the Ss were working under a different experimental set, and no psychedelic phenomena were reported.

Subjects

Two Ss participated in all three experimental sessions. They will be called Anne and Bill. A third S, Carol accidentally participated in the second experimental session, as will be explained below. All Ss were graduate students in psychology and in their twenties. Each had done some work as hypnotists, administering Form A, B, or C of the Stanford Hypnotic Susceptibility Scale (Weitzenhoffer & Hilgard, 1959, 1962). This procedure does not require much "skill" in the usual sense in which we think of a hypnotist being skilled, as verbatim reading of the induction and suggestibility items is all that is required for giving the test. None of the Ss had done much hypnosis other than this.

Each S was unusual in being moderately hypnotizable: although there are few studies of this, it is a common belief among investigators working with hypnosis that almost all hypnotists are very poor Ss themselves (LeCron, 1951; Moss & Riggen, 1963; Moss, Riggen, Cayne, & Bishop, 1965). The reason is unknown, but speculation usually runs along the line that the hypnotist really regards his "powers" as "magical," regardless of what he tells the S, and is not going to submit to anyone else's magical control. Thus it was a fortunate coincidence to find Ss who both had had some experience as hypnotists and were moderately hypnotizable themselves.

The Ss had never had any experience with psychedelic drugs.

Self-Report Depth Scale

If an S is asked to scale the degree to which he is hypnotized, under some conditions his estimate is very useful in that: (a) it correlates significantly with the usual suggestibility test criteria of hypnotic depth (Hatfield, 1961; Hilgard & Tart, 1966; LeCron, 1953; O'Connell, 1964; Tart, 1963, 1966c; Tart & Hilgard, 1966); (b) it discriminates between different qualities of experience reported by the S (Tart, 1966a, 1966b); and (c) the Ss feel they are making meaningful discriminations. Indeed, it will be argued elsewhere* that the degree to which an S reports feeling hypnotized may be used as the criterion of hypnosis, rather than his suggestibility.

An early form of self-report scale was used in the present study. It was being used concurrently in dissertation research (Tart, 1966c).

The Ss were instructed, while hypnotized in the preliminary session, that whenever I asked, "Trance depth?" a number would *instantly* flash into their mind indicating his or her hypnotic depth at the moment. The following illustrative values were read to the Ss for scaling: "(a) zero is

---

*Tart, C. Self-report scales of hypnotic depth. In preparation.

waking; (b) from 1 to 12 is a state in which you feel very relaxed and detached, and your arm can rise up or rotate (automatic motion) if I suggest it; (c) a depth of 20 or greater is required for your hand or any other part of your body to become numb (analgesia); (d) a depth of 25 or more is required for you to dream while in the hypnotic state; (e) a depth of 30 or more is required for you to develop amnesia, your mind is very quiet, and you pay almost no attention to anything besides my voice or things I direct your attention to, and you can see and hear anything I suggest; (f) at a depth of 40 or more your mind is absolutely still and everything I suggest to you is perfectly real, absolutely real, just as real as anything in the world; and (g) a depth of 50 or more is an extremely profound trance, so profound that your mind becomes naturally sluggish or slow." This scale thus extended to the level of trance commonly called "plenary" (Erickson, 1956), seldom encountered in practice. The usual "good" hypnotic S would be, a priori, expected to score between 30 and 40.

Because the depth of hypnosis can fluctuate from minute to minute, the Ss were frequently asked for depth reports.

Preliminary Training Sessions

The possibility was considered that if Anne and Bill were both hypnotists and Ss there might be no way of bringing the experiments to a halt at a convenient time. Further, since the procedure was altogether novel, complications could arise which I would be unable to deal with as the Ss could be completely *en rapport* with each other but oblivious to me or anyone else. Thus Anne and Bill were each given an individual hypnotic training session with me as the hypnotist, in order to (a) establish *rapport* with me; and (b) implant a post-hypnotic suggestion that this *rapport* would last into the later experimental sessions. Thus I could always intervene in the later sessions and take control of the situation (theoretically). Also, the role of hypnotist was temporarily transferred to Anne in Bill's training session and vice versa to establish initial *rapport* between them.

Anne was hypnotized with a hand lowering procedure (Erickson, 1956) and after several minutes of deepening procedures reported a maximum depth of 35. She responded positively to a suggestion that the room would be visually distorted when she opened her eyes. Bill had her walk around the room while hypnotized, and suggested that she would respond well to him in the later experimental sessions. I had her have a couple of dreams in hypnosis, one about hypnotizing Bill, the other about some topic she wanted but which she didn't have to tell to me or anyone (to encourage a sense of autonomy). She reached a maximum depth here of 39, then was dehypnotized.

Bill's training session was similar. He reported a maximum depth of 40, and was able to experience visual distortion of the room, but could not hallucinate a solid object with his eyes open.

First Mutual Hypnosis Session

Bill induced hypnosis in Anne to begin. He suggested that she concentrate on her breathing, that her eyes would close, that she would eventually see a blue vapor flowing in and out of her nostrils as she breathed, and that she would feel herself falling backwards into hypnosis. This was a radical departure from the standardized induction procedure of the SHSS. The instructions to concentrate on the breathing and see it as a blue vapor are an interesting parallel to some Yoga concentration exercises. Anne reported after the session that she did experience falling back in her chair, over and over again, during this induction, although she did not experience coming back up after each fall: just the falling back part. Anne reported a state of 27 at the end of this 7 minute induction procedure. Bill continued to deepen Anne by counting and various other techniques until she reached a reported depth of 40 several minutes later.

After the session Anne reported the following experience occurred during this deepening ". . . I had a sensation for the first time of actually relinquishing control. I had a most unusual physical sensation of my body disintegrating—with great chunks folding off like thick bark on a tree. I was momentarily threatened, almost resisted, reassured myself, and soon this feeling passed, after which my body was *gone*, and I felt like a *soul* or a big ball of *mind*."

Bill now instructed Anne to hypnotize him. Anne opened her eyes, held up a finger, told Bill to watch it, and hypnotized him with this eye fixation technique. After eye closure, Anne closed her eyes and began talking about how she and Bill were climbing down a manhole together, and that Bill would be deeply hypnotized by the time they reached the bottom. Anne said she was seeing bright, glowing crystals on the walls of the manhole as they descended and Bill said he was seeing them too when Anne questioned him. The bottom of the manhole was reached seven minutes after the start of Anne's induction, and Bill reported a depth of 13. I reminded Anne to hypnotize Bill much more deeply. She went through a hand lowering and then a hand levitation procedure with Bill. It was interesting to see Anne's hand show appropriate minor movements during this, suggesting that a high degree of empathy and *rapport* already existed. Bill reported a depth of 36 at the end of this.

I then told Anne to have Bill deepen her hypnotic state, and to remind him to respond to my suggestions whenever I put my hand on his shoulder and spoke to him. This was to keep up my *rapport* with the *S*s.

Bill's eyes kept blinking open and closed as he deepened Anne, but after a few minutes his eyes stayed open and his gaze was fixed and steady, a perfect "hypnotic gaze." He apparently stabilized in his role as hypnotized hypnotist. After about 10 minutes Anne reported a state of 43, and when I asked Bill for his state immediately after he also reported 43.

Anne now began deepening Bill again. Both reported a depth of 47 in a few minutes. Anne deepened Bill by suggesting that he would experience himself lying on a warm beach in the sun and listening to the waves rolling in. At the end of this I suggested to Anne that *she* dream a dream which would lead her into much deeper hypnosis and that she describe the dream aloud to Bill so that he would also go much deeper. Anne described dreaming of the two of them being in a car on the desert, watching the road unwind before them, seeing small lizards run over the sand, then walking along the desert road, feeling hot and sticky but with an overall feeling of pleasantness.

When asked by Anne, Bill indicated he was dreaming the same dream. From later questioning, both *S*s were by now completely oblivious to their actual surroundings and totally absorbed in their hallucinatory world(s). An interesting sidelight is that the laboratory room became very hot with sun shining on the roof shortly before this, and while both *S*s claimed no awareness in a late interview that the lab was hot this stimulus was apparently unconsciously incorporated into their shared dream world(s).

Bill became rather unresponsive at this point. Asked to deepen Anne's hypnotic state he rolled his head about, was silent and unresponsive. I asked his depth and he replied, after a long pause, 25. I then asked Anne to deepen him. Anne was silent for several minutes, and I finally asked her what she was doing. She replied, "Taking Bill down the steps." As she was apparently "hallucinating" that she was deepening Bill I asked her to do it *aloud*, so that Bill would be with her, to which she indignantly replied that Bill *was* with her!* So I asked Anne to get Bill's depth report when they were all the way down the steps. There was a silent period of several minutes, then Anne asked Bill for his depth and he replied, "I don't know." I placed my hand on Bill's shoulder and asked him why he couldn't give his depth and he replied that nothing came when he was asked. I suggested that he would give a depth report when I snapped my fingers, and he replied with a report of 57, beyond the deepest level defined in the scale. From his behavioral inert-

---

*In the post-session interview, Bill said he was with Anne in going down the steps. As will be discussed later, both Bill and Anne felt they had shared many detailed experiences which were not verbalized during the experimental sessions.

ness and depth report he was apparently in a plenary trance state, far deeper than anything he had ever reached before.

Because Anne and Bill were so deep I wondered if they could become behaviorally active without disrupting the hypnotic state, so I suggested (through Anne) that both she and Bill would simulate wakefulness in a minute. On signal they both opened their eyes, sat up, lit cigarettes, talked with me and a couple of observers in the room (one of whom was Carol, who had come into the room about this time), and claimed they were awake. I told them depth reports would indicate their true state when I snapped my fingers, and Anne reported 32 and Bill reported 48. Both Ss in the post-session interview reported that they were quite surprised to hear these depth reports automatically come from themselves. Anne felt she was just about normally awake. Bill felt he was awake but almost "turned off" and relapsed into hypnosis several times. Both Ss showed some psychomotor retardation and a lack of initiative.

After a few minutes of simulated wakefulness I suggested they go back into hypnosis again and cease simulating. Anne reported a depth of 38, Bill a depth of 53 at this time. At my suggestion, Bill dehypnotized Anne by counting backwards, and after Anne was fully awake (eyes open and depth report of zero) she dehypnotized Bill by getting his depth report (48) and counting backwards from that with the suggestion that he would be fully awake when she reached zero. At zero Bill still reported a depth of 12, so Anne counted bacwards from 12 to fully rouse him. We then talked about the experiment for a while until the Ss had to go off to other business. The session had lasted a little over an hour.

Several major themes emerged in this first session which reappeared in the later ones. Both Ss began to resent my intervening and suggesting that they do anything in particular. Both Ss also felt they had been much more deeply hypnotized than ever before and, in addition, I and one of the observers felt that Anne was a far more dramatic (and presumably effective) hypnotist than she had ever been before: her voice became "hypnotic," she improvised effective techniques instead of sticking to the SHSS forms, and clearly showed great empathy and *rapport* with Bill's reactions. Both Ss were pleased and excited over this mutual hypnosis technique, and wanted to continue working with it, although Bill admitted many months later that he had been ambivalent about further exploration.

Second Mutual Hypnosis Session

This session was held about one month later. The entire session was tape recorded. Anne began by hypnotizing Bill with a hand levitation technique followed by several suggestions of various automatic movements of the hands for deepening. Bill reported a depth of 9 at the end of this, a rather slow beginning.

At this point Carol entered the room to observe and Anne mentioned this to Bill, commenting that "Carol is going to come in and sit down in the corner, but it will not bother you and you will not pay any attention to her." The phrasing of this remark is significant in the light of later events.

Anne improvised further deepening analogies (watching clock hands turning, seeing a pendulum swing,* etc.) which she used until a report of 18 was given by Bill. She then suggested that he dissociate and watch himself being hypnotized, watch himself perform various hypnotic phenomena, such as his hand becoming light and floating up. She also suggested he have a dream of becoming more deeply hypnotized, and after 13 minutes Bill gave a depth report of 29. As Anne appeared discouraged at this slow progress I suggested that she tell Bill to think about whatever he wanted to that would help him become more hypnotized, and she suggested this to Bill: ". . . imagine whatever you feel will make you the most relaxed, the most drowsy, the most hypnotized . . ." Anne was silent then for five minutes and Bill's depth report at the end of this was 38. I then suggested (through Anne) that Bill begin to hypnotize her. This elicited some sighs, long silences, and a depth report of 43 from Bill. Anne questioned him as to what he was experiencing and found that he had spontaneously regressed and was reliving a pleasant experience that had happened to him two years before. Anne suggested that he come to the present.

The change that then came over Bill was dramatic. He began mumbling typical induction suggestions about relaxing, but over the course of a few minutes his voice became dramatic and forceful. He suggested that Anne see a diamond in her hand and concentrate on it and then almost immediately suggested that it would disappear and her mind would go blank. Then he very forcefully suggested physical relaxation as he counted her into hypnosis: when he reached 20 his whole manner changed and became relaxed and soothing. Anne reported a depth of 22.

Bill then began talking about a "hallucinatory" journey that he and Anne were on together. His voice was confident, smooth, relaxed, and completely convincing that he was describing actual events that were happening rather than anything "unreal." They were standing on a mountain slope, in front of the entrance to a tunnel. They walked hand-in-hand down this tunnel, with the explicit suggestion by Bill that they would be going deeper into hypnosis as they walked deeper into the dark tunnel. It was quiet in the tunnel, all outside noises had vanished, and an ineffable feeling of pleasantness and

---

*I could see rapid eye movements under Bill's closed lids when the vision of the swinging pendulum was suggested to him.

significance pervaded the tunnel. Anne reported a depth of 35 after a few minutes of this, and Bill continued describing their walk down the tunnel.

At this point I noticed that Carol had spontaneously gone into hypnosis and was apparently sharing the hallucinatory journey with Anne and Bill: her eyes were closed and her facial expressions seemed to follow Bill's words. I put my hand on Bill's shoulder (the hypnotically implanted signal to put him *en rapport* with me) and told him that Carol was hypnotized and was coming along too. Bill shook his head no, and Carol reported in the post-session interview that she knew she was rejected then, but she stayed hypnotized and in the tunnel. Bill completely lost conscious touch with me and the laboratory environment for the rest of this session and, as indicated in later interviews, strongly resented my attempts to "intrude" into his and Anne's hypnotic world.

Bill soon suggested that Anne guide him deeper into the tunnel (which was equated in both Ss' minds with the depth of hypnosis as well as possessing total experiential reality for them at the time). Anne reported a depth of 40 at this time, then was silent. After a few minutes I suggested that she continue to take Bill deeper into the tunnel. She began speaking in a dramatically smooth and confident manner about continuing the journey into the tunnel. As with Bill's voice, there was a quality that gave absolute reality to what she was describing. She mentioned faintly hearing music as they went deeper into the tunnel, and wondering if it were angels singing. She frequently suggested that the experience was very peaceful, very relaxing and refreshing. When she asked Bill for his depth, he reported 45.

At this point I wondered if I could suggest a post-hypnotic hallucination that would serve as a behavioral check on the deep hypnotic state indicated by the depth reports, so I put my hand on each Ss' shoulder and suggested: "Why don't you both continue going down the tunnel together, each going deeper into hypnosis, and I want you each to find some sort of object, like a rock or something, that you can bring back to this laboratory and look at here." Bill reported in the post-session interview that he had not heard this suggestion from me. Anne immediately asked Bill if he had found the diamond (which Bill had suggested Anne hallucinate in the induction) in the tunnel, but Bill sternly replied that anything found in the tunnel *belonged* there and could not be taken away.

I continued to suggest to Anne that she bring back something, perhaps a rock from the mouth of the tunnel, and that it would be good if Bill would bring back something too. Anne wanted to go further into the tunnel and to bring something back, very badly: Bill insisted they could do neither and then forcefully took them out of the tunnel. Anne was very distressed at this, she wanted so much (according to later interview) to see what was at the end of the tunnel, and to bring something back. With his voice extremely forceful and loud, Bill took them both from the tunnel and attempted to dehypnotize Anne. As Bill finished his attempt to dehypnotize Anne I asked her for a depth report. She replied with 25, so I then dehypnotized her. Upon inquiry, Anne told me she was mostly awake now. When I asked her if she had remembered to bring a rock back she unhappily replied no. She then dehypnotized Bill, who was already back to a very light state (depth report of 9), and Carol also awakened by herself about this time.

The immediately ensuing interview brought out a number of important points about the experience.

The tunnel was absolutely real to Anne and Bill (and to Carol), as real as any experience in life. Although it was dark they could "see" its walls in a strange way: Anne said it felt as if she had a "light" coming out from under her eyebrows, and ". . . it wasn't illuminating anything I was seeing, yet it helped me to know that things were there without seeing them." Both Ss reported feeling the texture of the rock walls, which ranged from soft and slippery at places where it seemed moss-covered to quite hard where the bare rock was exposed.

A second important quality about the tunnel was that it was clearly Bill's personal property: Anne felt she was there only by virtue of Bill's permission and guidance, and Carol, as discussed below, felt she was trespassing. Bill said that the tunnel had rules of its own, that last time it had been Anne's hole in the ground but this time it was his tunnel and very important and personal to him. Further, Bill felt *he* knew what was at the end of the tunnel that Anne wanted to see so much, but he would not let her (or Carol) see it.

Carol's experience is of great interest. She found herself hypnotized and standing near the mouth of the tunnel at about the time when I asked Bill if she could come along. She felt rejected by him (although her eyes were closed and she did not see him nod his head no), but stayed in the tunnel. She followed Anne and Bill into the tunnel, staying out of "sight" behind them, and feeling like a child following its parents when its parents have forbidden it to come. She also wanted to go all the way to the end, as Anne did. When I suggested that Anne and Bill find something to bring back she found a picture of a (unidentified) person, in a small, wooden frame: whenever Bill told Anne that she couldn't bring anything back the picture would twist in her hand and face away from her! When Bill began forcing Anne back out of the tunnel she ran along ahead of them to avoid being caught, and lost the picture while running.

Bill stated that he knew Carol might be back in the tunnel somewhere, but while he didn't like anyone else in *his* tunnel he deliberately paid no attention to her.

Bill reported he was no longer aware of me after I told him that Carol was along, although he seemed to remain vaguely aware of me as an intruding influence. Anne had resented my voice intruding in the previous mutual hypnosis session. This time she perceived my voice as a small, tiny voice, far off, like the voice of conscience inside her head, while she was in the tunnel. She felt that this served the function of making me distant and unimportant, and therefore easy to ignore if she did not like what I was saying.

Anne and Carol were intensely curious as to what lay at the end of the tunnel, the end that Bill would not let them reach. This resulted in an interesting aftermath. About a month after this session, Anne was a subject in a group hypnosis test. As she knew what the induction procedure was, she decided to "go" back to the tunnel and explore it as soon as she was hypnotized but before the suggestibility test items were administered. She found herself running along the tunnel, hurrying to reach the end before the test items. At the end of the tunnel she found a cave, blazing with brilliant white light, and occupied by an old man of angelic appearance. The room was filled with music from an unseen source. Anne repeatedly asked him what this experience meant: he ignored her at first, and finally told her, very sternly, that he could not answer her question because Bill was not with her. Anne then found herself back at the group hypnosis testing.

Following this second session, Anne and Bill developed an intense friendship, spending a great deal of time together. They felt extremely close to one another as a result of their shared experience. Anne wanted to continue experimenting with mutual hypnosis, but Bill was very ambivalent about it. It was almost three months before they agreed to try one more session. Bill insisted that neither Carol nor any other observer be present.

Third Mutual Hypnosis Session

Neither Anne nor Bill felt like hypnotizing the other to begin the session, so they asked me to hypnotize them both to start. I did so with a very permissive eye fixation technique, stressing relaxation, detachment, and feelings of peace. After 10 minutes of this Anne reported a depth of 31 and Bill of 25. I then suggested that they each have a dream, one that they would not have to say anything about, but which would take them much deeper. Both were silent for several minutes. Then both of their hypnotic dreams ended within a couple of seconds of each other (they had each kept an index finger raised during the dream and lowered it at the end, according to a prearranged plan). After the session, both reported dreams which had begun quite differently, but each dream ended with the S climbing upward on a swaying support, a rope ladder in Bill's case, a golden rope for Anne. I got depth reports of 48 for Bill and 42 for Anne at this moment, and suggested that they "go exploring" together, describing it aloud. I did not know at the time that they both experienced being together in a hallucinatory world at this point, and that they both felt they had each climbed up into this world on a rope ladder or golden rope, so I was surprised at how quickly the Ss began talking as if they were seeing similar things.

The Ss experienced themselves as standing together in a place that they described as a "heaven" of some sort. Their conversation sounded like a continuous description of a drug-induced psychedelic experience. The Ss expressed wonderment at the beauty surrounding them. Almost immediately Bill instructed Anne to appreciate what was around them but not to look *too* closely, not to interfere with them, to let them change as they would. Bill's instructions to Anne to not grasp at the phenomena, to accept them without trying to possess them, are remarkably parallel to the sorts of instructions given in psychedelic "trip manuals" which came into print years later, such as Leary, Metzner, and Alpert's (1964), and are now widely disseminated as psychedelic lore. There were elaborations of these instructions later in the session.

The first thing the Ss remarked about in this heaven world was the water in front of them: it was like champagne and had beautiful, huge bubbles in it. They swam in it together and found it to be remarkably bouyant and "bouncy," as well as tasting delicious.

Then Anne heard a distant voice calling to Bill, a voice from an "inhabitant of up there." Bill told her to ignore the voice though, and reminded her not to grasp at anything, to simply let events flow as they would. Anne then asked Bill if he had gotten here on a golden rope as she had, but Bill told her not to worry about how they had gotten here but just *be* there. As with the tunnel in the previous session, this place is clearly felt by Bill to be *his*: he didn't want anyone else to know about how to get to it, and he knew what the rules of the place were and insisted that Anne obey them.

The Ss then wandered around looking at beautiful, translucent, glowing, multicolored rocks on the ground for a while. Then Bill suddenly announced that it was time for them to go.

Although asked about it at length in the post-session interview, Bill could not (or would not) explain why he suddenly *knew* it was time for them to leave. Anne was not ready to go, and, as in the previous session, Bill forced her to. I attempted to contact Bill at this point, but he did not respond to me and in the post-session interview claimed he had not heard me at all. Anne stalled, saying it looked as if it were going to rain and they should stay to see if the rain were like champagne. Bill suggested it would rain, all right, but that it would *thunder** and be *cold*, so when this rain occurred it was very unpleasant.

*At about this time a jet plane flew over and shook the building. Both Ss denied consciously hearing any plane in the post-session interview. Anne heard the thunder in the place she was at. Bill heard neither the thunder nor the plane: he felt he had created the thunder to frighten Anne and get her out of there, but there was no need for him to hear the thunder or be bothered by it.

Bill counted back from 50 with instructions that this would dehypnotize Anne.

When Bill reached a count of one I asked each S for a depth report. Anne reported 10, Bill reported 20, so I spent a couple of minutes rousing them to full wakefulness.

The interview clarified a number of things about the experience. As with the tunnel in the previous session, the place they felt they were at possessed complete experiential reality. It was different, however, in being obviously "unworldly," much more so than the tunnel. Anne had wondered during the session if it was "God's house," and Bill agreed afterward that it was heaven, but it wasn't the heaven of the Christians, it was the heaven of the Greeks, it was a heaven without finality.

As with the tunnel, Anne felt it to be very much Bill's "possession." Bill was the one who knew how they had gotten there, what the rules of the place were, and how to get back, so Anne didn't think it would be a good idea to insist on staying or doing anything Bill didn't approve of, much more so than in the tunnel of the second session.

The quality of the place they were in was difficult for the Ss to describe. When they first "opened their eyes" and looked about things were "gray," yet it was not an obscuring grayness, and there were many vivid colors and glowing lights. Ordinary concepts of space seemed poorly applicable, for sometimes things were definitely "nearer and further," but at other times the concept of spatial distance between the perceiver and the perceived simply did not fit the experience. The setting was consistently described as beautiful by both Ss, except for the rain. The rain was simply a warm rain falling on his skin to Bill, but to Anne it came with the thunder that frightened her away. Instead of a delightful rain like champagne that she expected, Anne found the rain as cold as ice, freezing and frightening her. The rocks referred to were more like translucent crystals, not tactually hard, and filled with glowing, pulsing colors.

I asked the Ss about their perceived bodies during the experience and found that they were curiously disembodied much of the time. They mentioned having heads or faces but no bodies at times, and Anne reported that they walked *through* each other sometimes. When Bill commanded Anne to give him her hand so he could lead her back, Anne reported that she had to "crawl back into my body, sort of. It was almost as if we were moving around with just heads. When Bill said give him my hand, I had to kind of conjure up a hand."

It also came out in conversations some weeks later that this passing through each other was also accompanied by a sense of merging identities, of a partial blending of themselves quite beyond the degree of contact human beings expect to share with others.

Anne asked Bill about the voice that had been calling him early in the session. Bill replied that he purposely ignored it, which had disappointed Anne, as she was sure it was the voice of someone who "lived up there" trying to contact them.

This was the last experiment with mutual hypnosis for Anne and Bill. Anne was ambivalent about the experiences, but would have tried more. Bill was strongly opposed to any further exploration and, like one of Erickson's (1964) Ss, lost his interest in hypnosis a few months afterward.

DISCUSSION

This section will discuss three main topics. First, the question of how the procedure affected the hypnotizability of the Ss and their functioning as hypnotists; second, the psychedelic qualities of this experience; and third, some possible dangers of this mutual hypnosis procedure.

Hypnotizability

I had hoped to administer some of the most difficult suggestibility test items from the SHSS to the Ss at the end of the later mutual hypnosis sessions, but they acquired a dynamic of their own each time, with the Ss terminating their own hypnotic states, which precluded this. I did attempt to have the Ss give themselves the post-hypnotic suggestion for a positive visual hallucination (bringing back the rock), but this was not accepted. Indeed, my desire to produce "objective" suggestibility phenomena made me rather insensitive to the dynamics of the situation at times.

In terms of their self-reports of hypnotic depth, both Ss reached much deeper levels than ever before. My clinical impression and that of another observer supports this: the Ss achieved a much deeper level of hypnotic experience than they had ever shown previously. In addition, Anne has continued experimenting with hypnosis, both self-induced and induced by others for several years and reports that she is far more hypnotizable than she was before these mutual hypnosis sessions.

Thus, although this is a limited case study, it certainly suggests that hypnotizability may be dramatically increased by this mutual hypnosis technique, and further research is warranted along this line.

With respect to their functioning as hypnotists, both Ss changed. Bill was a fairly forceful and dynamic person before this experiment, but his performance as a hypnotist definitely became more dramatic and confident. The

ange in Anne was even more striking: she dropped the relatively bland
yle of the SHSS procedures and became confident, inventive, and dramatic.
'hen both Ss gave hypnotic suggestions their voice quality possessed such
ality that one could hardly doubt that the suggestion would work.

Whether the increase in hypnotizability and more effective functioning
hypnotists resulted only from an increase in *rapport* is unknown. Certainly
e two Ss showed a great sensitivity and empathy to the other's experiences
ut not necessarily an agreement). Subsequent conversations revealed that
e Ss felt so much *rapport* with each other that it seemed telepathic, although
ere was no objective evidence to support the idea of telepathic contact
ere.

sychedelic Characteristics

A variety of experiences reported by the Ss are frequently reported in
njunction with drug-induced psychedelic experiences (Cohen, 1965; de
opp, 1957; Master & Houston, 1966; Solomon, 1964). These included
arked perceptual changes, changes in self-concept and body image, feel-
gs of greatly enhanced empathy and paranormal communication, and a
nse of immediate significance to the experiences.

The perceptual changes were not changes in perception of the external
orld but rather changes in the quality of internal imagery. *Imagery*, how-
ver, is too mild a word for the Ss' experiences, as it connotes something
ss intense than perception of external qualities, less "real," yet for the
s their internal perceptions were in no way less real or less vivid than their
rdinary sensory perceptions. They were also much more vivid and real than
eir usual imagery. Further, the "sensory" qualities of the internal imagery
ere often *more* vivid than ordinary sense perceptions: thus Anne talked
out colored light glowing as if it were alive. This sort of sensory enhance-
ent is almost always reported from psychedelic experiences. More difficult
convey, but just as real to the Ss, were times in which they "sensed"
ings in their internal environments but in a way which could not be equated
ith any usual sensory modalities: thus the Ss would talk about "seeing"
ings in their shared world but indicate to me that they were simply using
analogy with vision because they could not find words for the actual
perience.

Changes in self-concept and body image were usually together. The
s at times perceived themselves as bodiless, or possessing just parts of a
ody. They also felt there were changes in psychological functioning over
d above the alterations in body image. An example of this would be the
se of modes of communication between themselves that they did not know

they possessed. The alteration that most impressed (and later frightened the Ss, however, was the feeling of *merging* with each other at times, especially in the final mutual hypnosis session. This seemed like a partial fusion of identities, a partial loss of the distinction between I and Thou. This was felt to be good at the time, but later the Ss perceived this as a threat to their individual autonomy.

Several times during the sessions the Ss said nothing for a time, but when questioned them replied that they were communicating, so there was a feeling at the time of the experience that paranormal communication of some sort was going on. Even more striking material regarding the Ss' feeling about this heightened empathy and communication was obtained a couple of months after the final session when the tapes of the sessions had been transcribed. Anne and Bill read the transcripts over and were both shocked. They had been talking about their experiences to each other for some time and found they had been discussing details of the experiences they had shared for which there were no verbal stimuli on the tapes, i.e., they felt they must have been communicating telepathically or that they had actually been "in" the nonworldly locales they had experienced. This was frightening to both Ss, for what had seemed a lovely shared *fantasy* now threatened to be something *real*. This feeling of the Ss does not constitute any sort of proof for genuine telepathic interaction, of course, for there were no independent records of the details of the Ss' experiences made before they had an opportunity to talk with each other, but the feeling of the Ss that there was telepathic interaction and their reaction to it was one of the most impressive aspects of the experience.

The final psychedelic quality of the experiences to be noted was the feeling of *immediate significance* that most of the experiences had for the Ss, i.e. the experience was self-validating, it did not need to be checked against some other reference system because it was significant in and of itself.

In the broad sense of the term, these experiences were "hypnotic dreams," dream-like experiences induced under hypnosis. However, they were not at all like the usual hypnotic dream in quality, intensity, or after-effects (Moss 1967; Tart, 1965).

Possible Dangers

Because of the intensity of the phenomena produced with this mutual hypnosis procedure, it could be dangerous in some cases and caution should be taken in future experimentation.

The Ss used in this study were quite mature persons. If this procedure were to be used with psychologically unstable persons and experiences of compaable intensity were obtained, they could be quite unsettling to the $S(s)$, in the same way that an LSD-25 experience is psychologically disturbing to unprepared or immature persons. I have heard indirectly of two college students who tried mutual hypnosis on each other after hearing one of the present Ss mention something about it at a social function. One of the boys was not very stable to begin with and was unable to be fully dehypnotized after the session until professional help was called in.

A complication and possible danger in the present study was introduced in conjunction with my taking a "master of ceremonies" role. I attempted to maintain ultimate hypnotic control of both Ss, both as a precautionary measure and to direct them toward the planned suggestibility testing. This resulted in my being resented by both Ss and losing this control with Bill. It is possible that with highly stable and mature Ss this external control might not be needed and the experimenter could act merely as an observer, but it would seem necessary to retain the "master of ceremonies" hypnotist until much more is known about mutual hypnosis. As profound as the experience was for the Ss, both felt that it had not reached its limit, yet experimental control had already been lost.

A final possible danger to be mentioned is that the "forced" intimacy produced by this technique may be unsettling. The Ss in the present study felt they had become quite close to each other quite suddenly as a result of their shared experiences, although they were able to handle these feelings. Our culture does not prepare people for sudden, intense intimacy. I know of a roughly comparable case of two married couples who took LSD-25 together: each experienced an intense merging of identities with the three others. Because of the sudden and unexpected intensity of these feelings the couples had a great deal of difficulty in their emotional relationships to each other for several months afterwards, all centered around feelings that they had seen too much of each other's real selves, more than their previous relationship had prepared them to handle comfortably.

Further explorations of the potentialities of this mutual hypnosis technique should bear these possible psychological dangers in mind. Until more is understood of the phenomena I would recommend that Ss for such experimentation be selected as carefully and the same experimental safeguards for the Ss' welfare be applied as one would use in administering LSD-25 to Ss.

Conclusions

Although this report is based on only two Ss, the results with them were dramatic enough to warrant considerable research on mutual hypnosis. The technique seems very powerful: it might offer a way to produce psychedelic experiences in the laboratory without the use of drugs and with more flexibility and control than is possible with drugs. As a way of exploring inner fantasy worlds it seems more potent than psychosynthesis techniques (Assagioli, 1965) or the ordinary hypnotic dream. And the possibilities of substantially increasing hypnotizability in Ss who are moderately responsive are worth looking into.

20

AUTOGENIC TRAINING: METHOD, RESEARCH, AND APPLICATION IN MEDICINE

WOLFGANG LUTHE

INTRODUCTION

Autogenic training is a psychophysiologic form of psychotherapy which the patient carries out himself by using passive concentration upon certain combinations of psychophysiologically adapted stimuli. In contrast to the other methods of psychotherapy, autogenic training approaches and involves mental and bodily functions simultaneously. Passive concentration on Autogenic Standard Formulas can be so tailored that a normalizing influence upon various bodily and mental functions will result. From a neurophysiologic point of view there is clinical and experimental evidence indicating that certain changes of corticodiencephalic interrelations are the functional core around which autogenic training revolves (Schultz & Luthe, 1959).

About 40 years ago the founder of the method, J. H. Schultz, psychiatrist and neurologist in Berlin, wrote the first publications about clinical and experimental observations of what he called "autogenic organ exercises" (1926). In 1932, the first edition of *Autogenic Training* became available (Schultz, 1932). Since then, 10 German editions have appeared (Schultz, 1961), translations into Spanish (1954), Norwegian (1956), and French (1958),

---

Reprinted by permission from *Amer. J. Psychotherapy*, Vol. 17, 1963, pp. 174–195.

as well as a recent American edition (1959). During the last three decades autogenic training has become widely known in Europe and today it is regarded as a valuable standard therapy in various fields of medicine. It has also been integrated into the training programs of many universities (Schultz, 1959; Durand de Bousingen, 1961, 1962; Luthe, 1961; Muller-Hegemann, & Kohler, 1961; Muller-Hegemann & Kohler-Hoppe, 1962).

The steady increase of interest in autogenic training is reflected by the progressively increasing number of publications of a clinical and experimental nature (Luthe, in Stokvis, Ed., 1960). During each of the last three years more than 100 articles on the subject were published in medical journals and books. It is interesting, however, that only about 1 per cent of a total of about 1,000 publications were written by English speaking authors (Schultz, 1959).

BACKGROUND OF THE METHOD

The beginning of autogenic training stems from research on sleep and hypnosis carried out in the Berlin Institute of the renowned brain physiologist Oskar Vogt during the years 1890 to 1900. Vogt observed that intelligent patients who had undergone a series of hypnotic sessions under his guidance were able to put themselves for a self-determined period of time into a state which appeared to be very similar to a hypnotic state. His patients reported that these "autohypnotic" exercises had a remarkable recuperative effect (Schultz, 1959, 1932, 1961).

At the time he observed that these short-term mental exercises, when practiced a few times during the day, reduced stressor effects like fatigue and tension. Other disturbing manifestations, as, for example, headaches, could be avoided and the impression was gained that one's over-all efficiency could be enhanced. On the basis of these observations Vogt considered such self-directed mental exercises to be of definite clinical value. He called them "prophylactic rest-autohypnoses" (*Prophylaktische Ruhe-Autohypnosen*).

Stimulated by Vogt's work (Schultz, 1951) J. H. Schultz became interested in exploring the potentialities of autosuggestions. His aim was to find a psychotherapeutic approach which would reduce or eliminate the unfavorable implications of contemporary hypnotherapy, such as the passivity of the patient and his dependency on the therapist.

During subsequent years, while investigating the question of hallucinations in normal persons, Schultz collected data which appeared to link up with Vogt's prophylactic mental exercises (1932). Many of Schultz's hypnotized subjects reported to have experienced, almost invariably, two types of sensations: a feeling of heaviness in the extremities often involving the whole body and frequently associated with a feeling of agreeable warmth.

Schultz concluded that the psychophysiologic phenomena related to the experience of heaviness and warmth were essential factors in bringing about the changes from the normal to a hypnotic state.

The next question was whether a person could induce a psychophysiologic state similar to a hypnotic state by merely thinking of heaviness and warmth in the limbs. The systematic pursuit of this question was the actual beginning of autogenic training. Under certain technical circumstances and by the use of passive concentration on verbal formulas implying heaviness and warmth in the extremities, Schultz's subjects were able to induce such a state, which appeared to be similar to a hypnotic state.

The self-directed nature of the approach had a number of clinical advantages over the conventional techniques of hypnosis, among them, the active role and the responsibility of the patient in applying the treatment and the elimination of dependence on the hypnotist.

METHOD

From Schultz's clinical work a number of useful verbal formulas gradually evolved which, according to their more bodily or mental orientation, formed two basic series of mental exercises: the *Standard Exercises* and the *Meditative Exercises*.

The six *standard exercises* are physiologically oriented. The verbal content of the standard formulas is focused on the neuromuscular system (heaviness) and the vasomotor system (warmth); on the heart, the respiratory mechanism, warmth in the abdominal area, and cooling of the forehead.

The *meditative exercises* are composed of a series of seven exercises which focus primarily on certain mental functions and are reserved for trainees who master the standard exercises.

Later, as more clinical and experimental data became available, a number of complementary exercises specifically designed for normalization of certain pathofunctional deviations evolved. These were called *special exercises*.

Psychophysiologically, autogenic training is based on three main principles: (a) reduction of exteroceptive and proprioceptive afferent stimulation; (b) mental repetition of psychophysiologically adapted verbal formulas; and (c) mental activity conceived as "passive concentration."

A reduction of afferent stimuli requires observation of the following points: the exercise should take place in a quiet room with moderate temperature and reduced illumination; restricting clothes should be loosened or removed; the body must be relaxed, and the eyes closed, before the mental exercises are begun. Three distinctive postures have been found adequate: (a) the horizontal posture; (b) the reclined arm-chair posture; and (c) the simple sitting posture. All three training postures require careful consideration of a number of points. When certain details are not observed, disagreeable side-effects or after-effects and ineffective performance of the exercises have been reported.

The first exercise of the *autogenic standard series* aims at muscular relaxation. The functional theme of the verbal formula is heaviness. Right-handed persons should start out with passive concentration on "My right arm is heavy." Left-handed persons should begin with focusing on the left arm.

During the very first exercises about 40 per cent of all trainees will experience a feeling of heaviness predominantly in the forearm. During subsequent periods of regular training, the whole arm becomes heavy and the feeling of heaviness will spread to other extremities. This spreading of a certain sensation (the heaviness, tingling, warmth) to other parts of the body is called the "generalization phenomenon." Along with the development of the generalization phenomenon, passive concentration on heaviness will be extended to the other arm or the homolateral leg. Usually the heaviness training continues until heaviness can be experienced more or less regularly in all extremities. This may be achieved within two to eight weeks. Clinical investigations of larger groups of trainees, however, indicate that about 10 per cent of the patients do not experience a sensation of heaviness. This fact is one of the reasons why patients should be told that the *Heaviness Formula* (and others) functions merely as a technical key to bring about many different functional changes in the brain and bodily system, and that a sensation of heaviness may or may not occur.

Furthermore, it has been found helpful to tell a patient that many changes of bodily functions occur (see section on experimental data) which one cannot feel. It is also important for the patient to know that according to experimental observations, the exercises are effective as long as they are performed correctly, even if one does not feel anything at all. Apart from this it is necessary that the therapist is familiar with the therapeutic problems resulting from different forms of *autogenic discharges* which may start while the patient is in an autogenic state (Geissmann & Luthe, 1961; Luthe & Geissmann, 1962).

Subsequently, passive concentration on warmth is added, starting, for example with "My right arm is warm." This formula aims at peripheral vasodilation. Depending on the generalization of the feeling of warmth in other limbs, the training progresses until all extremities become regularly heavy and warm. This training may take another period of from two to eight weeks.

After having learned to establish the feeling of heaviness and warmth, the trainee continues with passive concentration on cardiac activity by using the formula "Heartbeat calm and regular." Then follows the respiratory mechanism with "It breathes me," and warmth in the abdominal region:

"My solar plexus is warm." The final exercise of the physiologically oriented standard exercises concerns the cranial region which should be cooler than the rest of the body. Here, one applies the formula "My forehead is cool."

The time usually needed to establish these exercises effectively varies between four and ten months.

The trainee's attitude, while repeating a formula in his mind, is conceived as "passsive concentration." Passive concentration may best be explained in comparison with what is usually called "active concentration." Concentration in the usual sense has been defined as "the fixation of attention," or "high degrees of intensity of attention," or "the centering of attention on certain parts of experience." This type of mental activity involves the person's concern, his interest, attention, and goal-directed investment of mental energy and effort during the performance of a task and in respect to the functional result.

In contrast, passive concentration implies a casual attitude during the performance and with regard to the functional result. Any goal-directed effort, active interest, or apprehensiveness must be avoided. The trainee's casual and passive attitude toward the psychophysiologic effects of a given formula is regarded as one of the most important factors of the autogenic approach. Furthermore, the effectiveness of passive concentration on a given formula depends on two other factors namely (a) the mental contact with the part of the body indicated by the formula (for example, the right arm); and (b) keeping up a steady flow of a filmlike (verbal, acoustic or visual) representation of the autogenic formula in one's mind. Passive concentration on a formula should not last more than 30 to 60 seconds in the beginning. After several weeks the exercises may be extended to three or five minutes; after a few months up to 30 minutes and longer.

The state of passive concentration is terminated by applying a three-step procedure, namely (a) flexing the arms energetically, then (b) breathing deeply, and (c) opening the eyes. Usually three exercises are performed in sequence, with about a one minute interval between each of them.

After the standard exercises have been mastered satisfactorily, one may train to modify the pain threshold in certain parts of the body or train the time sense for waking up at a specific time. The therapy may be continued by applying autogenic principles for approaching specific functional disorders or even certain organic diseases. A number of special formulas and procedures have been worked out for meeting the therapeutic requirements of various functional and organic disorders like bronchial asthma, writer's cramp, hemorrhoids, brain injuries, esophagospasm, pruritus and others.

The meditative exercises should not normally be started until after six to 12 months of standard training, and the trainee should be able to prolong the autogenic state up to 40 minutes without experiencing any disagreeable side-effects or after-effects.

The meditative series begins with passive concentration on phenomena of visual imagination, as, for example, the spontaneous experience of certain colors. Later, the trainee may focus on seeing all colors at will. When that is achieved, the meditative series continues with visual imagination of objects This training phase may take several weeks before results are obtained. It is followed by imagining abstract concepts like "happiness" or "justice" in different sensual modalities (musical, chromatic, plastic). Still later, one may meditate on one's own feelings and, in contrast, try to evoke the image of another person. Finally, at the deepest level of meditation, an interogatory attitude may be assumed in expectation of answers from the unconscious.

Autogenic training at the meditative level may be applied as what has been called "Nirvana Therapy" (Schultz, 1932, 1961) in clinically hope-less cases (for example, advanced cancer) or in monotonous and desperate situations as may occur under exceptional circumstances. The meditative exercises have also been found to be of particular value in depth-dimensional psychotherapy. In general, it has been observed that the effects of the more physiologically oriented standard exercises are reinforced by the medi-tative training. However, the meditative exercises are not introduced to the average patient. The average clinical therapy centers on the standard for-mulas in combination with special exercises and intentional formulas speci-fically designed to meet the therapeutic requirements of relevant functional or organic disorders.

EXPERIMENTAL DATA

From experimental data and clinical results we know that passive con-centration on the standard formulas induces multidimensional changes of a mental and organismic nature. In principle, two categories of effects may be distinguished: immediate effects, occurring during passive concentration on the different formulas, and effects resulting from practice of autogenic exercises over periods of weeks and months. Information about the im-mediate effects during the exercises is still incomplete. However, the experi-mental data available indicate clearly that each of the standard formulas induces physiologic changes of certain autonomic functions which are co-ordinated by diencephalic mechanisms.

During passive concentration on heaviness, Siebenthal (1952; Schultz, 1952), Wittstock (1956), and Eiff and Jorgens (1961) recorded a significant decrease of *muscle potentials*. Along the same lines Schultz found a significant reduction of the patellar response during passive concentration of heaviness in both legs (1932, 1961). Determinations of motor chronaxie (musc. extensor digit. comm. dexter) by Schultz, Lewy, and Gaszmann (1932, 1961) indicated that the intensity of the stimulus has to be increased during the heaviness exercise because the excitatory threshold rises from its resting value.

Changes in peripheral circulation during passive concentration on heaviness and warmth have been verified by a number of independent authors (Schultz, 1959, 1926, 1932; Binswanger, 1929; Stovkis, Renes & Landmann, 1961). The most extensive study was carried out at the University of Wurzburg by Polzien (1955, 1959, 1961). Polzien found that the rise of the skin temperature was more pronounced in distal parts of the extremities than in the more proximal areas. Simultaneously variable changes in the rectal temperature were recorded. Depending upon the subject, and the duration of passive concentration, the increase of skin temperature in the fingers varied between 0.2 and 3.5°C. These findings are in accordance with other results reported by Siebenthal (1952) and Muller-Hegemann (1956). Using special devices, both authors independently recorded an increase of weight in both arms during passive concentration on heaviness. The measured increase of weight has been ascribed partly to the relaxation of regional muscles and partly to an increase of blood flow in the arm (Schultz, 1959).

More recently, Marchand (1956, 1961) demonstrated that the standard exercises and passive concentration on warmth in the liver area induce certain changes in the trainee's blood sugar level. During the first three standard exercises there is a slight increase of blood sugar. The fourth standard exercise (It breathes me) coincides with a slight drop in blood sugar, which is followed by another slight increase during passive concentration on "My solar plexus is warm" (fifth standard exercise). Subsequently passive concentration on warmth in the liver area is associated with a significant rise. The control values obtained after termination of the exercises indicate a sharp drop of blood sugar values, which, however, are slightly higher than the control values determined before starting the standard exercises. *White cells counts* during this investigation (24 subjects) indicated that the first four standard exercises are associated with a slight but progressive decrease in white cell values. This trend was reversed during the fifth standard exercise and during passive concentration on warmth in the liver area which was associated with a marked increase. The highest white cell values were obtained three minutes after termination of the exercises. Subsequent determinations corresponded to values obtained before starting the exercises (Marchand, 1956, 1961).

Various electroencephalographic studies (Schultz, 1959; Geissmann & Luthe, 1961; Luthe & Geissmann, 1962; Granek & Thren, 1948; Heimann & Spoerri, 1953; Israel & Rohmer, 1958; Israel, Geissmann, & Noel, 1960;

Jus & Jus, 1960; Geissmann & Noel, 1961, Jus & Jus, 1961; Luthe, 1962) during passive concentration on the standard formulas revealed that the different standard exercises and the autogenic state were associated with certain changes which are similar to, but not identical with, patterns occurring during sleep or hypnosis (Luthe, Jus, & Geissmann, 1962; Luthe, 1962).

According to the observations reported by P. Geissmann and C. Noel (1961) no true psychogalvanic reactions appeared during the standard exercises in completely relaxed trainees; certain reactions which were observed in a number of subjects seemed to be due to difficulties related to the experimental arrangement.

A systematic study of the respiratory changes occurring during the standard exercises revealed a significant decrease of the respiratory frequency which was associated with a gradual and significant increase of the thoracic and abdominal respiratory amplitude and a corresponding significant augmentation of the inspiration/expiration ratio (Luthe, 1958; 1962; Luthe, in Stovkis, Ed., 1960; Schultz & Luthe, 1959). Furthermore, it was observed that passive concentration on heaviness in the limbs is associated with a significant decrease of the respiratory volume and that the different standard formulas may produce a number of qualitative changes of the trainee's respiratory pattern. In asthmatic patients an almost instantaneous normalization of a disturbed pattern of respiratory innervation has been observed frequently (Schultz, 1959).

The close physiologic and topographic relations between respiratory and circulatory mechanisms stimulated further studies of the effect of the standard exercises on cardiac activity (Schultz, 1959), blood pressure (Schultz, 1959; Luthe, 1960), the electrocardiogram (Schultz, 1959; Luthe, 1960; Polzien, 1961) and certain variables more closely related to metabolic processes (Hiller, Muller-Hegemann & Wendt, 1961; 1962; Marchand, 1956; 1961; Polzen, 1955; 1959; 1961; Schultz & Luthe, 1959). In a group of normotensive subjects it was found (Schultz, 1959; Luthe, in Stokvis, Ed., 1960) that passive concentration on heaviness produces a slight but significant decrease of the heart rate (5 to 10%) and a tendency toward lowering of the blood pressure. In hypertensive patients regular practice of the two first standard exercises usually produces a significant drop of the systolic (10–25%) and the diastolic (5–10%) blood pressure (Schultz, 1959; Luthe, in Stokvis, Ed., 1960).

Electrocardiographic changes during autogenic standard therapy were reported by various authors (Schultz, 1959; Luthe, in Stokvis, Ed., 1960; Jus & Jus, 1960; Geissmann & Noel, 1960; Polzien, 1961; Schultz & Luthe, 1961). The relevant observations may be summarized as follows: during passive concentration on heaviness (and warmth) the heart rate usually decreases. In relatively few cases an increase of the heart rate has been observed.

This paradoxic reaction is regarded as resulting from *autogenic dischàrges* (Luthe, 1961; 1962; Luthe, Jus, & Geissmann, 1962).

During the Third World Congress of Psychiatry in Montreal (1961), Polzien reported that 28 out of a group of 35 patients with confirmed ST-depressions showed an elevation of the ST-curve and an increase of the T-wave by ·05mV or more during the first standard exercise. In five cases the ECG remained unchanged and two patients reacted with further deterioration. In a control group of 20 patients with normal curves, an elevation of the ST-curve or the T-wave by ·05mV or more was observed in 10 trainees. It is of particular interest that a correlation between the heart rate and the ST and T-wave changes did not exist. This finding is in contrast to the physiologic correlation which normally exists between the heart rate and the elevation of the "ST segment-T wave phase." In other words, it is not possible to explain the elevation of the "ST segment-T wave phase" as observed during autogenic training, by the simultaneously occurring changes (decrease, increase) of the trainee's heart rate (Polzien, 1940).

More recent investigations carried out at the University of Wurzburg have verified the normalizing effect of the standard exercises on certain hyperthyroid conditions (Polzien, 1961). Other experimental studies dealing with the effect of autogenic training on bodily work and subsequent recuperation have been carried out at the University of Leipzig (Hiller, Muller-Hegemann, & Wendt, 1961; 1962).

Briefly, the experimental data indicate that passive concentration on physiologically oriented formulas influences autonomic functions which are coordinated by diencephalic mechanisms. Both clinical results and experimental data indicate that autogenic training operates in a highly differentiated field of bodily self-regulation and that with the help of autogenic principles it is possible to use one's brain to influence certain bodily and mental functions effectively. It is evident that this type of psychophysiologic manipulation requires proper training, adequate medical background knowledge, critical application, and systematic control of the effects of the treatment (Luthe, 1961). Furthermore, I hope it is quite clear that autogenic training is neither a simple relaxation technique nor a self-persuasive approach as applied by Coue.*

*Dr. Luthe stated in a letter accompanying this article, that "Passive concentration on autogenic standard formulas (or any others) is a very potent 'interference' with 'normal' functions. Even the trial of the First Standard Formula should be thoroughly discouraged unless a careful medical and psychodynamic evaluation has been carried out before, and unless the trainee is under supervision by a physician who himself has adequate practical experience with the method. Undesirable and regrettable consequences may result in case autogenic techniques are applied without careful adaptation to each individual case."—*Editor*.

The long-range effects resulting from regular practice of the standard exercises are manifold and depend largely on the psychophysiologic constellation of the individual and the nature of the patient's condition. Briefly, one could say that a gradual process of multidimensional optimalization develops. This process is reflected in psychodynamic changes which can be verified by physiologic measurements and projective tests.

In line with reports on gradual changes in the patient's behavior (Schultz, 1959; Luthe, in Stovkis, Ed., 1960; Luthe, in Speer, Ed., 1958; 1962), I have observed a characteristic pattern of projective changes, for example, in the Drawing-Completion test: Progressive differentiation of the projective responsiveness, increase of output, more shading, elaboration of details, stronger pressure of lines, increase of dynamic features, better integration and composition of the drawings, less rigidity, fewer inhibitions, faster performance, and better adaptation to the different stimuli. Corresponding changes have been observed in the Draw-A-Person test (Luthe, in Speer, Ed., 1958).

Our observation that a patient's progressive improvement jumps ahead after four to eight months of regular practice of the standard exercises is reflected objectively by the patient's performance in the control tests which I administer at regular intervals during autogenic standard therapy. With respect to these clinical observations it is of particular interest that the EEG also reveals significant differences between trainees who have practiced autogenic exercises for two to four months and others who have practiced the standard exercises for much longer periods (Geissmann, Jus, & Luthe, 1961; Luthe, Jus, & Geissmann, 1962). Subjects practicing two to four months show an EEG pattern similar to the EEG pattern seen in states of "predrowsiness," for example, bursts of anterior theta waves with a tendency to spatial generalization in anterior posterior direction in association with a preserved alpha activity. In contrast, subjects with longer training periods (6 to 36 months) pass very rapidly from the pattern of a normal state to a pattern characterized by (a) a flattening of the baseline pattern with theta oscillations; (b) the alpha main frequency shows an increase of rapidity (1 unit/sec.); and (c) brief paroxysmal bursts of theta waves in temporal-posterior derivations (Geissmann, Jus, & Luthe, 1961; Luthe, Jus, & Geissmann, 1962; Franek & Thren, 1948; Heimann & Spoerri, 1953; Israel & Rohmer, in Aboulker, Chertok, & Sapir, Eds., 1958; Israel, Geissmann, & Noel, 1960; Jus & Jus, 1960; Geissmann & Noel, 1961; Jus & Jus, 1961; Luthe, 1962; Schultz & Luthe, 1961; Luthe, 1962).

These electroencephalographic differences between short-period and long-period trainees seem to indicate that the regular practice of the standard exercises over longer periods of time brings about certain functional changes in the trainee's brain.

Clinical and experimental observations gathered over the past 35 years have indicated that the physiologic changes occurring during autogenic exercises are of a highly complex and differentiated nature, involving autonomic functions which are coordinated by diencephalic mechanisms. The physiologic changes which occur during the standard exercises coupled with the fact that the regular practice of autogenic training over longer periods of time has a normalizing influence on a great variety of bodily and mental disorders led to the conclusion that autogenic training exerts a therapeutic action on certain mechanisms which are of pathofunctional relevance for many different types of bodily and mental disorders. In summarizing my experimental and clinical findings I hypothesized (Schultz, 1959; Luthe, in Stovkis, Ed., 1960; Luthe, Jus, & Geissmann, 1962) that the therapeutic key factor lies in a self-induced (autogenic) modification of cortico-diencephalic interrelations, which enables natural forces to regain their otherwise restricted capacity for self-regulatory normalization. The hypothesis implies that the function of the entire neurohumoral axis (cortex, thalamus, reticular system, hypothalamus, hypophysis, adrenals) is directly involved and that the therapeutic mechanism is not unilateraly restricted to either bodily or mental functions.

INTRODUCTION TO SECTION 6 MINOR PSYCHEDELIC DRUGS

===

The term "psychedelic" was coined by Humphrey Osmond and literally means *mind-manifesting*. Osmond felt that terms like "hallucinogenic" or "psychotomimetic," commonly used to describe the effects of LSD-25, were misleading: they described drug effects obtained under special psychological circumstances which were *not* the most characteristic effects of the drug.

The term was intended to be emotionally neutral but has since acquired a positive emotional bias: psychedelic is "good." However, since no better term has achieved general usage, psychedelic will be used broadly here to indicate ASCs that may show us something about the (potential) ways in which the mind can function. In this and the following section the psychedelic ASC is usually drug-induced, but it is clear from many sources, including those in the earlier sections of this book, that psychedelic experiences can be produced by a variety of techniques other than drugs.

The division of psychedelic drugs into "minor" and "major" drugs in this and the following section is somewhat artificial, because there can be great overlaps in the effects produced by the drugs put in these two classes. Nevertheless the distinction is useful. The sort of drugs I have here classified as minor psychedelics are characterized by one or more of the following characteristics: (1) the effects are felt to be under a fair amount of volitional control by most individuals who use the drugs; (2) the duration of action is typically short; (3) aftereffects are generally mild or nonexistent; (4) the effect of the drug experience is rarely strong enough to cause the user to actively prosely-tize and try to convince others that they *must* have this experience them-selves; and (5) these characteristics make them highly suitable for research—because the *S*s welfare is not appreciably threatened in most cases, elaborate and costly schemes for protecting *S*s are not as necessary as with the major psychedelics.

To make the distinction between minor and major psychedelic drugs clearer, I would classify the following as minor psychedelics: marijuana, Scotch Broom, carbon-dioxide, and nitrous oxide. Typical examples of major psychedelic drugs would be LSD-25, mescaline, psilocybin, harmaline (yage, telepathine), dimethyltryptamine (DMT), and diethyltryptamine (DET).

One can easily sum up the current level of scientific knowledge about the minor psychedelics with the statement that they are vastly underresearched, considering their potential applications. The account of the effects of nitrous oxide in Chapter 24, for example, is from an article written in 1882 by William James; there simply has not been, to my knowledge, anything better written on the effects of this drug in the last 86 years.

I believe the lack of research on the minor psychedelics represents a great loss, for the potential usefulness of knowledge about these is very high. They often make *S*s report being directly aware of certain mental functions that are normally nonconscious, for example. This is a most intriguing source of hypotheses about mental functioning, and it constitutes important phenome-nological data in its own right. Further, some of the minor psychedelics seem to loosen up the associative process, making unlikely associations more probable. This could be a very practical way of enhancing creativity or by-passing some defense mechanisms in the course of psychotherapy. Also, many Americans are now using the minor psychedelics, particularly mari-juana, for recreation; the ASCs induced by these drugs are considered highly pleasurable. Many view this situation with alarm, others with joy, but in terms of society making a response to regulate this trend, we are so ignorant of the basic effects of most of the minor psychedelics that we can only legis-late or "educate" in ignorance and emotional hysteria at present.

This section cannot deal with all drugs that might be classed as minor psychedelics, but I have selected papers which cover a fairly broad range, from the mild effects of Scotch Broom to the fairly strong effects of mari-juana and nitrous oxide.

Chapter 21 is a compilation of facts about marijuana by the Bruin Humanist Forum, "Marijuana (Cannabis) Fact Sheet." I believe this rather lengthy discussion of what is scientifically known about marijuana, scanty though this knowledge is, is very necessary, for most scientists have heard nothing but the very biased and factually incorrect propaganda put out by the Narcotics Bureaus. In spite of the incredibly harsh legal penalties for the mere possession of marijuana in all states,* reliable investigators now estimate that somewhere between one and five million Americans have smoked marijuana, and the trend seems to be rapidly accelerating. (Fort, 1965; Goldstein, 1966). The marijuana laws in this country were passed with no attempt to incorporate the available scientific evidence on the effects of marijuana. There is a clear trend toward legalizing the smoking of marijuana, particularly because it is now used by many middle-class, politically influential people.

Chapter 22, "The Effects of Marijuana on Consciousness," describes the subjective effects of marijuana intoxication (what it's like to be "stoned," in current terminology) and relates many of the effects to current theoretical work in language, thought, and communication. The author of this chapter, a professor in the social sciences at a major American university, prefers to remain anonymous: he has been systematically observing the effects of marijuana on himself and acquaintances for several years and, understandably, feels his opportunities to continue his observations would be sharply curtailed in prison. This chapter is particularly valuable because of the author's ability to describe the marijuana experience in psychological terms. Most first-hand accounts of the effects of marijuana are of the order of, "Gee Whiz!" I saw beautiful visions and it was great!"

---

*At the time of this writing, legal research with marijuana is practically impossible, with the exception discussed here. I recently wrote the Federal Narcotics Bureau asking how a reputable scientist could obtain whatever permits were necessary to do marijuana research. The reply stated that it was possible under Federal law (not mentioning, however, the ridiculous record-keeping procedures required, so that an investigator could be heavily fined or jailed for minor bookeeping errors), but that the Federal law also required compliance with state law, and no one had been able to comply with California law in this area in 30 years. The major exception is federally sponsored research. In fiscal 1967, the Federal government spent over 700,000 dollars for marijuana research. Some of this was research on the active ingredient of tetrahydrocannabinol, marijuana that is classified as an investigational new drug, whose possession has not (yet) been prohibited in state and Federal legislation. Much of the rest of this research, judging by abstracts of it, is oriented around the theme, "What sort of mental illness would turn a person to smoking marijuana?" I suspect this research money is largely wasted, for it is investigating the *secondary* variables that affect marijuana use. The primary factor which would account for almost all the variance in the data is simple pleasure. It is very enjoyable to smoke marijuana, as any marijuana smoker will tell you. The sort of investigations being carried out would be similar to studying why people eat steaks by studying family background, manifest anxiety, birth order, personality correlates, and so forth without ever realizing that steak tastes good. Thus the outlook for effective research on marijuana is quite poor at present, but I hope that increasing social pressures for legalizing marijuana will make research possible.

This is fine as a start, but they seldom go any further; Chapter 22 does. I particularly hope this article will stimulate other investigators to work with marijuana when it is legally possible to do so,* for the kind of hypotheses advanced here make it clear how important an understanding of marijuana effects are to theories of thought, cognition, emotion, time estimation, problem solving, etc.

The next article, by James Fadiman, "Psychedelic Properties of Genista Canariensis," deals with a common American plant, Scotch Broom (*Genista canariensis*). Smoking the plant produces very mild psychedelic effects. Their mildness, and the fact that the plant is not illegal, makes its use in properly conducted laboratory settings quite feasible.

In Chapter 24, "Subjective Effects of Nitrous Oxide," I have presented an account by William James on the nitrous oxide experience, including James' speculations regarding its nature and meaning. I do not know of any better account of the phenomenology of the nitrous oxide experience. Research with nitrous oxide is legally possible in a medical setting, and the brevity of the effects (fading out within minutes after inhalation of the nitrous oxide is stopped) makes it easy to handle in the laboratory.

The final article in this section, by Frederick Glaser, "Inhalation Psychosis and Related States," deals with the negative effects of a variety of substances which are mind-altering, such as glue sniffing. It provides some overview of a wide variety of drugs used to produce ASCs, some of their effects, and the dangers inherent in the use of many of them. Many of the preceding papers have been emotionally positive in tone; this final chapter provides some balance: don't run off and smoke, inhale, or ingest just *anything* in order to experience an ASC.

For further reading about marijuana, I cannot recommend too highly David Solomon's book, *The Marijuana Papers* (1966). An interesting anthology, *The Book of Grass*, has recently appeared (Andrews & Vinkenoog, 1967), as well as a collection of articles edited by Simmons (1967). Many of the references in Chapter 32, "Guide to the Literature on Psychedelic Drugs," contain much material on minor psychedelic drugs, in addition to the references in other articles of this section.

---

*A mandatory sentence of 5–20 years for a first conviction of possessing even minute amounts of marijuana is *typical* in most states.

Note added in press: A definitive study of the effects of marijuana on psychological and motor processes has just appeared: A. Weil, N. Zinberg, & J. Nelsen, Clinical and psychological effect of marijuana in man, *Science*, 1968, **162**, 1234–1242. The authors confirm many of the statements in Chapters 21 and 22.

21

MARIJUANA (CANNABIS) FACT SHEET

ISSUES STUDY COMMITTEE OF
THE BRUIN HUMANIST FORUM

Marijuana is not a narcotic. Although California laws calls it a narcotic, it is pharmacologically distinct from the family of opium derivatives and synthetic narcotics. (Wolstenholme, 1965; Watt, 1965; Garattini, 1965; 1 Crim 5351 Calif. District Court of Appeal, 1st Appel. Dist.)

Marijuana is not addicting. The use does not develop any physical dependence (see p. 329). (Mayor's Committee on Marihuana, New York City, 1944; Allentuck & Bowman, 1942; Freedman, 1946; Fort, 1965a, 1965b; Panama Canal Zone Governor's Committee, 1933; Phalen, 1943; Indian Hemp-Drug Commission, 1894; Watt, 1965; 1 Crim 5351 Calif. District Court of Appeal, 1st Appel. Dist.; United Nations, 1964a, 1946b).

In a small percentage of individuals, a "psychological dependence" can develop, but a predisposition must be present. In his paper, "Dependence of the Hashish Type," Watt (1965, p. 65) concludes: The habit is gregarious and is easily abandoned. Personality defect and incipient or existing psychotic disorder are the essential factors underlying the formation of the habit.

Marijuana is not detrimental to the user's health. Even when used over long periods of time, it does not appear to cause physical or psychological impairment. (Mayor's Committee on Marihuana, New York City, 1944; Freedman, 1946; Fort, 1965a, 1965b; Panama Canal Zone Governor's

Committee, 1933; Phalen, 1943; Indian Hemp-Drug Commission, 1894; Becker, 1963)

Marijuana does not tend to release "aggressive behavior." On the contrary, its use inhibits aggressive behavior; it acts as a "tranquilizer." (Mayor's Committee on Marihuana, New York City, 1944; Fort, 1965a, 1965b; Panama Canal Zone Governor's Committee, 1933; Phalen, 1943; Garattini, 1965)

Marijuana does not "lead to" or "promote" the use of addicting drugs. "Ninety-eight percent of heroin users started by smoking tobacco and drinking alcohol *first*!" (Mayor's Committee on Marihuana, New York City, 1944; Fort, 1965a, 1965b; Panama Canal Zone Governor's Committee, 1933; Phalen, 1943; Garattini, 1965)

Marijuana comes from the Indian hemp plant, which was formerly grown widely in the United States for the making of rope, and which still grows wild in many areas. Up until a few years ago it was a main ingredient in commercial bird-seed. Leaves and flowering tops provide the cannabis (commonly known in the Western Hemisphere as marijuana, grass, or pot); the resin and pollen, in which the active ingredients are highly concentrated, are the source of "hashish." (Wolstenholme, 1965).

The effects of smoking marijuana have been described as follows: "euphoria, reduction of fatigue, and relief of tension ... [It will] also increase appetite, distort the time sense, increase self-confidence, and, like alcohol, can relax some inhibitions." (Fort, 1965) A heightened awareness of color and of esthetic beauty, and the production of rich and novel mental associations are also commonly reported effects. Some users report that the marijuana experience is "psychedelic": can result in heightened awareness, or in a consciousness-expanding change in perspective, ideas about the self, life, etc. Marijuana is not, however, like LSD— a very powerful psychedelic. Whereas LSD drastically alters thoughts and perspective, often "jarring" the user into heightened awareness, marijuana "suggests" or points the way to a moderately deepened awareness. The user is free to follow these potentials or not, as they present themselves. (Mayor's Committee on Marijuana, New York City, 1944; Fort, 1965a, 1965b; Panama Canal Zone Governor's Committee, 1933; Goldstein, 1966; Becker, 1963; De Ropp, 1957; Indian Hemp-Drug Commission, 1894)

Pharmacological studies of marijuana and tetrahydrocannabinol (the major active ingredient) are as yet inconclusive, both because of insufficient research and because of the subtlety and complexity of its effect on the human mind. Grattini (1965) tested maze-learning in rats and found that marijuana caused no change or very slight impairment; Carlini and Kramer (1965) found that maze-learning was significantly improved by an injection of a marijuana extract. Multiple active ingredients are present in the marijuana plant, and these could vary in concentration (e.g., one of the components is sedative, and another is euphoric/psychedelic). (Wolstenholme, 1965; Watt, 1965; Carlini & Kramer, 1965)

As with other psychedelics, the effects of marijuana depend in part on how one interprets, uses, and learns to develop them. As pointed out by many researchers in the area of philosophical/psychological effects, the environment ("setting") is of great importance. Many people have no effects whatever the first time they smoke a marijuana cigarette, but do the second or third time—and thereafter. Everyone has to learn the effects before he can use them to his own benefit. (Becker, 1963; Fort, 1965a, 1965b; Indian Hemp-Drug Commission, 1894).

Some years ago it was estimated that marijuana users numbered "several hundred thousand people in the United States, including many from the middle-class." (Fort, 1965a, 1965b) During the 1960's, however, there has been a rapid increase in the use of marijuana, particularly among "respectable" people: those in the professions, non-bohemian high school and college students, artists, writers, intellectuals, etc. One report on campus use (Goldstein, 1966) estimates that approximately 15% of college students have used or are using marijuana, with the percentage at some large, metropolitan campuses as high as 30–60%. This same report also held that marijuana use is now becoming "respectable," and indulged in by members of student government, campus groups, and fraternities and sororities. (Fort, 1965a, 1965b; Irwin, 1966; Goldstein, 1966)

Marijuana smoking does not constitute a social hazard. Four separate official studies have been conducted on this question, as a part of a larger study: New York City Mayor's Committee in 1944; a committee of the health department of the U.S. Army; another U.S. Army committee, concerned with discipline effects; and a very thorough study by a committee established by the British Government to study the effects in India where it is—and was—in as widespread use as is alcohol here. All of these studies came to the conclusion: marijuana is not damaging to the user or to society, and therefore should not be outlawed. Political and economic pressures prevented authorities in New York from carrying out the recommendations of the Mayor's Committee—the greatest part of the political pressure from Harry J. Aslinger, former U.S. Commissioner of Narcotics. (Mayor's Committee on Marijuana, New York City, 1944; Panama Canal Zone Governor's Committee, 1933; Phalen, 1943; Indian Hemp-Drug Commission, 1894)

On the grounds that marijuana is safer and more beneficial than tobacco or alcohol (both of which are physically toxic; both of which are addicting), and that there is no basis for legalizing these two dangerous drugs while outlawing one which is not dangerous, attorneys are challenging the present laws. In the wording of one such legal brief: "The appellant contends that the classification of marijuana as a narcotic in Section 1101 (d) of Health and Safety Code and the marijuana prohibition law is based upon an arbitrary and unreasonable classification having no reasonable relation to the public health, safety, welfare, and morals. . . . The classification of marijuana as a narcotic is unconstitutional and void in violation of the Eighth Amendment provision against cruel and unusual punishment, and the Due Process clause of the Fourteenth Amendment of the Constitution of the United States." (1 Crim 5351 Calif. District Court of Appeal, First Appel. Dist., pp. 61–62 and Appendix 1, p. 6)

Among the authorities favoring legalization of marijuana, there have been medical doctors, lawyers, psychologists, sociologists, and even some religious leaders. Bishop Pike, for example, supports re-legalization. *Lancet* (1963), the British journal of medicine, in an editorial in 1963, found no good reason for marijuana being prohibited, but good reason why it should be legal. (Irwin, 1966)

Many authorities, however, remain opposed to the re-legalization of marijuana. Predominantly, these are "law-enforcement" authorities, or politicians (e.g., Attorney General Lynch of California). Although these authorities rarely give verifiable reasons for their insistence that marijuana be illegal, the ones which have been offered prove to be either unsubstantiated "opinions" or out-and-out mistaken data. In this same area, there was a time when law-breakers—taking their cue from the law-enforcement officials—claimed marijuana use as an excuse for their crimes. The fiction of a marijuana-crime relationship has been thoroughly detailed (if there is any correlation at all, it is in a negative direction—crimes of violence are drastically lower than would be statistically expected among marijuana users). (Fort, 1965a, 1965b; Phalen, 1943; Anslinger, 1932; 1 Crim 5351 Calif. District Court of Appeal, First Appel. Dist.; Irwin, 1966; Blum & Wahl, 1965; Boyko, Rotberg, & Disco, 1967; Laurie, 1967) See also below, pages 329 and 331.

Harry J. Anslinger, not one to be daunted by mere facts, included the following comments—both of which are in diametric contradiction to statements by him before committees of the U.S. Congress: "The section noting that many criminals coming before the courts who allege that they were under the influence of marijuana when a crime was committed, and that this defense is usually without foundation and is used with the idea of obtaining lenient treatment by the courts, recommends that a defense of being under the influence of marijuana during the commission of a crime should not mitigate the penalty for a criminal act." (Anslinger, 1932) "The Narcotic Section recognizes the great danger of marijuana due to its definite impairment of the mentality and the fact that its continuous use leads direct [sic] to the insane asylum." Even without the aid of Anslinger, arguments opposed to free marijuana use are contradictory, confused, and grossly innocent of verifiable facts. (Fort, 1965a, 1965b; Phalen, 1943; Anslinger, 1932; 1 Crim 5351 Calif. District Court of Appeal, First Appel. Dist.; Irwin, 1966; Blum & Wahl, 1965; Washington Bulletin, 1963)

In a study of police attitudes and reasoning on "drugs," Blum and Wahl (1965) found much disagreement as to reasons why marijuana should be suppressed. Some officers simply felt that, although marijuana was less dangerous than alcohol, society (and the law) disapproved of marijuana. Reasons given for suppressing marijuana ran from claims that it caused criminal behavior [which is, ex post facto, correct—so long as marijuana use is "criminal"], to the claim that it is more dangerous than alcohol because it *isn't* as disruptive of behavior and is therefore harder to detect.

Many "expert" groups such as WHO Expert Committee on Addiction Producing Drugs have tended to perpetuate misinformation on marijuana because of poor data [Anslinger was the U.S. spokesman for many, many years at the U.N.], and a conservative reluctance toward "softening" or changing previous policies. In the last few years, however, the World Health Organization has progressively modified its view on marijuana. In 1964 the Expert Committee proposed revised definitions of types of drug dependence, which were subsequently adopted. The new definition of "dependence of the Cannabis type" was as follows: "(1) a desire (or need) for repeated administrations of the drug on account of its subjective effects, including the feeling of enhanced capabilities; (2) little or no tendency to increase the dose, since there is little or no development of tolerance; (3) a psychic dependence on the effects of the drug related to subjective and individual appreciation of those effects; (4) absence of physical dependence so that there is no definite and characteristic abstinence syndrome when the drug is discontinued." (United Nations, 1964b) The Committee actually is saying that there is no reason to keep marijuana on its list: Its definition of dependence of the marijuana type would easily satisfy for a definition of "liking" (i.e., the natural tendency to repeat a pleasant and rewarding, non-harmful experience). Actual dependence on marijuana is extremely rare, and depends entirely on a pre-existing psychological problem—and even this is not "addicting." [See above, p. 1] (Watt, 1965; United Nations, 1964b)

As has been noted by many researchers, scientific as well as governmental groups which have seriously investigated the effects of marijuana on the individual and on society have consistently refused to condemn it or support legislation aimed at suppressing it; law-enforcement-oriented groups, on the other hand, including the Narcotics Experts, are very slow indeed to admit any of this evidence into the debate. In spite of this, the Proceedings of the White House Conference on Narcotic and Drug Abuse, 27–28 September 1962, states: "It is the opinion of the Panel that the hazards of marijuana per se have been exaggerated, and the long criminal sentences imposed on an occasional user or possessor of the drug are in poor social perspective. Although marijuana has long held the reputation of inciting individuals to commit sexual offenses and other antisocial acts, the evidence is inadequate to substantiate this. Tolerance and physical dependence do not develop, and withdrawal does not produce an abstinence syndrome." (United Nations, 1965; United States, 1963)

The following, from an editorial in the *Washington Bulletin*, is given here both for the illuminating facts uncovered, and as an example of the more modern approach to the "problem" of marijuana. "Seventy years of institutional documentation indicate that this vision [of marijuana's "dangers"] was a big American fib. Latest such document is the New York County Medical Society Narcotics Sub-committee Report of May 5, 1966: 'There is no evidence that marijuana use is associated with crimes of violence in the United States ... marijuana is not a narcotic, nor is it addicting ... New York State should take the lead in attempting to mitigate the stringent federal laws in regard to marijuana possession.' Well, everybody knew that 10 years ago. [U.S.] House Marijuana Hearings, Ways and Means Committee, 1937, page 24, Rep. John Dingall: 'I'm just wondering whether the marijuana addict [sic] graduates into a heroin, an opium, or a cocaine user?' *Anslinger:* 'No sir. I have not heard of a case of that kind. I think it's an entirely different class. The marijuana addict [sic] does not go in that direction.' Nowadays the Narcotics Bureau [headed during this entire period by Anslinger] propagandizes the idea that marijuana leads directly to heroin, which is obviously silly, as millions of college boys can inform their parents. But the Narcotics Bureau has raised such an unscientific scream on this point that nothing will suffice to prove the obvious except a giant survey of comparative statistics showing that millions of pot smokers are not junkies. When such documents are at hand, timid but sympathetic medical authorities in key places have declared themselves ready to move toward legislation, licensing or reduction of punishment for marijuana possession to the status of a parking violation." (*Washington Bulletin*, 1966)

The UCLA Law Review, in March of 1967, published an article on California's anti-marijuana laws, from which the following is quoted. "... the purpose of this article is to outline the defects in one area of both federal and state criminal law: the control of marijuana—specifically, treatment of possession of the drug, without more, as criminal. The pattern in California, perhaps more than in any other state, has been one of legislative intransgence and increasingly harsh penalties for possession and use of marijuana. The authors take the position that at least a portion of the existing legislation in California against marijuana—Health and Safety Code section 11530, imposing stringent penalties for possession of the drug irrespective of abuse—is an unwelcome disruption of the delicate balance between reason and emotion in the state's drug control laws. . . . Although the United States Supreme Court normally has given the state legislatures an extended opportunity to clean their own houses, judicial finger-tapping where marijuana is concerned has all the signs of continuing indefinitely. But, unbridled legislative and police suppression of all uses of marijuana, together with savage sentences for even the most innocent uses, might prove to be the source of earlier constitutional review. . . . The characteristics attributed to marijuana by law enforcement agencies, legislative reports and the communications media are markedly different from, or not supported by, available scientific information. . . . In this country, the only comprehensive publication at a local or state level scientifically describing the effects of marijuana is the so-called 'LaGuardia Report' . . . reactions which are natively alien to the individual cannot be induced by the ingestion or smoking of the drug. . . . An even more subtle claim, asserted primarily by law enforcement agencies, is that marijuana is a 'stepping stone' to addictive and disabling drugs. Not only is the alleged causal relationship unsupported in fact, but even the California Attorney General's Office has suggested that the evidence leads to a contrary conclusion. . . . In addition to the 'stepping stone' thesis, the widely promoted claim that marijuana use causes crime is also lacking in factual support. The LaGuardia researchers, in direct conflict with the routine alarms from law enforcement officials, found that the alleged causal connection does not exist. . . . Indeed, in several subsequent studies it has been shown that there is a *negative* correlation between crime and the use of marijuana. . . . Unlike 'plain drunk' reckless driving and drunk driving statutes, protecting only against the abuses of alcohol, section 11530 [marijuana] declares a crime even when there is no abuse or victim. Ironically, although it is unlawful to drive under the influence of any narcotic or any drug within the separate statutory classification of 'restricted dangerous drugs' (barbiturates, amphetamine and LSD), these driving offenses are alternatively punishable as misdemeanors, and the penalties are less severe than for possession, without use, of marijuana. And it is only a misdemeanor to 'use' or 'be under the influence of' marijuana." (Boyko et al., 1967)

"These 'new' drugs, however, were neither physically addicting nor illegal; the dangers were considered moderate. In fact, this *moderate* element of danger might have added an intriguing dimension to the undertaking. The increased use of marihuana on college campuses appears to have a similar background with one added factor: the legal penalties are quite severe, even though, like LSD, the drug is not physically addicting. Students, therefore, rationalize that it is a 'bad' law which they are not obligated to obey (an attitude somewhat similar to the reaction to Prohibition)." (Kleber, 1967)

R. D. Laing, M.D., writing in *Sigma* (Vol. 6), states: "I would be far happier if my own teenage children would, *without breaking the law*, smoke marijuana when they wished, rather than start on the road of so many of their elders to nicotine and ethyl alcohol addiction."

"Summary of conclusions regarding effects. The Commission have now examined all the evidence before them regarding the effects attributed to hemp drugs. It will be well to summarize briefly the conclusions to which they come. It has been clearly established that the occasional use of hemp [marijuana] in moderate doses may be beneficial; but this use may be regarded as medicinal in character. It is rather to the popular and common use of the drugs that the Commission will now confine their attention. It is convenient to consider the effects separately as affecting the physical, mental or moral nature. In regard to the physical effects, the Commission have come to the conclusion that the moderate use of hemp drugs is practically attended by no evil results at all. There may be exceptional cases in which, owing to idiosyncracies of constitution, the drugs in even moderate use may be injurious. There is probably nothing the use of which may not possibly be injurious in cases of exceptional intolerance. ... In respect to the alleged mental effects of the drugs, the Commission have come to the conclusion that the moderate use of hemp drugs produces no injurious effects on the mind. ... In regard to the moral effects of the drugs, the Commission are of the opinion that their moderate use produces no moral injury whatever. There is no adequate ground for believing that it injuriously affects the character of the consumer ... for all practical purposes it may be laid down that there is little or no connection between the use of hemp drugs and crime. Viewing the subject generally, it may be added that the moderate use of these drugs is the rule, and that excessive use is comparatively exceptional." (Indian Hemp-Drug Commission, 1894)

"The psychic habituation to marihuana is not so strong as to tobacco or alcohol. ... There is no evidence to suggest that the continued use of marihuana is a stepping stone to the use of opiates. Prolonged use of the drug does not lead to mental, physical, or moral degeneration, nor have we observed any permanent deleterious effects from its continued use." (Allentuck & Bowman, 1942)

"There are no apparent reasons for cannabis' status as a Dangerous Drug. It is not addictive, its use does not in Western society cause crime or unacceptable sexuality, and it does not lead to addiction to the hard drugs. The major problem with this drug is that it is illegal. This has three undesirable effects: first, an underground, cannabis-using sub-culture is created and maintained that puts the potential heroin addict one step nearer access to the hard drugs; second, it lessens respect for D.D.A. [Dangerous Drug Act] drugs in the thousands of young people who have tried marihuana or hashish and know from personal experience how harmless the drug is; third, it causes considerable waste of man-power, either through creative and educated people being sent to prison for possession of the drug—a Glasgow doctor was sentenced to six months recently—or through the use of policemen who would be better otherwise employed, to track down the drug and its users." (Laurie, 1967)

"The smoking of the leaves, flowers and seeds of *Cannabis sativa* [marijuana] is no more harmful than the smoking of tobacco or mullein or sumac leaves. . . . The legislation in relation to marihuana was ill-advised . . . it branded as a menace and a crime a matter of trivial importance. . . . It is hoped that no witch-hunt will be instituted in the military service over a problem that does not exist." (Phalen, 1943)

"The controls over marihuana under federal [law] and state laws are dissimilar. Under the federal law, marihuana is not considered a narcotic drug. On the other hand, many states have covered marihuana by including it within the definition of 'narcotic drug' since adoption of the Uniform Narcotic Drug Act in 1932. Marihuana is equated in many state laws with the narcotic drugs because the abuse characteristics [under current laws, *all* use is 'abuse'] of the two types of drugs, the methods of illicit trafficking [*all* exchange of pot is 'illicit'], and the types of traffickers have a great deal in common. . . . Because marihuana does not result in physical dependence, the physician need not apply himself to physical complications of withdrawal. . . . No physical dependence or tolerance has been demonstrated. Neither has it been demonstrated that cannabis causes any lasting mental or physical changes." (A.M.A. Committee on Alcoholism and Drug Dependence, 1967)

"Two of the most common and widely used psychic modifiers are cannabis and alcohol. . . . First, marijuana is most often used in a social setting, in a group of users who mutually enjoy the effects of the drug. Second, the intent is to heighten enjoyment of outer experiences, e.g., conversation, listening to or performing music, dancing, joking. Unlike the Brahman priest, whose vocabulary during his intoxication is limited to repeating one of the names of his God, the marijuana devotee laughs, giggles, eats without restraint, tells jokes, participates in sexual relationships, and takes pleasure in the company of both men and women, especially if they are also using marijuana. Third, the effects are interpreted by a marijuana-user as analogous to those of alcohol. He prefers marijuana because the effects are more rapid and 'neater'; there is no hangover, and no debilitating physical consequences of chronic use. Thus, the use of cannabis in our society is to attain an experience which, far from renouncing the active life in favor of contemplative, ascetic ideal, affirms the pleasures of sex, music, food, laughter, and human companionship." (Chein et al., 1964)

"A characteristic marihuana psychosis does not exist. Marihuana will not produce a psychosis *de nova* . . ." "But even excessive marijuana use is less likely to lead to aggressive or anti-social conduct than immoderate consumption of alcohol." (Allentuck & Bowman, 1942; Boyko et al., 1967; Murphy, 1963)

The following excerpt is from a letter to *The Princetonian*, Princeton University, by the Director of Counseling Services at Princeton. "If and when the severe laws governing marijuana are to receive the review they probably deserve, this will come about only after a significant level of public interest and influential desire has been achieved. . . . In the meantime the underground tide of illegal use will continue to swell and 'lamentable affairs' [arrests] will occur. In judging the reasonableness of current laws, and indeed current clandestine marijuana use, the individual should probe the facts, rather than merely harbor widespread and misinformed assumptions which often yield a sort of sociological hysteria whenever the subject is raised. In the confidential settings of the Counseling Services and the Health Services, whenever the subject of marijuana is discussed we are pleased to find that factual information usually helps clear away much of the undue anxiety stemming from the popular myths surrounding this subject in our society at-large. Recognizing the reality of existing laws, and recognizing the fact that every individual must come to terms with such realities in his own way, we hope we may find ways to be helpful to students currently faced with such quandaries." (MacNaughton, 1967)

22

THE EFFECTS OF MARIJUANA ON CONSCIOUSNESS

ANONYMOUS

A marijuana high usually lasts two or three hours, during which a wide range of effects may occur, varying both in intensity and quality. The usual, most noticeable effect is intensification of sensation and increased clarity of perception. Visually, colors are brighter, scenes have more depth, patterns are more evident, and figure-ground relations both more distinct and more easily reversible. Other sense modalities do not have the variety of visual stimuli, but all seem to be intensified. Sounds become more distinct, with the user aware of sounds he otherwise might not have noticed. Music, recorded and live, is heard with increased fidelity and dimension, as though there were less distance between the source and the listener. Taste and smell are also enhanced under marijuana. The spice rack is a treasure of sensation, and food develops a rich variety of tastes.

Skin receptors are also effected. Heat, cold, and pressure receptors become more sensitive. Pain produces paradoxical effects. If attention is not on the area of pain, there is a reduced sensitivity to the hurt. But awareness of pain from a lesion, such as a burn or cut, will often persist for a longer period than usual, even allowing for the changed perception of time under marijuana.

Awareness of proprioceptive responses is enhanced. The person using marijuana may become aware of usually automatic, non-conscious, muscle tensions, small movements, feedback and control processes, and feelings of physical comfort and discomfort. These can be perceived with great clarity and distinctness.

Such effects vary with the individual and the situation. Sometimes one modality will predominate; sometimes a sequence of effects will occur; sometimes nothing will seem to happen. The direction or modality of effect can be often manipulated by the individual if he deliberately exposes himself to the stimulus, such as music, or paintings. However, such setting may not affect the perception if the person is not otherwise ready to respond in that way. Effects more often call attention to themselves; the user observes what he is experiencing in the situation and realizes it is not how he usually experiences the stimuli. On the other hand, some sense modalities may function in a straight pedestrian manner, neither being enhanced nor diminished.

The person himself is the most important determinant of how the enhancement will appear. Some persons orient primarily to visual stimuli and visual thinking, others to sound, others to tactile impressions. Visual orientation seems to predominate among persons in our culture; audile and tactile thinking is less common. It seems likely that sensory enhancement of a marijuana high would be most noticed in the predominant sense modality of the user; it certainly should have a differential response in relation to less used ways of perceiving.

Another factor which affects the response is that persons unfamiliar with the marijuana state frequently must "learn" that they are perceiving experience in a different way. That is, someone makes them aware of changed perception by showing them objects, playing music, and calling their attention to the difference in sights and sounds. Then they become consciously aware of the perceptual changes. This initiation procedure has led sociologist H. S. Becker (Becker, 1963; partially reproduced in Solomon, 1966) to suggest that most of the effects of marijuana are learned, not spontaneous. He says (accurately, I am sure) that the user must learn to notice the effects, categorize them, and connect them to the total experience of using the drug. What is learned in most cases is not a new way of perceiving, but the awareness of a change in perception. Few persons observe what they are doing in the sense of observing their seeing, and it is not surprising that many should have to learn how to become aware of themselves experiencing by checking current perception against memory and expectations.

The user's internal psychological needs will also influence his response. A fear of being overwhelmed by too much input will often reduce any changes to only those which the user can cope with or to changes only in certain modes. A fear of losing control over the perception of experience may suppress most of the effects and even shut down responses to below normal. On the other hand, emotional involvement with some part of the environment may enhance its perception. Internal physical needs also affect the response, e.g., hunger may be intensified so the person finds himself ravenous on getting high.

For a person using marijuana for the first few times sensory changes occur sequentially, rather than all at once. First he may notice increased brightness and clarity of colors, then sounds, then visual structures, such as paintings or designs. (Two dimensional photographs and motion pictures may be seen in three dimensions in the marijuana high, a perception which can be transferred to the normal state under certain conditions.) Then proprioceptive sensations may present themselves. Any order of the effects may occur during one high state or several. Often effects will develop to particular levels and then stabilize without further elaboration. I know some individuals who listen to music during a high, and this is their major use and apparently their only enhancement.

There are two states of awareness which relate to these sensory effects. The basic one can be called pure awareness. In this state the person is completely and vividly aware of his experience, but there are no processes of thinking, manipulating, or interpreting going on. The sensations fill the person's attention, which is passive but absorbed in what is occuring, which is usually experienced as intense and immediate. Pure awareness is experiencing without associations to what is there.

The other state of awareness is one which can be termed conscious awareness, in which the sensory experience is connected to meanings, plans, functions, decisions, and possible actions. This is our normal way of perceiving and how we usually go about our daily lives. We do not sense the world directly, but with the incorporation of our memories, meanings, and uses. In the state of pure awareness objects are experienced as sensory qualities, without the intrusion of interpretation. There are examples of this in normal life. The sensation of sexual orgasm may be (and hopefully is) experienced with pure awareness. Natural beauty, such as flowers, mountains, oceans, and sunsets, is sometimes experienced from a point of awareness without adding conscious thinking.

These two processes of awareness have been described by Charles Solley and Gardner Murphy (1960, Chapter 14) as nonreflective consciousness and reflective consciousness. Alan Watts compares the awareness state to a floodlight of attention, which shows a broad area and lights up anything that is there. Consciousness awareness he compares to a spotlight, which is focused and can be directed, though on a narrower area. This is a good analogy in pointing out that no deliberate directing is done in the awareness state, although it is sometimes the case that the area perceived in awareness may be a small one seen in great detail.

The awareness state can be called "choiceless" because choice is a part of consciousness functions. Decisions made outside of consciousness are not called "by choice" since choice implies conscious action. In a state of direct awareness there are no choices made and no decisions or actions occur. The stream of sensation flows and the person is aware of what is happening; if he acts he does so without consciously deciding to move. (That is, action is handled by some process other than the consciousness monitoring the awareness experience.) When complicated action becomes necessary conscious attention is activated and the sensation is used as stimuli, criteria, or information for the choices, plans, or action.

The awareness is not always experienced purely under marijuana, but often is mixed with some, though reduced, conscious attention. Consciousness, conscious awareness, or conscious attention involves a connecting function which observes experience in relation to past experience, memory images, memory recording, expectancies, plans, goals, etc. This type of consciousness may intrude on the awareness state at a low level. However, when awareness fills the attention there is a "becoming lost" in the experience, in which there is often not even a memory of what occurred. This seems to be a state in which consciousness functions are not present, and all experience is at the level of awareness. Consciousness, attention, and memory recording are apparently not active. (It is possible that attention was present and either was not remembered or the memory is not accessible to consciousness.) Such a state of pure awareness is at one end of a continuum of varying degrees of conscious activity, with the other end at a state in which the contents of awareness are used for decisions, plans, inferences, etc., and are not experienced for their primary sensory qualities; they are information rather then experiences.

This analysis suggests a reason for sensory enhancement under marijuana, a movement of attention from consciousness processes to awareness processes. We usually think of attention as synonomous with consciousness, but it is an uneasy synonomy. Consciousness seems to be more than attention, but we cannot describe a consciousness without attention. Perhaps it is possible for attention energy to move into sensory processes and operate less in the decisional, deliberative processes of consciousness. If this happens it would provide much more energy for attending to sense data, and we could expect the sensory experience to be more vivid and more detailed.

Intensity of sensory experience seems related to the total proportion or amount of attention which is involved in the process. If attention is used in conscious or unconscious processes in making decisions, remembering, evaluating, etc., then this much is removed from the awareness of the sense experience. Thus it may be that one of the causes of sensory enhancement under marijuana is that attention energy moves from consciousness processes into awareness processes, which amplifies the experience.

TIME DISTORTION

Besides sensory enhancement, the other most immediate effect of marijuana is a change in the perception of time: events take longer to occur. Bach's first Brandenburg Concerto lasts hours. An hour seems to have passed, but the clock records 25 minutes. The person's internal fantasies are long and involved, but only a few minutes have passed in government time. In this state the fantasies and music do not move at a faster pace—they move at their own usual rate, though often more fluently and more clearly. The impression is that external time must have slowed down, while the internal experience continues at the same rate. There is not the impression of speed or rapidity, but that the time available to the user is magnified.

There are similar effects in normal experience. Time spent at a boring talk seems to pass more slowly, and one thinks in dismay, "What, only five minutes have passed since I looked at my watch?"

A method used by Linn Cooper (1958) to induce time distortion under hypnosis is useful to note here. A metronome set at one beat per second is used. The hypnotized subject is told that the metronome is slowing down to one beat every two seconds, every five seconds, once a minute. Verbally or conceptually we can now say that the subject's internal rate has remained the same, but external time relative to the subject has slowed down. Has the subject's own pace actually speeded up? I do not know, and I can think of no reliable criteria for determining this. Brain wave research shows that the basic alpha rhythmn can be speeded up by a flickering light (called photic driving), but not very much, and not even to twice its normal rhythmn. Cooper's subjects report that they do mentally imagine the amount of thoughts appropriate to the expanded time available, including counting imagined objects. This may be a convenient hallucination or it may be an accurate description of what they do. (Even calculation of real problems would not be a valid test because calculating geniuses can answer complex mathematical problems almost instantaneously, and this ability may be available under hypnosis, though it has never been reported to my knowledge under marijuana or hypnosis.) In this procedure under hypnosis and also in marijuana the subjective experience of time is disconnected from the marking of social or government time.

The effect under marijuana is analogous to effects in visual and sound modalities. Visual scenes often have more depth, sounds are heard with more dimension; so too with time—there is an expansion of the fabric of time so there is a feeling of depth instead of the usual two dimensional flow.

The explanation of this sometimes given by marijuana users is that more is happening: they are thinking faster or more thoughts are occuring in the same time period. This could cause external time to be relatively slower. Although it need not be the case that internal processes change at a faster rate it is possible that a person is aware of more perceptions in a given amount of time as a result of the enhancement of sensory data. With visual enhancement more details of the movements of the self and others are attended to. This means that more information is perceived in the same amount of time. This is also true of proprioceptive and tactile responses. Time is somewhat conditioned to a normal rate of information input in particular contexts. One has a "standard rate of intake" and if the amount of information is increased for a unit of time, then one of the responses may be that time is going slower. To be conscious of any change in experience there must be a comparison with previous similar situations. Thus if the time experience while high is compared with a similar normal experience or with a time pace constructed from normal experience, it may be perceived as slower.

A more important cause for time distortion under marijuana can be found by noting how persons normally judge the passage of time, then investigating the changes in these criteria caused by marijuana. This is rather difficult because no one knows how we judge time. Nevertheless, there are some relevant observations which can be made.*

Notice the situations in which time seems to alter for many persons in everyday experience and out-of-the-ordinary experience. These are situations in which the experience itself is the focus of attention; they are not means to extrinsic goals. Persons totally involved in making love seem to have no awareness of how much time may pass. Persons in a state of anger do not become aware of time lapse until the emotion subsides or ego controls are invoked. Psychotherapy hours in which emotional material is covered seem to be out of time awareness. Mystics become unaware of the passage of time during meditation, as do persons having peak experiences (Maslow, 1964). In dreams, day dreams, fantasies, ecstasy, and strong emotional states, the sense of time is absent or changed. And in the state of pure awareness, as I have used the term, there is no perception of the rate of time. These are all personal experiences in which conscious attention

*See "Time and the Unconscious" by Marie Bonaparte (1940) for speculation on this problem from the framework of psychoanalysis.

is not dominant, and immediate experience, rather than goals, expectancies, plans, and decisions, is predominant. Time perception is a socially reinforced response. The experiences and states I have described are not states which are socially conscious; they are not internally subordinated to social time or schedules. Anger cannot be paced with conscious control, nor can ecstasy. Feelings, fantasies, dreams, and awareness do not incorporate the sense of time which is built up by and maintained in the consciousness. Thus when one is experiencing such content there is no marking of the passage of time, and to the extent this material is the content of awareness, the less social time is noted. Immediate experience is always timeless; time is perceived in relation to the uses of experience in controlling or predicting the future or interpreting the past, the present being perceived in relation to past or future. This is one of the major functions of consciousness. In a normal conscious state when the internal or external input is to be changed or manipulated the time required is automatically projected, based on past experience. This imposes the knowledge of time on the consciousness. One of the effects of marijuana is to reduce the strength of expectancies and goals which are socially reinforced. Thus non-time experiences are increased in relative strength and time oriented associations are decreased, which creates the sense that time is expanded.

Some indication that this is what occurs may be seen in reports of marijuana users that time passes instantaneously. One girl reported that when high she suddenly discovered 45 minutes had passed without her realization of this. And there are reports of listening to music when the individual realizes the music had stopped, without his remembering hearing the selection as it was playing. What happens in these cases is that most of the person's attention is in non-time processes, so that time passage is not noted until the social consciousness returns. Then it seems that no time has passed, since there was no process noting its passage. Just as in sleep, amnesic hypnosis, or anaesthesia, there is no consciousness of the duration of the state, and the conscious time flow seems unbroken from the moment of falling asleep to the moment of waking.

When observing sensory stimuli, listening to music, fantasying, etc., there is the feeling of expanded time because the outside experiences are overwhelmed by the mental, internal experience which is not marking time and there is no way to gauge their pace. The quantity of the time change varies. If the user is almost totally involved with the awareness processes, with little conscious attention, then there will be little sense of duration, and long periods of clock time will go by quickly.

Events themselves are timeless, in that they are always in the present— they do not echo their past nor presage their future states; we alone do that to them, for ourselves. And we ourselves do not experience the past or the future; we experience memories or expectancies, which may be realistic or fantasies. So our experience of the passage of time is based on our comparison of present experience with our remembrance of the past, usually the immediate past, or our anticipation of the future and how we get there.

Marijuana decreases the strength of the automatic memory, expectancy, and anticipation processes; thus the perception of an experience is not surrounded by the usual multitude of past encounters, future possibilities, and potential uses. In contexts requiring action on the basis of expectations and plans, such as driving an automobile, they are available and often with more focused attention. Given a situation not requiring activity or decisions, the penumbra of response patterns, functions, and potentials surrounding experience decreases, and the immediate experience *per se* is perceived, rather than its position in a pattern of change. This decreases comparison of the present with the past, and again reduces the feeling of duration or passing of time. ("Passing of time" is a curious phrase, because time passing cannot be empirically observed. One may conclude the passage of time by observing changes in experience, but it is not really an inference either. What seems to be described is the mental reviewing of the preceding changes which led up to the present point. Re-running the succession in memory from some point up to the present gives the sensation of passing time. We are aware of events which are different from the ones we now experience but that are connected by physical changes in which we have participated (directly or through observation). This awareness may be "awareness of the passage of time."

In summary, under marijuana, the sense of time is distorted. First, because mental contents and awareness processes which are not connected to time needs or markers are strengthened. These include daydreams, fantasies, event memories, peak experiences, emotions, and the pure awareness state. Second, because goals, anticipations, and expectancies are decreased in prominence, reducing attention given to possible changes in the environment, which decreases awareness of future states. Third, memory of immediate past experience is decreased in strength, which reduces knowledge of change and moves attention to the present. If consciousness is completely passive, and non-time elements fill attention, then the experience seems timeless. If some consciousness processes and associations are maintained time will seem to have slowed, as attention moves among the various contents.

EXPECTANCIES

Both the intensification of sensory experience and the expansion of time are part of an increased attentiveness to immediate experience in contrast to memories of the past or plans for the future. Memories and plans *are* experienced but only as they arise out of the immediate content and needs of the person's internal and external experience; they do not automatically operate as in normal consciousness. Every action and potential action, in the normal state, is evaluated according to its consequences: what results will follow. Mental processes imagine as many consequences as they have experience to do so, both immediate and long range, testing these consequences against criteria or goals of valued states. The consequences which are most valued control the action. For example, if a person feels angry toward another he may want to insult him verbally. He mentally anticipates the possible consequences of this action, which may include the release and satisfaction of the anger, feelings of masculinity, enhanced self concept of strength, etc., on the positive side, and the anger or disapproval of the other person, loss of self control, fear of his own impulses, what his mother would think of the action, etc. on the negative side. Depending on the person's past experience, his needs and strengths of various values, the action will be taken, modified, or inhibited. Every action a person engages in is surrounded and extended mentally (consciously and unconsciously) by such expectancies, and every situation experienced by a person is responded to by anticipating its potential consequences and relating them to desirable and undesirable conditions. (Of course, the opposite of such action—its inhibition—is also subject to the same processes.) Some of this process is conscious, especially when the situation is new, unfamiliar, very important, or ambiguous, but most of the expectancy and anticipation process is done preconsciously. Normally persons are not aware of the activity which occurs to determine an action; expectancies have become incorporated into automatic responses.

The mind is efficient in making its activities automatic. First an action is consciously made in response to a need or situation. If it is successful (reinforced) it becomes habitual, and is taken automatically without the need of conscious attention, much as driving a car, sewing, tying your shoes, and smoking a cigarette are all composed of large blocks of now automatic actions which once had to be done with conscious attention at every point. Later only the major elements must be controlled with conscious attention, such as changing lanes when driving, searching for an ashtray, etc. How can an action be released without conscious attention? What must happen is that criteria for action and the particular action are connected by the conscious mind; then the process can be made automatically. When the criteria are fulfilled, then the action is made.* This suggests that there is

*This is the behavior structure described insightfully in *Plans and the Structure of Behavior*, by George Miller, Eugene Galanter, and Karl Pribram (1960).

some process or energy which releases action but which does not need *conscious* attention. Similarly, most of the expectancies around experiences are not conscious—only the more important ones or ones which are so complex as not to be automatically used.

Such expectancies and anticipations function to keep behavior consistent, goal directed, and reasonably integrated. They help avoid conflicts within the personality and with the environment, including other persons. They have obvious survival value and undoubtedly are reinforced by our society and our own needs. The function of reinforcement is clear: The reinforcement value of the projected consequences of an action come to affect our decision to take or not to take the action. These expectancies are responses to possible futures, and orient our actions to the future, not the present.

One of the major effects of marijuana is to decrease the strength of these expectancies and anticipations, on both conscious and preconscious levels. Thus in the high state the expectancy processes decrease their influence on behavior. Since these are always oriented to future states, they take attention away from perception of immediate experience and turn it to following imagined states. Thus when attention given to imagined states is reduced, the perception of the present experience will increase in strength or intensity, either because more energy is available for such awareness or because there are fewer processes to attend to, and present experience becomes relatively more predominent in the mental field. This enhancement of immediate experience is reflected in the effects of marijuana on sense data and time perception. Indeed, the decrease in expectancies, which are connected to goals, may be one of the reasons for the change in the awareness of time, since time is perceived in terms of changes, including changes in relation to a potential state of affairs. If the knowledge provided by expectancies is reduced, then the immediate experience will not be seen as a point in time with a future, but more as an event, per se.

The reduction in the strength of expectancies also contributes to the increase in intensity of sensory experience. Objects as well as situations and actions are surrounded by our potential responses to them, such as our past experiences with them, how we might use them, other forms they have taken, how they are made, their qualities in other sense modalities, etc. When we perceive an object, whether a fire in a fireplace, a photograph of a fire, a fire engine, or a fiery speaker, not only are we aware of the object, but also we have incorporated in our awareness these other elements which give structure and meaning to the sense data. Thus we know that the object is a bird cage or a rib cage, and we know its qualities, functions, and potentials. Usually these are keyed to our verbal response, our classification, but they are known non-verbally as well (e.g., we can have emotional responses or motor responses without verbal responses).

FUNCTIONAL ASSOCIATIONS

Particularly important to us is the function of objects.* One sees this in a child's definition: a hole is to dig. A bridge is to walk over to get to the other side. Someone said that home is "A place where when you go there, they have to take you in." There is an essential effect of these operational definitions: they force classifications rather than specificity. Any hole is to dig and how hole X differs from hole Y is not important so long as each can be dug. My home is not different from your home, since they will both take us in. Such definitions attempt to capture some particular criteria of whatever they define. The criteria of definition are the only characteristics which need to be observed in perceiving the object, and we are trained to perceive in this way. We learn as children to see the function of objects and to see the similarities of objects, rather than experience them in all possible ways. The advantage of this is obvious: we survive because we can use the environment, we can generalize, we can cooperate within a socially constructed reality. The disadvantages are obvious: we may not see reality except in terms of functions, which shuts out an enormous amount of reality (some of which would be functional in various contexts). And often persons see objects only in terms of their own functional needs, which narrows their perspective considerably. (Psychologists might see persons as experimental subjects, an insurance salesman might see one as a prospect, etc.)

This leads, incidentally, to failures of discrimination in perception, illustrated by the classical occidental observation that all Chinese look alike, and no doubt Chinese observe the same about occidentals. One of my friends took an astronomy course and discovered that stars were not all the same color, as he had previously perceived, but were red, blue, yellow, and white. This led him to realize that all trees looked alike to him. Of course he would not have said that they were identical, but I doubt if he could have told the differences between an elm and an oak, even standing in front of them, because a tree is with leaves and to be shaded by. And after all, which of us could easily describe essential differences between two holes dug by a child in the sand at the beach? Though the child probably could.

Under marijuana the functional associations of objects are decreased in strength. In addition to this specific association, other associations such as verbal labeling and memory constructs of such objects are decreased in strength. Normally all these elements are imposed on the conscious experience of the object, some incorporated into the perception (such as seeing

*An excellent discussion of this and other relations of language to perception is in *Semantics and Communication*, by John C. Condon (1966, chapter 3).

the object as a teapot) and some claiming attention on the periphery of consciousness (such as knowing it is hot and not touching it). When these associations are decreased there are fewer mental impositions on the sensory perception of the object. Aspects which would normally be shut out (such as a blemish on the teapot or the shape of the handle) are given equal attention, and hence are seen instead of being ignored. When attention is directed by goals, as it usually is in the normal state, it is simply not given to non-functional stimuli, i.e., elements that do not have anything to do with what the person wants at the moment.

The person under marijuana is not seeing this object as "flowers" with a mental image of flowers and his memories of flowers being confirmed by these flowers, which are to look at and smell and if one can look at and smell these one has confirmed that they are flowers and that settles that part of reality, and so on to another. Rather he has a great deal of time and it is not urgent what uses these have or what consequences could result and much more of his awareness is filled by these flowers. And there are textures, colors, shades, shapes, feels, crevices, shadows, smells; all things that are there; experienced rather than used.

An important principle is that you can *experience* something only if you do not think in terms of its function. You can know what it is only if you do not impose what it will be or could be or ought to be. This often becomes quite evident under marijuana.

This suggests a principle regarding processes of attention. When attention is reduced for some elements in perception, the amount given to other elements increases, as though attention is a mobile amount of energy, and when a quantity is not needed at one point it moves to another point. This is consistent with Freudian theory, which holds that as energy is released from conflict points it becomes available to the general system. With marijuana, when association processes reduce their demands on attention, it flows to whatever else is in the consciousness. (I am using a fluid metaphor, but other models will do equally well. Electrically one can speak in terms of activation. Cybernetically we could refer to homeostatic balancing of elements. Or we could talk of homunculi leaving the study and going to the patio.)

ASSOCIATIONS

This reduction of associations is an important basic effect of marijuana. It contributes to the expansion of time, to sensory enhancement, and to the increase in attention which is given to the focus of consciousness.

However, not all association patterns are decreased in strength in the high state. Well known are the flights of fantasy and dreaming stimulated by hashish and cannabis.* And in non-fantasy high states users have reported that they can perceive connections and associations of ideas that were not accessible to them in the non-high state (usually called "straight" by users). This seems inconsistent with what I have just said about the decrease in association strength. However, while associations, particularly those based on social learning, are reduced in strength, any association may gain in strength if it becomes the focus of the detailed attention possible under marijuana. Thus fantasies and creative thinking may have increased associations and may be more fully developed than in the normal state of consciousness.

The associations which are reduced in strength seem to be those which are learned through social reinforcement: meanings and behaviors which are taught by society. Functions of objects are socially taught. Patterns of communication are social. Language and verbal knowledge (Columbus discovered America in 1492) is social in origin. Inhibitions and controls on behavior are socially reinforced, and are often incorporated into the verbal system through "should" and "should not" statements. When social norms are the same as personal needs, desires, and meanings, there is consistency in the response to a situation or object. When conflict between social and personal directions occurs it must be resolved, and usually it is resolved in favor of social meanings, functions, and approved behavior (usually called rational). Thus the social perception of a situation may exclude many of the potential meanings, behaviors, and emotions. Under marijuana this excluding function of socially learned associations is reduced in strength. The excluding function has certain survival value. It keeps our consciousness from being clogged up with unnecessary and distracting contents. Thus a scholar looks at a book and notices the title but not the binding; for a book binder the opposite is the case. Associations which contribute to the goals of society are learned by persons through social reinforcement, and one effect of these associations is to inhibit other associations. Marijuana desreases this inhibition and lowers the reinforcement value of the association. In effect this makes all associations more equal, and the network of associations is less guided or channeled in socially reinforced directions. A person who is high may be aware that an object is a pencil, but he may successively also see it as a shape, a phallic metaphor, a geometrical solid, the printing on it, etc. He has more associations once they are away from the strict control of social perception.

---

*Accounts of such experiences can be found in *The Drug Experience* (Ebin, 1965).

INHIBITIONS

The same pattern can be seen in expectancies and anticipations. Socially oriented behavior makes great use of expectancies to control behavior in an effort to maximize approval and minimize or avoid disapproval, which are social reinforcers.* Such behavior thus involves a large amount of inhibition. By inhibition I mean any kind of control to prevent activity from reaching a certain level. The activity can be thoughts, action, fantasies, or emotions. Inhibitions in Freudian terms are controlled by anti-cathexes, in learning theory by aversive stimuli, and in terms used here, by expectations of aversive stimuli. Inhibitions need not be on anti-social acts, but are often to direct behavior into patterns normal in our society. Persons maintain appropriate social distances (which are arbitrary), you do not tug at the beard of someone you have just met (though the thought may cross your mind), and a man does not cry in public. These may seem minor but they are controlled with great power by social reinforcement, as can be seen by the strong rejection of the behavior if it occurs. Of course, inhibitions are also placed on behavior which would be dangerous to society, such as aggressive or destructive acts.

When behavior is inhibited, the psychological tendency is to inhibit any mental activity which might lead to such behavior. Feelings, impulses, images, fantasies, etc., may be inhibited and decreased in strength, or even prevented from entering consciousness. Such inhibited feelings and impulses may appear in consciousness in the high state, often without effort of the person. This may cause anxiety and the person may use ego defense measures to block their appearance or diminish their threat. On the other hand, he can also use methods of analysis and self-therapy in the high state to deal with conflict material, and may free himself from neurotic responses.

The effects of the reduction of social inhibitions can be seen in various ways. At marijuana social gatherings persons may not feel pressure to participate in conversational games, play behavior increases, physical activity may increase. The decrease of socially reinforced inhibitions also accounts for the actions of users which claim public attention: jumping over fireplugs and parking meters, uninhibited dancing (erotic and non-erotic), and playful behavior (which is subtley taboo in our society). Here the person is expressing impulses in behavior which would usually be inhibited by expectancy of negative social reinforcement (frowns, rejection, blame, punishment and other expressions of disapproval). However, this reduction in strength of social inhibitions does not usually result in anti-social

*Julian B. Rotter (1955) discusses this process in "The Role of the Psychological Situation in Determining the Direction of Human Behavior."

acts (unless jumping fireplugs is considered anti-social). This is curious because social inhibitions are usually considered the bulwark against committing crimes, aggressing against others, raping women, etc. But we do not have cases of contemporary users of marijuana burglarizing or attacking others, though such effects are evident in the use of alcohol, where users are much more likely to express violent and aggressive behavior.

Why then if inhibitions are reduced in strength do not users become violent and aggressive? One reason may be that aggression is usually specific to situations and expectancies about situations, and the use of marijuana today rarely is in a conflict situation. With reduced pressure from memories and expectancies one would also expect less non-relevant feeling. Beyond this, one of the psychological effects of marijuana is euphoria. Thus anger and aggressive impulses are less strong and do not draw much support from the rest of the personality. This effect may also be related to the decrease in the strength of social reinforcers, since chronic anger is often the result of conflicts between social requirements and personal desires.

ATTENTION

The process of attention is clearly affected by marijuana. The most obvious effect is to narrow the amount of diverse contents in the focus of attention. The person under marijuana usually perceives fewer objects of attention, which may mean physical objects, actions, social elements, emotions, etc. We have already noted this effect: a person who is high may become absorbed in an object, event, or process to the exclusion of everything else. A train of fantasy may occupy all of a person's attention. This is a psychological analogy of tunnel vision, with the contents of the tunnel expanded.

In the normal, straight state, conscious and non-conscious processes give continual attentiveness to many internal and external stimuli, with responses such as awareness, memories, expectancies, and the many associations we have already noted. Many of these are conscious, especially those on which decisions are necessary. Others, and probably the bulk of the responses, autonomously operate without being consciously attended to, and come to consciousness only when necessary. These are in a preconscious state, but nevertheless involve perception, associations, memories, and expectancies.* Such processes often regulate behavior when consciousness

---

*By preconscious processes, I mean a state of mental functioning which goes on outside of conscious attention. Lawrence Kubie describes this foggy territory in *Neurotic Distortion of the Creative Process* (1961).

does not intervene (as in driving a car automatically). But whenever novel stimuli appear or more than routine decisions must be made, the contents become part of the conscious state.

In the consciousness processes connections can be made among several types of information, and in different contexts of meaning—making connections with the many factors relevant to a decision or the resolution of conflict. Conscious attention moves easily from one interpretation to another interpretation of information, with the various memories and expectancies which go with each interpretation, thus obtaining more information for the decision. These interpretations and associations are drawn from the preconscious processes, which, alone, cannot make interconnections among themselves as fluidly as can consciousness. Connections of ideas are made in preconscious states, but these seem based on almost any relation, from contiguity to puns. Consciousness can select the significant or realistic connections and systematize their use.

We can regard the conscious system as the system which does just that: selects and interprets information in relation to a goal or purpose. It does this when it is activated by attention energy. It may be that attention is the activating energy of awareness. Attention usually is in the conscious system, which consists of processes which select information to make decisions. It can also be activated in preconscious contents, which contain information, emotional values, and random associations. Most of the time awareness is of the conscious processes.

Under marijuana attention-awareness energy may move into the preconscious system and be less in consciousness processes. Since there are fewer elements in attention the person is more strongly aware of any individual element of meaning, memory, emotion, etc., and less of its relation to other elements which would be relevant in the conscious system. Whatever is in the center of attention occupies all of awareness: this may be sensory data, such as visual stimuli, or imagery, such as fantasies. The effect can be termed a unity of attention, in that all attention is focused on one subject. In normal conscious states, several channels can be used at once, e.g., reading a book while listening to music. Attention may alternate, but even so keeps all channels of input on the edge of attention. This does not occur with marijuana, which so far as awareness goes, fills the attention with one thing at a time. If one is recalling an experience from the memory, then almost all attention is on the event, and almost none on the external environment, expectancies or plans. Processes in normal states which seem to parallel this would be extreme concentration on a book or television, exciting conversations, and the state of romantic love.

It is not the case that there is less attention, for the quantity seems at least the same. Analogically it is as though a portion of a photograph were blown up to the size of the original picture, thus maintaining the size of the print but increasing the magnification of a smaller relative section.

Some of the processes which contribute to this effect are obvious. The reduction in expectancies and associations reduces peripheral contents of consciousness. Many of these elements are maintained continuously at a low level, appropriate to the environment and needs of the person. Some items are continuously monitored, much as a hostess may habitually check how each of her guests is getting along. Such monitoring takes some attention away from any central content, just as the hostess may not concentrate fully on her own conversation if she is attending to the state of her party. However, without the need for these side glances, attention flows to the central subject. This means that the plans, anticipations, etc., are not automatically attended to, although if such an element enters the central position it receives the intense central attention and is attended to in great detail.

Peripheral attention and its contents are reduced in the high state; central attention receives the energy which would otherwise be used in peripheral attention. This could be because each type of attention is different, and thus differentially affected, or because the peripheral contents are reduced in strength because of the reduction in the strength of associations. The latter seems to be true; the former may be also.

MEMORY

One of the processes important in perception is the comparing of current input with similar past experience. When we see a friend, a memory image of his face is presented to our consciousness along with the sensation of his actual present appearance. This memory image (which can be called a schema) blends with the current sensation, so that the perception is a combination of the two. The relative strengths of each source of information probably vary from person to person. Some primarily perceive the memory image, with the sensory input serving as confirmation of the identification. For others, the memory image may be so weak that reorientation and identification is continually necessary. Though the construction and recall of this image is not clearly understood, it must be partially constructed from previous experience of the stimulus (including verbal knowledge) up to a point where the person knows all he needs to know for purposes of his response. After this, encounters with the stimulus do not add to the memory image appreciably; further discrimination is unnecessary and the image stabilizes. (Of course, the person may continue to make discriminations.

One of the valued behaviors in science is to make perceptual discriminations for which we have no functional need, assuming that such information is valuable per se or may be valuable later.)

Most persons rely principally on memory images in perception unless there are evident differences in the immediate situation, and their responses are keyed to the memory image. Consequently we do not respond only to immediate experience. We identify current experience according to past experience and then respond on the basis of past experience, modified by whatever differences we perceive to be significant in the current information. Our actions originate from past experience, they are connected to the structures built up in our memories, and these memories are elicited by the immediate stimulus. In unfamiliar settings, no memory image is available. Then we must deliberately and consciously act, randomly act, follow instructions or models, or act according to the most similar memory image. Any situation is a combination of elements, and may call for complex combinations of memories and response patterns, some new, some familiar.

Marijuana has two effects on this process. The first is to reduce the general automatic availability of memory images; the second is to increase the strength of memories when they are relevant to central needs. We have already discussed the general reduction in strength of memories in response to current experience, which is principally in the automatic recall of memory schema. The strength or visibility of the mental image is reduced, with a resulting increase in the brightness of the data themselves (there being nothing else to look at). This explains also why experiences seem new: they are observed without the feeling of familiarity caused by memory images. For most persons in straight consciousness it is likely that sensation is checked against a memory image (at a preconscious level) and what is seen from the current stimulus is what is necessary to fulfill the criteria for identification, based on the memory schema. The relevant elements, the criteria, are affected by the goals or functions which are important to the person. We do not perceive dust on a typewriter when we look for something to type on. When we look for a friend in a crowd we do not look at his face, we identify it. Similarly, in conversation and daily life we generally know what we are seeing, so perception is more identification than observation. However, when fewer memory images are available, as when high, one must respond to the sense data as unfamiliar material. This may cause anxiety, depending on the individual and the environment, or it may result in pleasure at the enhancement or challenge of current perception. It may also increase the potential responses, since there is less pressure for a learned habitual response, which would normally inhibit other responses.

(This may, incidentally, suggest an explanation for the *jamais vu* sensation, a which there is the feeling that a normally familiar situation is totally unfamiliar. Several experiences of *jamais vu* reported to me seem to have occurred when there are unfamiliar emotional elements present, as though the usual memory schema and their associated responses were not available.)

At the same time, some memory images may be strengthened if they are emotionally salient. A person having paranoid fears, for example, may find his imagery increased in strength. One person reports that once when high he observed a friend sitting to one side of him staring directly at him. He turned to face his friend and found him looking in another direction, his face turned partially away from him. Apparently a fear activated the image of a full staring face, which was superimposed on the profile of the other person. It may be that psychotic or schizophrenic perceptual projections are partially caused by increased internal imagery. Under marijuana, at least, emotional force may activate internal imagery which is used to search for, identify, or interpret incoming stimuli.

So also if the person deliberately attempts to recall past experiences there will often be increased recall, either of events in great detail or flashes of experiences. This is particularly true if there is salient emotional content. Recall which appears to be eidetic may occur under marijuana, and images which are like playbacks of the original perceptual experience may become accessible at will to conscious attention. If the conscious attention is allowed to unfocus, so that only monitoring is going on, almost instantaneous images can be obtained of visual and sometimes auditory or tactile stimuli. The image must be seen when it occurs; if there is an attempt to hold it in consciousness a mental composite image takes its place. It is possible that what occurs is an activation of the actual memory record, selected from the stream of consciousness which is recorded in the brain.* Only one flash comes at a time. This ability, incidentally, has been transferred to straight, non-high control after it has been observed under marijuana. The essential feature seems to be in allowing the conscious attention not to try to hold on to the image when it appears. One must learn to see rather than look.

Another type of memory which is strengthened is that for emotion laden events. Strong emotional responses, such as grief, fear, guilt, etc., often arise under marijuana. These are responses to remembered events, responses which might normally be suppressed. Usually the person's sense of identity is functioning, so he can either accept the emotion and be a

---

*This kind of recall can be obtained by electrical stimulation of the brain. See Wilder Penfield and Lamar Roberts' book *Speech and Brain Mechanisms* (1959), Chapter 3.

part of it, which is usually therapeutic, or reject it, which may produce dissonance and anxiety. "Bad trips" are sometimes caused by emotions or pressures which threaten the person's self concept or his sense of control. While suppression processes are usually not too effective as defenses, distraction is, because of the mobile flow of attention under marijuana. For this reason, movement such as dancing, running, exercise, showers, etc., will usually change the emotional tone.

One other effect on memory should be noted. Normally we have a short-term recall process which holds memories in access for about 20 minutes, and then a long-term storage, which is permanent. In the high state, short-term memory becomes shorter, and in very high states the sequence of thoughts is not remembered past one or two transitions. The sequence can sometimes be recalled with an effort, or reconstructed, but there is no automatic remembering as there is normally . On the other hand, after the high, events within it can be remembered, indicating that at least some of the experiences are being filed in long-term memory.

Partly due to the reduction in strength of memory there is less intellectual control over the stream of consciousness. Memory seems to be needed to maintain concepts or goals under which to manipulate thoughts. Another cause of the reduced control is the lowered inhibition processes, which are used in thinking to filter irrelevant material and keep it from cluttering the conscious attention. Logical ideas and connections may also be enforced by such inhibitions; these would be loosened by the decrease in association strength.

VARIABLES

In general for marijuana to have effects the user must cooperate with it and facilitate the effects. He must learn to allow himself to respond. There are some persons whose response to marijuana is almost unnoticeable: their consciousness seems not to change. These may be persons who have fears about and strong defenses against losing control, and elements of their feeling, thoughts, or action which threaten their control are strongly rejected. Such personality systems are endangered by marijuana effects and often maintain their structure against these effects. Sometimes they will respond, but what effects are occurring will be blocked from their conscious awareness. The most noticeable effect is often time distortion, indicated by long silences and broken often by a comment that nothing is happening.

The effect of the physical and interpersonal setting on the response to marijuana is strong and usually controls the tone of the experience. The basic fact is that the individual creates the reaction, not the drug. If the erson feels under pressure, then the drug will enhance his feeling of stress, nd the effect will depend on how the person can deal with the stimulus. If e feels energetic, the drug will enhance his willingness to be active. Some ersons become less self-conscious, others more self-conscious. Some move hysically, others sit quietly. Some talk, others are silent. Users of marijuana re as individual as they are. For this reason, one must expect different ffects to occur from different times and varying physical and interpersonal urroundings. For some the effect is quite different when smoked alone han with other persons, probably because social situations elicit different ersonality elements and present various pressures.

These variable factors should be noted in considering research and nvestigation of the effects of marijuana. The plant probably does every-hing anybody has claimed for it, but only in a situation which enables it to lo whatever is claimed for it. One highly respectable philosopher and uthor, who has explored a variety of chemicals, says that marijuana will ake a person as far as LSD. To which I would add, especially if you can o as far as LSD on it. This is not tautologous, for it cannot be said of offee or orange juice; even if you are ready, coffee will not take you there.

There are further effects of marijuana which relate to complex structures f association, learning, values, intra-personality communication, inter-ersonal perception, and consciousness. It is difficult to separate the aware-ess of these effects from the effects of the awareness. It seems best to top at this point, having discussed what seems verbalizable at present.

Given facilitating conditions, the effects I have described will develop. ensations are enhanced and clarified: sight, hearing, taste, touch. Time erception changes. Attention becomes more unified, and moves more into reconscious material and the state of pure awareness. The many broad rocesses of association, such as social meanings, memory images, ex-ectancies, and plans are reduced in number and relevance. Inhibitions nd suppressions relax, allowing emotions, thoughts, fantasies, and nemories to flow more freely. The development and strength of these ffects will depend on the individual, the times he has used marijuana, how e has used marijuana, and the environment.

23

PSYCHEDELIC PROPERTIES OF
GENISTA CANARIENSIS

JAMES FADIMAN

The recent work of ethnobotanists Richard Evans Schultes (1963, 1965) and Gordon Wasson (1962) in uncovering the use in America of new psychedelic plants encourages one to further investigation of the herb lore of the American Indian.

A shaman of the Yaqui tribe of Northern Mexico was told in a psychedelic-induced vision to smoke the blossoms of a plant which he erroneously identified as Scotch Broom (*Cytisus scoparius, Genista scoparia, Spartium scoparium*).

Following the shaman's method of preparation, samples of these flowers as well as blossoms of two similar plants, Spanish Broom (*Spartium junceum*) and Canary Island Broom (*Genista canariensis*), were collected near Palo Alto, California. All samples were aged for ten days in sealed sterile glass jars. The blossoms of Scotch Broom and Spanish Broom turned dark brown during this period, while Canary Broom blossoms retained much of their characteristic yellow color. The blossoms were dried at low heat and prepared for smoking in hand-rolled cigarettes.

Of the three plants investigated, *Genista canariensis* proved to be the most

Reprinted by permission from *Economic Botany*, Vol. 19, 1965, p, 383. I wish to thank Dr. Michael Harner whose initial discovery and reports led directly to this study.

pleasant and effective. Subsequently, it was learned that *Genista canariensis* was the plant used by the shaman informant.

Effects were dependent on the amount smoked. To maximize effects, subjects were told to inhale and to retain the smoke for about ten seconds to increase the amount of active principle absorbed. When less than a single cigarette was smoked, the subjects reported feeling more relaxed. They felt good about themselves and friendly toward the others in the room. These feelings lasted up to two hours. There was no subsequent letdown. Rather, they reported an imperceptible lessening of the effect until it could no longer be noticed.

When several cigarettes were smoked, the effects were longer lasting and more intense. In addition to the amiable relaxation mentioned at the lower dose, subjects reported increased intellectual clarity and flexibility. The first few hours were characterized by physical ease followed by a period of psychological arousal and alertness.

A heightened awareness of color and contrast was often reported. Neither visual distortions nor hallucinations were reported. Some people experienced imagery with their eyes closed, and one subject reported extensive hypnogogic imagery before falling asleep. The effects lasted no more than five hours. No subject reported any effects the following day.

Since this initial work was completed, there have been reports of persons experiencing headaches after smoking these blossoms. It is possible that the headaches are a result of smoking improperly prepared blossoms (allowing mold to form, etc.) or it may be a side-effect of the active principles.

The reported effects class this plant among the mildest psychedelics known. The extreme mildness of the effects allowed a second set of experiments with potential economic import. Naive subjects were given cigarettes or pipefulls of the prepared blossoms. They were told that this was a tobacco substitute used by some American Indians. They were then asked to compare it with what they usually smoked. There were no special instructions given.

Smokers found it to be as mild or milder than some commercial cigarettes and reported that it had a sweet aftertaste, in contrast to the slightly bitter aftertaste of tobacco.

These preliminary results indicate that *Genista canariensis* might be a potential substitute or adjunct to tobacco. With the mounting pressure to find less carcinogenic alternatives to tobacco, *Genista canariensis* may be worth more critical chemical, pharmacological and medical investigation.

24

SUBJECTIVE EFFECTS OF NITROUS OXIDE

WILLIAM JAMES

Some observations of the effects of nitrous-oxide-gas-intoxication which I was prompted to make by reading the pamphlet called *The anaesthetic revelation and the gist of philosophy* (Blood, 1874), have made me understand better than ever before both the strength and the weakness of Hegel's philosophy. I strongly urge others to repeat the experiment, which with pure gas is short and harmless enough. The effects will of course vary with the individual, just as they vary in the same individual from time to time; but it is probable that in the former case, as in the latter, a generic resemblance will obtain. With me, as with every other person of whom I have heard, the keynote of the experience is the tremendously exciting sense of an intense metaphysical illumination. Truth lies open to the view in depth beneath depth of almost blinding evidence. The mind sees all the logical relations of being with an apparent subtlety and instantaneity to which its normal consciousness offers no parallel; only as sobriety returns, the feeling of insight fades, and one is left staring vacantly at a few disjointed words and phrases, as one stares at a cadaverous-looking

Reprinted by permission from *Mind*, Vol. 7, 1882, pp. 186–208. This account of James' experiences with nitrous oxide is taken from a lengthy note to an article of his on the philosophy of Hegel, concerning the resolution of thesis and antithesis. Some of the material pertinent only to his discussions of Hegelianism has been deleted—*Editor*.

snow-peak from which the sunset glow has just fled, or at the black cinder left by an extinguished brand.

The immense emotional sense of *reconciliation* which characterizes the "maudlin" stage of alcoholic drunkenness—a stage which seems silly to lookers-on, but the subjective rapture of which probably constitutes a chief part of the temptation to the vice—is well known. The centre and periphery of things seem to come together. The ego and its objects, the *meum* and the *tuum*, are one. Now this, only a thousandfold enhanced, was the effect upon me of the gas: and its first result was to make peal through me with unutterable power the conviction that Hegelism was true after all, and that the deepest convictions of my intellect hitherto were wrong. Whatever idea of representation occurred to the mind was seized by the same logical forceps, and served to illustrate the same truth; and that truth was that every opposition, among whatsoever things, vanishes in a higher unity in which it is based; that all contradictions, so-called, are but differences; that all differences are of degree; that all degrees are of a common kind; that unbroken continuity is of the essence of being; and that we are literally in the midst of *an infinite*, to perceive the existence of which is the utmost we can attain. Without the *same* as a basis, how could strife occur? Strife presupposes something to be striven about; and in this common topic, the same for both parties, the differences merge. From the hardest contradiction to the tenderest diversity of verbiage differences evaporate; *yes* and *no* agree at least in being assertions; a denial of a statement is but another mode of stating the same, contradiction can only occur of the same thing—all opinions are thus synonyms, are synonymous, are the same. But the same phrase by difference of emphasis is two; and here again difference and no-difference merge in one.

It is impossible to convey an idea of the torrential character of the identification of opposites as it streams through the mind in this experience. I have sheet after sheet of phrases dictated or written during the intoxication, which to the sober reader seem meaningless drivel, but which at the moment of transcribing were fused in the fire of infinite rationality. God and devil, good and evil, life and death, I and thous, sober and drunk, matter and form, black and white, quantity and quality, shiver of ecstasy and shudder of horror, vomiting and swallowing, inspiration and expiration, fate and reason, great and small, extent and intent, joke and earnest, tragic and comic, and fifty other contrasts figure in these pages in the same monotonous way. The mind saw how each term *belonged* to its contrast through a knife-edge moment of transition which *it* effected, and which, perennial and eternal, was the *nunc stans* of life. The thought of mutual implication of the parts in the bare form of a judgment of opposition, as "nothing—but," "no more—than," "only—if," etc., produced a perfect delirium of theoretic rapture. And at last, when definite ideas to work on came slowly, the mind went through the mere *form* of recognizing sameness in identity by contrasting the same word with itself, differently emphasized, or shorn of its initial letter. Let me transcribe a few sentences:

What's mistake but a kind of take?
What's nausea but a kind of -ausea?
Sober, drunk, -unk, astonishment.
Everything can become the subject of criticism—how criticise without something *to* criticise?
Agreement—disagreement!!
Emotion—motion!!!!
By God, how that hurts! By God, how it *doesn't* hurt! Reconciliation of two extremes.
By George, nothing but *oth*ing!
That sounds like nonsense, but it is pure *on*sense!
Thought deeper than speech . . . !
Medical school; divinity school, *school*! SCHOOL! Oh my God, oh God; oh God!

The most coherent and articulate sentence which came was this:

There are no differences but differences of degree between different degrees of difference and no difference.

But now comes the reverse of the medal. What is the principle of unity in all this monotonous rain of instances? Although I did not see it at first, I soon found that it was in each case nothing but the abstract *genus* of which the conflicting terms were opposite species. In other words, although the flood of ontologic *emotion* was Hegelian through and through, the ground for it was nothing but the world-old principle that things are the same only so far and no farther than they *are* the same, or partake of a common nature—the principle that Hegel most tramples under foot. At the same time the rapture of beholding a process that was infinite, changed (as the nature of the infinitude was realized by the mind) into the sense of a dreadful and ineluctable fate, with whose magnitude every finite effort is incommensurable and in the light of which whatever happens is indifferent. This instantaneous revulsion of mood from rapture to horror is, perhaps, the strongest emotion I have ever experienced. I got it repeatedly when the inhalation was continued long enough to produce incipient nausea; and I cannot but regard it as the normal and inevitable outcome of the intoxication, if sufficiently prolonged. A pessimistic fatalism, depth within depth of impotence and indifference, reason and silliness united, not in a higher synthesia, but in the fact that whichever you choose it is all one—this is the upshot of a revelation that began so rosy bright.

Even when the process stops short of this ultimatum, the reader will have noticed from the phrases quoted how often it ends by losing the clue. Something "fades," "escapes"; and the feeling of insight is changed into an intense one of bewilderment, puzzle, confusion, astonishment. I know no more singular sensation than this intense bewilderment, with nothing particular left to be bewildered at save the bewilderment itself. It seems, indeed, a *causa sui*, or "spirit become its own object."

My conclusion is that the togetherness of things in a common world, the law of sharing, of which I have said so much, may, when perceived, engender a very powerful emotion; that Hegel was so unusually susceptible to this emotion throughout his life that its gratification became his supreme end, and made him tolerably unscrupulous as to means he employed; that *indifferentism* is the true outcome of every view of the world which makes infinity and continuity to be its essence, and that pessimistic or optimistic attitudes pertain to the mere accidental subjectivity of the moment; finally, that the identification of contradictories, so far from being the self-developing process which Hegel supposes, is really a self-consuming process, passing from the less to the more abstract, and terminating either in a laugh at the ultimate nothingness, or in a mood of vertiginous amazement at a meaningless infinity.

25

INHALATION PSYCHOSIS AND RELATED STATES

FREDERICK B. GLASER

It has long been known that affect and cognition may be considerably influenced by the inhalation of various substances. Both natural and artificial perfumes are prized for this very reason. Recently, however, attention has been drawn in both the professional and the popular press to persons who have become frankly psychotic while inhaling such substances as gasoline and model airplane glue. Because of the general concern in various quarters about these phenomena, a review of what has been learned appears to be indicated. It is quite possible that the further study and understanding of the states produced by the inhalation of such substances may reveal more differences than similarities, but in the present state of our knowledge it is more convenient to consider them together. In this discussion the pathological end point of these practices will be referred to as inhalation psychosis, and clinical syndromes due to inhalation but falling short of this end point will be referred to as related states.

The materials and techniques currently being used to induce inhalation psychosis and related states will be discussed, and both the acute and chronic states which may result will be considered. An attempt will be made to draw a composite picture of the person who inhales, and finally certain theoretical

Reprinted by permission from *Arch. Gen. Psychiat.*, Vol. 17, 1966, pp. 315–322.

matters will be briefly explored. It must be emphasized that this report is not a statistical analysis of the studies in the literature. Because of variable reporting and difference of emphasis, such an analysis would not be highly meaningful.

MATERIALS AND TECHNIQUES

By far the most popular substances used for the induction of inhalation psychosis are gasoline (Clinger & Johnson, 1951; Easson, 1962; Edwards, 1960; Faucett & Jensen, 1952; Anon., 1961; Grant, 1962; Lawton & Malmquist, 1961; Nitsche & Robinson, 1959; Pruitt, 1959; Quintanilla, 1961; Tolan & Lingl, 1964) and model airplane glue (Brewer, Picchioni, & Chin, 1960; Dodds & Santostefano, 1964; Glaser & Massengale, 1962; Anon., 1962a; Anon., 1962b; Jacobziner & Raybin, 1962; Jacobziner & Maybin, 1963; Massengale et al., 1963; Merry & Zachariadis, 1962; Press, 1963; Sokol & Robinson, 1963; Sterling, 1964; Verhulst & Crotty, 1962, 1964). Both are mixtures. Gasoline is a mixture of petroleum hydrocarbons and contains paraffins, olefins, napthenes, and aromatics; the aromatic hydrocarbons are chiefly benzene, toluene, and the xylenes. The proportions vary with the type of manufacturing process and the geographic origin of the crude petroleum (Machle, 1941). Model airplane glues may contain a wide variety of substances including hexane, benzene, toluene, xylene, carbon tetrachloride, chloroform, ethylene dichloride, acetone, cyclohexanone, methyl ethyl ketone, methyl isobutyl ketone, amyl acetate, ethyl acetate, tricresyl phosphate, butyl alcohol, ethyl alcohol, and methyl cellosolve acetate (Anon., 1961).

Paint thinner and lighter fluid have also been used (Ackerly & Gibson, 1964; Andersen & Kaada, 1953; Christiansson & Karlsson, 1957). Thinner generally contains butyl acetate, toluene, and ethyl alcohol, while lighter fluid is a mixture of aliphatic hydrocarbons, naphtha being the principal one. The use of toluene, chloroform, diethyl ether, and carbon monoxide in their pure state has been mentioned (Grabski, 1961; Lawton & Malmquist, 1961; Satran & Dodson, 1963; Schneck, 1945). Such other materials as paint, nail polish remover, and laundry marking pencils have received brief notice. It is to the clinical states produced by most of the foregoing chemicals, singly and in their various combinations, that we shall turn our attention in what follows.

Similarities are at once noticeable among these substances. With the exception of carbon monoxide they are all fat-soluble organic solvents. As such, they would be expected to pass the blood-brain barrier very rapidly.

Their fat solubility also hints at myelin as a possible site of action, and one study of gasoline intoxication in a commercial setting mentioned both peripheral and central alterations of myelin (Machle, 1941). However, the studies which have been done on industrial exposure to these solvents (Greenburg et al., 1942; Lawrence, 1945; Machle, 1941; Von Oettinger, Neal & Donohue, 1942; Wilson, 1943) do not approximate the conditions of acute, intermittent exposure to high levels of the vapors, and hence their applicability is open to question. The detailed pathologic physiology of inhalation psychosis and related states is clearly unknown at present.

Inhalation techniques of a considerable variety have been reported. Most commonly, a handkerchief or rag is saturated with the material and then either held over the face or placed directly into the mouth. If the latter technique is perfected, it can be done surreptitiously and in such public places as school. Simple inhalation from a container of the substance is also employed. Model airplane glue is often evacuated into a paper or plastic bag which is then placed over the face or head to provide a high concentration of vapors. The dangers of this practice are quite considerable. Nine deaths from glue inhalation had been reported up to mid-1964, and of these six were definitely and one probably due to suffocation from the plastic bag (Verhulst & Crotty, 1964). In spite of this, merchants in some instances offered plastic bags for an additional penny with a purchase of model airplane glue, and refused to stop this practice when approached by health officials (Jacobziner & Raybin, 1963).

Inhalers have proven resourceful in varying their technique. Some have found that heating most of these materials will result in higher vapor concentrations (Glaser & Massengale, 1962). One child used a dispersion principle, distributing gasoline over the surface of a large salad bowl and then inhaling, somewhat after the technique of the brandy snifter (Quintanilla, 1961). Most enterprising of all have been certain Swedish school-children who placed paint thinner in perfume sprayers and sold sniffs to their habituated classmates (Christiansson & Karlsson, 1957).

Reported schedules for inhalation vary considerably. Some users will inhale briefly but intensely, others for long periods which occasionally exceed 24 hours. In these cases inhalation is not usually constant but is returned to again and again over the 24-hour period. There is some suggestion that considerable individual variation exists as to which effects are considered to be desirable, and in the time required to produce them. Learning an adequate technique and becoming familiar with the effects of the inhalant are probably necessary before finding inhalation pleasurable, though some seem to find it so from the very first. In this, there are considerable parallels with the smoking of marijuana and the use of narcotics (Becker, 1953; Cameron, 1963; Felix, 1944).

THE NATURE OF INHALATION PSYCHOSIS

Virtually all of what is known of the acute state produced by inhalation is derived from retrospective reports. Inhalation is generally not performed publically, and the acute effects are short-lived. However, in one instance an attempt was made to simulate inhalation psychosis under experimental conditions, using paint thinner as the inhalant.

With the beginning of sniffing significant coughing appeared. A pleasant excitation was achieved after 15 to 25 "drags." After another 10 some odd drags, the maximum excitation was achieved. One of the experimental subjects fell afterwards into a deep sleep but of short duration. Pleasant drowsiness followed the sniffing. During continuous experimentation, neurological examination revealed a high degree of nystagmus, a positive Romberg, and a slurring of the speech. The experimental subjects were subjectively and objectively without signs and symptoms one hour after they had ceased sniffing (Christiansson & Karlsson, 1957).*

These experimenters also took serial electroencephalographic tracings on one of their subjects; they are the only such acute state recordings reported. The authors describe "clear electroencephalographic changes" which they were able to correlate with alterations in the consciousness of their subject. The major finding was a decrease in frequency from 8–10/second waves to 4–6/second waves, and a decrease in regularity. These findings and the reproduced tracings are similar to what have been described as the stage 2 to stage 3 electroencephalographic changes of delirium (Romano & Engel, 1944).†

Thus, it is possible that, in some cases at least, inhalation psychosis may be a delirium (Engel & Romano, 1959; Romano & Engel, 1944), similar to that induced by barbiturates and alcohol. If this is so, it is important to note that it therefore differs from the psychosis induced by LSD-25 and related compounds, which is not felt to be a delirium and which can be differentiated from deliria both objectively and subjectively (Unger, 1963; Engel & Romano, 1959; Ditman & Whittlesley, 1959). Statements to the contrary which have appeared may be due to the fact that they are based solely on retrospective data (Tolan & Lingl, 1964).

Bleuler (1950) pointed out that the more evident clinical characteristics of a mental illness might consist of the reaction of the organism to the disease

*Dr. Oliver Massengale supplied me with a translation of this article.

†Since this manuscript was submitted a report containing EEG tracings in the acute phases of intoxication from glue sniffing has appeared. In my opinion it supports the interpretation of the EEG changes in inhalation psychosis as being indicative of delirium (Brozovsky & Winkler, 1965).

process, rather than the direct primary manifestations of the disease process itself. He was concerned chiefly with the delusions and hallucinations of schizophrenia. The same phenomena—both visual and auditory hallucinations and paranoid delusions—are the most characteristically reported clinical manifestations of inhalation psychosis. As is the case in schizophrenia they may be a reaction of the organism to the basic ego-weakening process, in this case a delirium. It is known that delusions and hallucinations may occur in deliria, and it has been suggested that they are more likely to occur in those whose psychic economy was in precarious balance prior to the delirium (Engel & Romano, 1959). The same may be found to be true in inhalation psychosis. Other interesting clinical phenomena which have been reported in inhalation psychosis include tactile hallucinations, spatial distortions, macropsia and micropsia, and body image distortions. It must be emphasized again that not all persons who inhale develop this type of symptomatology.

Inhalation may become a chronic practice. Most writers believe that many more persons experiment with inhalation than become chronic users. But the degree of chronicity which may be achieved is considerable. In five reported cases, the duration of inhalation was in the neighborhood of ten years (Clinger & Johnson, 1951; Easson, 1962; Edwards, 1960; Nitsche & Robinson, 1959; Satran & Dodson, 1963). One is struck in many of the chronic cases by the strength of the need to inhale the preferred substance. Instances are reported independently from Ohio and Texas of parents literally chaining their children to prevent them from inhaling (Ackerly & Gibson, 1964; Clinger & Johnson, 1951). Both children broke free by dint of remarkable effort, and resumed inhalation; the boy in the latter case achieved newspaper notoriety as "The Sniffer."

Whether or not chronic inhalers can be said to be addicted is a question of some interest. If the strength of the urge to use is taken as the criterion, there can be little argument. Rado (1956), for example, noted that "not the toxic agent, but the impulse to use it, makes an addict of a given individual," and Fenichel (1945) added that "the word addiction hints at the urgency of the need and the final insufficiency of all attempts to satisfy it." Chein and his co-workers (1964) felt that "craving" was a most important component of addiction. If additional criteria of tolerance and physical dependence are added, however, the picture is less than clear. Such phenomena have been claimed to be present in inhalation by a number of authors but have never been convincingly documented.

The question of organic damage to the CNS, liver, kidneys, bone marrow and other systems of the body due to chronic inhalation appears in like fashion not to have been definitively settled. Studies in which routine laboratory tests have been done have been equivocal in their results, and even more sophisticated techniques have produced no clear-cut answer. Neurological examinations have been infrequently reported but when given are negative, excepting only one instance of cerebellar disorder which was felt to be secondary to the inhalation of toluene (Grabski, 1961). Electroencephalograms of 19 cases in the chronic state are reported by 14 authors; in only five cases were abnormalities found (Easson, 1962; Faucett & Jenson, 1952; Lawton & Malmquist, 1961; Satran & Dodson, 1963; Tolan & Lingl, 1964). None of the abnormalities was marked, and in one case there was a prior history of epilepsy. The applicability of industrial studies has already been noted to be questionable. Psychologists working with glue sniffers having a median number of 82 intoxications found no significant differences between them and a matched control group on psychological tests measuring a wide variety of cognitive functions, particularly those which they felt would be most vulnerable to organic brain disease (Dodds & Santostefano, 1964). Whether or not it is found that a certain amount of direct toxicity to various organ systems does exist, the practice of inhalation is dangerous and occasionally fatal, as in the cases where death was due to plastic bag suffocation. Further, the grandiose notions of invulnerability and of the power of flight which have been observed in some chronic cases (Verhulst & Crotty, 1964) may have fatal outcomes, and the susceptibility of delirious individuals to such dangers as automobile accidents is also clear.

THE INHALER

We have considered the material currently used for inhalation and the techniques employed, and surveyed the acute and chronic states associated with it. We may now consider certain characteristics of the inhaler himself, and attempt to draw a composite picture.

Age

When first seen the inhaler is likely to be between the ages of 11 and 15, with the average age in most of the larger series being in the neighborhood of 13 years (Christiansson & Karlsson, 1957; Glaser & Massengale, 1962; Massengale et al., 1963; Sterling, 1964). Since the average duration of inhalation practices is roughly one year, the average age of onset also falls within this range. In general this is a younger age than is reported for either juvenile alcoholics or juvenile drug addicts (Sterling, 1964; Meyer, 1952). It may thus be an earlier indication of a difficult adolescence.

Of some interest are those who go beyond the limits of this age range in either direction. Nine cases began inhalation in their 10th year or arlier, and three of these (Easson, 1962; Faucett & Jensen, 1952; Nitsche & Robinson, 1959) were 5 years old or less. This includes the case of a oy whose inhalation of gasoline began at the age of 18 months (Nitsche & Robinson, 1959). It was encouraged by the parents because it pacified he child; when seen by the reporting psychiatrists, he had achieved a uration of 10.5 years of inhalations. At the other end of the spectrum re three cases which were first seen when the patients were more than 20 ears of age (Grabski, 1961; Satran & Dodson, 1963; Schneck, 1945); n one case (Schneck, 1945) the patient had begun inhaling at the age of 3. These cases comprise all of the reports of persons who have inhaled hemically pure substances, which would be expected to be more available o older persons. Such inhalants as model airplane glue are more available o youngsters. Studies of child alcoholics and of drug addicts in general, nd particularly of physician addicts, have suggested that a factor of availa-ility is of some importance in these conditions as well (Quintanilla, 1961;)'Donnell, 1963, 1964; Modlin & Montes, 1964).

ex

All reports state that inhalation is far more frequently a practice of males han of females. In 276 cases surveyed in which the sex of the inhaler is pecified, there are but 22 females. A similar preponderance of males has een noted in both alcoholism and drug addiction (Sterling, 1964; Lisansky, 957; Kolb, 1962; Meyer, 1952). Theories as to why this should be so either avor certain special psychological characteristics of females (Abraham, 953; Chein et al., 1964) or point to the greater strictures which society places n female activities in all spheres (Kolb, 1962). Neither answer by itself is erhaps wholly satisfactory, and the study of female inhalers may shed some ew light on this problem.

Minority Group Status

Three studies have reported a high percentage of cases among Spanish-American minority groups (Ackerly & Gibson, 1964; Glaser & Massengale, 962; Sokol & Robinson, 1963). On the other hand, there are reports of only ight Negro inhalers (Clinger & Johnson, 1951; Simmel, 1948), and in a Chicago study which found Negroes to be well represented among juvenile lcoholics and in the city population, there were no Negro inhalers. Such lata are suggestive of historical trends among minority groups with respect o specific antisocial activities; for example, the percentage of Negro admissions for narcotics addiction to the USPHS Hospital at Lexington has fluctuated from 8.9% in 1936 to 52% in 1955 (Pescor, 1943; Lowry, 1956) to approximately 41% in 1964.*

Concurrent Use of Other Addicting Substances

Narcotic drugs are rarely ever reported as being used together with inhalants (although the sniffing of heroin and cocaine has long been known). With one exception (Sterling, 1964), however, most studies report that tobacco and alcohol are often employed by inhalers, sometimes to a rather unusual degree (Edwards, 1960; Glaser, 1962; Schneck, 1945). Along possibly related lines it is amusing to note an Australian boy of 11 years who was seen because of gasoline inhalation. "He said he had been eating rubber erasers at school for the last four years, had run out of them, had 'wanted something nice to do,' and so decided to sniff petrol, of which he had always liked the smell." (Grant, 1962)

Status of Home

In ten individual cases in the literature, the home of the inhaler was physically broken by death, abandonment, or divorce. But since this datum is not given for many cases, it is difficult to arrive at an estimate of its significance. A comparative study showed no difference in the incidence of physically broken homes between glue-sniffers and juvenile alcoholics (Sterling, 1964).

Antisocial Activities

Two groups contained within roughly the same temporal and spatial area, one of glue-sniffers and one of juvenile alcoholics, exhibited an identical rate of recidivism with respect to arrests, although the glue-sniffers were more likely to have been arrested previously for intoxication than were the alcoholics (Sterling, 1964). There were no differences between the groups as to type of crimes (conduct versus property offenses); as to the seriousness of the crimes, as judged by police juvenile specialists; or as to the incidence of group versus solitary offenses. Thus, in most respects, the two groups were indistinguishable in their antisocial activities.

There has been a continuing question as to whether glue, alcohol, and other agents have a direct effect in driving persons to commit antisocial acts, or whether their use is simply one characteristic of persons who also commit antisocial acts. The inhalation literature gives some support to both of these

*Personal communications, USPHS Hospital, Lexington, Ky., May 5, 1965.

ypotheses (Merry & Zachariadis, 1962; Tolan & Lingl, 1964; Ackerly & Gibson, 1964). It is important to note that most authorities hold that narcotic drugs do not produce crimes directly, since they have a marked quieting effect upon their users (Kolb, 1962; Wikler, 1952). It is in connection with obtaining funds to purchase narcotics that crimes are committed by narcotics addicts, and these are generally crimes against property and not violent crimes against persons.

Intelligence

In a well-controlled study no significant differences were found between glue-sniffers and normals (Massengale et al., 1963). Many of the inhalers do poorly in school, but this is not necessarily due to lack of intelligence. Moreover, it appears that inhalation practices of long duration are not incompatible with high academic attainment, including professorship at medical schools (Schneck, 1945). With respect to the 14 individual cases in which intelligence quotients are reported, eight scored less than 100, and two of the eight less than 70. In those cases in which intellectual impairment existed it appeared to bear some relationship to the patient's general difficulties, but in the overall picture intelligence does not appear to be highly significant. This accords with studies in alcoholics and narcotics addicts (Peters, 1956; Kolb, 1925; Meyer, 1952).

Diagnosis

Only in nine surveyed cases had a diagnosis been made which was consistent with the standard nomenclature of the American Psychiatric Association. In five of these cases, the diagnosis was either schizoid personality or schizophrenia, but to draw valid conclusions from this small number of cases is difficult. Inspection of all cases surveyed appears to indicate that inhalation cuts across the whole spectrum of psychiatric diagnoses. If there is any preponderance, it is likely to be in the category of personality disturbances. There are parallel findings in alcoholism and narcotics addiction (Peters, 1956; Felix, 1944; Kolb, 1962; Pescor, 1943). Felix's statement is perhaps apropos of all three groups: "The addict is not a creature apart from the psychiatric point of view. He differs from other psychiatric cases of the same class chiefly in his presenting symptom." (Felix, 1944)

Natural History

What is the incidence and prevalence of inhalation? What percentage of experimenters go on to chronic use? Do inhalers eventually "graduate" into alcoholism and drug addiction? What is their fate, psychologically and socially? At present the answers to these and related questions are entirely unknown. There is only one report which includes a follow-up period of more than a year (Clinger & Johnson, 1951). The careful application of epidemiological techniques is urgently needed.

THE ETIOLOGY OF INHALATION PSYCHOSIS

At the present time, no single factor which is both necessary and sufficient to result in inhalation psychosis and related states may be identified, beyond those components which are necessary simply in terms of its definition, i.e., an inhalant of some type and a means of inhaling it. The comparative data cited above indicate that etiologic factors operative in alcoholism and narcotics addiction might also be influential here. But this is not of great assistance, since there is considerable disagreement as to the causes of alcoholism and narcotics addiction. Disputes over whether social or psychological factors are more important would seem to be of little value in any of these problems. The literature clearly indicates that neither factor can be excluded with any justice in any case, though their relative degrees of importance may vary somewhat.

A rather intriguing problem with respect to etiology is the relationship between inhalation and smell. What role does the sense of smell play in leading to inhalation psychosis and related states? It would seem highly unlikely that no connection would exist. But one is struck by the paucity of reports by inhalers of the nature of the olfactory experience in inhalation. Nevertheless, if we accept it as part of the total phenomenon, we find an interesting situation in looking at the psychoanalytic literature concerning the sense of smell. Several authors have stressed the determining importance of oral factors in those who seek olfactory experiences (Fenichel, 1953; Fitzherbert, 1959; Wayne & Clinco, 1959). Most of the writers of the classic period of psychoanalysis viewed such interests in the light of transmutations of coprophilia, an anal stage phenomenon (Freud, 1930; Abraham, 1953; Ferenczi, 1950; Anon., 1962). The rather extraordinary relationship between smells and genital sexuality was noted by Havelock Ellis and earlier researchers whose work he summarizes (Ellis, 1937). It has been noted that:

> Smell, as a special sense, is present from birth onward. As such it has an autonomy of its own. . . . It comes into association from the beginning with oral, anal, urethral and genital levels of psychosexual development. Smell experiences may be drawn into conflict at any or all of these levels, and as a result may serve to express the particular material of the conflict (Sandler & Nagera, 1963).

Thus, even if smell were to prove to be intimately related to inhalation psychodynamically, it would provide no positive clues as to the involvement of a particular phase of development.

On a rather impressionistic level it may be noted that a general feeling of eroticism pervades many reports of inhalation. This has long been noted with respect to alcoholism and narcotics addiction as well, and its highly narcissistic quality has led some to view these phenomena in a light of auto-erotic activity (Romano & Engel, 1944; Simmel, 1948). Masturbation is one of the earlier and more common situations in which the organism deals with impulses toward self-gratification. How it copes with this situation may be a paradigm of how it will cope with similar situations later in life. Spitz (1962) noted a direct relationship between the type of mothering received by an infant and the type of autoerotic play the infant engaged in. He found that "in the case of the infants where the relationship between mother and child was a problematic one, genital play was much rarer and other autoerotic activities tended to replace it. . . ." It remains to be seen whether addiction, inhalation, and alcoholism may be the later representatives of those "other autoerotic activities."

Finally, one cannot but be impressed with the wealth of fantasy material reported in cases of inhalation. The following intriguing report concerns the case of a 5-year-old child.

Initially, he breathed the gasoline fumes only occasionally. Each time, however, he had a pleasant hallucination of friendly, gnomelike men who were fond of him and spoke kindly to him. At this time parental discord was intense. The patient felt that father was abusive and severe with him. "Father heckled me and gave my mother and me heck at everything we did." Because of this, he began to plot with the men of his hallucinations to remove his father. He said, "I want to make my father go away, so I can go off someplace with mom and we can make a living together and be happy on a farm." His hallucinations promised to help him if he would never call again. Quite by coincidence the father left on a three weeks' trip about this time. The patient interpreted this as the fulfillment of his wishes and believed the hallu-cinations helped him to do away with his father (Faucett & Jensen, 1952).

The function of fantasy had been viewed as being "to create a wish-fulfilling situation which allows a certain amount of instinctual discharge—a dis-charge which would not be permitted in the existing circumstances of external reality—and which also corrects and modifies that reality in the imagination" (Rosenbaum, 1961). Since there is some evidence that inhala-tion facilitates such fantasies, one might speculate that it would appeal to those whose ability to fantasy is impaired. There is evidence that this is the case with narcotics addicts (Chein, et al., 1964), and it can be shown experi-mentally that narcotics increase the ability of an addict to fantasy (Brown,

1943). It might also be the case that inhalation facilitates fantasies in those who are cut off from other avenues of instinctual discharge. For example, the circumstances of an isolated rural environment, a schizoid personality, limited intellectual endowment, or membership in a minority group might block certain of the commonly used paths to instinctual discharge and lead to a search for others, including discharge through fantasies facilitated by inhalation. All of these circumstances may be found among the cases of inhalation psychosis and related states.

TREATMENT

Because of its relatively brief duration it is unlikely that the acute form of inhalation psychosis will present itself for treatment. If it does, the general principles of the management of an acute delirium should probably be followed. This would include the elimination of ambiguous and misleading stimuli like shadows and whispered voices; the protection of the patient and others from his hostile outbursts; and the provision of a supportive and familiar environment in which continuous professional observation of the patient may be made. Because of the lack of evidence that a withdrawal syndrome exists, provision for gradual abstinence from the offending material does not appear to be necessary. The home or the hospital might serve as the locus for this treatment, though the latter would facilitate access to laboratory methods of assessment of organic damage to the bone marrow, liver, kidneys, and central nervous system. It would also lead more naturally to the thorough psychological and psychiatric examination which should follow. The case of the chronic inhaler has generally been managed on an outpatient basis, except when the patient's psychiatric condition necessitated hospitalization.

With respect to the overall problem preventive measures are clearly indicated and have been initiated along certain lines. Several laws have been passed in an effort to control inhalation practices, and conferences to share what has been learned have taken place (Verhulst & Crotty, 1964). The manufacturers of some of the products involved have experimented with the substitution of relatively nontoxic solvents and the addition of various irritants which would discourage inhalation. Public education programs may be expected to be helpful, if carried out in a judicious fashion; it has been cautioned that "while one is warning some youths, he may be instructing others" (Sterling, 1964). It may also be reasonably expected that general social improvements may have an ameliorating effect on the incidence and prevalence of inhalation, as well as upon narcotics addiction and alcoholism. A very convincing demonstration has recently appeared which indicates that the potentially remediable condition of overcrowding may affect the mother-child relationship and result in such illnesses in the child (Spitz, 1964). Basic to all these approaches is the need for much more data concerning all of these problems. Rarely, if ever, may we be satisfied with the current state of our knowledge on any subject, and certainly not in the case of those under discussion here. Sir Thomas Browne, himself a physician, once wrote:

> The wisedome of God receives small honour from those vulgar heads that rudely stare about, and with a grosse rusticity admire his workers; those highly manifie him, whose judicious enquiry into his acts, and deliberate research of his creatures, return the duty of a devout and learned admiration (*Religio Medici*).

SUMMARY

The practice of deliberate inhalation of a wide variety of substances containing organic solvents, especially gasoline and model airplane glue, has of late been widely reported. A number of techniques are employed in achieving an acute intoxication from these substances, which appears to be a toxic delirium. The impulse to engage in such practices may be very strong and may result in chronic usage, which resembles in some respects addiction to narcotics and alcohol. Despite some dispute about the direct toxic effects of these substances on various organs, a number of deaths have been associated with the practice. Most cases reported are in their early teens, though the spread is considerable. The intoxicant used may bear some relationship to age-determined availability. There is a high preponderance of males, and broken homes and minority group status may also be seen. In some cases diminished intelligence is present. Unusual accessory utilization of tobacco and alcohol, but not of narcotics, is reported. The practice appears to be conducive to the performance of antisocial acts as well as being a favored outlet of those already antisocially inclined. The natural history of these practices is essentially unknown. A multifactorial approach to the etiology, treatment, and prevention of inhalation psychosis and related states seems most likely to prove valuable.

INTRODUCTION TO SECTION 7. MAJOR PSYCHEDELIC DRUGS

In 1943 a Swiss chemist, Albert Hoffman, accidentally ingested a minute quantity of a newly developed chemical compound, lysergic acid diethylamide-25 (LSD-25).* With the onset of marked perceptual changes, intense fantasy activity, and cognitive changes, the most powerful mind-altering drug known to man was discovered: as little as 100 micrograms can produce an extremely strong ASC.

There have been many other psychedelic chemicals, usually constituents of various plants, known to man throughout his history, for example the peyote cactus and the Amanite Muscaria mushroom. It was the widespread research with LSD-25 and the publicity resulting from it, however, that has brought on the "psychedelic revolution" of our time. Various sources estimate that, as of 1967, between one and three million Americans have taken LSD-25 or a similar psychedelic chemical. Usage is particularly high among college students (Hollander, 1967).

It would take a series of books to begin to adequately cover what is known about the effects of the major psychedelic drugs, much less the cultural innovations of the "hip" world. Many such books have been written and the better ones are referenced in the "Guide to the Literature on Psychedelic Drugs," Chapter 32. In this section the psychedelics are treated as another way of producing ASCs, and I have selected a series of papers that provide

---

*The suffix 25 simply indicates that it was the twenty-fifth compound in this series, and has no intrinsic chemical meaning.

a good overview of the psychedelic drug phenomena and relate it to other material on ASCs.

Specifically, this section will cover the current status of research with the major psychedelics, the phenomenology of the psychedelic state, considerations in the use of psychedelic drugs, and the relation of psychedelic states to some other ASCs.

The state of our scientific knowledge about the effects of the major psychedelics is very difficult to assess, not for lack of experimental literature (there are well over a thousand studies) but because much of what were considered to be drug-specific effects (statements that "LSD causes so and so") have been found to be a mixture of drug *plus* psychological factors. Indeed, one could argue, for heuristic purposes, that the major psychedelic drugs have *no* specific psychological effects, they simply produce phenomena in accordance with the expectations of *S*s and experimenters, acting as a sort of psychological "amplifier." Thus LSD-25 was initially called a "psychotomimetic" drug and study after study showed that *S*s acted in a psychotic manner. These findings appear to be primarily a result of the use of the drug by white-coated psychiatrists in a sterile hospital setting. Until this entanglement of drug effects and set and setting effects is resolved by future research, it is hard to say exactly what the psychedelic drugs "normally" do, although we can say that they create a very wide variety of ASCs in accordance with the psychological pressures applied to the *S*.

At the time of this writing, the prospects for future research in this area are poor. The last two years saw a wave of hysteria about the terrible effects of LSD sweep the nation, based almost entirely on false data worked up by journalists into juicy horror stories that would sell newspapers and magazines. Highly restrictive legislation has been enacted on a Federal level and by a number of states, including jail sentences for the mere possession of LSD-25. The number of Federally supported or state supported research projects has dropped to a small fraction of what it was. The legislation has generally been enacted with no heed to testimony of scientists, a situation parallel to the introduction of restrictive marijuana legislation three decades ago (Ginsberg, 1967). The effect of the legislation has been to make it difficult for the legitimate researcher to carry on research: apparently anyone else can easily buy LSD-25 on the black market for his own use in most major cities.

The first article in this section, "Current Status and Future Trends in Psychedelic (LSD) Research," by Robert Mogar, surveys current scientific knowledge on psychedelics and reviews the research situation. Although written in 1965, it is quite up-to-date at the time of this writing (1967), since restrictive legislation has virtually ended research.

Chapter 27, "Implications of LSD and Experimental Mysticism," by

Walter Pahnke and William Richards, is an excellent description of the phenomenology of the psychedelic state. Comparisons are made with the ASCs described in the mystical experience.*

Chapter 28, "Attitude and Behavior Change through Psychedelic Drug Use," by Joseph Downing, discusses the various technical considerations involved in giving LSD-25 to psychiatric patients, such as dosage, patient preparation, and follow-up. While the discussion centers around the use of psychedelics in an out-patient treatment setting, it is generally applicable to the use of psychedelic drugs in a variety of settings.

The next article, "*Ipomeoa Purpurea*: A Naturally Occurring Psychedelic," by Charles Savage, Willis Harman, and James Fadiman, deals with the use of and psychedelic effects obtained from the ingestion of morning glory seeds. Many students and others are using morning glory seeds to produce "trips," but there has been no really good source of scientific information on their effects. This previously unpublished paper is the only source of scientific data available on morning glory intoxication other than the Fink et al. (1966) report on some psychotic reaction.

In the section on minor psychedelics, I indicated that marijuana might be useful for enhancing creativity because of its seeming loosening of associative processes. Chapter 30, "Psychedelic Agents in Creative Problem Solving," by Willis Harman, Robert McKim, Robert Mogar, James Fadiman, and Myron Stolaroff, is a concrete illustration of the use of psychedelics to enhance creativity. This article was intended to be a pilot study, but the results were overwhelmingly positive and should provoke a great deal of research in this area that is not only of theoretical interest but of so much practical importance.

"'Psychedelic' Experiences in Acute Psychoses," by Malcolm Bowers and Daniel Freedman, links the psychedelic states with ASCs in general and psychotic episodes in particular. The case material presented by these authors suggests that any event which "loosens up" the organization of the normal state of consciousness may produce a number of effects usually associated with the psychedelic experience. In the cases reported, however, a psychotic break resulted after a short period of psychedelic experiences. One wonders what would have happened to these patients if they had been immediately cared for and "guided" by someone who understood the psy-

---

*The degree to which various religions have been influenced by drug-induced psychedelic experiences is a fascinating and important question. The priests of the Temple in Jerusalem, for example, apparently used an annointing oil (Exodus 30:23–25) which has been rumored to be mildly psychedelic, although I know of no modern research on the effects of this oil.

chedelic aspects of the experiences they were having: might they have improved instead of having the psychotic break?

Finally, the last article in this section is a guide to the vast literature on psychedelics. Many other references are included in the articles of this section. Other relevant papers in this book are Aaronson's (Chapter 17), Krippner's (Chapter 18), and my own (Chapters 10 and 19).

26

CURRENT STATUS AND FUTURE TRENDS IN PSYCHEDELIC (LSD) RESEARCH

ROBERT E. MOGAR

Since the discovery of d-lysergic acid diethylamide (LSD-25) in 1943, a voluminous literature has accumulated concerning its effects on a variety of animals, including man. Despite the mass of published reports, definitive evidence is generally lacking, particularly with regard to the subjective and behavioral effects both during and subsequent to the LSD induced state. It is well established that this powerful agent produces major alterations in cerebral processes and central autonomic functions. There is also ample evidence indicating a markedly lowered threshold for arousal (Key & Bradley, 1960) and an increased sensitivity to stimuli in all modalities (Klee, 1963). These psychopharmacological effects parallel the findings of clinical and behavioral studies at least on the molar descriptive level. Pronounced perceptual changes have been almost invariably demonstrated with concomitant alterations in affect, ideation, and the relationship between subject and environment (Hoffer, 1965). Beyond these rather global findings, results have been inconsistent and often contradictory, even within species far less complex than man (Cohen, 1964).

The well-known methodological problems encountered in research with centrally acting drugs are at least partly responsible for the slow progress thus far (Zubin & Katz, 1964). This has been especially true with

Reprinted by permission from *J. Human Psychol.*, Vol. 2, 1965, pp. 147–166.

human subjects. Systematic study of human reactions to LSD poses unique problems associated with greater organic complexity, shortcomings of currently available measuring devices, the ubiquity of individual differences, lack of an adequate theoretical model, and the influence of non-drug variables such as set and setting. In addition to these experimental obstacles, LSD has until recently been the center of a complicated medico-legal-social controversy (Harman, 1964). This has tended to obscure the relevant empirical questions and inhibit investigations which are both imaginative and reasonably objective.

AMBIVALENCE IN A PERIOD OF TRANSITION

The short but illustrative history of LSD-25 (a) as a subject of research, (b) as a psycho-social phenomenon, and (c) as a theoretical or philosophical enigma may be viewed as a case study of significant trends in contemporary psychology and psychiatry. It is equally instructive to reverse the process by viewing the growing interest and fascination with altered states of consciousness from the perspective of recent shifts in psychological theory and research. As young disciplines lacking stable direction, self-scrutiny and constant revision characterize the social sciences. And in the light of their subject-matter, these fields are particularly attuned to the wider culture. In this connexion, recent developments in the philosophy and sociology of science emphasize the transactional interplay between theory, observer, and actuality. Rather than laws of nature, theory and evidence are more accurately viewed as working fictions or convenient myths and reflect the belief system of a given time and place (Holten, et al., 1965). A rather extreme version of this "Indeterminacy Model" of science has been described by Alfred de Grazia (1963, p. 56):

> The model suggests that the spirit of the times and customs dictate what will and will not be science.... Scientists operate under the indeterminacy system by various myths—primarily of rationality, of causation, and of power of choice—but in fact do not know what they are seeking, what is available, or what are solutions. That their compensation, whether in esteem, position, or money, is related to performance is only an illusion. What is accepted and what is rejected are therefore only a product of chance encounters of purpose and provision.

A growing body of empirical evidence supports the view that science as a branch of human endeavor is socially and psychologically conditioned just as any other human activity (Rosenthal, 1963). From this perspective, contemporary theoretical issues and recent shifts in psychological research become a sensitive barometer of the present social climate and also a timetable of significant cultural trends. A case in point is the recent emergence of a "third force" in American psychology with its emphasis on personal growth and greater realization of human potentialities. The third force in psychology has counterparts in each of the arts and science.* Collectively, they represent a concerted effort to counteract the progressive subordination of personal identity to what Erik Erikson calls the "technological superidentity" (1962). Interestingly, they also share a highly positive vision of modern man's foreseeable possibilities. This ambivalent, somewhat paradoxical position suggests that contemporary humanistic thinking has been inspired not only by the dehumanizing effects of the scientific-industrial complex, but also by its capacity for making the lives of men healthy, safe, and reasonably secure for the first time in history.

Traditionally, the motive power of western cultures has necessarily focused on survival and environmental mastery—human strivings which are highly congenial to a behavioristic or psychoanalytic frame of reference. In contrast to these orientations, Maslow views the organismic equilibrium made possible by satiated bodily needs, physical safety, and some measure of psychological security as merely prerequiste to more uniquely human pursuits. This hierarchical conception of man's strivings depicts him as a self-directed creature with impulses toward creative expression and self-enhancement as well as homeostatic maintenance (Maslow, 1962).

It is too early to gauge the extent to which Maslow's humanistic image of man meshes with the modern temper. On the other hand, considerable evidence has already accumulated indicating that behaviorism and psychoanalysis, in their orthodox forms, no longer have what Bruner describes as "an immediate resonance with the dialectic of experience" (1962). Yet their continuing impact on our self- and world-view is clearly substantial. Thus, three divergent orientations occupy the same stage concurrently— reflecting and in turn effecting social values and individual conduct. Viewed comparatively, these equipotent theories of man and the research they generate give testimony to the preoccupations and uncertainties of our time.

Placed within this broader context, the diverse descriptions and interpretations of the LSD experience become more understandable. And since psychedelic, "mind-manifesting," substances have been known and ingested throughout man's history (Barnard, 1963), the current fascination with this class of experiences seems particularly significant. Although presently unclear, one general reason for the increasing interest in psychedelic phenomena can be identified: either as a means of investigating higher thought processes or as a potentially valuable personal experience, the

*See Rene Dubos' excellent account of "Humanistic Biology" (1965). Similar trends in contemporary fiction, poetry, and drama have been summarized by Mogar (1964).

LSD-induced state is intriguing because it meshes with the *zeitgeist* in the social sciences and with major trends in the larger culture. There is convincing evidence from a variety of quarters which supports this contention.

EXPERIMENTAL PSYCHOLOGY: THE RETURN OF THE OSTRACIZED

In a recent issue of the *American Psychologist*, an incisive paper by a well-known research psychologist is entitled, "Imagery: The Return of the Ostracized" (Holt, 1964). After examining the traditional scientific and cultural resistances to such phenomena as pseudohallucinations, hypnogogic and dream images, extrasensory perception, and hypnosis, the author goes on to describe the current status in these fields. Echoing Hebb's manifesto as president of the American Psychological Association (1960), he points to a number of recent breakthroughs in a variety of research areas which signal the second phase of a psychological revolution. The first phase, covering the first half of this century, was characterized by the scientific extremism of psychoanalysis and behaviorism; movements which purged psychology of the unique and the private. While both psychoanalysis and behaviorism in their orthodox forms have made valuable contributions to our understanding of man, it seems evident now that these orientations can no longer exclude altered states of consciousness and novel perceptual experiences from the *primary* subject-matter of a *normal* psychology.

Significantly, some of the leading exponents of both theories such as B. F. Skinner (1963) and H. Hartmann (1958) have recognized these omissions and indicated a need for revision. Consistent with theoretical developments, behavioristic research shows an increasing concern with internal processes including sensations, images, and cognitions (London & Rosenhan, 1964). Similarly, psychoanalytic studies focus more on normal or superior functioning and less on pathology (Frosch & Ross, 1960). These trends are not surprising since some of the most exciting developments during the past decade have occurred in experimental work with dream activity, sensory deprivation, creativity, hypnosis, and the psychedelic drugs. Viewing this rich array of research activity as occurring within a broader cultural context, one convergent finding seems of major significance; namely, that richness of imagination and so-called regressive experiences are not the exclusive privilege of madmen and artists. Instead, this work indicates quite conclusively that under favorable circumstances, most eople can greatly expand their experiential horizons without sacrificing ffectiveness in dealing with conventional reality.

The significant parallels among relatively independent lines of investigation are most striking. First it should be noted that each of these phenomenon (psychedelic, dreams, creativity, sensory isolation, and hypnosis) have traditionally been associated with the negative, bizarre, and abnormal. Until recently dreams and hypnosis have generally been linked with magic and the occult. Similarly, "hallucinogenic" drug states, sensory confinement, and inordinate creativeness have strong historical associations with defective character and insanity. As a result, these classes of experience have typically been treated as isolated phenomena, discontinuous with other psychological processes and inexplicable in terms of known principles.

Although presently accepted as legitimate areas of study, the tainted heritage of novel experiences has continued to exert strong influence. For example, recent findings indicate that the main features of creativity and the necessary conditions for its development run counter to prevailing ideologies (Getzels & Jackson, 1962; Gruen, 1964). Similar cultural and professional resistances have been documented regarding the psychedelic drugs with particular reference to their presumed "psychotomimetic" properties (Savage & Stolaroff, 1965). The same biases have been noted in perceptual isolation research. In their recent critique, Arnhoff and Leon (1964) conclude that most studies of sensory deprivation effects have grossly misapplied the concepts and terms of pathology. In much the same vein, Shor's (1960, p. 162) work on "hypnotic-like" experiences in normal subjects indicates that:

> In our culture naturally-occurring hypnotic-like experiences tend to be regarded with some misgivings if not as outright pathology. Consequently they are little talked about, but this does not mean that they occur with less frequency or profundity than in cultures where they are encouraged or institutionalized. In many cultures such experiences are seen as a vital source of creative inspiration and gratification.

A second significant parallel concerns the remarkable subjective and behavioral similarities of these experiences. Consistent findings in research on hypnotic, psychedelic, and dream states, certain phases of the creative process, as well as sensory and dream deprivation indicate an almost complete overlap of major effects. Reported communalities include significant alterations in perception, dominance of sensation and imagery over verbal-associative thinking, relaxed ego boundaries, changes in bodily feelings, and the suspension of conventional reality-orientation to space, time, and self.

Theoretical accounts of these psychological changes have also ru
parallel. Whether self-induced or situationally induced by means of fatigue
drugs, or some form of stress, such states have typically been viewed a
regressive, infantile, or primitive, indicating sudden loss of ego contro
and the eruption of unconscious forces. Until very recently, the effect
have been interpreted as disturbing, incapacitating, quasi-psychotic, dis
sociative, or depersonalizing. Consistent with these interpretations, person
prone to altered states of awareness have generally been described a
poorly adjusted, suggestible, irrational, passive, and low in ego strength.

Perhaps the most important parallel concerns the current status an
direction of research in these areas. At the present time, work in eac
area reveals a discernible shift away from investigating the condition o
phenomenon per se, focussing instead on the situation- and subject
determined variables. This significant turning point calls attention to th
key importance of the psycho-social context in which these experience
are inextricably embedded. Related to this new research strategy, recen
findings and shifts in theorizing about altered states of consciousness hav
taken a more positive turn.

As a case in point, the aftereffects of dream deprivation, both positiv
and negative, vary widely across subjects. Dement (1960) found that "th
kinds of alterations represent extensions or revelations of tendencies nativ
to the individual personality" and that their form, degree, and dynami
meaning were influenced by the setting and by interpersonal transactions
With regard to hypnotic susceptibility, Barber (1964) has established th
central importance of attitudinal and motivational variables. Similarly
recent findings indicate that the nature and intensity of hypnotic experience
are strongly influenced by the socio-psychological milieu, particularly th
mutual expectancies of subject and experimenter (Sarbin & Lim, 1963).

The same trends are found in sensory deprivation research. Considerabl
evidence has accumulated indicating that greatly reduced sensory inpu
can impair or facilitate mental functioning depending on the particula
interaction of set, setting, and personality (Brownfield, 1964). For example
Leiderman (1964) found that "with the element of fear removed, th
imagery of sensory deprivation becomes like the imagery of daydreams
quite familiar and usually not anxiety-producing." Interestingly, sensory
deprivation is reportedly therapeutic for some patients (Zuckerman, 1964)

---

*The comparable effects and interpretations described here are well documented
in the research literature. Representative and recent reports may be found in
Barron (1963) on creativity, Zuckerman (1964) on sensory deprivation, Cohen
(1964) on psychedelic states, Weitzenhoffer (1963) on hypnosis, and Dement (1960)
on dream deprivation.

he direction of thinking in this area is perhaps best summed up by uedfeld (1964). Noting that some experimentally isolated subjects reveal riking creativity in solving problems, he poses the question, "What would appen if creative behavior were externally reinforced by the experienter?"

Turning to the psychedelics, it has become apparent that adverse psychogical or behavioral effects are not drug-specific. More generally, the ature, intensity, and content of the experience are the result of complex ransactions between the subject's past history and personality, the set nd expectancies of both subject and administrator, and the physical and sychological setting in which the experience takes place (see e.g., Unger, 964). As in the case of related phenomena, most of these determinants f response to LSD can be intentionally arranged and manipulated so as o foster either a propitious or a stressful experience. In the search or relatively invariant or "drug-specific" reactions, much of the esearch until recently has failed to assess, control, or systematically ary relevant non-drug variables.

Laboratory studies of behavioral effects during the LSD-induced state ave been particularly insensitive to situation- and subject-determined ariables. Changes in performance levels on a wide variety of tasks have een extensively investigated with inconclusive results. Instrumental learning has been found to be impaired (Krus et al., 1963), enhanced (Rosenbaum t al., 1959), and unchanged (Kornetsky, 1957). Both impairment and nhancement of color perception have been reported (Wapner & Krus, 1960; Hartman & Hollister, 1963). Similarly, studies of the effects of LSD on ecall and recognition, discrimination learning, concentration, symbolic hinking, and perceptual accuracy have yielded contradictory results (see .g., Trouton & Eysenck, 1961). It is perhaps significant that most of the aboratory research has used the drug as a stressor with the intention of imulating psychotic-like performance-impairment (psychotomimetic rientation). In contrast, well over three-hundred clinical studies on the herapeutic effectiveness of LSD have reported almost uniformly positive esults (Hoffer, 1965; Mogar, 1965). This more recent line of investigation iews the drug as a liberator which facilitates accurate perception, self-nsight, and performance-enhancement (psychedelic orientation). Consistent with their objectives and positive findings, clinical studies have generally (a) optimized the context of the drug experience and (b) been particularly attentive to individual differences in personality and set.

A number of studies have demonstrated that personality differences are as important as preparation and setting in determining response to LSD. n a study of immediate and long-term effects of the psychedelic experience, Mogar and Savage (1964) found that post-LSD changes were related to personality styles and modal defense patterns. The results indicated that subjects with a well-defined but flexible self-structure responded most favorably to the drug, while those with either under-developed or overly-rigid ego defenses responded less favorably. Similar differential findings have been obtained recently in work with sensory deprivation and hypnosis. For example, both neuroticism and "field-dependence" correlate significantly with disturbing, stressful reactions to sensory deprivation (Zuckerman & Cohen, 1964). Other isolation studies have found positive relationships between "field- independence" and performance-enhancement (Brownfield, 1964), and between "self-actualizing maturity" and enjoyment of sensory deprivation (Blazer, 1963). Particularly relevant to the psychedelics is the finding that positive visual imagery during isolation correlates highly with (a) intellectual flexibility, breadth, and richness, (b) acceptance of one's passive, feminine side, and (c) freedom from emotional disturbance and constriction (Holt & Goldberger, 1961).

Comparable results in research on individual differences in hypnotic susceptibility have seriously undermined long-standing interpretations. Specifically, a host of studies recently found that hypnotic susceptibility was negatively correlated with neuroticism and placebo-responsiveness, and positively correlated with emotional stability (Bentler, et al., 1963; Lang & Lazovik, 1962). Although generally unrelated to specific personality attributes in normal subjects, independent work by Shor (1962) and As (1963) indicate a consistently high relationship between hypnotizability and the freqeuncy of *naturally occurring* altered states, particularly ecstatic and peak experiences. The range of personal history experiences inventoried in these studies were characterized by constructive use of regression, tolerance for logical paradoxes, willingness to relinquish ego control, and the ability to suspend disbelief or adopt an "as if" attitude. It is worth noting that these correlates of hypnotic susceptibility are also associated with propitious psychedelic states, certain aspects of creativity, and self-actualization.*

Current findings and theorizing in the various areas considered here can be summarized briefly. Whether self-induced, stress-induced, or drug-induced, altered states of consciousness will be welcomed and valuable rather than feared and harmful to the degree that the sociopsychological demands of such experiences are congenial to the "kinetic" needs and values of a given individual. Based on an analysis of imagery in Rorschach responses, Holt and Havel (1960, p. 311) reach a similar conclusion:

*The extensive research by Theodore R. Sarbin and his co-workers indicates that the same "as-if" dimension is central to both acting and hypnosis. The as-if attitude prominent in hypnotic states is viewed as analogous to the "creative-if" proposed by Stanislavsky as the very essence of acting talent (Sarbin & Lim, 1963).

We find primary process thinking in conscious subjects either out of strength r out of weakness. In the former case, it is more likely to appear in a playful r esthetic frame of reference, accompanied by pleasant affect. If, on the other and, primary thinking breaks through the usual defenses uninvited and unwanted, he subject may feel anxious or threatened and is likely to act defensively.

This view is consistent with recent developments in personality theory, articularly the current emphasis on latent creative potential and self-ctualizing tendencies. Representative of this trend, the opposing dualisms n psychoanalytic theory have undergone major revision so as to include egression in the service of the ego and creative fusions of primary and econdary process thinking (Hilgard, 1962). In a similar vein, Maddi (1963,). 193) refers to the id as "the breeding ground of love and worship, as well s of the novel imaginations which are eventually applauded, instituted, and herished by society." Stated simply, recent theoretical innovations ecognize that greater access to unconscious resources is a cardinal feature f psychedelic, creative, and other novel perceptual experiences, as well s psychosis. And that in contrast to hallucinatory states, creative or evelatory experiences involve a *temporary* and *voluntary* breaking up of erceptual constancies, permitting one "to shake free from dead literalism, o re-combine the old familiar elements into new, imaginative, amusing, or eautiful patterns" (Holt & Havel, p. 304).

PSYCHEDELIC EXPERIENCES AND CONTEMPORARY PSYCHOTHERAPY

Consistent with the scene in experimental psychology, a similar trend way from viewing psychedelic phenomena as undesirable or pathological s also apparent in clinical psychology and psychiatry. A growing ecognition of the potential value of psychedelic experiences is especially iscernible in contemporary psychotherapy. Recent theorizing in psycho-herapy reveals an increasing awareness of the restraints imposed by onventional modes of thought and perception. As suggested earlier, urrent developments in psychoanalytic theory correct the previous over-mphasis on maintaining impulse-control and a sharp distinction between elf and non-self. Instead, present formulations recognize the relative latness of consensual reality as well as the creative potential of novel houghts and impulses. Representative of this trend, the conditions of nental health proposed by Heinz Hartman (1958) include the ability to 'deautomatize" stereotyped perceptions and the ability to maintain luid subject-object boundaries. It is noteworthy that similar attributes ave been found to characterize highly self-actualized persons. More ignificantly, a number of studies have found that novel states of awareness

including loss of distinction between self and non-self, transcendenta
or peak experiences, and oceanic feeling states are fairly common in th
normal college population (As, 1962; Shor, 1960). Furthermore, ther
has been a greater willingness in recent years to acknowledge and repor
such experiences without apology or embarrassment.

These conceptual revisions and empirical findings also call attentio
to the well-documented shortcomings of orthodox therapies and th
critical need for more effective techniques. In a recent critique of th
status of psychotherapy, Colby (1964) concludes that our current para
digms have demonstrably failed and urges a major transition from ordinar
to extraordinary innovation. Certainly many therapists readily acknow
ledge what Colby calls an impending crisis. However, Astin (1961) note
that "the principle of functional autonomy will permit psychotherap
to survive long after it has outlived its usefulness." A similar view is ex
pressed by Korn (1964, p. 38) after examining previous reactions to nev
methods of treating psychopathology.

It is notorious that virtually no nostrum has ever been abandoned merely becaus
it failed to work. The old method had always to be overthrown by the new—an
it is also notorious that the practitioners of the traditional way will attempt t
prevent even the first trial of the method on the strange grounds that it has neve
been tried and proven—a criterion not applied in their own case.

Despite the reluctance to abandon the old and embrace the new, disil
lusionment with traditional techniques finds expression in the curren
upsurge of interest among therapists of *all* persuasions in Zen Buddhisn
(Maupin, 1962), existentialism (Lyons, 1961), and transcendental or peak
experiences (Maslow, 1962). Also indicative of present developments i
the host of studies establishing personal and cultural belief systems as key
variables in psychotherapy. The representative work of Hollingshead anc
Redlich (1958) demonstrated a significant relationship between social class
incidence and type of mental illness, and the form of treatment received
The relationships found were remarkably consistent with middle-clas
American values. Numerous studies have indicated that improvement i
therapy involves a basic change in the patient's core belief system, tha
therapists' values influence both the process and outcome of therapy, anc
that in "successful" outcomes, the patient's value orientation change
in the direction of the therapist's (see, e.g., London, 1964; Schofield, 1964)

These trends are relevant to what is perhaps the major issue in psychotherapy today, namely, the search for positive criteria of mental health o
personal growth which are explicitly based on humanistic values. It is now
generally recognized that psychological health or self-fulfillment involve
more than the absence of illness or emotional disturbance. These develop-

nents in mental health concepts have paralleled the recent discovery that most recipients of psychotherapy are *not* suffering from the traditional forms of neurosis and character disorder. While certainly self-dissatisfied and unfulfilled, the person seeking therapy today is generally not unproductive, ineffective, or crippled with neurotic symptoms. Many writers have described the typical therapy patient as one who is relatively free of physical complaints, neurotic anxiety and depression, failures of achievement, and interpersonal conflicts (Strupp, 1963). In short, the hallmarks of emotional disorder are conspicuously absent. Rather, the central struggle for an increasing number of successful and relatively well-adjusted people seems to be a "a loss of meaning in life, an absence of purpose, or a failure of faith" (Schofield, 1964). Modern discontent tends to take the form of alienation. In William Barrett's terms, alienation from God, from nature, from the human community, and ultimately, alienation from self (1958). While recognizing that the person with problems in personal identity and life outlook deserves help, some investigators have concluded that the psychotherapist is ill-equipped for such a *priestly* task (Wheelis, 1958). This belief is somewhat substantiated by the disappointment which many patients of this type experience in psychotherapy. Yet a dearth of alternative resources seem open to the person in this predicament.

In the light then of what seems to be an incompatibility between psychotherapy, as traditionally conceived, on the one hand, and the nature of modern discontent, on the other, it is certainly less than a coincidence that many people who fit this description express an interest in the psychedelic experience and find their way to LSD. It should perhaps be emphasized that the only sentiment these people share with the stereotyped beatnik is a sense of alienation from traditional values.

The attitudes and reactions to LSD, both positive and negative, become more understandable when viewed against this background of present-day trends in psychology and psychiatry. Within this broader context, it is not surprising that the major application of LSD today is to *treat* mental illness rather than *produce* it. Beyond this shift in emphasis, the use of LSD for therapeutic purposes clearly reflects the ambivalence among therapists toward the ever-growing number of meaning- and identity-seekers who request their services. The research and clinical literature concerning LSD as a therapeutic agent reveals two major view points which seem representative of this ambivalence. These two orientations are associated with greatly dissimilar methods of administration. One emphasizes the use of LSD periodically and in small doses as an adjunct to traditional techniques of psychotherapy (Crockett et al., 1963). The other major approach employs LSD in a single, large dose, producing an intense and prolonged psychedelic experience. Applied in this manner, LSD serves as a catalyst for inducing rapid and profound changes in the subject's value-belief system and in his self-image (Sherwood et al., 1962). While recognizing the therapeutic benefits of LSD, this latter technique places greater emphasis on its more unique potentialities and value, namely, as a means of facilitating personal growth and self-actualization. Rather than freedom from emotional symptoms, the primary objective of the psychedelic experience becomes a major reorganization of one's beliefs and life outlook. In short, the first method is essentially illness-oriented, the second, health or growth-oriented.

When employed as an adjunct to psychotherapy, most investigators have associated the beneficial effects of LSD with reduced defensiveness, the reliving of early childhood experiences, increased access to unconscious material, and greater emotional expression. In contrast, when used as a primary vehicle for rapid personality change, emphasis is usually placed on the transcendental quality of the experience, the resynthesis of basic values and beliefs, and major changes in the relationship between self and environment.

With regard to effectiveness, both orientations have reported impressive results. Since over three-hundred studies have been reported, only the most salient and consistent findings will be summarized.* Despite great diversity in the conduct of these studies, high improvement rates have been almost uniformly reported, with both adults and children, and in group as well as individual psychotherapy. Used either as an adjunct or as a primary treatment method, LSD has been found to facilitate improvement in patients covering the complete spectrum of neurotic, psychosomatic, and character disorders. Particularly noteworthy are the positive results obtained with cases highly resistant to conventional forms of therapy. High remission rates among alcoholics, for example, have frequently been reported following a single, large dose LSD session. Based on their findings with over one thousand alcoholics, Hoffer and his co-workers concluded that LSD was twice as effective as any other treatment program (1965). Other chronic conditions carrying a poor prognosis which have responded favorably to psychedelic therapy include sexual deviations, criminal psychopathy, autism in children, and adolescent behavior disorders.

Since most reports have been based on clinical judgments of unknown reliability, it is worth noting that comparable results have been obtained by investigators in many other countries. Furthermore, Freudian therapists, Jungians, behaviorists, existentialists, and a variety of eclectic therapists have reported positive findings with LSD. It seems safe to conclude from the

*For more detailed and referenced critiques of the extensive applications of LSD as a therapeutic agent, see the reviews compiled by Hoffer (1965), Mogar (1965), and Unger (1964).

breadth and consistency of the clinical evidence that LSD can produce far-reaching beneficial effects in some people, under some conditions. However, controlled studies of the process variables involved have yet to be conducted. Specifically, in what particular ways do various kinds of people respond to LSD, both during the experience and afterward? What are the optimal conditions of preparation, administration, and follow-up for given objectives, and for given subjects? How can we account for the various kinds and extent of change which follow an LSD experience? In short, despite the mass of accumulated data on the *outcome* of psychedelic therapy, relationships among *process* variables remain obscure.

Primarily because of the controversy surrounding these chemical agents (which interestingly is confined to the United States), controlled research aimed at maximizing their safety, their effectiveness, and their human value has barely begun. In addition to questions concerning the possible uses of LSD as a therapeutic or educative device, its potential value as a basic research tool for investigating higher mental processes has also been minimally explored. Although clinical evidence and testimonial reports indicate that LSD promises to be a valuable tool for both the study and enhancement of cognitive and perceptual functioning, such claims have been neither supported nor refuted by means of controlled studies. Other hypotheses readily testable include the suggested similarities noted earlier between psychedelic, hypnotic, and dream states, the inspirational phase of creativity, as well as sensory and dream deprivation experiences.

PSYCHEDELIC, NADIR, AND PEAK EXPERIENCES

The nature, extent, and duration of effects both during and subsequent to the LSD-induced state has been a major focus of study in the psychedelic research program conducted at the International Foundation for Advanced Study, Menlo Park, California. Over a three-year period, extensive assessments were obtained on almost four-hundred subjects before, during, and at various points following a psychedelic experience. Each subject underwent a single, large dose LSD session conducted in a comfortable, aesthetically pleasing setting. Although trained staff members were present throughout the session day, primarily for emotional support and human contact, no attempt was made to direct or interpret the experience. Rather, the subject was urged to explore himself and his universe without external guidance or intrusion. Prior to the LSD experience, each subject was given a physical and psychiatric examination followed by a series of preparatory interviews. These interviews were designed to help the individual examine or re-examine his reasons for taking LSD, to clarify whatever problems or questions he wished to explore, and to become accustomed extensive follow-up evaluations were made covering a minimum of six months.

The design of this research program was based on the assumption that significant changes would occur along three major dimensions; values and beliefs, personality, and actual behavior in major life areas. More specifically, it was hypothesized that a profound psychedelic experience tends to be followed by a major reorientation of one's value system and life outlook. It was further hypothesized that this change in basic beliefs would in terms be followed by *slower* alterations in personality as well as changes in modal behavior patterns.

The findings so far provide considerable support for the general hypothesis concerning parallel changes in values, personality, and behavior (Mogar and Savage, 1964; Savage et al., 1965a; Savage et al., 1965b). Three days following the LSD session, a consistent and reliable increase was found in the extent to which an individual agrees with test items reflecting a deep sense of meaning and purpose in life, open-mindedness, greater aesthetic sensitivity, and sense of unity or oneness with nature and humanity. Decreases were found on values pertaining to material possessions, social status, and dogmatism. Also significant was the finding that changes in personal beliefs either remained constant or became still more prominent at later follow-ups. These were consistent results cutting across such factors as age, sex, religious orientation, or personality type. Thus, it seems safe to conclude that a rapid and extensive change in values does tend to occur in most subjects, and importantly, is maintained over time.

The additional hypothesis that slower modifications in personality and behavior would occur has also received considerable support. For example, the data show that if a person values human brotherhood more after his psychedelic experience, his personality and behavior reflect this new conviction. He tends to be less distrustful and guarded with others, warmer and more spontaneous in expressing emotion, and less prone to feelings of personal inadequacy. With regard to modal behavior patterns, parallel changes tend to occur in such areas as marital relations and work effectiveness (Savage et al., 1965a).

Although the overall results indicate that almost all subjects derived some degree of benefit along the lines hypothesized, it is important to emphasize that the nature, extent, and the stability of changes varied considerable. Specific sources or correlates of this variability included pre-LSD personality structure, the type of presenting problem, and variations in the psychedelic experience itself. With regard to pre-LSD individual differences subgroups were objectively defined according to (a) personality structure (anxiety neurotics, borderline psychotics, nonconforming normals, manic-impulsives, and normal depressives), and (b) major defense pattern (hystericil, intellectual-compulsive). Despite the brevity of the LSD program, all subgroups displayed positive personality changes at two and six months following the psychedelic experience. The nature and extent of improvement compared most favorable with longer-term orthodox therapies (Mogar & Savage, 1964).

Although each subgroup maintained significant improvement, subjects varied considerably in their capacity to translate profound insights into attitudes, feelings, and conduct. Individual differences were particularly apparent at six months since by this time a leveling off had generally occurred, that is, most subjects had in large part come to terms with their rapidly altered self-world image. For six months habitual patterns of response to situations had been scrutinized and repeatedly challenged. Dissonance between thought, feeling, and action had generally been reconciled and a higher level of integration achieved. At six months some individuals maintained and consolidated the gains demonstrated at two months (Nonconforming Normals, Manic-Impulsives, Normal Depressives). Others displayed further personal growth which was still in progress (Anxiety Neurotics, Intellectual-Compulsives). Still others showed a tendency to regress from the level of improvement indicated at two months (Borderline Psychotics, Hysterics). In these subjects, either the pull of well-entrenched maladaptive defenses and/or an uncongenial life environment undermined to some extent the favorable personality alterations demonstrated earlier.

With regard to the nature of changes characterizing different personality types, shifts tended to occur consistent with the symptoms and defense pattern of a given group. Anxiety neurotics were less anxious, compulsive, and withdrawn while close relationships were more gratifying. In contrast, impulsive, hyperactive subjects led a more orderly, less hectic existence and displayed greater impulse control.

The "illness-oriented" nature of these findings reflects the fact that two-thirds of the total sample resembled the typical case load of an out-patient psychiatric clinic. The remaining one-third did not present complaints of a psychiatric nature and revealed minimal emotional disturbance according to both diagnostic evaluation and psychological test data. Instead, the interest expressed by these subjects seemed to be "growth-motivated" rather than "deficiency-motivated." Some were dimly aware of potentialities which they hoped to activate and develop more fully. Others expressed a feeling of emptiness and lack of meaningful purpose while adequately meeting the exigencies of life. Still others sought a deeper understanding or more satisfying resolutions to problems of an existential nature.

As a result of their stable life circumstances and relative freedom from neurotic disturbance, these subjects were more likely to grapple with ultimate problems during the LSD experience. In addition to self-identity and personal worth, questions of love, death, creation and rebirth, and the resolution of life paradoxes received frequent attention. Unlike the neurotic group, childhood memories, intrapsychic conflicts, and specific inter-personal relations were explored minimally. Accounts of the experience written shortly afterward revealed that healthier subjects were less likely to view the psychedelic state as fantastic or totally dissimilar from previous experience. These personal reports together with clinical evaluations and ratings also indicated that this group benefited considerably from the psychedelic experience along the lines of self-actualization, richer creative experience, and enhancement of specific aptitudes and talents. At the present time, these tentative findings are being investigated more objectively with measures appropriate for a normal sample. Thus it will be possible to compare individuals, differing in personality and presenting problems, with regard to health-growth dimensions as well as decreases in pathology.

Since most subjects in this series of studies were college trained and psychologically sophisticated, it is noteworthy that the frequency of occurrence of transcendental-like experiences is apparently as great in "naive" prisoners and alcoholics (Unger, 1964). Such communalities are not surprising in view of the key role placed by universal and personal symbolism in psychedelic experiences and the relatively weak role of the conscious self (including verbal facility, accumulated knowledge, and intelligence). What seems to be affected by subject-differences is the *content* of the experience, rather than its *form*, *intensity*, or *profundity*.

Differences in the thematic content of the experience were found among subjects with diverse cultural backgrounds. For example, wide individual differences were demonstrated with respect to content in the frequent experience of unity. However, the fact that the majority of subjects experienced a sense of unity or oneness seems far more significant than whether the unity was felt with self, nature, the universe, God, or some combination of these. This is merely another way of saying that to the degree an individual can verbalize the experience, he will draw on his own particular semantic framework and belief system. One can only speculate on the dis-crepancy between this communicated account of the experience and the experience itself.

These findings suggest that the profundity or intensity of a psychedelic experience is more crucially related to subsequent change than thematic content. More specifically, the hypothesis currently being tested is that subsequent transformations in values, personality, and conduct are a function of the experience's intensity, either positive or negative—or both. In other words, painful experiences can be as personally revealing and permanently beneficial as experiences of great joy and beauty.

The hypothesis that a profound and intense psychedelic experience, regardless of its emotional valence, can serve as a catalyst for rapid personal growth is consistent with current interpretations of both *nadir* and *peak* experiences. Concerning nadir experiences, Erikson's brilliant analysis of the post-adolescent identity crisis (1959) has recently been extended to include periodic "crisis of maturation" (Kahn, 1963), naturally occurring "desolation experiences" (Laski, 1961), and the therapeutic value of "existential crises" (Bugental, 1965). In each case, these writers emphasize that although negative and painful, a personal crisis is: (a) not pathological, (b) a critical choice point in life necessitating a "leap of faith," (c) an essential condition of growth and psychological change, and (d) often a catalyst for an emerging inner conviction or new awareness. The potential value of nadir experiences has been well-stated by Forer (1963, p. 280): "Crisis as a psychological experience is a part of any creative effort, scientific, artistic, therapeutic, or inter-personal."

With regard to positive revelatory experiences, Maslow recently developed the thesis that experiences referred to as religious, mystical, or transcendental actually denote special cases of the more generic "core-religious" or peak experience, described as the hallmark of highly self-actualized people (Maslow, 1964). Similarly, the extensive research on creativity by MacKinnon and his associates indicates that the truly creative person is distinguished from the noncreative individual by his capacity for "transliminal experience" (MacKinnon, 1964). Following Harold Rugg's study of creative imagination, the transliminal experience is characterized by an illuminating flash of insight occurring at a critical threshold of the conscious-unconscious continuum. MacKinnon's description of the transliminal experience bears a striking resemblance to the more inclusive peak experience. Interestingly, Maslow (1964) suggests that psychedelic drugs may offer a means of producing a controlled peak experience under observation, particularly in "non-peakers."

Although tentative at this point, these lines of investigation seem highly significant and certainly suggestive of future directions in LSD research. And if the historical perspective described earlier is relatively accurate, the exploration of ways of expanding human consciousness will soon occupy a prominent position in the mainstream of contemporary psychology. Should this prediction materialize, we can look forward to a far more extensive application of these powerful agents as a means of facilitating social as well as individual potentialities. For the present, research with the psychedelics will continue to seek those conditions which maximize their safety, their effectiveness, and their human value.

27

IMPLICATIONS OF LSD AND EXPERIMENTAL MYSTICISM

WALTER N. PAHNKE and WILLIAM A. RICHARDS

Mirrored in the sensationalistic array of recent magazine and newspaper articles focusing upon the past, present, and future uses of drugs like LSD is a blurred spectrum of attitudes ranging from an indignant desire to destroy a terrifying plague of drug-induced psychoses to a naive belief that the keys to Utopia have finally been placed into the hands of man. In the light of this complex controversy, the need soberly to consider the potential dangers and values inherent in this field of research from theological, psychiatric, and societal perspectives has become crucial. The special class of drugs in question, including lysergic acid diethylamide (LSD), psilocybin, and mescaline, to name the major examples, has been given many names, from psychotomimetic to mysticicomimetic, but the two terms that are gaining acceptance are *psycholytic* (mind-releasing) in Europe and *psychedelic* (mind-opening) in the United States. These drugs are not narcotics, sedatives, or energizers, but have the unique effect on the human psyche of bringing into awareness forms of consciousness that are usually hidden or unconscious.

At the outset, it must be stated that since the statistics of the first major attempts at controlled experimentation in this field are still being compiled, none of the proposed uses of these drugs can at present be supported by conclusive empirical data. The high hopes that constructive uses of these drugs may be validated empirically, however, are reflected in the formation

Reprinted by permission from *J. Religion & Health*, Vol. 5, 1966, pp. 175–208.

of the International Association for Psychodelytic Therapy; in international conferences on the use of LSD in psychotherapy, held in New York City in 1959 (Abramson, 1960), in London in 1961 (Crochet, Sandison, & Walk, 1963), and on Long Island in 1965 (Abramson, 1967); and in the two days devoted to the psychedelics in March, 1966, by the *Collegium Internationale Neuro-psychopharmacologicum* in Washington. In the midst of this experimental ferment, however, we are confronted by the very real possibility that the known and unknown uses of these drugs that could prove to be legitimate and beneficial for individual persons and society may be suppressed until some future century when investigation will be permitted to proceed unhampered by popular hysteria and over-restrictive legislation. In the United States, interested and capable scientists are hesitating to investigate this field because of the abundance of unfavorable publicity and the threat of condemnation by identification with irresponsible researchers. Even among those who are willing to risk their reputations, some are finding it difficult to obtain the governmental approval now prerequisite for the legal acquisition of these drugs for research purposes. Paradoxically, a significant danger confronting our society may lie in losing out on the values that the responsible use of these drugs may offer. Hypnosis, for example, is only beginning to recover from the sensationalistic publicity and irrational reactions that surrounded Mesmer and subsequently suppressed its legitimate use for almost a century.

The first section of this article attempts to define and illustrate a specific form of psychedelic experience that is frequently reported when relatively high dosage is administered to normal subjects or selected mental patients in supportive settings. For want of a better term, we have called this form of experience *mystical consciousness*. A second section then briefly surveys other forms of altered consciousness associated with the ingestion of these drugs, illustrating how they differ from mystical consciousness. A third section presents and discusses the research findings that have suggested the similarity, if not the identity, between the psychedelic experience of mystical consciousness and spontaneously occurring experiences recorded in the literature of mysticism. A final section considers some of the theological, psychiatric, and societal implications arising out of such research, stressing promise for the future as well as the very definite hazards of irresponsible experimentation.

THE PSYCHEDELIC EXPERIENCE OF MYSTICAL CONSCIOUSNESS

The form of psychedelic experience here called *mystical consciousness* can best be described as a dimension of experience that, when expressed on paper by an experimental subject and subsequently content-analyzed, corresponds to nine interrelated categories, each of which is described below. These categories were derived by Pahnke (1963) from a historical survey of the literature of spontaneous mysticism, including the commentaries of scholars such as William James (1902) and W.T. Stace (1960). As Stace has emphasized, such categories attempt to describe the core of a universal psychological experience, free from culturally determined philosophical or theological interpretations. Some of the categories described below are illustrated by excerpts from phenomenological descriptions of psychedelic experiences. The ontological status of such descriptions may, of course, be debated. Our concern here is simply to present examples of the psychological phenomena being reported.

1. Unity

Experience of an undifferentiated unity, we suggest, is the hallmark of mystical consciousness. Such unity may be either *internal* or *external*, depending upon whether the subject-object dichotomy transcended is between the usual self and an "inner world" *within* the experiencer, or whether it is between the usual self and the external world of sense impressions *outside* the experiencer. Both forms of unity are known to occur within the same person, even in the same psychedelic session. Although each form of unity occurs in a different manner, the states of consciousness ultimately experienced may be identical.

Internal unity reportedly occurs in the following manner: Awareness of all normal sense impressions (visual, auditory, cutaneous, olfactory, gustatory, and kinesthetic) cases, and the empirical ego (i.e., the usual sense of individuality) seems to die or fade away while pure consciousness of what is being experienced paradoxically remains and seems to expand as a vast inner world is encountered. A sense of movement is experienced within this inner world through numerous so-called "dimensions of being" towards a goal that is felt to have the status of ultimate reality. Internal unity occurs when consciousness merges with this "ground of being," beyond all empirical distinctions. Although awareness of one's empirical ego has ceased, one does not become unconscious.

I found myself grunting in agreement or mumbling, "Of course it has always been this way" over and over again as the panorama of my life seemed to be swept up by this unifying and eternal principle... I seemed to relinquish my life in "layers:" the more I let go, the greater sense of oneness I received. As I approached what I firmly believed to be the point of death, I experienced an ever greater sense of an eternal dimension to life.

In contrast, external unity generally seems to occur as follows: Awareness of one or more particular sense impressions grows in intensity until suddenly the object of perception and the empirical ego simultaneously seem to cease to exist as separate entities, while consciousness seems to transcend subject and object and become impregnated by a profound sense of unity, accompanied by the insight that ultimately "all is One." The subject-object dichotomy transcended may be between the empirical ego and (1) an animate visual object such as another person or a rose; (2) an inanimate visual object such as the leg of a table (Huxley, 1963) or even a grain of sand; or (3) an auditory object such as the music of a symphony. Theoretically, objects of other sensory modalities could stand in polar relation to the empirical ego and be incorporated into experiences of external unity as well.

When looking at the rose as an object, it seemed to "come alive" before my eyes. Its petals seemed to "breathe" as, slowly and gracefully, then unfolded, seeming to express the ultimate in beauty. Fascinated, I watched these movements of "cosmic gentleness" until, suddenly, I *knew* the rose; that is to say, transcending the dichotomy of subject and object, I somehow became One with the rose, no longer existing as an ego passively viewing an object in its environment. Although in the objectivity of my critical mind, I knew there were no physical changes in the flower, subjectively I seemed to see it in a totally new perspective, a perspective which elicited tears and deep feelings of reverence. . . . Supporting the ancient monistic school of thought, I expressed the philosophical insight that, "We are all the same thing." . . . Another time I commented that, "There is more to beauty than we know."

2. Objectivity and Reality

Intrinsic to this second category are two interrelated elements: (1) insightful knowledge or illumination about being or existence in general that is felt at an intuitive, nonrational level and gained by direct experience, and (2) the authoritativeness or the certainty for the experiences that such knowledge is truly or ultimately real, in contrast to the feeling that the experience is a subjective delusion. These two elements are connected because the knowledge through participation in ultimate reality (in the sense of being able to *know* and *see* what is *real*), carries its own sense of certainty. It is to this facet of mystical consciousness that William James assigned the term "noetic quality," writing: "Although so similar to states of feeling, mystical states seem to those who experience them to be also states of knowledge. They are states of insight into depths of truth unplumbed by the discursive intellect" (James, 1902, p. 371). Such insight is intuitively felt to be of a more fundamental form of reality than either the phenomena of everyday consciousness or the most vivid of dreams or hallucinations.

I was experiencing directly the metaphysical theory known as emanationism in which, beginning with the clear, unbroken and infinite light of God, the light then breaks into forms and lessens in intensity as it passes through descending degrees of reality... Bergson's concept of the brain as a reducing valve I now saw to be precisely true.... The emanation theory, and especially the elaborately worked out layers of Hindu and Buddhist cosmology and psychology had heretofore been concepts and inferences. Now they were objects of the most direct and immediate perception. I could see exactly how these theories would have come into being if their progenitors had had this experience. But beyond accounting for their origin, my experience testified to their absolute truth.

Experience of the contents of this category may be expressed in many ways, among which are assertions of having known the origin and goal of history, of having found the answer to the ancient query, "What am I?", of having intuited the harmonious structure of the universe, of having experienced the primacy of love and the brotherhood of man, or of having realized the reality of life that transcends temporal death.

3. Transcendence of Space and Time

This category refers on one hand to the loss of a person's usual orientation as to where he is during the experience in terms of the usual three-dimensional perception of his environment, and on the other hand, to a radical change in perspective in which he suddenly feels as though he is outside of time, in eternity or infinity, beyond both past and future. In this state of consciousness, space and time are generally meaningless concepts, although one may feel that one can look back upon the totality of history from this transcendent perspective.

From the perspective of the Timeless, I could see my life in retrospect and prospect. It was as if it had all been lived through before, as if we had all been here before, and would be here again. There was a strong pre-ordained feeling about this. I began to see a bit into the future. I understood that I should go back and try to work through some unresolved problems in my relationships with others, and that there would be considerable suffering ahead. My own death was also dimly sensed and strangely accepted. I saw the unbroken *continuity* of my past with my future, which was not contradicted by the feeling that this present experience would remain with me and bring about deep changes. The fact that all was pre-ordained did not contradict living in freedom, fighting for truth and against evil...

4. Sense of Sacredness

Sacredness is here defined as a nonrational, intuitive, hushed, palpitant response in the presence of inspiring realities. It is that which a person feels to be of special value and capable of being profaned. Inherent in the nondifferentiated unity of mystical consciousness is a profound sense of holiness and sacredness that is felt to be at a more basic level than any religious or philosophical concepts held by the experiencer. Furthermore, an acute awareness of unfinitude is reported, as though one had stood before the Infinite in profound humility, overwhelmed by feelings of awe and reverence. This aspect of mystical consciousness is well reflected in Rudolf Otto's term, the *mysterium tremendum* (Otto, 1958, pp. 12–40).

The most impressive and intense part of this experience was the *white light* of absolute purity and cleanness. It was like a glowing and sparkling flame of incandescent whiteness and beauty, but not really a flame—more like a gleaming white-hot ingot, yet much bigger and vaster than a mere ingot. The associated feelings were those of *absolute awe, reverence*, and *sacredness*. Just before this experience I had the feeling of going deep within myself to the self stripped bare of all pretense and falseness. It was the point where a man could stand firm with absolute integrity—something more important than mere physical life. The white light experience was of *supreme importance*—absolutely self-validating and something worth staking your life on and putting your trust in. The white light itself was so penetrating and intense that it was not possible to look directly at it. It was not in the room with me, but we were both somewhere else—and my body was left far behind.

5. Deeply-Felt Positive Mood

This category focuses upon the feelings of joy, love, blessedness, and peace inherent in mystical consciousness. Joy may be exuberant or quiet. Love may vary in intensity from feelings of tenderness, through deeply felt nonsensual feelings of ultimate concern for other persons, to a state resembling prolonged intense sexual orgasm. The latter degree of intensity is generally dissociated from any stimulation or excitation of the sexual organs, being "spiritual" rather than "erotic" in nature. Peace is "the peace which passes understanding" and entails not only deep relaxation, but a conviction that ultimately there is no ground for anxiety.

The feelings I experienced could best be described as cosmic tenderness, infinite love, penetrating peace, eternal blessing and unconditional acceptance on one hand, and on the other, as unspeakable awe, overflowing joy, primeval humility, inexpressible gratitude and boundless devotion. Yet all of these words are hopelessly inadequate and can do little more than meekly point towards the genuine inexpressible feelings actually experienced.

6. Paradoxicality

This category reflects the manner in which significant aspects of mystical consciousness are felt by the experiencer to be true in spite of the fact that they violate the laws of Aristotelian logic. For example, the subject claims to have died or ceased to exist, yet obviously continues to exist and even writes about his experiences. He may claim to have experienced an empty unity that at the same time contains all reality. He may write about non-being that is more than being. He may claim to have felt "out of the body" while he was still "in the body." He may envision a universal self that is both unqualitied and qualitied, both impersonal and personal, and both inactive and active.

There was awareness of undifferentiated unity, embracing the perfect identity of subject and object, of singleness and plurality, of the One and the Many. Thus I found myself (if indeed the words "I" and "myself" have any meaning in such a context) at once the audience, the actors and the play! Logically the One can give birth to the Many and the Many can merge into the One or be fundamentally but not identical with it; they cannot be *in all respects* one and many simultaneously. But now logic was transcended . . . I doubt if this statement can possibly be made to seem meaningful at the ordinary level of consciousness. No wonder the mystics of all faiths teach that understanding comes only when logic and intellect are transcended! . . . Logic also boggles at trying to explain how I could at once *perceive* and yet *be* those colours and those forms, how the *seer*, the *seeing* and the *seen*, the *feeler*, the *feeling* and the *felt* could all be one; but, to me, all this was so clearly self-evident as to suggest the words "childishly simple" (Blofeld, 1966, p.29).

7. Alleged Ineffability

When a subject attempts to communicate mystical consciousness verbally to another person, he usually claims that the available linguistic symbols— if not the structure of language itself—are inadequate to contain or even accurately reflect such experience. Perhaps the reason such experience is felt to be beyond words is to be found in a frustration with language, which, in turn, arises out of the paradoxical nature of the essential phenomena and the incomparable uniqueness of the experience itself. One subject likened himself to a cave-man who was momentarily transported into the bustling center of Manhattan and then returned to his cave, suggesting that, when subsequently interrogated by his wife, such a cave-man could not claim that his experience was ineffable in spite of the fact that it seemed intrinsically logical at the time, as though it could be discussed with words by some future generation.

To seek to condense any of my experiences into words is to distort them, rendering them finite and impure . . . What is a "transcendent dimension of being?" Such words on paper are little more than metaphysical poetry. Somehow I feel I could better communicate my experience by composing a symphony or by molding a twisted piece of contemporary sculpture, had I the talents required for either form of artistic expression. In no sense have I an urge to formulate philosophical or theological dogmas about my experience. Only my silence can retain its purity and genuineness.

8. Transiency

This category refers to the temporary duration of mystical consciousness in contrast to the relative permanence of the level of usual experience. The special and unusual forms of consciousness discussed above appear, remain for anywhere from a matter of seconds to a few hours and then disappear, returning the experiencer to his usual state of everyday consciousness. The characteristic of transiency indicates that the mystical state of consciousness is not sustained indefinitely and marks one of the important differences between it and psychosis.

9. Positive Changes in Attitude and/or Behavior

Persons who have experienced the contents of the eight categories discussed above are also known to report concomitant changes in attitudes (1) toward themselves, (2) toward others, (3) toward life, and (4) toward mystical consciousness itself. Increased personality integration is reported, including a renewed sense of personal worth coupled with a relaxation of habitual mechanisms of ego defense. It is as though Paul Tillich's assertion that "It is the power of being-itself that accepts and gives the courage to be" (Tillich, 1952, p. 185) has been immediately experienced as true, and one thus is able to "accept oneself as accepted in spite of being unacceptable" (Tillich, 1952, p. 164). One feels as though personal problems can now be so confronted that they may finally be reduced or eliminated. One's faith in one's own potential for creative achievement tends to be increased, at least at the subjective level. In one's relationships with other persons, greater sensitivity, increased tolerance, and more real compassion are reported. Theologically trained persons frequently feel that they have acquired new and profound insights into the meaning Martin Buber sought to convey in his term "the I-Thou relationship," finally knowing the meaning of genuinely meeting another person without the subtle masks that separate man from man. Changed or enlarged attitudes towards life are reported in the areas of deeper sensitivity to values that are felt to be eternal, increased sensitivity to an inner imperative that seeks expression through other-centered behavior, increased vocational commitment, loss of a fear of death coupled with an expanded awareness of the significance of historical existence, and an enriched appreciation for the whole of creation. As an expression of these attitudes, more time may be spent in meditation. The memory of mystical consciousness itself is regarded as deeply meaningful and similar experiences may be sought as a source of growth and strength.

Although attitudinal and behavioral changes such as these are subjectively reported by psychedelic subjects who have experienced the contents of the preceding eight categories, the duration and permanence of such changes and the extent to which they are manifested in everyday existence are topics in need of extensive research. Only after such research is completed can the degree of correspondence between the positive changes claimed by psychedelic subjects and the effects of spontaneous life-enhancing mystical experiences be determined.

NONMYSTICAL FORMS OF ALTERED CONSCIOUSNESS

We now turn our attention to other forms of drug-facilitated altered consciousness that cannot be classified as *mystical* as this term has been defined above. According to the standards here suggested, many experimental subjects who have only seen visionary imagery and felt powerful emotions may be understood to have had nonmystical experiences of an aesthetic, psychodynamic, psychotic or cognitive nature. In advancing his hypothesis that mystical consciousness is ultimately one and the same, irrespective of the culture, era, or childhood traumas associated with any given mystic, W. T. Stace (1960, pp. 50–51) emphasizes that, "On the essential point of distinguishing between visions and mystical experiences the Christian mystics and the Hindu mystics are in complete accord". In non-mystical forms of consciousness, the empirical ego generally exists as the subject viewing objects of a visionary nature, or pondering objects of a cognitive nature; only in mystical consciousness and some psychotic reactions is the subject-object dichotomy transcended and the empirical ego extinguished.

Aesthetic Phenomena.

One of the first effects noted by many persons after ingesting a psychedelic drug is a change in spatial perception. Distances suddenly seem to be different. A person sitting across the room may suddenly seem to be sitting only a few feet away. The ceiling may seem to bulge at the corners of the room and the walls may undulate as though they were breathing. It may actually seem possible to step inside a picture of a woodland scene on the wall and walk among the trees. Such distortions of perception are often quite amusing and may be temporary. To the person of artistic temperament,

THEN ⑨

they may be especially intriguing. Although such phenomena are usually seen as delightful illusions, occasionally reality-testing is impaired in a delusory manner.

As other changes in the nervous system occur, a person is likely to become increasingly sensitive to color and to form. Colors often grow richer and deeper, while the contours of objects in the room may stand out in sharp relief. The whole environment may seem to come into sharper focus, as though the person had just discarded a dirty, incorrectly ground pair of glasses for a clean, perfectly ground pair.

Also, near the beginning of an experience, one frequently sees geometric patterns of multi-colored abstract lines that are visionary in nature. Although such patterns are often more clearly visible when one's eyes are closed, they may be seen superimposed upon objects in the external world when one's eyes are open. These abstract patterns are generally three-dimensional and constantly change in a steady, rhythmic flow, resembling the view through a kaleidoscope.

Objects in the room or parts of such objects may be symmetrically incorporated into this visionary pattern. Thus, instead of being composed merely of abstract lines, it may contain any number of objects such as candles, flowers, human eyes, reels from a tape-recorder, etc. At this point an experience may be seen to have overtones of psychodynamic significance, although such overtones usually are not consciously recognized by the experiencer, unless he is trained in psychoanalysis. A symmetrical pattern of candles and rosebuds, for example, may be seen to have definite psychoanalytic significance. Even if those objects are present in the room, one may ask why those particular objects and not others were incorporated into the pattern. If faces of people not present in the room or foreign objects become involved, the experience may definitely be seen to be moving in a psychodynamic direction.

If music is being played, synesthesia often develops. The pattern thus seems to flow with the music, even changing color at appropriate places. If the music is slow and minor, the lines may move slowly and be darkly colored; if the music is fast and major, the lines may swoop almost violently and be brightly colored. When a new theme is introduced, a new pattern may emerge in the midst of the old pattern.

This level of experience is, of course, very shallow. If the experience progresses beyond this level, one may seem to *go through* the pattern towards mystical consciousness, experience more definite psychoanalytic imagery and feelings, or enter states of more profound aesthetic imagery.

In the latter case, common objects in the room may suddenly become transformed into works of considerable beauty and artistic value. Similarly, visions of objects not present may suddenly appear. At times, in a dreamlike state, one may enter one's visions and seem to be walking through gardens, art museums, medieval castles, futuristic cities, etc. Archetypal imagery may appear, and one thus finds oneself encountering mythological characters such as angels, demons, dragons, and Grecian gods. On the boundary of mystical consciousness, it is not uncommon for Christians to encounter an image intuitively identified as the Christ.

Again, such imagery may have significance for psychotherapy, but is not necessarily recognized as such. A beautiful golden column in the majestic corridor of a visionary castle, covered with mosaics of intricate design, may well be considered a glorified phallic symbol. Needless to say, such connotations do not distort the beauty of the imagery; rather the imagery may be understood to elevate the polarity of the masculine and the feminine into its rightful place in the nature of reality. The following quotation is illustrative of this general level of experience:

I lay on my stomach and closed my eyes and brilliantly colored geometrical patterns of fantastic beauty collided, exploded, raced by. Other things too: teeth and pearls and precious stones and lips and eyes. Outside of the window the branches of the tree were gigantic arms with transparent muscles, now threatening, now embracing. Glasses started rolling on the table, the bookcase was full of swimming books, the door bulged like a balloon, the carpet in the other room was full of thousands of little green snakes. The dial on the telephone was a huge pearl-studded wheel. The shapes and colors of objects got more and more intense, the outlines etched with luminous clarity and depth. Anything with a polished metal surface turned into gleaming gold or silver ... The faces of other people became clear and beautiful and open. At one point all faces were colored green.

Associated with such imagery, the experiencer may live through the whole spectrum of human feelings. He may experience a variety of intriguing somatic sensations, feeling as though his body is melting, falling apart, or exploding into minute fragments. On occasion sexual pleasure may be experienced; it is not uncommon for persons to giggle or laugh uproariously.

Although some aspects of aesthetic experience may be very beautiful and inspiring, they are hardly to be considered mystical. It is easy to understand why persons who frequently experience aesthetic phenomena may take psychedelic drugs for "kicks." The artist may enter this world in search of new inspiration and improved perception. As mystical consciousness is seldom entered without serious preparation and a quiet, reverent atmosphere, we may suggest that the experiences of most people at "LSD parties" are of an aesthetic nature. It may be of significance that many, if not most, of the persons who experience mystical consciousness show little interest in taking a psychedelic drug again for a period of at least several months, claiming that they have many profound experiences to ponder and assimilate.

Psychodynamic Phenomena.

Although many of the aesthetic phenomena discussed above may have definite psychodynamic significance, the significance is purely symbolic and must be interpreted for the experiencer, unless he happens to be alert to various forms of archetypal imagery and their meaning during the drug session. There are other forms of altered consciousness, however, in which the psychodynamic nature of the phenomena is obvious to the experiencer at the precise time that the experience occurs.

One of the clearest forms of such psychodynamic experience is actual regression to infancy or early childhood. Writing of his work, employing psychedelic drugs in psychotherapy, Spencer (1963, p. 37) states: "Not only did LSD enable unconscious memories to be recovered easily, but their being relived was extremely realistic to the patient, as they were frequently accompanied by changes in the body image, so that the patient felt he was of the physical size and age he had been when the traumatic experience occurred." This form of experience has been especially common in clinics where reasonably small doses of the drugs have been employed in the treatment of neurotic patients. The following two descriptions are typical of such experience:

I then fell much deeper into the experience and lay in a bassinet as a baby about a quarter-year old. I felt very comfortable. Then suddenly coldness broke out within me and all around me. (Fernandez-Cerdeno, 1964, p. 18)

I had a memory of tremendous sexual excitement. I felt that I was about six and that somebody had been "playing" with me sexually . . . I could remember being held down and the uncontrolled lustful look on my uncle's face absolutely vividly. It was as though it had happened yesterday. (Ling & Buckman, 1964)

Another type of experience that may be strongly therapeutic involves the unexpected confrontation of guilt. The following illustration is taken from the report of a person who had been seriously neglecting his wife and children:

I opened my eyes and there was a picture over the mantle . . . There seemed to be in front of this picture many veils hanging and I pushed each veil aside one by one, knowing that as I got the last veil aside I would finally see God . . . Finally the last veil was to be removed. I knew it was the last veil and tried to prepare myself for the great experience of seeing God. I raised my hand over my head and then leaned backwards to make myself more receptive in order to feel the full force of

God. And finally the last veil was pulled aside and there were my three children crying for their father . . . Before me was going all the selfish feelings—all the selfish attitudes that I had had throughout my entire married life.

In contrast to aesthetic experiences, even those consisting of visions that obviously portray psychoanalytic themes, these experiences generally involve abreaction, being marked by intense struggle and suffering. Feelings such as guilt, grief, or hostility may be experienced in great intensity. Such experiences may be useful in facilitating psychotherapy if a competent therapist is available both at the time these experiences occur and in the following weeks to help the patient integrate feelings and insights. Without competent psychiatric supervision, such experiences may, at best, remain frightening memories and, at worst, cause a person to decompensate under the stress.

Psychotic Phenomena.

Although some researchers would hold that all phenomena occurring in altered states of consciousness should be labelled "psychotic," here we reserve the term for experiences of paranoia, of panic, or of extreme disorientation and confusion. Paranoia, usually manifested in systematized delusions of reference, generally occurs when one attempts to control the experience instead of passively yielding to whatever develops. Similarly, panic seems to be associated with an attempt to escape from emerging experiences instead of accepting and confronting them. Because the crucial importance of this sense of unconditional trust was not realized until recently, much of the early work with psychedelic drugs was called "psycho-mimetic" (psychosis-mimicking). When subjects were given a psychedelic drug without knowing what to expect or how to respond, often being left alone in a dark room or threatened by unfamiliar researchers demanding cooperation in psychological testing, it is easy to understand why many experiences quickly became psychotic. If nonpsychotic experiences are desired, subjects must be prepared, must feel secure in a friendly environment, and above all must be willing and able to trust in a reality greater than themselves.

Besides paranoia and panic, the experience of feeling as though one is separated from the world by a thick, glass wall, being trapped in a silent, unreal room where no activity whatsoever is occurring has been reported. This form of experience may be associated with the presence of penicillamine in the body (Hoffer, 1965), and may result when one has recently taken penicillian. Further, one may become thoroughly disorientated and confused—symptoms that may well be labelled psychotic. Generally, one can vacillate almost at will from experiential depths to the clarity of usual, rational consciousness; that is to say, one can "go in" and have an experience and then "come out" and discuss the experience with other people or speak about it into the microphone of a tape-recorder—after which, of course, one can "go in" again. When aesthetic, psychodynamic, or mystical phenomena occur, consciousness is usually clearer than normal, a sharp contrast to any sense of confusion.

Cognitive Phenomena

There is a form of psychedelic experience that occasionally occurs when small dosage is administered or just before returning to usual consciousness when one feels capable of thinking unusually sharply, quickly, and clearly. Such experience is *cognitive* as opposed to *intuitive*; that is, it is the process we usually call *thinking*. Visionary imagery is seldom seen during this time and few changes in feeling-tone are manifested. One often feels acutely sensitive to the meaning of words and to very fine differentiations between similar words. Further, one seems to be conscious of the presuppositions underlying one's thoughts and of the interrelations between different ideas. Chain reactions of associations and inferences may occur, and one may feel as though one is able to think on several different levels of discourse all at once. Since paranoic thinking can follow a similar pattern, the validity of this feeling of cognitive excellence is subject to serious questioning. As yet no experiment has been designed to test it.

Miscellaneous Phenomena

Some phenomena do not seem to fit into any of the preceding categories and thus are briefly mentioned here for the sake of comprehensiveness. *Photic phenomena* are often, but not always, reported by persons who experience mystical consciousness, usually in the sense of seeing a brilliant white light, perhaps similar to the light experienced by Saint Paul at the time of his conversion. *Electrical phenomena* occur fairly frequently as subjects seem to become aware of the flow of electrical energy in their bodies. At times electrical energy may seem to flow in a pattern corresponding to the peripheral nervous system; at times it may seem to ascend the spinal column from its base, bursting into the brain—an experience also described by adepts of Yoga as the kundalini force. *Psychosomatic phenomena* such as nausea, rapid heartbeat, clammy coldness, or contractions of the stomach occasionally occur, usually being associated with an attempt of the experiencer to resist and control the experience. *Evolutionary phenomena* occasionally occur, in which the subject feels as though he is reliving part of the evolutionary process or, more probably, reliving part of his own foetal development. Some *parapsychological phenomena* of a telepathic, clairvoyant or precognitive nature have been reported, but none have been conclusively validated at this stage of research. *Phenomena of somatic change* occur as people experience changes in kinesthetic and cutaneous reception. Claims of merging with floorboards or feeling unity with the walls of a room that have been misinterpreted as mystical belong in this category. Such experiences entail intriguing changes in perception, but do not necessarily involve the extinguishing of the empirical ego. Similarly, there are experiences of *altered perception of time* that do not entail the mystical transcendence of time. Experiences may occur with such rapidity that a minute may seem like several hours to a subject. On the other hand, a subject may feel that only an hour has passed when he has been in the psychedelic state for several hours. Such slowing down or speeding up of time experience may precede or follow entry into mystical consciousness, but in themselves should not be considered mystical in nature. As mentioned above, the mystical transcendence of time and space involves an experience described as eternity or infinity. Finally, mention of *consciousness of bodily processes* may be made, including those experiences in which one becomes acutely aware of various aspects of the body's physiological mechanism as it functions.

In summary, we see that no person is ever justified in speaking of *the* psychedelic experience, as there is great variation among individual experiences. In any single psychedelic session, of course, any number of the forms of consciousness discussed above may be experienced. The person who enters mystical consciousness, for example, will almost undoubtedly also experience some aesthetic phenomena between the time the mystic intensity wanes and the moment of his return to usual consciousness. Furthermore, psychological problems may have to be encountered before a "breakthrough" into mystical consciousness is possible. It thus becomes obvious that studies of behavioral and attitudinal changes in persons who have ingested these drugs must be correlated with the types of phenomena experienced before any significant conclusions can be drawn. The findings of Blum and his co-workers (1964) in their study of persons who have ingested psychedelic drugs would have been much more relevant and meaningful had such a correlation been made.

A STUDY IN EXPERIMENTAL MYSTICISM

Of all the varieties of psychedelic experiences, the type that has elicited the most enthusiastic interest as well as the most indignant rebuttal from both psychiatric and theological spokesmen is the mystical experience. The claim that spontaneous mystical experiences are similar to, if not identical with, psychedelic experiences of drug-facilitated mystical consciousness has caused considerable apprehension and dismay among some religious professionals, and the possible therapeutic potential of experiences of mystical consciousness has been somewhat embarrassing to those therapists who pride themselves on their scientific objectivity and lack of religious involvement. Whether or not the mystical experience is "religious" is naturally dependent upon one's definition of "religion," and to raise this point only confuses the issue, although such experiences may well have religious implications. In order to provide some evidence in a systematic and scientific manner, Pahnke (1963) in 1962 designed and executed a controlled, double-blind experiment to investigate the relationship between the experiences recorded in the literature of spontaneous mysticism and those reportedly associated with the ingestion of psychedelic drugs. Prior to the experiment, from a study of the writings of the mystics and commentaries upon them, a phenomenological typology of the mystical state of consciousness was formulated, with which experimental descriptions subsequently could be compared. The categories of this typology were the same as those presented above in the definition of mystical consciousness.

Twenty subjects were chosen for the experiment, all graduate-student volunteers with middle-class Protestant backgrounds from one denominational seminary, none of whom had ever taken any of the psychedelic drugs prior to the experiment. Screening procedures had included psychological tests, a physical examination, a psychiatric interview and questionnaires inquiring medical history and previous religious experiences. These subjects were divided into five groups of four students on the basis of compatibility and friendship. Ten leaders who knew the positive and negative possibilities of psychedelic experience then assisted in preparations for the experiment, two leaders meeting with each group of four subjects to encourage trust, dissipate fears, and establish group rapport. Subjects were encouraged to relax and cooperate with the drug effects, but no mention was made of the characteristics of the typology of mystical consciousness.

On the day of the experiment, Good Friday, 1962, the subjects and leaders met in a lounge beside a private chapel into which the service in the main sanctuary would subsequently be transmitted over loudspeakers. There, ninety minutes before the service began, capsules identical in appearance were administered, some contained thirty milligrams of psilocybin and some containing two-hundred milligrams of nicotinic acid, a vitamin that causes feelings of warmth and tingling of the skin, but has no effect upon the mind. Half of the subjects and one of the leaders in group received psilocybin. Because double-blind technique was employed, neither the experimenter nor any of the participants (leaders or subjects) knew the contents of any given capsule. Further, as the use of an inactive placebo had been anticipated by the subjects as a control substance, suggestion was maximized for the control group when the nicotinic acid began to act.

Inside the private chapel, the subjects and leaders listened to a two-and-one-half-hour religious service consisting of organ music, four solos, readings, prayers, and personal meditation. The experimental design presupposed that in order for experiences most likely to be mystical, the atmosphere should be broadly comparable to that achieved by tribes who use natural psychedelic substances in their religious ceremonies, and that the particular content and procedure of the ceremony had to be applicable (e.g., familiar and meaningful) to the participants.

Immediately following the service, tape-recordings were made both of individual reactions and of the group discussions that followed. As soon after the experiment as was convenient, each subject wrote a detailed phenomenological account of his experience. Within a week all subjects had completed a 147-item questionnaire designed to measure phenomena of the typology of mystical consciousness on a qualitative, numerical scale. The results of this questionnaire were used as the basis for a ninety-minute tape-recorded interview that followed immediately. Six months later each subject was interviewed again after completion of a follow-up questionnaire in three parts with a similar scale. The first part was open-ended; the participant was asked to list any changes that he felt were a result of his Good Friday experience and to rate the degree of benefit or harm of each change. The second part (52 items) was a condensed and somewhat more explicit repetition of items from the post-drug questionnaire. The third part (93 items) was designed to measure both positive and negative attitudinal and behavioral changes that had lasted for six months and were felt to be due to the experience. The individual, descriptive accounts and the first part of the follow-up questionnaire were then content-analyzed with a qualitative, numerical scale by judges who were independent from the experiment.

When the data from (a) the post-drug questionnaire, (b) the follow-up questionnaire, and (c) the content-analysis of the written accounts were analyzed, the conclusion was drawn that, under the conditions of this experiment, those subjects who received psilocybin experienced phenomena that were apparently indistinguishable from, if not identical with, certain categories defined by the typology of mystical consciousness. Statistically, the scores of the experimental subjects from all three methods of measurement were significantly higher than those of the control subjects in all categories except "sense of sacredness." In all the other eight categories there were less than two chances in one hundred that the difference was due only to chance rather than to psilocybin, and in more than half of the categories, less than two chances in one thousand. Even sacredness showed a statistically significant difference in score (chance expectation of no more than five chances in one hundred) from both questionnaires, but not from the content-analysis. The degree of completeness or intensity of the various categories was presented and discussed by comparing the consistency of score levels on individual items and groups of items among the three methods of measurement. Not all categories were experienced in the most complete way possible, although there was evidence that each category had been experienced to some degree. A more detailed description of this experiment, including statistical analysis of the data, has been published elsewhere (Pahnke, 1966, 1967).

INTERDISCIPLINARY IMPLICATIONS

Implications for Theology.

On the basis of the research findings discussed above, it now appears possible to select almost any normal, healthy person and, combining a sufficient dose of a psychedelic substance with a supportive set and setting, enable that person to experience various altered forms of consciousness. The mystical experience seems the most difficult to facilitate, perhaps because of the as yet undetermined roles of personality variables; but nonetheless, these phenomena are now sufficiently reproducible to allow mysticism to be studied scientifically under laboratory conditions. Thus at long last, research into mysticism need no longer be limited to the scholarly scrutiny of various devotional or metaphysical documents left behind by such historic personages as Shankara, Plotinus, Meister Eckhart, William Blake, and Teresa of Avila. Persons can be studied extensively both before and after the experience of mystical consciousness in controlled settings. As noted above, experimental subjects who have experienced this form of consciousness have made powerful claims of increased personality-intergration, of greater sensitivity to the authentic problems of other persons, of a responsible independence of social pressures, of both sensing deeper purposes in life and losing anxieties about death, guilt, and meaning lessness, and so forth. If research continues, there is no reason why such claims cannot be studied empirically and then either accepted as valid or dismissed as instances of emotional exaggeration and wishful thinking.

To some theologians, the awareness that it appears possible to experience mystical consciousness (*samadhi* in advaitan Hinduism, *satori* in Zen Buddhism, the *beatific vision* in Christianity) with the help of a drug on a free Saturday afternoon at first appears ironic and even profane. Such experience is the goal of life for most followers of the Hindu, Buddhist, and Taoist religions. In Christianity, Judaism, and Islam, it has generally been viewed as a gift bestowed by God upon certain saints and prophets who have lived lives of exceptional stature. It is understandable that throughout Christian history, certain leaders have responded defensively whenever such bio-chemical aids to mystical consciousness have been encountered. Padre Nicolas de Leon, a Spanish missionary in Mexico who found that the Aztecs were using peyote (the natural source of mescaline), for example, included the following questions in the confessional that priests were instructed to employ in their examinations of penitent Indians:

Art thou a sooth-sayer? Dost thou foretell events by reading omens, interpreting dreams, or by tracing circles and figures on water? . . . Dost thou suck the blood of others? Dost thou wander about at night calling upon demons to help thee? Hast thou drunk peyote or given it to others to drink . . . ? (LaBarre, 1938, p. 23)

More recently, a very able professor of comparative religions at Oxford, R. C. Zaehner, has responded to the psychedelic drugs in a similarly irrational and defensive manner. Zaehner even submitted himself to "artificial in-terference with consciousness" at one time for the purpose of proving that "this state . . . has nothing at all to do with what Christians . . . mean by the Beatific Vision. (Zaehner, 1954)" As might be expected, Zaehner did not experience mystical consciousness in this session, but had a rather shallow aesthetic experience, typical of subjects with considerable anxiety and resistance. Unfortunately the publication of his experience did not prove the existence of the Thomistic gulf between the natural and the super-natural as he had hoped, but rather reflected the mental set of a dedicated Roman Catholic convert (Zaehner, 1961, pp. 212–226).

Perhaps one of the reasons mysticism has come to be considered other-worldly in the sense of being an escape from social responsibilities lies not in the nature of mystical consciousness itself, but rather in the poor methods that have been used by men to gain such experience. The medieval monk in his darkened cell and the hermit in the deep recesses of his cave, for example, used not psychedelic substances, but the tools of sensory deprivation, sleep deprivation, meditative disciplines, and fasting to elicit biochemical changes and unlock the door to unconscious levels of mind. The Hindu yogin uses similar methods in addition to autohypnosis and breath control, the latter increasing the amount of carbon dioxide in the blood and triggering unconscious levels of mind (see Meduna, 1950). Altered forms of consciousness often occur unexpectedly and spontaneously when one is undergoing great mental stress and is exhausted physically. It would appear logical to suggest that whenever altered forms of consciousness occur, whether they are anticipated or come as a complete surprise, under-lying biochemical activity may be involved. Thus the Hindu yogin practicing breath control or the Christian monk spending long hours in solitary prayer may be seen to be influencing body chemistry in the same direction as the modern man who ingests a psychedelic drug. In all seriousness, one may ask if the yogin or monk has much time for social action when perhaps a major portion of his life is spent in withdrawal from the world. Furthermore, such ascetic practices are poor means of unlocking the unconscious and may be similar to the ingestion of extremely small doses of the psychedelics. One thus enters aesthetic realms of experience more often than mystical consciousness itself. It is granted that other nonmystical forms of experience that may be considered "religious" are also known to occur, with and without the assistance of drugs. There is reason to think that other-worldliness may be a result, not of going too deep into the unconscious mind, but rather of not going deep enough. It seems significant that persons who have experienced mystical consciousness generally feel thrown back into the very heart of life in this world and feel also that they have been given the inner strength to cope with suffering and struggle in society. It would seem better for a person to have a drug-facilitated experience of mystical consciousness, enjoy the enriched life that may follow, and serve other persons during the greater part of his life than to live a life that may be inauthentic and withdrawn until old age, when such an experience may occur by means of ascetic practices.

Some persons concerned with religion are disturbed by drug-facilitated mystical experiences because of the apparent ease of production, implying that they are "unearned" and therefore "undeserved". Perhaps the Puritanical and Calvinistic element of our Western culture, especially in the United States where most of the controversy about psychedelic drugs has centered, may be a factor in this uneasiness. Although a drug-facilitated experience might seem unearned when compared with the rigorous discipline that many mystics describe as necessary, the available evidence suggests that careful preparation and expectation play an important part, not only in determining the type of experience attained, but in determining the extent of later fruits for life. By no means is positive mystical experience with the psychedelic drugs automatic. It would seem that this specific "drug effect" is a delicate combination of psychological set and setting in which drug itself is only the trigger or facilitating agent. Rather than a psychedelic experience being an easy way to achieve growth, many subjects report that the subjective sense of work done during the drug session entails as much suffering and exhaustion as would be encountered in several years of living. But perhaps the hardest work comes after the experience when insights must be integrated. Unless such an experience is integrated into the on-going life of a person, only a memory remains rather than the growth of an unfolding process of renewal that may be awakened by the mystical experience. If the person has a religious framework and discipline within which to work, the integrative process is encouraged and stimulated. In this respect, Huston

Smith's (1964, p. 165) distinction between "religious experiences" and "religious lives" is especially noteworthy. Many persons may not need the drug-facilitated mystical experience, but there are others who would never become aware of the undeveloped potentials within themselves or become inspired to work in this direction without such experience. "Gratuitous grace" is an appropriate theological term in this connection, for the psychedelic mystical experience can lead to a profound sense of inspiration, reverential awe and humility, perhaps correlated with the feeling that the experience is essentially a gift from a transcendent source, a gift that can never be earned or deserved by any man.

In a paper of this scope, it is impossible to deal adequately with any of the theological questions raised by this field of research. Suffice it to say that there is an increasing need for contemporary theologians to include mystical consciousness in their rational reflections. Among experimental subjects who have known this dimension of experience, some have reported an enrichment of their understanding of Christianity, claiming that dead dogmas have suddenly come alive; others with less theological sophistication have despaired at the seeming indifference of dogma-centered churches to mystical experience and have turned towards the religions of the East. Tillich has perceptively noted that "The alliance of psychoanalysis and Zen Buddhism in some members of the upper classes of Western society (those within the Protestant tradition) is a symptom of dissatisfaction with a Protestantism in which the mystical element is lost" (Tillich, 1963, p. 243). Perhaps basically, theologians need to acknowledge the reality of other worlds, other dimensions of Being, to which man has access through the mystery of mind, but which no man would claim as his own personal property any more than the tourist who once visited Paris would claim that Paris was part of himself. Besides the works of Tillich, the recent impassioned attempt of Karl Jaspers (1962, 1963) to relate his *Existenzphilosophie* to Christian theology could prove valuable to theologians concerned with this creative area of thought.

In general, mysticism and *inner* experience have been stressed much more by Eastern than by Western religions. Perhaps Western culture is as far off balance in the opposite direction with its manipulation of the *external* world as exemplified by the emphasis on material wealth, control of nature, and admiration of science. As mentioned above, mysticism has been accused of fostering escapism from the problems of society, indifference to social conditions, and disinterest in social change. While the possibility of such excesses must be considered, the beneficial potential of mystical experience in stimulating the ability to feel and experience deeply and genuinely with the full harmony of both emotion and intellect has been indicated in the course of psychedelic research.

Further, the experience of mystical consciousness may enable Western scholars better to understand the so-called elusive "Eastern mind". In the approaching era of unprecedented cultural interaction, this possibility could be of profound significance. Not only the religious systems of Hinduism, Buddhism, and Taoism, but also Eastern political traditions and even Eastern forms of architecture may be seen to have largely originated in various forms of altered consciousness. After such experience, contemplation may take on new meaning for the Western man who finds little time to ponder the meaning of his own existence and the philosophical presuppositions upon which his religious, political, scientific, and ethical convictions rest.

It is also possible that psychedelic drug experiences carefully employed in a religious setting (as in the experiment described above) could illumine our understanding of the dynamics and significance of worship. Increased understanding of the psychological mechanisms involved might lead to more meaningful worship experiences for those who have had neither spontaneous nor drug-facilitated experiences. Light might be shed upon doctrines of the Holy Spirit and the efficacy of sacraments, for example, thus enriching worship through psychological understanding. Such considerations raise the question of the place of emotion as opposed to cognition in religious worship. An even more basic question inquires into the validity of mystical consciousness in terms of religious truth. Reactions to such questions and possibilities will vary with theological positions and presuppositions, but the field under discussion invites thoughtful examination by those persons concerned with the lack of meaning reported by many contemporary church members in conjunction with religious worship.

The ethical implications relevant to this field of inquiry also merit careful examination. Any research that uses human volunteers must examine its motives and methods to make certain that human beings are not being manipulated like objects for purposes that they neither understand nor share. But in research with powerful mental chemicals that may influence the most cherished human functions and values, the ethical problem is even more acute. Historically, mystical experience has filled man with wondrous awe and has been able to change his style of life and values; but it must not be assumed that increased control of such powerful phenomena will automatically result in wise and constructive uses. Potential abuses are equally possible. The degree to which brainwashing techniques could be enhanced by the psychedelics is at present unknown. As persons in the deeper states of altered consciousness are so hypersensitive to the fine nuances of interpersonal communication, especially in terms of love and honesty, deception and manipulation may be minimized. In this sense, the drugs may be seen to have a "built-in control." Yet there are many varieties of psychedelic experience that do not entail such Buberic communication and may certainly be prone to suggestive influences, either for good or evil.

Implications for Psychiatry.

Turning from the religious implications of these drugs to their possible applications in psychiatry, we find that in the more than twenty years during which LSD has been investigated under medically controlled conditions, two major methods of therapeutic application have evolved. The first, called psycholytic therapy and predominant in Europe, involves a small-dose technique (e.g., 25 to 100 mcg. of LSD) in weekly or bi-weekly sessions order to facilitate the release of unconscious material and aid psychotherapy or group therapy. Sandison and Spencer (Sandison, Spencer, & Whitlaw, 1954) in England and Leuner (1962) in Germany have pioneered in this method. Leuner in particular uses a psychoanalytic approach in working through the material during the drug sessions themselves as well as during the time between subsequent sessions. Mascher (1967) recently reviewed the research presented in forty-two scientific papers that describe the method and results of psycholytic therapy in sixteen-hundred patients during the past fifteen years. LSD sessions are considered superior to Amytal interviews, for example, insofar as the patient remains alertly conscious during the experience and has much less amnesia afterwards.

The second method, called psychedelic therapy and used mainly in the United States and Canada, involves a much smaller number of sessions, or even a single session, but at a higher dosage in order to produce an experience with such an overwhelming impact that the patient's view of the world and himself may be radically changed in a healthful and therapeutic manner. The primary aim is to achieve a breakthrough to a "psychedelic peak" that has the characteristics described above in the definition of mystical consciousness. Relatively high dosage is a necessary, but not a sufficient, condition for eliciting a psychedelic peak. Through careful preparation, a trustful bond of rapport with the therapist must be established as in any effective therapy. Special skill on the part of an experienced psychedelic therapist must be used for guiding the patient during the actual drug session. Careful planning of both the emotional atmosphere and the physical environment is important. Stimuli such as classical music (symphonic and choral) with long, flowing phrases, beautiful flowers, and reproductions of great works of art have proved helpful. After the drug session, the therapist must accept the crucial task of helping the patient integrate what he has learned during this intense, existential experience. Frequently this entails the direct confrontation of problematic situations in the patient's everyday world. Descriptions of this method have been written by Chwelos and co-workers (Chwelos, Blewett, Smith, & Hoffer, 1959), MacLean and co-workers(MacLean, MacDonald, Byrne, & Hubbard, 1961), and Sherwood and co-workers (Sherwood, Stolaroff, & Harmon, 1962). Also instructive is Unger's excellent review article (1963) and his description of the English language literature (1964).

If the claims of therapeutic help from such experiences are substantiated in the controlled, clinical trials now being conducted, the need for, and relevance of, interdisciplinary discussion in this area between psychiatry and religion is accentuated. At the Spring Grove State Hospital in Baltimore, two projects that have been supported by the National Institute of Mental Health are in progress. There the effects of psychedelic therapy are being investigated on two groups of hospitalized patients: chronic alcoholics and severe psychoneurotics. Although the final results must be judged by the statistical evaluation of long-term follow-up studies in comparison with control groups, the early reports are encouraging (Kurland, Unger, & Shaffer, 1967; Savage, 1966). Mystical consciousness is being experienced by these patients, many of whom were not previously interested in either religion or mysticism.

A project in Massachusetts began to investigate the possible effectiveness of psychedelic therapy in the rehabilitation of prisoners, but unfortunately was interrupted and remains incomplete and inconclusive (Leary, Metzner, Presnell, Weil, Schwitzgebel, & Kinne, 1965; Leary, & Clark, 1963). It is probable that such a procedure would have the highest chance of success if it were co-ordinated with a treatment program that included job placement.

At the Federal Narcotics Hospital in Lexington, Kentucky, drug addicts have been treated with a combination of LSD and hypnosis—so-called hypnodelic therapy. This technique is now also being applied to chronic alcoholics in a study at the Mendota State Hospital in Madison, Wisconsin (Levine & Ludwig, 1967; Ludwig, 1966).

When LSD was compared with narcotics as a pain-relieving agent for terminal cancer patients at the Cook County Hospital in Chicago (Kast, 1964), a marked analgesic effect was noted; but of greater significance, it appears possible that psychedelic therapy can provide an opportunity for the dying patient to view his life and death in a new perspective (Cohen, 1965). Useful possibilities of working with such experiences by those who care for and minister to the dying open up an area for investigation that has all too often been a depressing embarrassment to physicians in spite of the triumphs of modern medicine and surgery. Because of the unique effects of mystical consciousness upon attitudes and interpersonal relationships, not only the patient, but also his family may be able to approach and view death in a new way. Old barriers and defenses can crumble within the patient, making possible meaningful dialogue with family members and friends concerning issues and feelings of mutual importance. This as yet relatively unexplored area of psychedelic research needs much more attention and careful study. Again the obvious religious implications highlight the intersection of psychiatry and religion.

Even if the therapeutic effectiveness of psychedelic therapy is eventually demonstrated empirically in carefully controlled clinical research, a further problem still remains. As yet there is no adequate theory to explain why the experience of mystical consciousness should facilitate therapy. Some of the researchers have claimed that "the root of the therapeutic effectiveness of the LSD experience is its potential for producing self-acceptance" (Chwelso et al., 1959, p. 589). This view has definite parallels with aspects of Paul Tillich's thought. The renewed sense of self-esteem noted in some patients after such experience may be due to a realignment of ego defenses and boundaries. Alcoholics who have experienced psychedelic mystical consciousness are surprised to discover that they have some internal, intrinsic worth as members of the human race and seem to gain a new self-concept involving goodness and love.

In trying to account for the phenomena associated with mystical consciousness, the concept of regression has been proposed (Prince & Savage, 1965). Such aspects of mystical consciousness as "unity" and "deeply felt positive mood" are certainly suggestive of the prenatal life of a foetus. Theories that dismiss mystical consciousness as "mere regression" or "an oceanic feeling of primary process," however, fail to wrestle with the noetic aspects of "objectivity and reality" and "transcendence of space and time." The mind appears to gain the ability of operating on many levels at once, while grasping interrelations of psychic functioning. The concept of time does not merely lose meaning, but, more impressively, is seen in a new perspective. Subjects assert that they felt "outside of" time, beyond both past and future, as though they were viewing the totality of history from a transcendent vantage point. The feeling of profundity and truth that insights acquire under the influence of psychedelic drugs may be a delusion: but this quality seems to provide the motivation for the patient to affect behavior change, especially if the insight gained holds true for the particular person when examined and tested later when the rational mind is again in full command. Because the life experience and learning acquired over the years are retained while in this altered state of consciousness, perhaps the term "regression in the service of the ego" is more appropriate.

Implications for Society

As is unfortunately true with many potentially beneficial but powerful discoveries, such as fire or atomic energy, misuse and abuse are possible if the discoveries are improperly handled. The psychedelic drugs are no exception, as the growing black market ominously testifies. There are an increasing number of people who are obtaining these drugs illegally and ingesting them without psychiatric screening, preparation, supervision, or follow-up therapy.

Such practices will inevitably lead to psychiatric casualties as have already been reported in the medical literature (Frosch, Robbins, Stern, 1965). When certain borderline or pre-psychotic persons take psychedelic drugs without capable psychiatric supervision, there is a risk of prolonged psychosis, irresponsible behavior, or suicide. Even persons who are in good physical and mental health can become quite emotionally shaken when they discover that their usual sense of control is suspended. Fighting to overcome the drug effect can lead to intense fear and a psychotic reaction.

Most of the cases coming to psychiatric attention are acute panic reactions that are usually reversible with proper drug treatment and temporary hospitalization. There are also some persons who seem to experience a spontaneous recurrence of the LSD effect months after having last taken the drug. Usually these persons are under stress when the symptoms recur. Although much more rare, the cases of prolonged psychosis following LSD and lasting more than a week are more alarming. A direct, causal relation to LSD cannot always be determined, however, because an examination of the case histories usually reveals severely disturbed persons who probably were in severe psychological trouble prior to taking the drug. Not all persons who seek psychiatric help after LSD, however, are in acute distress or in need of hospitalization. There are also a growing number of persons who mistakenly thought they were in good mental health, but discovered during their drug experience that many repressed problems came to the surface. This realization may encourage such persons to work out their problems, whereas previously they may have denied their reality or sought some form of escape. Paradoxically enough these are people who probably should have been in psychiatric treatment before, but only now are motivated to do so. In the long run, with proper help, many of them may be guided towards better mental adjustment, but at best this is a risk-filled method of self-diagnosis.

In any discussion of the dangers of psychedelic drugs, it is essential to consider the incidence rates of harmful effects. Cohen has collected the only statistics of this nature published to date and found that, in a survey of 5,000 persons who had taken psychedelic drugs a total of 25,000 times, there was a suicide rate of one per 2500 persons among psychiatric patients undergoing treatment, and no attempted or completed suicides among experimental subjects. Psychotic reactions lasting longer than forty-eight hours had an incidence of one per 555 among patients and one per 1200 among experimental subjects (Cohen, 1960).

In commenting on Cohen's statistics, Levine and Ludwig (1964) have emphasized the relative safety of LSD when compared with other methods of psychiatric treatment. Since Cohen's survey was published in 1960, much more has been learned about treatment procedures with LSD-type drugs and the art of avoiding psychotic reactions. With this increased knowledge, coupled with improved therapist training, the use of LSD should become even safer. It must be emphasized, however, that Cohen gathered his data from a survey of doctors engaged in clinical research with these drugs. These statistics and comments, therefore, refer only to the properly controlled, medical use of LSD.

The current increase in dangerous after-effects is almost entirely caused by the indiscriminate use of LSD among untrained persons. Such use takes place outside legitimate research auspices without medical supervision. These very real dangers must not be allowed to obscure the potentials of a powerful therapeutic tool. To offer an analogy, little benefit would be expected to come from an x-ray machine if an untrained person were allowed to shoot x-rays in all directions indiscriminately. In fact, unless the intensity and frequency of the x-rays were carefully controlled, much harm could result in the form of radiation sickness and permanent damage.

Although neither physiological addiction nor tissue damage has been reported in the case of LSD, psychological dependence might be expected if the experience were continually repeated. The intense subjective pleasure and enjoyment, at least of aesthetic forms of experience, could lead to escapism and withdrawal from the world. An experience capable of changing motivation and values might cut the nerve of achievement. Wide spread apathy toward productive work and accomplishment could cripple a society. It is unfortunate that, at present, public opinion concerning these drugs is being molded primarily on the basis of the response of the beatnik dimension of society, a dimension that contains many persons already in poor states of mental health. Such persons are accused of numerous forms of irresponsible behavior, and also the sin of quietism—of claiming inspiration, but producing few concrete works of social, literary, or artistic promise.

There are relatively few experimental studies that provide information concerning the possible continuing benefits of psychedelic drug experiences in normal, mentally healthy persons who have already established a responsible and creative position in society. In fact, these people cannot legally take the drugs unless they happen to live near one of the few qualified research projects. Increased legitimate opportunities for both average and gifted people to take these drugs under adequate supervision will be needed before the possible beneficial effects for individual persons and society can be assessed.

Practically speaking, the reality of the black market must be confronted. LSD can take the form of a clear, odorless, tasteless liquid. It can be quite easily and inexpensively manufactured in a home laboratory by any good organic chemist. Two hundred millionths of a gram constitutes a powerful dose that is no larger than a drop of water. At present there is a 1000% to 3000% mark-up from manufacturer to consumer. So it is that attempts to control the black market by police force face serious obstacles and almost certainly will prove futile. There is, in fact, a growing demand for these drugs, not only among the rebellious element of society, but also among our future leaders who are now attending universities. Many of the sensationalistic articles in the popular press that have presented somewhat slanted accounts of the bizarre and lurid effects of these drugs rather than their potential usefulness have only attracted more interest and curiosity from the very people who should not take the drugs, and have tended to decrease support for responsible investigation.

If the recent estimate is correct that one million doses of LSD will be consumed in the United States in 1966 (Rosenfeld & Farrell, 1966), the usage will probably grow at an even faster rate because each person who has a positive experience will introduce at least one or two of his friends to the drug. Positive experiences are much more common than negative ones, and it is a human fallacy to believe that a bad reaction "won't happen to me". How then can we deal constructively with the problems posed by the black market?

It would seem that not suppression, but informed education and an expanded program of research with an interdisciplinary approach is urgently needed. Education needs a basis of empirically derived facts on which to draw. To gather such facts, concerning both dangers and possible benefits, increased, responsible research in all realms of application is needed before research is stopped because of the growing public hysteria in the face of the black market. We propose carefully controlled studies in which drug dosage, setting, personality variables, experimenter expectation, experimental procedure, and follow-up can be regulated. Only then can answers be found to questions concerning the personality characteristics or disturbances that contraindicate the use of the drugs, the optimal treatment procedures to insure the most beneficial effect, and the best screening procedures to identify persons most likely to be harmed or those who should be singled out for special handling. Patients with various symptoms and relatively normal subjects both need to be intensely studied in such experiments.

Because persons who take the drugs on their own are most interested in aesthetic and mystical experiences, research needs to be focused on the possible benefit or harm resulting from such experiences. Another variable needing elucidation the effect of frequency of ingestion. It is conceivable that benefit might result from an experience once or twice a year, whereas weekly exposures might cause chronic deleterious changes in personality.

Because these drugs are without a doubt the most powerful psychoactive agents known to man, their use needs to be supervised by persons who have received specialized training. In view of the wide range of potential applications, an interdisciplinary approach to their use is essential. A training and research center for psychedelic therapists will probably need to be established. The staff of such a center should include psychiatrists, clinical psychologists, and professional religious personnel.

The results of increased knowledge from such research on the drugs may provide an answer to the problem of the black market. If legitimate medical uses and methods are confirmed and the dangers and benefits are determined accurately, socially sanctioned centers for persons desiring this form of human experience can be establised. Most persons would then probably prefer the safety of medical supervision to the risk of black-market usage. Admittedly, this kind of solution may lie a long way in the future and will depend upon the results of careful yet imaginative and daring research. But this may be the only way to deal effectively with this problem.

What would be the effect of relatively broad use of the psychedelics in some future decade? Would people become more creative than ever before? If the garbage collector experienced mystical consciousness, would he collect garbage more passionately than ever before, or would he escape to the forest or the university? Could these drugs enrich society or do they threaten to destroy it? If the latter should prove to be the case, are there ways in which this threat can be lessened? These are questions whose crucial answers are at present unknown. Not only are they unknown, but research aimed at finding answers to them is severely limited in the United States.

Religion has long been accused by sociologists of being a prime illustration of the phenomenon of the "cultural lag." Bruno was burned at the stake for his adherence to the Copernican view of the universe. For the same heretical belief, Galileo was condemned and forced to recant, even though the truth of the panoramas he had seen through his telescope were indelibly fixed upon his mind. Similarly, Darwin was condemned for his heretical theory of evolution. Yet, in retrospect, Christian theology, including biblical interpretation, has been greatly enriched by the convictions of these men. New glimpses into the nature of reality always seem first to evoke defensive reactions of fear and, only later, reactions of wonder and praise.

With these drugs, science stands on an awesome threshold. Some religious leaders would undoubtedly consider it improper for man to tread upon the holy ground of the unconscious, protesting against the exploration of "inner space" as they have campaigned against the exploration of outer space. But man's apparent destiny to seek an ever greater comprehension of the nature of reality cannot be thwarted or suppressed. The importance of research proceeding in harmony with the highest known ethical principles, however, is clear. Those who undertake such research carry a heavy responsibility.

28

ATTITUDE AND BEHAVIOR CHANGE THROUGH PSYCHEDELIC DRUG USE

JOSEPH DOWNING, M.D.

Five years ago, 1962, a sensible, balanced review of psychedelic drugs in the treatment of mental conditions was possible. Experienced clinicians were conducting controlled experiments or making closely observed clinical studies. This phase of work, extending over a fifteen year period in Europe and the United States, was adequately represented in the Ciba Symposium publications.

The review by Sidney Unger (1963) summarized these results. Broadly, promising remission of symptoms was found in a broad variety of non-psychotic disorders including psychosomatic conditions, addictions, neuroses and character problems. The psychotic disorders appeared to show little change, although borderline schizoid personalities occasionally showed improvement. Most studies were easily criticized by methodological purists for lack of comparability of case material, inadequate or absent control, faulty study design, lack of rigorous observational variables, and so forth. In fact, they reflected the general problems of behavioral change research in a clinical setting and were neither better or worse than the prevailing climate of psychotherapy results assessment.

FACTORS IN THE THERAPEUTIC EXPERIENCE

This clinical report aims at the means whereby a favorable result from the psychedelic experience can be assured. It does not purport to deal with research design, or the variables cogent to research evaluation.

It appears that the wide variability of reported experiences and results associated with psychedelic drug use depends on the interaction of the following eight variables: (a) the patient or subject's problems and personality, (b) the therapist's or research guide's personality and purpose, (c) the purpose of the experience, whether experimental, therapeutic, or experience-seeking, (d) the physical and social setting in which the experience takes place, (e) the nature of the preparation given the person taking the drug, (f) the person's expectations, particularly those based on suggestions made by the therapist, either purposely or inadvertently, (g) the companions present during the experience, and (h) the specific drug and the dosage administered.

At higher dosage levels (2-plus micrograms LSD per pound of body weight), the successful treatment experience appears to be associated with a religious "enlightenment" similar to religious conversion. The subject's basic ethical and religious attitudes are reoriented, in the direction of a greater unity with his total world and reduction in dualistic strains and entanglements. A deeper sense of personal security and lessened fear and anxiety results. Whether or not the therapist is personally sympathetic to this seemingly worthwhile change, such profound spiritual reorientation should not be undertaken lightly even for valid therapeutic goals. This phenomenon has been well described by Aldous Huxley (1954) and Allan Watts (1962) so will not be elaborated here.

PROBLEMS AND PRECAUTIONS IN THERAPY

In general, the structured psychedelic experience as given here has been favorable. This contrasts to the occasionally harmful experiences of persons having such experiences in unstructured settings. This favorable impression for structured experiences is confirmed by others using similar techniques. For best, most safe results, the person administering the drug, whether therapist or researcher, should have had a psychedelic experience be a stable person, and be aware of the possible profound, long-range, post-drug effect on the subject.

Generally, persons who have a positive, supportive, satisfying, anxiety-alleviating drug "enlightenment" experience, have a good chance of viewing their subsequent life experience in similar terms. Equally important, those who have a "bad trip", an anxious, perplexing, unsupported experience leading to temporary pathological defenses such as projection, hallucinations and paranoia occasionally have a persistent negative, insecure and sometimes bewildered life orientation. With proper preparation and support, however, an unpleasant experience may not be "bad," on the contrary, may represent working out old fears, to a new, more balanced personality level. This difference in results is not certain, and remains to be investigated. In either case, post-drug interviews and discussion are necessary for adequate integration and resolution of newly uncovered material.

Illustrative of a presumptively poor result is the following example: a social psychologist told of taking LSD eighteen years ago as a graduate student in a prominent eastern university to earn ten dollars. Given no preparation at all, and experiencing the usual perceptual distortions, he experienced anxiety and near panic, despite which he was left alone or in the company of a disinterested laboratory assistant. Due to profound but incomplete personal insights, he was perplexed and experienced anxiety for some months afterward. A fellow subject became confused, wandered out of the building and ended in the local psychopathic hospital! Reflecting on the experience today, he characterizes it as "the most frightening experience of my life." Nevertheless, he feels that this single experience changed both his personality and his entire life pattern (in an unspecified manner).

So, these drugs are not short-term or temporary in their effects, at least for some subjects. They should be used with caution and respect. Early lack of researcher understanding and responsibility was due to ignorance of lasting effects. This excuse is not acceptable today, yet studies of casual use continue to be reported, without any apparent recognition of the profound immediate consequences, and possible permanent changes, for ill as well as good. Regarding toxic, physical ill effects from drug administration, personal inquiry of a number of experimenters has uncovered only two cases of concurrent physical problems, one a mild asthmatic-like attack and one instance of moderate hypotension and shock. Neither was fatal. Reports of one investigator suggest caution in persons who have a history of coronary artery disease (Tenenbaum, 1961). In our previous work, we have had injectable and oral Thorazine available as well, in case the drug effect needs to be terminated quickly. Nicotonic acid (Niacin) also is useful for ending LSD drug effects, in dosages of $\frac{1}{2}$ gram and up. This nonprescription vitamin should always be available for terminating drug experiences which are overly anxiety producing.

THE DRUG EFFECT

The psychedelic drug effect is similar in some ways to that of a hypnotic state. There is a marked lowering of the threshold of perception, both external and internal, together with a marked heightening of symbolic integration, emotional responsiveness, and intuitive insight into oneself and others. Light, speech and noise become difficult to tolerate, one's own internal percepts highly pleasant and important. The personality defenses seem to soften, become plastic, as the subject becomes concurrently more suggestible. As one psychiatrist described the experience, "My personality and its defenses became absolutely transparent." At the same time, there is a drastic reduction of capacity to perceive, integrate and act realistically on external stimuli; i.e., there is selective ego regression along with increased ego function in other areas resulting in introspection and intense preoccupation with intra-psychic processes.

Allowing for individual variability and susceptibility, as with any drug, these effects generally occur about at the level of 0.5 to 1.5 microgram LSD per pound of body weight. At lower levels, 0.5 microgram LSD per pound or less, the ego regressive effects are less prominent and the heightened perception relatively more prominent. This is the marijuana effect of about one-half "joint" or cigarette. At higher levels, that is, approximately 2 micrograms LSD per pound or higher, ego integration is lost and consciousness of individual personality, the "I", disappears like a drop of water merging with the ocean. This ineffable experience cannot be described, being at other than the verbal level, but the patient is panic stricken, usually. It is retrospectively interpreted as "union with God" or the universe, or a "descent into hell," or death and rebirth. The "descents into hell" are rather infrequent, having been estimated to be about 15% of such experiences.

Speculatively, the integration of the individual's unique life experience or memories constitutes the "self," the unique "me." The temporary disorganization produces these "ego-death" and "union with the universe" effects. I do not recommend entering this level of experience lightly although for some patients it was a strongly positive experience. It should be noted that during the period of the drug-induced "illumination experience" the person is extremely dependent on the environment for support of all types, including cues as to proper behavior, explicit reassurance as to reality or unreality, satisfaction of emotional and bodily needs, and general support and protection. If the person engaged in the "illumination" experience does not receive the necessary understanding and protection, the chain of events so often described as "psychotomimetic" may take place: first, overwhelming ego stress (in this case the drug); second, a reduction in ego defenses and bizarre perceptual integration; third, anxiety resulting from the feeling of being defenseless in a confusing unreal world; fourth, pathological secondary defenses such as hallucinations, delusions, paranoid projections and so forth; finally, fear and estrangement from the environment and a disorganized attempt to fight, escape, or otherwise resolve the intolerable situation.

This pathological sequence happens most often in quasi-therapeutic, thrill seeking, and occasional research situations. The persons taking the drug have not been given adequate preparation before the drug was administered, sufficient support, understanding and protection during the drug experience, and finally opportunity to understand and reintegrate the experience following recovery from the drug. It seems likely that there would be few therapeutic benefits in an experience which involves regression to lower ego integration, extreme anxiety and secondary psychotic-like defense formation. On the other hand, when the environment is understanding and supportive, the subject feels free and safe to enter into a profoundly reflective, beneficial, primarily intrapersonal experience without exhibiting pathological personality defenses.

There is the question of single or multiple LSD experiences and individual or group experiences. Multiple experiences carry the subjects deeper into their conflicts. They are carried out as described previously, with most personality change occurring when the introspective drug effect is enhanced by concurrent psychotherapy. The use of low dosage, 25 to 75 gamma, has been investigated. My experience has been with higher dosages, the pre- and post-drug psychotherapy focusing on this. Having no experience with multiple low-dosage concurrent therapy, my only opinion would be concern with the problems of arranging proper settings of emotional security for so many periods. (I am personally convinced that persons receiving low dosages need concurrent companionship and support, just as do the higher amounts.)

Group therapy with LSD has distinctive advantages, when strictly structured in a protected environment. The following is the structure developed by one competent clinician.

STRUCTURE FOR GROUP EXPERIENCES

The group members agree *in advance* to this structure:

1. All that is not prohibited by structure is permitted.
2. No physical harm or violence to self or others during the experience. (Usually a two-day "marathon" period.)

3. Not to leave the treatment area of house and yard without permission.

4. No sexual intercourse is permitted.

5. Every individual is to be responsible to himself, to members of the group, and to the group as a whole.

6. Anything the therapist states *under structure*, will be done. Anything the therapist states should not be done, *under structure*, will not be done.

7. The more the subject can set aside judgement and control, and trust the therapist's control and judgement, the better his experience.

8. The penalty for breaking structure is instant dismissal from the group, after receiving the appropriate antidote.

ADDITIONAL POINTS OUTSIDE OF "STRUCTURE"

1. The first three to five hours are usually individual, try to relax and let go.

2. Spouses' problems; usually we like spouses separate for first group treatments. If both are present, it is better if you start in different areas, but if you both want to be together, okay.

3. Don't be surprised at anything you may see the therapist doing—he knows what he is doing.

4. A person who is having trouble breaking through needs something to resist against—the therapist may hand wrestle, or be on top and have three to six others on top as well. The person then can exert all his strength to break loose.

5. Anytime you are in trouble, don't hesitate to ask for help.

6. As people make break-through you'll hear laughing, crying, screaming. Don't worry about it, or get concerned.

7. *Nothing is expected of you, don't expect anything of yourself*—most people have a glorious trip.

8. Try to avoid impressing anybody—you'll have a better trip.

9. Around three to four hours after beginning, a stimulant will be brought around to keep your energy level up.

10. Anytime you want to stop the trip, take some niacin, 500 to 1000 mgm at a time. Niacin is good for bad re-entry, will make it easier.

11. During the experience, if you want to come together, touch the other person or ask him. He may shake his head "no," or else turn and touch you. Don't have hurt feelings, or guilt if they don't want to be with you, be free to be yourselves.

PATIENT SELECTION

Treatment results to date show what would be expected; the better integrated and more capable the person before treatment, the more benefit received by it. For example, of 12 alcoholics who received LSD in dosages from 200–900 micrograms, the two functioning at the highest social level at time of LSD treatment made spectacular improvement, four who had reasonably well integrated lives at an earlier period although currently desocialized, made a fair social recovery, and six who had been life-long "inadequates" showed little or no change. Of this latter "inadequate" group, one might speculate on the possibly beneficial effects of repeated "illumination" experiences in a highly structured, highly controlling social therapeutic community.

Therapeutic indications for the drug are yet undetermined. It should be used with caution with thrill-seekers, volunteers and persons with defective ego formation such as those predisposed to schizophrenic reactions. Nonetheless, one young man undergoing long-term psychotherapy had an excellent experience less than two years after a paranoid schizophrenic episode.

DOSAGE LEVEL

For therapeutic purposes it seems generally best to use the higher dosages, between one and two micrograms orally per pound of body weight. With alcoholics, who seem to be somewhat more resistant to this as to other drugs, 2–3 micrograms per pound seems indicated. The extremely high dosages, up to 10–12 micrograms per pound, are extremely likely to produce continuing "flashbacks" and possible panic and injury.

PATIENT PREPARATION

The preparation of the patient is of considerable importance. Confidence in the therapist is essential. The therapist should have a good working understanding of the general personality structure, and of specific conflicts and relationship problems, both past and present which are likely to preoccupy the patient. In pre-drug interviews, the patient should be acquainted with what is likely to be encountered in the drug experience, both directly by the therapist and by reading such works as Watts' *Joyous Cosmology* (1962, p. 2) and Huxley's *Doors of Perceptions* (1954, p. 2). He should also be told that the drug experience is only a part of a total treatment program, including at least three pre-drug and three post-drug interviews. The other elements in the treatment are still not fixed, as we try various patterns of experience. Currently the patient is asked to agree to perform the following for three months after the drug experience: at least one hour of solitary meditation a week and one concert or religious service a week. Some patients have gone to a religious retreat for a long weekend before and after the experience. They felt this preparation was valuable in the actual experience.

In the interviews prior to the drug and on the day of treatment, the patient is told that the therapist has taken the drug, knows himself what the effects are, and that there is no reason to be anxious. Most particularly, emphasis should be made that if the patient becomes confused as to reality, the therapist knows what it is, and should be followed. Further, the therapist will remind him of this pre-drug conversation, if necessary. Since consciousness and memory are retained, if told this in advance the patient finds a secure orientation point in a world where seemingly all security is lost. Further, he is told that a drug, Thorazine, is available which will quickly counteract the drug and make everything normal again.

If he wishes the return to normal during the experience, Thorazine, 100 mgm, or Niacin, 500 mgm, will be given. The therapist will maintain control at all times and interrupt the experience if he feels it best. The fear of losing verbal or motor control with resultant embarrassing confession or violent destructive behavior needs to be allayed. None of our patients have shown any aggressive, violent or "acting out" behavior. Few have talked more than a few words, and none have said anything other than what they would have said without the drug. The patient can be absolutely reassured on this point. All these points are highly reassuring to the drug-perplexed patient, and promote an externally uneventful and therapeutic experience.

MUSIC

Music is valuable but should not be used continuously. Compositions should be carefully selected due to the heightened perception and aesthetic awareness of the patient. Banal or poorly performed compositions may be intolerable.

It is valuable to present the patient with a fresh rose to hold and experience. The beauty of the rose, its exquisite form and scent further guarantee a deep appreciation and personal identity with the total grandeur and beauty of nature.

THE TREATMENT SETTING

The setting should be comfortable, familiar and beautiful. After unsatisfactory trials at using a hospital room, which turned out to be both unnecessary in terms of patient security and therapeutically inhibiting, a special room was furnished. This works fairly well, but has musical limitations. For optimal results, in the future a quiet, specially designed non-hospital, tree and nature surrounded special clinical setting would be best. We have no anxiety about uncontrolled, violent or disorganized behavior, using present preparations and reassurance.

THE COMPANIONS

Obvious problems of dependency, fear, aggressive and erotic transference and counter-transference are minimized by the presence of two companions, one of each sex. It might be added that three companions have been found mildly uncomfortable to the patient, and four to be a definite distraction. Unless there are exceptional circumstances, two companions have been found generally the best.

Somewhat to my surprise, the companions present during the long, drawn out, hence fairly intimate treatment experience are even more important than I first realized. Following the experience of Sherwood et al. (Sherwood, Stolaroff, & Harman, 1962), we began with two companions, a man and a woman, one of whom was the therapist. Experimenting with administering the drug in the most familiar environment, the patient's home, the spouse was found of unexpected importance in acting to focus the patient's current emotional tensions, whatever their genetic origin.

Often patients are afraid they will "spill the beans" and confess something which will wound the spouse and be used against them. The element of distrust is pointed out, together with the reassurance that they will retain control of their tongue, and the therapist will assist where needed. No bad "confessional" effects have been seen. Also, in view of this and of the strong positive transference created by the beneficial drug experience I now insist on the spouse being present. If the therapist and spouse are of the same sex, an added, third person of the other sex is needed. This may be a friend or close relative but in any case should be of high ethical qualities. Some patients seem to identify with and retain the characteristics of their companions during the experience, although this is hard to evaluate.

THE TREATMENT EXPERIENCE

Having been told to dress informally and comfortably, the patient arrives about 8:00 to 9:00 A.M. He is shown the treatment room, the way to the toilet, and in general made familiar with the treatment setting. The companions are told to find comfortable seats, and that they may read or do as they like.

The LSD is given orally with as much or little ceremony as the therapist wishes.

The three stages of evasion, symbolism and immediate perception are well described by Sherwood, et al. (1962, p. 12). During the first, or evasive phase, the patient tries to maintain ego control by talk, distraction, walking about, etc. They should be permitted to do so, but encouraged to lie down. It is found well to put on a black eye shade such as sometimes used by restless sleepers, or to wring out a hand towel in warm water and place this over the eyes. This minimization of external incident light cuts down on the number of distracting visual images, and leads into the second or symbolization stage.

After the fifth hour, the patient is usually sitting up. It is well to encourage him to use the toilet if he's not done so before. If he feels like talking, the therapist should be receptive but not probing because he will be so deeply introspective that even simple questions will tend to confuse the patient.

After the initial three to four hour stages of profound drug involvement, there is a wave-like effect with periods of normal environmental contacts. Withdrawn introspective periods steadily lessen and the normal periods lengthen, but these waves of introspection continue up to twelve hours. The therapist may suggest a brief walk, preferably in a garden. He should always accompany the patient and look for uneasiness as soon as they are out into the general world. The patient will have a great reduction in ability to integrate even minor interaction, such as passing other pedestrians on the walk. If the therapist sees him feeling tense and anxious, he should gently but firmly suggest returning to the protective environment of the treatment setting. When the patient appears generally normal and integrated and is talking easily about the experience, the therapist can let him go home. This occurs between six and eight hours, occasionally sooner. However, there must always be a companion to do the driving, and define advance planning so the patient will not be alone the rest of the evening.

At the time of leaving the treatment setting, the patient's companion is given 25 mg of Thorazine plus one and one-half gr of Nembutal with instructions that the patient is to take these at the normal time of retiring, if desired. There are no limitations as to activity other than that the patient should not drive a car or go out that evening. If he wishes to take one or two alcoholic drinks at home he may do so. After the usual admonitions to call the therapist if needed, the patient is allowed to leave with the companion. The following day he can engage in all normal activities, including driving.

FOLLOW-UP

Following the experience, the therapist schedules an interview within the next day or two if at all possible, to include both the patient and companion, whether the spouse or not. The patient will want to discuss some aspect of the experience and will find it helpful to relate it to the people present during the experience. Gentle probing is sometimes indicated but most times a fairly superficial survey of experience seems to be best at the first immediate treatment interview. The therapist should be aware that there tends to be the great increase of positive transference described previously and where indicated, to make allowances for this phenomena. In many instances, the patient will feel no further need for discussion after the first interview since there is generally a marked alleviation of anxiety and tension symptoms after the experience. Several facts also should be stated: first, that the patient should be told to guard against over-enthusiasm for the drug experience—a conversion-like proselytizing; second, he should know that in from one-and-a-half to three months there tends to be a return towards previous level of tension or symptom formation although never to the degree present before; lastly, that some emotional release may lead to over-emphatic statement of views or feelings during the first two to three weeks, that could be embarrassing and should be held under control.

CONCLUSION

This LSD treatment experience combines the conscious use of psycho-therapeutic techniques and principles, with direct life experience, all intensified by the LSD "enlightenment" effect. The therapy model outlined has been designed to give the patient explicit support, instruction and assurance. He is told that his inner motives and feelings are valuable and can be trusted, that the powerful and protective therapist desires that he should have them and approves them, and that in this crucial interpersonal situation, love, protection and appropriate gratification are available.

Although it is too early to be certain, it appears that for most patients as a result of having this experience, there is a growth of self-confidence and security in the self. There is the added certainty that the world is a safe and rewarding place which takes care of the patient to a worthwhile degree. From the experience narrated by persons taking the drug in a non-supporting and less favorable environment, the opposite situation can produce a deep and lasting insecurity, wariness and mistrust of the world and of the patient's environment in general. It is difficult to coin a name for this particular kind of supportive, reassuring, rewarding therapy. It is not unique, having been tried repeatedly with various types of withdrawn and usually institutionalized persons. The possible unique application described here is in its conscious use with non-psychotic and non-institutionalized patients whose receptivity has been heightened with the use of a particular drug, LSD-25.

29

morning glory seeds

IPOMOEA PURPUREA: A NATURALLY OCCURRING PSYCHEDELIC

CHARLES SAVAGE, WILLIS W. HARMAN and JAMES FADIMAN

Of the naturally occurring plant alkaloids used in ancient and modern religious rites and divination one of the least studied is ololiuqui. The earliest known description of its use is by Hernandez, the King of Spain's personal physician, who spent a number of years in Mexico studying the medicinal plants of the Indians and "accurately illustrated ololiuqui as a morning glory in his work which was not published until 1651" (Schultes, 1960). In his words, "When a person takes ololiuqui, in a short time he loses clear reasoning because of the strength of the seed, and he believes he is in communion with the devil" (Alacon, 1945). Schultes (1941) and Wasson (1961) have reported in detail on the religious and divinatory use of two kinds of morning-glory seeds, *Rivea corymbosa* and *Ipomoea violacea*, among the Mazatec and Zapotec indians. The first of these is assumed to be the ololiuqui of the ancient Aztecs.

In 1955 Osmond described personal experiments with *Rivea corymbosa* seeds and reported that the effects were similar to those of d-lysergic acid diethylamide (LSD-25). He suggested (1957) that the word psychedelic (meaning mind-manifesting) be used as a generic term for this class of substances to refer to their consciousness-expanding and psychotherapeutic function as contrasted with the hallucinogenic aspect. In 1960 Hofmann

By permission of the authors.

reported that he had isolated d-lysergic acid amide (LA) and d-isolysergic acid amide from the seeds of both *Rivea corymbosa* and *Ipomoea violacea.* LA is very similar to LSD in its psychological and physiological manifestations but is reported to have about one twentieth the psychological effectiveness of LSD (Cerletti & Doepfner, 1958).

The work of these investigators led us to a preliminary study of the psychedelic properties of species of *Ipomoea* which are commonly found within the continental United States. The seeds of *Ipomoea purpurea*, the common climbing morning glory, resemble the seeds of *Ipomoea violacea* and have been found to have similar psychedelic properties. Recent analysis by Taber et al., (1963) has verified that LA is present in the varieties used and is probably the primary active agent.

The effects of the seeds of *Ipomoea purpurea* (varieties Heavenly Blue and Pearly Gates) in a total of 45 cases are summarized below. The subjects are all normally functioning adults and the majority had previous experience with LSD. The onset of effects is about half an hour after the seeds have been chewed and swallowed and they last from five to eight hours.

Low Dose, 20–50 Seeds (11 Subjects)

This dosage rarely produces any visual distortions, although with eyes closed there may be beginning imagery. Restlessness, evidenced by alternating brief periods of pacing about and lying down, may be present. There tends to be a heightened awareness of objects and of nature, and enhanced rapport with other persons. A feeling of emotional clarity and of relaxation is likely to persist for several hours after other effects are no longer noticeable.

Medium Dose, 100–150 Seeds (22 Subjects)

In this range the effects resemble those reported for medium-dose (75–150 micrograms) LSD experiences, including spatial distortions, visual and auditory hallucinations, intense imagery with eyes closed, synesthesia and mood elevation. These effects, which occur mainly during the period of 1 to 4 hours after ingestion, are typically followed by a period of alert calmness which may last until the subject goes to sleep.

High Dose, 200–500 Seeds (12 Subjects)

In this range the first few hours may resemble the medium-dose effects described above. However, there is usually a period during which the subjective states are of a sort not describable in terms of images or distortions, states characterized by loss of ego boundaries coupled with feelings of euphoria and philosophical insight. These seem to parallel the published descriptions of experiences with high doses (200–500 micrograms) of LSD given in a supportive, therapeutic setting as reported by Sherwood et al. (1962).

All the subjects who had previous experience with LSD claimed the effects of the seeds were similar to those of LSD. Transient nausea was the most commonly reported side effect, beginning about one half hour after ingestion and lasting a few minutes to several hours. Other reported side effects not commonly found with LSD were a drowsiness or torpor (possibly due to a glucoside also present in the seeds) and a coldness in the extremities suggesting that the ergine content of the seeds may be causing some vascular constriction. (If this is the case, there may be some danger of ergot poisoning resulting from excessive dosages of the seeds.) The only untoward psychic effect was a prolonged (eight hours) disassociative reaction which was terminated with chlorpromazine. The possibility of prolonged adverse reactions to the psychological effects of the seeds is essentially the same as with LSD, and the same precautions should be observed (Cohen & Ditman, 1963).

30

PSYCHEDELIC AGENTS IN
CREATIVE PROBLEM SOLVING:
A PILOT STUDY

WILLIS W. HARMAN, ROBERT H. McKIM, ROBERT E. MOGAR,
JAMES FADIMAN, and MYRON J. STOLAROFF

In recent years, psychedelic agents such as LSD-25, mescaline, and psilocybin, have been used in the treatment of a variety of emotional disorders (Hoffer, 1965; Mogar & Savage, 1964). Researchers have noted similarities between the drug-induced state and certain phases of the creative process (Barron, 1963; Mogar, 1965). Wallis (1926) had defined the stages of creation as (1) preparation, (2) incubation, (3) illumination, and (4) verification. With reference to the illumination phase of creativity, Barron (1963) reported that creative people "deliberately induce in themselves an altered state of consciousness in which the ordinary structures of experience are broken down. The ordinary world may thus be transcended." Further, Barron recommended the application of psychedelic drugs to the study of creativity: "Certain aspects of the creative process, although by no means the creative process as a whole, are analogous to the kind of breaking up of perceptual constancies that is initiated mechanically by the ingestion of the drug."

A more comprehensive rationale for the use of psychedelic agents as facilitative of creative activity is suggested by Rogers' conditions for fostering creativity (1959, condensed from the original):

Reprinted by permission from *Psychol. Rep.*, Vol. 19, 1966, pp. 211–227.

445

The *inner conditions* are three: (a) low degree of psychological defensiveness; lack of rigidity and permeability of boundaries in concepts, beliefs, perceptions, and hypotheses; tolerance for ambiguity where it exists, ability to receive and integrate apparently conflicting information; sensitive awareness of feelings and openness to all phases of experience; (b) evaluative judgement based primarily, not on outside standards or prejudices, but on one's own feelings, intuition, aesthetic sensibility, sense of satisfaction in self-expression, etc.; (c) the ability to "toy" with ideas, colors, shapes, hypotheses; to translate from one form to another; to think in terms of analogues and metaphors.

External conditions are two: (a) an atmosphere of psychological safety, in which the individual feels accepted as of unconditional worth; in which he feels he can be spontaneous without fear that his actions or creations will be prematurely evaluated by rigid external standards; in which he feels empathic understanding; (b) an atmosphere of psychological freedom; of permissiveness to think, to feel, to be whatever is discovered within oneself.

Within this framework, the psychedelic state would be expected to enhance creativity *temporarily* insofar as the "external conditions" were present in the session milieu and to the extent that the "inner conditions" were induced or facilitated by the experience. In addition, *long-term* changes would be expected to occur if the "inner conditions" were permanently altered by the experience and/or if S became less affected by non-ideal "external condition."

As noted earlier, a number of specific attributes and abilities related to creativity are often observed to be heightened *during* the psychedelic experience. This is the case if the session is so oriented and when S is prepared to expect such intensification. In studies of the therapeutic efficacy of psychedelic drugs, the *long-term* changes bear a striking similarity to behavior under creativity-fostering conditions. In a study of nearly 400 patients, Savage et al. (1966) reported the following changes in values and personality based on extensive test data, observer ratings, follow-up interviews, and subjective reports: greater spontaneity of emotional expression, more adequate ego resources, reduction in depression and anxiety, less distance in interpersonal relations, more openness to experience, increased aesthetic appreciation, deeper sense of meaning and purpose in life, and an enhanced sense of unity with nature and humanity. Such results suggest that, used in an appropriate context, psychedelic agents may facilitate lasting change in the direction of increased creative expression and self-actualization.

With regard to the apparent creativity-fostering potential of psychedelic agents, it is essential to recognize the crucial importance of the expectations of all persons involved in the session, and of the psychosocial milieu in which the session is conducted. If expectations and intentions are primarily therapeutic, S is likely to find that his personal problems occupy the center of his experience. If an ingestant expects "kicks," then euphoria and visions may be the result. But, if S is prepared to expect that distractions will be at a minimum and that he will be able to focus his attention and resources on creative problem-solving, then the likelihood of enhancement of performance will be greatly increased. The confidence of E, based on personal experience, that the process "works," is an essential ingredient. The psychedelic S is extremely sensitive in his heightened state of empathic awareness to doubt conveyed by E.

TABLE 1
Some Reported Characteristics of the Psychedelic Experience

Those Supporting Creativity	Those Hindering Creativity
1. Increased access to unconscious data.	1. Capacity for logical thought processes may be diminished.
2. More fluent free association; increased ability to play spontaneously with hypotheses, metaphors, paradox, transformations, relationships, etc.	2. Ability to consciously direct concentration may be reduced.
3. Heightened ability for visual imagery and fantasy.	3. Inability to control imaginary and conceptual sequences.
4. Relaxation and openness.	4. Anxiety and agitation.
5. Sensory inputs more acutely perceived.	5. Outputs (verbal and visual communication abilites may be constricted).
6. Heightened empathy with external processes, objects, and people.	6. Tendency to focus upon "inner problems" of a personal nature.
7. Aesthetic sensibility heightened.	7. Experienced beauty may lessen tension to obtain aesthetic experience in the act of creation.
8. Enhanced "sense of truth," ability to "see through" false solutions and phony data.	8. Tendency to become absorbed in hallucinations and illusions.
9. Lessened inhibition, reduced tendency to censor own by premature negative judgment.	9. Finding the best solution may seem unimportant.
10. Motivation may be heightened by suggestion and providing the right set.	10. "This-wordly" tasks may seem trivial, and hence motivation may be decreased.

These important aspects of the drug-induced state help reconcile otherwise contradictory findings. Studies indicate that many kinds of performance tend to deteriorate or remain unchanged during the acute phase of the experience (cf., Trouton & Eysenck, 1961). Other investigators report enhancement of various kinds of performance during and subsequent to the psychedelic state (Hoffer, 1965). The preliminary findings of the present exploratory study suggest that, when performance impairment occurs, it may be attributed at least partially to an anxiety-provoking setting and/or the negative expectations of S and E.

Other specific characteristics of the psychedelic experience are listed in Table 1. The left-hand column includes frequently reported attributes which would tend to facilitate creative activity. The right-hand column contains features which might operate to hinder creativity or make communication difficult, especially in a group-conducted problem-solving situation.

When the problem is viewed in terms of complex transactions between pharmacologic psychosocial variables, it becomes apparent that the enhancement of creativity by means of psychedelic substances requires that the facilitating characteristics be carefully cultivated and the hindering characteristics minimized or eliminated. The key to this task is the establishment and maintenance of an appropriate set in S, both prior to and during the psychedelic problem-solving session.

The exploratory study reported here is an initial attempt to obtain data relevant to three empirical questions: (1) Does the psychedelic experience enhance creativity and if so, what is the evidence of enhancement? (2) Does the experience result in the production of concrete, valid, and feasible solutions, as viewed by the pragmatic criteria of industry and science? (3) Does the psychedelic experience result in demonstrable long-term personality changes in the direction of increased creativity and self-actualization?

One further point requires elucidation. For reasons explained immediately below, the design of this and further research involves comparison of an S's performance during a problem-solving session with the same S's performance at other times and with other Ss' performance under "normal" or no-drug conditions. It does not include comparison with the same S's performance when expectancy is eliminated or when the psychedelic drug is eliminated, other factors being presumably the same.

The aim of this research was to devise a way to using drugs to optimize conditions for creative problem-solving by humans. It is not conceived as an attempt to establish experimentally the psychological effects of a psychedelic drug. In fact previous research with the psychedelic agents has shown (Mogar, 1965) that this latter is an extremely difficult if not a rather futile question. There are no specific psychological reactions to these drugs; there are, rather, various reactions depending upon such variables as expectancies of S and E, S's degree of trust, the over-all setting, S's personality characteristics, etc. The psychedelic agent in this case is part of the complex, including the expectancy and motivation of S, which is being investigated. Reduction or elimination of any one of these three main ingredients of expectancy, motivation, or psychedelic agent clearly alters the efficacy of the procedure. The question under scrutiny is to what extent performance can be enhanced when all factors are optimized.

The question of the relative contribution of the various elements of this procedure is valid. It is not under study here, partly because the matter of separating out one of the factors is much more difficult than may appear superficially to be the case. To eliminate the psychedelic agent, for example, without at the same time affecting the expectancy variable is very difficult, if not impossible. Neither the experienced investigator nor the naive S is easily fooled on the matter of whether he has received a psychedelic substance or merely a psychoactive placebo such as amphetamine. Thus, even if the research design ostensibly uses a double-blind technique, expectancies of E and of S vary according to their appraisals (fairly accurate) as to whether or not S has received a psychedelic drug.

METHOD

Selection of Subjects

The participants were 27 males engaged in various professional occupations, i.e., engineers, physicists, mathematicians, architects, a furniture designer, and a commercial artist. Most Ss had no previous experience with psychedelic agents.* They were selected from local industries and academic institutions according to the following criteria: (1) Participant's occupation normally requires creative problem-solving ability. (2) Participant is psychologically normal with stable life circumstances as determined by psychiatric interview-examination. (3) Participant is adequately motivated to discover, verify, and apply problem-solutions within his industrial or academic work capacity.

*Eight Ss (Nos. 103, 104, 204, 207, 211, 212, 214, 220) had two or more previous LSD sessions with dosages of 200 mcg. or more. One of these (No. 212) participated in earlier trial sessions. The remaining 19 had no previous psychedelic experience.

Procedure Prior to Sessions

As indicated previously, considerable attention must be paid to establishing the appropriate expectancy, or more generally, to the careful preparation of each S prior to his participation in an experimental session.

Ss were instructed to select one or more problems of professional interest which require a creative solution. A number of participants had worked weeks or months on their chosen problems without obtaining a satisfactory solution. In addition to the psychiatric examination (with the psychiatrist who would supervise the psychedelic session) at least one presession interview was conducted with each S plus a minimum of one meeting attended by those Ss who would participate simultaneously, i.e., as a group. The focus of these preliminary meetings was twofold: first, to allay apprehension and establish rapport and trust among all persons involved; and second, to structure in considerable detail the conduct of the session. Instructions emphasized that the experience could be directed as desired. Ss were told that they would not experience difficulty with such distractions as visions, involvement with personal problems, and so on. Instead, they would find that, following an initial period of 2 or 3 hours for "getting into" the psychedelic state, they would be able to concentrate on the assigned tasks with ease and would be able to work more effectively than usual. The agenda and sequence of events to be followed in the study were outlined in detail. Thus, before engaging in the problem-solving session, participants were generally positively and enthusiastically expectant, with a clear picture of what would take place and under what conditions, and had information on how to cope with various exigencies that might arise.

Procedure during Sessions

The first step in testing the hypothesis that psychedelics could be used to enhance creativity was to conduct trial group sessions to work out techniques and gain experience. A group-size of four was decided upon as being both economical and manageable. (If at the last minute an S dropped out, n was 3.) In each group were also two observers who did not take any drugs. Initially it had been anticipated that the group would be difficult to manage if the dosage was too high. Preliminary informal trials with varying dosages indicated that up to 200 mg. of mescaline sulfate (or the approximate equivalent, 100 mcg. of LSD) could be used without difficulty. For the 7 sessions reported here (involving basically 27 Ss) the drug regime included as primary active agent 200 mg. of mescaline.* During the session an initial period of about 3 hours was spent quietly listening to music with stereo earphones. Ss were advised to "turn off" their analytic faculties, to relax and accept whatever form of experience came their way, to refrain from attempting to control the sequence or nature of the events. The declared aim was to stop using one's cognitive and perceptual processes in the familiar way and to heighten the likelihood of discovering new ways.

After this initial "quiet period" Ss were roused and encouraged to talk with one another briefly. Snacks were available. Approximately an hour was then devoted to psychological testing. (Alternate forms of the tests had been administered during the pre-session meeting.)

Following the testing, S spent 3 to 4 hours solving the problem he had previously chosen. During this main problem-solving period, the participants worked by themselves, usually in total silence. Toward the end of the afternoon Ss often shared experiences and sometimes worked together on a problem brought in by one of the participants. Ss were driven home about 6 P.M., with a sedative which they could take if difficulty in sleeping occurred. In many cases they preferred to stay up as late as 4 A.M., working out insights discovered earlier in the day.

Assessment Procedures

In addition to the psychological test data obtained before and during the session, each participant was asked to submit a subjective report of his experience within several days after his experimental session. Each was also asked to answer a questionnaire concerning various aspects of the experience. Three to 6 weeks after the session, S was interviewed by the psychiatrist and asked to respond to a questionnaire related to (a) the effect of the psychedelic experience upon post-session creative ability and (b) the validity and acceptance of solutions conceived during the session, according to the pragmatic criteria of industry and science.

From the data of this exploratory study, the effects of a psychedelic agent on creative performance were evaluated in three ways: (a) an analysis of change scores on tests of creative ability administered several days prior to and again during the acute phase of the experimental session; (b) a content analysis of subjective reports for evidence of generally recognized components of the creative process and distinguishing features of creative solutions; and (c) subjection of the solutions derived in the session (theories,

*Research psychologists interested in a more exact description of procedures used should contact the author directly. Mescaline sulfate was procured from F. Hoffmann LaRoche Co., Basel, Switzerland.

inventions, designs, etc.) to the pragmatic test of scientific, industrial, and/or commercial endorsement.

RESULTS AND DISCUSSION

Psychometric Data*

Three objective tests of creativity were administered several days prior to and again during the acute drug phase of the problem-solving sessions. (For two of the tests data were not obtained from all Ss.) All three tests have reported split-half reliabilities of over 0.90. In the pre-drug session and in the drug session, the order of taking the two forms was reversed for half the Ss. Test-retest reliability data was not available; however, published research with these tests indicates that practive effects are not significant.

Purdue Creativity Test. S's ($n = 18$) task is to find as many uses as possible for each of a variety of pictured objects (Lawshe & Harris, 1960). The test is scored for two subscales, fluency of ideas under time pressure and flexibility or range of solutions. Net positive change on the fluency scale was significant (13 of 18 males; $\chi^2 = 5.88$, $df = 12$, $p < 0.02$). Change on the flexibility score was not statistically significant (10 of 18 males increased their scores). Mean change of combined score from pre-session testing to the testing during the session was $+15$ percentile points (matched against engineering-student norms). Individual shifts ranged from -30 to $+60$ percentile points for 14 of the Ss. Further inference cannot be drawn in the absence of more complete validation data.

Miller Object Visualization Test. S's ($n = 27$, 8 females* and 19 males) task is to envision a two-dimensional outline figure folded into a solid (Miller, 1955). Approximately half the Ss reported that the alternate form taken during the psychedelic session seemed easier and averaged about half the time taken for the earlier testing. About a third of the Ss reported using a more visual approach, and each of these improved his score on the second testing (or took less time to achieve the same score). One S reported experiencing greater difficulty on the second test and indicated that he

---

*A transcript of raw data has been filed with the American Documentation Institute, Auxiliary Publications Project, Photoduplication Service, Library of Congress, Washington, D.C. 20540 as Document No. 8953. Remit $1.25 for photocopies or 35-mm microfilm.

*Scores of female Ss were obtained in sessions structured exactly like those of the male Ss except that the nature of their problems was somewhat different. These few scores are included here since test results are at best rather skimpy.

had attempted purely analytical solutions. Improvement in performance was significant ($\chi^2 = 26$, $p < 0.02$). A ceiling effect limited the change scores for this instrument.

Witkin Embedded Figures Test. S's ($n = 14$, 4 females* and 10 males) task is to distinguish a simple geometrical figure embedded in a complex colored figure (Watkin, 1950). Every S but one male improved on this measure. Mean time for locating the 12 figures was 404 seconds for the pre-session testing and 234 seconds for the testing during the session. Performance enhancement was significant ($\chi^2 = 8.64$, $df = 13$, $p < 0.01$). These are extremely high and significant changes (individual improvements in speed up to 200%) compared with changes observed in previous research with this instrument (Witkin et al., 1962).

The implications of these data are twofold. First, it is clear that scores on a stable test can shift dramatically upward under the drug condition and second, this shift is in the direction of enhanced ability to recognize patterns, to isolate and minimize visual distraction, and to maintain visual memory in spite of confusing color and spatial forms. Viewed as personality change, these Ss showed a shift from "field dependence" to "field independence," as defined by Witkin et al., (1962). Research has related this dimension to numerous performance variables, including autonomic stability, concept formation, resistance to suggestion in reporting illusions, and resourcefulness in ambiguous situations (e.g., Elkind et al., 1963; Elliott, 1961). As measured by the embedded figures test, field-dependence has been reported to be resistant to a variety of experimental interventions including stress, training, sensory isolation, hypnosis, and the influence of a variety of drugs (Witkin et al., 1962).

Subjective Ratings

Following the experimental session, each S completed a brief questionnaire in which he rated his experience with respect to nine characteristics relevant to creative problem-solving. Each characteristic was rated along a 5-point scale from -2 (marked impairment) through 0 (no change) to $+2$ (marked enhancement). The nine characteristics with average ratings are listed below:

1. Lowering of defenses, reduction of inhibitions and anxiety $+1.7$
2. Ability to see the problem in the broadest terms $+1.4$
3. Enhanced fluency of ideation $+1.6$
4. Heightened capacity for visual imagery and fantasy $+1.0$
5. Increased ability to concentrate $+1.2$
6. Empathy with external processes and objects heightened $+0.8$

7. Empathy with other people heightened   +1.4
8. Data from "unconscious" more accessible   +0.8
9. Enhanced sense of "knowing" when the right solution appears   +1.0

These results may be summarized by noting that selected visual and verbal skills were enhanced for some and that this enhancement was objectively measurable. It cannot be concluded that all mental functioning will be subject to the same enhancement; however, it apears that performance levels on specific creative abilities can be temporarily improved if the psychedelic session is specifically focused appropriately.

The increased intuitive skills reflected in these test results are consistent with the cardinal features of psychedelic therapy, including reduced defensiveness, reliving early memories, increased awareness of unconscious material, and greater emotional expression. These results strengthen the proposition that it is important to define set and setting accurately in interpreting the results of research with psychedelic agents.

Subjective Reports

The literature on creativity includes analytical description of the components of creative experience, the personal characteristics of creative individuals, and the distinguishing features of creative solutions. From the participants' reports it was possible to extract 11 strategies for creative problem-solving, or experiential modes related to creativity, which were reported as heightened during the session. These 11 aspects of the creative process, their correspondence with current theory and research on creativity and representative quotations from subjective reports are detailed below.

A. *Low inhibition and anxiety*. Examples of comments are:

There was no fear, no worry, no sense of reputation and competition, no envy, none of these things which in varying degrees have always been present in my work.

Diminished fear of making mistakes or being embarrased.

Each of the four major theoretical orientations—psychoanalytic, behavioristic, Gestalt, and existential—emphasizes the necessity of this condition of creativity. Also, a mass of empirical evidence indicates that inhibition and anxiety narrow perception, reduce the breadth of conscious-unconscious awareness, and impair cognitive and psychomotor performance. Bruner's (1962) criterion, "Freedom to be dominated by the object," means specifically, "free of the defenses that keep us hidden from ourselves." Maslow's "self-actualizing person" and Rogers' "fully-functioning person" stress the importance of being unfrightened by the unknown, the mysterious, the puzzling (Mackler & Shontz, 1965). Getzels and Jackson (1962) found that the homes of creative persons are relatively threat-free and uninhibited. It seems apparent that circumstances that reduce anxiety will facilitate experience.

B. *Capacity to structure problems in a larger context.* Sample comments from Ss are:

Looking at the same problem with (psychedelic) materials, I was able to consider it in a much more basic way, because I could form and keep in mind a much broader picture.

Ability to start from the broadest general basis in the beginning . . .

I returned to the original problem. . . . I tried, I think consciously, to think of the problem in its totality, rather than through the devices I had used before.

The Gestalt position views creativity in terms of reorganization or restructuring of the *total* stimulus field. Wertheimer (1945) notes that each step in the creative process is taken by surveying the whole situation, the total dynamic field. The importance of seeing a problem from a larger perspective is given explicit expression in G. Murphy's principle of *progressive mastery* (1963). A behavioristic concept of creativity formulated by Mednick (1962) emphasizes the associative hierarchy of elements; the ability to bring remote ideas into contiguity to form creative matrices. The larger context also finds expression in Koestler's (1964) concept of "bisociation" and in Guilford's (1959) primary trait, *divergent thinking*, which denotes viewing the molecular from the vantage point of the molar.

C. *High fluency and flexibility of ideation.* Illustrative comments by Ss are:

I began to draw . . . . my senses could not keep up with my images . . . . my hand was not fast enough . . . . I was impatient to record the picture (it has not faded one particle). I worked at a pace I would not have thought I was capable of.

My mind seemed much freer to roam around the problems, and it was these periods of roaming around which produced solutions.

. . . I dismissed the original idea entirely, and started to approach the graphic problem in a radically different way. That was when things began to happen. All kinds of different possibilities came to mind.

Based on extensive research and quantification of creative abilities, Guilford (1959) considers fluency and flexibility the two crucial attributes. His primary factors include (1) word fluency, associational fluency, and ideational fluency; and (2) flexibility of thinking, composed of spontaneous flexibility and figural adaptive flexibility. These same attributes are included in the psychoanalytic condition of creativity, "deautomatization" (Hartmann, 1958) or the relaxing of ego boundaries.

D. *High capacity for visual imagery and fantasy.* Three examples of *S*s' comments are:

I tried to relax and create a completely white and clear mental image. Suddenly I was not in the present but experienced very vivid technicolor, dreamlike mental pictures.

I began to see an image of the circuit. The gates themselves were little silver cones linked together by lines. I watched this circuit flipping through its paces. . . . The psychedelic state is, for me at least, an immensely powerful one for obtaining insight and understanding through visual symbolism.

I began visualizing all the properties known to me that a photon possesses. . . . The photon was comprised of an electron and a positron cloud moving together in an intermeshed synchronized helical orbit. . . . This model was reduced for visualization purposes to a black and white ball propagating in a screw-like fashion through space. I kept putting the model through all sorts of known tests. . . .

This cardinal feature of the psychedelic experience has been associated with creativity since man's earliest history. It is not surprising then that this attribute occupies a central position in current theories of creativity supported by a large body of empirical evidence (Holt, 1964). The psychoanalytic view formalizes the importance of retaining the child's capacity for fresh, free-flowing perception and thought. Among the conditions conducive to creativity, Kris (1952) lists capacity for regressive experiences, richness of imagination, and ability to convert fantasy into creative products. These conditions are embodied in the term, "regression in the service of the ego"—the hallmark of creative inspiration. The notion of creative regression has been further elaborated by Schachtel (1959) with particular emphasis on the key roll of visual imagery as a mode of thought. The same attributes are embraced in Rorschach's concept of *inner creation,* Bleuler's account of constructive *autistic thinking*, Werner's *physiognomic perception*, and Adler's *creative self* (Stark, 1964).

E. *High ability to concentrate.* Examples from *S*s' comments follow:

I was impressed with the intensity of concentration, the forcefulness and exuberance with which I could proceed toward the problem.

The drug appeared to maintain motivation to pursue what is aesthetically intriguing to a point far beyond what I would do normally.

I was amazed at the four hours that had passed and would have guessed that it was only one and one-half hours.

In what seemed like 10 minutes, I had completed the problem, having what I considered (and what I still consider) a classic solution.

The importance of sustained focus of attention, separating the essential from the nonessential and eliminating irrelevant elements, has been particularly emphasized in behavioristic formulations. Considerable laboratory research indicates a direct positive relationship between ability to concentrate and enhanced performance in problem solving (Mednick, 1962). Roe (1953) found that prolonged concentration was a prominent characteristic in the lives of creative thinkers. From a more dynamic standpoint, the existential position also emphasizes concentration. The word "absorption," "involvement," "being caught up in," seem to catch the intense enrapturement of heightened awareness and occur frequently in existential writings (Mackler & Shontz, 1965).

F. *High empathy with external processes and objects.* Illustrative remarks are:

The sense of the problem as a living thing that is growing toward its inherent solution.

I spent a productive period climbing down my retina, walking around and thinking about certain problems, relating to the mechanism of vision.

Ability to grasp the problem in its entirety to "dive" into without reservations, almost like becoming the problem.

According to Schachtel (1959), creativity occurs when allocentric (in contrast to autocentric), perception is dominant, i.e., there is openness to the world in its inexhaustible being. Lowenfeld (1947) refers to an intense concern with the environment; with the *tactual space* in which the person is embedded. A number of theorists including Adler, Erich Fromm, Rank, Maslow, and Barron stress that the creative individual is highly sensitive to his environment (Mackler & Shontz, 1965). Two of Murphy's (1963) conditions of creativity are relevant to empathic communion with the world: receptivity to the outer world and the capacity to love or move outgoingly toward it. *Canalization* or *cathexis* means forming an emotional line of communication from the self to the stimulus value of outer things.

G. *High empathy with people.* This may be illustrated with selected comments:

It was also felt that group performance was affected in subtle ways. This may be evidence that some sort of group action was going on all the time.

Only at intervals did I become aware of the music. Sometimes, when I felt the other guys listening to it, it was a physical feeling of them listening to it.

Sometimes we even had the feeling of having the same thoughts and ideas.

Adequate trust and mutuality in interpersonal relations are emphasized in psychoanalytic and self theories of creativity. Rogers (1959) more than any other theorist gives empathy with people a central place in his hierarchy of conditions fostering creativity. It is only through such empathy that the necessary psychological safety and freedom can occur. It is especially central to creative problem-solving in areas that involve interpersonal relationships.

H. *Accessibility of unconscious resources*. Comments from *S*s are:

... brought about almost total recall of a course that I had had in thermodynamics; something that I had never given any thought about in years.

I was in my early teens and wandering through the gardens where I actually grew up. I felt all my prior emotions in relation to my surroundings.

This is another feature of creativity that has been recognized since early times. Harold Rugg's classic work on *Imagination* (1963) refers to the transliminal experience, the illuminating flash of insight occurring at a critical threshold of the conscious-unconscious continuum. MacKinnon (1964) has elaborated on this concept in order to account for his results of intensive studies of creative individuals. He concludes that the truly creative person is distinguished from the noncreative individual by the greater ease with which he moves from more conscious and active to more unconscious and passive states. His results and interpretation are consistent with psychoanalytic views of creativity, particularly the emphasis on access to preconscious material, primary process activity, and ego regression.

I. *Ability to associate seemingly dissimilar elements in meaningful ways.* Sample comments are:

The next insight came as an image of an oyster shell, with the mother-of-pearl shining in different colors. I translated it (into) the idea of an interferometer.

Most of the insights come by association.

It was the last idea that I thought was remarkable because of the way in which it developed. This idea was the result of a fantasy that occurred during Wagner. I put down a line which seemed to embody this (fantasy). . . . I later made the handle which my sketches suggested and it had exactly the quality I was looking for. . . . I was very amused at the ease with which all of this was done.

The concepts of Mednick, Koestler, and Guilford described above embrace also the ability to restructure in novel, useful, amusing, or elegant ways. Murphy (1963) refers to this attribute as combinatory skill, the capacity to form structure whether architectural, musical, verbal, spatial, or in other media. Few writers on the creative process have failed to make some reference to the reintegrative element usually present. Mednick (1962) emphasizes that "the more mutually remote the elements of the new combination, the more creative the process or solution."

J. *High motivation to obtain closure; an appetite for elegance. Ss'* comments may be given:

> Had tremendous desire to obtain an elegant solution (the most for the least).

> All known constraints about the problem were simultaneously imposed as I hunted for possible solutions. It was like an analog computer whose output could not deviate from what was desired and whose input was continually perturbed with the inclination toward achieving the output.

> It was almost an awareness of the "degree of perfection" of whatever I was doing.

The extensive work on problem solving by the Gestalters led to the concept of closure. Closure is the end product of creative thinking involving changes in the functional meaning, grouping, and reorganization of the items in the field until the gaps and difficulties in the problem are resolved. The field is restructured to restore harmony (Mackler & Shontz, 1965) Closely related to the closure principle, Mackworth (1965) emphasizes the passion for excellence characteristic of original thinkers. Murphy (1963) call attention to the urge or *will* to create elegant solutions to problems.

K. *Capacity to visualize the completed solution in its entirety.* Illustrative examples of *Ss'* comments are:

> I looked at the paper I was to draw on. I was completely blank. I knew that I would work with a property of 300 ft. square. I drew the property lines. . . . Suddenly I saw the finished project. I did some quick calculations. . . . It would fit on the property and not only that . . . it would meet the cost and income requirements . . . it would park enough cars . . . it met all the requirements.

> I visualized the result I wanted and subsequently brought the variables into play which could bring that result about. I had great visual (mental) perceptibility; I could imagine what was wanted, needed, or not possible with almost no effort. In what seemed like ten minutes I had completed the problem. . . . I was amazed at my idealism, my visual perception, and the rapidity with which I would operate.

Bertrand Russell once remarked that in the discovery of the theory of relativity, Einstein began with a kind of mystical or poetical insight into the truth which took the form of visualizing the totality of the law in all its ramifications. The Gestalt view conceives creativity as an action which produces a new idea or "insight" full-formed; it comes to the individual in a flash of insight in which the completed solution is grasped in its entirety constitutes the most distinctive feature of Rugg's "transliminal experience" and Maslow's "peak experience."

Pragmatic Utility of Solutions

The practical value of obtained solutions is a check against subjective reports of accomplishment which might be attributable to temporary euphoria. The nature of these solutions was varied; they included: (a) a new approach to the design of a vibratory microtome, (b) a commercial building design accepted by client, (c) space probe experiments devised to measure solar properties, (d) design of a linear electron accelerator beam-steering device, (e) engineering improvement to magnetic tape recorder, (f) a chair design modeled and accepted by manufacturer, (g) a letterhead design approved by customer, (h) a mathematical theorem regarding NOR-gate circuits, (i) completion of a furniture line design, (j) a new conceptual model of a photon which was found useful, and (k) design of a private dwelling approved by the client.

The over-all tally, obtained by questionnaire, showed out of 44 problems attempted: 1 on which there had been no further activity for a month or more after the date of the problem-solving session, 20 on which new avenues for further investigation had been opened, 1 on which a developmental model to test the solution had been authorized, 2 on which a working model had been completed, 6 for which the solution had been accepted for construction or production, 10 for which the partial solution obtained was being developed further or being applied in practice, and 4 for which no solution was obtained.

Long-term Enhancement of Creative Ability

The present exploratory study included a relatively short follow-up evaluation 2 weeks after the psychedelic session. Most Ss reported significant changes in their modes of functioning which were continuous with the enhancement experienced during the acute phase of the psychedelic state. For example:

I feel there has been a general improvement, maintained to date, in my ability to concentrate on specific problems, in my visual perceptibility of problems, and a general reduction of inhibitions.

I find that I can dwell upon a problem without distractions creeping in.

I have an energy and decisiveness I have never known before.

Pending more objectives, systematic confirmation of possible long-term behavioral changes, these tentative findings suggest that various kinds and degrees of creative abilities tend to persist for a while subsequent to a single psychedelic experience that is conducted according to the carefully structured regimen described above. A significant accomplishment of the present effort was the development of an effective set of procedures for observing the effects of psychedelic agents on creative problem-solving. Extension of this work should permit a more comprehensive, reliable description of these effects, both immediate and long-term. Specifically, further research should include (a) a larger sample of Ss who represent more varied specialties within the arts and sciences, (b) an expanded battery of performance tests of creativity which have been pretested and have alternate forms, and (c) a second battery of standardized paper-and-pencil tests which may be given before and at various points subsequent to the psychedelic session.

Summary

Based on the frequently reported similarities between creative and psychedelic (drug-induced, consciousness-expansion) experiences, a preliminary study was conducted to explore the effects of psychedelic agents (LSD-25, mescaline) on creative problem-solving ability. Twenty-seven professionally employed males were given a single psychedelic experience in 1 of 7 small groups (ns = 3 or 4) following extensive selection and preparatory procedures. This drug-induced problem-solving session was carefully structured with particular focus on establishing Ss' expectancies and a psychosocial milieu conducive to creative activity. Tentative findings based on tests of creativity, on subjective reports and self ratings, and on the utility of problem solutions suggested that, if given according to this carefully structured regimen, psychedelic agents seem to facilitate creative problem-solving, particularly in the "illumination phase." The results also suggest that various degrees of increased creative ability may continue for at least some weeks subsequent to a psychedelic problem-solving session.

31

"PSYCHEDELIC" EXPERIENCES IN ACUTE PSYCHOSES

MALCOLM B. BOWERS, JR., AND DANIEL X. FREEDMAN

The disease which thus evokes these new and wonderful talents and operations of the mind may be compared to an earthquake which by convulsing the upper strata of our globe, throws upon its surface precious and splendid fossils, the existence of which was unknown to the proprietors of the soil in which they were buried (Rush, 1962).

This paper is concerned with subjective experience in the early phases of some psychotic reactions and has been prepared with two problems in mind. First, in the experimental production of altered states of awareness in man, the most common source of information is the self-report; yet when data obtained in this way are compared to clinical conditions it becomes clear that we have very little comparable information from patients. As a result, when studies in experimental psychopathology are related to clinical states, comparisons may be confusing and can give rise to spurious controversy as to whether or not a particular experimental state actually resembles a certain clinical syndrome. Thus precise information about subjective experience in clinical conditions might help to clarify some of these issues. Secondly, altered experiences of self and external world have not been easily accounted for in psychodynamic theories of psychosis. Arlow and Brenner have recently emphasized that some of the observations on which dynamic theories of psychosis have been based require more

Reprinted by permission from Arch. Gen. Psych., Vol 15, 1966, pp. 240–248.

careful scrutiny (1964) and the observations recorded in this report are a part of such an ongoing attempt.

There are some noteworthy observations in the literature focused on subjective experience in early psychosis. Jaspers, Mayer-Gross, Binswanger, Straus, and Minkowski have written about self-experience interpreted from the viewpoint of existentialist theories or phenomenology (Jaspers, 1964; May, Angel, and Ellenberger, 1958) McGhie and Chapman have characterized some of the perceptual alterations in early schizophrenia (1961). Their clinical findings have led to several experimental approaches to perceptual and cognitive processes in schizophrenia (McGhie, Chapman, and Lawson, 1965). Norman Cameron has written in detail about the subjective world of the incipient paranoid psychotic (1959). Arieti has described schizophrenic panic, and his description is similar to many of the cases we will cite (1961).

We have obtained information from two sources. First in clinical work with psychotic patients over a two year period, an attempt was made to elicit information about their earliest recognition of "changes." This was done either at the time they were acutely disturbed (e.g., "What are you feeling now?") or in retrospect. Whenever possible, a patient was encouraged to write a brief statement describing his earliest subjective experiences when he fell ill. In several instances it turned out that patients had written down their feelings during the early stages of their psychosis, and we asked permission to read these accounts (Bowers, 1965). As our second source, we reviewed most of the available self-reports by psychotic patients in a rather restrictive way (Sommer & Osmond, 1960; Sommer & Osmond, 1961). That is, we in essence asked of each document the question, "Is there included in this account any clear description of the writer's earliest and/or most consistently experienced alteration in subjectivity?" In a number of instances—some classic, some relatively unfamiliar—we found material pertinent to this question.

REPORT OF CASES

CASE 1. A 38-year-old music teacher, pressed by debts and family problems and concerned with a very real national crisis, began to feel that life was taking on an emotional intensity which was new. He noted a cross on a familiar church for the first time and felt that it had profound, exciting meaning for him. He felt close to nature, emphatically understanding human and subhuman life. A few nights later he described a sensation that "God actually touched my heart. The next day was horror and ecstasy. I began to feel that I might be the agent of some spiritual reawakening." The emotional intensity of the experience became overpowering. Gradually, anxiety and persecutory delusions out-stripped the ecstatic elements and the patient made a serious suicide attempt. Even much later in psychotherapy he recalled "the experience" as one of profound meaning for him, one which he would always cherish.

CASE 2. A 21-year-old college student, concerned about his parents and about a love affair, became guilt-ridden after a sexual experience with his girlfriend. Soon thereafter, he felt that his life was completely changed. He felt a sense of mission in the world which he now saw "as a completely wonderful place" and stated, "I began to experience goodness and love for the first time." Life for him took on an intense benevolent quality which he had never felt before. He talked with friends fervently about the "new life" and about the way he could now care for and understand people. The feelings progressed to frank delusions that he was a religious messiah and heralded an acute catatonic psychosis.

CASE 3. Another 21-year-old college student had been ruminating for some time about "personality problems" and difficulties in the choice of a vocation. The following is essentially a verbatim account of the week prior to his admission.

Before last week, I was quite closed about my emotions; then finally I owned up to them with another person. I began to speak without thinking beforehand and what came out showed an awareness of human beings and God. I could feel deeply about other people. We felt connected. The side which had been suppressing emotions did not seem to be the real one. I was in a higher and higher state of exhilaration and awareness. Things people said had hidden meaning. They said things that applied to life. Everything that was real seemed to make sense. I had a great awareness of life, truth, and God. I went to church and suddenly all parts of the service made sense. My senses were sharpened. I became fascinated by the little insignificant things around me. There was an additional awareness of the world that would do artists, architects, and painters good. I ended up being too emotional, but I felt very much at home with myself, very much at ease. It gave me a great feeling of power. It was not a case of seeing more broadly but deeper. I was losing touch with the outside world and lost my sense of time. There was a fog around me in some sense, and I felt half asleep. I could see more deeply into problems that other people had and would go directly into a deeper subject with a person. I had the feeling I loved everybody in the world. Sharing emotions was like wiping the shadow away, wiping a false face. I thought I might wake up from a nightmare; ideas were pulsating through me. I became concerned that I might get violent so I called the doctor.

On admission, this patient was severely agitated; delusional and self-referential thoughts were prominent.

CASE 4. 31-year-old housewife wrote a description of the week prior to her hospitalization for an acute paranoid psychosis.

Thoughts spun around in my head and everything—objects, sound events—took on a special meaning for me. I felt like I was putting the pieces of a puzzle together. Childhood feelings began to come back, as symbols and bits from past conversations went through my head. The word *religious* and other words from other past conversations during the fall and summer months came back to me during this week and seemed to take on a new significance. I increasingly began to feel that I was experiencing something like mystical revelations . . . at the gas station, the men smiled at me with twinkles in their eyes, and I felt very good, I saw smiling men's faces in the sky and the stars twinkling in their eyes. I felt better than I ever had in my life.

CASE 5. A 21-year-old student, progressively agitated by homosexual concerns and fears of nuclear disaster, walked all night long with a friend. He described his experience as a "revelation." Sights and sounds possessed a keenness that he had never experienced before. He felt an unusual sense of empathy with his friend and spoke of spontaneous understanding "like that of a little child." Stars in the sky seemed to have special significance, and at one point he felt that his friend resembled Christ. This state proceeded rapidly to an acute catatonic reaction.

CASE 6. A 35-year-old housewife sought psychiatric assistance because of her uneasiness over an impending move to another city. In the course of the evaluation she began to wonder about the "meaning of my whole life." She reported sensations of "being a spectator while the procession of life goes by." Over a two-day period her anxiety mounted as she attempted to deal with her guilt about a long-standing affair of which her husband had no knowledge. Rather abruptly she noted "my senses were sharpened, sounds were more intense and I could see with greater clarity, everything seemed very clear to me. Even my sense of taste seemed more acute. Things began to fall together and make sense. Words I would repeat had particular significance for my life." She began to feel that God was asking to give her life to tell other people about religion. The subjective changes were associated with intense fright and acute insomnia.

CASE 7. A 20-year-old artist subsequently followed for seven years in psychotherapy has frequently referred to his states of altered awareness. Such subjective feelings occurred during each of two acute psychotic episodes and throughout psychotherapy. He describes a mystic or "cryptic state" from which the solutions to various problems seem obvious. Colors become impressive to him, they lose their boundaries, and seem to flow. In these states, his sense of communion and community is enhanced; he feels capable of bringing together the arts and sciences, his separated parents, and himself into harmonious "oscillation" with the world. Going without sleep heightens the mystic states and improves his "freedom and vision" in painting. In this state he cannot tell whether he is "thrilled, frightened, pained, or anxious—they are all the same."

Amphetamine and Alcohol Withdrawal States.

We have seen several patients in these categories whose symptomatology suggested similarities to the previous cases. The phenomenon of "amphetamine psychosis" is well known, and our experience suggests that the full-blown syndrome often develops out of a state of hyperawareness (Connell, 1958). One patient, having taken small doses of amphetamine for only three days in the post-partum period, began to have the subjective feeling that God was trying to help her. Colors and normally trivial observations began to take on ominous significance. Things that would not usually be noticed seemed to be "connected." Another patient, chronically sleepless and taking high doses of amphetamines over several months phoned and reported he was feeling better, "released," and productive; the world looked beautiful and bright, he could see "how to repair my marriage" and had new ideas for his work. The next day he reported at length that it was fascinating to note "reflections" from polished cars and the following day announced that huge parabolic mirrors were placed on top of a newspaper building and as a hoax were reflecting images of naked women off windows and onto bodies. He thus moved from an absorption in the reflections and in his subjective state of "seeing solutions" to problems, to a fullfledged paronoid psychosis. Another patient who experienced delirium tremens on several occasions noted that prior to the full-blown state he would often become hyperaware of sounds and would find himself suddenly distracted by insignificant items such as a leaf or a bird in a tree. He added that the difference in such a state and delirium tremens was that in the latter he could not "come back."

CASE 8. The final case presented a unique opportunity in that one of us treated for four months a young man who had taken lysergic acid diethylamide (LSD-25) two years prior to his psychotic episode. He frequently compared the two experiences and found a number of similarities. In the following account, the first part was written down after a few weeks of treatment when he was considerably calmer and was reflecting upon the prior LSD-25 experience. The last part is taken from his admission interview.

In the half hour for the drug to take effect, the drugged person has a psycho-sommatic terror of madness. He seeks to retain some small part of his former existance unchanged . . . he desires to repeat things for the assurance such repetition gives of a return to normality. The tendency to repeat is compulsive and persistent. There is yet another resistance and that is verbosity. The drugged person, like the insane, feels that weeding out what was previously wrong—an attempt to perfect an earlier feeling—is necessary. There is a paranoid fear of certain places . . . the feeling is that such places are in some way taboo. There are manic feelings under the drug. There are moments when the feeling of omniscience is not omnipotence becomes dominant. The feeling of omnipotence under LSD-25 corresponds directly in intensity to the drugged person's sense of guilt as the drug wears off. The guilt felt afterward can be terribly profound to the point that the depressed person (drugged and/or insane) will do almost anything to bring himself out of the depression. The drugged person, like the insane, is quite vulnerable to suggestion. The experience also involves feelings such as the conviction that one can go through walls. Colors seem to hold great and uncanny significance. All of them are providential and mean something . . . now (on the day hospitalized for psychosis) everything takes on significance and patterns. You feel lost and you try to repeat. I feel surges of warmth and great terror of myself. Walls start to move at the periphery of my vision. I feel my tactile senses are enhanced as well as my visual ones, to a point of great power. Patterns and designs begin to distinguish themselves and take on significance. This is true for the LSD-25 experience also. It's the same now as it was with the drug, only then I knew I was coming back. Now there is nothing to hold onto.

LITERARY ACCOUNTS*

John Custance (1952). First and foremost comes a general sense of intense well-being . . . the pleasurable and sometimes ecstatic feeling tone remains as a sort of permanent background . . . closely allied with this permanent background is . . . the "heightened sense of reality". If I am to judge by my own experience, this "heightened sense of reality" consists of a considerable number of related sensations, the net result of which is that the outer world makes a much more vivid and intense impression on me than usual. . . . The first thing I note is the peculiar appearances of the lights. . . . They are not exactly brighter, but deeper, more intense, perhaps a trifle more ruddy than usual. Certainly my sense of touch is heightened. . . . My hearing appears to be more sensitive, and I am able to take in without disturbance or distraction many different sound impressions at the same time. . . . It is actually a sense of communion, in the first place with God, and in the second place with all mankind, indeed with all creation. . . . The sense of communication extends to all fellow creatures with whom I come in contact; it is not merely ideal or imaginative but has a practical effect on my conduct.

*A number of these accounts has been compiled and edited by B. Kaplan in *The Inner World of Mental Illness*, Harper and Row, 1964.

Anonymous Account (Anonymous, 1955). I experienced a sudden feeling of creative release before my illness, was convinced that I was rapidly attaining the height of my intellectual powers, and that for the first time in my life, I would be about to function up to the level of my ability in this direction. . . . On several occasions my eyes became markedly oversensitive to light. Ordinary colors appeared to be much too bright, and sunlight seemed dazzled in intensity. . . . I also had a sense of discovery, creative excitement, and intense, at times mystical inspiration in intervals where there was relief from fear. . . . My capacities for aesthetic appreciation and heightened sensory receptiveness, for vivid grasp of the qualities of living, and for imaginative empathy were very keen at this time. I had had the same intensity of experience at other times when I was perfectly normal, but such periods were not sustained for as long, and had also been integrated with feelings of well-being and happiness that were absent during the tense disturbed period.

Schreber (Macalpine & Hunter, 1955). Dr. Weber, who was in charge of the asylum where Schreber was hospitalized wrote the following in his court testimony:

At the beginning of his stay there he (Schreber) mentioned mostly hypochondrical ideas . . . but ideas of persecution soon appeared in the disease picture, based on hallucinations, which at first appeared sporadically while simultaneously marked hyperesthesia, great sensitivity to light and noise made their appearance. Later the visual and auditory hallucinations multiplied and, in conjunction with disturbances of common sensation, ruled his whole feeling and thinking. . . . Gradually, the delusions took on a mystical and religious character . . . he saw "miracle", heard "holy music.". . . I have in no way assumed a priori the pathological nature of these ideas, but rather tried to show from the history of the patient's illness how the appellant first suffered from severe hyperesthesia, hypersensitivity to light and noise . . . and particular disturbances of common sensation which falsified his conception of things : . . . and how from these pathological events, at last the system of ideas was formed which the appellant has recounted . . . in his memoirs.

Clifford Beers (1908). No man can be born again, but I believe I came as near it as ever a man did. . . . It seemed as though the refreshing breath of some kind goddess of wisdom were being gently blown against the surface of my brain. . . . So delicate, so crisp and exhilarating was it that words fail me in my attempt to describe it. Few, if any, experiences can be more delightful. . . . For me, however, this experience was liberation, not enslavement.

Norma McDonald (1960). What I do want to explain, if I can, is the exaggerated state of awareness in which I lived before, during, and after my acute illness. At first it was as if parts of my brain "awoke" which had been dormant, and I became interested in a wide assortment of people, events, places, and ideas which normally would make no impression on me. Not knowing that I was ill, I made no attempt to understand what was happening, but felt that there was some overwhelming significance in all this, produced either by God or Satan, and I felt that I was duty-bound to ponder on each of these new interests, and the more I pondered, the worse it became. The walk of a stranger on the street could be a "sign" to me which I must interpret. Every face in the windows of a passing streetcar would be engraved on my mind, all of them concentrating on me and trying to pass me some sort of message. Now, many years later, I can appreciate what had happened. Each of us is capable of coping with a large number of stimuli invading or being through any one of the senses . . . it is obvious that we would be incapable of carrying on any of our daily activities if even one hundredth of all these available stimuli invaded us at once. So the mind must have a filter which functions without our conscious thought, sorting stimuli and allowing only those which are relevant to the situation in hand to disturb consciousness. And this filter must be working at maximum efficiency at all times, particularly when we require a high degree of concentration. What had happened to me in Toronto was a breakdown in the filter . . . new significance in people and places was not particularly unpleasant, though it got badly in the way of my work, but the significance of the real or imagined feelings of people was very painful . . . . In this state, delusions can very easily take root and begin to grow . . . . By the time I was admitted to hospital I had reached a stage of "wakefulness" when the brilliance of light on a window sill or the color of blue in the sky would be so important it could make me cry. I had very little ability to sort the relevant from the irrelevant. The filter had broken down. Completely unrelated events became intricately connected in my mind.

COMMENT

Characterization and Comparison

It will be clear that we have been struck by certain repetitive aspects in these accounts and have abstracted from them to clarify our argument. In brief it seems that these patients are describing a state, early in their illness, in which they recognize an altered way of experiencing themselves, others, and the world. They report having stepped beyond the restrictions of their usual state of awareness. Perceptual modes seem heightened and the emotional response evoked is singularly intense. Such experiences are frequently felt to be a kind of breakthrough, words and phrases such as *release* or *new creativity* being used to characterize them. Individuals experience feelings of getting to the essence of things—of the external world, of others, and of themselves. On the other hand, there is usually a vague disquieting, progressive sense of dread which may eventually dominate the entire experience.

In some accounts the experience of perceptual alterations seems to be dominant; others emphasize the intense affectivity, and still others the inner experience of revelation or creative clarification. In most of the accounts— but not in all—the experience comes as a kind of surprise and is apprehended as happening *to the subject* and not *within him*. Others, however, seem to recognize the process as basically an inner change which in turn "makes all things new" (case 3, anonymous account, Beers, McDonald).

Given such an altered *experience*, formal processes of thought and cognition are likely to be altered. Wynn, for example, has suggested that schizophrenia be broadly understood as an "experience disorder," and that formal thought processes are studied as an indicator of altered experience (Wynn, 1963).

When seen from the point of view of subjective experience, early psychotic experiencing becomes less discontinuous with other altered modes of experiencing. For instance LSD-25 and mescaline may induce a very comparable perceptual and affective condition. It is clearly a multipotential state with many factors influencing the final outcome which can range from excruciating anxiety and paranoid delusions to an experience of intense self-knowledge. Space does not permit detailed excerpts from the drug literature but Terrill's summary of "The Nature of the LSD Experience" can serve as a comprehensive statement of the phenomenon (Terrill, 1962). Such characteristics as increased perceptual sensitivity and portentousness, intensification of interpersonal experience, feelings of unique insight into life, and personal clarification—all well-documented in the LSD reaction—are clearly shared by the accounts we have listed. More recent reviews have made it clear that the drugs induce a kind of fluid state in which a number of variables act to fashion the final result along the psychedelic-psychotomimetic continuum. Freedman has characterized this state from the viewpoint of the clinician (Giarman & Freedman, 1965).

Psychotomimetic drugs such as d-lysergic acid diethylamide ... reliably and consistently produce periods of altered perception and experience without clouded consciousness or marked physiological changes; mental processes that are usually dormant and transient during wakefulness become "locked" into a persistent state. The usual boundaries which structure thought and perception become fluid; awareness becomes vivid while control over input is markedly diminished; customary inputs and modes of thought and perception become novel, illusory, and portentous; and with the loss of customary controlling anchors, dependence on the surroundings, on prior expectations, or on a mystique for structure and support is enhanced. Psychiatrists recognize these primary changes as a background state out of which a number of secondary psychological states can ensue, depending on motive, capacity, and circumstances. This is reflected in the terminology that has grown around these drugs; if symptoms endure, the term psychotomimetic or psychodysleptic is used;

and if mystical experience, religious conversion, or a therapeutic change in behavior is stressed, the term *psychedelic* or mind "manifesting" has been applied.

The drugs and clinical states set up a "search for synthesis," and the motives and capacities of subjects and patients to achieve this are obviously of importance if one is to assess outcomes and compare and contrast these states.

There are other intense self-experiences—unrelated to the use of drugs—which have elements in common with the accounts we have presented. William James' classic study of religious phenomena, for instance, is replete with accounts of conversion experiences that are strikingly similar to the cases we have described and to the experiences of some subjects under LSD-25 and mescaline (1958). James describes the characteristics of the affective experience in religious conversion as follows.

The central one is the loss of all worry, the sense that all is ultimately well with one, the peace, the harmony, the willingness to be, even though the outer conditions should remain the same.... The second feature is the sense of perceiving truths not known before. The mysteries of life become lucid ... and often the solution is more or less unutterable in words.... A third peculiarity of the assurance state is the objective change which the world often appears to undergo.... The most characteristic of all the elements of the conversion crisis ... is the ecstasy of happiness produced.

James himself seems to have been well aware of the similarity between the conversion experience and certain psychotic reactions.

But more remains to be told, religious mysticism is only one half of mysticism. The other half has no accumulated traditions except those which the textbooks on insanity supply. Open any one of these, and you will find abundant cases in which "mystical ideas" are cited as characteristic symptoms of enfeebled or deluded states of mind. In delusional insanity ... we may have a *diabolical* mysticism, a sort of religious mysticism turned upside down. The same sense of ineffable importance in the smallest events, the same texts and words coming with new meanings, the same voices and visions and leadings and missions, the same controlling by extraneous powers; only this time the emotion is pessimistic: instead of consolations we have desolations; the meanings are dreadful; and the powers are enemies to life. It is evident that from the point of view of their psychological mechanism, the classic mysticism and these lower mysticisms spring from the same level, from that great subliminal or transmarginal region of which science is beginning to admit the existence, but of which so little is really known. That region contains every kind of matter: "seraph and snake" abide there side by side. To come from thence is no infallible credential. What comes must be sifted and tested, and run the gauntlet of confrontation with the total context of experience, just like what comes from the outer world of sense.

The significance of religious feeling in psychosis has been earlier explored by Boisen (Boisen, 1952) and more recently by Laing (Laing, 1965).

Maslow has described the subjective phenomenology of "peak experiences" and emphasizes new modes of awareness which may be encountered at certain maturational milestones (Maslow, 1962). Similarly, in the course of psychotherapy crisis points and periods of intense insight may also be characterized by exhilaration, expressed new modes of experiencing and perceiving, transient fear mixed with intense happiness, and a sense of acceleration of intrapsychic activity (Arlow & Brenner, 1964; Carlson, 1961). Mystical experiences occurring as a culmination of intense intrapsychic conflict have recently been presented (Freemantle, 1965).

The utility of such insight, the extent to which it is delusional or adaptive, varies not only in psychotherapy but in psychoses, drug states, and religious and mystical practices experimentally and has advanced hypotheses to account for the intrapsychic phenomena in such procedures (Deikman, 1963; Deikman, to be published). Further, a number of creative individuals—including Blake, Coleridge, Brahms, and Rilke, to mention only a few—described comparable unique shifts in their subjective experience of perceptual processes which they held to be an integral part of their creative gifts (Schorer, 1959; Kris, 1939).

IMPLICATIONS

With the advent of psychotomimetic drugs there was renewed interest in the study of altered mental states, but the opportunity to catch "in situ" the formation and genesis of a variety of symptoms and modes of behaving and coping has not been extensively exploited. In part it was doubted that drug-induced experiences were sufficiently related to clinically encountered dysfunctions to be of interest (Hollister, 1962). Yet it is hardly surprising that temporary and experimentally induced states do not reproduce all the features characterizing clinical processes; the latter are neither bound as rigorously by time nor circumscribed by the highly socialized safeguards of the conventional laboratory situation. Rather, these differences only highlight those features of clinical disorders which require explanation in terms of developmental factors and restitutive and compensatory sequences. The patient experiencing and functioning in this altered state must cope overtime with a variety of life tasks, family and social interactions; his resilience and overall disposition to represent, identify, and differentiate "inside and outside" and to relate in a reality oriented way, will differentiate him from most experimental subjects.

Similarly, the fact that these drugs produce ecstatic states from which new learning, a shift in values, or subsequent behavior change purportedly ensue, was thought to isolate such states from their "psychotomimetic status" and perhaps to elevate them to a higher level of discourse. Some enthusiasts even appear to argue that this novelty is beyond psychological description and investigation. Yet the variety of contexts in which such mystic states occur includes clinical conditions as our data have reemphasized. It is also evident that this range of similar states differs not only in outcome but in the extent to which a variety of ego functions are operative—functions such as memory, self-reflective capacity, tolerance for ambiguity, selective attention, the ability to implement wishes and needs in reality, the ability to synthesize, to order, and to serially locate, and to integrate ongoing experiences with past and future. These differentiating features tend to be lost if all such states are described only in terms of loosened ego boundaries, regression in the service of the ego, altered ego autonomy, and deautomatization (Deikman, to be published; Federn, 1962; Federn, 1952). Such descriptions should properly apply only to certain aspects and attributes of certain of the ego operations altered during these conditions. During various phases of the clinical course of a psychosis one frequently can see fluid states in which elements of perceptual instability and psychedelic experience occur preceded or followed by more settled postures in which the patient, through either recognition, insight, withdrawal, or delusion and symptom formation tends to experience and cope in quite different ways. Similarly, in drug-induced psychedelic states, as the acute and vivid effects subside we and others (Salvatore & Hyde, 1956) can observe a variety of paranoid and defensive measures, mild ideas of reference, mood change, and inappropriate or highly imaginative interpretations of the ongoing or previous experience. From a descriptive and theoretical stand-point, then, the clinical and drug-induced psychedelic experience reflects a multipotential mental state which cannot easily be encapsulated or understood without careful scrutiny and study of the sequences of states and differentiation of primary and secondary reactions. It seems apparent that the reaction of the therapist or other significant persons in the environment could crucially affect the course and resolution of such states.

Descriptively, these states of heightened awareness but diminished control over input are frequently characterized by delusional mastery (either shared or idiosyncratic) or (as with dreams) by hallucinatory mastery of the ongoing experience with concomitant euphoria. One is reminded of Freud's "model psychosis." "A dream, then, is a psychosis," he remarked, beginning a chapter in the *Outline of Psychoanalysis* (Freud, 1949). The absurdities, lapses, hallucinatory mastery, and mental processes of psychoses are evident in dreams, Freud argued. Some of the differences between dream and psychosis cited by him were the short duration of the dream, its useful or adaptive function, and the fact that it is to some degree under the control of the dreamer. In the case of drug-induced states the onset and duration of changes (and to a great extent the intensity of effects) are dependent on dosage. On the other hand, as Freud noted, "the dream is brought about with the subject's consent and is ended by an act of his will." However, this might be translated into the language of ego psychology; the dream as an episode in a sequence of states is implied as is a normal, overall capacity to integrate this episode into the total fabric of living. Such autonomy or integrative control probably is present in widely varying degrees in the states we have reviewed, and in drug states the role both of altered body chemistry and the milieu is clearly great; all these features require differential assessment.

These states frequently appear almost to compel rationalization to interpretation as on occasion do dreams or any number of traumatic, infantile, or hypnoid states (Loewald, 1955) in which the ongoing intense experiences have yet to "run the gauntlet of confrontation" with total experience. That this is not easy and that delusional outcomes, conversion, or startling change in behavioral patterns can occur is apparent. The outcomes occur with varying degrees of dependency upon persons, groups, or authority. This fact indicates that drug-induced gaps in reality-coping confer a grave responsibility for the bridging of such gaps which should fall heavily upon the therapists using psychotomimetic drugs. One would expect, therefore, to have encountered considerable literature on the need for case supervision and on the characteristic countertransference problems evoked by such treatment, but with a few exceptions (Savage, 1955) this is relatively absent in the psychedelic-treatment literature.

The bearing of the phenomenological accounts such as those presented upon the various psychodynamic theories of psychosis, while complex, deserves at least brief comment. For instance, it is hard to conceive of all of these states as caused and preceded by a simple withdrawal of libidinal investment in the object world. Rather the outside world may be experienced in a highly intensified, albeit personalized manner. This kind of experience is highly narcissistic (in that it is referred to the self), but descriptively certain aspects of relatedness to objects remain and even attain a heightened personal significance; further, such relatedness assumes a heightened importance in regulating ego functions. In the drug experience, subjects characteristically depend on the therapist or "guide" not simply as an object but for elemental ego support—to diminish anxiety and to structure the experience or to sanction participation in it. Patients in acute psychotic states have similar narcissistic needs. From scrutiny of clinical and drug-induced states one might propose that there is a rearrangement of a number of ego functions (of which changes in the control of attention and perception are quite striking); these may lead subsequently *or* concomitantly to a narcissistically enchanced significance of the self and the world. Pious, for example, postulates a sudden ego breach-a "nadir experience," following which characteristic psychotic symptoms ensue (Pious, 1961). Obviously the question of conceptualizing and observing the sequence of initiating events (libidinal withdrawal or ego disruption or both) requires further differentiation and scrutiny.

The experimental production of experiences of heightened awareness can help both to differentiate and reveal the relatedness of many complex phenomena encountered in clinical psychiatry, with their intricate layering of social, motivational, compensatory, and regressive features. The wide range of contexts in which states of heightened awareness are found to occur and the variety of initiating causes indicate that this mode of functioning and experiencing reflects an innate capacity (like the dream) of which the human mind in a most general sense is capable. These states and the conditions which produce them create a number of unsolved research problems for experimental psychiatry. It is, for example, noteworthy that of the drugs which induce this particular kind of heightened awareness, the indole alkyl amines and certain derivatives of catecholamines are effective, whereas distinctly different pictures are found following other centrally active compounds related to the pharmacology of acetylcholine (Bowers, Goodman, & Sim, 1964; Abood, 1958). There are other unresolved research problems aside from reconciling the continuity between psychotomimetic and psychedelic experience, a major task is to stipulate the determinants of the various outcomes of both drug-induced and naturally occurring conditions.

SUMMARY

We have presented accounts of subjective experience in some early psychotic reactions from both our clinical work and the literature and have compared these accounts to certain natural and drug-induced experiences which have a certain experiential characteristic in common—that of heightened consciousness or awareness. *Psychedelic and psychotomimetic phenomena are closely related.* Our hypothesis is that these states demonstrate to varying degrees the subjective phenomena of intrapsychic alteration, that they are fluid states whose outcome is determined by both intrapsychic and environmental factors. There are clearly quantitative, interindividual differences in the way such experiences can be tolerated, interpreted, terminated, and assimilated into the ongoing context of experience. To account for such differences in terms of discrete ego liabilities *and* assets would be to explicate many crucial psychological phenomena, including certain forms of psychosis, therapeutic personality change, and creative insight.

32

GUIDE TO THE LITERATURE ON PSYCHEDELIC DRUGS

CHARLES T. TART

This chapter is designed to introduce the reader to the serious literature*
on psychedelic drugs. It is in no sense a comprehensive or exhaustive guide,
for the serious literature is too large and too varied: there are over
1000 articles on the effects of LSD-25 alone in the scientific periodicals.
Nor is there enough unanimity of research findings at the time for any
really comprehensive review articles to have been written. This guide
should enable the reader to get off to a good start in the psychedelic literature
and to follow up the references therein for more specialized reading.

I have classified references in ten major categories: Introductory Readings,
Dangers, Experimental Psychology, General, Legal Aspects, Personal
Accounts, Pharmacology and Botany, Religious Aspects, Sociology and
Anthropology, and Therapeutic Applications. This is a rough categorization
and many of the articles cited in one category would also be relevant in
another. Within each category I have included some basic books and articles,
as well as a few recent selections from the scientific literature to illustrate
research methodology in this area.

*There also exists an immense amount of popular and highly sensationalized
writing, primarily dealing with the alleged "dangers" of the nonmedical use of
LSD-25, which I have not attempted to reference. Most of this literature is
inaccurate and rather hysterical: the reader is particularly referred to the Dangers.
section of the references, where the few *objective* studies of the risks of LSD-25
use are referred to.

Various chapters in this book provide additional references to the literature on psychedelic drugs. The reader may consult the Sandoz annotated bibliography (available through NIMH) for articles published through mid-1965 dealing with LSD-25 and psilocybin experiments. Unger (1964) has also published a recent bibliography of the English-language literature on the therapeutic usage of LSD-25.

INTRODUCTORY READINGS

Cohen, S. *The beyond within: the LSD story.* New York: Athenium, 1965.

Debold, R., & Leaf, R. (Eds.) *LSD, man and society.* Middletown, Conn.: Wesleyan University Press, 1967.

DeRopp, R. *Drugs and the mind.* New York: Grove, 1957.

Harman, W. The issue of the consciousness-expanding drugs. *Main Currents in Modern Thought*, 1963, **20**, No. 1, 5–14.

Masters, R., & Houston, J. *The varieties of psychedelic experience.* New York: Holt, Rinehart, & Winston, 1966.

Mogar, R. (Ed.) Special issue on the psychedelic experience. *ETC: J. gen. Semantics*, 1965, **22**, No. 4.

Solomon, D. (Ed.) *LSD: the consciousness-expanding drug.* New York: G. P. Putnam's Sons, 1964.

Stafford, P. & Golightly, B. *LSD, the problem-solving psychedelic.* New York: Award Books, 1967.

DANGERS

Auerbach, R., & Rugowski, J. Lysergic acid diethylamide: effect on embryos. *Science*, 1967, **157**, 1325–1326.

Bender, L., & Sankar, D. Chromosome damage not found in leukocytes of children treated with LSD-25. *Science*, 1968, **159**, 747–748.

Cohen, M., Marinello, M., & Back, N. Chromosomal damage in human leukocytes induced by lysergic acid diethylamide. *Science*, 1967, **155**, 1417–1419.

Cohen, S. Lysergic acid diethylamide: side effects and complications. *J. nerv. ment. Dis.*, 1960, **130**, 30–40.

Cohen, S., & Ditman, K. Complications associated with lysergic acid diethylamide (LSD-25). *J. Amer. Med. Assoc.*, 1962, **181**, 161–162.

Cohen, S., & Ditman, K. Prolonged adverse reactions to lysergic acid diethylamide. *Arch. gen. Psychiat.*, 1963, **8**, 475–480.

Fink, M., Simeon, J., Hague, W., & Itil, T. Prolonged adverse reactions to LSD in psychotic subjects. *Arch. gen. Psychiat.*, 1966, **15**, 450–454.

Frosch, W., Robbins, E., & Stern, M. Untoward reactions to lysergic acid diethylamide (LSD) resulting in hospitalization. *New England J. Med.*, 1965, **273**, 1235–1239.

Geber, F. Congenital malformations induced by mescaline, lysergic acid diethylamide, and bromolysergic acid in the hamster. *Science*, 1967, **158**, 265–266.

Hensala, J., Epstein, L., & Blacker, K. LSD and psychiatric inpatients. *Arch. gen. Psychiat.*, 1967, **16**, 554–559.

Irwin, S., & Egorcue, J. Chromosomal abnormalities in leukocytes from LSD-25 users. *Science*, 1967, **157**, 313–314.

Loughman, W., Sargent, T., & Israelstam, D. Leukocytes of humans exposed to lysergic acid diethylamide: lack of chromosomal damage. *Science*, 1967, **158**, 508–509.

Prince, A. LSD and chromosomes. *Psychedelic Rev.*, 1967, No. 9, 38–41.

Savage, C., & Stolaroff, M. Clarifying the confusion regarding LSD-25. *J. nerv. ment. Dis.*, 1965, **140**, 218–221.

Savage, C., Stolaroff, M., Harman, W., & Fadiman, J. Caveat! The psychedelic experiences. *J. Neuropsychiat.*, 1963, **5**, 4–5.

Skakkebaek, N., Philip, J., & Rafaelsen, O. LSD in mice: abnormalities in meiotic chromosomes. *Science*, 1968, **160**, 1246–1248.

Slatis, H. Chromosome damage by LSD. *Science*, 1968, **159**, 1492–1493.

Sparkes, R., Melnyk, J., & Bozzetti, L. Chromosomal effect in vivo of exposure to lysergic acid diethylamide. *Science*, 1968, **160**, 1343–1345.

Ungerleider, J., Fisher, D., & Fuller, M. The dangers of LSD: analysis of seven month's experience in a university hospital's psychiatric service. *J. Amer. Med. Assn.*, 1966, **197**, 389–392.

Warkany, J., & Takacs, E. Lysergic acid diethylamide (LSD): no teratogenicity in rats. *Science*, 1968, **159**, 731–732.

EXPERIMENTAL PSYCHOLOGY

Amarel, M., & Cheek, F. Some effects of LSD-25 on verbal communication. *J. abnorm. Psychol.*, 1965, **70**, 453–456.

Haertzen, C. Addiction Research Center Inventory (ARCI): development of a general drug estimation scale. *J. Nerv. Ment. Dis.*, 1965, **141**, 300–307.

Hollister, L., & Hartman, A. Mescaline, lysergic acid diethylamide and psilocybin: comparison of clinical syndromes, effects of color perception and biochemical measures. *Comprehensive Psychiat.*, 1962, **3**, 235–241.

Jarvik, M., Abramson, H., & Hirsch, M. Comparative subjective effects of seven drugs including lysergic acid diethylamide (LSD-25). *J. abnorm. soc. Psychol.*, 1955, **51**, 657–662.

Levine, J., & Ludwig, A. Alterations in consciousness produced by combinations of LSD, hypnosis and psychotherapy. *Psychopharmacologia*, 1965, **7**, 123–137.

McGlothlin, W., Cohen, S. & McGlothlin, M. Short term effects of LSD on anxiety, attitudes and performance. *J. nerv. ment. Dis.*, 1964, **139**, 266–273.

Paul, I. The effects of a drug-induced alteration in state of consciousness on retention of drive-related verbal material. *J. nerv. ment. Dis.*, 1964, **138**, 367–374.

Sjoberg, B., & Hollister, L. The effects of psychotomimetic drugs on primary suggestibility. *Psychopharmacologia*, 1965, **8**, 251–262.

GENERAL

Blewett, D. Psychedelic drugs in parapsychological research. *Int. J. Parapsychol.*, 1963, **5**, 43–74.

Cavanna, R., & Ullman, M. (Eds.) *Psi and altered states of consciousness: Proceedings of an international conference on hypnosis, drugs, dreams, and psi.* New York: Parapsychology Foundation, 1968.

Efron, D., Holmstedt, B., & Kline, N. (Eds.) *Ethnopharmacologic search for psychoactive drugs.* Washington, D.C.: Public Health Service Publication 1967.

Garrett, E. (Ed.) *Proceedings of two conferences on parapsychology and pharmacology.* New York: Parapsychology Foundation, 29 W. 57th St., 1961.

Hoffer, A. D-lysergic acid diethylamide (LSD): a review of its present status. *Clin. Pharmacol. Therapeutics*, 1965, **6**, 183–255.

Hoffer, A., & Osmond, H. *The hallucinogens* New York: Academic Press, 1967.

Kluver, H. Mescal and the mechanisms of hallucination. Chicago: University of Chicago Press, 1966.

Leary, T., Metzner, R., & Alpert, R. *The psychedelic experience: a manual based on the Tibetan Book of the Dead.* New Hyde Park, N.Y.: University Books, 1964.

Lewin, L. *Phantastics, narcotic and stimulating drugs.* New York: Dutton, 1964.

Metzner, R., & Leary, T. On programming psychedelic experiences. *Psychedelic Rev.*, 1967, No. 9, 5–20.

Mogar, R. Psychedelic research in the context of contemporary psychology. *Psychedelic Rev.*, 1966, No. 8, 96–104.

Weil, G., Metzner, R., & Leary, T. *The psychedelic reader: selected from the Psychedelic Review*, New Hyde Park, N. Y.: University Books, 1965.

LEGAL ASPECTS

Alpert, R., Forte, J., Meyers, F., & Smith, D. Psychedelic drugs and the law: a symposium. *J. Psychedelic Drugs*, 1967, **1**, 8–27.

Barrigar, R. The regulation of psychedelic drugs. *Psychedelic Rev.*, 1964, **1**, 394–441.

Bates, R. Psychedelics and the law: a prelude in question marks. *Psychedelic Rev.*, 1964, **1**, 379–393.

Blum, R., & Funkhouser, M. A lobby for people? *Amer. Psychologist*, 1965, **20**, 208–210.

Lindersmith, A. *The addict and the law.* Bloomington, Ind.: Indiana University Press, 1965.

McGlothlin, W. Toward a rational view of hallucinogenic drugs. *J. Psychedelic Drugs*, 1967, **1**, 40–52.

Metzner, R. Two new laws relating to psychedelics. *Psychedelic Rev.*, 1966, No. 7, 3–10.

PERSONAL ACCOUNTS

Bishop, M. *The discovery of love: a psychedelic experience with LSD-25*. New York: Dodd Mead, 1963.

Burroughs, W., & Ginsberg, A. *The Yage letters*. San Francisco: City Lights Books, 1963.

Dunlap, J. *Exploring inner space: personal experiences under LSD-25*. New York: Harcourt, Brace, & World, 1961.

Ebin, D. *The drug experience: first-person accounts of addicts, writers, scientists and others*. New York: Orion Press, 1961.

Huxley, A. *The doors of perception*. New York: Harper Bros., 1954.

Michaux, H. *Light through darkness*. New York: Orion Press,1963.

Michaux, H. *Miserable miracle*. San Francisco: City Lights Books, 1963.

Newland, C. *Myself and I*. New York: Coward-McCann, 1962.

Ward, R. *A drug-taker's notes*. London: Victor Gollancz, 1957.

PHARMACOLOGY AND BOTANY

Buck, R. Mushroom toxins: a brief review of the literature. *New England j. Med.*, 1961, **265**, 681–686.

Freedman, D. Aspects of biochemical pharmacology of psychotropic drugs. *Psychedelic Rev.*, 1966, No. 8, 33–58.

Heim, R. *Champignons toxiques et hallucinogenes*. Paris: N. Boubée & Cie., 1963.

Metzner, R. The pharmacology of psychedelic drugs. *Psychedelic Rev.*, 1963, **1**, 69–114.

Schultes, R. Botanical sources of the new world narcotics. *Psychedelic Rev.*, 1963, **1**, 145–166.

Usdin, E., & Efron, D. *Psychotropic drugs and related compounds*. Washington, D.C.: Public Health Service Publication No. 1589, Supt. of Documents, 1967.

Wasson, R. The hallucinogenic fungi of Mexico: an inquiry into the origins of the religious idea among primitive peoples. *Psychedelic Rev.*, 1963, **1**, 27–42.

Wasson, R. Notes on the present status of Ololiuhqui and the other hallucinogens of Mexico. *Psychedelic Rev.*, 1964, **1**, 275–301.

RELIGIOUS ASPECTS

Blofeld, J. A high yogic experience achieved with mescaline. *Psychedelic Rev.*, 1966, No. 7, 27–32.

Clark, W. Religious aspects of the psychedelic substances and the law. *Int. J. Parapsychol.*, 1967, **9**, 32–36.

Huxley, A. *Visionary experience*. Paper, Int. Congress Applied Psychol., Copenhagen, 1961.

Leary, T. The religious experience: its production and interpretation. *Psychedelic Rev.*, 1964, **1**, 324–346.

Pahnke, W. Drugs and mysticism, *Int. J. Parapsychol.*, 1966, **8**, 295–320.

Watts, A. *The joyous cosmology: adventures in the chemistry of consciousness.* New York: Pantheon, 1962.

SOCIOLOGY AND ANTHROPOLOGY

Alpert, R., Cohen, S., & Schiller, L. *LSD.* New York: New American Library, 1966.

Blum, R., & Associates. *Utopiates: the use and users of LSD-25.* New York: Atherton Press, 1964.

Brand, S. The Native American Church meeting. *Psychedelic Rev.*, 1967, No. 9, 21–37.

Carstairs, G. Daru and Bhang: cultural factors in the choice of intoxicant. *Psychedelic Rev.*, 1965, No. 6, 67–83.

Dustin, C. *Peyotism and New Mexico.* Privately printed, P. O. Box 1661, Albuquerque, N. M., 1960.

Harman, W. Some aspects of the psychedelic-drug controversy. *J. Humanistic Psychol.*, 1963, **3**, 93–107.

Kusel, H. Ayahuasca drinkers among the Chama indians of northeast Peru. *Psychedelic Rev.*, 1965, No. 6, 58–66.

La Barre, W. *The peyote cult.* Hamden, Conn.: Shoestring Press, 1964.

McGlothlin, W. Hallucinogenic drugs: a perspective with special reference to peyote and cannabis. *Psychedelic Rev.*, 1965, No. 6, 16–57.

McGlothlin, W., & Cohen, S. The use of hallucinogenic drugs among college students. *Amer. J. Psychiat.*, 1965, **122**, 572–574.

Murphey, G., & Cohen, S. The search for person-world isomorphism. *Main Currents in Modern Thought*, 1965, **22**, 31–34.

Schur, E. *Crimes without victims.* Englewood Cliffs, N.J.: Prentice-Hall, 1965.

Simmons, J., & Winograd, B. *It's happening: a portrait of the youth Scene today.* Santa Barbara, Calif.: Marc-Laird, 1966.

THERAPEUTIC APPLICATIONS

Abramson, H. (Ed.) *The use of LSD in psychotherapy.* New York: Josiah Macy, Jr., Foundation, 1960.

Abramson, H. (Ed.) *Proceedings of the second international conference on the use of LSD in psychotherapy.* New York: Bobbs-Merrill, 1966.

Bender, L. D-lysergic acid in the treatment of the biological features of childhood schizophrenia. *Dis. Nerv. System*, 1966, **27**, No. 7, 39–42.

Cholden, L. (Ed.) *Lysergic acid diethylamide and mescaline in experimental psychiatry.* New York: Grune & Stratton, 1956.

Crockett, R., Sandison, A., & Walk, A. (Eds.) *Hallucingenic drugs and their psychotherapeutic use.* Springfield, Ill.: Thomas, 1963.

Fisher, G. Some comments concerning dosage levels of psychedelic compounds for psychotherapeutic experiences. *Psychedelic Rev.*, 1963, **1**, 208–218.

Lee, P., Metzner, R., & von Eckartsberg, R. The subjective after-effects of psychedelic experiences: a summary of four recent questionnaire studies. *Psychedelic Rev.*, 1964, **1**, 18–26.

Leuner, H. *Die experimentelle Psychose: ihre Psychopharmakologie, Phänomenologie un Dynamik in Beziehung zur Person.* Berlin: Springer-Verlag, 1962.

Levine, J. The hypnodelic treatment technique. *Int. J. clin. exp. Hyp.* 1966, **14**, 207–215.

Ling, T., & Buckman, J. *Lysergic acid (LSD-25) and ritalin in the treatment of neurosis.* London: Lambarde Press, 1963.

Ludwig, A., & Levine, J. A controlled comparison of five brief treatment techniques employing LSD, Hypnosis and psychotherapy. *Amer. J. Psychother.*, 1965, **19**, 417–435.

MacLean, J., MacDonald, D., Byrne, U., & Hubbard, A. The use of LSD-25 in the treatment of alcoholism and other psychiatric problems. *Quart. J. Stud. Alcohol.*, 1961, **22**, 34–45.

Mogar, R., & Savage, C. Personality change associated with psychedelic (LSD) therapy: a preliminary report. *Psychotherapy*, 1964, **1**, 154–162.

Savage, C., Fadiman, J., Mogar, R., & Allen, M. The effects of psychedelic (LSD) therapy on values, personality and behavior. *Int. J. Neuropsychiat.*, 1966, **2**, 241–254.

Savage, C., Savage, E., Fadiman, J., & Harman, W. LSD: therapeutic effects of the psychedelic experience. *Psychol. Rep.*, 1964, **14**, 111–120.

Sherwood, J., Stolaroff, M., & Harman, W. The psychedelic experience: a new concept in psychotherapy. *J. Neuropsychiat.*, 1962, **4**, 69–80.

INTRODUCTION TO SECTION 8 THE PSYCHOPHYSIOLOGY OF SOME ALTERED STATES OF CONSCIOUSNESS

Our knowledge of ASCs is based almost exclusively on verbal reports from those who have experienced them. There has been little systematic study of the actual behavior of people in ASCs, and practically nothing done on the psychophysiology of ASCs.

The psychophysiological correlates of ASCs are of great interest, not only in leading to a better understanding of ASCs per se, but, insofar as one considers some ASCs desirable, as a way of understanding how to produce them more effectively.

The three articles in this section illustrate both of these points. The article by Akira Kasamatsu and Tomio Hirai, "An Electroencephalographic Study on the Zen Meditation (Zazen)," on electroencephalographic (EEG) patterns of meditating Zen monks, and chapter 34 by B. K. Anand, G. S. Chhina, and Baldev Singh, "Some Aspects of Electroencephalographic Studies in Yogis," on the EEG patterns of meditating yogins, both indicate pronounced alterations in brain functioning during the ASCs produced by the practices of these venerable systems, Zen and Yoga. The adept practitioners of both forms of meditation show almost continuous alpha waves (normally associated with a state of relaxed alertness in ordinary Ss) during meditation. This is particularly startling in the case of the Zen monks because their eyes are open: one almost never sees alpha rhythm in the eyes-open condition in ordinary Ss. The Zen monks also show normal blocking of the alpha rhythm in response to stimulation which does not adapt with repeated trials as it does in ordinary Ss. The Yogins, on the other hand, show no response to stimulation at all. Although not pointed out by the authors, these differences may be quite consistent with the differing philosophical outlooks of Zen and Yoga. The Zen monks are striving to exist in the here-and-now, in the immediacy of the phenomenal world; thus if one interprets the adaptation to stimulation invariably see in ordinary Ss as the substitution of abstract cognitive patterns for the raw sensory experience, the Zen monks are apparently managing to stay in the here-and-now of immediate sensory experience. Yoga philosophy, on the other hand, has a strong world-denying quality, a belief that the phenomenal world is all illusion and ensnarement (*maya*), which the yogin must learn to transcend. Thus it makes sense that they show no EEG response to stimulation and also report being unaware of the stimulation when questioned after the meditative state is terminated.

Chapter 35 by Joe Kamiya, "Operant Control of the EEG Alpha Rhythm and Its Effects on Consciousness," indicates that ordinary Ss may be trained, by conventional operant techniques, to produce an EEG pattern similar to that found for the meditating Zen monks and yogins, viz., almost continuous alpha rhythm. Further, Kamiya's Ss prefer to produce this high alpha state as contrasted with a low alpha state; his Ss who have had some prior experience with meditation are more adept at producing it. While it would be naive to equate the state of consciousness of the meditating Zen monk or yogin with that of the college student producing almost continuous alpha rhythm, the fascinating possibility is suggested that *one* of the things that Zen monks and yogins learn to do in their years of meditation is to produce a high alpha state. If we can produce the high alpha state in just hours in a modern psychophysiological laboratory, would our Ss have a pronounced head start if they then attempted to learn the practice of meditation in the Zen or Yoga style? I have confirmed many of Kamiya's findings in my own laboratory, as have several other investigators who will be publishing shortly. Hart (1967) has already published confirmatory findings.

There has been very little work done on the psychophysiology of ASCs, but there are several other studies the reader may follow up in addition to the ones listed in the papers of this section. Two further studies on the physiology of the yogic state are those of Wenger & Bagchi (1961), and Wenger, Bagchi, & Anand (1961). Two studies of the mediumistic trance state have been reported by Evans & Osborn (1951), and Goldney (1938). Greatly enhanced alpha rhythm has also been reported in the case of a self-induced trance state showing multiple-personality phenomena (Thomson, Forbes, & Bolles, 1937) and in the case of a young woman who experienced her consciousness as being "located" at a point above her physical body (Tart, 1968).

EEG changes associated with acute alcoholic intoxication have been reported by Davis, Gibbs, Davis, Jetter, & Trowbridge (1941), Engle & Rosenbaum (1945), and Engel, Webb, & Ferris (1945).

It seems fairly certain that there are no EEG changes accompanying the normal hypnotic state unless sleep intervenes, in which case the hypnotist loses contact with the S.* For recent work on this subject see Chertok & Kramarz (1959), Crasilneck & Hall (1959), Diamont, Dufek, Hoskevic, Kristof, Pekarek, Roth, & Velek (1960), and Gorton (1962).

There have been a number of studies on physiological changes, especially EEG changes, as a function of the ASCs produced by various drugs, particularly the psychedelics. Since anxiety produces similar physiological changes to those reported, and almost all Ss were probably anxious because of having to cope with powerful drug effects for the first time, we currently have no valid knowledge of the general psychophysiological changes occurring in most drug-induced ASCs.

The psychophysiology of the hypnagogic state and of nocturnal dreaming has been touched on in earlier sections.

---

*There may be a startling exception to this, however, reported by Cobb, Evans, Gustafson, O'Connell, Orne, & Shor (1965), in which Ss carried out hypnoticlike behavior while showing a stage 1 sleep EEG pattern.

33

AN ELECTROENCEPHALOGRAPHIC STUDY ON THE ZEN MEDITATION (ZAZEN)

AKIRA KASAMATSU AND TOMIO HIRAI

INTRODUCTION

It is our common knowledge that EEG undergoes strikes changes in the transition from wakefulness to sleep, and has become one of the reliable ways to assess the state of wakefulness or sleep. In clinical practice, EEG often becomes a good neurophysiological method to find out the disturbance of consciousness. And many studies, both clinical and experimental, on the consciousness have been published during the past 30 years. In recent years electroencephalographic and neurophysiological studies on the consciousness are focused on an understanding of the relationship between the brain mechanisms and consciousness in general (Gastaut, in Adrian et al., Eds., 1954). These studies give rise to an attempt to relate the various electrographic findings with the psychological states and their behavioral correlates (Lindsley, 1952).

The authors have carried out the study on EEG changes during anoxia, epileptic seizures, the exogeneous disorders of the brain and other allied states from neurophysiological and psychological points of view (Kasamatsu & Shimazono, 1957). In the course of our study, it was revealed that a series

Reprinted by permission from *Folio Psychiat, & Neurolog, Japonica*, Vol. 20, 1966, pp. 315–336.

of EEG changes was observed in the state of attentive awareness during Zen-sitting (Zazen. And what Zazen is like will be explained later, Hirai, 1960; Kasamatsu & Shimazono, 1957). These findings deserve further investigation because of understanding EEG pattern to corresponding psychological state and of interpreting the neurophysiological basis of consciousness. The subject of the present paper is to describe the results of our experiments in detail and to discuss some of the electrographic characteristics in which the mental state in Zen-sitting will be reflected.

Zazen—Zen meditation means the sitting meditation which is a kind of religious exercise in Zen-Buddhism. In Japan there are two Zen sects named Soto and Rinzai. Both sects regard Zazen as the most important training method of their disciples to enlighten their minds. Zen sitting is performed in two basic meditation forms: A full cross-legged sitting and a half cross-legged sitting. During the Zen sitting, the disciple's eyes must be open and look downward about one meter ahead, and his hands generally join. In a quiet room the disciple sits on a round cushion and practices the meditation for about 30 minutes. Sometimes the intensive Zen training is performed 8 to 10 times a day for about one week. This is called *Sesshin* in Zen Buddhism. The disciples do not engage in daily activities but live the religious life following a strict schedule (Hirai, 1960).

By practising Zen meditation it is said that man can become emancipated from the dualistic bondage of subjectivity and objectivity, of mind and body and of birth and death. And he can be free from lust and self-consciousness, and be awakened to his pure, serene and true-self.

This mental state (Satori or enlightenment) will often be misunderstood as trance or hypnosis. It is said that Satori is not an abnormal mental state but one's everyday mind in the Zen sense. Dr. Erich Fromm describes it, "If we would try to express enlightenment in psychological terms, I would say that it is a state in which the person is completely tuned to the reality outside and inside of him, a state in which he is fully aware of it and fully grasps it. *He* is aware of it—that is, not his brain, nor any other part of his organism, but *he*, the whole man. He is aware of *it*; not as of an object over there which he grasps with his thought, but *it*, the flower, the dog, the man, in its or his full reality. He who awakes is open and responsive to the world, and he can be open and responsive because he has given up holding on to himself as a thing, and thus has become empty and ready to receive. To be enlightened means 'the full awakening of the total personality to reality'" (Fromm, Suzuki & de Martino, 1960).

If one asks what this state of mind is concerned with in psychotherapy, it may be said that Zen meditation is the method through which we can communicate with the unconscious. In this context, however, the unconscious does not mean Freud's "unconsciousness." Rather the "unconscious" in Zen is closely related to the unconscious which is stated by Jung, C. G. (Suzuki, 1960) or Fromm, E. (Fromm, Suzuki & de Martino, 1960). In regard to this problem Dr. Daisetsu Suzuki states the meaning of it as "the Cosmic unconscious" (Humphrey, Ed.).

At any rate the Zen meditation influences not only the mind but also the body as a whole organism. The authors want to investigate Zen meditation as a subject of psychophysiology, especially that of electroencephalography.

SUBJECTS AND METHODS

EEG was recorded continuously through all stages—before, during and after Zazen with opened eyes. All our EEG data were obtained in the eyes opened state.

As recording electrodes the silver-coated disc electrodes with thin (100μ to 200μ) copper wire in vinyl tube were used, and they were applied with collodion on the scalp of the frontal, central, parietal, and occipital regions in the middle line of the head. These electrodes did not disturb Zen meditation and long-lasting recordings were obtained.

Along with EEG, the pulse rate, respiration and GSR were polygraphically recorded on a San-ei 12 channel ink-writing electroencephalograph. The same experiments were performed for one week during Zen meditation's intensive training (Sessin). These results were useful to confirm the EEG changes in the whole course of Zen meditation.

In order to investigate the functional state of the brain, the responses to sensory stimuli with several modalities were examined. And the blocking time of alpha pattern to repeated click stimulations was measured.

Our experiments were made at the usual Zen-training hall with cooperations of the Zen priests and their disciples as our subjects. But the stimulation experiments were performed in the air-conditioned, sound-free shield room of our laboratory.

The cooperative 48 subjects were selected among the priests and disciples in both Soto and Rinzai sects. Their ages ranged from 24 to 72 years old. According to their experience in Zen training, these subjects could be classified into the following 3 groups:

Group I: 1 to 5 years experience (20 disciples).
Group II: 5 to 20 years experience (12 disciples).
Group III: over 20 years experience (16 priests).

As control subjects, we selected 18 research fellows (23 to 33 years of age) and 4 elderly men (54 to 60 years of age). They have had no experience in Zen meditation, and their EEGs were recorded under the same condition with opened eyes, as the Zen disciples.

RESULTS

1. EEG Changes of Zen-Masters during Zen Meditation

First we shall consider the typical EEG changes of a certain master in detail.* He is a priest with over 20 years' experience in Zen meditation. Before Zen meditation the activating pattern is predominant because his eyes are open (low voltage, fast activity). After Zen meditation has started, the well organized alpha waves of 40–50μV, 11–12/sec. appear within 50 seconds in all the regions and continue for several minutes in spite of opened eyes. After 8 minutes and 20 seconds, the amplitude of alpha waves reaches to 60–70 μV predominantly in the frontal and the central regions. Initially, these alpha waves alternate with the short runs of the activating pattern, but a fairly stable period of the persistent alpha waves ensues during the progress of Zen meditation. After 27 minutes and 10 seconds, rhythmical waves of 7–8/sec. appear for 1 or 2 seconds. And 20 seconds later rhythmical theta trains (6–7/sec., 70–100μV) begin to appear. However, it does not always occur. After the end of Zen meditation alpha waves are seen continuously and 2 minutes later alpha waves still persist. It seems to be the after-effect of Zen meditation.

In the control subjects, EEG changes are not observed; a control subject shows the long-lasting activating pattern of opened eyes. Another 2 control subjects of 58 and 60 years of age also show beta dominant type of EEG with short runs of small alpha waves. But neither increase of alpha amplitude nor decrease of alpha frequency are observed on their EEG of opened eyes. It is not likely that the aging process of the control subjects influences EEG changes during Zen meditation.

Sometimes the theta waves appear as Zen meditation progresses. These changes are clearly shown in the EEG of another Zen master of 60 years of age, large alpha waves with 70–100μV. in amplitude and 8–9/sec. in frequency appear after 24 minutes of his Zen meditation. And 30 seconds later, the rhythmical theta train (6–7/sec. 60–70μV.) begins to appear. The appearance

---

*Note: Figures illustrating the various EEG changes discussed in this paper have been deleted due to space limitations.—*Editor.*

of the theta train becomes distinct through the stable periods of large and slow alpha waves. From the above-mentioned results it is pointed out that a series of EEG changes in the course of Zen meditation are observed; the activating pattern (of opened eyes) before Zen meditation—appearance of alpha waves at initial stage—increase of alpha amplitude—decrease of alpha frequency—appearance of rhythmical theta train in later stage of Zen meditation.

This series of changes cannot always be observed in all Zen subjects. Some subjects only show the appearance of alpha waves through all the meditation period and others show the typical series of electrographic changes. But from our findings, the changes of electroencephalogram during Zen meditation are classified in the following four stages:

Stage I: a slight change which is characterized by the appearance of alpha waves in spite of opened eyes.
Stage II: the increase in amplitude of persistent alpha waves.
Stage III: the decrease of alpha frequency.
Stage IV: the appearance of the rhythmical theta train, which is the final change of EEG during Zen meditation but does not always occur.

2. EEG Changes and the Degree of Zen Training

In accordance with the subjects' years spent in Zen training, 23 Zen disciples were classified into 3 groups—within 5 years, 5–20 years and over 20 years. Also, the evaluation of the mental states in the Zen sense of these disciples were used and their Zen master divided them into 3 groups; low (L), middle (M) and high (H). This evaluation was made independently without regard to their EEG changes.

Then the authors attempted to relate these degrees of Zen training in the 4 stages (I, II, III and IV) of the EEG changes. Tables 1 and 2 show the results. In the vertical line the stages of EEG changes are plotted and the horizontal line shows the subjects' training years (Table 1). It is clear that the more years spent in Zen training, the more EEG changes are seen. The correlation of EEG changes with mental state, which was evaluated by the Zen master, is shown in Table 2. It shows the close relationship between the evaluation by the master and the degree of EEG changes. From these findings, it will be concluded that the degrees of EEG changes during Zen meditation are parallel with the disciples' proficiency in Zen training. The 4 stages of EEG changes reflect physiologically the mental state during Zen meditation. This will be discussed later.

TABLE 1

Relationship between Degree of EEG Changes and Years Spent in Zazen Training

Stage

Rhythmical theta waves	IV	0	0	3
Decrease in alpha frequency	III	3	2	3
Increased alpha amplitude	II	2	1	0
Alpha with eyes open	I	8	1	0
		0–5	6–20	21–40
		Years of Experience in Zazen		

TABLE 2

Relationship between Degree of EEG Changes and Ratings of Disciples' Proficiency at Meditation by the Zen Master.

Stage

Rhythmical theta waves	IV	0	0	3
Decrease in alpha frequency	III	0	7	1
Increased alpha amplitude	II	2	1	0
Alpha with eyes open	I	5	4	0
		Low	Medium	High
		Proficiency Rating		

3. EEG Changes during Zen Meditation and Hypnosis

The mental state in hypnosis is generally considered as "trance." Some may think that the mental state of Zen meditation will be a trance-like state. The authors compared the EEG changes in hypnotic trance with those of Zen meditation. In a hypnotized subject, a university student of 20 years, the catalepsy is manifested. Few alpha waves are seen, but the activating pattern is more prominent than EEG in Zen meditation. The series of EEG changes during Zen meditation is not observed in the course of hypnotic trance.

4. EEG Changes during Zen Meditation and Sleep

In the course of EEG recording during Zen training, the disciples sometimes fall into a drowsy state, which becomes clear on the EEG pattern. At this time the click stimulus is given, then the drowsy pattern turns into the alpha pattern and alpha arousal reaction is observed. This electrographical change is usually accompanied with a floating consciousness from sleep to wakefulness, according to the disciple's introspection. This state is different from the mental state in Zen meditation. The sleepiness, which is called "Konchin," is suppressed in Zen training.

As mentioned before the rhythmical theta train appears in some Zen priests during their Zen meditation. The theta train is also seen in the sleep pattern. But the electrographical difference exists between the theta waves in sleep and the rhythmical theta train in Zen meditation. This difference is evident in the following example: A rhythmical theta train is clearly seen on EEG during a certain Zen master's meditation. At this time, the click stimulus is given. The rhythmical theta train is blocked by the stimulation and reappears spontaneously after several seconds later. The alpha arousal reaction, which is often seen by the stimulation in a drowsy state, is not observed. Therefore the rhythmical theta train in this instance has an "alpha activity" (Brazier, 1960) which is similar to the waking alpha rhythm.

Just before falling into sleep or in the hypnagogic stage, large alpha waves are often seen. These waves are similar to that of Zen meditation. But the large alpha waves seen in stage II or III of Zen meditation persist much longer than the pre-sleep pattern. This difference will be discussed later in detail.

5. EEG Response to Click Stimulation in Zen Meditation

In the preceding sections a series of EEG changes in Zen meditation was described. In this section, the authors will deal with the results of alpha blocking to the repetitive click stimuli with regular intervals.

The click stimulation was performed at the stage of long persisting alpha waves of a certain Zen master. To the first stimulus the alpha blocking occurs for 2 seconds. With the regular intervals of 15 seconds, the click stimuli are repeated 20 times, the alpha blocking is always observed for 2–3 seconds. On the other hand the same stimulation is performed in alpha pattern of control subjects with closed eyes. The more the stimulation repeats, the less the alpha blocking time. The same experiments were performed on 3 Zen masters and 4 control subjects and the alpha blocking time to each stimulation was measured. The measurement of the alpha blocking time leads to the following results: In control subjects, the alpha blocking time decreases rapidly, but in Zen masters, the alpha blocking time is fairly constant, though some random changes are seen.

From the above mentioned results it is concluded that there is almost no adaptation of alpha blocking during Zen meditation.

DISCUSSION

It has become apparent in our study that the electrographic changes of Zen meditation are the appearance of alpha waves without regard to opened eyes. These alpha waves increase amplitude and decrease frequency with the progress of Zen meditation. And sometimes the rhythmical theta train appears in the later stage of the meditation. These findings are also parallel with the degree of Zen disciples' mental states in the Zen sense and their years spent in Zen training.

It is common that the mental activities of concentration, mental calculation and efforts to perceive the objects elevate the level of consciousness accompanied by the activating pattern (Adrian & Matthews, 1934; Bartley, 1940; Callaway, 1962; Glass, 1964; Slater, 1960; Walter & Yeager, 1956; Walter, 1950). Thus the activating pattern indicates the augmentation of level of consciousness (Lindsley, 1952; Mundy-Castle, 1959).

Zen meditation is the concentrated regulation of inner mind. It will be, therefore, expected that Zen meditation will bring about the activating pattern. Nevertheless the lowering of cortical potentials is confirmed by our electrographic findings. This is rather paradoxical but is of prime interest to consider a relationship between the physiology of the brain and the level of consciousness.

According to the instructions of Zen meditation, the regulation of inner mind is strongly emphasized. And by obeying the rules of Zen training the well-achieved meditation has been completed. In the well-achieved meditation, it will be said that "concentration" without tension (that is the true concentration) is going on in the utmost inner world of psychic life.

From the electroencephalographic point of view, our results are coincident with EEG changes of lowered consciousness or vigilance. A. C. Mundy-Castle (1953, 1958) states that the persistent appearance of alpha waves indicates the brain function at the time of lowered vigilance. And many empirical observations of alpha waves point out its being not of action but of hypofunction of the brain (Dynes, 1947; Lindsley, 1952).

In attempting to relate the various stages of the EEG pattern to corresponding psychological states and the behavioral correlates, D. B. Lindsley (1952) states that during more or less continuous relaxed state of wakefulness, amplitude modulated alpha waves are characteristic. The same concept is stated by H. Jasper (1941, 1941) in his sleep-wakefulness continuum; he introduces the concept of the cortical excitatory states reflected on these EEG patterns. According to Jasper's suggestion, it is said that the amplitude modulated alpha waves reflect the lowered level of the cortical excitatory states.

On the other hand, many agents which affect nerve cell metabolism, are known to alter the EEG (Brazier, 1945; Grunthal & Bonkalo, 1940; Jung, 1953). A. Kasamatsu and Y. Shimazono (1957) report that the large and slow alpha waves are observed in the earlier stage of N_2 gas inhalation, just before the loss of consciousness. In this state, subjects experience relaxed consciousness or slightly elevated mood-changes. In the acute alcoholic intoxication the same effects are seen in both the EEG and consciousness (Kasamatsu & Shimazono, 1957). T. Hirai (1960) points out a decrease of the respiratory rate accompanied with the slowing of EEG pattern during Zen meditation. Y. Sugi et al. (1964) report the results of measurements of the respiratory rate, tidal volume and O_2 consumption during Zen meditation. They find a decrease of energy metabolism which is lower than basic metabolism. According to Sugi's suggestion, it may be due to the decrease of energy metabolism in the brain. It is possible that the decrease of energy metabolism also alters the electrographic pattern in Zen meditation.

From the foregoing surveys and discussions, EEG changes during Zen meditation seem to indicate that the cortical excitatory level will be gradually lowered even by the "concentration" of inner mind.

From a psychological point of view, both Zen meditation and hypnotic trance bring about the changes of consciousness. But the trance is called "Sanran" (confusion) and is strictly suppressed in Zen meditation. Therefore, some discussions will be needed about the difference of EEG changes between Zen meditation and hypnotic trance. The authors discovered that there are no definite changes of subjects' electroencephalograms in hypnotic trance. There are many reports concerning the EEG changes in hypnotic trance but many of these indicate that the pattern does not differ from the waking EEG (Kleitman, 1963; Loomis & Habart, 1936). There are no similarities of the pattern in hypnotic trance to EEG changes during Zen meditation.

Some scholars state that the sleep-like changes of EEG, more or less slight, are observed in hypnotic trance. Goldie et al. (Kleitman, 1963) elicited a paradoxical electrographic effect in a drowsy hypnotized subject— the alpha pattern appearing in the opened-eyes condition D. J. Frank (1960) reports that slow activity seen in deep sleep is recorded during the hypnosis. D. B. Lindsley (1952) points out that in accordance with general relaxation, which occurs during hypnotic episodes, there is sometimes an increase in alpha pattern if slight drowsiness supervenes.

K. Fujisawa (1960) studies EEG in the hypnotic state caused by sleep suggestion ("hypnotic sleep") (Baker & Burgwin, 1949; Dynes, 1947) and reveals the low voltage theta pattern which is similar to the drowsy pattern. He also points out that the drowsy-like pattern continues for a fairly long time as far as the rapport with the hypnotized subject is not lost and true sleep ensues if the rapport is lost. It is noticed that the slow rhythm in hypnotic sleep is more similar to the drowsy pattern than the rhythmical theta activity seen in Zen meditation.

Zen meditation is not a sleep from the disciples' introspections. But during Zen training, sometimes the slight drowsiness also can be supervened in a hypnosis. In the transitory state from wakefulness to drowsiness, large alpha waves are prominently seen and are prone to decrease in frequency just before the subject shows slight drowsiness (Oswald, 1959). It may be said, therefore, that the large and slow alpha pattern during Zen meditation is a foregoing pattern of the drowsiness. Perhaps there is the lower threshold in a sweep or span of consciousness during Zen meditation. But in actual sleep, alpha waves recede, spindles burst and slow waves appear, and consciousness is lost. Such a series of electrographic changes does not occur in Zen meditation and consciousness is not lost, since in Zen meditation there is no lack of awareness of things going on externally and internally.

Even in the later stage of Zen meditation, in which the rhythmical theta train is seen on EEG, the sensibility is not lost and in fact the rhythmical theta train shows the marked blocking to sensory stimulation. From these findings, we will show the difference between both schematically in Fig. 1. A series of EEG changes is common at a limit of alpha activities, but the sleep pattern diverges from this series in a downward curve, and turns to deep sleep.

From the foregoing discussions, it can be said that during Zen meditation the level of the cerebral excitatory state is gradually lowered in a way that is different from sleep.

Next we will discuss the alpha blocking in Zen meditation. As described before,

EEG changes in Zazen and sleep

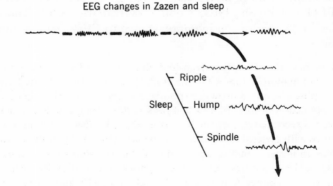

Figure 1 A schematical representation of the difference between EEG changes in Zen meditation and in sleep. A series of EEG changes is common at a limit of alpha activities but the sleep pattern diverges from above horizontal train in a downward curve and turns to deep sleep.

each click stimulus brings about a fairly constant alpha blocking continued for several seconds, even though the stimulation is repeated 20 times at regular intervals. But in control groups with closed eyes, the alpha blocking time is longer at 1st and 2nd stimulations but rapidly decreases and almost diminishes after 3rd or 4th stimulation. So the habituation of alpha blocking is clearly recognized in this ordinary awakening state.

In Zen meditation the alpha blocking is less susceptible to habituation to sensory stimuli than in ordinary waking state. This fact is noteworthy to clarify the arousal state of consciousness in Zen meditation. During Zen meditation "concentration" without tension is maintained in the inner mind of the disciple while keeping the correct sitting form. These mental and physical conditions naturally lead to production of the certain constant experimental circumstances: A kind of concentration subserves the maintenance of a certain level of the consciousness on the one hand, and the sitting meditation form supports the centripetal sensory inflows at a certain level on the other. In these circumstances, it would be supposed that the alpha blocking becomes less susceptible to habituation.

These findings are also supported by the introspection of our subjects in this experiment. The Zen masters reported to us that they had more clearly perceived each stimulus than in their ordinary waking state. In this state of mind one cannot be affected by either external or internal stimulus, nevertheless he is able to respond to it. He perceives the object, responds to it, and yet is never disturbed by it. Each stimulus is accepted as stimulus itself and treated as such. One Zen master described such a state of mind as that of noticing every person one sees on the street but of not looking back with emotional curiosity.

However, it seems to be impossible to consider separately the continuous appearance of alpha waves and the alpha blocking, which is less susceptible to habituation in Zen meditation. The alpha blocking depends upon the cortical excitatory state, conversely the cortical excitatory state closely related to the centrifugal sensory impulses brought about alpha blocking.

Using the arousal reaction of EEG as a criterion response, S. Sharpless and H. Jasper (1956) studied a great variety of characteristics of the habituation. They classified two types of arousal reaction: a longer lasting one more susceptible to habituation and a shorter lasting one less susceptible. This finding, in agreement with other studies (Jung, 1953; Lindsley, 1952) suggests that a longer lasting arousal reaction corresponds to the tonic activation on the cerebral cortex and a shorter lasting one to the phasic activation.

According to Jasper's suggestion, the alpha blocking, which is less susceptible to habituation, seems to be decided by the equilibrium of the tonic and phasic activation on the cerebral cortex. The authors want to postulate that there is an optimal activation mediated by the equilibrium of cortical excitatory state in a broad sweep or span of the waking consciousness. And perhaps its underlying neurophysiological basis may be an interaction between the cerebral cortex and the reticular activation systems of the diencephalic and mesencephalic portions in the brain stem (Moruzzi & Magoun, 1949).

The optimal preparedness for incoming stimuli, which conversely maintains the optimal level of the cortical excitatory state, is well reflected in both the alpha blocking, which is less susceptible to habituation, and in the series of EEG changes, which directs to the slowing of the pattern.

These EEG findings persist for a fairly long time and are constant though slight fluctuation is observed. Also these persistant alpha waves can be often seen even after the end of Zen meditation. These findings suggest that in the awakening consciousness, there will be the special state of consciousness, in which the cortical excitatory level becomes lower than in ordinary wakefulness, but is not lowered as in sleep, and yet outer or inner stimulus is precisely perceived with steady responsiveness.

Zen meditation is purely a subjective experience completed by a concentration which holds the inner mind calm, pure and serene. And yet Zen meditation produces a special psychological state based on the changes in the electroencephalogram. Therefore, Zen meditation influences not only the psychic life but also the physiology of the brain. The authors call this state of mind the "relaxed awakening with steady responsiveness."

SUMMARY

Zen meditation (Zazen) is a spiritual exercise held in the Zen sect of Buddhism. Apart from its religious significance, the training of Zen meditation produces changes not only in the mind but also in the body—these influences are of interest to scientific studies, from the standpoint of psychology and physiology.

In the present study the EEG changes accompanied with Zen meditation have been revealed and described in detail. The authors discussed further these electrographic changes in relation to the consciousness with its underlying neurophysiological background, compared with that of the hypnotic trance and sleep.

In our study, 48 priests and disciples of Zen sects of Buddhism were selected as the subjects and their EEGs were continuously recorded before, during, and after Zen meditation. The following results were obtained:

1. The appearance of alpha waves were observed, without regard to opened eyes, within 50 seconds after the beginning of Zen meditation.

These alpha waves continued to appear, and their amplitudes increased. And as Zen meditation progressed, the decrease of the alpha frequency was gradually manifested at the later stage. Further the rhythmical theta train with the amplitude modulated alpha-background was observed in some records of the priests. These EEG changes could be classified into 4 stages: the appearance of alpha waves (Stage I), an increase of alpha amplitude (Stage II), a decrease of alpha frequency (Stage III), and the appearance of rhythmical theta train (Stage IV).

2. These 4 stages of EEG changes were parallel with the disciples' mental states, which were evaluated by a Zen master, and disciples' years spent in Zen training.

3. These electrographic changes were also compared with that of the hypnotic trance and sleep. From the electroencephalographic point of view, the changes of Stages I, II and III could not be clearly differentiated from those seen in hypnagogic state or the hypnotic sleep, though the changes during Zen meditation were more persistent and did not turn into a deeper sleep pattern. The rhythmical theta train is suppressed by click stimulation and turns into a desynchronized pattern, whereas the drowsy pattern turns into alpha waves (the alpha arousal reaction).

4. The alpha blocking to the repeated click stimuli with regular intervals was also examined in Zen meditation with opened eyes and the ordinary conditions of control subjects with closed eyes. The former showed a fairly constant blocking time (3–5 seconds) to every stimuli repeated 20 times and the habituation was not recognized. On the other hand, in control subjects the habituation of alpha waves occurred very quickly. This alpha blocking, which is less susceptible to habituation, is of importance in considering the neurophysiological basis of the mental state during Zen meditation.

These electroencephalographic findings lead to the following conclusions: In Zen meditation, the slowing of the EEG pattern is confirmed on the one hand, and the dehabituation of the alpha blocking on the other. These indicate the specific change of consciousness. The authors further discussed the state of mind during Zen meditation from the psychophysiological point of view.

34

SOME ASPECTS OF ELECTROENCEPHALO-
GRAPHIC STUDIES IN YOGIS

B. K. ANAND, G. S. CHHINA and BALDEV SINGH

INTRODUCTION

Yogis practising *Raj Yoga* claim that during *samadhi* (meditation) they are oblivious to "external" and "internal" environmental stimuli although their higher nervous activity remains in a state of "ecstasy" (*mahanand*). Physiological and experimental studies have demonstrated that the basis of the conscious state of the brain is the activation of the reticular activating system through peripheral afferents (Magoun, 1958), without which higher nervous activity passes into the "sleep" state. Studies were, therefore, undertaken to investigate electroencephalographically the activity of the brain during *samadhi*. Some reports have already appeared on the subject (Das and Gastaut, 1955; Bagchi and Wenger, 1957), but the physiological mechanism of the state of *samadhi* still needs further elucidation.

EXPERIMENTAL SUBJECTS

Scalp EEG was used to study the brain activity of Yogis during *samadhi*. Two types of yoga practitioners, who volunteered for this study, were investigated.

Reprinted by permission from *Electroenceph. clin. Neurophysiol.*, Vol. 13, 1961, pp. 452–456.

1. Yogis practicing meditation. Four Yogis practicing *samadhi* had their EEG recordings taken before as well as during meditation. Two of them were exposed to "external" stimuli which were photic (strong light), auditory (loud banging noise), thermal (touching with hot glass tube) and vibration (tuning fork). The effect of these on the EEG activity was studied both before as well as during meditation. One Yogi during *samadhi* also practiced "pin-pointing of consciousness" (which means concentrating attention on different points of the vault of the skull).

2. Yogis with raised pain threshold. Two Yogis, who had developed increased pain threshold to cold water, were also investigated. They were able to keep their hand in water at 4°C for 45–55 minutes respectively without experiencing any discomfort. Their EEG records were obtained before and during the period when they kept their hand in cold water.

RESULTS

The changes observed in the EEG records of the Yogis investigated are presented below.

1. Yogis practicing meditation. All these Yogis showed prominent alpha activity in their normal resting records. During the stage of *samadhi* all of them and persistent alpha activity with well-marked increased amplitude modulation. In addition one of them showed occasional hump activity in the parietal zones, although he professed to remain awake throughout this period. In both the Yogis who were exposed to "external" stimulation, all the stimuli blocked the alpha rhythm and changed it to a low voltage fast activity when the Yogis were not meditating. This blocking reaction did not show any adaptation to repetition of the same stimuli. On the other hand, none of these stimuli produced any blockage of alpha rhythm, when the Yogis were in meditation (*samadhi*). In the Yogi who concentrated attention on different points of the vertex ("pin-pointing of consciousness"), these attempts were accompanied by well-marked "blinking" responses recorded from the frontal electrodes.

2. Yogis with raised pain threshold. The EEG records of these two Yogis also showed persistent alpha activity, both before and during the period in which the hand was immersed in cold water. No change in the electrical activity in the parietal leads was observed even when sensory afferents from the hand were expected to be projecting there.

3. EEG studies were also made on a number of beginners in the various yoga practices. It was observed that those who had a well-marked alpha

activity in their normal resting records showed greater aptitude and zeal for maintaining the practice of yoga.

DISCUSSION

In these experimental observations on Yogis, a persistent and well-modulated alpha activity, more marked during *samadhi*, was observed. This alpha activity could not be blocked by various sensory stimuli when the Yogi was in *samadhi*, although it could easily be blocked when he was not meditating. Even during deep meditation when the Yogis appeared quite relaxed and in a sleep-like condition, the EEG record showed only prominent alpha activity. Only in one Yogi was occasional hump activity observed, the alpha rhythm persisting in the rest of the period. Bagchi and Wenger (1957) also found the normal alpha pattern, sometimes with good amplitude modulation, in the EEG records of some Yogis during meditation. Okuma et al. (1958) observed in *Zen* practitioners that the alpha waves of these subjects increased remarkably with the progress of their performance, even if their eyes were kept open. Das and Gastaut's (1955) observations on high amplitude fast waves in the EEG records of Yogis during meditation have not been confirmed.

The significance of prominent alpha activity observed during meditation is not yet clear. Yogis generally claim that during *samadhi* they are oblivious to their external and internal environments, and in the present experiments their alpha rhythm could not be blocked by external stimuli. They also did not pass into delta activity. Although the reticular activating system (RAS) is activated by peripheral sensory inputs, it has also been reported that this system is capable probably of some spontaneous or autonomous discharge (Bremer, 1954; Dell, 1952). The alpha activity may be due to this discharge. Garoutte et al. (1958) have also observed that bilateral alpha and beta rhythms are probably under the control of a subcortical pacemaker, or system of pacemakers. It is, therefore, suggested that the brain activity of Yogis during the stage of *samadhi* has for its basis a type of consciousness which probably depends upon mutual influences between the cephalic RAS and the cortex, and which does not depend upon the activation of RAS through external and internal afferents.

The two Yogis, who could keep their hand without discomfort in ice cold water for long periods, showed alpha activity during this practice. This suggests again that these individuals were able to block the afferents from activating the RAS and thus remain in alpha activity.

Lastly the observation that those beginners who had a well-marked alpha activity in their resting records, showed greater aptitude for maintaining the practice of yoga, is quite important and may have some bearing on the problem under discussion.

SUMMARY

Four Yogis who practiced *samadhi* were investigated electroencephalographically. It was observed that their resting records showed persistent alpha activity with increased amplitude modulation during *samadhi*. The alpha activity could not be blocked by various sensory stimuli during meditation.

Two Yogis, who could keep their hand immersed in ice cold water for 45–55 minutes, also showed persistent alpha activity both before and during this practice.

The possible mechanism of these observations has been discussed.

what is this mechanism?

35

OPERANT CONTROL OF THE EEG ALPHA RHYTHM AND SOME OF ITS REPORTED EFFECTS ON CONSCIOUSNESS

JOE KAMIYA

The history of psychology seems to be a history, or a prehistory, of the mind-body problem. Modern psychology began by dealing with one aspect of this problem, epistomology, the question of how we come to know the outside world. The early psychologists, working in the 1870s, administered sensory stimuli to Ss and were concerned with seeing what kinds of responses the Ss gave under specific verbal instructions, and then trying to develop what they considered a psycho-physical relationship. But this wasn't satisfactory because there was too much disagreement among investigators concerning the theoretical structures. There were debates, for instance, as to whether thoughts could be thoughts without containing images. The whole picture of experimentation in learning and often in physiological psychology also was concerned with the question of what it is that makes the organism, human or the animal, interact with the world in the way it does. The concept of mind was with us long before any more sophisticated, philosophical, scientific, logical outlook had been developed, but as the psychologists, especially after the behaviorist revolution, began to think about this problem, they began to use concepts like mind not in the older, introspectively oriented sorts of ways but rather as hypothetical constructs. The hypothetical constructs, such as images, dreams, hopes, fears, etc., stood or fell according to how *useful* they were in ordering the data and making valid predictions.

The problem for the scientist of private experience—i.e., that you can sit there and all of a sudden become aware of the way the seat fits your pants—is the kind of problem to which I like to think psychology ought to be addressing itself. But it's a very difficult problem, and many of the attempts psychology has made in the past to become more "scientific" seem to me to have been detours which have left the undergraduate psychology student, after he has finished his first year of courses and has gotten properly brainwashed with the behavioristic routine, unsatisfied because he still *knew* that he had dreams, that he had these funny sensations inside, that he could let his mind wander, etc., etc. One of the chief difficulties is that it is very very difficult when an individual says, "I had a dream last night," to know whether in fact he is telling the truth. This emerges as a problem because we have no independent way of indexing the occurrence of a dream, or the occurrence of an image, or the occurrence of a hope, etc.

By and large, psychology is still dealing with the uttered word as the primary source of datum to make these inferences of a hypothetical sort about what went on behind those words, how those words emerged.

As psychology has been struggling with the problem of the usefulness of introspective reports, other disciplines, those of a more biological orientation, have been dealing with the relationship between behavior and brain function. This work has had important implications for psychology. It is now possible to index the activity of a variety of events within the brain: we can put electrodes on the scalp and observe patterns of electrical activity that reflect brain activity. It is the possibility of correlating the electrical activity of the brain with Ss' reports of their experience and their behavior which has intrigued me as a psychologist, for I feel it is a more solid approach than building hypothetical mental mechanisms on the basis of verbal reports alone.

Suppose we assumed that a particular brain process that we could identify was associated with some particular subjective state. Then we may ask: "Can people be trained to discern the comings or goings of brain rhythms, say the EEG alpha rhythm, just by using the standard learning procedures that have been developed for use with rats and pigeons?" What we did in our laboratory in Chicago several years ago was the following: We attached EEG electrodes on the scalp (occipital-to-ear lobe tracing) in order to detect the EEG alpha rhythm. Our experimental question was, if we set up the proper discrimination procedure, could we get individuals to say "A" when the alpha rhythm was present and to say "B" when the rhythm was absent? The S was told that from time to time he would hear a bell ring once; when he heard it, he was to make a guess as to whether at that time he was in brain wave state A or brain wave state B. And as soon as he made his response we told him if he was correct. You will recognize this as a pretty straightforward discrimination learning problem. The stimuli to be discriminated were not in the outside world, as is the conventional case with most experimental psychology, but were instead located inside the S, and were presumably correlated with the comings and goings of the alpha rhythm.

After a S had been given his task, he began to call out his guesses. Usually in the first hour or so there was essentially chance performance; in the second hour the S very often began to get about 60% correct. In the third hour, Ss typically got about 75 or 80% correct. Some Ss became 100% correct in naming their brain wave state. Thus Ss had learned to make correct discriminative responses to something that was going on inside their brains.

At a simple-minded level of thinking about correctness, one can say that the S here had learned to read his own brain, or his mind, if you will. In so far as that is true, one can argue that he has learned to make some kind of an introspective response. But that's perhaps primarily a pedantic lession in academic psychology. What may interest you more is what the Ss reported about how they carried out this task. Any particular S, even one who got nearly 100% correct, was not necessarily able to articulate in English just *how* he was able to do this. He may have felt that he should say "A" sometimes and "B" at other times, but not be able to give us any reasons, but this was the extreme case. Many Ss, however, did offer various kinds of verbal explanations on the basis for their discriminative responses. One thing that needs to be mentioned before discussing these reports, however, is this: any Ss who were sort of mid-way in the learning process, that is when they were getting more than 50% correct, but not yet 100% correct, were quite unable to tell us how they were able to do it. They would offer various verbalizations, but then immediately qualify them by saying they weren't all sure, and so on. I find this rather interesting; it suggests that we have succeeded in teaching individuals to make internal discriminations or perceptions about them-selves whose dimensions are so unfamiliar that they are unable to give a clear-cut verbal description.

Now let me report an important finding that we came upon quite by accident. We said to the S, "Look, obviously you've learned how to make this discrimination quite well. Let's see if you can produce those states that you have been calling 'A' and 'B' upon our command." The S was told that if he heard the bell ring twice, he was to enter into that state that he'd been calling "A"; and as soon as he heard the bell ring once, he was to change into the other state that he'd been calling "B." We found that having successfully gone through the discrimination training, most Ss seemed to have at the same time acquired the skills necessary for the control of the brain wave states that they had been discriminating. I think there may be other explanations possible to account for this finding, but they are not this striking, and certainly you do not see results like this in an untrained subject.

When I moved from Chicago to San Francisco, I asked myself the natural question, "Can people be trained to control their brain waves without this prior discrimination training?" The answer seems to be yes. The procedure I used is quite simple. I set up an electronic device which would turn on a sine-wave tone in the S's room whenever the alpha rhythm was present. The tone would disappear as soon as the alpha rhythm would disappear. The S was told: "Hear that tone? That's turned on by your brain wave." And after waiting for a few minutes for the S to settle down, I said: "Now let's see if you can learn how to control the percent of time that the tone is present. First we'll have you try and keep the tone *on* as much as you possibly can, and then we'll have you try to keep the tone *off* as much of the time as you can."

I did various kinds of experiments along these lines; sometimes I just trained people to suppress the alpha rhythm without any training for enhancing it. I found generally speaking, that most Ss had the ability to learn how to produce more alpha or to suppress it, although the extent to which they were able to suppress it is a little bit in question. Figure 1 illustrates the results of suppression training only. On the ordinate I have scaled the percentage of time that alpha was absent, i.e., suppressed. Consider only the section of the graph under Phase A for now. As you can see, for six of the seven individual curves of performance, there is a general upward trend. The lowest curve depicts the one exception, an S who seems to be going the opposite direction. We ran this individual several more trials with an added factor, discussed below, and he soon joined the group of individuals back up at the other end of the graph.

By this time I had found, especially for suppressing the alpha rhythm, a fair degree of agreement by the different Ss on their reports as to *how* it was done, especially as the Ss became more and more proficient in the task. I would often hear that visual imagery was the answer, that all they would have to do was to conjure up an image of a person's face, hold it, and look at it very *carefully*, so much so that they could actually see the features of the person's face. If the S was able to fixate something like this, or if he fixated the spots that float around in the visual field, the visual phosphenes, or if he engaged in other kinds of visual imagery activity, it seemed to be effective in turning alpha off.

Because of this agreement among the successful alpha-suppressors as to the value of visual imagery in suppressing the alpha rhythm, I decided to

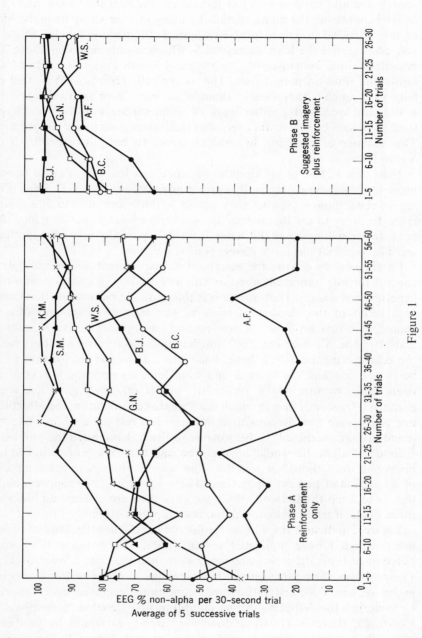

EEG % non-alpha per 30-second trial
Average of 5 successive trials

Phase A
Reinforcement
only

Phase B
Suggested imagery
plus reinforcement.

Figure 1

K.M.
S.M.
W.S.
G.N.
B.J.
B.C.
A.F.

B.J.
G.N.
A.F.
B.C.
W.S.

Number of trials

511

see what would happen with our less successful *S*s if they were instructed to try suppressing the alpha rhythm by using intense visual imagery. Most of the *S*s found it very helpful. In Figure 1, the portion labeled Phase B, you can see that the least successful *S*, who was only reaching about 20% non-alpha time, went up to 80%, and some of my other poor *S*s reached 100% non-alpha time on many trials. The *S*s typically reported, "Yes, that did help very much"; they *kind of* thought so, but weren't entirely sure that it did, and were trying other ways of alpha suppression they had hypothesized would be successful even after the instructions to use visualization. This manner of checking hypotheses seems to be quite essential if the *S* is to learn.

This area is full of all kinds of superstitious learning. Partial success brought on by some practically correct attempts inside the *S*'s head often are so rewarding to *S*s that they persist in these and plateau at a certain level. In order to get themselves up to a higher level of performance they have to be willing to shake loose from that partially correct hypothesis and find one that has more elements of correctness in it.

I want now to discuss the results of an experiment which attempts to control for one important question that is raised by this suppression-only experimental design. That question is this: it might be possible that simply as a result of the number of trials or the number of sessions of a repeated task that an *S* would get less and less alpha, i.e., that it is simply a shift in the *S*'s baseline EEG and has nothing to do with the tone or the reinforcement at all. I thought the best way to control for that would be to use one and the same *S* and train him, on opposite blocks of five trials each, to turn alpha on or to turn it off. So I gave five trials, each trial 30 seconds long in which the *S* was to keep alpha on, and after those five trials were over he was then instructed to rest for a while while "we tuned up our machine." Unbeknownst to the *S*, I recorded the number of seconds of alpha he would have gotten had the tone been switched into his room, even though it was not. This was an attempt to get some kind of a baseline of percent alpha time. Then, I asked him to suppress alpha, that is to keep the tone off. What we have then are alternating blocks of three kinds of trials: enhance alpha, rest, suppress alpha.

Figure 2 indicates the sort of results obtained from this kind of experiment, which I have replicated several times. The ordinate is scaled in percentage time alpha was present, rather than the time it was absent, as Figure 1 was. The three curves represent the average performances of a group of seven *S*s under the three conditions, enhance, rest, suppress. Considering the Suppress Alpha condition first (labeled "low alpha" in Figure 2), there is clearly a downward trend, as would be predicted, although it is not as pronounced as the curve in Figure 1. The increase

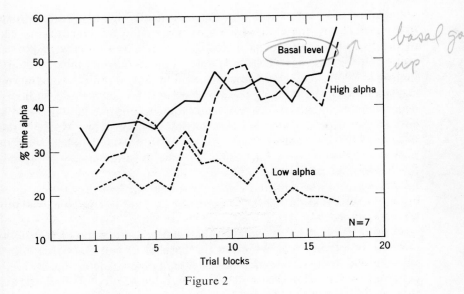

basal goes up

Figure 2

in the curve for the Enhance Alpha condition is much more striking, and it is clear that there is a very significant difference in percent alpha time between the enhance and suppress conditions for these Ss. Thus it's not merely a function of alpha decreasing with the passage of time; there does seem to be some measure of volitional control. Now, consider the third curve (labeled "basal level") which represents the percent alpha score Ss got in the rest periods when they weren't getting the tone: as a matter of fact they were specifically told *not* to try producing tones, they were told that the tones would be switched off and just merely to wait until we got our machine aligned. This curve shows a generally upward trend, yet if this were really *a baseline* sort of thing one would have expected it to have stayed level. My interpretation of this upward trend is that the Ss do not remain the same after having learned these two kinds of tasks; the experimental tasks apparently set them into certain *preferred* modes of waiting, and the preferred mode is the higher alpha state. There will be additional evidence for this later, but let me cite one important piece right now. If the Ss are asked which of the two tasks—enhance or suppress—they prefer, they almost invariably say they greatly prefer learning how to turn alpha *on*. A good many of them will say suppressing alpha is easy, all you have to do is conjure up an image, but it's not particularly fun or pleasant, and it's much more interesting to keep oneself in the high alpha state.

Let me report a few verbalizations about the high alpha state, besides its general pleasantness, that have been reported by Ss. First, they all seem to say that this seems to have to do with some kind of *relaxation* of the mental apparatus, not necessarily relaxation in the motor system, but a kind of a general calming-down of the mind. Second, it is a state in which it is good not to be thinking too much about the outside world, or how the experiment is going, or even how you're doing, but one in which you just sort of listen for the tone and just let it carry you along. Some of them have said in this context that it's one of those things where you stop being *critical* about anything, including the experiment. I will elaborate the description of the high alpha state in a moment, but it suffices to say now that I feel these reported characteristics of the high alpha state support my hypothesis that during rest periods the Ss tend to continue to produce high alpha, and thus the "baseline" goes up.

Another indirect bit of evidence that supports this interpretation of the increase of percent alpha time in the baseline condition is that with Ss who are given only suppression training, their percent alpha time in baseline conditions tends to decrease. That is, they seem to continue doing what they have been trained to do. But when they have been trained for both enhancement and suppression, they prefer enhancement, and baselines go up.

Now let me describe a little bit more fully what Ss say about this high alpha state, and what kinds of people seem to be especially good at producing it. Tentatively, I have found that there are certain kinds of individuals that do much better at learning how to control alpha, especially learning how to increase alpha; and these individuals so far seem to be those who have had some interest in and practice of what I shall loosely call "meditation." It doesn't necessarily have to be of the Zen or Yoga school, or any other formal school of meditation. If the individual has had a long history of introspection on his own, he seems to be especially good at enhancing the alpha rhythm. Also he is likely to be an individual who uses words like *images, dreams, wants,* and *feelings*. It have come to the conclusion that there are a large number of people who really don't know exactly what you are talking about when you talk about images and feelings. To such people the words describe something that *somebody else* might have; but these people do not seem to have any degree of sensitivity to such things themselves. These people do not do well in my experiments, they do not gain a high degree of control over their alpha rhythm.

Let me mention some other characteristics of people who are good at learning alpha control, although these are impressions that I don't consider well proven yet. Psychotherapists, of the type who lay great store by such techniques as sensitivity training and the other sorts of growth techniques used at such places as Esalen Institute, seem to be good at learning alpha control. People who look you in the eye and feel at ease in close interpersonal relationships, who are good at intuitively sensing the way you feel, are also good at this. Also I notice I generally tend to have more positive liking for the individual who subsequently turns out to learn alpha control more readily. I find this especially true of females, for some reason!

I mentioned that people who have practiced meditation are good Ss. I have been carrying on further experiments with these meditators, as I have come to call them, and have been pushing them to see how high they could go in percent time of alpha, and whether their testimony changes over a period of many sessions. I have run one or two of these Ss on sort of "marathon" runs, at one time attempting to do it on a 20-hour basis. I've been finding that these Ss do seem to continue to improve their skills by doing this over and over for as much as 20 and 30 hours total time. One S plateaued after about 50 hours and didn't improve much beyond that; but this individual started at about 15% alpha and got himself up to 85% alpha. That's a rather substantial change; certainly if you look at the EEG record before and after, it would look like the EEG records of two different people.

I think it's rather intriguing that those who practice meditation, are skillful at this task and it makes me listen with more interest to reports about the effects of meditation. For example, the ineffability of the meditative state, so often stressed in mystical writings is similar to statements many of my Ss make, e.g., "In this experiment, you keep asking me to describe this darned alpha state. I can't do it; it has a certain feel about it, sure, but really, it's best left undescribed; when I try to analyse what it is I don't do well."

The high alpha state is a desirable thing to my Ss. It used to be that to motivate Ss to participate in these experiments I payed them a certain flat rate per hour and threw in a bonus on some occasions. But now it's gotten to be the case that they're almost ready to pay *me* to serve as Ss, especially if I say I will let them turn on alpha for an extended period of time! I no longer pay Ss, and I have a list a mile long from various people who call me on the telephone or who write me from New York, and other places all over the country to ask if they can come over and serve as subjects! I think that perhaps this is somewhat indicative, although certainly not conclusively so, that the state itself is a nice one to be in. I have tried it myself for only a couple of hours, so I can't give you my own introspective reports on this. Before one can be sure that this is something that people really will strive for, one needs to see that this state works as a motivator in the conventional sorts of ways that are available for testing such a concept.

Finally let me briefly describe the latest experiment in this area. The experiments all have to do with changing the *amplitude* and *frequency of occurrence* of the alpha rhythm, the extent to which there were bursts of alpha rhythm of sufficient amplitude to trigger our tone device. But, is it possible to train Ss to vary the *frequency* of the alpha rhythm? My engineer devised a cycle period analyser and thus had a system whereby each EEG alpha wave cycle was compared against a standard duration: if the wave was *longer* in duration than the standard, the S heard a *high*-pitched click, while if the wave was *shorter* than the standard, he heard a *low*-pitched click. I chose a standard duration for each S in such a fashion that approximately half of his clicks would be high clicks and approximately half would be low clicks. I now told the S to try to increase the predominance of one kind of click over the other. Again we used the S as his own control, alternating blocks of trials in which he was to raise alpha frequency with blocks in which he was to decrease alpha frequency.

Figure 3 presents the mean performance of ten Ss on alpha *frequency* control. I have plotted the mean percent difference between the conditions when they were trying to produce high clicks in predominance on the one hand, and the condition in which they were trying to produce low

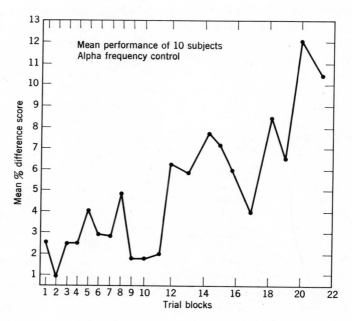

Figure 3

clicks on the other. As you can see, the difference between those two experimental conditions grows as a function of trial blocks and it's a rather striking change. One can actually see the difference in the raw EEG record in some cases, although I have yet to run the magnetic tape data through the computer to see exactly how much the frequency shifts. I can say that for some Ss the shift is as large as two cycles per second.

I do not know, and nobody really knows for sure what the significance of a change alpha frequency is. However, we can note that when individuals are drowsy, their alpha frequency tends to slow up a little. When they are asleep and in a stage 1 EEG state, with the eyes moving, there is some slowed alpha activity mixed in with the irregular theta rhythms. Recently I ran across a report that some Japanese investigators had been looking at the EEGs of Zen masters, and found that as they were doing their meditative exercises, their alpha rhythm became more abundant and tended to be slower. It's not just drowsiness that will bring this slowing about; as a matter of fact, any marked degree of drowsiness is almost always accompanied by a drop in the control that my Ss have over their alpha rhythm.

I shall refrain from speculating on where this work is going to lead. Clearly we have a rather strong effect, but many questions remain to be answered about it. My laboratory will be busy for many years to come working in this area.

REFERENCES

Aaronson, B. Hypnosis, time rate perception, and personality. Paper, Eastern Psychol. Assn. Atlantic City, 1965. (a)

Aaronson, B. Hypnosis, being, and the conceptual categories of time. Paper, N. J. Psychol. Assn. Princeton, 1965. (b)

Aaronson, B. Hypnosis, depth perception, and psychedelic experience. Paper, Soc. Sci. Study of Relig. New York, 1965. (c)

Aaronson, B. Hypnosis, time rate perception, and psychopathology. Paper, Eastern Psychol. Assn. New York, 1966. (a)

Aaronson, B. Behavior and the place names of time. *Amer. J. clin. Hyp.*, 1966, **9**, 1–18. (b)

Aaronson, B. Distance, depth and schizophrenia. *Amer. J. clin. Hyp.*, 1967, **9**, 203–207. (a)

Aaronson, B. Hypnosis, responsibility, and the boundaries of self. *Amer. J. clin Hyp.*, 1967, **9**, 229–245. (b)

Abell, A. *Talks with the great composers.* Garmisch-Partenkirchen: G. E. Schroder-Verlag, 1964.

Abood, L. A new group of psychotominetic agents. *Proc. Soc.*, 1958, **97**, 483–486.

Abraham, K. Remarks on the psychoanalysis of a case of foot and corset fetishism. In *Selected papers of Karl Abraham.* New York: Basic Books, 1953, **1**, 125–136.

Abraham, K. The psychological relations between sexuality and alcoholism. In *Selected papers of Karl Abraham.* New York: Basic Books, 1953.

Abramson, H. *The use of LSD in psychotherapy.* New York: Josia Macy Jr., Foundation publications, 1960.

Abramson, H. (Ed.) *The use of LSD in psychotherapy and alcoholism.* Indianapolis: Bobbs-Merrill, 1967.

Ackerly, W., & Gipson, G. Lighter fluid sniffing. *Amer. J. Psychiat.*, 1964, **120**, 1056–1066.

Adler, A. *What life should mean to you.* New York: Capricorn, 1968.

Adrian, E., & Matthews, B. The Berger rhythm. Potential changes from the occipital lobes in man. *Brain*, 1943, **57**, 355–385.

Agnew, H., Webb, W., & Williams, R. The effects of stage four sleep deprivation. *EEG clin. Neurophysiol.*, 1964, **17**, 68–70.

Alancon, H. Contribution toward the study of hallucination producing plants, particularly of Machoha, Cannibis sativa, known as marihuana in the United States. Quoted by Periera, *J. Rev. de Flora med.*, 1945, **12**, 3, 85–209.

Alexander, F. Buddhistic training as an artificial catatonia (the biological meaning of psychic occurrence). *Psychoanal.*, 1931, **19**, 129, 145.

Allport, G. *Personality: A psychological interpretation.* New York: H. Holt, 1937.

American Medical Association. Committee on alcoholism and drug dependence. Dependence on cannabis (marihuana). *Amer. Med. Assn. J.*, 1967, **201**, 108–111.

Anderson, E. Abnormal mental states in survivors, with special reference to collective hallucinations. *J. Roy, Nav. Med. Serv.*, 1942, **28**, 361–377.

Anderson, P., & Kaada, B. The electroencephalogram in poisoning by lacquer thinner (butyl acetate and toluene). *Acta Pharmacol. Toxicol.*, 1953, **9**, 125–130.

Andrews, G., & Vinkenoog, S. *The book of grass: an anthology of Indian hemp.* New York: Grove Press, 1967.

Anonymous. An autobiography of a schizophrenic experience. *J. Abnorm. soc. Psychiat.*, 1955, **51**, 677–680.

Anonymous. The cloud of unknowing. In D. Knowles, *The English mystical tradition.* London: Burnes & Oates, 1961, 77.

Anonymous. Gasoline intoxication. *Brit. med. J.*, 1961, **1**, 1477.

Anonymous. Gasoline intoxication. *Brit. med. J.*, 1962, **2**, 1043.

Anonymous. Glue sniffing by youngsters fought by department. *New Eng. J. Med.*, 1962, **267**, 993–994.

Anonymous. Washington Bulletin, August. 1966.

Anslinger, H. *Traffic in opium and other dangerous drugs for the year ended December 31, 1931.* Washington, D.C.: Govt. Printing Office, 1932.

Arieti, S. Introductory notes on the psychoanalytic therapy of schizophrenia. In Burton (Ed.), *Psychotherapy of the psychoses*, New York: Basic Books, 1961.

Arieti, S., & Meth, J. Rare, unclassifiable, collective and exotic psychotic disorders. In S. Arieti (Ed.), *American handbook of psychiatry.* New York: Basic Books, 1959, **1**, 546–566.

Arlow, J., & Brenner, C. *Psychoanalytic concepts and the structural theory.* New York: International Universities Press, 1964.

Arnhoff, F., & Leon, H. Psychological aspects of sensory deprivation and isolation. *Merrill-Palmer Quart.*, 1964, **10**, 179–194.

Arnold-Foster, M. *Studies in dreams.* New York: MacMillan, 1921.

Ås, A. A note on distractibility and hypnosis. *Amer. J. clin. Hyp.*, 1962, **5**, 135–1357.

Ås, A. Non-hypnotic experiences related to hypnotizability in male and female college students. *Scand. J. Psychol.*, 1962, **3**, 112–121.

Ås, A., Hilgard, E., & Weitzenhoffer, A. An attempt at experimental modification of hypnotizability through repeated individualized hypnotic experience. *Scand. J. Psychol.*, 1963, **4**, 81–89.

Aserinsky, E., & Kleitman, N. Two types of ocular motility occurring in sleep. *J. appl. Physiol.*, 1955, **8**, 1–10.

Aserinsky, E., & Kleitman, N. Regularly occurring periods of eye motility and concomitant phenomena during sleep, *Science*, 1953, **118**, 273–274.

Assagioli, R. *Psychosynthesis: A manual of principles and techniques.* New York: Hobbs & Dorman, 1965.

Astin, A. The functional autonomy of psychotherapy. *Amer. J. Psychol.*, 1961, **16**, 75–78.

Aurobindo, S. *On Yoga, I: The synthesis of Yoga.* Pondicherry. India: Aurobindo Ashram Press, 1955.

Bagchi, B., & Wenger, M. Electrophysiological correlates of some Yogi exercises. *EEG clin. Neurophysiol.*, 1957, **7**, 132–149.

Baker, W., & Burgwin, S. Brain wave patterns during hypnosis, hypnotic sleep, normal sleep. *Arch. Neurol. Psychiat.*, 1949, **62**, 412–420.

Baldwin, J. *Mental development in the child and the race.* New York: Mac-Millan, 1895.

Ban, T., Lohrenz, J., & Lehmann, H. Observations on the action of Sernyl—a new psychotropic drug. *Canad. Psychiat. Assn. J.*, 1961, **6**, 150–157.

Barber, T. Hypnotizability, suggestibility, and personality: V. A critical review of research findings. *Psychol. Rep.*, 1964, **14**, 299–320.

Barber, T. The effects of "hypnosis" on learning and recall: a methodological critique. *J. clin. Psych.*, 1965, **21**, 19–25.

Barber, T. Toward a theory of "hypnotic" behavior: the hypnotically induced dream. *J. nerv. ment. Dis.*, 1962, **135**, 206–221.

Barber, T. Measuring "hypnotic-like" suggestibility with and without hypnotic induction: psychometric properties, norms, and variables influencing response to the Barber Suggestibility Scale. *Psychol. Rep.*, 1965, **16**, 809–844.

Barber, T., & Calverley, D. Toward a theory of "hypnotic" behavior. *Arch. gen. Psychiat.*, 1964, **10**, 209–216.

Barnard, M. The god in the flowerpot. *Psychedelic Rev.*, 1963, **1**, 244–251.

Barron, F. *Creativity and psychological health.* Princeton: Van Nostrand, 1963.

Barry, H., MacKinnon, D., & Murray, H. Studies in personality: A. Hypnotizability as personality trait and its topological relations. *Hum. Biol.*, 1931, **13**, 1–36.

Bartlett, F. *Remembering.* London: Cambridge, 1932.

Bartlett, J. A case of organized visual hallucinations in an old man with cataract, and their relation to the phenomena of the phantom limb. *Brain*, 1951, **74**, 363–373.

Bartley, S. The relation between cortical responses to visual stimulation and changes in the alpha rhythm. *J. exp. Psychol.*, 1940, **27**, 627–639.

Becker, H. Becoming a marihuana user. *Amer. J. Social.*, 1953, **59**, 235–242.

Becker, H. *Outsiders: studies in the sociology of deviance.* New York: Free Press, 1963.

Becker, H. History, culture, and subjective experience: an exploration of the social bases of drug-induced experiences. In C. Hollander (Ed.), *Background papers on student drug involvement.* Washington, D.C.: U.S. National Student Assn., 1967, 69–86.

Beers, C. *A mind that found itself.* New York: Longmans, Green, 1908.

Behanan, K. *Yoga: a scientific explanation.* New York: Dover, 1937.

Belo, J. *The trance in Bali.* New York: Columbia University Press, 1960.

Ben-Avi, A. Zen Buddhism. In S. Arieti (Ed.), *American handbook of psychiatry.* New York: Basic Books, 1959, 2.

Bennett, A. Sensory deprivation in aviation. In P. Solomon et al. (Eds.), *Sensory deprivation.* Cambridge, Mass.: Harvard University Press, 1961, 6–33.

Benoit, H. *The supreme doctrine: psychological studies in Zen thought.* New York: Viking Press, 1959.

Bentler, P., O'Hara, L., & Krasner, L. Hypnosis and placebo. *Psychol. Rep.,* 1963, **12**, 153–154.

Benussi, V. Zur experimentellen Grundlegung Hypnosuggestiner Methoden psychischer analyse. *Psychologiche Forschung,* 1927, **9**, 197–274.

Berger, R. Tonus of extrinsic laryngeal muscles during sleep and dreaming. *Science,* 1961, **134**, 840.

Berger, R. Experimental modification of dream content by meaningful verbal stimuli. *Brit. J. Psychiat.,* 1963, **109**, 722–740.

Berger, R., & Oswald, I. Effects of sleep deprivation on behavior, subsequent sleep, and dreaming. *EEG clin. Neurophysiol.,* 1962, **14**, 297.

Berger, R., & Oswald, I. Eye movement during active and passive dreams. *Science,* 1962, **137**, 601.

Berlin, L., Guthrie, T., Weider, A., Goodell, H., & Wolff, H. Studies in human cerebral function: the effects of mescaline and lysergic acid on cerebral process pertinent to creative activity. *J. nerv. ment. Dis.,* 1955, 122, 487–491.

Bernheim, H. *Suggestive therapeutics.* New York: Putnam, 1889.

Bertini, M., Lewis, H., & Witkin, H. Some preliminary observations with an experimental procedure for the study of hypnogogic and related phenomena. *Archivo d. psicologia, Neurol. Psichiatria,* 1964, **25**, 493–534.

Binswanger, H. Beobachtungen an entspannten and versenkten Versuchspersonen: Ein Beitrag zu Moglichen Mechanismen der Konversionhysterie. *Nervenarzt,* 1929, **4**, 193.

Blackburn, N., & Benton, A. Revised administration and scoring of the digit span test. *J. consult. Psych.,* 1957, **21**, 139–143.

Blazer, J. An experimental evaluation of "transcendence of environment." *J. human. Psych.,* 1963, **3**, 49–53.

Bleuler, E. *Dementia Praecox, or the group of schizophrenias.* J. Zinkin (Trans. Ed.). New York: International Universities Press, 1950.

Blofield, J. A high yogic experience achieved with mescaline. *Psychedelic Rev.,* 1966, **7**, 27–32.

Blood, B. *The anaesthetic revelation and the gist of philosophy.* New York: Amsterdam, 1874.

Blum, R., et al. *Utopiates: the use and users of LSD-25.* New York: Atherton Press, 1964.

Blum, R. (Ed.) *Utopiates.* New York: Atherton Press, 1965.

Blum, R., & Wahal, J. Police views on drug use, section 12. In R. Blum, (Ed.), *Utopiates.* New York: Atherton Press, 1965.

Boisen, A. *The exploration of the inner world.* New York: Harper-Row, 1952.

Bonaparte, M. Time and the unconscious. *Int. J. Psychoanal.,* 1940, **21**, 427–468.

Bonhoeffer, D. *Letters and papers from prison.* New York: MacMillan, 1953.

Boss, M. *The analysis of dreams*. London: Rider, 1957.

Bowers, M. Friend or traitor. Hypnosis in the service of religion. *Int. J. clin. exp. Hyp.*, 1959, **7**, 205–217.

Bowers, M. The onset of psychosis—a diary account. *Psychiat.*, 1965, **28**, 346–358.

Bowers, M. Experimental study of the creative process by means of hypnoanalytic associations to a painting done in occupational therapy: the magic ring of Walter Positive. *Int. J. Clin. exp. Hyp.*, 1966, **14**, 1–21.

Bowers, M., Goodman, E., & Sim, V. Some behavioral effects in man following anticholinesterase administration. *J. nerv. ment. Dis.*, 1964, **138**, 383–389.

Bowers, P. The effect of hypnosis and suggestions of reduced defensiveness on creativity test performance. Unpublished doctoral dissertation, University of Wisconsin, 1965.

Boyd, D., & Norris, M. Delirium associated with cataract extraction. *J. Indiana med. Assn.*, 1941, **34**, 130–135.

Boyko, E., Rotberg, M., & Disco, D. Constitutional objections to California's marijuana possession statute. *U. C. L. A. Law Rev.*, 1967, **14**, 773–795.

Brauchi, J., & West, L. Sleep deprivation. *J. Amer. med. Assn.*, 1959, **171**, 11–14.

Brazier, M. *The electrical activity of the nervous system*. 2nd Ed. London: 1960.

Brazier, M., & Finesinger, J. Action of barbiturates on the cerebral cortex. *Arch. Neurol. Psychiat.*, 1945, **53**, 51–58.

Bremer, F. The neurophysiological problem of sleep. In *Symposium on brain mechanisms and consciousness*. Oxford: Blackwell Scientific Publications, 1954, 137–162.

Brenman, M. Dreams and hypnosis. *Psychoanal. Quart.*, 1949, **18**, 455–465.

Brenman, M. The phenomena of hypnosis. In H. Abramson (Ed.), *Problems of consciousness*. New York: Josiah Macy Jr. Foundations, 1950, 123–163.

Brenman, M., Gill, M., & Knight, R. Spontaneous fluctuations in depth of hypnosis and their implications for ego-functioning. *Int. J. Psychoanal.*, 152, **33**, 22–33.

Brewer, W., et al. Hazards of intentional inhalation of plastic cement fumes. *Arizona Med.*, 1960, **17**, 747.

Broad, C. Dreaming and some of its implications. *Proc. soc. psych. Res.*, 1959, **52**, 53–78.

Brown, R. The effect of morphine upon the Rorschach pattern in post-addicts. *Amer. J. Orthopsychiat.*, 1943, **13**, 399–342.

Brownfield, C. Deterioration and facilitation hypotheses in sensory-deprivation research. *Psych. Bull.*, 1964, **61**, 304–313.

Brozovsky, M., & Winkler, E. Glue-sniffing in children and adolescents. *N.Y. State J. Med.*, 1965, **65**, 1984–1989.

Bruner, J. *On knowing*. Cambridge, Mass.: Harvard University Press, 1962.

Brunton, P. *The secret path*. New York: E. P. Dutton, 1935.

Brush, E. Observations on the temporal judgment during sleep. *Amer. J. Psychol.*, 1930, **42**, 408–411.

Buck, L., & Geers, M. Varieties of consciousness. *J. clin. Psychol.*, 1967, **23**, 151–152.

Bucke, R. *Cosmic consciousness: a study in the evolution of the human mind*. New Hyde Park, N.Y.: University Books, 1961.

Bugental, J. The existential crisis in intensive psychotherapy. *Psychother.*, 1965, **2**, 16–20.

Burney, C. *Solitary confinement.* New York: Coward-McCann, 1952.

Byrd, R. *Alone.* New York: G. P. Putnam's Sons, 1938.

Calkins, M. Statistics of dreams. *Amer. J. Psychol.*, 1893, **5**, 311–343.

Callaway, E., III. Factors influencing the relationship between alpha activity and visual reaction time. *EEG clin. Neurophysiol.*, 1962, **14**, 674–682.

Cameron, D. Addiction—current issues. *Amer. J. Psychiat.*, 1963, **120**, 313–319.

Cameron, N. Paranoid conditions and paranoia. In S. Arieti (Ed.), *American handbook of psychiatry.* New York: Basic Books, 1959.

Cannon, W. Voodoo death. *Amer. Anthropol.*, 1942, **44**, 169–181.

Carlini, E., & Kramer, C. Effects of Canabis sativa (marihuana) on maze performance of the rat. *Psychopharm.* (Berlin), 1965, **7**, 175–181.

Carlson, H. The relationship of the acute confusional state to ego development. *Int. J. Psychoanal.*, 1961, **42**, 517–536.

Carrington, H. *Your psychic powers and how to develop them.* New York: Templestar Publishers, 1958.

Cerletti, A., & Doepfner, W. Comparative study on the serotonin antagonism of amid derivatives of lysergic acid and/or ergot alkaloids. *J. Pharm. exp. Therapeutics*, 1958, **122**, 124–136.

Chang, G. *Teachings of Tibetan Yoga.* New Hyde Park, N. Y.: University Books, 1963.

Chaudhuri, H. *Philosophy of meditation.* New York: Philosophical Library, 1965.

Chein, L. *The road to H: narcotics, delinquency, and social policy.* New York: Basic Books, 1964.

Chertok, L., & Kramarz, P. Hypnosis, sleep, and electroencephalography. *J. nerv. ment. Dis.*, 1959, **128**, 227–238.

Christensen, C. Religious conversion. *Arch. gen. Psychiat.*, 1963, **9**, 207–216.

Christiansson, G., & Karlsson, B. Sniffing: a means of intoxication among children. *Svenska Lakartidningen*, 1957, **54**, 33–44.

Chwelos, N., Blewett, D., Smith, D., & Hoffer, A. Use of LSD-25 in the treatment of chronic alcoholism. *Quart. J. Studies on Alcohol*, 1959, **20**, 577–590.

Clark, J., & Skinner, J. *Treatises and sermons of Meister Eckhart.* New York: Harper, 1958.

Claviere, J. La rapidité de la pensée dans le rêve. *Rev. phil.*, 1897, **43**, 507–509.

Clinger, O., & Johnson, N. Purposeful inhalation of gasoline vapors. *Psychiat. Quart.*, 1951, **25**, 555–561.

Cobb, J., Evans, F., Gustafson, L., O'Connel, D., Orne, M., & Shor, R. Specific motor responses during sleep to sleep-administered meaningful suggestion: an exploratory investigation. *Percept. mot. Skills*, 1965, **20**, 629–636.

Coe, G. *The psychology of religion.* 2nd Ed. Chicago: University of Chicago Press, 1917.

Cohen, J. Color adaptation of the human eye. *Amer. J. Psychol.*, 1946, **59**, 84–110.

Cohen, S. *The beyond within: the LSD story.* New York: Atheneum, 1964.

Cohen, S. Lysergic acid diethylamide: side effects and complications. *J. nerv. ment. Dis.*, 1960, **130**, 30–40.

Cohen, S. LSD and the anguish of dying. *Harper's Magazine*, 1965, **231**, 60–72, 77–78.

Cohen, S., & Ditman, K. Prolonged adverse reaction to lysergic acid diethylamide. *Arch. gen. Psychiat.*, 1963, **8**, 475–480.

Cohen, S., Silverman, A., & Shmavonian, B. Psychophysiological studies in Altered sensory environments. *J. psychosom. Res.*, 1962, **6**, 259–281.

Colby, K. Psychotherapeutic processes. *Ann. Rev. Psychol.*, 1964, **15**, 347–370.

Condon, J. *Semantics and communication*. New York: MacMillan, 1966.

Connell, P. *Amphetamine psychosis*. London: Oxford University Press, 1958.

Cooley, C. *Human nature and the social order*. New York: Scribners, 1902.

Cooper, L. Time distortion in hypnosis. In L. Cron (Ed), *Experimental Hypnosis* New York: MacMillan, 1956, 217–228.

Cooper, L., Banford, S., Schubot, E., & Tart, C. A further attempt to modify hypnotic susceptibility through repeated individualized experience. *Int. J. clin. exp. Hyp.*, 1967, **15**, 118–124.

Cooper, L., & Erickson, M. *Time distortion in hypnosis: an experimental and clinical investigation*. Baltimore: Williams & Wilkins, 1954.

Coue, E. *Die Selbstbemeisterung durch bewusste Autosuggestion*. Basel, Stuttgart: Schwabe Verlag, 1961.

Crasilneck, H., & Hall, J. Physiological changes associated with hypnosis: a review of the literature since 1948. *Int. J. Clin. exp. Hyp.*, 1959, **7**, 9–50.

1 Crim. 5351 California District Court of Appeal, First Appellate District; People v. Gilcrease, Appellant's Opening Brief.

Crochet, R., Sandison, R., & Walk, A. (Eds.) *Hallucinogenic drugs and their psychothereapeutic use*. Springfield Ill.: Thomas, 1963.

Crocket, R., Sandison, R., & Walk, A. (Eds.) *Hallucinogenic drugs and their psychotherapeutic use*. London: J. Q. Lewis, 1963.

Cubberly, A. The effects of tensions of the body surface upon the normal dream. *Brit. J. Psychol.*, 1923, **13**, 243–265.

Custance, J. *Wisdom, madness, and folly*. New York: Farrar, Straus, and Girous, 1952.

Das, N., & Gastaut, H. Variations de l'activité électrique du cerveau, de coeur et des muscles squelettiaues au cours de la méditation et de "l'extase" yoguique. *EEG clin. Neurophysiol.*, 1955, suppl. 6, 211–219.

Davidson, W. Psychiatric significance of trance cults. Paper, 121st annual meeting of the Amer. Psychiat. Assn., New York, May 3–7, 1965.

Davis, P., Gibbs, F., Davis, H., Jetter, W., & Trowbridge, L. The effects of alcohol upon the electroencephalogram. *Quart. J. Study Alcohol*, 1941, **1**, 626–637.

De Grazia, A. The scientific reception system and Dr. Velikovsky. *Amer. Behav. Scientist*, 1963, **7**, 48–67.

Deikman, A. Experimental meditation. *J. nerv. ment. Dis.*, 1963, **136**, 329–343.

Deikman, A. De-automatization and the mystic experience. *Psychiat.*, 1966, **29**, 329–343.

Deikman, A. Implication of experimentally induced contemplative meditation. *J. nerv. ment. Dis.*, 1966, **142**, 101–116.

Dell, P. Correlation entre le système vegetatif et le système de la vie de relation, mesencephale, diencephale et cortex cérébrale. *J. Physiol.* (Paris), 1952, **44**, 471–557.

Dement, W. The effect of dream deprivation. *Science*, 1960, **131**, 1705–1707.

Dement, W. Experimental dream studies. In J. Masserman (Ed.), *Science and Psychoanalysis*, New York: Grune and Stratton, 1964, 7, 129–162.

Dement, W., Kahn, E., & Roffwarg, H. The influence of the laboratory situation on the dreams of the experimental subject. *J. nerv. ment. Dis.*, 1965, **140**, 119–131.

Dement, W. & Kleitman, N. The relation of eye movements during sleep to dream activity: an objective for the study of dreaming. *J. exp. Psychol.*, 1957, **53**, 339–346.

Dement, W., & Kleitman, N. Cyclic variations in the EEG during sleep and their relation to eye movements, body motility, and dreaming. *EEG clin. Neurophysiol.*, 1957, **9**, 637–690.

Dement, W., & Wolpert, E. The relation of eye movements, body motility, and external stimuli to dream content. *J. exp. Psychol.*, 1958, **55**, 543–553.

Deren, M. Religion and magic in Haiti. In E. Garrett (Ed.), *Beyond the five senses*. New York: J. B. Lippincott, 1952, 238–267.

de Ropp, R. *Drugs and the mind.* New York: Grove Press, 1957.

De Sanctis, S., & Neyroz, U. Experimental investigation concerning the depth of sleep. *Psychol. Rev.*, 1902, **9**, 254–282.

Desoille, R. The waking dream in psychotherapy: an essay on the regulatory function of the collective unconscious. *Le rêve éveillé en psychothèrapie* Paris, Universitaire, 1945.

Devereaux, G. Cultural factors in hypnosis and suggestion: an examination of some primitive data. *Int. J. clin. exp. Hyp.*, 1966, **14**, 273–291.

De Vito, R., & Frank, I. Ditran: searchlights on psychosis. *J. Neuropsychiat.*, 1964, **5**, 300–305.

Diamont, J., Dufek, M., Hoskovec, J., Kristof, M., Pekarek, V., Roth, B., & Velek, M. An electroencephalographic study of the waking state and hypnosis with particular references to subclinical manifestations of sleep activity. *Int. J. clin. exp. Hyp.*, 1960, **8**, 199–212.

Dickes, R. The defensive function of an altered state of consciousness. *J. Amer. psychoanal. Assn.*, 1965, **13**, 356–402.

Ditman, K., & Whittlesly, J. Comparison of the LSD-25 experience and delirium tremens. *Arch. gen. Psychiat.*, 1959, **1**, 47–57.

Dittborn, J. Experimental recollection of dreams. *J. Psychol.*, 1963, **55**, 39—41.

Dodds, E. *The Greeks and the irrational.* Berkeley, Calif.: University of California Press, 1963.

Dodds, J., & Santostefano, S. A comparison of the cognitive functioning of glue-sniffers and non-sniffers. *J. Pediat.*, 1964, **64**, 565–570.

Dubos, R. Humanistic biology. *Amer. Scientist*, 1965, **53**, 4–19.

Durand de Bousingen, R. Enseignement du training autogene en France. *Proc. Third Int. Congress Psychiat.*, Montreal, 1961.

Dynes, J. Objective method for distinguishing sleep from the hypnotic trance. *Arch. Neurol. Psychiat.*, 1947, **57**, 84–93.

Eagle, M., & Klein, G. Fragmentation phenomena in the stabilized retinal image. Unpublished manuscript.

Easson, W. Gasoline addiction in children. *Pediat.*, 1962, **29**, 250–254.

Ebin, D. (Ed.) *The drug experience*. New York: Orion Press, 1961.

Edwards, R. A case report of gasoline sniffing. *Amer. J. Psychiat.*, 1960, **117**, 555–557.

Ehrenwald, H. Versuche zür Zeitauffassung des Unbewussten. *Archiv für die gesamte psychologie*, 1923, **45**, 144–156.

Ehrenzweig, A. The undifferentiated matrix of artistic imagination. In W. Neusterberger, & S. Axelrad (Eds.), *The psychoanalytic study of society*. New York: International Universities Press, 1964, 373–398.

Eiff, A., & Jorgens, H. Die Spindelelrregbarkeit beim autogenem training. In *Proc. Third Int. Congress Psychiat.*, Montreal, 1961.

Elder, J. A study of the ability to awaken at assigned hours. *Psychol. Bull.*, 1941, **38**, 693.

Elkind, D., Koegler, R., & Go, E. Field independence and concept formation. *Percept. mot. Skills*, 1963, **17**, 383–386.

Elliot, R. Interrelationships among measures of field dependence, ability, and personality traits. *J. abnorm. soc. Psychol.*, 1961, **63**, 27–36.

Ellis, H. *The world of dreams*. London: Constable, 1911.

Ellis, H. *Psychology of sex*. New York: Emerson Books. 1937.

Engle, G., & Romano, J. Delirium: a syndrome of cerebral insufficiency. *J. chron. Dis.*, 1959, **8**, 260–277.

Engle, G., & Rosebaum, M. Delirium III. EEG changes associated with acute alcoholic intoxication. *Arch. Neurol. Psychiat.*, 1945, **53**, 44–50.

Engel, G., Webb, J., & Ferris, E. Quantitative EEG studies of anoxia in humans: comparison with acute alcoholic intoxication and hypoglycemia. *J. clin. Investigation*, 1945, **24**, 691–697.

Erikson, E. Identity and the life cycle. *Psychol. Issues*, 1959, **1**, 1–119.

Erikson, E. Youth: fidelity and diversity. *Daedalus*, 1962, **91**, 5–27.

Erickson, M. Further observations on hypnotic alteration of visual perception. *Amer. J. clin. Hyp.*, 1966, **8**, 187–188.

Erickson, M. Deep hypnosis and its induction. In LeCron (Ed.), *Experimental Hypnosis*, New York: MacMillan, 1956, 71–112.

Erickson, M. The confusion technique in hypnosis. *Amer. J. clin. Hyp.*, 1964, **6**, 183–207.

Erikson, M. Pantomine techniques in hypnosis and the implications. *Amer. J. clin. Hyp.*, 1964, **7**, 64–70.

Erikson, M., & Erikson, E. Concerning the nature and character of post-hypnotic behavior. *J. gen. Psychol.*, 1941, **24**, 95–133.

Estabrooks, G. (Ed.) *Hypnosis: current problems.* New York: Harper & Row, 1962.

Evans, C., & Osborn, E. An experiment in the electroencephalography of the mediumistic trance. *J. soc. psych. Res.*, 1951–1952, **36**, 588–596.

Fadiman, J., Harman, W., McKim, R., Mogar, R., & Stolaroff, M. *Use of psychedelic agents to facilitate creative problem solving.* San Francisco: Inst. for Psychedelic Res. of San Francisco State College, 1965.

Faucett, R., & Jensen, R. Addiction to the inhalation of gasoline fumes in a child. *J. Pediat.*, 1952, **41**, 364–368.

Federn, P. *Ego psychology and the psychoses.* New York: Basic Books, 1955.

Felix, R. An appraisal of the personality types of the addict. *Amer. J. Psychiat.*, 1944, **100**, 462–467.

Fenichel, O. *Drug addiction in the psychoanalytic theory of neurosis.* New York: W. W. Norton, 1945.

Fenichel, O. Respiratory introjection. In O. Finichel & D. Rappaport (Eds.), *Collected papers: First series.* New York: W. W. Norton, 1953, 221–240.

Ferenczi, S. The ontogenesis of the interest in money. In *Selected papers.* New York: Basic Books, 1950, **1**, 319–331.

Fernandez-Cerdeno, A. Die reactivierung von Erlebnissen aus dem ersten Lebensjahr durch Halluzionogene (Altersregression). Gottingen: Georg-August University, unpublished dissertation, 1964.

Field, M. *Search for security: an ethnopsychiatric study of rural Ghana.* Evanston, Ill.: Northeastern University Press, 1960.

Fingarette, H. *The self in transformation: psychoanalysis, philosophy and the life of the spirit.* New York: Basic Books, 1963.

Fink, P., Goldman, M., & Lyons, I. Morning glory seed psychosis. *Arch. gen. Psychiat.*, 1966, **15**, 209–213.

Fisher, C. Studies on the nature of suggestion: I. Experimental induction of dreams by direct suggestion. *J. Amer. psychoanal. Assn.*, 1953, **1**, 222–255.

Fisher, C. Dreams and perception: the role of preconscious and primary modes of perception in dream formation. *J. Amer. psychoanal. Assn.*, 1954, **2**, 389–445.

Fisher, C. Subliminal and supraliminal influences on dreams. *Amer. J. Psychiat.*, 1960, **116**, 1009–1017.

Fiske, D. Effects of monotonous and restricted stimulation. In D. Fiske & S. Maddi (Eds.), *Functions of varied experience.* Homewood, Ill.: Dorsey Press, 1961, 106–144.

Fiss, H. The effects of experimentally induced changes in alertness on response to subliminal stimulation. *J. Person.*, 1966, **34**, 577–595.

Fitzherbert, J. Scent and the sexual object. *Brit. J. med. Psychol.*, 1959, **32**, 206–209.

Fogel, S., & Hoffer, A. The use of hypnosis to interrupt and to reproduce an LSD-25 experience. *J. clin. exp. Psychopathol.*, 1962, **23**, 11–16. (a)

Fogel, S., & Hoffer, A. Perceptual changes induced by hypnotic suggestion for the posthypnotic state. I. General account of the effect on personality. *J. clin. exp. Psychopathol.*, 1962, **23**, 24–35. (b)

Fogel, S., & Hoffer, A. Effects of hypnotically induced changes in perception. *J. clin. exp. Psychopathol.*, 1963, **23**, 24.

Foley, C. The legend of Rachmaninoff. *Music Guide*, 1963.

Forer, B. The therapeutic value of crisis. *Psychol. Rep.*, 1963, **13**, 275–281.

Fort, J. Giver of delight or ligeratory of sin: drug use and addiction in Asia. *Bull. Narc., UN*, 1965, **17**, 1–11.

Foulkes, D. Dream reports from different stages of sleep. Unpublished doctoral dissertation. University of Chicago, 1960.

Foulkes, D. Dream reports from different stages of sleep. *J. abnorm. & soc. Psychol.*, 1962, **65**, 14–25.

Foulkes, D. Theories of dream formation and the recent studies of sleep consciousness. *Psychol. Bull.*, 1964, **62**, 236–247.

Foulkes, D. *The psychology of sleep*. New York: Scribners, 1966.

Foulkes, D. & Rechtschaffen, A. Presleep determinants of dream content: the effects of two films. Paper read at Midwestern Psychol. Assn., St. Louis, 1964.

Foulkes, D., Spear, P., & Symonds, J. Individual differences in mental activity at sleep onset. *J. abnorm. Psychol.*, 1966, **71**, 280–286.

Foulkes, D. & Vogel, G. Mental activity at sleep onset. *J. abnorm. Psych.*, 1965, **70**, 231–243.

Franek, B. & Thren, R. Hirnelektriche Befunde bei aktiven hypnoseubungen. *Arch. psychiat. nervenkr.*, 1958, **181**, 360.

Frank, B. L'hypnos et l'EEG. *Electroenceph. clin. Neurophysiol.*, 1950, **2**, 107.

Frederking, W. Deep relaxation and symbolism. *Psyche.*, 1948, **2**.

Freedman, H., & Rockmore, N. Marihuana: factor in personality evaluation and Army maladjustment. Part 1. *J. clin. Psychopathol.*, 1946, **7**, 765–782.

Freedman, S., Grunbaun, H., & Greenblatt, M. Perceptual and cognitive changes in sensory deprivation. In P. Solomon et al. (Eds.), *Sensory deprivation.* Cambridge: Harvard University Press, 1961, 58–71.

Freedman, S., Grunbaun H., & Greenblatt, M. *Perceptual and cognitive deprivation: a symposium.* Cambridge, Mass.: Harvard University Press, 1961.

Freeman, T. Some comments on views underlying the use of ether and carbon-dioxide in psychotherapy. *Brit. J. med. Psychol.*, 1952, **25**, 148–156.

Freemantle, A. *Protestant mystics.* New York: New American Library of World Literature, 1965.

Freud, S. Formulations regarding the two principles in mental functioning. In collected papers. London: Hogarth, 1925, **4**, 13–21.

Freud, S. *An outline of psychoanalysis.* New York: W. W. Norton, 1949.

Freud, S. *Civilization and its discontents.* London: Hogarth, 1930.

Freud, S. *The interpretation of dreams.* London: Allen & Unwin, 1954.

Freud, S. The interpretation of dreams. In A. Brill (Ed.), *The basic writings of Sigmund Freud.* New York: Modern Library, 1938.

Freud, S. Standard edition of the complete psychological works. London: Hogarth, 1961, **21**, 64–73.

Freud, S. *The interpretation of dreams.* New York: Basic Books, 1956.

Freud, S. Dreams and telepathy. In collected papers, Vol. 4. New York: Basic Books, 1959, 408–435.

Friedlander, J., & Sarbin, T. The depth of hypnosis. *J. abnorm. soc. Psychol.*, 1938, **33**, 281–294.

Frobenius, K. Über die zeitliche Orientierung im Schlaf und einige Aufwach-phanomene. *Zeitschrift für die gesamte Psychologie*, 1927, **103**, 100–110.

Fromm, E. Psychoanalysis and Zen Buddhism. *Psychologia*, 1959, **2**, 79–99.

Fromm, E. *The forgotten language.* New York: Grove Press, 1957.

Fromm, E., Suzuki, D., & de Martino, R. *Zen Buddhism and psychoanalysis.* London: Allen & Unwin, 1960.

Frosch, J., & Ross, N. (Eds.) *Annual survey of psychoanalysis.* New York: International Universities Press, 1960.

Frosch, W., Robbins, E., & Stern, M. Untoward reactions to lysergic acid diethylamide (LSD) resulting in hospitalization. *New Engl. J. med.*, 1965, **273**, 23, 1235–1239.

Fujisawa, K. The psychophysiological studies of sleep. *Jap. psychol. Res.*, 1960, **2**, 120–134.

Gaines, R. LSD: Hollywood's status symbol drug. *Cosmopolitan*, 1963.

Galvin, J., & Ludwig, A. A case of witchcraft. *J. nerv. ment. Dis.*, 1961, **133**, 161–168.

Garattini, S. Effects of a cannabis extract on gross behavior. In, G. Wolstenholme (Ed.), *Hashish: its chemistry and pharmacology.* Boston: Little, Brown, & Co., 1965, 70–82.

Gardner, R., Holzman, P., Klein, G., Linton, H., & Spence, D. Cognitive control: a study of individual consistencies in cognitive behavior. *Psychol. Issues*, 1959, **1**, 1–186.

Garoutte, B., & Aird, R. Studies on the cortical pacemakers. Synchrony and asynchrony of bilaterally recorded alpha and beta activity *EE6 clin. Neurophysiol.*, 1958, **10**, 259–268.

Garrison, O. *Tantra: the yoga of sex.* New York: Julian Press, 1964.

Gastaut, H. The brain stem and cerebral electrogenesis in relation to consciousness. In E. Adrian, et al. (Eds.), *Brain mechanisms and consciousness.* Oxford: Blackwell, 1954.

Geissmann, P., Jus, A., Luthe, W., & Noel, C. Electroencephalographic study with frequency analysis and polygraphy of autogenic training. In *Proc. Third Int. Congress Psychiat.*, Montreal, 1961.

Geissmann, P., Jus, A. & Luthe, W. Neurophysiologic and psychophysiologic aspects of the autogenic state. In *Proc. Third Int. Congress Psychiat.*, Montreal, 1961.

Getzels, J., & Jackson, P. *Creativity and intelligence.* New York: John Wiley & Sons, 1962.

Ghiselin, B. *The creative process.* New York: New American Library, 1952.

Giarman, N., & Freedman, D. Biochemical aspects of the actions of psychotomimetic drugs. *Pharmacol. Rev.*, 1965, **17**, 1–25.

Gibson, W. *The boat.* Boston: Riverside Press, 1953.

Gill, M., & Brennan, M. *Hypnosis and related states: psychoanalytic studies in regression.* New York: International Universities Press, 1959.

Gill, M., & Brennan, M. *Hypnosis and related states.* New York: International Universities Press, 1958.

Ginsberg, A. Fact sheet: Small anthology of footnotes on marijuana. In C. Hollander (Ed.), *Background papers on student drug involvement.* Washington, D.C.: U.S. National Student Assn., 1967, 9–36.

Glaser, H., & Massengale, O. Glue-sniffing in children: deliberate inhalation of vaporized plastic cements. *J. Amer. med. Assn.*, 1962, **181**, 300–303.

Glass, A. Mental arithmetic and blocking of the occipital alpha rhythm. *EEG clin. Neurophysiol.*, 1964, **16**, 595–603.

Goddard, D. *A Buddhist Bible*, (2nd Ed.) Thetford, Vt.: Dwight Goddard, 1938.

Goldberger, L. Individual differences in the effects of perceptual isolation as related to Rorschach manifestations of the primary process. Unpublished doctoral dissertation. New York: New York University, 1958.

Goldney, K. An examination into physiological changes alleged to take place during the trance state. *Proc. soc. psych. Res.*, 1938–1939, **45**, 43–68.

Goldstein, K. *The organism*. New York: American Book Co., 1939.

Goldstein, R. *One in seven*. New York: Walker & Co., 1966.

Goodenough, D., Lewis, H., Shapiro, A., Jaret, L., & Sleser, I. Dream reporting following abrupt and gradual awakening from different types of sleep. *J. Pers. soc. Psychol.*, 1965, **2**, 170–179.

Gordon, J. *Handbook of clinical and experimental hypnosis*. New York: MacMillan, 1967.

Gorton, B. Current problems of physiologic research in hypnosis. In G. Estabrooks (Ed.), *Hypnosis: current problems*. New York: Harper & Row, 1962, 30–53.

Govinda, A. *Foundations of Tibetan mysticism*. New York: E. P. Dutton, 1959.

Grabski, D. Toluene sniffing producing cerebellar degeneration. *Amer. J. Psychiat.*, 1961, **118**, 461–462.

Granda, A., & Hammack, J. Operant behavior during sleep. *Science*, 1961, **133**, 1485–1486.

Grant, W. Inhalation of gasoline fumes by a child. *Psychiat. Quart.*, 1962, **36**, 555–557.

Green, C. Ecsomatic experiences and related phenomena. *J. soc. psych. Res.*, 1967, **44**, 111–130.

Green, W. The effect of LSD on the sleep dream cycle: an exploratory study. *J. nerv. ment. Dis.*, 1965, **140**, 417–426.

Greenburg, L. et al. The effects of exposure to toluene in industry. *J. Amer. med. Assn.*, 1942, **118**, 573–578.

Greifenstein, R., De Vault, M., Yoshitake, J., & Gajewski, E. A study of l-arylo-cyclohixylamine for anesthesia. *Anesthes. & Analges.*, 1958, **37**, 283–294.

Gresham, S., Webb, W., & Williams, R. Alcohol and caffeine: effect on inferred visual dreaming. *Science*, 1963, **140**, 1226–1227.

Gruen, W. *The composition and some correlates of the American core culture*. Canandaugua, N.Y.: Veterans Administration Hospital, 1964.

Grunthal, E., & Bonkalo, A. Über Ermudung und schlaf auf Grund hirnbioelektrischer Untersuchungen. *Arch. f. psychiat.*, 1940, **3**, 652–655.

Guilford, J. Traits of creativity. In J. Anderson (Ed.), *Creativity and its cultivation*. New York: Harper, 1959, 142–161.

Hall, C. *The meaning of dreams*. New York: Dell, 1959.

Hall, C., & Van de Castle, R. *The content analysis of dreams*. New York: Appleton-Century-Crofts, 1966.

Happich, C. *Anleitung zur meditation*. (Introduction to meditation.) (3rd Ed.) Darmstadt: E. Rother, 1948.

Happich, C. *Bildbewüsstsein und Schöpferische Situation*, (Symbolic consciousness and the creative situation.) *Dtsch. med. Wschr.*, 1939, **2**.

Happich, C. Das Bildbewüsstsein als Ansatzstelle psychischer Behandlung. *Zbl. Psychother.*, 1932, **5**, 663–677.

Harman, W. Some aspects of the psychedelic drug controversy. *J. human. Psychol.*, 1964, **2**, 93–103.

Harman, W., McKim, R., Mogar, R., Fadiman, J., & Stolaroff, M. Psychedelic agents in creative problem-solving: a pilot study. *Psychol. Rep.*, 1966, monograph supplement 2-V19.

Hart, J. Autocontrol of EEG alpha. Paper, Soc. psychophysiol. Res., San Diego, 1967.

Hartman, A., & Hollister, L. Effect of mescaline, LSD, and psilocybin on color perception. *Psychopharm.*, 1963, **4**, 441–451.

Hartmann, H. *Ego psychology and the problem of adaptation*. New York: International Universities Press, 1958.

Hatfield, E. The validity of the LeCron method of evaluating hypnotic depth. *Int. J. clin. exp. Hyp.*, 1961, **9**, 215–221.

Hawkins, D., Puryear, H., Wallace, C., Deal, W., & Thomas, E. Basal skin resistance during sleep and dreaming. *Science*, 1962, **136**, 321–322.

Hebb, D. The motivating effects of exteroceptive stimulation. *Amer. Psychol.*, 1958, **13**, 109–113.

Hebb, D. The American revolution. *Amer. Psychol.*, 1960, **15**, 735–745.

Heimann, H., & Spoerri, T. Elektroencephalographische Untersuchungen an Hypnotisierten. *Monatsschr. psychiat. Neurol.*, 1953, **4**, 261.

Henderson, L. *The fitness of the environment: an inquiry into the biological significance of the properties of matter*. Boston: Beacon Press, 1958.

Hennings, J. *Von den traumen und nachtwanglern*. 1874.

Heron, W. The pathology of boredom. *Sci. Amer.*, 1957, **196**, 52–56.

Heron, W. Cognitive and physiological effects of perceptual isolation. In P. Solomon (Ed.), *Sensory deprivation: a symposium*. Cambridge, Mass.: Harvard University Press, 1961.

Herrigel, E. *Zen in the art of archery*. New York: Pantheon, 1953.

Hervery de Saint-Denys. *Les rêves et les moyens de les diriger*. Paris: anonymous publisher, 1967.

Hildebrandt, F. *Der traum und seine verwertung fürs leben*. 1874. Leipsig: Schloamp. In G. Ramsey, Studies of dreaming. *Psychol. Bull.*, 1953, **50**, 432–455.

Hilgard, E. Impulsive versus realistic thinking: an examination of the distinction between primary and secondary processes in thought. *Psychol. Bull.*, 1962, **59**, 477–488.

Hilgard, E. *Hypnotic susceptibility*. New York: Harcourt, Brace, & World, 1965.

Hilgard, E., & Tart, C. Responsiveness to suggestions following waking and imagination instructions and following induction of hypnosis. *J. abnorm. Psychol.*, 1966, **71**, 196–208.

Hiller, J., Muller-Hegemann, D., & Wendt, H. Über Auswirkungen des autogenen trainings auf erholung und physische leistung. In *Proc. Third Int. Congress Psychiat.*, Montreal, 1961.

Hiller, J., Muller-Hegemann, D., & Wendt, H. Experimentelle untersuchungen über den einfluss des autogenen trainings auf die listung. *Med. sport.* 1962, **1**, 5.

Hilton, W. *The scale of perfection*. London: Burns & Coates. 1953.

Hilton, W. *The ladder of perfection*. Baltimore: Penguin Books, 1957.

Hinkle, L. The physiological state of the interrogation subject as it affects brain function. In A. Biderman & H. Zimmer (Eds.), *The manipulation of human behavior*. New York: John Wiley & Sons, 1961, 19–50.

Hirai, T. Electroencephalographic study on the Zen meditation. (Jap.) *Psychiat. Neurol. Jap.*, 1960, **62**, 76–105.

Hobson, J. The effect of LSD on the sleep cycle of the cat. *EEG clin. Neurophysiol.*, 1964, **17**, 52–56.

Hochberg, J., Triebel, W., & Seaman, G. Color adaptation under conditions of homogeneous visual stimulation. *J. exp. Psychol.*, 1951, **41**, 153–159.

Hoffer, A. LSD: a review of its present status. *Clin. pharmacol. Ther.*, 1965, **183**, 49–57.

Hofman, A. *Planta medica*, 1961, **9**, 354–366.

Hollander, C. *Background papers on student drug involvement*. Washington, D.C.: U.S. National Student Assn., 1967.

Hollingshead, A., & Redlich, F. *Social class and mental illness*. New York: John Wiley & Sons, 1958.

Hollingworth, H. The psychology of drowsiness: an introspective and analytical study. *Amer. J. Psychol.*, 1911, **22**, 99–111.

Hollister, L. Drug-induced psychoses and schizophrenic reactions: a critical comparison. *Ann. N.Y. Acad. Sci.*, 1962, **96**, 82–90.

Holt, R. Imagery: the return of the ostracized. *Amer. Psychol.*, 1964, **19**, 254–264.

Holt, R., & Goldberger, L. Assessment of individual resistance to sensory alteration. In B. Flahery (Ed.), *Psychophysiological aspects of space flight*. New York: Columbia University Press, 1961.

Holt, R., & Goldberger, L. Personalogical correlates of reactions to perceptual isolation. *W.A.D.C. tech. Rep.*, 1959, 59–375.

Holt, R., & Havel, J. A method for assessing primary and secondary process in the Rorschach. In M. Rickers-Ovsiankina (Ed.), *Rorschach psychology*. New York: John Wiley & Sons, 1960, 263–315.

Holton, G. Science and culture. *Daedalus*, 1965, **94**, 1–265.

Horowitz, M. The imagery of visual hallucinations. *J. nerv. ment. Dis.*, 1964, **138**, 513–523.

Hull, D. *Hypnosis and suggestibility*. New York: Appleton-Century, 1933.

Hutchinson, E. *How to think creatively*. New York: Abinton-Cokesbury, 1949.

Huxley, A. *The perennial philosophy*. New York: Harpers, 1945.

Huxley, A. *The doors of perception*. New York: Harper & Bros., 1954.

Huxley, A. *Heaven and hell*. New York: Harpers, 1956.

Huxley, A. *Island*. New York: Harper & Row, 1962.

Huxley, J. Psychometabolism. *Psychedelic Rev.*, 1963, **1**, 183–204.

Indian Hemp Drug Commission. *Report of the Indian hemp drug commission*. Simla. British Government, 1894.

Irwin, L. Down the up staircase. Radio documentary produced for Los Angeles radio station KRLA, February, 1966.

Isakower, O. A contribution to the pathopsychology of phenomena associated with falling asleep. *Int. J. Psychoanal.*, 1938, **19**, 331–345.

Israel, L., Geissmann, P., & Noel, C. Modifications des rhythmes electroencephalographiques au cours de la relaxation, observées a l'analyse de frequence. *Rev. med. psychosom.*, 1960, **3**, 133.

Israel, L., & Rohmer, F. Variations electroencephalographiques au cours de la relaxation autogene et hypnotique. In P. Aboulker, L. Chertok, & M. Sapir (Eds.), *La relaxation*. Paris: Expansion Scientif. Francaise, 1958, 88–98.

Jackson, C., & Kelly, E. Influence of suggestion and subjects' prior knowledge on sensory deprivation. *Science*, 1962, **135**, 211–212.

Jacobziner, H., & Raybin, H. Accidental chemical poisonings: glue-sniffing. *N.Y. State J. Med.*, 1962, **62**, 3294–3296.

James, W. *Collected essays and reviews.* New York: Longmans, Green, 1920, 500–513.

James, W. *Outline of psychology.* New York: Dover Pub., 1950.

James, W. *The varieties of religious experience.* New York: The New American Library of World Literature, 1958.

Jasper, H. In W. Penfield & T. Erikson (Eds.), *Epilepsy and Cerebral Localization.* Springfield: Thomas, 1941.

Jasper, H., & Shagass, C. Consciousness time judgments related to conditioned time intervals and voluntary control of the alpha rhythm. *J. exp. Psychol.*, 1941, **28**, 503–508.

Jaspers, K. *General psychopathology.* Chicago: University of Chicago Press, 1964.

Jaspers, K. *Der philosophische glaube angesichts der Offenbarung.* Munich: R. Piper & Co., 1962.

Jaspers, K., & Zahrnt, H. *Philosophie und Offenbarungsglaube: ein Zwiegsprach.* Hamburg: Furche-Verlag, 1963.

Jessen, P. *Versuch einer wissenschaflichen Begrundung der Psychologie.* Berlin, 1855. In S. Freud, *The interpretation of dreams.* Trans. by J. Strachey. London: Allen & Unwin, 1954, 23–24.

Jones, E. *On the nightmare.* New York: Grove Press, 1959.

Jones, E. The Madonna's conception through the ear: a contribution to the relation between anesthetics and religion. In *Essays in applied psychoanalysis.* London: Hogarth Press, 1951, **2**, 266–357.

Jouvet, M. Recherches sur les structures nerveuses et les mechanismes responsables des differantes phases du sommeil physiologique. *Arch. Ital. Biol.*, 1962, **100**, 125–206.

Jung, R. Neurophysiologische untersuchungmethode. In G. Bergmann (Ed.), *Handbuch d. inn. med. neurologie.* Berlin: Springer-Verlag, 1953.

Jus, A., & Jus, K. Etude polygraphique du training autogene. *Rev. med. Psychosom.*, 1960, **3**, 136.

Kahn, R. On crises. *Psychiat. Quart.*, 1963, **109**.

Kamiya, J. Behavioral, subjective, and physiological aspects of drowsiness and sleep. In D. Friske & S. Maddi (Eds.), *Functions of varied experience.* Illinois: Dorsey Press, 1961, 145–174.

Kasamatsu, A., & Hirai, T. Science of zazen. *Psychologia*, 1963, **6**, 86–91.

Kasamatsu, A., & Shimazone, Y. Clinical concept and neurophysiological basis of the disturbance of consciousness. (Jap.) *Psychiat. Neuro. Jap.*, 1957, **11**, 969–999.

Kast, E. Pain and LSD-25: a theory of attenuation of anticipation. In D. Solomon (Ed.), *LSD: The consciousness-expanding drug.* New York: Putnams, 1964.

Katz, S., & Landis, C. Psychologic and physiologic phenomena during a prolonged vigil. *Arch. Neurol. Psychiat.*, 1935, **34**, 307–316.

Key, B., & Bradley, P. The effects of drugs on conditioning and habituation to arousal stimuli. *Psychopharmac.*, 1960, **1**, 450–462.

King, C. *The states of human consciousness.* New Hyde Park, N.Y.: University Books, 1963.

Kirkpatrick, C. *Religion in human affairs.* New York: John Urley & Sons, 1929.

Kleber, H. Prolonged adverse reactions from unsupervised use of hallucinogenic drugs. *J. nerv. ment. Dis.*, 1967, **144**, 308–319.

Klee, B. LSD-25 and ego functions. *Arch. gen. Psychiat.*, 1963, **8**, 461–474.

Klein, D. The experimental production of dreams during hypnosis. *Univ. of Texas Bull.*, 1930, 3009.

Klein, G., Gardner, R., & Schlesinger, H. Tolerance for unrealistic experience: a study of generality of a cognitive control. *Brit. J. Psych.*, 1962, **53**, 41–55.

Kleitman, N. *Sleep and wakefulness.* Chicago and London: University of Chicago Press, 1939.

Kleitman, N. Patterns of dreaming. *Scientific American*, 1960, **203**, 81–88.

Kleitman, N. *Sleep and wakefulness.* (2nd Ed.) Chicago: University of Chicago Press, 1963.

Kline, M. *The nature of hypnosis: contemporary theoretical approaches.* New York: Institute for Research in Hypnosis, 1962.

Kluver, H. *Mescal.* London: Routledge, 1928.

Kluver, H. Mechanisms of hallucinations. In Terman, Kluver, & Merrill, (Eds.) *Studies in personality.* New York: McGraw-Hill, 1942, 10.

Knowles, D. *The English mystical tradition.* London: Burnes & Oates, 1961. 57.

Koestler, A. *The act of creation.* New York: MacMillan, 1964.

Kolb, L. Drug addiction among women. *Proc. Amer. Prison Assn.*, 1938, 340–357.

Kolb, L. Drug addiction and crime. In *Drug addiction: a medical problem.* Springfield, Ill.: Thomas, 1962, 16–37.

Kolb, L. Types and characteristics of drug addicts. In *Drug addiction: a medical problem.* Springfield, Ill.: Thomas, 1962, 38–49.

Kondo, A. Zen in psychotherapy: the virtue of sitting. *Chicago Review*, 1958, **12**, 57–64.

Korn, R. Psychopathology as experience and action. Unpublished manuscript. City University of New York, 1964.

Kornetsky, C., & Humphries, O. Relationship between effects of a number of centrally acting drugs and personality. *Arch. Neurol. Psychiat.*, 1957, **77**, 325–327.

Kramer, M., Whitman, R., Baldridge, B., & Ornstein, P. The pharmacology of dreaming: a review. In G. Martin & B. Kisch (Eds.), *Enzymes in mental health.* New York: Lippincott, 1966, 102–116.

Krippner, S. The hypnotic trance, the psychedelic experience, and the creative act. *Amer. J. clin. Hyp.*, 1964, **7**, 140–147.

Krippner, S. Creative production and "mind-manifesting" experience: a study of the "psychedelic artist." A paper presented at the annual convention of the Amer. Psychol. Assn., Washington, D.C., 1967.

Kris, E. On inspiration. *Int. J. Psychoanal.*, 1939, **20**, 377–389.

Kris, E. *Psychoanalytic explorations in art.* New York: International Universities Press, 1952.

Krishnamurti, J. *Discussions with Krishnamurti in Europe.* Ojai, Calif.: Krishnamurti Writings, Inc., 1966.

Krus, D., Wapner, S., Freeman, H., & Casey, T. Differential behavioral responsivity to LSD-25. *Arch. gen. Psychiat.*, 1963, **8**, 557–563.

Kubie, L. The use of induced hypnogogic reveries in the recovery of repressed amnesic data. *Bull. Menninger Clin.*, 1943, **7**, 172–182.

Kubie, L. The value of induced dissociated states in the therapeutic process. *Proc. Roy. Soc. Med.*, 1945, **38**, 681–683.

Kubie, L. *Neurotic distortion of the creative process.* New York: Noonday Press, 1961.

Kubie, L., & Margolin, S. A physiological method for the induction of states of partial sleep and securing free associations and early memories in such states. *Trans. of the Amer. Neurolog. Assn.*, 1942, 136–139.

Kubie, L., & Margolin, S. The process of hypnotism and the nature of hypnotic state. *Amer. J. Psychiat.*, 1944, **100**, 611–622.

Kurland, A., Unger, S., & Shaffer, J. Psychedelic psychotherapy (LSD) in the treatment of alcoholism (an approach to a controlled study). In H. Brill et al. (Eds.), *Neuro-Psycho-Pharmacology. Proceedings of the Fifth International Congress of the Collegium Internationale Neuropsychopharmalogicum.* Amsterdam: Excerpta Medica Found., 1967, 435–440.

LaBarre, W. *They shall take up serpents.* Minneapolis: University Press, 1962.

LaBarre, W. *The peyote cult.* Hamden, Conn.: Shoe String Press, 1964.

Ladd, G. Contribution to the psychology of visual dreams. *Mind*, 1892, **1**, 299–304.

Laing, R. Transcendental experience in relation to religion and psychosis. *Psychedelic Rev.*, 1965, **6**, 7–15.

Lancaster, H. The derivation and partition of x^2 in certain discrete distributions. *Biometrika*, 1949, **36**, 117–129.

Lang, P., & Laxovik, A. Personality and hypnotic susceptibility. *J. Consult. Psychol.*, 1962, **26**, 317–322.

Laski, M. *Ecstasy: a study of some secular and religious experiences.* London: Cresset Press, 1961.

Laurie, P. *Drugs: medical, psychological, and social facts.* Baltimore: Penguin Books, 1967.

Lawes, T. Schizophrenia, "sernyl" and sensory deprivation. *Brit. J. Psychiat.*, 1963, **109**, 243–250.

Lawrence, J. Acute poisoning due to petrol vapor. *Brit. J. Med.*, 1945, **1**, 871–873.

Lawshe, C., & Harris, D. *Purdue creativity test.* W. Lafayette, Ind.: Purdue Research Foundation, 1960.

Lawton, J., & Malmquist, C. Gasoline addiction in children. *Psychiat. Quart.*, 1961, **35**, 55–61.

Leaning, F. An introductory study of hypnagogic imagery. *Proc. soc. psych. Res.*, 1925, **35**, 289–412.

Leary, T. The religious experience: its production and interpretation. *Psychedelic Rev.*, 1964, **1**, 324–346.

Leary, T. & W. Clark. Religious implications of consciousness-expanding drugs. *Religious Education*, 1963, 251–256.

Leary, T., Metzner, R., Presnell, M., Weil, G., Schwitzgebel, R., & Kinne, S. A change program for adult offenders using psilocybin. *Psychotherapy*, 1965.

LeCron, L. A study of the hypnotizability of hypnotists. *Pers.*, 1951, **1**, 300–306.

LeCron, L. A method of measuring the depth of hypnosis. *J. clin. exp. Hyp.*, 1953, **1**, 4–7.

Leiderman, H. Sensory deprivation: clinical aspects. *Arch. Intern. Med.*, 1958, **101**, 389–396.

Leiderman, P. Imagery and sensory deprivation. *Proc. Third World Congress in Psychiat.*, 1964, 227–231.

Leishaman, J., & Spender, S. *Duino elegies-Rainer Maria Rilke.* New York: W. W. Norton, 1963.

Lesse, S. Experimental studies on the relationship between anxiety, dreams, and dream-like states. *Amer. J. Psychother.*, 1959, **13**, 440–455.

Leuner, H. *Die experimentalle psychose.* Berlin: Springer Verlag, 1962.

Levine, J., Ludwig, A., & Lyle, W. The controlled psychedelic state. *Amer. J. clin. Hyp.*, 1963, **6**, 163–164.

Levine, J., & Ludwig, A. The LSD controversy. *Comp. Psychiat.*, 1964, **5**, 314–321.

Levine, J., & Ludwig, A. Alterations in consciousness produced by combinations of LSD, hypnosis, and psychotherapy. *Psychopharm.*, 1965, **7**, 123–217.

Levine, J., & Ludwig, A. The hypnodelic treatment technique. *Int. J. clin. exp. Hyp.*, 1966, **14**, 207–215.

Levine, J., & Ludwig, A. Hypnodelic therapy. In H. Abramson (Ed.), *The use of LSD in psychotherapy and alcoholism.* Indianapolis: Bobbs-Merrill, 1967, 533–541.

Lewin, B. *The psychoanalysis of elation.* New York: W. W. Norton, 1950.

Lewis, H., Goodenough, D., Shapiro, A., & Slesser, I. Individual differences in dream recall. *J. abnorm. Psychol.*, 1966, **71**, 52–59.

Lhermitte, J. *Le sommeil.* Paris: Librarie Armand Colin, 1931.

Li, C., Jasper, H., & Henderson, L. The effect of arousal mechanisms on various forms of abnormality in the electroencephalogram. *EEG clin. Neurophysiol.*, 1952, **4**, 513–526.

Liberson, W., & Liberson, C. EEG records, reaction times, eye movements, respiration, and mental content during drowsiness. In *Recent advances in biological psychiatry.* New York: Plenum Press, 1966, **3**, 295–302.

Lichtensten, E. The relation of three cognitive controls to some selected perceptual and personality variables. Unpublished doctoral dissertation. University of Michigan, 1961.

Lidz, T. August Strindberg: a study of the relationship between his creativity and schizophrenia. *Int. J. Psychoanal.*, 1964, **45**, 399–406.

Lilly, J. Discussion. In *Illustrative strategies on psychopathology in mental health.* G. A. P. Symposium No. 2, 1956, 13–22.

Lindsey, D. Common factors in sensory deprivation, sensory distortion and sensory overload. In P. Solomon et al. (Eds.), *Sensory deprivation*. Cambridge, Mass.: Harvard University Press, 1961, 174–194.

Lindsley, D. Psychological phenomena and the electroencephalogram. *EEG clin. Neurophysiol.*, 1952, **4**, 443–456.

Ling, T., & Buckman, J. The treatment of frigidity with LSD and ritalin. *Psychedel. Rev.*, 1964, **1**, 450–458.

Linton, H., & Langs, R. Subjective reaction to lysergic acid diethylamide (LSD-25). *Arch. gen. Psychiat.*, 1962, **6**, 352–368.

Linton, H., & Langs, R. Placebo reactions in a study of lysergic acid diethylamide (LSD-25). *Arch. gen. Psychiat.*, 1962, **6**, 369–383.

Lisansky, E. Alcoholism in women: social and psychological concomitants. *Quart. J. Stud. Alcohol.*, 1957, **15**, 588–623.

London, P. Hypnosis in children: an experimental approach. *Int. J. clin. exp. Hyp.*, 1962, **10**, 79–91.

London, P. *The modes and morals of psychotherapy*. New York: Holt, Rinehart, & Winston, 1964.

London, P., & Rosenhahn, D. Personality dynamics. *Ann. Rev. Psychol.*, 1964, **15**, 447–492.

Loomis, A., Harvey, E., & Hobart, G. Brain potentials during hypnosis. *Science*, 1936, **83**, 239–241.

Lourie, R. Alcoholism in children. *Amer. J. Orthopsychiat.*, 1943, **13**, 322–338.

Lowald, H. Hypnoid states—repression, abreaction, and recollection. *Amer. J. psychoanal. Assn.*, 1955, **3**, 201–210.

Lowenfield, V. *Creative and mental growth: a textbook on art education*. New York: MacMillan, 1947.

Lowry, J. Hospital treatment of the narcotic addict. *Fed. Probation*, 1956.

Luby, E., Frohman, C., Grisell, J., Lenzo, J., & Gottlieb, J. Sleep deprivation: effects on behavior, thinking, motor performance, and biological energy transfer systems. *Psychosom. Med.*, 1960, **22**, 182–192.

Luby, E., Grissell, J., Frohman, C., Lees, H., Cohen, B., & Gottlieb, J. Biochemical, psychological, and behavioral responses to sleep deprivation. *Ann. N. Y. Acad. Science.*, 1962, **96**, 71–78.

Ludwig, A. Witchcraft today. *Dis. nerv. Syst.*, 1965, **26**, 288–291.

Ludwig, A. An historical survey of the early roots of mesmerism. *Int. J. clin. exp. Hyp.*, 1964, **12**, 205–217.

Ludwig, A. The trance. Paper, 121st. Ann. Meeting of the Amer. Psychiat. Assn., N. Y., May 3–8, 1965.

Ludwig, A. The formal characteristics of therapeutic insight. *Amer. J. Psychother.*, 1966, **20**, 305–318.

Ludwig, A. The trance. *Comp. Psychiat.*, 1967, **8**, 7–15.

Ludwig, A., & Levine, J. A controlled comparison of five brief treatment techniques employing LSD, hypnosis, and psychotherapy. *Amer. Psychother.*, 1965, **19**, 417–435.

Ludwig, A., & Levine, J. Alterations in consciousness produced by hypnosis. *J. Nerv. ment. Dis.*, 1965, **140**, 146–153.

Ludwig, A., & Levine, J. The hypnodelic treatment technique. Paper, 2nd conference on the use of LSD in psychotherapy, Amityville, L.I., New York, May 8–19, 1965.

Ludwig, A., & Levine, J. Clinical effects of psychedelic agents. Clin. Med., 1966, **73**, 21–24.

Luk, C. *Ch'an and zen teaching.* London: Rider, 1960.

Luthe, W. International coordination of autogenic training. In *Proc. Third Int. Congress of Psychiat.*, Montreal, 1961.

Luthe, W. Physiological and psychodynamic effects of autogenic training. In B. Stokvis (Ed.), *Topical problems of psychotherapy.* Basel, New York: S. Karger, 1960, **3**, 174.

Luthe, W. Signification clinique de diverse formes d'abreactions autogenes. *Rev. Med. Psychosom.*, 1962, **4**, 3.

Luthe, W. The clinical significance of various forms of autogenic abreaction. In *Proc. Third Int. Cong. of Psychiat.*, Montreal, 1961.

Luthe, W. Zür psychotherapeutischen Velaufskontrolle durch projektive tests bei Autogenem training. In E. Speer (Ed.), *Aktuelle psychotherapie.* Münich: J. F. Lehmanns, 1958, 159–168.

Luthe, W. Entrenaminto autgeno. Modificaciones psicofisologicas e indicaciones clinicas. *Rev. Lat. Amer. hipn. Clin.*, 1962, **2**, 61.

Luthe, W., Jus, A., & Geissmann, P. Autogenic state and autogenic shift: psychophysiologic and neurophysiologic aspects. *Acta Psychother.*, 1962.

Luthe, W. Autogenic training: method, research, and application in psychiatry. *Dis. nerv. Syst.*, 1962, **23**, 383.

Luthe, W. Experimentelle Untersuchungen über den Einfluss des Autogenen trainings auf die Atmung, I. Mittellungs: Frequenz und Amplitudenanderunger bei normalgesunden Personen. *Zaschr. Psychother. med. Psychol.*, 1958, **3**, 89.

Lyons, J. Existential psychotherapy: fact, hope, fiction. *J. abnorm. soc. Psychol.*, 1961, **62**, 242–249.

McCord, H., & Sherrill, C. A note on increased ability to do calculus posthypnotically. *Amer. J. clin. Hyp.*, 1961, **4**, 20.

McDonald, N. Living with schizophrenia. *Canad. med. Assn. J.*, 1960, **82**, 218–221.

McGhie, A., & Chapman, J. Disorders of attention and perception in early schizophrenia. *Brit. J. med. Psychol.*, 1961, **34**, 103–110.

McGhie, A., Chapman, J., & Lawson, J. The effect of distraction on schizophrenic performance. *Brit. J. Psychiat.*, 1965, **3**, 383–390, 391–398.

McGlothlin, W., Cohen, S., & McGlothlin, M. *Long-lasting effects of LSD on normals.* Los Angeles: Institute of Government and Public Affairs, 1967.

McGlothlin, W., Cohen, S., & McGlothlin, M. Short-term effects of LSD on anxiety, attitudes and performance. *J. nerv. ment. Dis.*, 1964, **139**, 266–273.

McKellar, P. The mental images which precede sleep. *J. Amer. soc. psych. Res.*, 1959, **53**, 23–27.

McReynolds, P. Anxiety, perception, and schizophrenia. In D. Jackson (Ed.), *The etiology of schizophrenia.* New York: Basic Books, 1960, 269.

Macalpine, I., & Hunter, R. *Daniel Paul Schreber—memoirs of my nervous illness.* London: William Dawson & Sons, 1955.

Mach, E. *Die Analyse der Empfindungen und das Verhaltness des psychischen zum Psysichen*. Jena: Gustav Fisher, 1903.

Machle, W. Gasoline intoxication. *J. Amer. med. Assn.*, 1941, **117**, 1965–1971.

MacKinnon, D. Creativity and transliminal experience. Unpublished paper given at the Amer. Psychol. Assn. Convention in Los Angeles, 1964.

MacLean, J., MacDonald, D., Byre, U., & Hubbard, A. The use of LSD-25 in the treatment of alcoholism and other psychiatric problems. *Quart. J. Studies Alcohol.*, 1961, **22**, 34–45.

Mackler, B., & Shontz, R. Life style and creativity: an empirical investigation. *Percept. mot. Skills.* 1965, **20**, 873–896.

Mackworth, N. Originality. *Amer. Psychol.*, 1965, **20**, 51–66.

MacNaughton, W. An education in pot. *Princetonian*, 1967.

Maddi, S. Humanistic psychology: Allport and Murray. In J. Wepman & R. Heine (Eds.), *Concepts of personality*. Chicago: Aldine Press, 1963.

Magoun, H. *The waking brain*. Springfield, Ill.: Thomas, 1958.

Malamud, W., & Linder, F. Dreams and their relationship to recent impressions. *Arch. Neurol. Psychiat.*, 1931, **25**, 1081–1099.

Malcolm, N. *Dreaming*. London: Routledge & Kegan Paul, 1959.

Malitz, S., Esecover, H., Wilkens, B., & Hock, P. Some observations on psylocybin, a new hallucinogen, in volunteer subjects. *Comp. Psychiat.*, 1960, **1**, 8–17.

Marchand, H. Die suggestion der warme im oberbauch und ihr einfluss auf blutzucker und leukozytem. *Psychother.*, 1956, **3**, 154.

Marchand, H. Das verhalten von blutzucker und leukozyten wahrend des autogenen trainings. In *Proc. Third Int. Congress of Psychiat.*, Montreal, 1961.

Marechal, J. *Studies in the psychology of the mystics*. Albany, N.Y.: Magi, 1964.

Margolin, S., & Kubie, L. An apparatus for the use of breath sounds as a hypnogogic stimulus. *Amer. J. Psychiat.*, 1944, **100**, 610.

Margolin, S., & Kubie, L. The therapeutic role of drugs in the process of repression, dissociation, and synthesis. *Psychosom. Med.*, 1945, **7** 147–151.

Marks, R. *The story of hypnotism*. New Jersey: Prentice-Hall, 1947.

Mescher, E. Psycholytic therapy: statistics and indications. In H. Brill et al (Eds.), *Neuro-Psycho-Pharmacology. Proc. Fifth International Congress of the Collegium internationale Neuro-Pharmacologicum.* Amsterdam: Excerpta Found., 1967, 441–444.

Maslow, A. Cognition of being in the peak experience. *J. genet. Psychol.*, in press.

Maslow, A. *Toward a psychology of being*. Princeton: Van Nostrand, 1962.

Maslow, A. *Religions, values, and peak experiences*. Columbus: Ohio State University Press, 1964.

Massengale, O., et al. Physical and psychologic factors in glue-sniffing. *New Eng. J. med.*, 1963, **269**, 1340–1344.

Masters, R., & Houston, J. *The varieties of psychedelic experience*. New York: Holt, Rinehart & Winston, 1966.

Maupin, E. Zen Buddhism: a psychological review. *J. consult. Psych.*, 1962, **26**, 362–378.

Maury, A. *Sommeil et les reves: etudes psychologiques sur ces phenomenes et les divers etats qui s'y rattachent*. Paris: Didier & Cie, 1878.

Mauz, F. The psychotic man in psychotherapy. *Archv. für psychiatrie*, 1948.

Max, L. An experimental study of the motor theory of consciousness. III: Action-current responses in deaf-mutes during sleep, sensory stimulations, and dreams. *J. comp. Psychol.*, 1935, **19**, 469–487.

May, R. Contributions of existential psychotherapy. In R. May, E. Angel, & H. Ellenberger (Eds.), *Existence: a new dimension in psychiatry and psychology*. New York: Basic Books, 1958.

May, R., Angel, E., & Ellenberger, H. *Existence*. New York: Basic Books, 1958.

Mayor's Committee on Marihuana, New York City. *The marihuana problem in the city of New York: sociological, medical, psychological, and pharmacological studies*. Lancaster, Pa.: Jacques Cattell, 1944.

Mead, G. *Mind, self and society*. Chicago: Chicago University Press, 1934.

Mednick, S. The associative basis of the creative process. *Psychol. Rev.*, 1962, **69**, 220–232.

Meduna, L. *Carbon dioxide therapy*. Springfield, Ill.: Thomas, 1950.

Meltzer, M. Solitary confinement. In *Factors used to increase the susceptibility of individuals to forceful indoctrination*. Group for the Advancement of Psychiatry Symposium No. 3, 1956.

Mendelson, J., et al. Hallucinations of poliomyelitis patients during treatment in a respirator. *J. nerv. ment. Dis.*, 1958, **126**, 421–428.

Menuier, R. A propos d'onirotherapia. *Arch. d. neurol.*, 1910. In H. Ellis, *The world of dreams*. London: Constable, 1910.

Merry, J., & Zachariadis, N. Addiction to glue-sniffing. *Brit. med. J.*, 1962, **2**, 1448.

Meyer, A. *Social and psychological factors in drug addiction: a review of research findings together with an annotated bibliography*. Bureau of Applied Social Research, Columbia University, 1952.

Michaux, H. *Light through darkness*. New York: Orion Press, 1963.

Miller, D. *Survey of object visualization*. Monterey, Calif.: California Test Bureau, 1955.

Miller, G., Galanter, E., & Pribram, K. *Plans and the structure of behavior*. New York: Holt, Rinehart & Winston, 1960.

Miller, S. Ego-autonomy in sensory deprivation, isolation, and stress. *Int. J. Psychoanal.*, 1962, **43**, 1–20.

Mirsky, A., & Carson, P. A comparison of the behavioral and physiological changes accompanying sleep deprivation and chloropromazine administration in man. *EEG clin. Neurophysiol.*, 1962, **14**, 1–10.

Mischel, W., & Mischel, F. Psychological aspects of spirit possession. *Amer. Anthropol.* 1958, **60**, 249–260.

Mischelet, J. *Satanism and witchcraft*. New York: Citadel Press, 1939.

Modlin, H., & Montes, A. Narcotics addiction in physicians. *Amer. J. Psychiat.*, 1964, **121**, 358–365.

Mogar, R. Value orientations of college students. *Psychol. Rep.*, 1964, **15**, 739–770.

Mogar, R. Psychedelic drugs and human potentialities. In H. Otto (Ed.), *Explorations in human potentialities*. Springfield, Ill.: Thomas, 1965.

Mogar, R. Current status and future trends in psychedelic research. *J. Human. Psychol.*, 1965, **4**, 147–166.

Mogar, R., & Savage, C. Personality changes associated with psychedelic therapy. *Psychother.*, 1964, **1**, 154–163.

Moller, H. Affective mysticism in western civilization. *Psychoanal. Rev.*, 1965, **52**, 115–130.

Monroe, L., Rechtscaffen, A., Foulkes, D., & Jensen, J. Discriminability of REM and NREM reports. *J. Pers. soc. Psychol.*, 1965, **2**, 456–460.

Monroe, W. A study of taste dreams. *Amer. J. Psychol.*, 1899, **10**, 326–327.

Mora, G. One hundred years from Lombroso's first essay—genius and insanity. *Amer. J. Psychiat.*, 1964, **121**, 562–571.

Morizzi, G., & Magoun, H. Brain stem reticular formation and activation of the EEG. *EEG clin. Neurophysiol.*, 1949, **1**, 455–473.

Moseley, A. Hypnogogic hallucinations in relation to accidents, abstr., *Amer. Psychol.*, 1953.

Moss, C. *The hypnotic investigation of dreams.* New York: John Wiley & Sons, 1967.

Moss, C., & Riggen, G. Personality and behavioral correlates of experienced psychotherapists relative to the use (or disuse) of hypnosis. Paper. Amer. Psychol. Assn., 1963.

Moss, C., Riggen, G., Cayne, L., & Bishop, W. Some correlates of the use (or disuse) of hypnosis by experienced psychologist-therapists. *Int. J. clin. exp. Hyp.*, 1965, **13**, 39–50.

Muller-Hegemann, D. Über die cortico-viscerale und die psychosomatische Betrachtungsweise in der psychotherapie. *Psychiatr. Neurol. med. Psychol.*, 1956, **2/3**, 33.

Muller-Hegemann, D., & Kohler, C. Eight years experience with autogenic training. In *Proc. Third Int. Congress of Psychiat.*, Montreal, 1961.

Muller-Hegemann, D., & Kohler-Hoppe, C. Über neue Erfahrungen mit dem autogenen training. *Psych. Neurol. med.*, 1962.

Mundy-Castle, A. An appraisal of electroencephalography in relation to psychology. Monogr. suppl. No. 2 of *J. nat. Inst. f. personnel Res.*, 1948, 1–43.

Mundy-Castle, A., & McKiever, B. The psychophysiological significance of the galvanic skin response. *J. exp. Psychol.*, 1953, **45**, 15–24.

Murphy, G. *Human potentialities.* New York: Basic Books, 1958.

Murphy, G. Creativity and its relation to extrasensory perception. *J. Amer. soc. Psych. Res.*, 1963, **57**, 203–214.

Murphy, H. The cannabis habit: a review of recent psychiatric literature. *Bull. Narcotics, UN*, 1963, **15**, 15–23.

Murphy, J. Psychotherapeutic aspects of shamanism on St. Lawrence Island, Alaska. In A. Kiev (Ed.), *Magic, faith, and healing.* New York: Free Press of Glencoe, 1964, 53–83.

Murray, E. *Sleep, dreams, and arousal.* New York: Appleton-Century-Crofts, 1965.

Muzio, J., Roffwarg, H., & Kaufman, E. Alterations in the nocturnal sleep cycle resulting from LSD. *EEG clin. Neurophysiol.*, 1966, **21**, 313–324.

Myers, F. *Human personality and its survival of bodily death.* New York: Longmans, Green, 1920, **1**.

Nachmansohn, M. Über experimentall erzeugte traueme nebst kritischen bemerkungen über die psychoanalytische methodik. In D. Rappaport (Ed.),

Organization and pathology of thought. New York: Columbia University Press, 1951, 257–287.

Narayana, R. *The dream problem and its many solutions in the search after ultimate truth*. Delhi, India: Pract. Med., 1922.

Nelson, J. A study of dreams. *Amer. J. Psychol.*, 1888, **1**, 367–401.

Newman, R., Katz, J., & Rubenstein, R. The experimental situation as a determinant of hypnotic dreams. *Psychiat.*, 1960, **23**, 63–73.

Nitsche, C., & Robinson, J. A case of gasoline addiction. *Amer. J. Orthopsychiat.*, 1959, **29**, 417–419.

Noyes, H. Meditation: the door to wholeness. *Main currents in modern thought*, 1965, **22**, 35–41.

O'Connel, D. An experimental comparison of hypnotic depth measured by self-ratings and by objective scale. *Int. J. clin. exp. Hyp.*, 1964, **12**, 34–46.

O'Donnell, J. A follow-up of narcotic addicts: mortality, relapse and abstinence. *Amer. J. Orthopsychiat.*, 1964, **34**, 948–954.

O'Donnell, J. A post-hospital study of Kentucky addicts—a preliminary report. *J. Kentucky State med. Assn.*, 1963, **604**, 553–557.

Ogata, S. *Zen for the west*. New York: Dial Press, 1959.

Okeima, T., Kogu, E., Ikeda, K., & Sugiyama, H. The EEG of Yoga and Zen pratitioners. *EEG clin. Neurophysiol.*, 1957, **9**, 51.

Omwake, K., & Lorenz, M. Study of the ability to wake at a specified time. *J. appl. Psychol.*, 1933, **17**, 468–474.

Opiel *The art and practice of astral projection*. San Francisco: Peach Publishing Co., 1961.

Orne, M. The nature of hypnosis: artifact and essence. *J. abnorm. soc. Psychol.*, 1959, **58**, 277–299.

Orne, M. On the social psychology of the psychological experiment: with particular reference to demand characteristics and their implications. *Amer psychol.*, 1962, **17**, 776–783.

Orne, M. The mechanism of hypnotic age regression: an experimental study. *J. abnorm. soc. Psych.*, 1951, **46**, 213–225.

Orne, M. Die Leistungsfahigkeit in hypnosis und im Wachzustand. *Psych. Rdsch.*, 1954, **5**, 291–297.

Orne, M. Implications for psychotherapy derived from current research on the nature of hypnosis. *Amer. J. Psychiat.*, 1962, **118**, 1097–1103.

Orne, M. *The nature of hypnosis: artifact and essence*. Doctoral dissertation. Social Relations Dept., Harvard, 1957.

Orne, M., & Scheibe, K. The contributions of nondeprivation factors in the production of sensory deprivation effects: the psychology of the "panic button." *J. abnorm. soc. Psychol.*, 1964, **68**, 3–12.

Osgood, C. *Method and theory in experimental psychology*. New York: Oxford University Press, 1956.

Osmond, H. *Ololiuqui: The ancient Aztec narcotic. Remarks on the effects of Rivea Corybosa (ololiuqui)*. Osmond, H. A review of the clinical effects of psychotominetic agents. *Ann. N. Y. Acad. Sci.*, 1957, **66** (3), 418–434.

Oster, G. *The science of moire patterns.* Barrington, N. J.: Edmund Scientific Co., 1964.

Ostfeld, A. Effects of LSD-25 and JB-318 on tests in visual and perceptual function in man. *Fed. Proc.,* 1961, **20**, 866–883.

Oswald, I. Experimental studies of rhythm, anxiety and cerebral vigilance. *J. ment. Sci.,* 1959, **105**, 269–294.

Oswald, I. *Sleeping and waking: physiology and psychology.* New York: Elsevier, 1962.

Oswald, I. Physiology of sleep accompanying dreaming. In *Scientific basis of medicine. Annual review,* 1964, 102–124.

Oswald, I., Berger, R., Jaramillo, R., Keddie, K., Olley, P., & Plunkett, B. Melancholia and barbiturates: a controlled EEG, body and eye movement study of sleep. *Brit. J. Psychiat.,* 1963, **109**, 66–78.

Otto, R. *The idea of the holy.* Tr. by J. Harvey New York: Galaxy Books, 1958, 12–40.

Pahnke, W. Drugs and mysticism: an analysis of the relationship between psychedelic drugs and the mystical consciousness. Unpublised thesis. Cambridge, Mass.: Harvard University, 1963.

Pahnke, W. Drugs and mysticism. *Int. J. Parapsychol.,* 1966, **8**, 295–320.

Pahnke, W. The contribution of the psychology of religion to the therapeutic use of the psychedelic substances. In H. Abramson (Ed.), *The Use of LSD in psychotherapy and alcoholism.* Indianapolis. Bobbs-Merrill, 1967, 628–652.

Panama Canal Zone Governor's Committee. Report of the Panama Canal Zone governor's committee: investigation of April-December, 1925. *Military Surgeon,* 1933.

Penfield, W., & Roberts, L. *Speech and brain mechanisms.* Princeton, N. J.: Princeton University Press, 1959.

Perls, F., Hefferline, R., & Goodman, P. *Gestalt therapy: excitement and growth in the human personality.* New York: Julian Press, 1951.

Pescor, M. A statistical analysis of the clinical records of hospitalized drug addicts. Publ. Hlth. Rep. Washington, D.C.: U.S. Govt. Printing Office, 1943, 143.

Peters, G. Emotional and intellectual concomitants of advanced chronic alcoholism. *J. consult. Psychol.,* 1956, **20**, 390.

Phalen, J. The marihuana bugaboo. *Military Surgeon,* 1943, **93**, 94–95.

Piaget, J. Principal factors determining intellectual evolution from childhood to adult life. In D. Rapport (Ed.) *Organization and pathology of thought.* New York: Columbia University Press, 1951.

Piaget, J. *The construction of reality in the child.* New York: Basic Books, 1954.

Pette, L., & Forrest, I. Electron paramagnetic resonance studies of free radicals in the oxidation of drugs derived from phenothiazine in vitro. *Biochem. biophys, acts.,* 1962, **57**, 419–420.

Pious, W. A hypothesis about the nature of schizophrenic behavior. In A. Burton (Ed.), *Psychotherapy of the psychoses.* New York: Basic Books, 1961.

Plutchik, R. *The emotions: facts, theories and a new model.* New York: Random House, 1962.

Poetzl, O. Experimentell erregte Traumbilder in ihren Beziehungen um indirekten

Sehen. *A. Neurophysiol. psychiat.*, 19!7, **37**, 278–349. In G. Ramsey, Studies of dreaming. *Psychol. Bull.*, 1953, **50**, 432–455.

Poincare, H. Mathematical creation. In B. Ghiselin (Ed.), *The creative process.* New York: New American Library, 1955.

Polzien, P. Therapeutic possibilities of autogenic training in hyperthyroid conditions. In *Proc. Third Int. Congress Psychiat.*, Montreal, 1961.

Polzien, P. Electrocardiographic changes during the first standard exercise. In *Proc. Third Int. Congress of Psychiat.*, Montreal, 1961.

Polzien, P. Respiratory changes during passive concentration on heaviness. In *Proc. Third Int. Congress Psychiat.*, Montreal, 1961.

Polzien, P. Die Anerdung der Temperaturregulation bei Gesamtumschaltung durch das autogene training. *Ztschr. exp. med.*, 1955, **125**, 469.

Polzien, P. *Uber die Physiologie des hypnotischen Zustands als die exakte Grundlage fur den Neurosenlehre.* Basel, N.Y.: Karger, 1959.

Poulain, A. *The graces of interior prayer: a treatise on mystical theology.* St. Louis: Herder, 1950.

Press, E. Glue sniffing. *J. Pediat.*, 1963, **63**, 516–518.

Prince, R., & Savage, C. Mystical states and the concept of regresion. Paper. 1st Annual Meeting of the R. M. Bucke Soc., Montreal, 1965. Also in *Psychedelic Rev.*, 1966, **8**, 59–81.

Pritchard, R. Visual illusions viewed as stabilized retinal images. *Quart. J. exp. Psychol.*, 1958, **10**, 77–81.

Pruitt, M. Bizarre intoxications. *J. Amer. med. Assn.*, 1959, **171**, 2355.

Puhl, L. Trans., *The Spiritual exercises of St. Ignatus.* Westminister, Md.: Newman Press, 1963.

Quintanilla, J. Gasoline sniffing. *Texas State med. J.*, 1961, **57**, 570–571.

Rado, S. The psychoanalysis of pharmacothymia (drug addiction). In *Psychoanalysis of Behavior.* New York: Grune & Stratton, 1956, **1**.

Raginsky, B. Creativity in hypnosis. *Psychosomatics*, 1963, **4**, 170–172.

Ramsey, G. Studies in dreaming. *Psychol. Bull.*, 1953, **50**, 432–455.

Rapaport, D. Consciousness: a psychopathological and psychodynamic view. In H. Abramson (Ed.), *Problems of consciousness.* New York: Josiah Macy Jr. Foundation, 1950, 18–57.

Rapaport, D. The autonomy of the ego. *Bull. Menn. Clin.*, 1951, **15**, 113–123.

Rapaport, D., Gill, M., & Schafer, R. *Diagnostic psychological testing.* Chicago: Year Book Publishers, 1945.

Rapaport, D. The theory of ego autonomy: a generalization. *Bull. Menn. Clin.*, 1958, **22**, 13.

Rapaport, D. Cognitive structures. In J. Bruner (Ed.), *Contemporary approaches to cognition.* Cambridge, Mass.: Harvard University Press. 1957, 157–200.

Rapaport, D., & Gill, M. The points of view and assumptions of metapsychology. *Int. J. Psychoanal.*, 1959, **40**, 153.

Ravenscroft, K. Voodoo possession: a natural experiment in hypnosis. *Int. J. clin. exp. Hyp.*, 1965, **13**, 157–182.

Rechtschaffen, A., & Dement, W. Studies on the relation of narcolepsy, cataplexy, and sleep with low voltage random EEG activity. In S. Kety (Ed.), *Sleep and altered states of consciousness.* To be published.

Rechtschaffen, A., & Monroe, L. The effect of amphetamine on the sleep cycle. *EEG clin. Neurophysiol.*, 1964, **16**, 438–445.

Reschtschaffen, A., & Verdone, P. Amount of dreaming: effect of incentive, adaptation to laboratory, and individual differences. *Percept. mot. Skills*, 1964, **19**, 947–958.

Rechtschaffen, A., Vogel, G., & Shaikin, G. Interrelatedness of mental activity during sleep. *Arch. gen. Psychiat.*, 1963, **9**, 536.

Rechtschaffen, A., Wolpert, E., Dement, W., Mitchell, S., & Fisher, C. Nocturnal sleep of narcoleptics. *EEG clin. Neurophysiol.*, 1963, 15, 599–609.

Rechtschaffen, A., Verdone, P., & Wheaton, J. Reports of mental activity during sleep. *Canad. Psychiat.Assn. J.*, 1963, **8**, 409–414.

Renneker, R. Dream thinking. *Psychoanal. Quart.*, 1952, **21**, 81–91.

Renneker, R. Presleep mechanisms of dream control. *Psychoanal.Quart.*, 1952, **21**,528–536.

Renshaw, S., Miller, V., & Marquis, D. *Children's sleep.* New York: MacMillan, 1933.

Reps, P. *Zen flesh, Zen bones.* New York: Anchor, 1961.

Ritter, C. *A woman in the polar night.* New York: E. P. Dutton, 1954.

Robin, E., Luby,E., & Gottlieb, J. The electroencephalogram during prolonged experimental sleep deprivation. *EEG clin. Neurophysiol.*, 1962, **14**, 544–551.

Roe, A. A psychological study of eminent psychologists and anthropologists and a comparison with biological and physical scientists. *Psychol. Monogr.*, 1953, **67**, 352.

Roffwarg, H., Dement, W., Muzio, J., & Fisher, C. Dream imagery: relationship to rapid eye movements of sleep. *Arch. gen. Psychiat.*, 1962, **7**, 235–258.

Rogers, C. Toward a theory of creativity. In H. Anderson (Ed.), *Creativity and its cultivation.* New York: Harper, 1959, 69–82.

Romano, J., & Engel, G. Delirium: I. Electroencephalographic data. *Arch. gen. neurophysiol. Psychiat.*, 1944. **51**, 356–377.

Rosenbaum, G., Cohen, B., Luby, E., Gottlieb, J., & Yelen, D. Simulation of schizophrenic performance with sernyl, LSD-25, and sodium amytal:attention, motor functions, and proprioception. *Arch. gen. Psychiat.*,1959, **1**, 651–688.

Rosenbaum, J. The significance of the sense of smell in the transference. *J. Amer. psychoanal. Assn.*, 1961, **9**, 312–324.

Rosenberg, S., & Feldberg, T. Rorschach characteristics of a group of malingerers. *Rorsch. Res. Exch.*, 1944, **8**, 141–158.

Rosenfeld, A. A remarkable mind drug suddenly spells danger. *Life*, March 25, 1965.

Rosenfeld, A., & Farrel, B. The spread and perils of LSD. *Life*, 1966, **60**, 28–33.

Rosenthal, R. On the social psychology of the psychological experiment: the experimenter's hypothesis as unintended determinant of experimental results. *Amer. Sci.*, 1963, **51**, 268–283.

Rotter, J. The role of the psychological situation in determining the direction of human behavior. In M. Jones (Ed.), *Nebraska Symposium on Motivation*. Lincoln, Neb.: University of Nebraska Press, 1955, 245–269.

Rousselle, E. Spiritual guidance in contemporary Taoism. In *Spiritual disciplines: papers from the Eranos yearbooks*. New York: Pantheon, 1960.

Rowland, V. Differential electroencephalographic responses to conditioned auditory stimuli in arousal from sleep. *EEG clin. Neurophysiol.*, 1957, **9**, 585–594.

Ruff, G., Levy, E., & Thaler, V. Factors influencing reactions to reduced sensory input. In P. Solomon (Ed.), *Sensory deprivation: a symposium*. Cambridge: Harvard University Press, 1961.

Rugg, H. *Imagination*. New York: Harper & Row, 1963.

Rund, J. Prayer and hypnosis. *J. hypn. psychol. Dent.*, 1957,**1**, 24.

Rush, B. *Medical inquiries and observations upon the diseases of the mind*. New York: Hafner Publishing, 1962.

St. John of the Cross. *The complete works of Saint John of the Cross*. Westminster: Newman Press, 1953, **1**.

Salvatore, S., & Hyde, R. Progression of effects of LSD. *Arch. Neurol. Psychiat.*, 1956, **76**, 50–59.

Sandison, R., Spencer, A., & Whitlaw, J. The therapeutic value of lysergic acid diethylamide in mental illness. *J. ment. Sci.*, 1954, **100**, 491–507.

Sandler, J., & Nagers, H. Aspects of the metapsychology of fantasy. *Psychoanal. Stud. Child.*, 1963, **18**, 159–194.

Sandoz. *Annotated bibliography: psilocybin*. No date, with supplement. Hanover, N.J. Sandoz Pharmaceutical.

Sandoz. *Catalog of the literature of delysid, d-lysergic acid diethylamide or LSD-25*. No date with two supplements. Hanover, N.J. Sandoz Pharmaceutical.

Sarbin, S., & Lim, D. Some evidence in support of the role-taking hypothesis in hypnosis. *Int. J. clin. exp. Hyp.*, 1963, **9**, 98–103.

Sarbin, T. Contributions to role-taking theory: I. Hypnotic behavior. *Psychol. Rev.*, 1950, **57**, 255–270.

Sargant, W. *Battle for the mind*. Garden City, N.Y. Doubleday, 1957.

Sato, E. Psychotherapeutic implication of Zen. *Psychologia*, 1958, **1**, 213–218.

Satran, R., & Dodson, V. Toluene habituation: report of a case. *New Eng. J. med.*, 1963, **268**, 719–721.

Saul, L. Dream scintillations. *Psychosom. Med.*, 1965, **28**, 286–289.

Savage, C. Variations in ego feelings induced by LSD-25. *Psychoanal.Rev.*, 1955, **42**, 1–16.

Savage, C. An outline of psychedelic therapy. Conference of the Collegium Internationale Neuro-psychopharmacologicum in Washington, 1966.

Savage, C., Fadiman, J., Mogar, R., & Allen, M. Process and outcome variables in psychedelic (LSD) therapy. Unpublished manuscript. 1965.

Savage, C., Fadiman, J., Mogar, R., & Allen, M. The effects of psychedelic therapy on values, personality, and behavior. *Int. J. Neuropsychiat.*, 1966, **2**, 241–254.

Savage, C., Hughes, M., & Mogar, R. The effectiveness of psychedelic (LSD) therapy. *Int. J. Soc. Psychiat.*, in press.

Savage, C., & Stolaroff, M. Clarifying the confusion regarding LSD-25. *J. nerv. ment. Dis.*, 1965, **140**, 218–221.

Schachtel, E. On memory and childhood amnesia, *Psychiat.*, 1947, **10**, 1–26.

Schachtel, E. *Metamorphosis: on the development of affect, perception, attention and memory*. New York: Basic Books, 1959.

Schatzman, M. *Reves et hallucinations*. Paris: Vigot Freres, 1925.

Schiff, S., Bunney, W., & Freedman, D. A study of ocular movements in hypnotically induced dreams. *J. nerv. ment. Dis.*, 1961, **133**, 59–68.

Schilder, P., & Kauders, O. *A textbook of hypnosis*. New York: International Universities Press, 1956.

Schilder, P., & Kauders, O. *A textbook of hypnosis*. New York: International Universities Press, 1956.

Schlesinger, H. Cognitive attitudes in relation to susceptibility to interference. *J. Pers.*, 1954, **22**, 354–374.

Schneck, J. Chloroform habituation with a case report of its occurrence in schizophrenia. *Bull. Menn. Clin.*, 1945, **9**, 12–17.

Schofield, W. *Psychotherapy: the purchase of friendship*. New Jersey: Prentice-Hall, 1964.

Schorer, M. *William Blake—the politics of vision*. New York: Heritage Books, 1959.

Schultes, R. *A contribution to our knowledge of Rivea Corymbosa*. Botanical Museum of Harvard University, 1941.

Schultes, R. The pharmaceutical sciences. Third lecture series, 1960.

Schultes, R. Botanical sources of the new world narcotics. *Psychedel. Rev.*, 1963, **1**, 145–167.

Schultes, R. Ein halbes jahrhundert ethnobotanik amerikanisher halluzinogens. *Planta medica*, 1965, **13**, 125–127.

Schultz, D. Sensory restriction: effects on behavior. New York: Academic Press, 1965, 95–97.

Schultz, J. Uber narkolyse und autogene organubunger, zwei neue psychotherapeuthische methoden. *Med. Klin.*, 1926, **22**, 952.

Schultz, J. Uber selbsttatige umstellungen der warmestrahlung der menschlichen Haut im autosuggestionen training. *Dtsch. med. wschr.*, 1926, **13**, 571.

Schultz, J. *Das Autogene training*. Stuttgart: Thieme Verlag, 1932.

Schultz, J. *Le training autogene*. Paris: Presses' Univ. de France, 1958.

Schultz, J. *Oringshefte for autogene training*. Oslo: Olaf Forlag, 1956.

Schultz, J. *Elentrenamiento autogeno*. Barcelona, Lisboa, Madrid: Ed. Cientifico medica., 1954.

Schultz, J. Oskar Vogt in der Geschichte der medizinischen psycholgie deutschlands. *Nervenarzt*, 1951, **2**, 41.

Schultz, J. Diskusionsbemerkungen zu den Arbeiten R. Kramer und V. Siebenthal. *Ztsch. Psychother. Med. psychol.*, 1956, **2**/3,85.

Schultz, J., & Luthe, W. Autogenic training. *In Proc. Third Int. Congress of Psychiat.*, Montreal, 1961.

Schultz, J., & Luthe, W. *Autogenic training: a psychophysiologic approach in psychotherapy*. New York: Grune & Stratton, 1959.

Schwartz, R., & Rouse, R. The activation and recovery of association. *Psychol. Issues*,1961, **3**, 1–140.

Shapiro, D. A perceptual understanding of color response. In M. Rickersman (Ed.), *Rorschach psychology*. New York: John Wiley & Sons, 1960, 154–201.

Sharpless, S., & Jasper, H. Habituation of the arousal reaction. *Brain*, 1956, **79**, 655–680.

Sherwood, J., Stolaroff, M., Harman, W. The psychedelic experience: a new concept in psychotherapy. *J. Neuropsychiat.*, 1962, **4**, 69–80.

Shor, R. Hypnosis and the concept of the generalized reality-orientation. *Amer. J. Psychother.*, 1959, **13**, 582–602.

Shor, R. The frequency of naturally occurring hypnotic-like experiences in the normal college population. *Int. J. clin. exp. Hyp.*, 1960, **8**, 151–163.

Shor, R., & Orne, E. *The Harvard Group Scale of hypnotic susceptibility. Form A: An adaptation for group administration with self-report scoring of the Stanford Hypnotic Susceptibility Scale, Form A*. Palo Alto, Calif.: Consulting Psychologists' Press, 1962.

Shor, R., & Orne, M. *The nature of hypnosis: selected basic readings*. New York: Holt, Rinehart & Winston, 1965.

Shor, R., Orne, M., & O'Connell, D. Validation and cross-validation of a scale of self-reported personal experiences which predicts hypnotizability. *J. psychol.*, 1962, **53**, 55–75.

Shor, R., Orne, M., & O'Connell, D. Psychological correlates of plateau hypnotizability in a special volunteer sample. *J. pers. soc. Psychol.*, 1966, **3**, 80–95.

Siebenthal, W. Eine vereinfachte Schwereubung des Schultz' schen autogenen trainings. *Ztschr. Psychother. med. Psychol.*, 1952, **2**, 135.

Siegel, S. *Nonparametric statistics for the behavioral sciences*. New York: McGraw-Hill, 1956.

Silberer, H. Report on a method of eliciting and observing certain symbolic and hallucination phenomena. In D. Rapaport (Ed.), *Organization and pathology of thought*. New York: Columbia University Press, 1951, 195–207.

Simmel, E. Alcoholism and addiction. *Psychoanal. Quart.*, 1948, **17**, 6–31.

Simmons, J. (Ed.) *Marijuana: myths and realities*. North Hollywood, Calif.: Brandon House, 1967.

Simons, C. Some immediate effects of drowsiness and sleep on normal human performance. *Human Factors*, 1961, 1–17.

Simons, C., & Emmons, W. Responses to material presented during various levels of sleep. *J. exp. Psychol.*, 1956, **51**, 89–97.

Sjoberg, B., & Hollister, L. The effects of psychotomimetic drugs on primary suggestibility. *Psychopharm.*, 1965, **8**, 251–262.

Skinner, B. Behaviorism at fifty. *Science*, 1963, **140**, 951–958.

Slater, K. Alpha rhythms and mental imagery. *EEG clin. Neurophysiol.*, 1960, **12**, 851–859.

Slocum, J. *Sailing alone around the world*. London: Rupert, Hart-Davis, 1948.

Smith, H. Do drugs have religious import. In D. Solomon (Ed.), *LSD: the consciousness-expanding drug*. New York: G. P. Putnams Sons, 1964, 165.

Snyder, E. *Hypnotic poetry*. Philadelphia: University of Pennsylvania Press, 1930.

Snyder, F. The new biology of dreaming. *Arch. gen. Psychiat.*, 1963, **8**, 381–391.

Sokol, J., & Robinson, J. Glue sniffing. *Western Med.*, 1963, **4**, 192–193, 196, & 214.

Solley, C., & Murphy, G. *Development of the perceptual world.* New York: Basic Books, 1960.

Solomon, D, (Ed.) *LSD: the consciousness-expanding drug.* New York: G. P. Putnam's Sons, 1964.

Solomon, D. *The marihuana papers*, New York: Bobbs-Merrill, 1966.

Solomon, P., Kubzansky, P., Leiderman, P., Mendelson, J., Trumbull, R., & Wexler, D. *Sensory deprivation.* Cambridge, Mass.: Harvard University Press, 1961.

Sommer, R., & Osmond, H. Autobiographies of former mental patients. *J. ment. Sci.*, 1960, **106**, 648–662.

Sommer, R., & Osmond, H. Autobiographies of former mental patients—addendum. *J. ment. Sci.*, 1961, **107**, 1030–1032.

Spencer, A. Permissive group therapy with lysergic acid diethylamide. *Brit. J. Psychiat.*, 1963, **109** (no. 458), 37.

Spiegelberg, F., Fadiman, J., & Tart, C. The concept of the subtle body. Lectures. Esalen Institute, Big Sur, Calif. June, 1964.

Spitta, H. *Die Schlaf und Traumzustande der menschlichen Seele.* Tubingen: Fuss, 1882.

Stace, W. *Mysticism and philosophy.* Philadelphia & New York: J. B. Lippincott, 1960.

Stark, S. Rorschach movement and Bleuler's three kinds of thinking: a contribution to the psychology of creativity. *Percept. mot. Skills*, 1964, **19**, 959–967.

Stepanow, G. Sogni indorristudio sperimentale sull'influeinze degli stimoli acustici sul sogno. Florence: Aldino, 1915. In G. Ramsey, Studies of dreaming. *Psychol. Bull.*, 1953, **50**, 432–455.

Sterling, J. A comparative examination of two modes of intoxication—an exploratory study of glue sniffing. *J. crim. law criminology, police Sci.*, 1964, **55**, 94–99.

Stovkis, B., Renes, B., & Landmann, H. Skin temperature under experimental stress and during autogenic training. *In Proc. Third Int. Congress of Psychiat.*, Montreal, 1961.

Stoyva, J. The effect of suggested dreams on the length of rapid eye movement periods. Unpublished dissertation University of Chicago, 1961.

Straecke, J. Neue Traumexperimente im Zusammenhang mit selteren und neuren Traumtheorien. In G. Ramsey, Studies of dreaming. *Psychol. Bull.*, 1953, **50**, 432–455.

Strupp, H. The outcome problem in psychotherapy revisited. *Psychother.: Theor. Res. and Pract.*, 1963, **1**, 1–13.

Suckling, E., Koeing, E., Hoffman, B., & Brooks, C. The physiological effects of sleeping on hard or soft beds. *Human Biol.*, 1957, **29**, 274–288.

Suedfeld, P. Toward greater specificity in evaluating cognitive and attitudinal changes in sensory deprivation. Unpublished paper given at the APA convention, 1964.

Sugi, Y., & Akutsu, K. *Science of Zazen—energy metabolism.* Tokyo, 1964.

Sully, J. *Illusions: a psychological study*. London: Kegan, Paul, Trench, & Trubner, 1905.

Suraci, A. Environmental stimulus reduction as a technique to effect the reactivation of crucial repressed memories. *J. nerv. ment. Dis.*, 1964, **138**, 172–180.

Sutcliffe, J. Credulous and skeptical views of hypnotic phenomena: experiments on esthesia, hallucination, and delusion. *J. abnorm. soc. Psychol.*, 1961, **62**, 189–200.

Suzuki, D. *The training of the Zen Buddhist monk*. New York: University Books, 1959.

Suzuki, D. *Zen and Japanese culture*. London: Routledge & Kegan, 1959.

Suzuki, D. *An introduction to Zen Buddhism*. C. Humphrey (ed.) Arrow-Books.

Taber, W., Vining, L., & Heacock, R. *Phytochemistry*, 1963, **2**, 65–70.

Tart, C. Frequency of dream recall and some personality measures. *J. consult. Psychol.*, 1962, **26**, 467–470.

Tart, C. Effects of posthypnotic suggestion on the process of dreaming. Unpublished doctoral dissertation University of North Carolina, 1963.

Tart, C. A comparison of suggested dreams occurring in hypnosis and sleep. *Int. J. clin. exp. Hyp.*, 1964, **7**, 163–170.

Tart, C. Hypnotic depth and basal skin resistance. *Int. J. clin. exp. Hyp.*, 1963, **11**, 81–92.

Tart, C. Hypnotic suggestion as a technique for the control of dreaming. Paper. Amer. Psychol. Assn., Los Angeles, 1964.

Tart, C. The hypnotic dream: methodological considerations and a review of the literature. *Psychol. Bull.*, 1965, **63**, 87–99.

Tart, C. Spontaneous thought and imagery in the hypnotic state: psychophysiological correlates. Paper. Amer. Psychol. Assn., New York, 1966 (a).

Tart, C. Types of hypnotic dreams and their relation to hypnotic depth. *J. abnorm. Psychol.*, 1966, **71**, 377–382.(b).

Tart, C. Some effects of posthypnotic suggestion on the process of dreaming. *Int. J. clin. exp. Hyp.*, 1966, **14**, 30–46.(c).

Tart, C. Toward the experimental control of dreaming: a review of the literature. *Psychol. Bull.*, 1965, **64**, 81–92.

Tart, C. Hypnosis, psychedelics, and psi: conceptual models. Paper. 2nd Inter. Conf. on Hypnosis, Drugs, & psi Induction, St. Paul de Vence, France, 1967.(a).

Tart, C. A second psychophysiological study of out-of-the-body experience in a gifted subject. *Int. J. Parapsychol.*, 1967, **9**, 251–258.(b).

Tart, C. The control of nocturnal dreaming by means of post-hypnotic suggestion. *Int. J. Parapsychol.*, 1967, **9**, 184–189.(c).

Tart, C. On influencing dream content. Paper. Conf. on Dream Psychol. and the New Biol. of Dreaming, Cincinnati, 1967.(d).

Tart, C. A psychophysiological study of out-of-the-body experiences in a selected subject. *J. Amer. soc. psych. Res.*, 1968, **62**, 3–27.

Tart, C., & Hilgard, E. Responsiveness to suggestions under "hypnosis" and "waking-imagination" conditions: a methodological observation. *Int. J. clin. exp. Hyp.*, 1966, **14**, 247–256.

Taylor, J. A comparison of delusional and hallucinatory individuals using field dependency as a measure. Unpublished doctoral dissertation. Purdue University, 1956.

Teilhard de Chardin, P. *The divine milieu.* New York: Harper, 1960.

Tenenbaum, B. Group therapy with LSD-25. *Dis. nerv. Syst.*, 1961, **22**, 459–462.

Terrill, J. The nature of the LSD experience. *J. nerv. ment. Dis.*, 1962, **125**, 425–439.

Thomas, E. The fire walk. *Proc. soc. psych. Res.*, 1934, **42**, 292–309.

Thomson, M., Forbes, T., & Bolles, M. Brain potential rhythms in a case showing self-induced apparent trance states. *Amer. J. Psychiat.*, 1937, **93**, 1313–1314.

Tillich, P. *The courage to be.* New Haven and London: Yale University Press, 1952.

Tillich, P. *Systematic theology.* Chicago: University of Chicago Press, 1963, **3**.

Tinnin, L. Cognitive activity without awareness. *Amer. J. clin. Hyp.*, 1963, **6**, 37–39.

Titchner, E. Taste dreams. *Amer. J. Psychol.*, 1895, **6**, 505–509.

Tolan, E., & Lingel, F. "Model psychosis" produced by inhalation of gasoline fumes. *Amer. J. Psychiat.*, 1964, **120**, 757–761.

Torrance, E. *Guiding creative talent.* Englewood Cliffs, N. J.: Prentice-Hall, 1962.

Trent, W. The demented world of KY Izumi. *Weekend Magazine*, Feb., 1966.

Trouton, D., & Eyesenck, H. The effects of drugs on behavior. In H. Eyesenck (Ed.), *Handbook of abnormal psychology.* New York: Basic Books, 1961, 634–696.

Tyler, D. Sleep deprivation. In *Factors used to increase the susceptibility of individuals to forceful indoctrination.* GAP Symposium No. 3, 1956, 103–109.

Uhr, L. Learning under hypnosis: What do we know? What should we know? *J. clin. exp. Hyp.*, 1958, **6**, 121–135.

Ullman, M. Dreaming, life-style, and physiology: a comment on Adler's view of the dream. *J. indiv. psychol.*, 1962, **18**, 18–25.

Underhill, E. *Mysticism: a study in the nature and development of man's spiritual consciousness.* New York: Meridian, 1955.

Unger, S. Mescaline, LSD, psylocybin, & personality change: a review. *Psychiat.*, 1963, **26**, 111–125.

Unger, S. LSD and psychotherapy: a bibliography of the English language literature. *Psychedel. Rev.*, 1964, **1**, 442–449.

Unger, S. Mescaline, LSD, psylocybin, and personality change. In D. Solomon, (Ed.), *LSD: the consciousness-expanding drug.* New York: G.P. Putnam's Sons, 1964.

United Nations. Evaluation of dependence-producing drugs: report of a W.H.O. scientific group. *W.H.O. tech. Rep.*, 1964, **287**, 1–25.

United Nations. Thirteenth report of the World Health Organization expert committee on dependence-producing drugs. *W.H.O. tech. Rep.*, 1964, **223**.

United Nations. Fourteenth report of the World Health Organization expert committee on dependence-producing drugs. *W.H.O. tech. Rep.*, 1965, 312.

United States. Proceedings of the White House conference on narcotic and drug abuse. Washington, D.C.: Govt. Printing Office, 1963.

van Eeden, F. A study of dreams. *Proc. soc. psych. Res.*, 1913, **26**, 431–461. 17, 75–115.

van Eeden, F. A study of dreams. *Proc. soc. psych. Res.*, 1913, **26**, 431-461.

van Eeden, F. *The bride of dreams.* New York: Mitchell Kennerly, 1918.

Vaschide, N. Les recherches experimentelles sur les reves. *Rev. psychiat.*, 1902, **5**, 145–164.

Verdone, P. Variables related to the temporal reference of manifest dream content. Unpublished doctoral dissertation. University of Chicago, 1963.

Verhulst, H., & Cotty, J. Glue-sniffing: II. *National clearing house for Poison Control Centers Bull.*, July–Aug., 1964.

Vinacke, W. *The psychology of thinking.* New York: McGraw-Hill, 1952.

Vogel, G. Studies in psychophysiology of dreams: II. The dream of narcolepsy. *Arch. gen. Psychiat.*, 1960, **3**, 421.

Vold, J. *Uber den Traum.* (Ed. by Ol Klem) Leipzig: Barth, 1912.

Von Oettinger, W., Neal, P., & Donohove, D. The toxicity and potential dangers of toluene: Preliminary report. *J. Amer. med. Assn.*, 1942, **118**, 579–584.

Von Senden, M. *Space and sight.* Glencoe, Ill.: Free Press, 1960.

Wallace, A. Cultural determinants of response to hallucinatory experience. *Arch. gen. Psychiat.*, 1959, **1**, 58–68.

Wallis, G. *The art of thought.* New York: Harcourt, 1926.

Walsh, W. *The psychology of dreams.* New York: Dodd, Mead, 1920.

Walter, R., & Yeager, C. Visual imagery and electrographic changes. *EEG clin. Neurophysiol.*, 1956, **8**, 193–199.

Walter, W. The twenty-fourth Maudsley lecture: the functions of electrical rhythms in the brain. *J. ment. Sci.*, 1950, **86**, 1–31.

Wapner, S., & Krus, D. Effects of LSD and differences between normals and schizophrenics on the Stroop color-word test. *J. neuropsychiat.*, 1960, **2**, 76–87.

Warrack, G. *Julian of Norwich, revelations of divine love.* London: Methuen, 1952.

Wasson, R. *Botanical museum leaflets.* Harvard University, 1961, **19**, 7.

Wasson, R. A new Mexican psychotropic drug from the mint family, *Botanical museum leaflets.* Cambridge, Mass.: Harvard University Press, 1962, **20**, 77–84.

Watt, J. Drug dependence of the hashish type. In G. Wolstenholm (Ed.), *Hashish: its chemistry and pharmacology.* Boston: Little, Brown, 1965, 54–66.

Watts, A. *The joyous cosmology: adventures in the chemistry of consciousness.* New York: Pantheon Books, 1962.

Wayne, G., & Clinco, A. Psychoanalytic observations on olfaction: with special reference to olfactory dreams. *Psychoanal. rev.,* 1959, **46** No. 4, 64–79.

Weisman, A. Reality sense and reality testing. *Behav. Sci.*, 1958, **3**, 228–261.

Weitzenhoffer, A. The nature of hypnosis: II. *Amer. J. clin. Hyp.*, 1963, **6**, 40–72.

Weitzenhoffer, A. *Hypnotism.* New York: John Wiley & Sons, 1953.

Weitzenhoffer, A., & Hilgard, E. *Stanford Hypnotic Suggestibility Scale, Forms A and B.* Palo Alto, Calif.: Consulting Psychologists' Press, 1959.

Weitzenhoffer, A., & Hilgard, E. *Stanford Hypnotic Susceptibility Scale, Form C.* Palo Alto, Calif.: Consulting Psychologists' Press, 1962.

Weitzenhoffer, A., & Hilgard, E. *Stanford Profile Scales of Hypnotic Susceptibility, Forms I and II.* Palo Alto, Calif.: Consulting Psychologists' Press, 1963.

Wells, F., & Ruesch, J. *Mental examiners' handbook.* New York: Psychol. Corp., 1945.

Wenger, M., & Bagchi, B. Studies of autonomic function in practitioners of Yoga in India. *Behav. Sci.*, 1961, **6**, 312–323.

Wenger, M., Bagchi, B., & Anand, B. Experiments in India on "voluntary" control of the heart and pulse. *Circulation*, 1961, **24**, 1319–1325.

Werner, H. *Comparative psychology of mental development.* New York: International Universities Press, 1957.

Wertheimer, M. *Productive thinking.* New York: Harper, 1945.

West, L., Janszen, H., Lester, B., & Comelisoon, F. The psychosis of sleep deprivation. *Ann. New York Acad. Sci.*, 1962, **96**, 66–70.

Wheelis, A. *The quest for identity.* New York: W. W. Norton, 1958.

White, R. A preface to a theory of hypnotism. *J. abnorm. soc. Psychol.*, 1941, **36**, 477–506.

White, R. Two types of hypnotic trance and their personality correlates. *J. Psychol.*, 1937, **3**, 279–289.

Whitman, R., Pierce, C., & Maas, J. Drugs and dreams. In L. Uhr & J. Miller (Eds.), *Drugs and behavior.* New York: John Wiley & Sons, 1960, 591–595.

Whitman, R., Pierce, C., Maas, J., & Baldridge, B. Drugs and dreams. II: Imipramine and prochlorperazine. *Comprehen. psychiat.*, 1961, **2**, 219–226.

Whitman, R., Pierce, C., Maas, J. & Baldridge, B. The dreams of the experimental subject. *J. nerv. ment. Dis.*, 1962, **134**, 431–439.

Wienpahl, P. *The matter of Zen: a brief account of zazen.* New York: New York University Press, 1964.

Wikler, A. Psychodynamic study of a patient during experimental self-regulated re-addiction to morphine. *Psychiat. Quart.*, 1952, **26**, 270–293.

Williams, G. Hypnosis in perspective. In L. LeCron (Ed.), *Experimental hypnosis.* New York: MacMillan, 1958, 4–21.

Williams, H., Granda, A., Jones, R., Lubin, A., & Armington, J. EEG frequency and finger pulse volume as predictors of reaction time during sleep loss. *EEG clin. Neurophysiol.*, 1962, 64–70.

Williams, H., Hammack, J., Daly, R., Dement, W., & Lubin, A. Responses to auditory stimulation, sleep loss, and the EEG stages of sleep. *EEG clin. Neurophysiol.*, 1964, **16**, 269–279.

Williams, H., Lubin, A., & Goodnow, J. Impaired performance with acute sleep loss. *Psychol. Monographs*, 1959, 73.

Williams, H., Morris, G., & Lubin, A. Illusions, hallucinations, and sleep loss. In L. West (Ed.), *Hallucinations.* New York: Grune & Stratton. 1962, 158–165.

Williams, H., Tepas, D., & Morlock, H. Evoked responses to clicks and electro-encephalographic stages of sleep in man. *Science*, 1962, **138**, 685–686.

Wilson, R. Toluene poisoning. *J. Amer. med. Assn.*, 1943, **123**, 1106–1108.

Winer, B. *Statistical principles in experimental design.* New York: McGraw-Hill, 1962.

Witkin, H. Experimental manipulation of the cognitive and emotional content of dreams. Paper. Conf. on Dream Psychol. and the New Biol. of Dreaming, Cincinnati, 1967.

Witkin, H., Dyk, R., Faterson, H., & Karp, S. *Psychological differentiation: studies of development.* New York: John Wiley & Sons, 1962.

Witkin, H., Lewis, H., Hertzman, M., Machover, K., Meissinger, P., & Waper, S. *Personality through perception.* New York: Harper, 1954.

Witkin, H., & Lewis, H. The relation of experimentally induced pre-sleep experiences to dreams: a report on method and preliminary finding. *J. Amer. Psychoanal. Assn.*, 1963, **13**, 819–849.

Witkin, H., & Lewis, H. Presleep experiences and dreams. In H. Witkin & H. Lewis (Eds.), *Experimental studies of dreaming.* New York: Random House, 1967, 148–202.

Wittstock, W. Untersuchungen uber cortikale Einflusse auf korperienene Aktionsstrome. *Psychiat, neurol. med Psychol.*, 1956, **2**/3, 85.

Wollman, L. Influence of hypnosis on the learning process. *J. Amer. Soc. psychosom. dentistry & med.*, 1965, **12**, 75–79.

Wolpert, E. Studies in psychophysiology of dreams: II. An electromyographic study of dreaming. *Arch. gen. Psychiat.*, 1960, **2**, 231–241.

Wolstenholme, G. (Ed.) *Hashish: its chemistry and pharmacology.* Boston: Little, Brown, 1965.

Wood, P. Dreaming and social isolation. Unpublished doctoral dissertation. University of North Carolina, 1962.

Woodruffe, S. *The serpent power.* Madras, India: Ganesh, 1931.

Woods, J. *The Yoga-system of Patanjali.* Harvard oriental series. Cambridge, Mass.: Harvard University Press, 1914, 42.

Woolley, V. Some auto-suggested visions as illustrating dream-formation. *Proc. soc. psych. Res.*, 1914, **27**, 390–399.

Wordsworth, W. Intimations of immortality from recollections of early childhood. In *Complete poetical works of William Wordsworth.* New York: Houghton Mifflin, Riverside Press, Cambridge edition, 1904, 353.

Wynne, L. Thought disorder and family relations of schizophrenics. *Arch. gen. Psychiat.*, 1963, **9**, 199–206.

Yeats-Brown, F. *Yoga explained: a simple approach to a fuller and richer life.* New York: Vista House, 1958.

Zaehner, R. The menance of mescalin. *Blackfriars*, 1954, **35**, 310.

Zaehner, R. *Mysticism: sacred and profane; an inquiry into some varieties of praeternatural experiences.* New York: Galaxy Books, 1961.

Zegans, L., Pollard, J., & Brown, D. The effects of LSD-25 on creativity and tolerance to regression. *Arch. gen. Psychiat.*, 1967, **16**, 740–749.

Zimmer, H. On the significance of the Indian Tantric Yoga. In *Spiritual disciplines: papers from the Eranos yearbooks.* New York: Pantheon, 1960.

Ziskind, E. Isolation stress in medical and mental illness. *J. Amer. med. Assn.* 1958, **168**, 1427–1430.

Ziskind, E., & Augsburg, T. Hallucinations in sensory deprivation: method or madness. *Science*, 1962, **137**, 992.

Zubeck, J., Pushkar, D., Sanson, W., & Gowing, J. Perceptual changes after prolonged sensory isolation (darkness and silence). *Canad. J. Psych.*, 1961, **15**, 83–100.

Zubin, J., & Katz, M. Psychopharmacology and personality. In P. Worchel & D. Byrne (Eds.), *Personality change.* New York: John Wiley & Sons, 1964.

Zuckerman, M. Perceptual isolation as a stress situation. *Arch. gen. Psychiat.*, 1964, **11**, 255–276.

Zuckerman, M., & Cohen, N. Sources of reports of visual and auditory sensations in perceptual-isolation experiments. *Psychol. Bull.*, 1964, **64**, 1–20.

Zuckerman, M., & Hopkins, T. Hallucination or dreams? A study of arousal levels and reported visual sensations during sensory deprivation. *Percept. mot. Skills.*, 1966, **22**, 447–459.

AUTHOR INDEX

Aaronson, B., 230, 263–270, 291, 380
Abood, L., 476
Aboulker, P., 318
Abraham, K., 369, 372
Abrams, I., 288, 289
Abramson, H., 400, 479, 482
Ackerly, W., 364, 367, 369, 371
Adler, A., 118, 119, 121, 122, 127–131, 456, 457
Adrian, E., 496
Agnew, H., 139
Alancon, H., 441
Alexander, F., 30
Allen, M., 483
Allentuck, S., 325, 332, 334
Allport, G., 239
Alpert, R., 302, 480, 482
Amarel, M., 479
American Medical Association Committee on Alcoholism and Drug Dependence, 333
Anand, B., 485, 486, 503–506
Anderson, E., 11
Anderson, P., 364
Andrews, G., 324
Angel, E., 464
Anonymous, 335–356, 364, 372, 469, 471
Anslinger, H., 328, 329
Arieti, S., 12, 464
Arlow, J., 463, 473
Armington, J., 139
Arnhoff, F., 385
Arnold-Foster, M., 115, 170
As, A., 279, 389, 390
Aserinsky, D., 75, 77, 85, 95, 113, 117, 130, 134

Assagioli, R., 176, 308
Astin, A., 390
Auerbach, R., 478
Aurobindo, S., 185

Back, N., 478
Bagchi, B., 486, 503, 505
Baker, W., 497
Baldridge, B., 138, 139, 174
Baldwin, J., 239
Ban, T., 264
Banford, S., 292
Barber, T., 137, 138, 230, 275, 281, 386
Barnard, M., 383
Barrett, W., 391
Barrigar, R., 480
Barron, F., 284, 386, 445, 457
Bartlett, J., 11, 240
Bartley, S., 496
Bates, R., 480
Becker, H., 326, 327, 336, 365
Beers, C., 264, 469, 471
Behanan, K., 185
Belo, J., 8, 11, 21
Ben Avi, A., 273
Bender, L., 478, 482
Bennett, A., 11
Benoit, H., 184
Bentler, P., 388
Benussi, V., 137
Berger, R., 134, 135, 137, 139, 140, 143
Bergson, H., 403
Berlin, L., 283
Bernheim, H., 241
Bertini, M., 74, 93–112
Binswanger, H., 315, 464

Bishop, M., 481
Bishop, W., 293
Blacker, K., 479
Blake, W., 32, 416
Blazer, J., 388
Bleuler, E., 366
Blewett, D., 422
Blofield, J., 405, 481
Blood, B., 16, 359
Blum, R., 328, 329, 413, 480, 482
Bolles, M., 486
Bolsen, A., 472
Bonaparte, M., 340
Bonhoeffer, D., 179
Bonkalo, A., 497
Boss, M., 115
Bowers, M., 273, 274, 275
Bowers, M. B., Jr., 11, 379, 463–476
Bowers, P., 277, 278
Bowman, K., 325, 332, 334
Boyd, D., 11
Boyko, E., 328, 331, 334
Bozzehi, L., 479
Bradley, P., 381
Brahms, J., 273
Brand, S., 482
Brauchi, J., 139
Bray, B., 32
Brazier, M., 495, 497
Bremer, F., 505
Brenman, M., 8, 13, 14, 30, 200, 213, 214, 231, 258, 259
Brenner, C., 46, 473
Brewer, W., 364
Broad, C., 151
Brooks, C., 140
Brown, D., 285
Brown, R., 373
Browne, T., 375
Brownfield, C., 386, 388
Brozovsky, M., 366
Bruin Humanist Forum, 322, 325–334
Bruner, J., 383, 454
Brunton, P., 184
Brush, E., 141
Buber, M., 406
Buck, L., 74
Buck, R., 481
Bucke, R., 8, 12, 16, 36
Buckman, J., 410, 483
Bugental, J., 397

Bunney, W., 138
Burgwin, S., 497
Burney, C., 11
Burroughs, W., 481
Busby, J., 272
Byrd, R., 11
Byrne, U., 422, 483

Calkins, M., 141
Callaway, E., 496
Calverley, D., 281
Cameron, N., 365, 464
Campbell, R., 175
Carlini, E., 326, 327
Carlson, H., 473
Carrington, H., 74
Carson, P., 139
Carstairs, G., 482
Cayne, L., 293
Cerletti, A., 442
Chang, G., 170
Chapman, J., 464
Chaudhuri, H., 183
Cheek, F., 479
Chein, L., 333, 367, 369, 373
Chertok, L., 318, 487
Chhina, G. S., 485, 503–506
Chin, L., 364
Cholden, L., 482
Christiansson, G., 364, 365, 366, 368
Chwelos, N., 422, 423
Clark, J., 28
Clark, W., 422, 481
Claviere, J., 136
Clinco, A., 372
Clinger, O., 364, 367, 369, 372
Cobb, J., 487
Coe, G., 11, 16, 215
Cohen, M., 478
Cohen, S., 110, 213, 264, 284, 290, 305, 381, 384, 388, 422, 424, 425, 443, 478, 479, 482
Colby, K., 390
Condon, J., 345
Connell, P., 467
Cooley, R., 239
Cooper, L., 280–281, 292, 339
Copeland, A., 273
Cornelisoon, F., 139
Coue, E., 317
Crasilneck, H., 487

Crochet, R., 400
Crockett, R., 38, 391, 482
Crotty, J., 364, 365, 368, 374
Cubberly, A., 137
Custance, J., 468

Dahl, N., 271
Daly, R., 139
Dante, 153
Darwin, C., 273
Das, N., 503, 505
Davidson, W., 20, 21
Davis, H., 487
Davis, P., 487
Deal, W., 134
Debold, R., 478
De Grazia, A., 382
Deikman, A., 7, 23–44, 175, 176, 184,
    199–218, 473, 474
Dell, P., 505
De Martino, M., 490, 491
Dement, W., 74, 75, 77, 78, 85, 95, 117,
    122, 123, 125, 126, 130, 134–137, 139,
    140, 386
Deren, M., 21
De Ropp, R., 264, 305, 326
De Sanctis, S., 136
Desoille, R., 223, 224, 227
De Vault, M., 269
Devereaux, G., 8
De Vito, R., 264
Diamont, J., 487
Dickes, R., 19
Disco, D., 328
Ditman, K., 366, 443, 478
Dittborn, J., 141
Dodds, E., 11
Dodds, J., 364
Dodson, V., 364, 367, 368, 369
Doepfner, W., 442
Donohue, D., 365
Downing, J., 379, 429–440
Dubos, R., 383
Dufek, M., 487
Dunlap, J., 481
Durand de Bousingen, R., 310
Dustin, G., 482
Dyke, R., 109
Dynes, J., 496, 497

Eagle, M., 213

Easson, W., 364, 367, 368, 369
Eastman, M., 151
Ebin, D., 16, 347, 481
Eckhart, M., 28, 416
Edwards, R., 364, 367, 370
Efron, D., 480, 481
Egorcue, J., 479
Ehrenwald, H., 141
Ehrenzweig, A., 41
Eiff, A., 314
Elder, J., 141
Elkind, D., 453
Ellenberger, H., 464
Elliot, R., 453
Ellis, H., 136, 147, 151, 153, 372
Emmons, W., 142
Engle, G., 366, 367, 373, 487
Epstein, L., 479
Erickson, M., 7, 8, 45–71, 231, 247, 280,
    281, 291, 292, 294, 304
Erikson, E., 383, 397
Esecover, H., 264
Estabrooks, G., 231
Evans, C., 486
Evans, F., 487
Eyesenck, H., 387, 448

Fadiman, J., 3, 286, 324, 357–358, 379,
    441–443, 445–461, 483
Farrel, B., 4, 426
Faterson, H., 109
Faucett, R., 464, 368, 369, 373
Federn, P., 36, 93, 103, 474
Felix, R., 365, 371
Fenichel, O., 89, 90, 367, 372
Ferenczi, S., 372
Fernandez-Cerdeno, A., 410
Ferris, E., 487
Field, M., 11, 20, 21
Fingarette, H., 30
Fink, M., 379, 478
Fisher, C., 135, 137, 138
Fisher, D., 479
Fisher, G., 482
Fiske, D., 128
Fiss, H., 74
Fitzherbert, J., 372
Fogel, C., 272
Fogel, S., 291
Forbes, T., 486
Forer, B., 397

Fort, J., 323, 325–329
Forte, J., 480
Foulkes, D., 75–92, 114, 115, 117–131, 134, 169
Fox, O., 115
Franek, B., 315, 318
Frank, B. L., 497
Frank, I., 264
Frederking, W., 225, 227
Freedman, D., 138, 379, 463–476, 481
Freedman, H., 325
Freedman, S., 87, 88, 216
Freeman, T., 19
Freemantle, A., 473
Freud, S., 30, 78, 90, 118, 119, 120, 121, 122, 125, 126, 128–131, 149, 222, 239, 272, 346, 348, 372, 392, 474, 475, 490
Frobenius, K., 141, 142
Frohman, C., 139
Fromm, E., 115, 121, 122, 188, 457, 490, 491
Frosch, W., 384, 424, 478
Frost, R., 272
Fujisawa, K., 497
Fuller, M., 479
Funkhouser, M., 480

Gaines, R., 283
Gajewski, E., 269
Galanter, E., 343
Galvin, J., 12, 19
Garattini, S., 325, 326
Gardner, R., 192, 194
Garoutte, B., 505
Garrett, E., 480
Garrison, O., 185
Gastaut, H., 489, 503, 505
Geber, F., 479
Geers, M., 74
Geissmann, P., 312, 315, 316–319
Getzels, J., 385, 455
Ghiselin, B., 239
Giarman, N., 471
Gibbon, E., 41
Gibbs, F., 487
Gibson, G., 364, 367, 369, 371
Gibson, W., 11
Gilbert, R., 283
Gill, M., 8, 14, 30, 31, 81, 200, 213, 214, 231, 258, 259
Ginsberg, A., 378, 481

Glaser, F., 324, 363–375
Glass, A., 496
Goddard, D., 26, 28, 29
Goethe, 224
Goldberger, L., 110, 194, 216, 388
Goldie, L., 497
Goldney, K., 486
Goldstein, K., 241, 323, 326, 327
Golightly, B., 478
Goodenough, D., 74, 110, 169
Goodman, E., 476
Goodman, P., 178
Gordon, J., 231
Gorton, B., 487
Gottlieb, J., 139
Govinda, A., 185
Grabski, D., 364, 368, 369
Granda, A., 139, 142
Grant, C., 283
Grant, W., 364, 370
Green, C., 74
Green, W., 174
Greenblatt, M., 87
Greenburg, L., 365
Greifenstein, R., 269
Gresham, S., 133, 140
Grisell, J., 139
Gruen, W., 385
Grunbaun, H., 87
Grunthal, E., 531
Guilford, J., 455, 458
Gustafson, L., 487

Habart, G., 497
Haertzen, C., 479
Hague, W., 478
Hall, C., 115, 121, 122
Hall, J., 487
Hammack, J., 139, 142
Happich, C., 220, 221, 226
Harman, W. W., 286, 379, 382, 390, 422, 437, 441–443, 445–461, 478, 482, 483
Harner, M., 357
Harris, D., 452
Hart, J., 486
Hatfield, E., 293
Hartman, A., 387
Hartmann, H., 30, 200, 384, 389, 455
Havel, J., 193, 388, 389
Hawkins, D., 134
Hebb, D., 10, 384

Hefferline, R., 178
Hegel, 359, 360, 361, 367
Heider, J., 176
Heim, R., 481
Heimann, H., 315, 318
Henderson, L., 41, 142
Hennings, J., 136
Hensala, J., 479
Heron, W., 11, 12, 87, 88
Herrigel, E., 182, 188, 191
Hertzman, M., 109
Hervey de St. Denys, Marquis, 147
Heyer, G., 228
Hildebrandt, F., 136
Hilgard, E., 230, 231, 256, 291, 292, 293, 389
Hiller, J., 316, 317
Hilton, W., 26, 28, 29, 200
Hinkle, L., 12
Hinsie, L., 175
Hirai, T., 34, 485, 489–502
Hirsch, M., 479
Hobson, J., 174
Hoch, P., 264
Hochberg, J., 94, 213
Hoffbauer, J., 136
Hoffer, A., 291, 381, 387, 392, 411, 422, 445, 446, 480
Hoffman, A., 377, 441
Hoffman, B., 140
Hollander, C., 377
Hollingshead, A., 390
Hollingwirth, H., 74
Hollister, L., 292, 387, 473, 479, 480
Holmstedt, B., 480
Holt, R., 110, 193, 216, 384, 388, 389, 456
Holton, G., 382
Hopkins, T., 74
Horowitz, M., 264
Housman, A., 273
Houston, J., 305, 478
Hubbard, A., 422, 483
Hull, D., 241
Hunter, R., 469
Hutchinson, E., 239
Huxley, A., 8, 16, 45, 46–71, 231, 239, 264, 267, 282–283, 402, 430, 435, 481
Huxley, J., 283
Hyde, R., 474

Indian Hemp-Drug Commission, 325, 326, 332
Irwin, L., 327, 328, 329
Irwin, S., 479
Isakower, O., 93, 103
Israel, L., 315, 318
Israelstam, D., 479
Itil, T., 478
Izumi, K., 272

Jackson, P., 385, 455
Jacobziner, H., 364, 365
James, W., 8, 16, 21, 24, 25, 32, 38, 41, 210, 239, 270, 322, 324, 359–362, 401, 402–403, 471
Janinger, 286
Janszen, H., 139
Jaramillo, R., 139
Jaret, L., 74, 169
Jarvik, M., 479
Jasper, H., 142, 419, 496, 499
Jaspers, K., 464
Jensen, J., 169
Jensen, R., 364, 368, 369, 373
Jessen, P., 136
Jetter, W., 487
Johnson, N., 364, 367, 369, 372
Jones, E., 12, 19
Jones, M., 348
Jones, R., 139
Jorgens, H., 314
Joskevic, J., 487
Jouvet, M., 130
Julian of Norwich, 25
Jung, C., 3, 222, 491, 497, 499
Jus, A., 316, 318, 319
Jus, K., 316, 317, 318

Kaada, B., 364
Kahn, E., 139, 140, 397
Kamiya, J., 134, 135, 176, 486, 507–518
Karlsson, B., 364, 365, 366, 368
Karp, S., 109
Kasamatsu, A., 34, 485, 489–502
Kast, E., 422
Katz, J., 138, 381
Katz, S., 13
Kauders, O., 251, 261
Kaufman, E., 174
Keddie, K., 140

Kekule, A., 273
Key, B., 381
King, C., 8
Kinne, S., 9
Kirkpatrick, C., 11
Kleber, H., 331
Klee, B., 381
Klein, D., 137
Klein, G., 192, 193, 213
Kleitman, N., 75, 77, 78, 85, 95, 113, 115, 117, 122, 123, 125, 126, 130, 134, 136, 497
Kline, M., 231
Kline, N., 480
Kluver, H., 479
Knight, R., 214
Knowles, D., 24, 25, 211
Koening, E., 140
Koestler, A., 12, 20, 455, 458
Kohler, C., 310
Kohler-Hoppe, C., 310
Kolb, L., 369, 371
Kondo, A., 179, 188, 189
Korn, R., 390
Kornetsky, C., 387
Kramarz, P., 487
Kramer, C., 326, 327
Kramer, M., 174
Kretschmer, W., 176, 219–228
Krippner, S., 230, 271–289, 380
Kris, E., 18, 30, 37, 239, 258, 456, 473
Krishnamurti, J., 178
Kristof, M., 487
Kroger, W., 270
Krus, D., 387
Kubie, L., 12, 13, 14, 19, 93, 349
Kurland, A., 422
Kusel, H., 482

LaBarre, W., 11, 16, 21, 417, 482
Ladd, G., 74, 141
Laing, R., 331, 472
Lancaster, H., 197
Landis, C., 13
Landmann, H., 315
Lang, P., 388
Laski, M., 38, 397
Laurie, P., 328, 333
Lawes, T., 264
Lawrence, J., 365
Lawshe, C., 452

Lawson, J., 464
Lawton, J., 364, 368
Lazovik, A., 388
Leaf, R., 478
Leaning, F., 74
Leary, T., 37, 302, 422, 480, 481
LeCron, L., 293
Lee, P., 483
Lehmann, H., 264
Leiderman, H., 11, 386
Lenzo, J., 139
Leon, H., 385
Lesse, S., 139
Lester, B., 139
Leuner, H., 421, 483
Levine, J., 13, 16, 290, 291, 422, 425, 479, 483
Levy, E., 87
Lewin, B., 30
Lewin, L., 480
Lewis, H., 74, 93–111, 115, 169
Lhermitte, J., 136
Li, C., 142
Liberson, C., 74
Liberson, W., 74
Lichtenstein, E., 192, 193
Lilly, J., 11
Lim, D., 386, 388
Linder, F., 137
Lindersmith, A., 480
Lindsey, D., 10
Lindsley, D., 489, 496, 497, 499
Ling, T., 410, 483
Lingl, F., 364, 366, 368, 371
Lisansky, E., 369
Loewald, H., 475
Lohrenz, J., 264
London, P., 276, 384, 390
Loomis, A., 497
Lorenz, M., 141
Loughman, W., 479
Lowenfeld, V., 457
Lowry, J., 370
Lubin, A., 139
Luby, E., 139
Ludwig, A., 7, 8, 9–22, 290, 291, 422, 425, 479, 483
Luk, C., 184
Luthe, W., 179, 219, 231, 309–319
Lyle, W., 11, 291
Lyons, J., 390

Maas, J., 138, 139
MacAlpine, I., 469
McCord, H., 275
MacDonald, D., 422, 483
McDonald, N., 469, 471
McGhie, A., 464
McGlothlin, M., 284, 479
McGlothlin, W., 284, 479, 480, 482
Mach, E., 150, 152, 156
Machle, W., 364, 365
Machover, K., 109
McKellar, P., 74
McKim, R., 379, 445–461
MacKinnon, D., 397, 458
Mackler, B., 455, 457, 459
Mackworth, N., 459
MacLean, J., 422, 483
MacNaughton, W., 334
McReynolds, P., 35
Maddi, S., 389
Magoun, H., 500, 503
Malamud, W., 137
Malcolm, N., 113
Malitz, S., 264
Malmquist, C., 364, 368
Marchand, H., 315, 316
Marechal, J., 27
Margolin, S., 12, 13, 14, 19, 93
Marinello, M., 478
Marks, R., 11
Maron, L., 140
Marquis, D., 137
Marquis d' Hervey, 147
Mascher, E., 421
Maslow, A., 239, 249, 340, 383, 390, 397, 454, 457, 459, 473
Massengale, O., 364, 365, 366, 368, 369, 371
Masters, R., 281, 282, 305, 478
Matthews, B., 496
Maupin, E., 176, 177–186, 187–197, 390
Maury, A., 136, 146, 147
Mauz, F., 226, 227
Max, L., 136
May, R., 464
Mayer-Gross, W., 464
Mayor's Committee on Marijuana, 325, 326, 327
Mead, G., 239
Mednick, S., 455, 456, 458
Meduna, L., 417

Meier, G., 136
Meissner, P., 109
Meligi, M., 265
Melnyk, J., 479
Meltzer, M., 11, 17
Mendelson, J., 11
Menuier, R., 136
Merry, J., 364, 371
Mesmer, A., 400
Meth, J., 12
Metzner, R., 302, 422, 480, 483
Meyer, A., 368, 369, 371
Meyers, F., 480
Michaux, H., 37, 38, 481
Miller, G., 343, 452
Miller, V., 137
Minkowski, E., 464
Mirsky, A., 139
Mischel, F., 20
Mischel, W., 20
Mischelet, J., 11, 12
Modlin, H., 369
Mogar, R., 378–380, 381–397, 445–461, 478, 480, 483
Moller, H., 40
Monroe, L., 76, 85, 89, 169
Monroe, W., 137
Montes, A., 369
Morlock, H., 134, 142
Morolock, J., 134
Moruzzi, G., 500
Morris, G., 139
Moseley, A., 11
Moss, C., 231, 293, 306
Muller-Hegemann, D., 310, 315, 317
Mundy-Castle, A., 496
Murphey, G., 482
Murphy, G., 277, 337, 455, 457, 458, 459
Murphy, H., 334
Murphy, J., 11, 19
Murray, E., 115
Muzio, J., 135, 174

Nachmansohn, M., 138
Nagera, H., 372
Narayana, R., 170
Neal, P., 365
Nelson, J., 141
Newland, C., 481
Newman, R., 138
New York County Medical Society Narcotics Sub-Committee Report, 330

Neyroz, U., 136
Nitsche, C., 364, 367, 369
Noel, C., 315, 316, 318
Noone, H., 160, 161
Norris, M., 11
Novalis, 152
Noyes, H., 176

O'Connell, D., 292, 293, 487
O'Donnell, J., 369
Ogata, S., 185
Okuma, T., 505
Olley, P., 140
Omwake, K., 141
Ophiel, 74
Orne, M., 13, 17, 138, 215, 231, 248, 291, 292, 487
Ornstein, P., 174
Osborn, E., 486
Osgood, C., 213
Osmond, H., 265, 270, 272, 321, 441, 464, 480
Oster, G., 264
Ostfeld, A., 264
Oswald, I., 106, 115, 129, 134–136, 139, 140, 142, 498
Otto, R., 404

Pahnke, W., 16, 379, 399–428, 482
Panama Canal Zone Governor's Committee, 325–327
Patanjali, 28, 200, 211
Paul, I., 479
Pekarek, V., 487
Penfield, L., 353
Perls, F., 178
Pescor, M., 370, 371
Peters, G., 371
Phalen, J., 325, 326, 327, 328, 329, 333
Philip, J., 479
Piaget, J., 239
Picchioni, A., 364
Pierce, C., 138, 139
Pike, J., 328
Pious, W., 476
Platman, S., 265
Plotinus, 416
Plunkett, B., 140
Plutchik, R., 265
Poetzl, O., 137
Poincaré, H., 273

Pollard, J., 285
Polzien, P., 315–317
Poulain, A., 25, 27
Powell, B., 110
Presnell, M., 422
Press, E., 364
Pribram, K., 343
Prince, A., 423, 479
Prince, R., 30
Pritchard, R., 213
Pruitt, M., 364
Puhl, L., 29
Puryear, H., 134

Quintanilla, J., 364, 365, 369

Rachmaninoff, S., 271
Rado, S., 367
Rafaelsen, O., 479
Raginsky, B., 273
Rank, O., 457
Rapaport, D., 13, 31, 34, 81, 89, 286
Ravenscroft, K., 11, 21
Raybin, H., 364, 365
Rechtschaffen, A., 74, 75, 77, 85, 89, 124, 125, 127, 135, 140, 141, 169
Redlich, F., 390
Renes, B., 315
Renneker, R., 141
Renshaw, S., 137
Reps, P., 176
Richards, W., 399–428, 379
Riggen, C., 293
Ritter, C., 11
Robbins, E., 424, 478
Roberts, L., 353
Robin, E., 139
Robinson, J., 364, 367, 369
Roe, A., 457
Roffwarg, H., 135, 139, 140, 174
Rogers, C., 445–446, 454, 457
Roheim, G., 104
Rohmer, F., 315, 318
Rolle, R., 25, 210
Romano, J., 366, 367, 373
Rorschach, H., 456
Rosenbaum, M., 373, 387, 487
Rosenfeld, A., 4, 272, 426
Rosenhahn, D., 384
Rosenthal, R., 547
Rotberg, M., 328

Roth, B., 384, 487
Rotter, J., 348
Rouse, R., 209
Rousselle, E., 182
Rowland, V., 143
Rubenstein, R., 138
Ruff, G., 87
Rugg, H., 397, 458, 459
Rugowski, J., 478
Rund, J., 12
Rush, B., 463
Russell, B., 459

St. Ignatius, 29
St. John of the Cross, 25, 26, 28
St. Theresa of Avila, 25
Salvatore, S., 474
Sandison, R., 400, 421
Sandler, J., 372
Sankar, D., 478
Santostefano, S., 364, 368
Sapir, M., 318
Sarbin, S., 386
Sarbin, T., 13, 235, 236, 247, 249, 388
Sargant, W., 11, 19
Sargent, T., 479
Sato, E., 179, 188
Satran, R., 364, 367, 368, 369
Saul, I., 74
Savage, C., 30, 264, 379, 385, 387, 394, 395, 422, 423, 441–443, 445, 446, 475, 479, 483
Schachtel, E., 40, 239, 246, 456, 457
Schatzman, M., 136
Schiff, S., 138
Schilder, P., 251, 261
Schiller, L., 482
Schlesinger, H., 192
Schneck, J., 364, 369, 370, 371
Schofield, W., 390, 391
Schorer, M., 473
Schrotter, K., 138
Schubot, E., 292
Schultes, R., 357, 441, 481
Schultz, D., 35, 179, 219, 220, 231, 309, 310, 311, 314, 315, 316, 318, 319
Schur, E., 482
Schwartz, R., 209
Schwitzgebel, R., 422
Seaman, G., 94
Shaffer, J., 422

Shaikun, G., 89, 127
Shankara, 416
Shapiro, A., 74, 110, 169
Shapiro, D., 39
Sharpless, S., 499
Sherrington, C., 18
Sherwood, J., 38, 422, 437, 438, 443, 483
Shimazono, Y., 489, 490, 497
Shmavonian, B., 110, 264
Shontz, R., 455, 457, 459
Shor, R., 10, 18, 230, 231, 233–250, 251–261, 291, 292, 385, 388, 390, 487
Siebenthal, W., 314, 315
Siegel, S., 195
Silberer, H., 37, 90, 93
Silverman, A., 110, 264
Sim, V., 476
Simeon, J., 478
Simmel, E., 369, 373
Simmons, J., 324, 482
Simon, C., 139, 142
Singh, B., 485, 503–506
Sjoberg, B., 292, 480
Skakkeback, N., 479
Skinner, B., 384
Skinner, J., 28
Slater, K., 496
Slatis, H., 479
Sleser, I. 74, 110, 169
Slocum, J., 11
Smith, D., 422, 480
Smith, H., 419
Snyder, E., 12, 20, 134, 140
Snyder, G., 185
Sokol, J., 364, 369
Solley, C., 33, 37
Solomon, D., 305, 324, 336, 478
Solomon, P., 216
Sommer, R., 464
Sparkes, R., 479
Spear, P., 74
Speer, E., 318
Spencer, A., 410, 421
Spiegelberg, F., 3
Spitta, H., 136
Spitz, R., 373, 375
Spoerri, T., 315, 318
Stace, W., 401, 407
Stafford, P., 478
Stark, S., 456
Stekel, W., 127

Stepanow, G., 136
Sterling, J., 364, 368, 370, 374
Stern, M., 424, 478
Stewart, K., 115, 156, 159–168
Stolaroff, M., 379, 385, 392, 422, 437,
    445–461, 479, 483
Stolberg, H., 265
Stovkis, B., 315, 316, 318, 319
Stoyva, J., 138, 140
Straecke, G., 136
Straus, E., 464
Strupp, H., 391
Suckling, E., 140
Suedfeld, P., 387
Sugarman, A., 265
Sugi, Y., 497
Sully, J., 136
Suraci, A., 40
Sutcliffe, J., 17
Suzuki, D., 28, 176, 490, 491
Symonds, J., 24, 74

Taber, W., 442
Takacs, E., 479
Tart, C., 1, 7, 73, 74, 113, 133–144, 151,
    169–174, 175–176, 229–231, 291–308,
    321, 377–380, 477, 485, 519
Taylor, J., 110
Teilhard de Chardin, P., 179
Tenenbaum, B., 431
Tepas, D., 134
Teresa of Avila, 416
Terrill, J., 471
Thaler, V., 87
Thomas, E., 11
Thomas, E., 134
Thompson, E., 136
Thomson, M., 486
Thren, R., 315, 318
Tillich, P., 406, 419, 423
Tinnin, L., 276, 277
Titchener, E., 138
Tolan, E., 364, 366, 368, 371
Tolstoy, 41
Torrance, E., 272, 276
Trent, W., 272
Trevor, J., 24
Triebel, W., 94
Trosman, H., 74, 75–92
Trouton, D., 387, 448
Trowbridge, E., 487

Tyler, D., 13

Uhr, L., 275
Ullman, M., 121, 122, 480
Underhill, E., 32, 76
Unger, S., 366, 387, 392, 396, 422, 429
Ungerleider, J., 479
U.S. House Marijuana Hearings, Ways and
    Means Committee, 330
Usdin, E., 481

Van de Castle, R., 115
van Eeden, F., 114, 115, 145–158, 170
Vaschide, N., 136
Velek, M., 487
Verdone, P., 75, 85, 89, 124, 125, 126,
    127, 135, 140, 141, 169
Verhulst, H., 364, 365, 368, 374
Vinacke, W., 272
Vinkenoog, S., 423
Vogel, G., 74, 75–92, 127
Vogt, O., 310
Vold, J., 136, 137
von Eckartsberg, R., 483
Von Oettinger, W., 365
Von Senden, M., 39, 212, 217

Wagner, R., 272
Wahl, J., 328, 329
Walk, A., 400
Wallace, A., 13
Wallace, C., 134
Wallis, G., 445
Walsh, W., 136
Walter, R., 496
Walter, W., 496
Wapner, S., 109, 387
Ward, R., 481
Warkany, J., 479
Warrack, G., 25
Washington Bulletin, 329
Wasson, R., 357, 440, 481
Watt, J., 325, 327, 329
Watts, A., 25, 38, 430, 435, 482
Wayne, G., 372
Webb, J., 487
Webb, W., 133, 139, 140
Webster, D., 175
Weil, G., 422, 480
Weisman, A., 36
Weitzenhoffer, A., 230, 256, 291, 292, 293,
    386

Wendt, H., 316, 317
Wenger, M., 486, 503, 505
Werner, H., 31, 32, 33, 39, 239, 456
Wertheimer, M., 455
West, L., 13, 139
Wheaton, J., 75, 85, 89, 124, 125, 127, 135, 169
Wheelis, A., 391
White, R., 13, 233, 234, 235, 236, 238, 249, 250, 251
White House Conference on Narcotic & Drug Abuse, 329
Whitlaw, J., 421
Whitman, R., 138, 139, 174
Whittlesly, J., 366
Wienpahl, P., 183
Wikler, A., 371
Wilkens, B., 264
Williams, G., 11
Williams, H., 134, 139, 142
Williams, R., 133, 139, 140
Wilson, R., 365
Winer, B., 82
Winkler, E., 366
Winograd, B., 482

Witkin, H., 74, 93–111, 115, 453
Wittstock, W., 314
Wollman, L., 281
Wolpert, E., 119, 135, 137
Wolstenholme, G., 325, 326, 327
Wood, P., 136, 138, 140
Woodroofe, S., 185
Woods, J., 26, 29, 200, 211
Woolley, V., 74
Wordsworth, W., 33
Wynn, L., 471

Yeager, C., 496
Yeats-Brown, F., 185
Yoshitake, J., 269

Zachariadis, N., 364, 371
Zaehner, R., 417
Zegans, L., 285
Zimmer, H., 185
Ziskind, E., 11
Zubeck, J., 35
Zubin, J., 381
Zuckerman, M., 74, 386, 388

SUBJECT INDEX

Absent-mindedness, 244–245
Adaptation to stimulation, 495–501, 504–
  506
Addiction, drug, 325, 329, 333, 367
Adlerian theory of dreams, 121–131
Aftereffects of ASCs, see Long-term ef-
  fects
Alcoholic intoxication, 133, 146, 360,
  486–487, 497
Alcoholism, 392, 422, 423, 435, 467
Alienation, 391
Alpha rhythm, 80–85, 318, 339, 492–501,
  504–517
Altered states of consciousness, see ASCs
Amanita muscaria, 377
Amnesia, 48–49, 56, 57, 59, 60, 64–65,
  68, 229–230, 294; see also Memory
Amphetamine psychosis, 467–468
Analgesia, 50, 56, 58–59, 60, 294, 313,
  335, 422, 504–506
Anticipation, see Expectancies
Antisocial behavior, 326, 327, 328, 347–
  349, 370–371, 422
Archaic involvement, 254–261; see also
  Transference
Archetypal symbolism, 223–224, 409–
  410
Artists, 283–290
  psychedelic, 287–290
ASCs, adaptive uses, 18–21
  definition, 1–2, 9–10
  maladaptive uses, 18–19, see also Pathology of ASCs
  physiological correlates, 263–264; see
  also specific ASCs

Asleeping, see Hypnagogic state
Associations, 344–349, 412, 447, 453,
  455, 458; see also Cognitive
  processes
Astral projection, see Out-of-the-body experiences
Attention, 195, 196–197, 199–200, 204–
  205, 211–212, 237–241, 253, 279–280,
  313, 337–338, 346, 349–351, 353, 453,
  456–457, 474, 496, 499–500
Autogenic discharges, 312, 317
Autogenic training, 177, 219–220, 309–
  319
  physiological changes, 309–319
Autohypnosis, 310; see also Autogenic
  training
Autokinetic phenomena, 193, 195
Automatization, see Deautomatization
Awakening, false, 156–158
  see also Hypnopompic state
Aztecs, 441–443

"Bad trips," see Dangers of ASCs
Barriers, intrapsychic, see Attention
B-cognition, 239
Beauty, see Perception, experiential en-
  hancement
Belief systems affecting ASCs, 29, 39, 181–
  182; see also Cultural determinants and
  functions
Black market in psychedelic drugs, 426
Body-field dimension, see Differentiation
Body image, 14, 151, 182–183, 191, 213–
  214, 258, 266, 295, 303, 305–306, 312–
  313, 367, 385, 409, 413

Body position, see Meditation, instructions
Borderline state, see Hypnagogic state
Boredom, 11
Brainwashing, 11, 420
Breakoff phenomena, 11, 218

Canary Island broom, 357–358
Cancer, therapy with LSD, 422–423
Carbon dioxide inhalation, 28, 417
Cardiovascular changes, 55, 61, 443; see
 also Autogenic training, physiological
 changes
Catalepsy, 59–60
Catatonia, 264
Childbirth, 38
Chloroform, 24–25
Chromosomal damage, allegedly resulting
 from LSD, 478–479
Clairvoyance, 412
Climbing, symbolism of, 222, 223–224,
 295, 301–302
Cloud of darkness (unknowing), 199, 211
Cognitive processes, 13, 31–33, 36, 41,
 56–57, 181–182, 201, 275, 337–339,
 343–354, 359–362, 385, 387, 404–
 405, 412, 447, 453–459; see also
 Creativity; Generalized reality
 orientation
Collective unconscious, 220, 224, 225
Color, see Light; Perception, experimental
 enhancement
Communication with others during ASCs,
 16, 50–51, 184, 305–306, 406, 437,
 447, 479
 literalness, 57–58, 59
Concentration, see Attention; Cognitive
 processes; and Distraction
Confusion technique for inducing hypnosis,
 63
Consciousness, definition, 1–2, 3
Contemplation, 27–30, 31–34, 177; see
 also Meditation
Control, motor, loss of, 14, 17, 294
Control of depth and nature of ASCs, 53,
 54, 63, 74, 76–77, 141, 159–167, 202,
 214, 216, 227, 249, 253, 321, 354,
 438, 450, 474–475, 507–517
Creativity, 20, 47–71, 163–167, 217–218,
 220, 239, 271–290, 322, 326, 345–349,
 385, 389, 396, 397, 445–461, 470–476
Cultural determinants and functions of

ASCs, 2–3, 20–21, 39, 159–167, 177–
 179, 200, 215, 249–250, 290, 383–389,
 401, 419–420, 482; see also Belief systems affecting ASCs
Cytisus scoparius, 357–358

Dangers of ASCs, 306–307, 317, 353–355,
 363–375, 424–427, 432–433, 472, 478–
 479; see also Long-term effects; Psychosis
Dangers of meditation, 178–179, 182, 219,
 223, 226, 227–228, 317
Daydream, guided (Desoille), 223–225
Day residue, see Dreams, presleep stimulation
Death and dying, 422–423
Deautomatization, 23–43, 200, 212, 217–
 218, 389–390, 455, 474
Dedifferentiation, 207–208; see also
 Perception
Deep reflection (Huxley), 47–52, 55, 56,
 60, 62, 65–66, 68–69
Deep relaxation and symbolism (Frederking),
 225
Defenses, see Inhibitions
Delerium, 366–367
Delusions, see Paranoia
Demand characteristics, 58, 215–216, 378,
 382–383, 386–387, 421, 430, 432–433,
 435–436, 437, 446–448, 450, 471, 473
Depersonalization, see Self-concept
Depth of hypnosis, see Hypnosis, depth of
Depth perception, 263–270
Derealization, see Self-concept
Destructuralized ego state, 81–91
Developmental processes and ASCs, 159–
 167, 276–277
Differentiation, 109–111, 453
Dissociation, 47–48, 245–248; see also
 Self-concept
Distraction, 181–182, 200, 201–202, 205,
 209–210, 279–280, 354, 456–457
Divergent thinking, 455; see also Creativity
Doctrines, see Belief systems affecting ASCs
Dreams, content, 123–131, 245, 474
 control of, 115, 133–167
 demoniacal, 149, 152, 155–156
 deprivation of, 139–140, 386
 effects of drugs on, 133, 139, 140, 169–
 174
 falling and flying, 153, 162–163
 high, 169–174
 hypnotic, 137, 294–308; see also Dreams,

posthypnotic
initial, 146
interpretation, 161–162, 164, 165
lucid, 1, 114–115, 145–158, 170
physiological correlates, 77, 117–118,
134–136, 316
posthypnotic, 138, 140–142
presleep stimulation effects, 110, 120,
126
recall of, 113, 117–118, 129, 133
stimulus incorporation, 136–138, 140–
141, 142–143, 146–147, 148, 296, 302n
theories about, 113, 117–131, 146–148,
161–162
Dream work, 120, 126
Drowsiness, see Hypnagogic state
Drugs, sedative, 140, 326–327, 421
stimulant, 140; see also Amphetamine
psychosis
tranquilizing, 139, 140, 326, 431, 436,
443

EEG, 37n, 366, 491–517; see also Autogenic
training, physiological changes
EEG feedback, 507–517
Electroencephalogram, see EEG
Electrooculogram, see EOG
Emotion, 14, 361, 404, 411, 442, 470–476
Empathy, 447, 453–454, 457–458, 468;
see also Communication with others
during ASCs
Energy, experience of, 412; see also Radia-
tion, experience of
EOG, see Rapid eye movements
Ergot, 443
Ethical considerations in working with
ASCs, 420–421
Euphoria, 404, 442, 447; see also Emotion
Evolution, experience of, 412
Expectancies, 342–344

Fantasy, 373–374; see also Imagery
Fatigue, use in inducing ASCs, 234, 238,
417
Field dependence-independence, see Dif-
ferentiation
Fire walk, 11
Free association, 108–109, 194
Freudian, see Psychoanalytic theory

Gasoline sniffing, 363–375

Generalized reality orientation, 53, 233–
261, 337–338, 341–344; see also
Expectancies
Genista canariensis, 357–358
Genista scoparia, 357–358
Gestalt theory, 455, 459
Glue sniffing, 363–375
Good Friday experiment, 414–416
Grass, see Marijuana
Group LSD experiences, 433–434, 450–451
Guided daydream, 223–225
Guru, see Teachers

Hallucinations, 54–56, 61, 367, 442
Hashish, see Marijuana
Healing, 19–20; see also Psychotherapy
Highway hypnosis, 238
Holiness, see Sacredness
Humanistic psychology, 383–384
Hyperalert states, 11, 12
Hypermnesia, see Memory, enhancement
of
Hypnagogic state, content, 76–111, 234
content versus physiology, 80–91, 146
physiological correlates, 75–76, 318, 494–
495, 498, 517
presleep stimulation and, 74, 93–111
recall of, 73n, 93–94, 100
and Zen meditation state, 494–495
Hypnodelic therapy, 290n, 422
Hypnopompic state, 73
Hypnosis, 17, 52–71, 213–216, 229–319,
310–311, 386, 388, 432, 490, 494
definition, 229, 233–234, 243–244
depth of, 53–71, 214, 245, 247, 249, 251–
261, 292–308
depth of, self-reports, 293–308
induction, 234, 258–259
mutual, 291–308
physiological correlates, 316, 487 and n,
494, 497–498
simulation of, 248n, 264–270
theoretical explanation of, 233–261
Hypnotic dreams, see Dreams, hypnotic
Hypnotizability of hypnotists, 293–308
Hypoalertness, 12

Identity, see Self-concept
Illumination, see Creativity
Imagery, 31–32, 194–195, 254, 305, 384,
408–410, 442, 447, 453, 456, 459, 510–
512

eidetic, 31–32, 288, 353
Individual differences in ASC experiences,
    89–90, 103, 109, 169, 187–197, 221–
    222, 286, 327, 336, 354–355, 365,
    387–388, 394–395, 413, 435, 449,
    471, 514–515; see also Training
Individuation, 222
Ineffability, 16, 20, 23, 35, 40–41, 204,
    215, 405–406, 509, 515
Inhibitions, 348–349, 447, 453, 454–455;
    see also Antisocial behavior; Control of
    depth and nature of ASCs
Intact ego state, 81–91
Intuition, see Cognitive processes
Involvement, see Attention
Ipomoea purpurea, 441–443
Ipomoea violacea, 441–443
Isolation, sensory, see Sensory deprivation
I-thou relationship, see Communication
    with others during ASCs; Self-concept;
    and Unity experience

Jamais vu, 352–353
Joy, see Euphoria; Emotion

Kayak disease, 11
Knowledge, transcendent, 20, 26–27, 39–
    40, 41–42, 359–362; see also Cognitive
    processes
Koan, 185; see also Zen
Konchin, 494–495
Kundalini yoga, 185, 412

LA (lysergic acid amide), 441–443
Learning, 387
Learning to use ASCs, see Training
Light, experience of, 37–38, 50–51, 55,
    153, 204, 207, 210, 212–213, 266, 300,
    303, 412, 468, 469; see also Perception,
    distortion, experiential enchancement
Long-term effects, of ASCs, 35–36, 171,
    173–174, 179, 189, 197, 215, 245–247,
    284–290, 301, 304, 310, 314–319,
    321, 325–326, 394–397, 406–407,
    411, 417–419, 424–427, 431, 439,
    446, 460–461
Lotus posture, see Meditation, instructions
Love, 163–164, 199
LSD, 38, 281–290, 355, 366, 377–483
    dosages, 432, 435
    legal status, 378, 400, 480

physiological correlates, 381
psychotherapeutic use, see Psychotherapy,
    and psychedelic drugs
usage frequency, 377, 426
Lysergic acid amide, 441–443
Lysergic acid diethylamide, see LSD

Mahanand, 503
Mandala, 222–223
Mantra, see Meditation, word
Marijuana, legal status, 322–324, 327–334,
    480
    psychological effects, 326–355, 432
    research opportunities, 322–323, 323n
    usage frequency, 322, 327
Meaning, 15–16; see also Cognitive processes
Meditation, 28–29, 31–34, 175–228, 311,
    340, 486, 514–515
    chapel, 221, 222
    design (mandala meditation), 222–223
    instructions, 28–29, 180–186, 189–190,
        200–202, 219–228, 313–314, 490
    meadow, 220–222
    mountain, 221, 222
    physiological correlates, 183; see also Yoga
        meditation; Zen meditation
    word, 223
    see also Contemplation; Yoga meditation;
        Zen meditation
Mediumistic trance, 147, 486
Memory, during ASCs, 148, 351–354, 387,
    410, 436, 458, 474
    enhancement of, by ASCs, 56–57, 61–62,
        108, 353
Memory of ASCs in normal state, 25, 28, 51–
    52, 73, 171, 209–210, 241, 338, 351–354,
    359–360; see also Amnesia; Ineffability
Memory of previous ASCs during ASCs, 51–
    52, 57, 338, 342, 351–154
Mental hospital, design of, 272
Merging, see Self-concept; Unity experience
Mescaline, 377, 450, 471
Metabolic rate in meditation, 497
Morning glory seeds, 441–443
Motivation, 235; see also Values
Motor activity, use to produce ASCs, 10–11
Multiple personality, 486
Mysterium tremendum, 404; see also Sacred-
    ness
Mystical experience, 23–43, 199–218, 399–
    428; see also Self-concept; Unity
    experience

Nadir experience, 393–397, 475–476
Narcolepsy, 77
Narcotics, 325
Niacin, see Nicotinic acid
Nicotinic acid, 414, 431, 434, 436
Nightmares, see Dreams, demoniacal
Nirvana therapy, 314
Nitrogen inhalation, 497
Nitrous oxide, 16, 359–362
Nonstriving attention and volition, see Attention; Passivity
NREM sleep, 75, 123–131, 149–150, 170n, 236–237, 245

Ololiuqui, 441–443
Out-of-the-body experiences, 151 and n, 486

Pain, see Analgesia
Paradoxes, resolution and transcendence, see Cognitive processes
Paranoia, 38, 353, 367, 394, 411–412, 467
Passive concentration, 313; see also Attention; Autogenic training
Passivity, 27, 29, 177, 180, 196, 353, 388, 411, 514
Pathology of ASCs, 18–19, 178–179, 221–222, 386–387; see also Dangers of ASCs
Peak experiences, 239, 249, 288, 340, 388, 393–397, 473
Penicillamine, 411
Perception, 15, 24–25, 36–38, 48–52, 57, 193, 207–208, 209–210, 385, 499
distortion, 15, 36–38, 204
experiential enhancement, 24–25, 32–33, 36–40, 171–174, 200, 265, 267, 305, 326, 335–336, 338–339, 344, 358, 407–410, 442, 447, 468, 469, 470–476
visual, 57–58, 203–204, 263–270, 305, 336–337, 387, 408, 452–453; see also Light
Perceptual isolation, see Sensory deprivation
Peyote, see Mescaline
Physiological correlates of ASCs, 485–517; see also specific ASC names and specific physiological variable names
Placebo, 414, 449
Plans, see Expectancies
Plenary trance state, 296–297
Pot, see Marijuana

Precognition, 154–155, 413
Preparation for experiencing ASCs, see Demand characteristics; Training
Primary process, 13, 119–120, 246–247, 389
Primitivation of mental structure, 31–33
Psilocybin, 414–421, 478
Psychedelic experiences, creation without drugs, 51, 62, 263–270, 291–308, 463–476
and psychosis, 463–476
Psychoanalytic theory, and ASCs, 29–30, 36, 196, 239 and n, 272, 340n, 346, 389, 454
Psychodynamic phenomena, 410–411
Psychodysleptic, see Demand characteristics
Psychological processes, awareness of, 37–39, 52, 236–237, 246–247, 322, 471
Psycholytic therapy, 399, 421
Psychosis, 226, 245, 378, 411–412, 424, 463–476
inhalation, 363–375
Psychotherapy, and meditative techniques, 219–228
and psychedelic drugs, 283, 348, 387, 389–397, 410–411, 421–423, 429–439, 482–483
Psychotomimetic, see Demand characteristics

Radiation, experience of, 207, 210, 412; see also Light
Rapid eye movements, 75–76, 135, 298, 504
Rapport, 292, 294, 296, 305; see also Transference
Reality, external, orientation to, 52–53, 54, 58, 76–77, 79–91, 142–143, 499–500; see also Perception
Reality of ASCs to experiencer, 35–36, 39–40, 43, 60–61, 66, 154, 229, 245, 253, 255–261, 300, 303, 305–306, 401, 402–403, 423
Rebirth experience, 16; see also Self-concept
Regression, 40, 79–91, 193–194, 196, 217–218, 221, 239, 388, 410–411, 423, 432
hypnotic, 62–68, 69–71, 257, 258, 274–275, 298
see also Regression in the service of the ego
Regression in the service of the ego, 258–259, 388, 423, 456, 474

Religious conversion, 11, 32, 472
REMs, see Rapid eye movements
Renunciation, 27–30, 34–35, 178–179, 486
Repression, 246, 258
Respiration, using to induce ASCs, 182–183, 189–190, 220, 295
Respiratory changes in ASCs, 55, 63, 191, 497; see also Autogenic training, physiological correlates
Restructuralized ego state, 81–91
Reticular activating system, 500, 505–506
Rivea corymbosa, 441–443
Role-taking, 235–236, 248–249, 252–253

Sacredness, 403–404
Samadhi, 416–417, 503–506; see also Yoga
Sanran, 497
Satori, 180, 185, 188, 196, 416–417, 490; see also Zen
Schizophrenia, 35n, 264, 269–270, 353, 435
Scientific methods and the study of ASCs, 5, 382–383, 507–508
Scotch broom, 357–358
Self-actualization, 388, 392, 396, 446, 455
Self-concept, 17, 32, 33, 50, 63, 66–68, 69–71, 184, 217, 236–237, 240, 242, 303, 305–306, 307, 360, 385, 389–390, 432, 442, 474; see also Unity experience
Self-hypnosis, see Autohypnosis
Self-observation, 183; see also Self-concept
Self-surrender, see Passivity
Senoi, 159–167
Sensory deprivation, 11, 34–35, 87–88, 110, 128, 194, 216–217, 386–387, 388, 417
Sensory input, reduction or patterning as a technique for producing ASCs, 10–11, 28, 83–84, 87–90, 93–94, 216
Sensory overload, 11
Sensory phenomena, see Perception
Sensory translation, 37–38; see also Perception
Sernyl, 268
Sesshin, see Zen
Set and setting, see Demand characteristics; Training
Sexuality, 20, 38, 163–164, 184–185, 207, 210–211, 330, 337, 340, 372–373, 409,

410, 437
Shamanism, 11
Sleep, EEG patterns of, 75–76
see also Dreams; NREM sleep
Sleep deprivation, 417
Smell, 372–373
Social isolation, 138, 140; see also Sensory deprivation
Somnambulists, 257–258
Space, perception of, 263–270, 272, 303, 337, 385, 403, 407, 423, 442
Spanish broom, 357–358
Spartium junceum, 357–358
Spartium scoparium, 357–358
Spirit possession, 11; see also Mediumistic trance
Spiritual advisors, see Teachers
Stabilized retinal images, 213
Stimulation during meditation, 495–501, 504–506
Stimulus barriers, see Attention
Structures, psychological, 31; see also Psychological processes, awareness of
✓Subject-object split, see Self-concept, Unity experience
Suggestibility, 16, 241, 432, 468; see also Demand characteristics
Suggestion, indirect, 52, 59, 60
Symbolic consciousness, 220–223
Synesthesia, 15, 408, 442

Tantric yoga, 185
Teachers, 29, 202, 224–225, 289
Telephathy, 305, 306, 412; see also Rapport
Temple sleep, 11
Terminating LSD states, 431, 434, 436, 438–439
Tetrahydrocannabinol, see Marijuana
Theta waves, 492–501
Third-force psychology, see Humanistic psychology
✓Time, contraction, 13–14, 204, 257, 341, 344, 385, 403, 413, 423
expansion, 13–14, 56, 66–68, 70, 204, 257, 280–283, 339–342, 344, 385, 403, 413, 423
Tohats, 160
Tolerance for unrealistic experience, 192–193, 195–196, 216–217, 446, 474
Training, effects of, 24–25, 210, 270, 318, 336–337, 365, 409, 485, 490, 493–494,

504–506
Trance, 3, 241–242, 248–261; *see also*
     Hypnosis
Transiency of mystical states, 406
Transference, 227; *see also* Archaic involve-
     ment
Transfiguration, 208; *see also* Light; Per-
     ception, experiential enhancement
Trans-sensate experience, 41–42, 215, 305
Trust, 394, 411; *see also* Paranoia

Unconscious processes, *see* specific headings
     such as cognitive processes, Creativity,
     Dreams, Regression, Repression
Unity experience, 32, 38–40, 199, 205–
     207, 215, 360–361, 396, 401–402, 407

Values, 219–220, 222, 224, 362, 390–391,

394–396, 446, 447
Visualization, *see* Imagery
Volition, *see* Control of depth and nature of
     ASCs

Wakefulness, simulation of, 297
Waking at a preselected time, 141, 313

Yoga, 28–29, 185, 200, 211, 295, 485–486,
     503–506
Yoga meditation, physiological correlates,
     503–506

Zazen, *see* Zen
Zen, 178, 182, 183, 185, 187–197, 273,
     485–486, 489–501
Zen meditation, physiological correlates,
     489–501, 505